HALO REACH

TABLE OF CONTENTS

WELCOME TO REACH 2

UNSC TRAINING 6

THE CAMPAIGN 28

01: Winter Contingency 28
02: ONI 46
03: Nightfall 64
04: Tip of the Spear 78
05: Long Night of Solace 96
06: Exodus 112
07: New Alexandria 130
08: The Package 142
09: The Pillar of Autumn 158

FIREFIGHT BASICS 176

FIREFIGHT MAPS 194

01: Beachhead 194
02: Corvette 198
03: Courtyard 202
04: Glacier 206
05: Holdout 210
06: Outpost 214
07: Overlook 218
08: Waterfront 222

MULTIPLAYER BASICS AND TACTICS 226

MULTIPLAYER ARSENAL 236

MULTIPLAYER VEHICLES 256

MULTIPLAYER GAME MODES 266

MULTIPLAYER MAPS 288

01: Boardwalk 288
02: Boneyard 290
03: Countdown 294
04: Powerhouse 296
05: Reflection 298
06: Spire 300
07: Sword Base 302
08: Zealot 304
09: Forge: The Cage 306
10: Forge: Pinnacle 308
11: Forge: Hemorrhage 310
12: Forge: Paradiso 312
13: Forge: Asylum 314

FORGE MODE 316

REFERENCE 326

01: Ordnance 326
02: Vehicles 340
03: Enemy Forces 349
04: Credits, Commendations, and Medals 360
05: The Armory 374
06: Skulls and Scoring 380
07: Achievements and Avatar Awards 389
08: Data Pads 395

WELCOME TO REACH

It is our esteemed pleasure to welcome you to Reach, a world our team of authors and multiplayer experts have had the privilege of inhabiting for much of this summer. Reach is a planet whose fate has been foretold for years, yet one we grew to love as no other in the *Halo* universe. It is here on Reach where the events leading up to *Halo: Combat Evolved* take place, and it is on this planet where the wizards at Bungie have decided to set their grand opus. Make no mistake about it, Bungie's decade of experience in crafting this best-selling franchise has lead to the creation of what is absolutely the biggest and best *Halo* game ever made.

As fans of the series, it was indeed a privilege to be given the opportunity to write this strategy guide—one we took very seriously. Few videogames can sniff the heights of which the *Halo* franchise has soared, and we worked tirelessly to ensure that the readers of this book received a guide that matched the caliber of the game it covers. Just as Bungie strove to develop a game that outshone all the others in the *Halo* series, we too aimed to make the most comprehensive *Halo* strategy guide ever published.

Naturally, you'd expect us to say nothing less, so let us share with you a bit of what makes this book special...

UNSC TRAINING

As surprising as it may sound to long-time fans, there are players who have never played a *Halo* game before now. This chapter is primarily for them. We designed this chapter to pick up where the user's manual leaves off and provide players—both veterans and rookies alike—with a comprehensive explanation of every fundamental aspect of the game, with extra attention devoted to what's new. This is where you'll find the lowdown for on-foot and vehicle controls, using weapons, the HUD, and game options, as well as the new Armor Abilities and Fireteam features.

CAMPAIGN

Most strategy guides provide a one-size-fits-all walkthrough that covers the game's default difficulty setting. There is nothing wrong with this approach, but *Halo's* various difficulty modes—particularly Heroic and Legendary—are nearly as famous as the games themselves. To accommodate this, we set out to provide a level of coverage that will be helpful to players on Normal, Heroic, and Legendary. Those playing on Easy mode should simply kick back and enjoy the sensation of being a hot knife slicing through so much Covenant butter.

Normal: Consult the "Battle Tactics" section at the start of each chapter for a general plan of attack. This, along with the maps and screenshot captions, will carry you through. Much of the strategy text is applicable also, though you may not need it.

Heroic: The walkthrough's primary strategy is based on Heroic mode. The tactics are centered on the major clashes that accompany each objective throughout the game, with details on where to go, which weapons to use, and how to take down the toughest foes. Together with the maps and tips, we are positive that the walkthrough will help you complete *Halo: Reach* "as it was meant to be played."

Legendary: Legendary mode is for experienced players only. We recommend playing through the game at least once on Heroic mode while following along with our base strategy. We've added a series of "Legendary Tactics" sidebars throughout the walkthrough that contain an extra level of detail, proven to work against the toughest Covenant threats.

FIREFIGHT

The Firefight mode fans enjoyed playing in *Halo: ODST* is but a fraction of what Bungie has packed into *Halo: Reach*. We've accepted the challenge of bringing you complete coverage of all seven Firefight variants and the myriad custom games and settings that are available, in addition to the detailed maps and battle tactics you expect in a book by BradyGames. Firefight coverage includes Covenant breakdown per wave, ordnance drops, scoring rules, and Skull modifiers per round, and these are just a few of the details that you'll find inside this section.

MULTIPLAYER

Fans may come to *Halo* for the single player experience, but it's the franchise's massively successful multiplayer mode that has kept them—and us—playing for years. Our team of expert players, helmed by key members of the Sea Snipers clan, not only compiled proven tactics and map-specific strategies for each of the game's modes, but they've delved deeper into the minutia of *Halo* data than ever before.

Maps: Detailed maps show every weapon, Medkit, vehicle location, and capture point for all nine maps that ship with the game.

Tactics: Proven strategies for the dozens of individual gameplay modes accompany map-specific tactics to help you lead your team to victory, no matter what playlist you find yourself enjoying.

Forge: Come with us as we guide you down the rabbit hole of the most ambitious map editing toolset ever included in a console game.

AND SO MUCH MORE...

Here's a sample of some of the additional information we would want in a strategy guide for *Halo: Reach*.

- Full explanation with data tables for the new **Credits** system, including how to earn Rank promotions and Commendations.
- Tactics on how to deal with every **Covenant** unit, including weapons and health data for each variant encountered in the campaign and Firefight.
- **Vehicle** controls, weapons, speed, and health data for each gameplay mode.
- Comprehensive **weapons analysis** with ratings, and tactics for campaign and Firefight.
- Player customization options shown in a comprehensive **Armory** appendix.
- **Achievement Guide** shows you how to unlock all 1000 Gamerscore.

Our goal when setting out to work on this book was to create not only a strategy guide that we would be proud of, but one that would answer every question we suspect the demanding *Halo* fanbase might ask. It is our hope that this effort shines through, and that the book you now hold helps you get the most out of this amazing game. Thank you.

MAP LEGEND

WEAPONS

Icon	Name	Page #
	ASSAULT RIFLE	326
	DMR	327
	MAGNUM	327
	SNIPER RIFLE	328
	SHOTGUN	328
	GRENADE LAUNCHER	329
	ROCKET LAUNCHER	329
	SPARTAN LASER	330
	TARGET LOCATOR	330
	MACHINE GUN TURRET	331
	FRAG GRENADE	331
	PLASMA PISTOL	332
	PLASMA RIFLE	333
	PLASMA REPEATER	333
	NEEDLER	334
	NEEDLE RIFLE	335
	CONCUSSION RIFLE	335
	FUEL ROD GUN	336
	FOCUS RIFLE	336
	PLASMA LAUNCHER	337
	PLASMA CANNON	337
	ENERGY SWORD	338
	GRAVITY HAMMER	338
	PLASMA GRENADE	339

VEHICLES

Icon	Name	Page #
	MONGOOSE	340
GUN	WARTHOG (GUN)	341
GAUSS	WARTHOG (GAUSS)	341
ROCKET	WARTHOG (ROCKET)	341
	SCORPION	342
	FALCON	343
	GHOST	345
	REVENANT	346
	WRAITH	347
	BANSHEE	348

ARMOR ABILITIES

Icon	Name	Page #
	ACTIVE CAMOUFLAGE	20
	ARMOR LOCK	21
	DROP SHIELD	21
	HOLOGRAM	22
	JET PACK	22
	SPRINT	23

CAMPAIGN

Icon	Name
	AMMO
	COVENANT AMMO
H	MEDKIT
A	MISSION OBJECTIVE

FIREFIGHT

Icon	Name
	COVENANT DROPSHIP
	MONSTER CLOSET

UNSC TRAINING

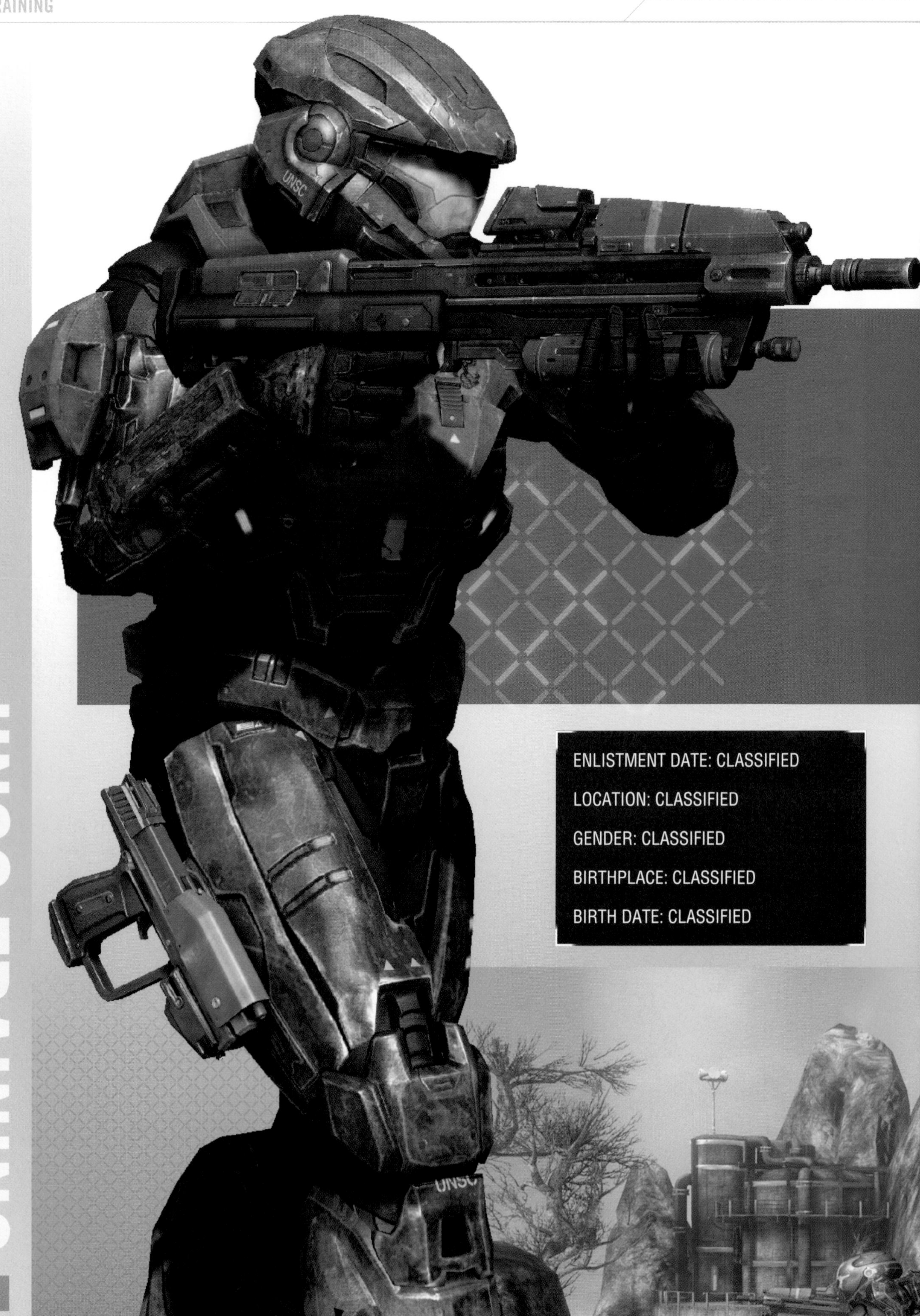

ENLISTMENT DATE: CLASSIFIED

LOCATION: CLASSIFIED

GENDER: CLASSIFIED

BIRTHPLACE: CLASSIFIED

BIRTH DATE: CLASSIFIED

UNSC TRAINING

So you want to be a Spartan, eh, soldier? Well, we're going to assume you've already done your homework and read the field manual that shipped with your copy of *Halo: Reach*, or else you wouldn't be here, right? *Right?* So forgive us if we don't repeat what the fine men and women at Bungie already wrote. Instead, we're going to expand on that field manual and impress upon you the lessons learned over countless hours spent living and dying on the battlefields of this great planet. This chapter is primarily geared for the greenhorns, but you veterans might learn a thing or two as well.

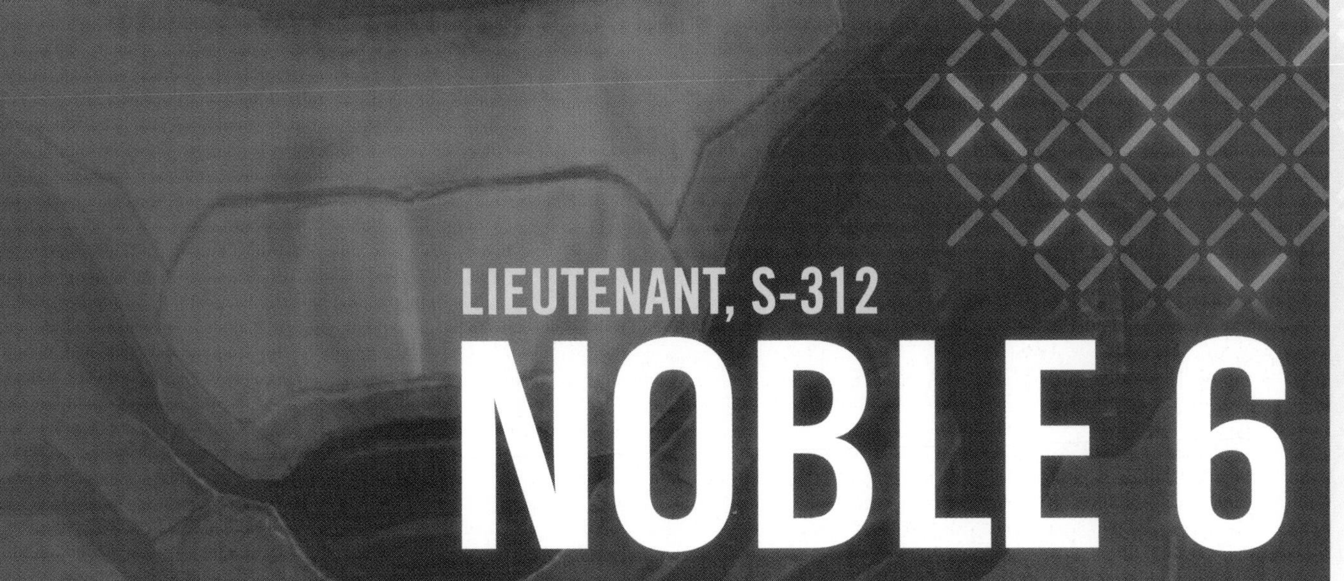

From Colonel Holland's Report:

"What little information I have been able to glean from around all of the redaction [note—I was quite literally expecting the ONI to start redacting page numbers] gives the impression that S-312 is more akin to a hyper-lethal vector than a soldier. A lone wolf assassin that has broken organizations and made entire militia groups disappear. At first glance, S-312 doesn't sound like the best fit for a team environment like NOBLE. However, we've been down a man for over a month—and frankly, there are hidden benefits to a XXX like S-312. Call it the luck of the draw. S-293's 1156 has been filed since 22/04/2552, every active duty Spartan-II is on XXX for special training, and it seems that XXX wasn't able to keep his own private grim reaper out of the pool—only time will tell if this luck is of the good or bad variety."

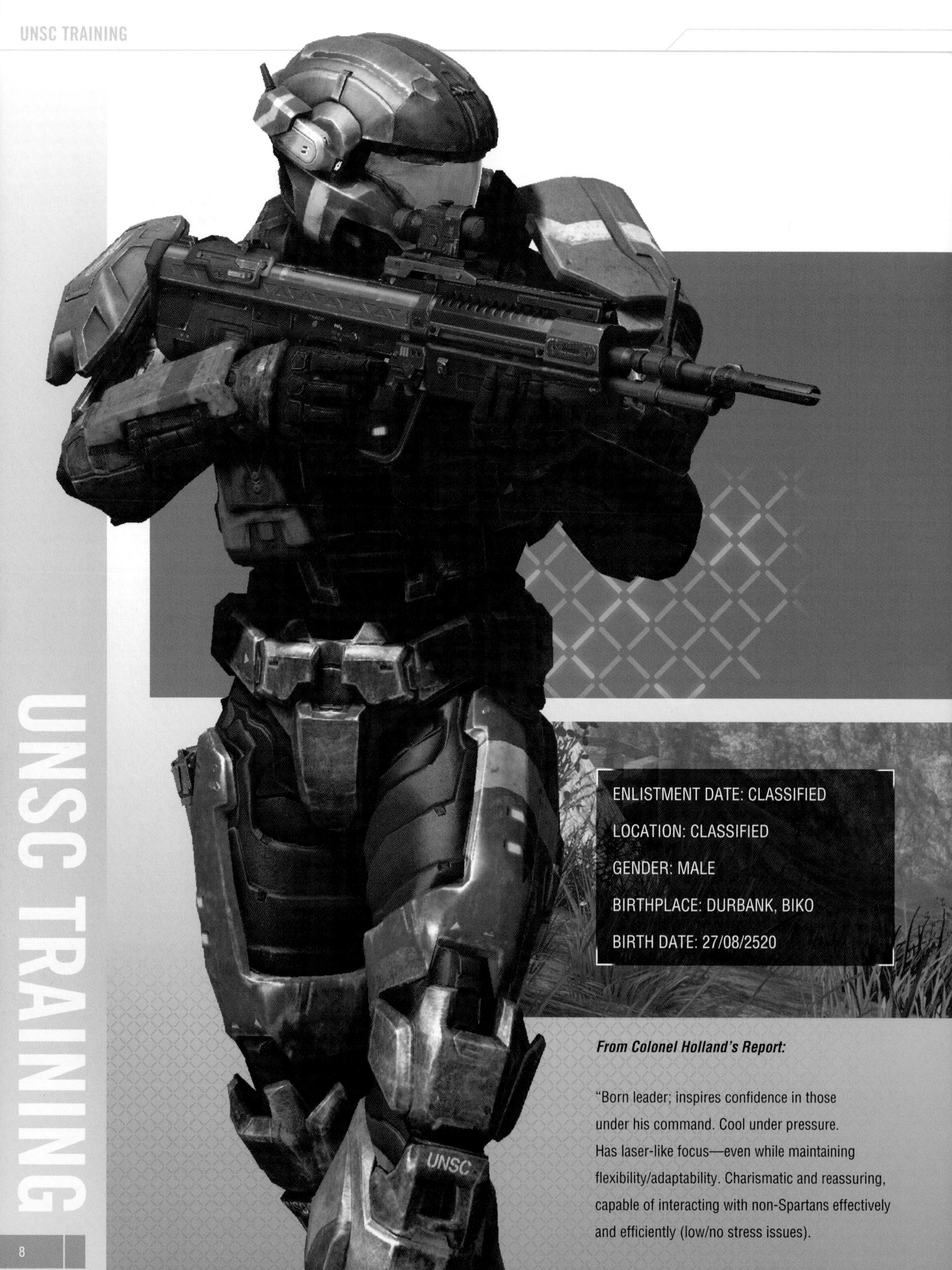

UNSC TRAINING

ENLISTMENT DATE: CLASSIFIED

LOCATION: CLASSIFIED

GENDER: MALE

BIRTHPLACE: DURBANK, BIKO

BIRTH DATE: 27/08/2520

From Colonel Holland's Report:

"Born leader; inspires confidence in those under his command. Cool under pressure. Has laser-like focus—even while maintaining flexibility/adaptability. Charismatic and reassuring, capable of interacting with non-Spartans effectively and efficiently (low/no stress issues).

MEET THE TEAM

You won't be taking on this mission alone. Whether you're playing the game co-op or by yourself, Campaign mode pits you in the role of Noble Six. Like many of your files, your birth name is classified, so the original five members just call you Noble Six. We have been granted limited access into the personnel files of each member of Noble Team. It's an impressive bunch, Spartan, you should be proud to join them.

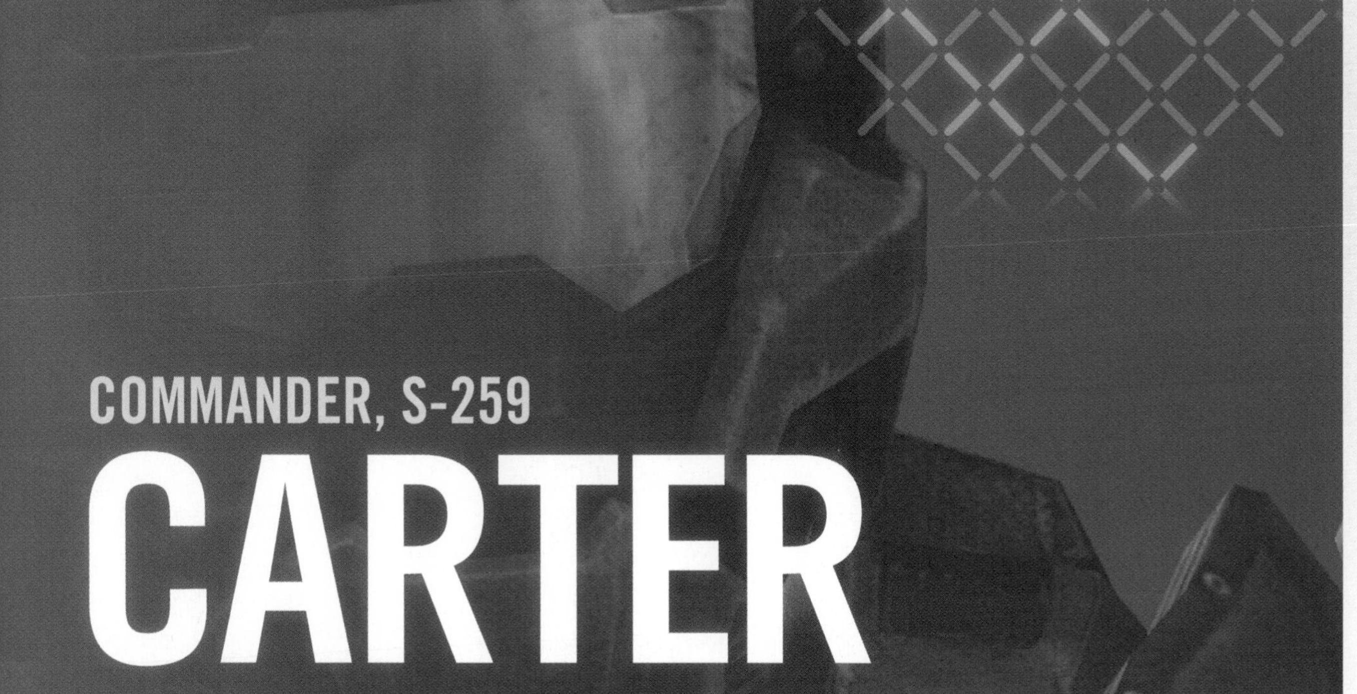

COMMANDER, S-259
CARTER

Minor trust issues; not severe enough to warrant psychiatric reevaluation, but enough to be noted—stems from operator [S-293] under his command being KIA 22/04/2552. He attributes S-293's death to his own "inadequate team preparation," not to enemy action or S-293's own lapse in situational awareness. Whether this is the source of his hesitation to commit to one of the replacements is unconfirmed at this time.

Perhaps replacing S-293 with the *1T271 from XXX group will get him back on track—he's always at his best while building a team."

From Colonel Holland's Report:

"Exemplary combatant, brilliant cryptanalyst—there hasn't been a system yet she hasn't been able to crack. However, she does tend to dig a little deeper than mission parameters require on occasion—and there have been times when NOBLE's proximity to classified matériel has made me rather nervous.

S-320 is an inspired tactician; this is certainly related to her ability to acquire and digest information. There are times when S-320's ability to read a situation—even with what many would consider cripplingly limited INTEL—could be described as supernatural. Unfortunately, even having MAGICAL INTEL can't protect you against a fatal lapse of situational awareness. To wit: S-293 was KIA during an OP that S-320 had put together [22/04/2552]; S-320 is now convinced that S-293's death rests solely on her own shoulders (S-259 is likewise convinced that he is solely responsible for S-293's death). Eventually, I hope to be able to get it through their thick Spartan skulls that Thom is dead because he chose to pursue a group of enemy combatants ON HIS OWN rather than wait for backup.

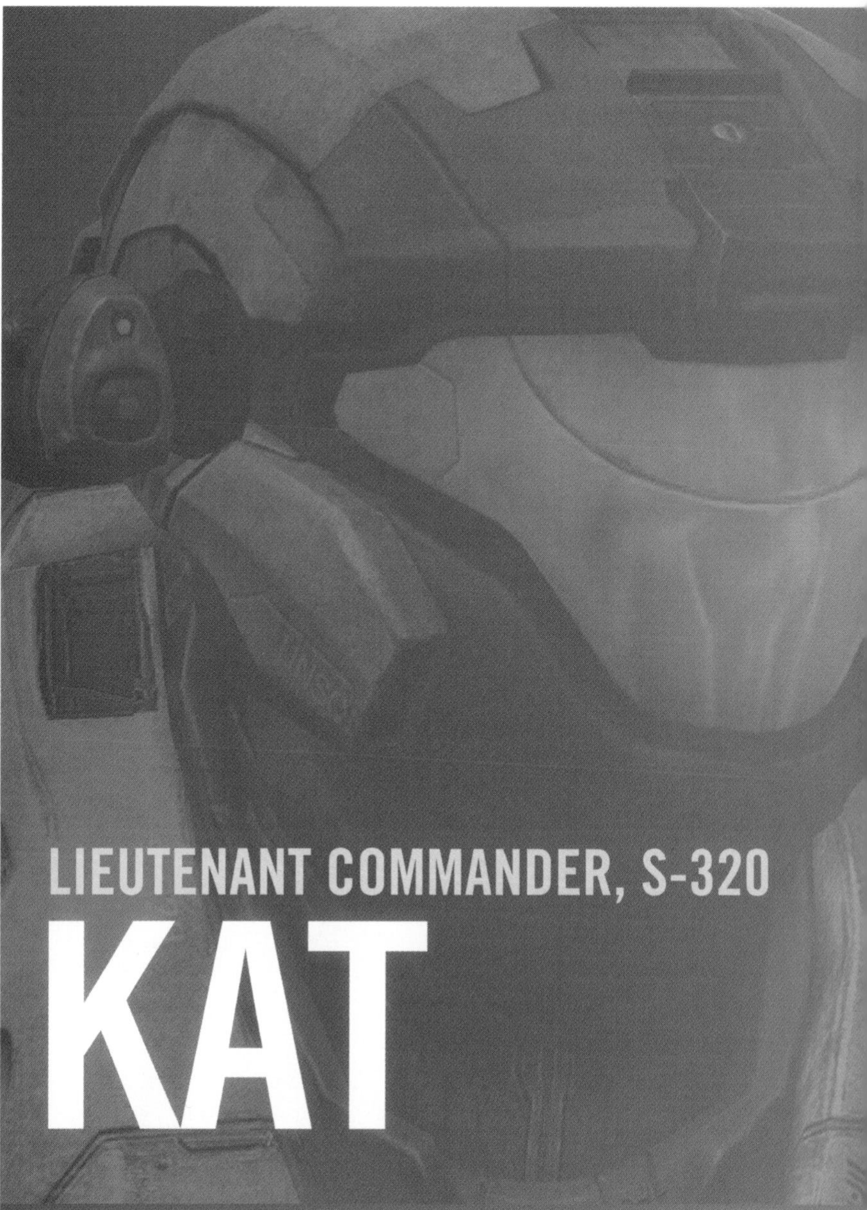

LIEUTENANT COMMANDER, S-320

KAT

ENLISTMENT DATE: CLASSIFIED

LOCATION: CLASSIFIED

GENDER: FEMALE

BIRTHPLACE: MONASTIR, NEW HARMONY

BIRTH DATE: 30/01/2530

S-320's refusal to resubmit her certification for the P_A(r)/NCSI-AMA is more than a little frustrating. She says she submitted her certification papers on 04/08/2551 and refuses to budge. My records show that she qualified expert level with the P_A(r)/NCSI-AMA [04/07/2551], but LOGistics/ Matériel Command claim they never received said notification and state that unless they receive said certification in a timely manner, the P_A(r)/ NCSI-AMA needs to be returned immediately. In the meantime, there is no way for me to stop getting spammed from LOG/MC with reminders. This has been going on entirely too long."

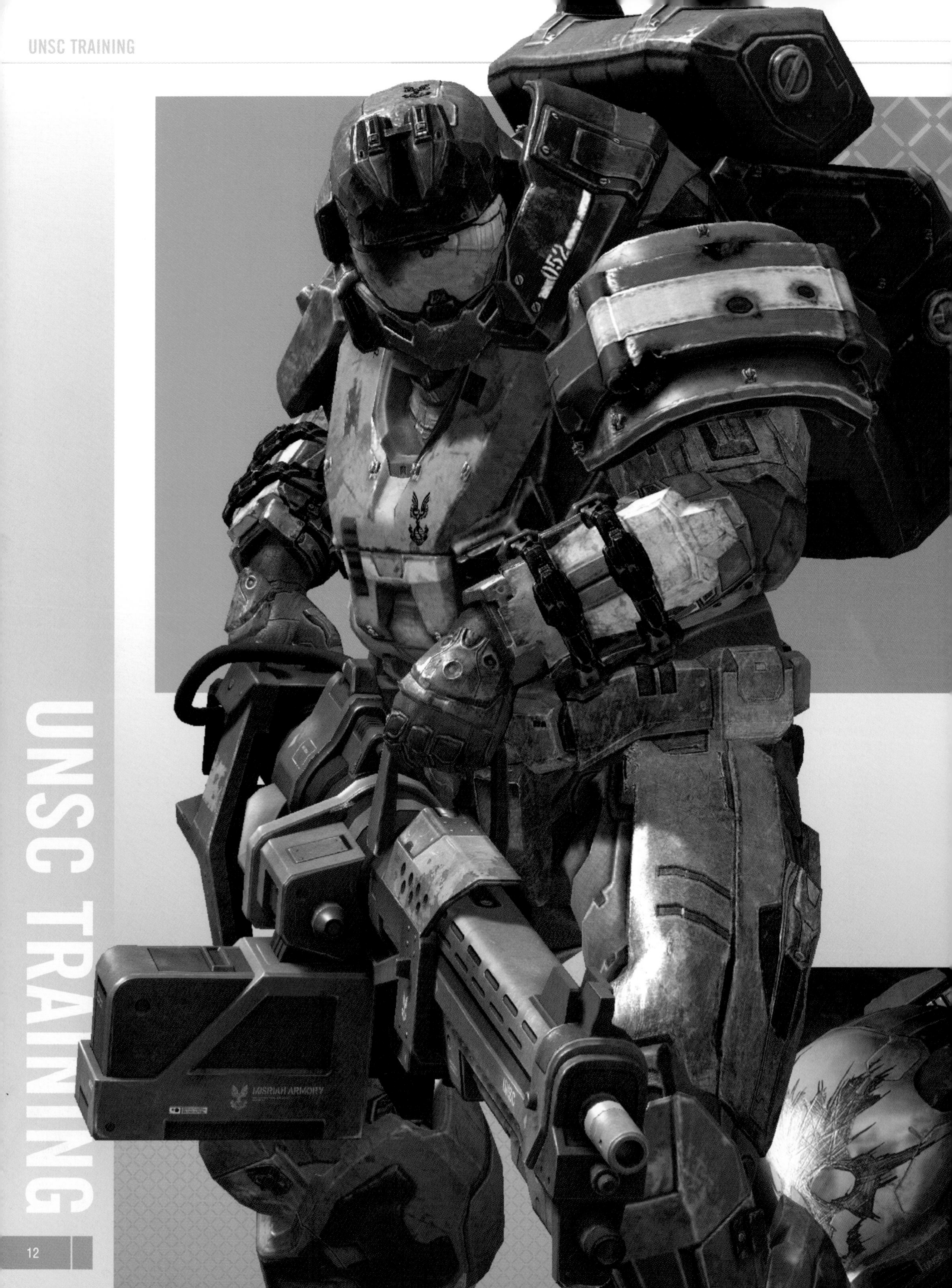
UNSC TRAINING
052
MISRIAH ARMORY
UNSC

CHIEF WARRANT OFFICER, S-052

JORGE

From Colonel Holland's Report:

"Career soldier—but then all the Spartans are, aren't they; inspires confidence in those around him—he is a combat multiplier! Rock solid, almost thirty years in the saddle and shows no signs of breaking or slowing, easygoing for someone from the class of '25, need to keep an eye on him around XXX as he tends to be pretty free with his opinions.

Vocal in his support of provincial self-rule, just as vocal in his condemnation of the separatist and insurrectionist movements. Only member of the team that has seen as much action, if not more, against human militants as Covenant forces. Very difficult to read. ((NOTE: never play cards with JORGE.))"

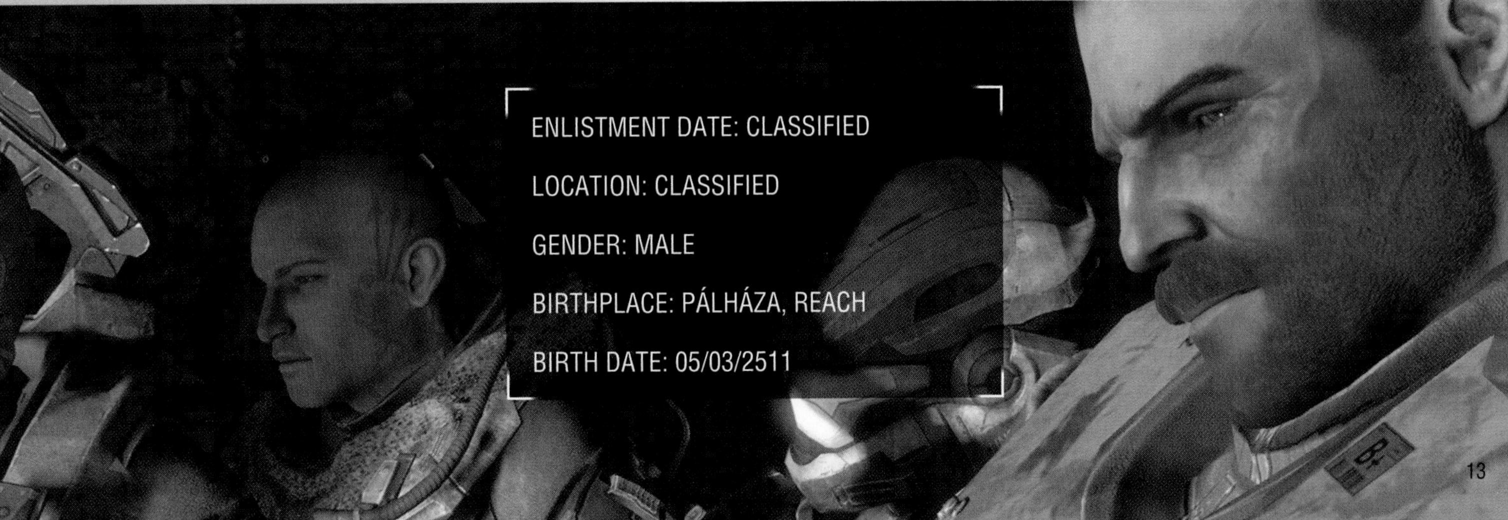

ENLISTMENT DATE: CLASSIFIED

LOCATION: CLASSIFIED

GENDER: MALE

BIRTHPLACE: PÁLHÁZA, REACH

BIRTH DATE: 05/03/2511

From Colonel Holland's Report:

"Respected by his peers, detail oriented, unbreakable. There's not a whole lot more to mention; he is an effective member of the unit while in the field and maintains strict discipline off the field. It does seem that he tends to have more difficulty interacting with non-Spartans than others within NOBLE, however.

I wish he would reel his audacity in the field back about 24%. His behavior makes it difficult to field him against insurrectionists; it's hard enough dealing with the stories of UNSC excess manufactured by the civilian media without S-239 providing them with hard evidence of said excess. That being said: it's an odd feeling to be relieved that you are sending your people out against hostile aliens.

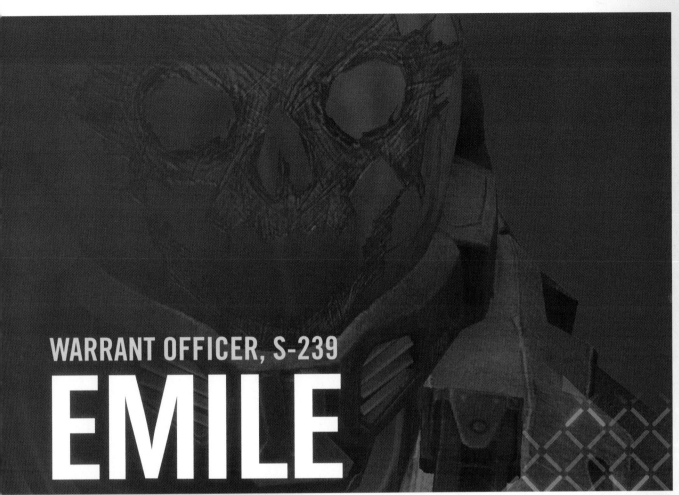

WARRANT OFFICER, S-239

EMILE

I may have to consider rotating S-344 into his spot if another IN/OP comes up before S-239's next mandatory psychiatric reevaluation [REF:03/09/2552]. S-239's collection of alien contraband is truly impressive. However, the existence of said collection is in direct violation of NAVCOM General Order 098831A-1/Sub_7. Good thing we're ARMY."

ENLISTMENT DATE: CLASSIFIED

LOCATION: CLASSIFIED

GENDER: MALE

BIRTHPLACE: LUXOR, ERIDANUS II

BIRTH DATE: 11/03/2523

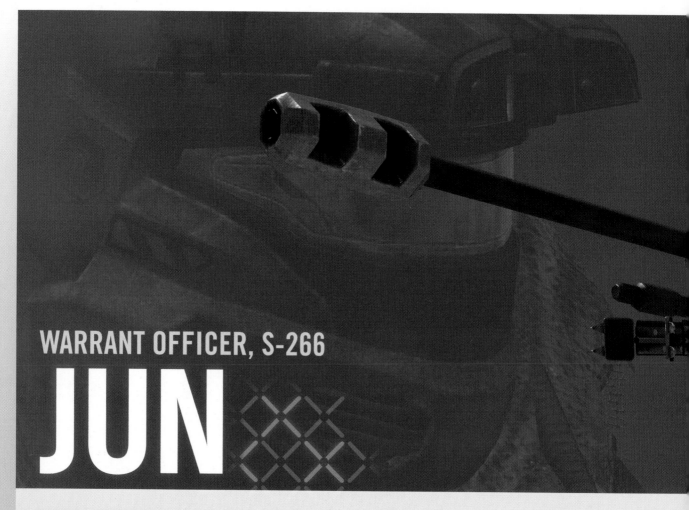

WARRANT OFFICER, S-266

JUN

From Colonel Holland's Report:

"Rock solid under pressure. Better than he has any right to be, but at least he isn't cocky—which is a good thing because he's chatty. This does tend to put him at odds with noise discipline protocols—his behavior in this regard is often overlooked by the other operators in the field because of the informational bent of his chatter.

During mandatory psychiatric evaluation [15/12/2549], it was noted by XXX that S-266 had "an unhealthy emotional detachment in regards to the consequences of his actions"—I can only suggest that this was done without any metric by which to measure said detachment. By my estimation, Jun is a rationalist. He is also a Spartan.

Although it is noted in his medical records that he has exhibited symptoms of PTSD in the past, there have been no indications of a relapse post-therapy [05/01/2550]."

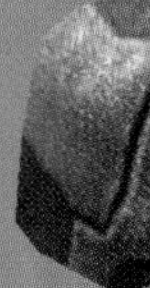

ENLISTMENT DATE: CLASSIFIED
LOCATION: CLASSIFIED
GENDER: MALE
BIRTHPLACE: TYUMEN, NEW HARMONY
BIRTH DATE: 28/02/2524

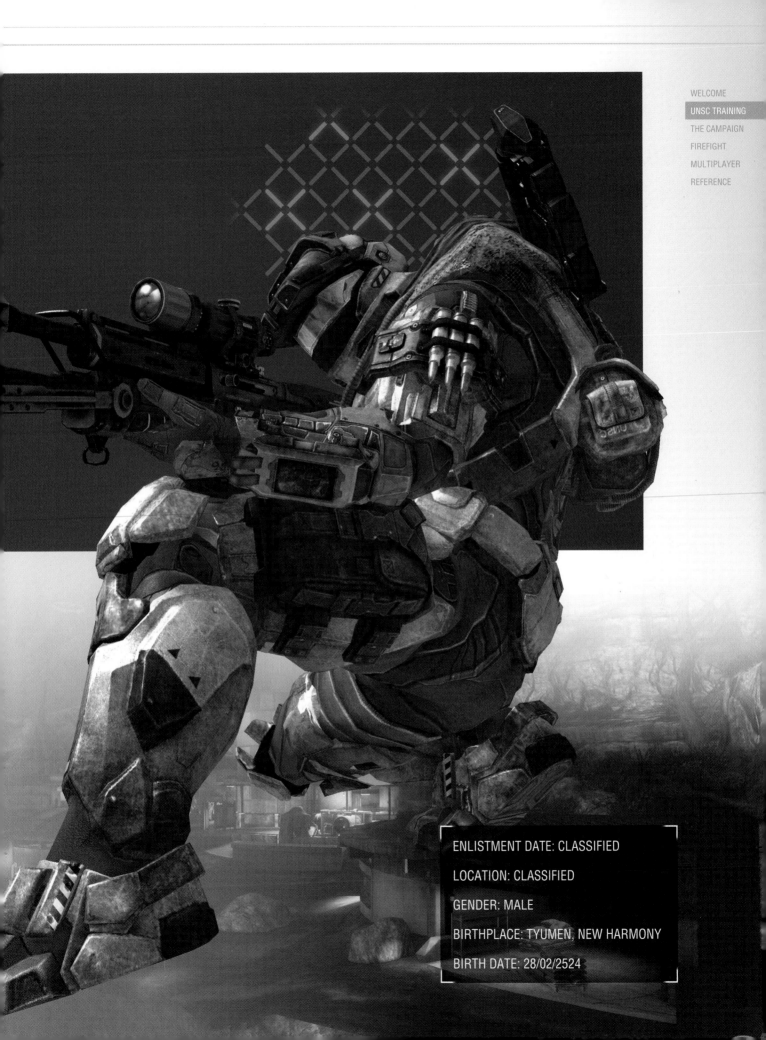

THE BASICS

CONTROLS

The default controls for *Halo: Reach* are a little bit different than what fans of *Halo 3* and *Halo 3: ODST* are used to. The game includes a number of alternative control configurations (accessed via the Back button, then selecting "Controller"), but most players prefer using the default configuration.

ON-FOOT CONTROLS (DEFAULT)

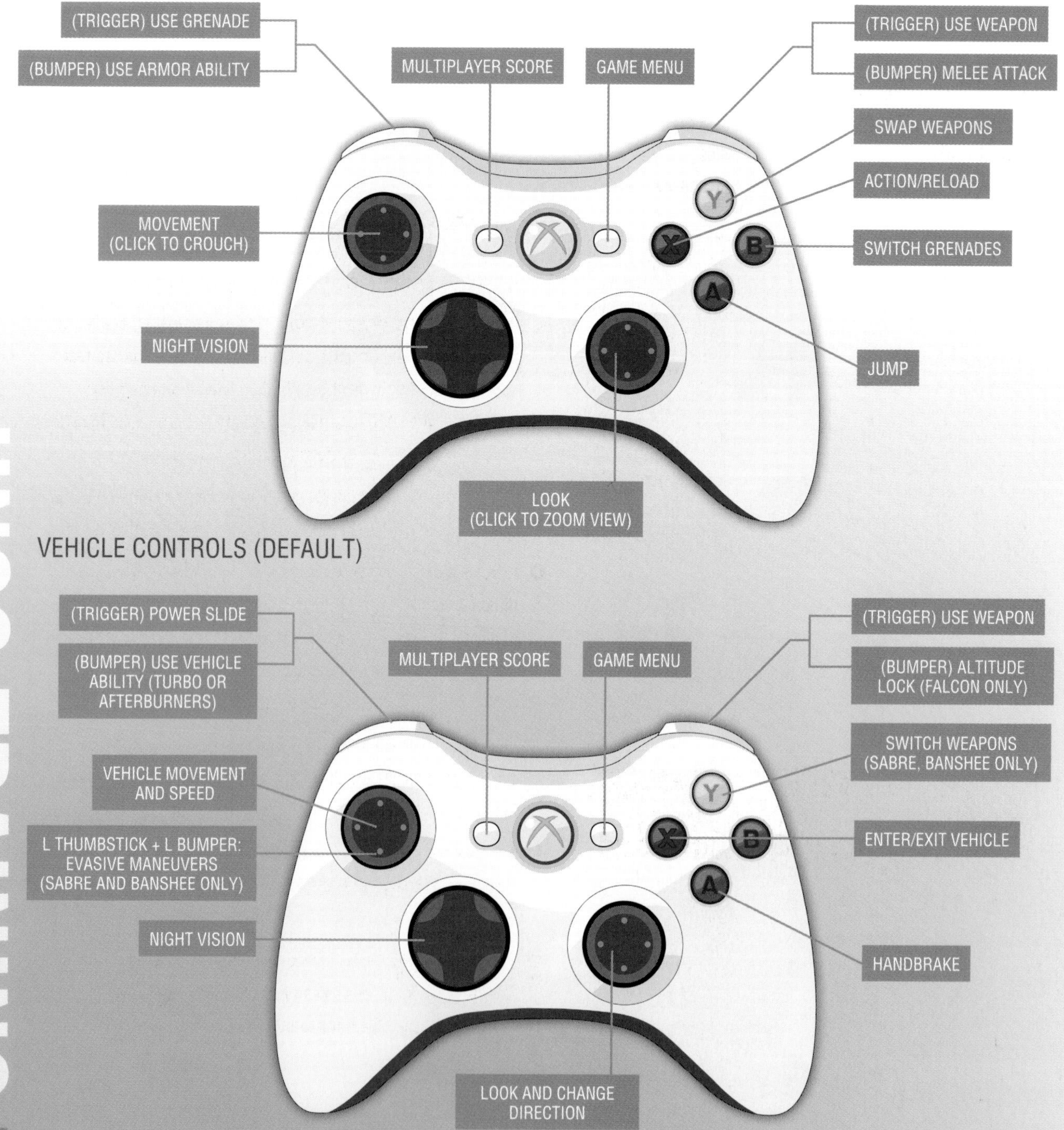

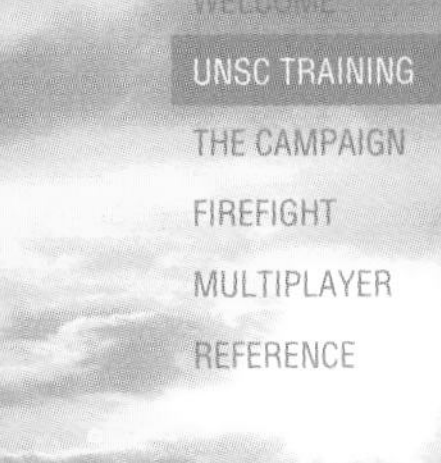

DIFFICULTY MODES

The *Halo* franchise has long been famous for its sophisticated A.I. and brutally hard difficulty settings. However, unlike a lot of games, increasing the difficulty doesn't just mean enemies have more health and inflict more damage to you. There are dozens of little tweaks made to the enemy behavior and stats behind the scenes to dial in the right feel for the given difficulty setting. As mentioned in the introduction, the majority of the walkthrough portion of this strategy guide is based on the Heroic difficulty setting, because that is *Halo* "as it is meant to be played." Nevertheless, obviously there are those of you out there who will want to play on one of the other settings (Easy, Normal, or perhaps even Legendary). Though this guide can't provide any specific numbers, the lead designers at Bungie were kind enough to pull back the covers and detail the major "knobs" that account for the increased difficulty between the modes. This information helps you know exactly what to expect each time you take that deep breath and start a new game on a higher setting.

First-time players, particularly those new to first-person shooters, should start with Normal difficulty. If this proves to be too difficult, go ahead and start over on Easy. Veterans of the series (or genre) should give Heroic a try the first time through the game. It's not advised to play through on Legendary without first experiencing the full Campaign on Heroic.

FIREFIGHT-SPECIFIC DIFFICULTY ADJUSTMENTS

Everything you'll read in this section pertains to both Campaign and Firefight with one exception: enemy units are not upgraded in Firefight based on difficulty. For example, bumping the difficulty from Normal to Heroic will not force an upgrade from blue Elite Minors to red Elite Majors in Firefight. All other tweaks are applicable to both Firefight and Campaign.

ENEMY ABILITIES

- Auto-upgrade character types based on difficulty. Blue Elites become red, red become white, etc. Not applicable to all enemy types in every encounter, but most experience this upgrade.
- All enemies have increased health and more shields, but "hard pings" remain static across all difficulties. Hard pings are real numbers, not fractions of health. If an enemy requires two shots from the DMR to trigger a hard ping on Normal difficulty, those same two shots trigger a hard ping on Legendary.
- The number of Covenant enemy that can be "berserking" at any one moment is increased as the difficulty setting is increased.
- Covenant attack behavior and skill is improved for each difficulty uptick. Enemies fire in longer bursts, with possibility of shorter delays between bursts. Covenant ability to track, lead, and hit moving targets is improved. Damage done by projectiles is increased, while overall accuracy is improved.
- The enemy's ability to target you as you exit cover is improved on higher settings. The delay between you exiting cover and being shot is diminished.
- Enemies tend to overcharge the Plasma Pistol more frequently, throw more grenades, and attempt to use vehicles to ram the player more often.
- The time between repeat melee attempts is decreased. Similarly, the time between an A.I. enemy throwing one grenade and then throwing another is also reduced.

PROJECTILE BEHAVIOR

- The speed of each projectile fired at the player is increased.
- The amount that the projectile tracks the player scales per difficulty. This makes it that much harder to evade enemy attacks—use cover!
- The damage to the player caused by enemy attacks and those from friendly fire is increased.

CO-OP CHANGES

Additional changes are made to scale the experience even further for those playing Campaign and Firefight with friends. These adjustments first scale up when two players are present, and then even further when four players are in the game.

- Enemy shield recharge rate is improved while the player's shield recharge rate is decreased.
- Enemies dive to avoid grenades more frequently and also employ Armor Lock more often. Both the chance of them evading an attack and the rate at which they can repeatedly evade increase.
- Length of enemy attack bursts increases while the delay between bursts diminishes. Projectiles fired by the Covenant travel faster and inflict more damage.

ARMOR ABILITIES

It's time to discuss the biggest addition to the *Halo* universe, and that's undeniably Armor Abilities. Unlike the equipment used in previous games, Armor Abilities are essentially "installed" directly into the Spartan's MJOLNIR armor and can be used repeatedly and on-demand whenever the player requires it. Sprint is the default Armor Ability that Noble Six begins the Campaign with, but others can be found throughout Reach, both on the ground and at UNSC supply cabinets delivered to key locations. You'll select a loadout based on a combination of Armor Ability and weaponry each time you respawn when playing Firefight.

ACTIVE CAMOUFLAGE

Renders the operator virtually invisible. Overall effectiveness depends on operator discipline—rapid or sudden movement tends to overtax the system.

- Lasts 40 seconds if motionless, 15 seconds while walking slowly.
- Requires four seconds of recharge between uses; it takes 15 seconds to fully recharge an empty meter.

Active Camouflage is one of the rarest Armor Abilities in Campaign mode, but can be extremely useful in Matchmaking and Firefight to a lesser extent. Nevertheless, those who like to mix some stealth into their *Halo* experience will certainly enjoy the opportunity to turn invisible. The key to using Active Camouflage is to move very slowly and avoid firing your weapons where you can be spotted, since sudden movements and weapons fire reduce the cloaking effect. It's also vital that you monitor the Armor Ability gauge and don't let it run empty during an inopportune time. Moving slowly while crouched or crouching in place slows the drain rate of the Armor Ability meter. The other key feature to Active Camouflage, especially in Versus modes on Firefight or Matchmaking, is the disturbance to the Motion Tracker. Triggering Active Camouflage causes the Motion Tracker to go haywire.

ARMOR LOCK 

Fairly effective even in this early prototype stage, it has internal components nearly identical to the Covenant gear that spawned it. The biggest drawback is that the local gravitic effect essentially immobilizes the operator.

- Lasts five seconds with a full meter.
- Requires five seconds of recharge between uses; it takes 13 seconds to fully recharge an empty meter.

Armor Lock lets you invoke temporary invulnerability at a moment's notice whenever and wherever you need to escape a sticky situation. Not only does this keep you safe from all types of attacks—even a direct hit from a Wraith's plasma bomb—but exiting Armor Lock also inflicts a short-range EMP blast to those around you. This EMP blast can deplete shields and short-circuit vehicles, the latter of which makes them that much easier to hijack. Lastly, Armor Lock can be used against speeding Ghosts or Revenants to completely obliterate oncoming vehicles, provided they ram you at full-speed. Armor Lock does lock you in one place and can't be used in quick succession, so use it sparingly in Matchmaking, or your opposition could just stand back and wait for it to run out, then lob a grenade at you.

DROP SHIELD 

An evolution of the bubble shield employed by ß5 Strike Teams, it creates a temporary, semi-spherical protective shield that also provides a curious restorative effect (still under investigation).

- Lasts up to 15 seconds depending on damage absorbed, and fully empties the meter.
- Drop Shields can be redeployed every 20 seconds, including recharge time.

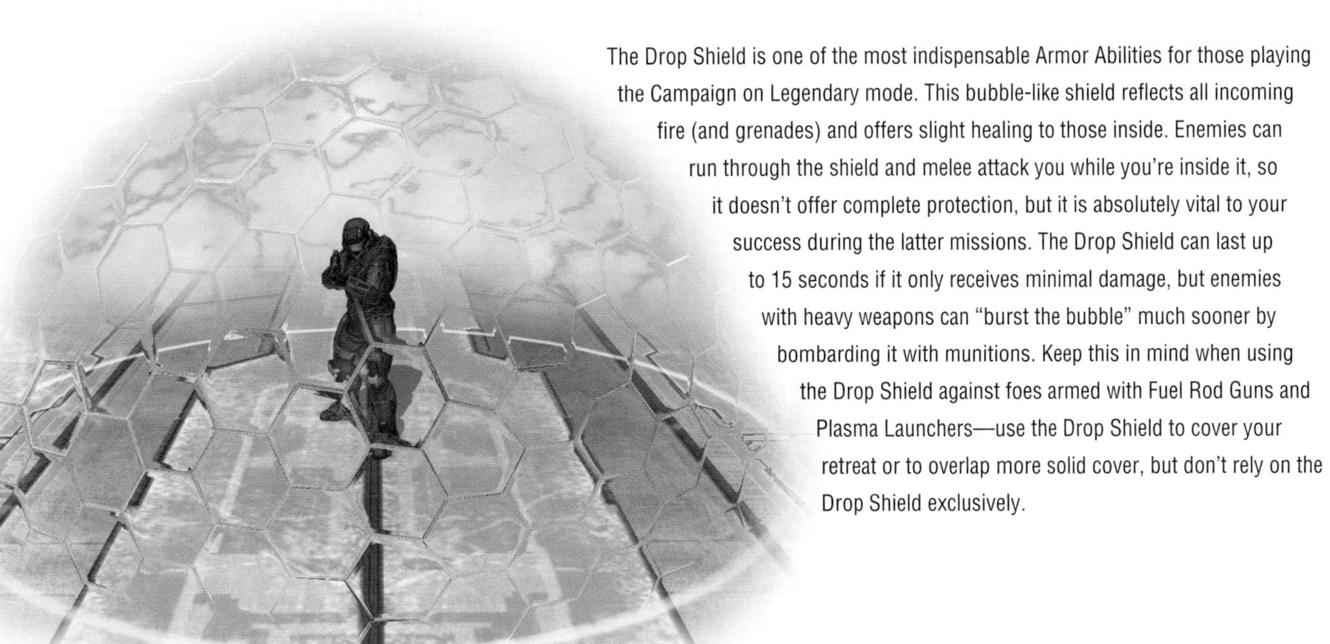

The Drop Shield is one of the most indispensable Armor Abilities for those playing the Campaign on Legendary mode. This bubble-like shield reflects all incoming fire (and grenades) and offers slight healing to those inside. Enemies can run through the shield and melee attack you while you're inside it, so it doesn't offer complete protection, but it is absolutely vital to your success during the latter missions. The Drop Shield can last up to 15 seconds if it only receives minimal damage, but enemies with heavy weapons can "burst the bubble" much sooner by bombarding it with munitions. Keep this in mind when using the Drop Shield against foes armed with Fuel Rod Guns and Plasma Launchers—use the Drop Shield to cover your retreat or to overlap more solid cover, but don't rely on the Drop Shield exclusively.

HOLOGRAM

This gives the operator the ability to create a virtual, holographic projection, which can be used as a decoy to draw enemy fire. The decoy has a regular lifespan of 10 seconds, but it may be canceled at any time.

- Lasts up to 10 seconds, but can be destroyed if it suffers too much damage.
- Hologram completely drains the meter, but it can be interrupted and redeployed after seven seconds.

Sure to be a lightning rod for what is definitely a *lively* discussion when it comes to Matchmaking; there is no debating the usefulness of Hologram in Campaign and Firefight. Point the reticule wherever you wish to send your holographic clone and press the Left Bumper to send your Hologram running across the map. Your Hologram looks exactly as you do—same armor, weapon, and color—but it's just a decoy. Hologram is extremely useful against Hunters: get a Hunter to turn and chase your Hologram, then open fire on its exposed back. The Hologram then runs across the map to reach the point where you aimed, provided it doesn't hit any obstacles. Otherwise, it runs in place against the obstacle and looks quite obviously like a fake. That said, a surefire way to trick opponents in Matchmaking is to imitate the Hologram. Try running against a wall when an enemy is coming (preferably one that doesn't look at the Motion Tracker too closely) to trick him into thinking you're a decoy, then turn around and blast him. Another trick is to deploy a Hologram straight down at the floor so it stands still while you imitate the Hologram and run across the map in a straight line. Turn and fire!

JET PACK

This newest model portable jump-jet finally has the power to lift a Spartan in the latest-generation MJOLNIR armor.

- Lasts four seconds under consistent use.
- Jet Pack takes five seconds to fully recharge after being depleted.

Another new way for Spartans to get around is via the Jet Pack. This Armor Ability can be used for on-demand airborne propulsion, and helps players cover ground faster than ever before. Though its noise and relative lack of maneuverability while airborne make it somewhat dangerous to use in Matchmaking, it comes in handy against the Covenant in Campaign and Firefight. Use it to cross large gaps, or to get a great destructive angle on groups of foes. The Jet Pack ability recharges very quickly, and prolonged flights are possible by pulsing the thrusters just enough to keep from falling too far while the meter recharges in short bursts.

SPRINT

S-320 is largely responsible for this plug. While not quite a hack, it does temporarily override the safety limiters on actuators and "muscles"—cheating the system regulators to keep the operator cool as well.

- Provides up to four seconds of Sprint, but can be cancelled.
- Sprint takes four seconds to recharge from an empty meter.

This long-desired ability has finally arrived and is every bit as straightforward as you would expect. It allows Spartans to cover distance faster and also makes it possible to leap greater distances. It's particularly useful in Firefight when trying to beat your teammates to an Ordnance drop, provided they don't have Jet Pack, which is even faster. Sprint is also helpful for escaping an attack, moving in behind a stunned enemy for an Assassination, and getting back to a safe zone during Firefight matches.

EVADE (ELITES ONLY) 

This appears to be a dummy module or terminator plug. While it is critical for operating the Elites' armor, its precise function is unknown. Spartans are encouraged to acquire it in the field if possible.

- Can Evade twice in quick succession before depleting the meter.
- Evade takes five seconds to recharge from a depleted meter; a half-empty meter takes four seconds to fully recharge.

Evade allows Elites to perform evasive maneuvers including forward and backward somersaults and side rolls. Evade cannot be triggered while airborne (whether from a jump or fall), but it is possible to leap immediately after using Evade to carry the momentum from the roll into the air. This is a great evasive tactic to escape gunfire aimed where the enemy expects you to finish your roll. Evade not only grants Elites a way to compact their stature and present a smaller target, but it is also gives the Elites a way to traverse ground faster. Evade isn't used during Campaign for obvious reasons, but it can be used in Matchmaking and Firefight.

BASIC TRAINING

This book contains well over 300 pages of strategy, tips, and information designed to help you master every nuance of *Halo: Reach*, but it's important to understand a few key gameplay elements before moving on to specific tactics. If you're new to the *Halo* universe, or if it's been awhile since you last took up arms against the Covenant, then these next few pages are for you.

SHIELDING AND HEALTH

The first rule to understand when playing *Halo: Reach* is you must acknowledge that you are mortal. Spartans have incredible abilities and are shrouded in the most advanced armor the human race has ever known, but beneath that armor is a man or woman made of flesh and bones "just like" us. And Covenant weaponry isn't designed to tickle—it's designed to kill.

The Spartan's armor flashes as the shields become disabled, and the screen bursts red as subsequent attacks damage the Spartan's health.

There are some attacks that are simply too powerful to survive even with full health and shield, but the Spartan's MJOLNIR armor and energy shield protect against most damage. As your Spartan is attacked, the shield gradually decreases in proportion to the amount of damage it is absorbing. Under normal situations (i.e., the Black Eye skull isn't active), the energy shield automatically recharges as soon as the player manages to avoid further damage. It takes roughly three seconds for the energy shield to replenish itself. Take cover and wait for the shield to replenish before stepping back into harm's way.

Sometimes, the enemy attacks are just too powerful for the shield to fully absorb, and the Spartan takes physical damage. The segmented blue health bar turns yellow as damage is taken (only once the shield is depleted), then eventually flashes red as the Spartan nears death. This health gauge automatically replenishes once the energy shield is recharged, depending on how much damage was suffered. The health gauge fully replenishes if only a small amount of damage was taken. On the other hand, the health gauge only partially replenishes (to roughly half-strength) if substantial damage was taken. The health gauge does not replenish lost health when a medium amount of damage is taken.

Fortunately, the Spartan needn't rely on health regeneration alone to heal. Medkits are scattered throughout Reach. Consult the maps in the walkthrough portion of this book, locate a Medkit, and press and hold ⊗ while standing next to it to fully replenish the health gauge. Medkits are single-use items, however, so don't use one unless you must. The other way to heal is by using a Drop Shield Armor Ability. Stand within the bubble for a few moments to gradually heal.

WEAPONS AND GRENADES

It should come as no surprise that a first-person shooter like *Halo: Reach* grants players an assortment of powerful weapons and grenades. Any weapon on the battlefield, whether it be UNSC or Covenant, can be picked up and used by anyone, regardless of race. The challenge lies in knowing which weapon is best for any given situation. This book's "Ordnance" and "Multiplayer Weapons" chapters provide a comprehensive analysis of each weapon in the game, along with pointers on how to get the most out of each of them. Nevertheless, there are a few basic rules regarding weapons usage worth knowing.

- Players can carry two weapons simultaneously. One is typically referred to as a primary weapon and the other as a secondary, but any combination of weapons is permissible. Players cannot, however, carry two identical weapons—moving over a weapon that you already carry automatically transfers the ammo from the weapon on the ground to the one you're carrying, if there is available ammo capacity. Players can also pick up a turret (Plasma Cannon or Machine Gun Turret) without dropping either of their equipped weapons—this is the only time players can carry a third weapon.

- There are two types of grenades in the game: Frag Grenades and Plasma Grenades. Both types inflict splash damage over a small area, but Frag Grenades bounce and slide across the ground, whereas a Plasma Grenade sticks to whatever it contacts first, whether it be an enemy, the ground, or even a vehicle. You can only carry up to two of each grenade type (four total) except in very specific situations during the Campaign, so use them wisely. Enemies are quite adept at evading grenades on the higher difficulty modes.
- The Designated Marksman Rifle (DMR) is one of the most lethal weapons ever issued by the UNSC, and its combination of precision, power, and rate of fire makes it an excellent weapon to carry for almost any situation. Regardless of the mode you're playing, the DMR should occupy one of your two weapon slots every chance you get. Get to know this weapon. *Love* this weapon. Be kind to it, and it will be kind to you. But most importantly of all, aim for the head of your enemies with it. The DMR grants the shooter sniper-like precision against medium-range enemies (and longer, in the right hands).
- One of the most longstanding tenets of *Halo* gameplay—and one certain to escape first-time players—is knowing to use weapons like the DMR or Magnum in partnership with plasma-based weapons. Weapon pairing is a critical aspect of *Halo*. Use a charged Plasma Pistol or the rapid-fire Plasma Repeater to quickly deplete an enemy's energy shield, then switch to a UNSC weapon and shoot that enemy in the head. Outside of heavy weapons and grenade-sticks, this is the most efficient way to kill a shielded enemy at range, such as an Elite, Brute Chieftain, or opponent in Matchmaking.
- Conservation of ammo and strategic reloading is another principal component of smart gameplay. Unless you're firing either of the turret guns, there is simply no reason to ever hold down the trigger and fire a steady barrage of bullets. Doing so only wastes ammo and gives your enemy the perfect opportunity to collect a "Load This!" medal when he snipes you while you're reloading. Every weapon—yes, even the Assault Rifle, Needler, and Spike Rifle—is most effective when firing individual rounds or in short, controlled bursts. It's also a good idea to get in the habit of reloading your weapon after every encounter. You never want to be caught with a partially loaded weapon, so reload often, and try to do so behind cover just in case.

STEALTH KILLS

One of the other new additions to the *Halo* world is the addition of stealthy Assassinations. Sneak up behind an enemy and press and hold the Right Bumper to perform an elaborate assassination. Stealth kills earn medals when playing in Firefight, Matchmaking, and in Campaign when scoring is turned on, but they are primarily designed to add a little extra flair to melee kills. Stealth kills are context-sensitive based on your position to the enemy, the type of enemy about to be killed, and whether or not you're running, jumping, or crouching. They range from a simple breaking of a Grunt's neck to an elaborate stabbing of an Elite.

Stealth kills are a useful tool in Firefight and Campaign, since they give you the opportunity to conserve ammo and silently kill enemies ranging from Grunts to Elites with a single melee attack. Their usefulness in Matchmaking is far less cut and dry. Though they are a fantastic way to stylishly eliminate—and humiliate—your opponents, performing an Assassination leaves you vulnerable to attacks from other players. It's impossible to interrupt a stealth kill once you initiate it, and the one to two seconds it takes for the animation to play out is more than enough time for a skilled opponent to headshot you. Worse yet, another player may even steal your kill by sniping the enemy you're in the midst of assassinating. This kill-stealing earns the thief the "Yoink" medal, effectively confirming their kill-stealing ways. But karma wins in the end...

RALLY POINTS AND CHECKPOINTS

There are a total of 11 named missions in the Campaign, nine of which constitute the bulk of the game. Each of these core nine missions is broken into two to four named sub-chapters, just as in *Halo 3*. When using the Campaign menu to choosing a mission to play, you are given the choice of selecting the mission start or a rally point, typically Rally Point Alpha or Rally Point Beta. These rally points do not necessarily sync up with the sub-chapter breaks within the mission, but they come relatively close. Consult the maps within the walkthrough to see where each Rally Point is located—this gives you a chance to replay portions of a mission to fine-tune your approach.

Rally points provide a place to load a portion of the mission, but that is not your only option for saving your progress. Every mission is chock-full of checkpoints, at which time your progress is automatically saved. You will respawn at the last checkpoint whenever you die during the Campaign. Some checkpoints trigger as you cross a certain location in the map, while others trigger after defeating a pre-determined set of enemies or by clearing a room or flipping a switch. Select "Continue Campaign" from the Main Menu to resume play right where you left off.

VEHICLE USAGE AND HIJACKING

One of the signature aspects of *Halo* combat has always been the inclusion of a diverse fleet of vehicles. Both the UNSC and Covenant sides boast a selection of vehicles that any player can use (Covenant won't drive UNSC vehicles in Campaign and Firefight, but they may use the a Warthog's turret) to travel faster across the map and deliver allies into battle. Vehicles not only provide transportation, but many of them are equipped with weapons systems far more powerful than the handheld ones you primarily rely on. Every vehicle, excluding the Ghost, can also carry at least one passenger or gunner. Gunners can either fire the vehicle's weapon or their own in certain instances—always give the A.I. controlled passenger the best weapon you have, since he or she is privy to unlimited ammo and excellent aim. Of course, one of the best vehicular attacks is the vehicle itself—driving straight into a crowd of unsuspecting enemies almost always nets you a few splatter kills.

Vehicles are not without their drawbacks. For starters, they present a pretty large target for the enemy and are typically a magnet for attacks. Stay on the move and maintain a safe distance (unless going for splatter kills) to avoid being targeted with a barrage of grenades and other explosives. Depending on the vehicle, those on board may or may not be protected from bullet and plasma fire, so keep in mind the direction the attacks are coming from and where your character is exposed.

Lastly, many of the vehicles can be hijacked. This is something that you can do to steal an enemy-driven vehicle, but also something the Covenant are capable of doing in Campaign and Firefight. It can be dangerous to get too close to a speeding vehicle, but hijacking is done by getting in close proximity to a vehicle and pressing ⓧ when prompted. Your character boards the vehicle, tosses the enemy driver out of it, then slips behind the wheel and takes over driving duties.

ALLIES AND FIRETEAMS

The Covenant army is a fearsome enemy, and far too numerous for one Spartan to handle alone. Fortunately, you won't have to. As part of Noble Team, you have as many as five other Spartans alongside you in combat. You needn't give your Noble Team allies any commands, nor worry about them taking damage and falling in battle. They are invincible and boast unlimited ammo. Listen to their instructions, watch how they engage the enemy, use them to your advantage.

You also encounter numerous UNSC Troopers (and even some members of an ODST team) during the Campaign who join you as part of a new feature called Fireteams. Approach these men to have them join your Fireteam. You can have up to five individual Troopers fighting alongside you as a Fireteam. Unlike the Noble Team members, these Fireteam troopers can—and will—perish in combat. You can't give them specific instructions, and you won't be penalized for their death, but you should try to keep them alive. Fireteam members are listed on-screen beside the Motion Tracker and can really help you suppress the enemy force. They are particularly helpful aboard vehicles, whether they are manning a gun or simply providing some additional firepower from the passenger seat.

WINTER CONTINGENCY

THERE'S A DISTURBANCE ON THE FRONTIER.

INTELLIGENCE BRIEFING

BASIC TACTICS

I Take point and descend the terraced bluffs to the distress beacon. Investigate the source of the smoke, then move east to the barn. Covenant soon enter the basement from the east; grab the Frag Grenades in the stairwell and use them to take out the Skirmishers on the lower floor. A small army of Grunt Infantry follows moments later. Stay inside the basement and take out the Grunts with headshots and a well-tossed grenade. Keep close to Noble Team and push on across the river and through the woods, eliminating any remaining Covies in the area.

II Drive the truck eastward towards the relay outpost. Carter and Jorge provide plenty of firepower, allowing you to focus on driving. Follow the main road to the southeast and clear out the Skirmishers and Grunts holing up in the structures along the way. Continue counter-clockwise along the road encircling the mountain to join up with a team of UNSC Troopers. Take cover near the barn and behind vehicles and clear an evacuation site. Covenant dropships then deploy teams of Jackals, Grunts, and Elites.

III Lead the team to the communications terminal inside the outpost. Activate night vision and accompany Jorge further inside. Swap the Assault Rifle for the DMR and advance past the Grunts and Jackals to a large room ahead. Take out the Grunts to flush out the Elite Hero in the area. Keep your distance and lure it into view of Jorge. Flip the switch on the junction terminal to reestablish communications.

CHAPTER-SPECIFIC ACHIEVEMENTS

WE'RE JUST GETTING STARTED: Complete the second mission on Normal or harder.

KEEP IT CLEAN: Kill seven moa during the first mission of the Campaign.

THEY'VE ALWAYS BEEN FASTER: Clear the first mission without setting foot in a vehicle.

MISSION OBJECTIVES

- Locate distress beacon.
- Investigate local structures.
- Engage hostile forces.
- Recon east valley.
- Locate missing trooper squad.
- Defend evac zone.
- Evac to relay outpost.
- Advance into relay outpost.
- Defend outpost entrance.
- Fallback into outpost.
- Eliminate hostiles inside outpost.

II

III

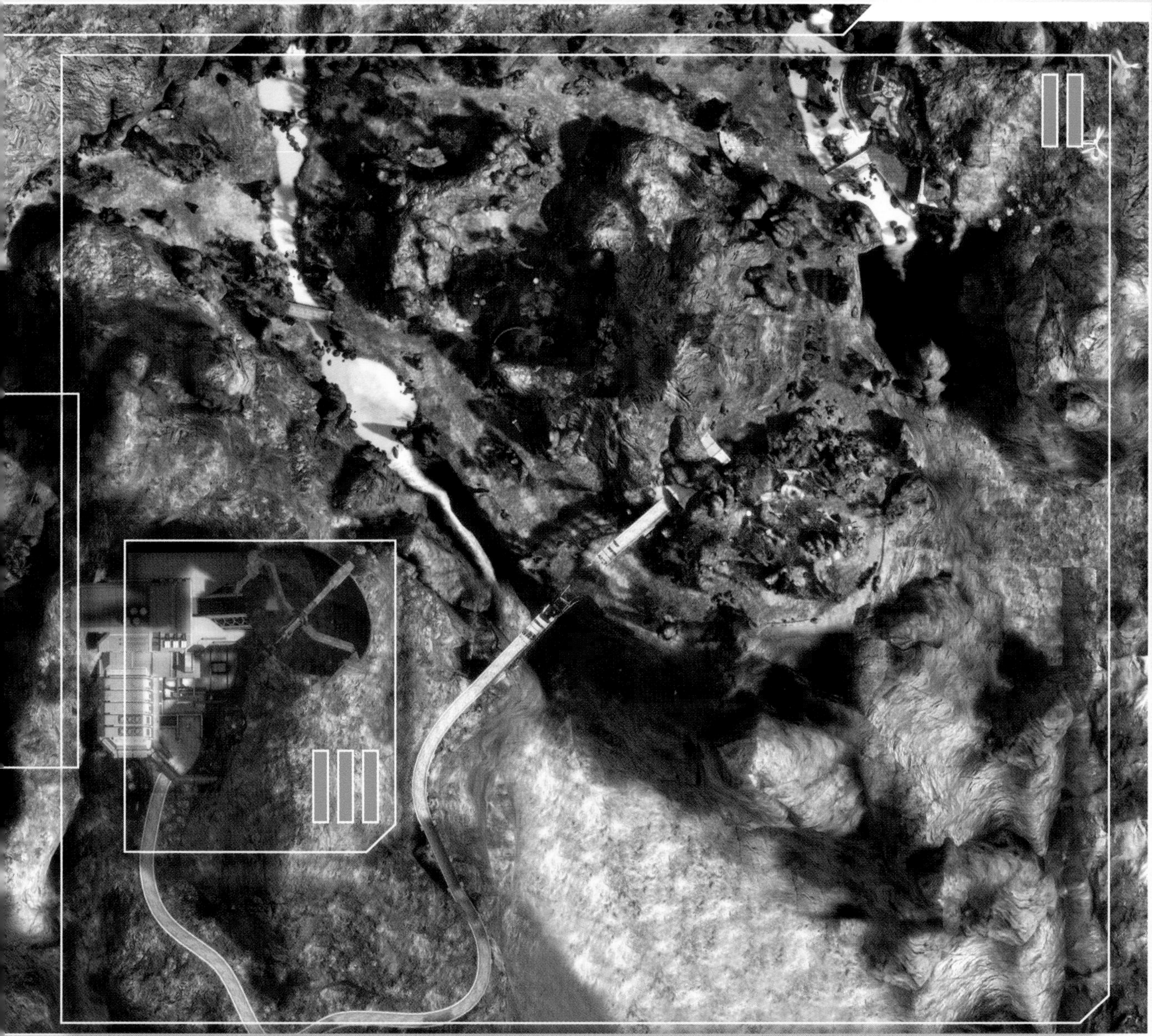

NOBLE ACTUAL

The "Noble Actual" mission listed in the campaign setup screen consists entirely of the opening cinematic that plays at the start of the campaign. Chances are you've already watched it, but we're not going to spoil anything for you on the outside chance you haven't. But if you were wondering why this guide begins with what appears to be the second mission, that's why. The first contains no gameplay. "Winter Contingency" is the true start of the campaign. Good luck, Spartan!

NOBLE TEAM

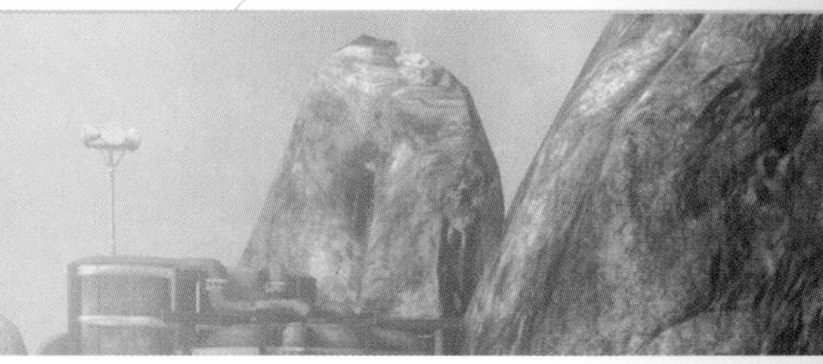

RECOMMENDED EQUIPMENT

M6G
MAGNUM

MA37
ASSAULT RIFLE

EASY/NORMAL

M6G
MAGNUM

MA37
ASSAULT RIFLE

HEROIC

M6G
MAGNUM

MA37
ASSAULT RIFLE

LEGENDARY

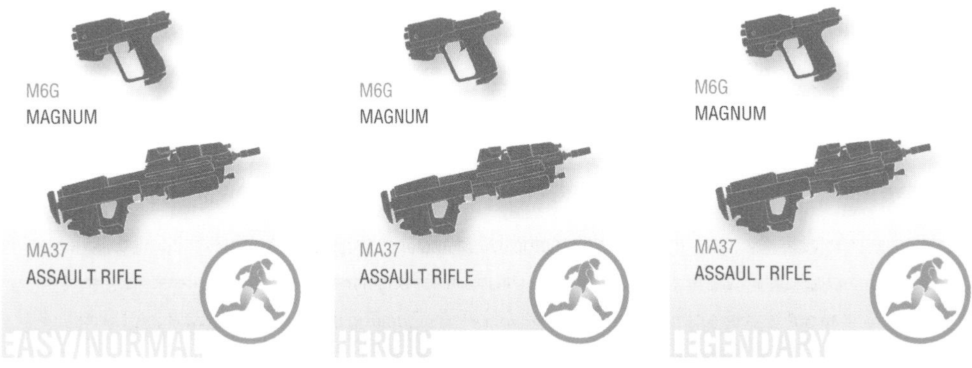

ENEMY FORCES

Covenant
Grunt Infantry
Grunt Specialist
Skirmisher Infantry
Skirmisher Specialist
Elite Specialist

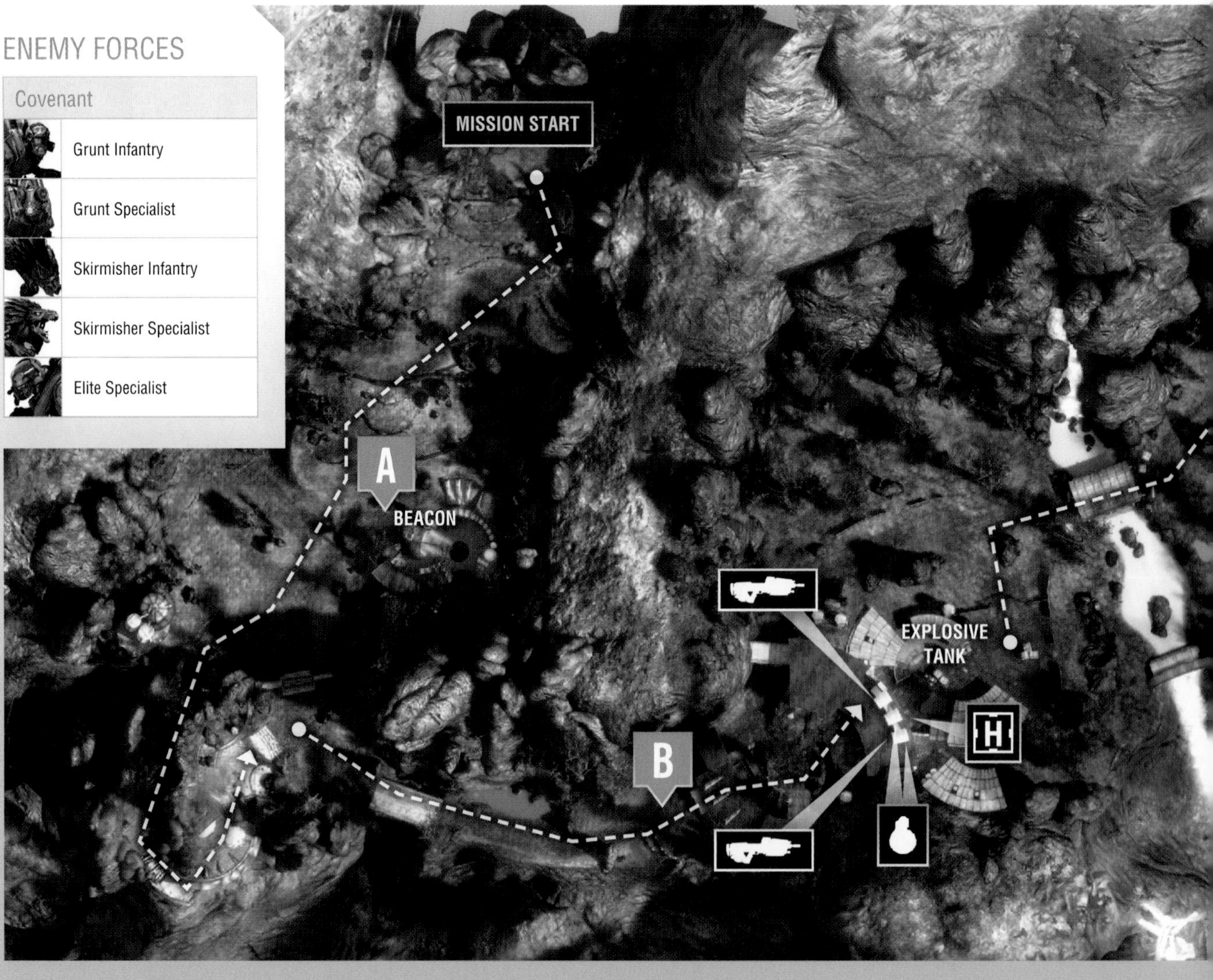

MISSION START
A
BEACON
B
EXPLOSIVE
TANK
H

CAMPAIGN

WELCOME
UNSC TRAINING
THE CAMPAIGN
M1: WINTER CONTINGENCY
M2: ONI
M3: NIGHTFALL
M4: TIP OF THE SPEAR
M5: LONG NIGHT OF SOLACE
M6: EXODUS
M7: NEW ALEXANDRIA
M8: THE PACKAGE
M9: THE PILLAR OF AUTUMN
FIREFIGHT
MULTIPLAYER
REFERENCE

OBJECTIVE

A: LOCATE DISTRESS BEACON

A distress beacon has been detected near Visegrad Relay Outpost. Investigate area and locate the beacon.

The Falcons set Noble Team down atop a terraced bluff, about 50 clicks from the outpost. Jun and Jorge stay on board to provide a set of eyes in the sky. Take point and descend the hillside to the south, where the distress beacon seems to be originating from. Follow the dirt path as it switchbacks its way down the terraces or you may opt to take a more direct approach. The choice is yours, but remember that Noble Six can suffer falling damage.

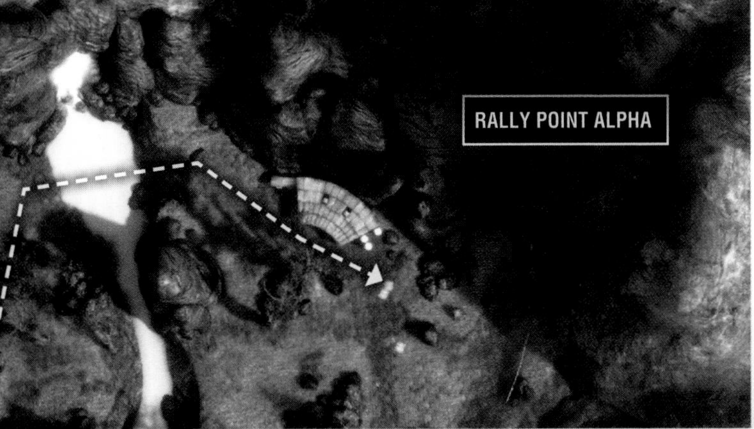

Regroup at the flaming Warthog near the base of the slope. Emile soon locates the beacon beneath the wooden pallets.

OBJECTIVE

B: INVESTIGATE LOCAL STRUCTURES

A military distress beacon has been discovered near Visegrad Relay. Investigate structures in the area and locate possible hostiles responsible.

Continue in the direction of the smoke billowing up from the distant structure. A gate blocks direct access, so you'll have to follow the narrow path along the cliffs to the southwest. Enter the circular house via the deck and exit through the gaping hole where its eastern wall used to be. Jun detects heat signatures inside the adjacent structure and sets Jorge down to help communicate with those inside—Jorge remains with you throughout the remainder of the mission.

Your team detects additional heat sources to the east. Use the Sprint Armor Ability to double-time it across the bridge and up the slope to the next building. Locate the bodies and continue through the building to the courtyard behind it. Move quickly and you may notice a pair of enemy blips on your motion tracker. Cross the courtyard into the barn where the rest of Noble Team awaits. And they're not alone...

Approach the window and use the Magnum to drop the Skirmisher standing atop the barn outside.

OBJECTIVE

C: ENGAGE HOSTILE FORCES

Covenant troops are responsible for attacking Visegrad Relay Outpost. Neutralize hostile forces in the area.

A Covenant force is approaching from the south, making their way into the basement of the building you occupy. Move down the stairs to the right, grab the Frag Grenades on the landing, and toss them at the lower entrance to catch the Skirmishers and Grunts as they approach. Stay inside the basement to maximize protection from incoming fire until all visible Covenant troops have been dispatched, and until Jun manages to chase off the Banshees overhead. Use the Medkit on the wall beside the door (if needed) and try to scavenge any Plasma Grenades the Grunts may have dropped before advancing. Look for enemies that wander near the red fuel tank outside the basement, on the left, and target it to detonate it for an environmental kill.

Play the angles from within the basement of the barn and eliminate the Grunts with headshots from either the Magnum or by detonating the fuel tank on the left.

EXPLODING GRUNT-PACKS

Grunts breathe a methane mixture and they carry a supply of this gas in tanks on their back. This air supply is volatile and can explode on impact. Aim for the packs to potentially detonate the methane tank and kill the Grunt. The explosion can be powerful enough to cause a chain-reaction with other Grunts, if they are standing side by side. For this reason, you must also be extra careful when using a melee attack against a Grunt, so you don't detonate the pack at close range.

Follow Jorge and Kat's lead out of the basement and take up a position behind the rocks that overlook the covered bridge to the northeast. A Phantom then deploys a number of additional Grunts and Skirmishers across the river, along with a single Elite. The Covenant forces often use the elevation to their advantage and hang back behind the rocks and trees uphill from the bridge. Push across the bridge with the rest of your team and throw grenades at the feet of any bunched-up Grunts or Skirmishers. The Skirmishers scamper amongst the trees and rocks, moving quickly in and out of cover while trying to outflank you. Stay near the mountains on the left and circle around to get the drop on them while they focus on your allies. A second drop ship soon deposits another batch of Grunts and multiple Elites. Hunt them down as you proceed on foot towards the relay outpost to the east. Use a Plasma Pistol dropped by a Grunt to deplete the Elites' shields prior to shooting them with the Magnum or Assault Rifle.

Maintain a safe distance from the Elites and use the Plasma Pistol to drain their shields. Use the rocks and bales of hay for cover.

"Get to work Noble, the war just came to Reach."

REBELS DON'T LEAVE PLASMA BURNS...

RECOMMENDED EQUIPMENT

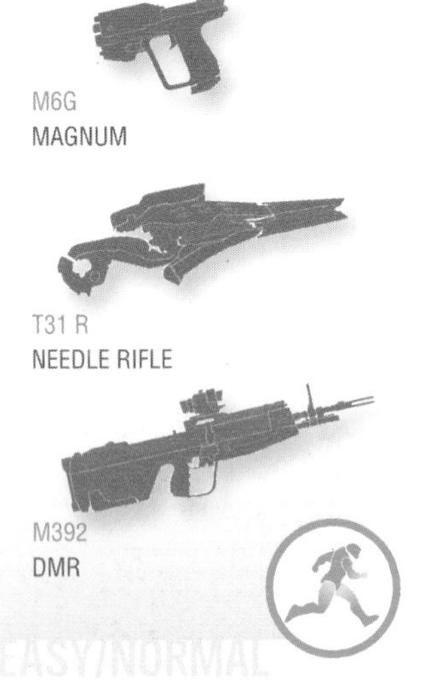

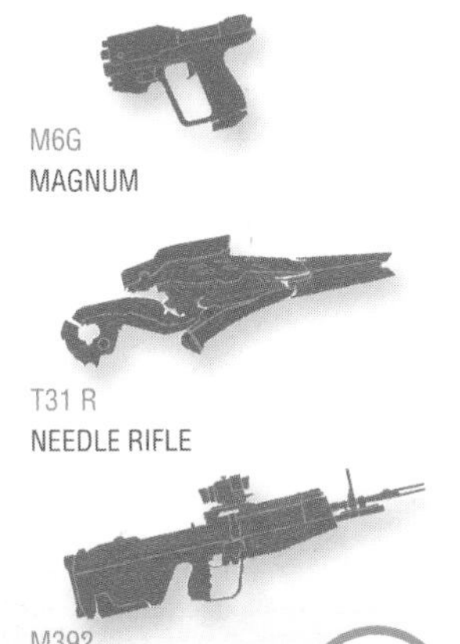

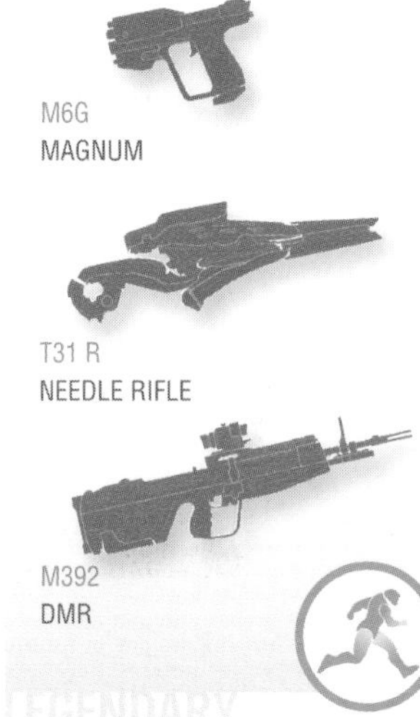

OBJECTIVE I

D: RECON EAST VALLEY

More hostile forces have been sighted to the southeast. Recon the east valley and draw the attention of Covenant forces while Kat and Emile infiltrate the relay outpost.

Slip behind the wheel of the truck (unless you are trying to earn the "They've Always Been Faster" Achievement) and let Carter and Jorge climb aboard—Emile and Kat arranged a pickup to get working on restoring the relay. The valley to the east is roughly shaped like a figure-eight, with several branching paths and loops. Covenant forces have taken hold of three primary structures located in the area. Even though the hostiles occupying these areas can be dealt with in any order, it's best to follow the path shown on the accompanying route map. This route is a bit circuitous but helps you maintain a full complement of Needle Rifle ammunition and eliminates any chance of you being caught in crossfire later on.

TRUCK
E
F
G
D
TRUCK
TRUCK
FORKLIFT

ENEMY FORCES

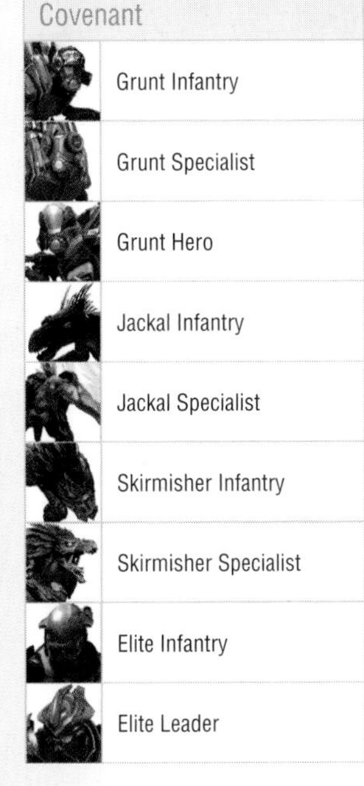

Covenant
Grunt Infantry
Grunt Specialist
Grunt Hero
Jackal Infantry
Jackal Specialist
Skirmisher Infantry
Skirmisher Specialist
Elite Infantry
Elite Leader

The valley tightens and turns to the east before opening up near a riverside barn. Follow the main road downhill to the southeast and cross the bridge near the flock of ostrich-like birds (called moa). Take the first left after crossing the bridge and follow the road back along the river to another fork that contains more Skirmishers. Eliminate this group so they don't flank your position later on, then take the right-hand fork to enter a narrow gorge that bisects the mountains in the center of the map.

Drive slowly so Jorge and Carter can eliminate the bands of Skirmishers encountered along the road. Hop out of the truck and steal all the Needle Rifle ammo you can find.

Drive the truck up and over the hill to the right of the drive-through basement and take up position on the roof of the building on the west side of the road. Strafe in and out of cover behind the mushroom-shaped chimney while using the Needle Rifle to pick off the Covenant holed up in the building on the other side of the road.

An elevated position with cover (like this chimney) makes a great vantage point for culling Covenant forces.

The path rejoins the main road near the river up ahead. Turn left and proceed under the ruined highway bridge. The road begins to curve to the northeast right where the second structure is located. Several farmers have survived the Covenant attack so far; try not to kill them while you gun down the Grunts and Elite in the vicinity. Again, keep your distance and use the Magnum and/or Needle Rifle to eliminate your enemies. The Needle Rifle delivers a super-combine explosion after just three direct hits, so aim carefully and fire quickly—the resulting explosion is usually enough to take out multiple enemies when they are clustered together.

LEGENDARY TACTICS

Play it safe when engaging Skirmishers and other enemies while you are in the truck on Legendary difficulty. Drive slower and try to keep the passenger side of the truck facing the Skirmishers so Carter can be most effective—and so Noble Six isn't catching any incoming projectiles. Hop out to collect the Needle Rifle ammo only when it's clear that Jorge and Carter have dispatched all the enemies in the area. Clearing the structures of Covenant requires a bit more patience and long-range targeting with the Needle Rifle and Magnum (if you have any ammo for it), but is otherwise similar to lesser difficulties. You'll also face some additional Elites, so consider having a Plasma-based weapon on hand.

OBJECTIVE

E: LOCATE MISSING TROOPER SQUAD

You've picked up a distress call from a squad of troopers. Locate the troopers and wait for evac.

Return to your truck (or commandeer the one parked by the structure) and follow the main perimeter road to the north where a dropship is hovering above a squad of UNSC Troopers. Eliminate any Skirmishers encountered en route and descend the path to the river. Spot the carcass of the Warthog on the left of the river and join the troopers there, but be careful not to park the truck over the DMR lying on the ground behind the Warthog; that's valuable UNSC property, Spartan!

Park the truck uphill from the Warthog, between the bales of hay and large boulder. This effectively extends the wall of cover for the troopers and Noble Team and puts you right next to the DMR when you exit the truck.

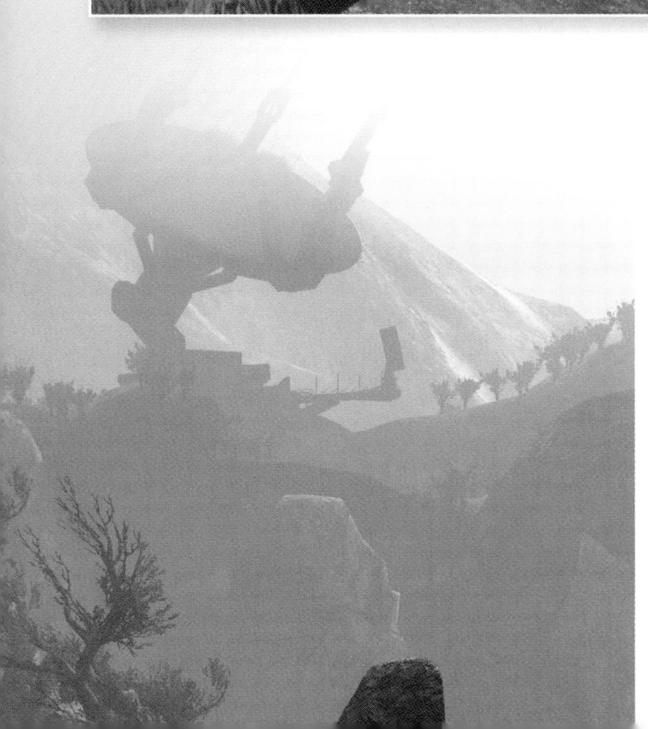

Designated Marksman Rifle

The weapon you see lying on the ground behind the burned-out Warthog is the Designated Marksman Rifle, known as the DMR. This piece of UNSC equipment may be the single best firearm ever sent into battle. The DMR is a high-powered, semi-automatic rifle that offers 2x zoom and pinpoint accuracy. The DMR combines the best of the Assault and Sniper Rifles into one all-purpose weapon that has the power, capacity, and rate-of-fire to down nearby enemies from the hip, as well as the precision and range to headshot distant foes. There are plenty of powerful weapons scattered across the world of Reach, but there's only one that should be on your person at all times. That's the DMR! Consult the Ordnance section of the Appendices on page 327 for additional stats and details about the DMR.

OBJECTIVE

F: DEFEND EVAC ZONE

The missing UNSC Trooper squad has been located. Defend evac zone.

Equip the DMR lying on the ground behind the Warthog and note the location of the two Medkits in front of the ruined vehicle. Leave the Grunts near the river for Jorge and the others to deal with, and circle around to the northwest to climb up onto the rocks high above the barn where the troopers are taking cover. This perch provides an excellent vantage point for sniping. And, thanks to the slight detour made while performing recon of the valley earlier, you won't need to worry about an outlying band of Skirmishers sneaking up on your rear.

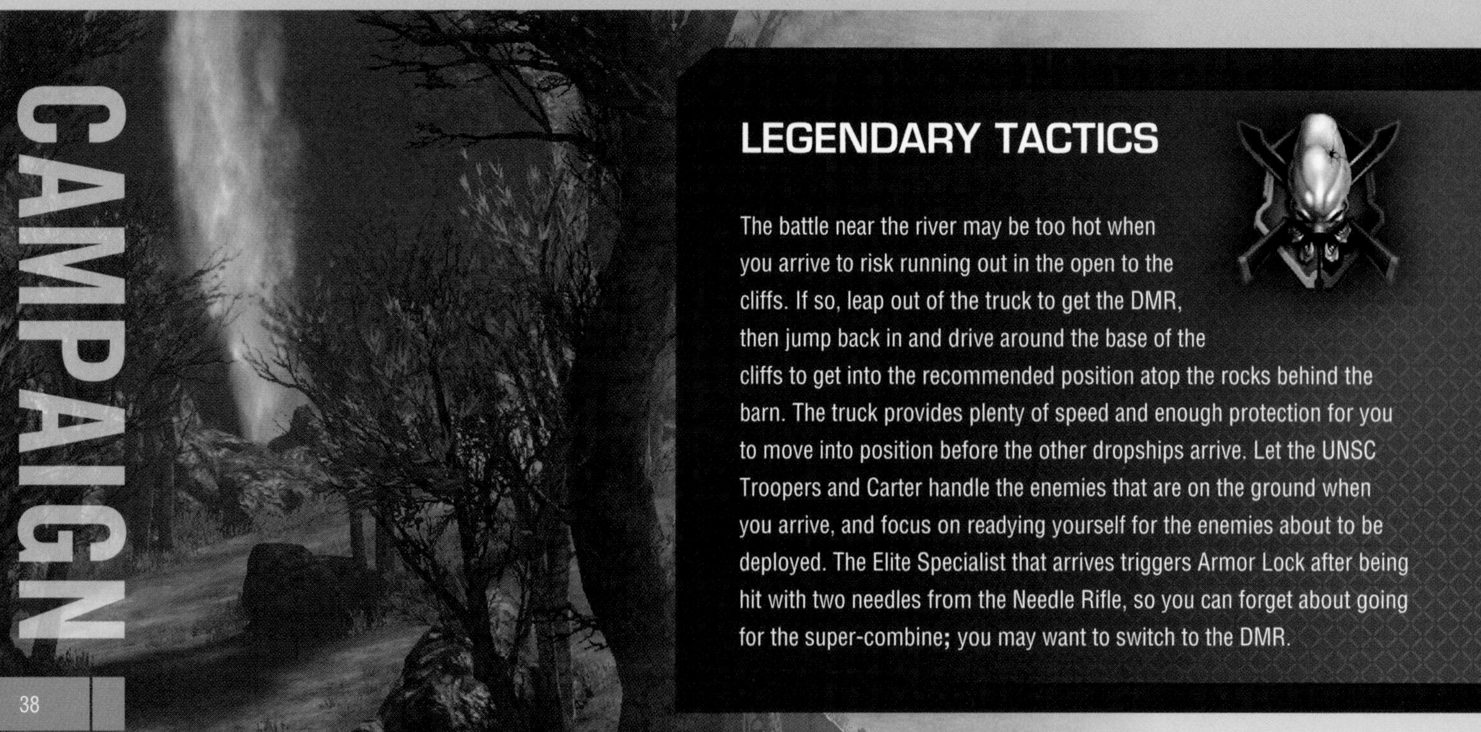

LEGENDARY TACTICS

The battle near the river may be too hot when you arrive to risk running out in the open to the cliffs. If so, leap out of the truck to get the DMR, then jump back in and drive around the base of the cliffs to get into the recommended position atop the rocks behind the barn. The truck provides plenty of speed and enough protection for you to move into position before the other dropships arrive. Let the UNSC Troopers and Carter handle the enemies that are on the ground when you arrive, and focus on readying yourself for the enemies about to be deployed. The Elite Specialist that arrives triggers Armor Lock after being hit with two needles from the Needle Rifle, so you can forget about going for the super-combine; you may want to switch to the DMR.

You don't have the necessary firepower to contend with the inbound dropships, so take cover behind the rocks until they depart the area, otherwise you are likely draw some very unwanted attention. The dropships deposit a large contingent of Covenant forces in and around the river. Maintain your position on the cliffs and use the DMR and any remaining Needle Rifle ammo in your possession to eliminate as many Covies as you can from that range. You may need to strafe to the edge of the cliff to the left in order to get a clean shot on the Jackals. Let your allies draw their attention towards the hay bales, then fire when their shields are turned.

Crouch behind the rocks atop this cliff and use the DMR to snipe enemies as they make their way up the riverbank.

SHOOTING AROUND THE SHIELD

Though it may seem as if there's no way to hit the Jackal head-on, thanks to their massive energy shield, you can actually target the Jackal's gun hand and blast them in the fingers. It takes a precise shot and is best done with the DMR, Magnum, Sniper Rifle, or Needle Rifle. Shoot the Jackal in the hand protruding beyond the side of the shield to get it to spin sideways in pain, thus opening up a clean line of sight at its head and chest.

The Elite Leader is sure to utilize the cover afforded it by the rocks and fallen log near the river and outlast the others. Leap down onto the roof of the barn and look for Plasma Grenades near the Grunt corpses—Plasma Grenades are great for depleting energy shields. Elites can evade grenade tosses fairly well by rolling to the side, so quickly throw one directly at the Elite in hopes of sticking it to him, then throw the other a few feet to the side, in the direction he's rolling.

Keep your distance and wait to engage the final Elite until the rest of the Covies have been eliminated.

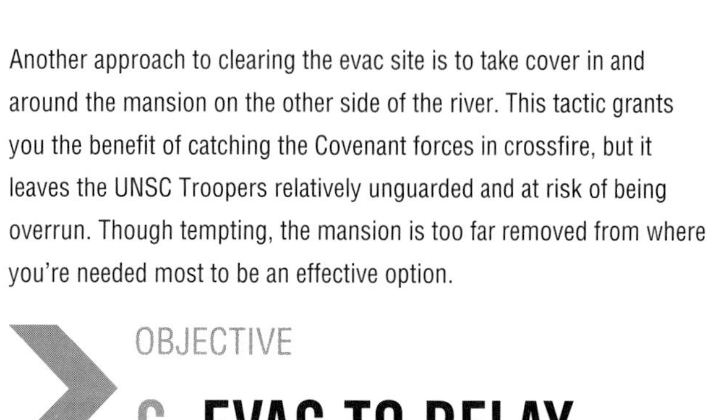

Another approach to clearing the evac site is to take cover in and around the mansion on the other side of the river. This tactic grants you the benefit of catching the Covenant forces in crossfire, but it leaves the UNSC Troopers relatively unguarded and at risk of being overrun. Though tempting, the mansion is too far removed from where you're needed most to be an effective option.

OBJECTIVE

G: EVAC TO RELAY OUTPOST

Evac site secure. Get aboard the Falcon and meet up with NOBLE Team at Visegrad Relay Outpost.

You've fulfilled your duty to never leave a soldier behind. The UNSC Troopers will be forever indebted to Noble Team. Now gather up any loose ammo or grenades near the river and use a Medkit to heal any injuries you've suffered during the firefight. The Falcon will come in for a landing any moment. Buckle in and enjoy the view as you fly around the cliffs to the Visegrad Relay Outpost.

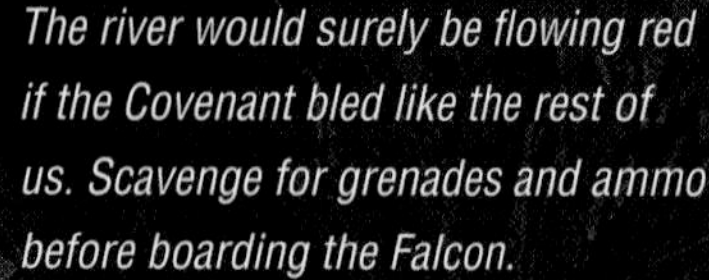

The river would surely be flowing red if the Covenant bled like the rest of us. Scavenge for grenades and ammo before boarding the Falcon.

OBJECTIVE

H: ADVANCE INTO RELAY OUTPOST

You've arrived at the Visegrad Relay Outpost. Advance inside.

The Falcon sets you, Carter, and Jorge down just in time to catch a number of Jackals and Grunts in crossfire. The rest of Noble Team is at the entrance to the outpost, where Kat was busy cutting through the door. Jorge then marches down the ramp, gunning down enemies as he proceeds forward. Take a moment to assassinate any nearby Covies facing down the hill towards the outpost, then make a beeline for the stairs leading up to the balcony on the left. Grab the DMR and Frag Grenade there, and jump down to assist the others near the entrance to the outpost. You can find additional DMR ammo and a Medkit inside the outpost entranceway.

Head up onto the balcony to get the DMR and Frag Grenade. Toss a Plasma Grenade down at the Jackals below.

OBJECTIVE

I: DEFEND OUTPOST ENTRANCE

Defend the entrance to Visegrad Relay Outpost until Kat can access to the front door.

That initial wave of Covenant wasn't the only one you'll encounter here. You and the rest of Noble Team must hold off two additional dropships' worth of Grunts, Jackals, and Elites (a similar mix to that of the riverbank battle) while Kat finishes hacking the controls to get into the base. Gather the maximum amount of DMR ammo from within the outpost entrance, then head back outside for battle.

LEGENDARY TACTICS

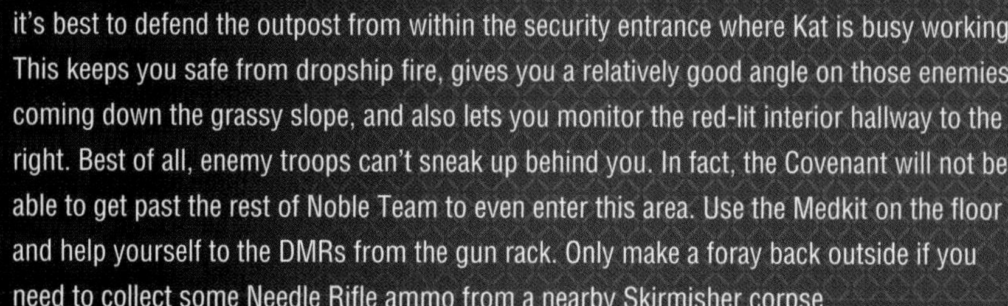

The firepower from the dropships, not to mention the greater aggressiveness and accuracy of the Grunts and Jackals, makes sticking near the barricade in front of the entrance too risky. Instead, it's best to defend the outpost from within the security entrance where Kat is busy working. This keeps you safe from dropship fire, gives you a relatively good angle on those enemies coming down the grassy slope, and also lets you monitor the red-lit interior hallway to the right. Best of all, enemy troops can't sneak up behind you. In fact, the Covenant will not be able to get past the rest of Noble Team to even enter this area. Use the Medkit on the floor and help yourself to the DMRs from the gun rack. Only make a foray back outside if you need to collect some Needle Rifle ammo from a nearby Skirmisher corpse.

Use the small green crate to leap onto the much larger bundle of crates behind the pillar. This provides you with the height needed to snipe the Covy units as they disembark the dropships, and also gives you plenty of cover. Sidestep in and out of cover behind the pillar to target enemies as they descend the ramp leading down to the base. Most of the enemies descend the right-hand side of the ramp and make their way towards the entrance where the rest of Noble Team is posted, but some try to flank to the left of the truck and barrels (if you didn't block that route with the other truck). It's these latter enemies that are your top concern—be sure to watch your motion tracker and peer around the left-hand side of the pillar to take out any would-be flankers before they get too close.

Standing atop this stack of crates gives you just enough of a height advantage to be able to snipe across the entire approach.

Try to put any grenades you have to good use by lobbing one or two at the very top of the sloping driveway just as the Covenant leap out of the dropship. Frag Grenades may very well bounce up and over their heads if thrown straight at them, so try to ricochet one off the wall on either side of the driveway. If you're going to use a Plasma Grenade instead, wait until the enemies descend past the parked truck before making the throw.

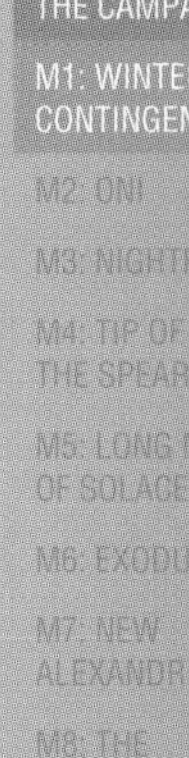

Once the majority of the enemies from the second dropship have descended the ramped driveway, leap down off the crates, but don't go far! The horizontal beams of the barrier are spaced just far enough apart to provide an excellent line of fire while offering plenty of protection from the opposition. Emile and the others cover the area near the entrance, so focus your fire on those enemies coming around from the left. Some of the Covenant will probably make their way through the red-lit structure to the far right—past the operable forklift truck—so don't overlook this area entirely.

OBJECTIVE

J: FALLBACK INTO OUTPOST

Noble Team has gained access to Visegrad Relay Outpost. Get inside and neutralize hostile forces.

Kat finishes hacking the controls just as a third dropship arrives on the scene. Keep count with how many dropships have deployed Covenants and get ready to run inside as soon as the third dropship makes its deposit. Go ahead and fire off a few shots if you like (again, for scoring purposes only), then head inside. Restock your DMR ammunition supplies and use the Medkit on the floor if necessary. It's time to head inside.

A wise Spartan knows when it's best to retreat. As soon as the third dropship deploys its alien cargo, retreat inside the outpost.

The lights are out inside the outpost, but Noble Six's helmet is equipped with night vision. Tap left on the Control Pad to toggle night vision on and off. Lead the way to the computer terminals around the corner to the left so Kat can get to work.

SKELETON CREW

RECOMMENDED EQUIPMENT

EASY/NORMAL

M392
DMR

MA37
ASSAULT RIFLE

HEROIC

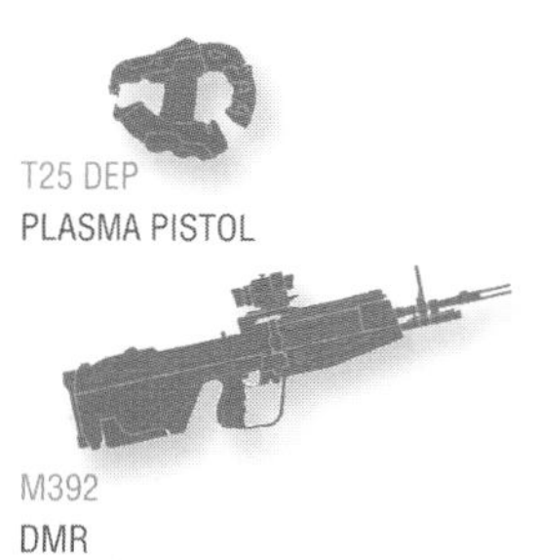

T25 DEP
PLASMA PISTOL

M392
DMR

MA37
ASSAULT RIFLE

LEGENDARY

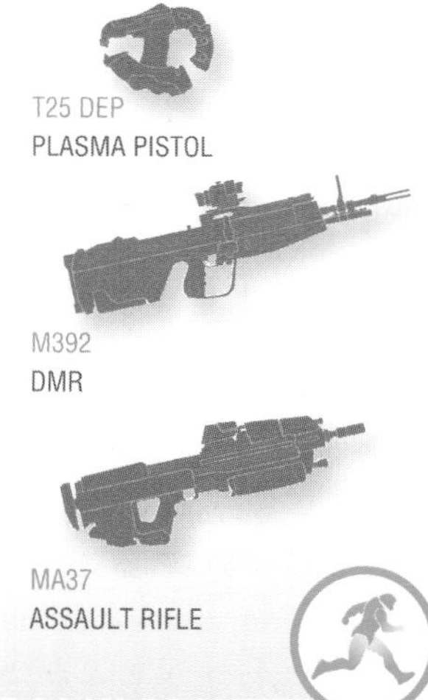

T25 DEP
PLASMA PISTOL

M392
DMR

MA37
ASSAULT RIFLE

ENEMY FORCES

Covenant
Grunt Infantry
Grunt Specialist
Grunt Hero
Jackal Infantry
Jackal Specialist
Skirmisher Infantry
Skirmisher Specialist
Elite Infantry
Elite Leader

OBJECTIVE I

K: ELIMINATE HOSTILES INSIDE OUTPOST

Neutralize enemies inside Visegrad Relay Outpost.

Accompany Jorge into the darkened corridor leading deeper into the outpost and immediately swap out the Magnum for the DMR on the rack near the door. An Elite and several Grunts and Jackals, are lying in wait at the end of the hall. They'll open fire as soon as you round the corner, so stay low and make use of the crates and barrels for cover. Stay close to Jorge and advance slowly. Target the fuel tanks on the right to both take out the early rushers and weaken the Elite. Jorge pushes up the center of the room, giving you the opportunity to swing wide and follow the left-hand side of the room. This gives you plenty of opportunity to rack up a string of headshots with the DMR. Just remember to return to the gun rack to grab a fresh supply of ammo before pushing deeper into the base.

Use the DMR to soften up the Elite from afar before targeting the fuel tanks. Allow the lesser enemies to approach before detonating the combustibles.

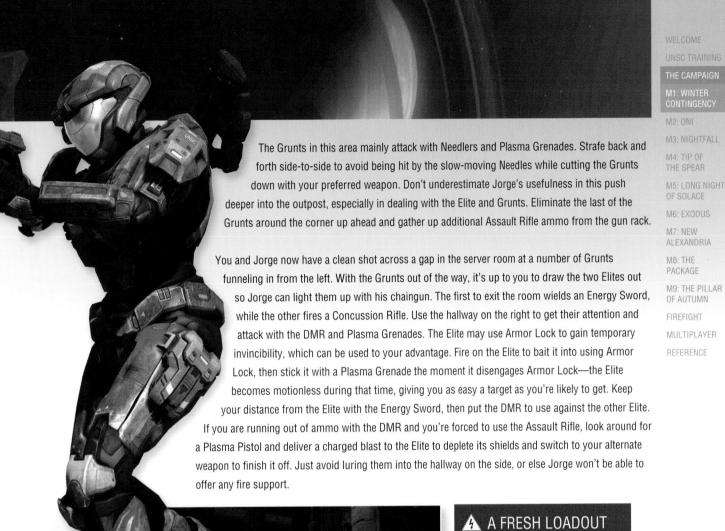

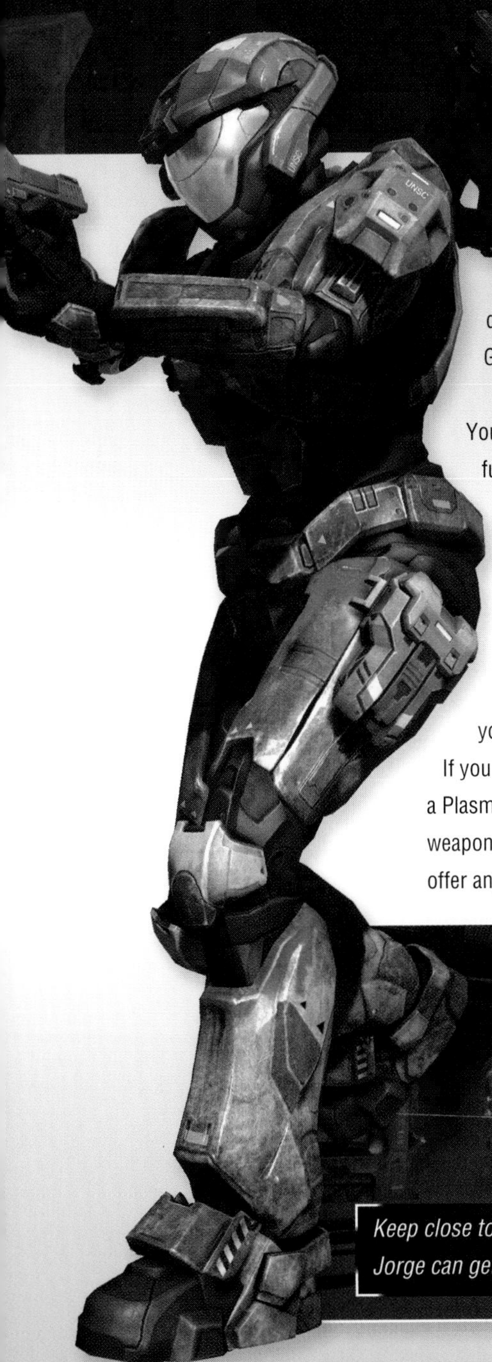

The Grunts in this area mainly attack with Needlers and Plasma Grenades. Strafe back and forth side-to-side to avoid being hit by the slow-moving Needles while cutting the Grunts down with your preferred weapon. Don't underestimate Jorge's usefulness in this push deeper into the outpost, especially in dealing with the Elite and Grunts. Eliminate the last of the Grunts around the corner up ahead and gather up additional Assault Rifle ammo from the gun rack.

You and Jorge now have a clean shot across a gap in the server room at a number of Grunts funneling in from the left. With the Grunts out of the way, it's up to you to draw the two Elites out so Jorge can light them up with his chaingun. The first to exit the room wields an Energy Sword, while the other fires a Concussion Rifle. Use the hallway on the right to get their attention and attack with the DMR and Plasma Grenades. The Elite may use Armor Lock to gain temporary invincibility, which can be used to your advantage. Fire on the Elite to bait it into using Armor Lock, then stick it with a Plasma Grenade the moment it disengages Armor Lock—the Elite becomes motionless during that time, giving you as easy a target as you're likely to get. Keep your distance from the Elite with the Energy Sword, then put the DMR to use against the other Elite. If you are running out of ammo with the DMR and you're forced to use the Assault Rifle, look around for a Plasma Pistol and deliver a charged blast to the Elite to deplete its shields and switch to your alternate weapon to finish it off. Just avoid luring them into the hallway on the side, or else Jorge won't be able to offer any fire support.

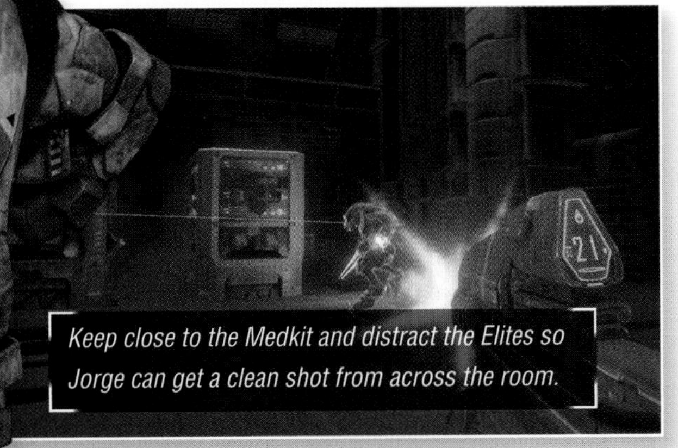

Keep close to the Medkit and distract the Elites so Jorge can get a clean shot from across the room.

A FRESH LOADOUT DOWN BELOW

If your current loadout just isn't working for you, leap over the railing into the lower storage area to find a Shotgun and Drop Shield equipment. This pairing of weaponry and Armor Ability makes it easier to take on the Elite with the Energy Sword.

The room where the Elites were located houses a junction box that Kat needs activated. Head inside and power it on so she can restore the relay. Colonel Holland is anxiously awaiting your report.

"There are no rebels. The Covenant are on Reach."

ONI: SWORD BASE

COVENANT ARE ATTACKING A VITAL ONI BASE. DRIVE THE BASTARDS OFF.

INTELLIGENCE BRIEFING

BASIC TACTICS

I Fight alongside Kat as you advance northward towards the bulk of the Covenant forces. Locate the Sniper Rifle on the walkway in the northwest corner and retreat to the bridge, so you can get a clear line of sight on many of the enemies. Eliminate the forces that deploy from the Phantom and advance down the road towards the eastern gate. Use the DMR or Concussion Rifle to eliminate the Skirmishers.

II Use the Target Locator to destroy the twin Wraiths outside the eastern gate, then drive west to the Airview Outpost and activate the anti-air gun positioned there. Continue the drive eastward along the cliffs to the Farragut Station and activate the comm. array. Use the long-range weapons at Farragut to eliminate the Covenant forces occupying the structure with the generator. Only then can you power on the equipment and activate the comm. array.

III Use the Gauss Warthog to destroy the Revenants and Ghosts on your way back to the eastern gate, and slowly proceed into the basement of Sword Base. Use the DMR and Frag Grenades to eliminate the Hunters from a safe distance. Or, if you're out of DMR ammo, use the Shotguns that are available in conjunction with Armor Lock to take them on at close range.

IV Work with your Fireteam and Jorge to clear Sword Base of enemies on your ascent up the atrium. Use the Plasma Pistol and DMR to take out the Elite Hero with the Fuel Rod Cannon, then carry the powerful weapon up to the roof where Covenant with Active Camouflage await. Defeat the final foes on the rooftop before equipping one of the Rocket Launchers near the UNSC corpses and blasting the Banshees out of the sky.

CHAPTER-SPECIFIC ACHIEVEMENTS

PROTOCOL DICTATES ACTION: Complete the 3rd mission on Normal or harder.

TWO CORPSES IN ONE GRAVE: Kill 2 vehicles at once with the Target Locator during the 3rd mission.

MISSION OBJECTIVES

- Defend courtyard.
- Protect exterior outposts.
- Activate anti-air gun.
- Find Farragut Outpost.
- Activate comm. array.
- Return to base.
- Find top floor breach.
- Secure breach and eliminate air forces.

II

IV

I

III

THE BEST DEFENSE...

RECOMMENDED EQUIPMENT

OBJECTIVE

A: DEFEND COURTYARD

The Covenant forces are assaulting the entrance to Sword Base. Confront them before they can breach it.

Noble Six and Kat are set down in the courtyard outside Sword Base just in time to assist a squad of UNSC Troopers who are repelling the first wave of Covenant. The enemies primarily arrive from the north, beyond a row of regenerating energy shields. Most foes stick to the ground, but some (including multiple Elites and several Jackals) may ascend to the upper walkway and push forward towards the bridge. The Covenant troops then spread out between the shields on the ground to the north of the bridge and the road curving downhill to the east.

Charging up the road guns blazing is a surefire way to trigger the end of Noble Six. To that end, this battle is best fought from a distance. Use the DMR to eliminate the four Grunts near the barricades under the bridge, then slowly move up the left-hand ramp. A fallen trooper near the door that leads inside has left behind additional DMR ammo, Frag Grenades, and a Medkit. Eliminate any enemies in the vicinity of the bridge and bide your time under cover until the Phantom vacates the area. The Phantom deploys additional enemies, including an Elite Specialist wielding a Concussion Rifle. Kat and the others definitely help eliminate the lesser foes, but the Elite Specialist and other Elites are probably yours to fight.

Proceed north along the western walkway and swap out the Assault Rifle for the Sniper Rifle on the balcony. Retreat to the area near the bridge and bombard the enemies taking cover behind the energy shields with the four Frag Grenades from the start of your mission. Aim your throws so that you kill a few enemies, but also disable the stationary energy shields. This temporarily opens up a clean line of sight for you to fire on the others with the Sniper Rifle. Focus your shots on the Elite Specialist first, then tear up the rest. The stragglers may withdraw out of sight from the bridge. Reposition yourself to the northwest corner of the upper walkway to finish them off.

Continue along the western walkway to the ramp at the far end to lure the remaining Elites towards the forklift truck. Open fire on the forklift to catch the Elites in a massive explosion.

CAMPAIGN

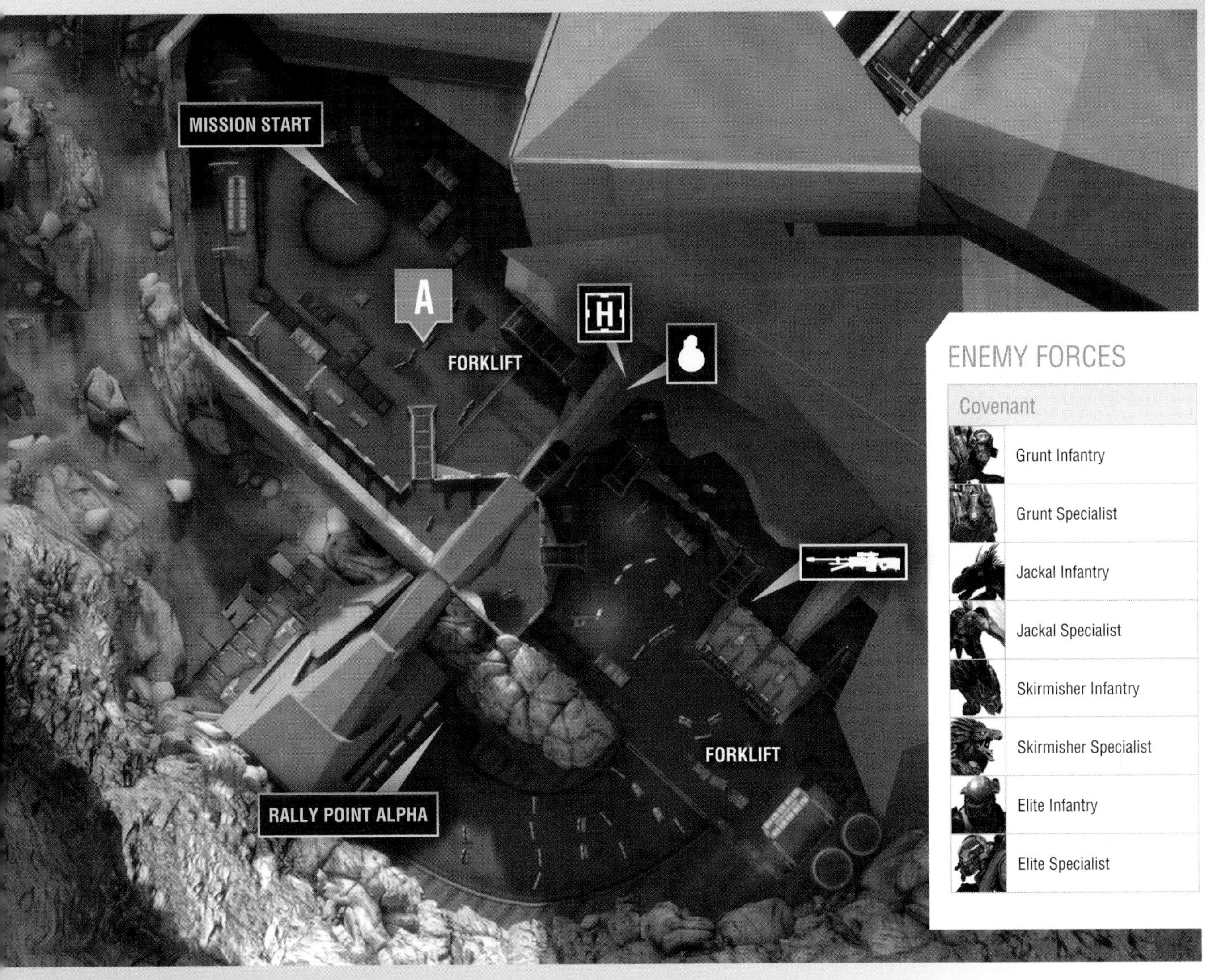

MISSION START
A
H
FORKLIFT
FORKLIFT
RALLY POINT ALPHA

ENEMY FORCES

Covenant
Grunt Infantry
Grunt Specialist
Jackal Infantry
Jackal Specialist
Skirmisher Infantry
Skirmisher Specialist
Elite Infantry
Elite Specialist

The Concussion Rifle dropped by the Elite Specialist may have a few useful rounds left in it. If so, swap out an empty Sniper Rifle for it and approach the curving road that descends to the southeast. You should be able to find a few Plasma Grenades on the ground as well. An Elite Infantry and band of Skirmishers are hiding beyond the barricades halfway down the road. Toss a grenade to flush them out and rapidly fire the Concussion Rifle to hit the fast-moving Skirmishers, or use the DMR to target their heads. You can also target the green fusion coil and trigger a minor detonation that could severely harm, or even kill, any Covenant troops adjacent to it. If you are in trouble, fall back up the hill to lure the Covenant towards Kat and the UNSC Troopers hanging back. Descend the ramp towards the Ordnance icon on the HUD and the gate leading east.

The Covies down the road move in and out of cover behind the barriers around the bend. Fire the Concussion Rifle rapidly to increase your odds of a direct hit.

GET THE HELL OFF MY LAWN!

RECOMMENDED EQUIPMENT

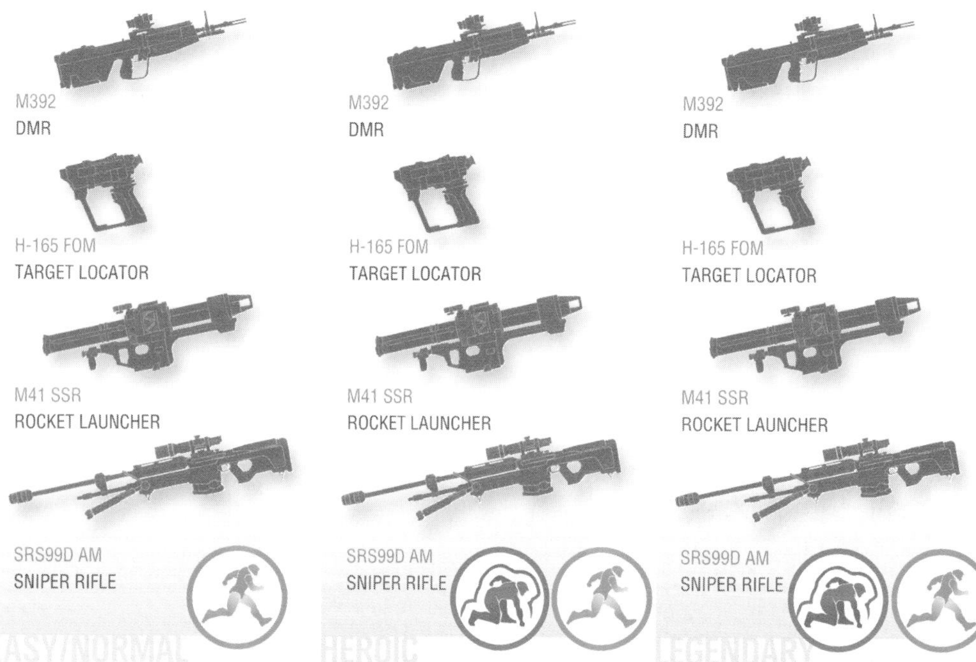

OBJECTIVE

B: PROTECT EXTERIOR OUTPOSTS

Two outposts to the east and west are under attack. To the east—Farragut Station and a vital comm. array. To the west—Airview and a powerful anti-air cannon. Get them both up and running.

Find the Target Locator in the weapon case inside the gate area (near the supply of Armor Lock pickups and DMRs) and equip it alongside the DMR. This is a good time to take up position behind the large boulder on the right outside the gate and use the Target Locator to trigger an orbital strike on the first of two Wraiths to enter the area. The first Wraith emerges from the southwest and blows up the Warthog downhill from Sword Base. Aim the targeting reticule at the Wraith (or slightly behind it in hopes that the second Wraith will also enter the target area) and hold the Fire Weapon button until target-lock is achieved. Immediately switch to the DMR—you don't need to continue holding the Target Locator after it turns red. Switch to your alternate weapon and pick off the Grunts and Elite moving in on foot from the southeast.

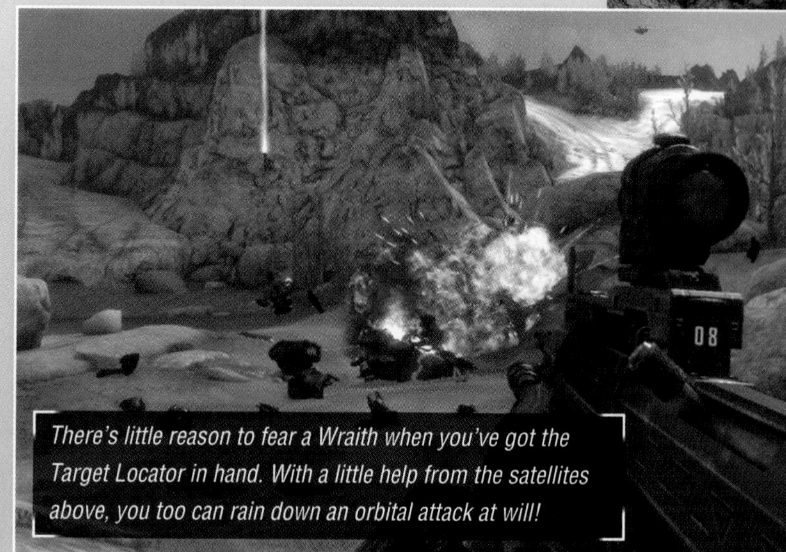

There's little reason to fear a Wraith when you've got the Target Locator in hand. With a little help from the satellites above, you too can rain down an orbital attack at will!

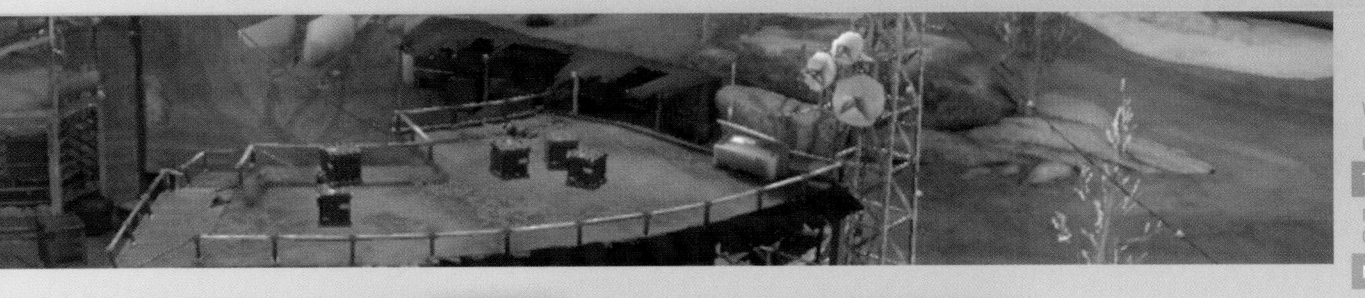

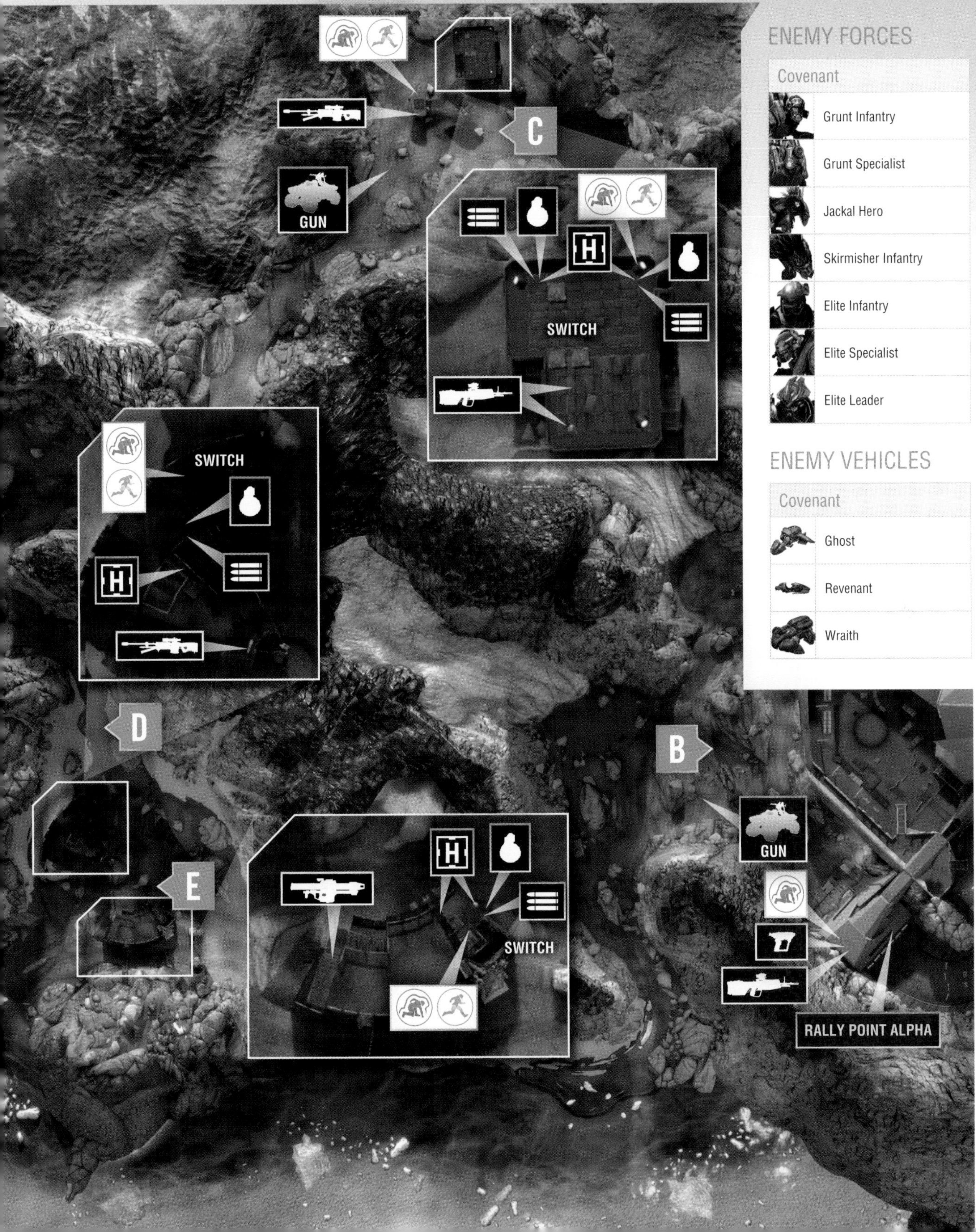

C
GUN
H
SWITCH
SWITCH
H
D
B
GUN
E
H
SWITCH
RALLY POINT ALPHA

ENEMY FORCES

Covenant
Grunt Infantry
Grunt Specialist
Jackal Hero
Skirmisher Infantry
Elite Infantry
Elite Specialist
Elite Leader

ENEMY VEHICLES

Covenant
Ghost
Revenant
Wraith

WELCOME
UNSC TRAINING
THE CAMPAIGN
M1: WINTER CONTINGENCY
M2: ONI
M3: NIGHTFALL
M4: TIP OF THE SPEAR
M5: LONG NIGHT OF SOLACE
M6: EXODUS
M7: NEW ALEXANDRIA
M8: THE PACKAGE
M9: THE PILLAR OF AUTUMN
FIREFIGHT
MULTIPLAYER
REFERENCE

TWO CORPSES IN ONE GRAVE

It's possible to unlock this Achievement right outside the eastern gate when the two Wraiths start making their way up the hill on Normal mode. It's risky because it takes awhile for them to get close enough to one another, but it is possible. Make sure you have Armor Lock equipped to withstand the bombardment from the Wraiths as you lure them towards one another. Another opportunity to unlock this Achievement—and one with a higher success rate on tougher difficulty settings—comes on the drive back to the eastern gate during the "Minimum Safe Distance" portion of the mission. Save one strike with the Target Locator for the drive back from Farragut Station and hop out of the Warthog as soon as you spot the three Revenants. Achieve lock-on upon the middle Revenant and hope it stays close to one of the others. You may even get lucky and take out three vehicles with a single strike!

A second Wraith appears moments after the first. Try to destroy it by shooting the gunner, hopping aboard, and planting a grenade to conserve the Target Locator's final strike. Otherwise, maintain your distance while the Target Locator recharges and keep your eyes skyward to watch for incoming plasma shots from the Wraith. Even though these attacks can be easily avoided with the Sprint ability equipped, those playing with scoring turned on can earn extra Medals by using Armor Lock to absorb the blast. Eliminate all Covy forces and vehicles in the vicinity.

Target Locator

The Target Locator is a brand-new weapon in the *Halo* universe that makes it possible to unleash an artillery attack on a given target. Once lock-on has been achieved, orbital satellites in the vicinity fire a barrage of over a half-dozen deadly blasts, effectively neutralizing anything and everyone within a radius of roughly 20 feet. The Target Locator has an LED display that shows the number of strikes current conditions allow for, as well as its recharge status. The Target Locator takes more than ten seconds to recharge before it can be used for a subsequent attack. The Target Locator makes a rather limited appearance in the Campaign, but is a vital and much-used addition to Firefight mode. Refer to the Ordnance section of the Appendices on page 320 for additional information and statistics about the Target Locator.

Now you must accompany Kat to two outposts—a comm. array to the east and an anti-aircraft gun to the west—and get them both online. Although you can tackle these objectives in either order, it's best to head west first, especially if you managed to save the second strike with the Target Locator. Slip behind the wheel of the Warthog and wait for Kat and a UNSC trooper to hop aboard. Turn right at the piles of Wraith debris and head west to Airview Base first. Drive alongside the exterior wall of Sword Base to be in position to run over the Grunts beyond the boulders up ahead, then hit the brakes and buy some time for your gunner to take out the Grunt driving the Ghost over the hill.

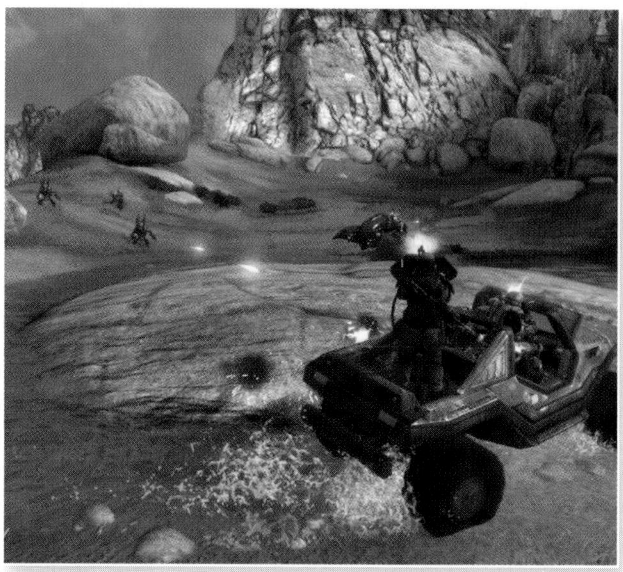

A road that forms a loop from Sword Base to the south connects these two outposts. Give your gunner and Kat a clear shot at the Ghost's driver by circling around it.

BE THE WHEELMAN

Learning to drive the Warthog in combat effectively takes practice and an understanding of not only the vehicle's handling and off-road capabilities, but also an understanding of the situation through the eyes of your gunner. One of the most common rookie mistakes is driving straight towards the enemy. Not only does this risk a head-on collision (not good for anybody), but the driver of the other vehicle is also shielded from your gunner's attacks by his vehicle's cowl. Instead, it's much more effective—and safer—to circle around enemy vehicles in a smooth, broad clockwise turn. This keeps the Warthog (and driver, in particular) safe from direct fire and allows the gunner and passenger to get a clean shot on the enemy driver.

OBJECTIVE

C: ACTIVATE ANTI-AIR GUN

WELCOME
UNSC TRAINING
THE CAMPAIGN
M1: WINTER CONTINGENCY
M2: ONI
M3: NIGHTFALL
M4: TIP OF THE SPEAR
M5: LONG NIGHT OF SOLACE
M6: EXODUS
M7: NEW ALEXANDRIA
M8: THE PACKAGE
M9: THE PILLAR OF AUTUMN
FIREFIGHT
MULTIPLAYER
REFERENCE

Airview's AA gun can help clear the skies and fend off the Covenant invasion. Reset the gun and defend the base from the remaining invaders.

Park the Warthog behind the boulders atop the hill on the left to avoid any plasma fire from the Phantom lurking overhead. You can find the control terminal for the anti-air gun on top of the large structure on the west side of the clearing, a structure heavily crawling with Covenant. If possible, use the Target Locator to lock-on either the Elite Specialist on the roof or the Elite Leader near the entrance to the outpost—the blast radius can encircle the entire facility and all but wipes out the initial Covenant contingent. This is a great use of the second Target Locator strike and should give you a rather hefty multi-kill Medal if you are playing with scoring turned on.

Take cover behind the rocks atop the hill and either use a final Target Locator strike or the DMR to eliminate those Elites!

STRATEGIC PARKING

It's not unheard of for an ambitious (some may say heretic) Grunt or Elite to climb aboard a parked Warthog and use the turret against you. Limit the damage they can do by parking the Warthog on the far side of objects (boulders, walls, etc.) opposite from the direction you're heading. Covenant forces will not drive the Warthog, so you needn't worry about them jacking your ride.

A second Phantom deploys a pair of Ghosts after another deposits a number of reinforcements. Use the time in between to run (Kat and the trooper may use the Warthog to engage other Covies in the area) across the clearing and enter the base from the south. There is a Medkit and extra munitions on the west exterior wall of the facility, as well as inside in the southwest corner. Be patient and deal with any immediate Covenant threats before going onto the roof to activate the guns. Beware of the two Elite Specialists that likely enter the outpost's main floor or fly up to meet you on the roof—one may even have a Plasma Launcher! Hit them with any Plasma Grenades you scavenged to deplete their shields, then finish them off with the DMR.

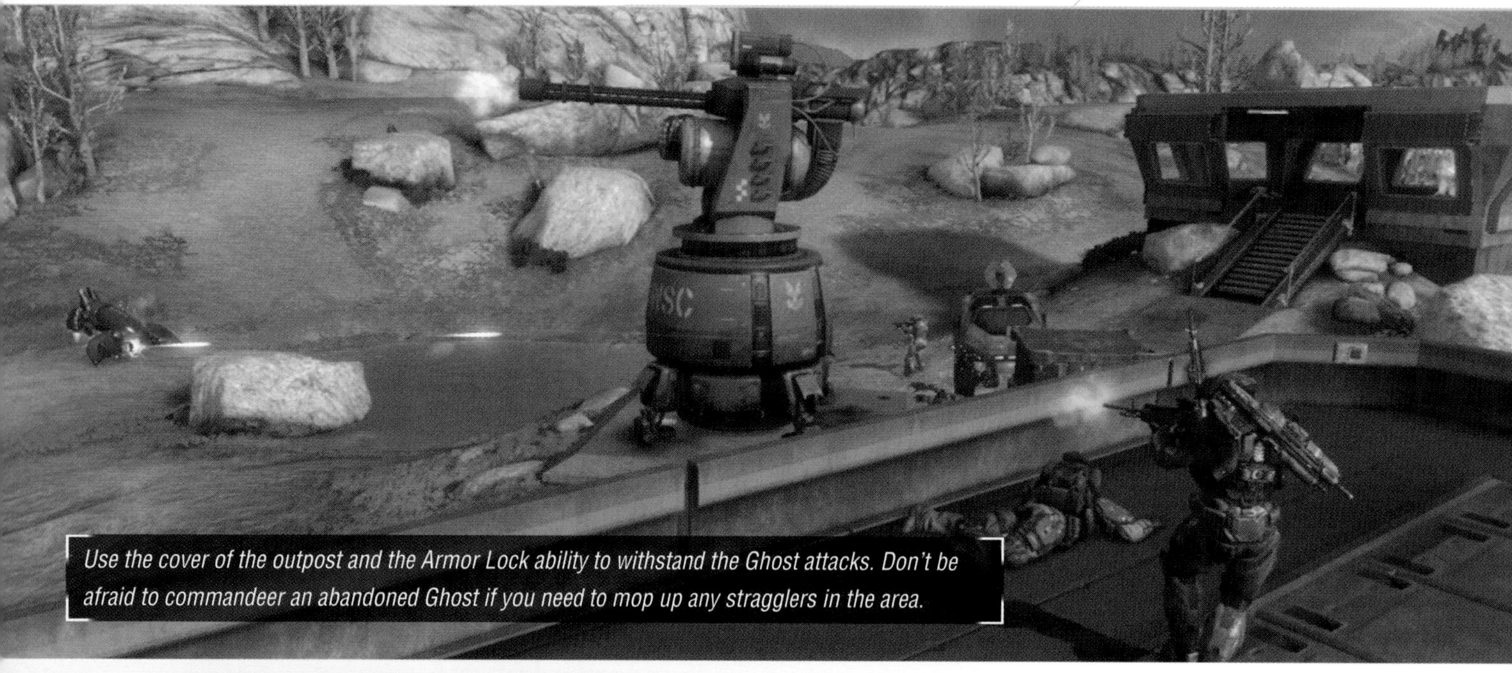

Use the cover of the outpost and the Armor Lock ability to withstand the Ghost attacks. Don't be afraid to commandeer an abandoned Ghost if you need to mop up any stragglers in the area.

Activate the anti-air guns via the controls on the roof of the outpost and eliminate any remaining Covenant. The guns soon come to life and open fire on the Phantom hovering off the coast to the north, knocking it out of the sky and clearing the way for a Pelican to deliver another Warthog. Stay on the roof of the structure and use the DMR to take out the drivers of the Ghost before heading back out into the open. Take a moment to collect the Sniper Rifle and Sprint ability in the watchtower south of the AA gun.

OBJECTIVE

D: FIND FARRAGUT OUTPOST

Find Farragut Outpost to the east.

Use the Warthog to continue the drive east to Farragut Outpost and the communications array that needs powering on. The road twists and turns, forming a counter-clockwise loop from Sword Base, past Airview Base, to Farragut Outpost. You'll encounter at least one Ghost en route, as well as a number of Grunts just before the road seemingly disappears at the base of a rockslide. Take out the enemies and enter the narrow valley uphill from where the two streams join. The comm. array is just around the corner.

A drop ship unloads a small squad of Covies and a pair of Ghosts near the base of the glacier. Run over the Grunts and swing wide to give your gunner a clear shot at the Ghost.

OBJECTIVE

E: ACTIVATE COMM. ARRAY

Farragut Station houses a comm. array that helps relay word of the attack. Power it up and switch it on.

Covenant forces heavily guard Farragut Outpost, but the biggest threat comes from the two Elites piloting the Revenant. The Revenant is not unlike a Ghost in appearance and mobility, but it packs the firepower of the Wraith—eliminating the Revenant upon arrival at this outpost is your top priority when playing on Heroic or Legendary difficulty. Skilled drivers can do it with the Warthog, but this is a risky proposition. As luck would have it, there's a Rocket Launcher perfectly suited for the job that has been left in the structure near the radio tower.

Drive the Warthog straight across the outpost to the east and park behind the building, near the radio tower. Enter from the rear and head up the stairs to the second floor and temporarily swap out the Sniper Rifle for the Rocket Launcher. Use the Rocket Launcher to destroy the Revenant, then return to where you found it and swap it for the Sniper Rifle. Stay inside this wooden shelter on the second floor of the outpost and aim between the gap in the boards to snipe the Jackals and Elites on the walkway across the yard.

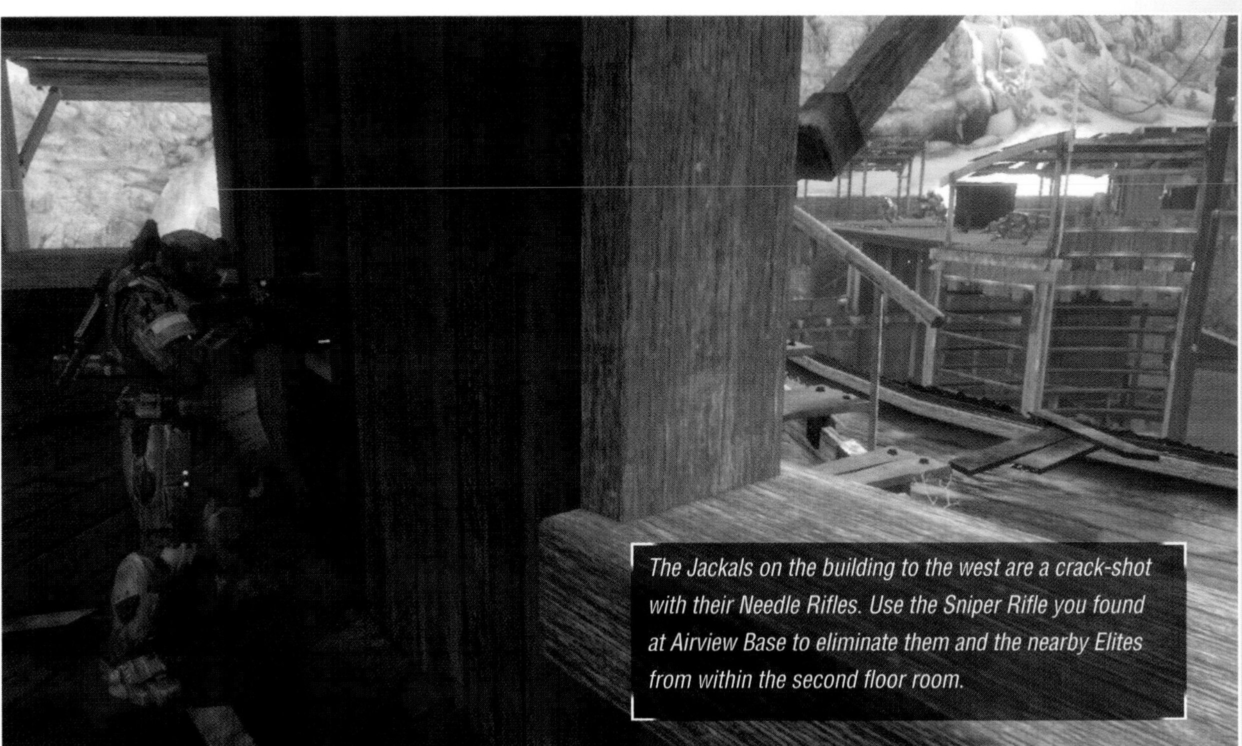

The Jackals on the building to the west are a crack-shot with their Needle Rifles. Use the Sniper Rifle you found at Airview Base to eliminate them and the nearby Elites from within the second floor room.

The building with the Rocket Launcher does indeed contain the controls for the comm. array, but you must first power the system on. This means crossing the yard to the other building and flipping the switch inside. Grab the Rocket Launcher and make your way across the clearing to the other structure in a clockwise looping direction, and ascend the stairs on the left. Pause to eliminate any Elites or Grunts near the snow behind the building with the Rocket Launcher, then head inside and throw the lever to power-up the comm. array.

Sprint back across the clearing to the building you were in earlier and scale the steps to the uppermost level where the comm. array controls are located. A drop ship arrives within moments to set down an army of Skirmishers and Grunts. Aim the Rocket Launcher at the drop zone on either side and kill as many as you can the moment they land. Locate the Sniper Rifle on the second floor deck of the building with the generator before leaving the area—it comes in handy in an upcoming battle. Finish off the remaining hostiles with Kat and the Warthog.

MINIMUM SAFE DISTANCE

RECOMMENDED EQUIPMENT

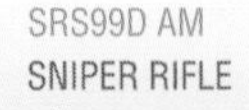

M392
DMR

SRS99D AM
SNIPER RIFLE

EASY/NORMAL

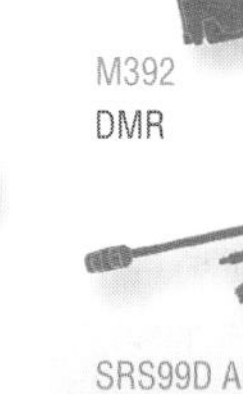

M392
DMR

SRS99D AM
SNIPER RIFLE

HEROIC

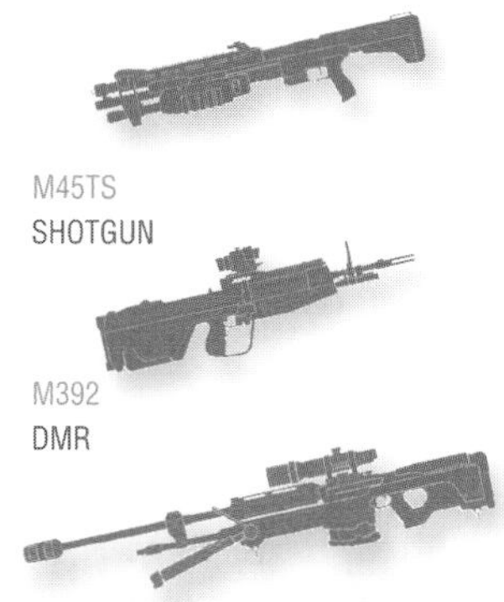

M45TS
SHOTGUN

M392
DMR

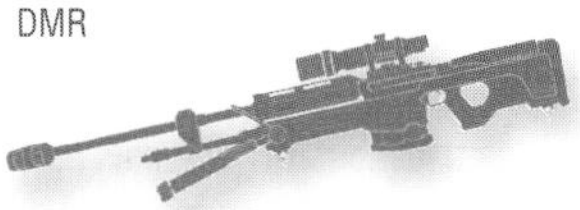

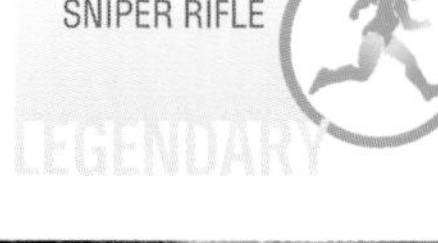

SRS99D AM
SNIPER RIFLE

LEGENDARY

RALLY POINT BRAVO

GAUSS

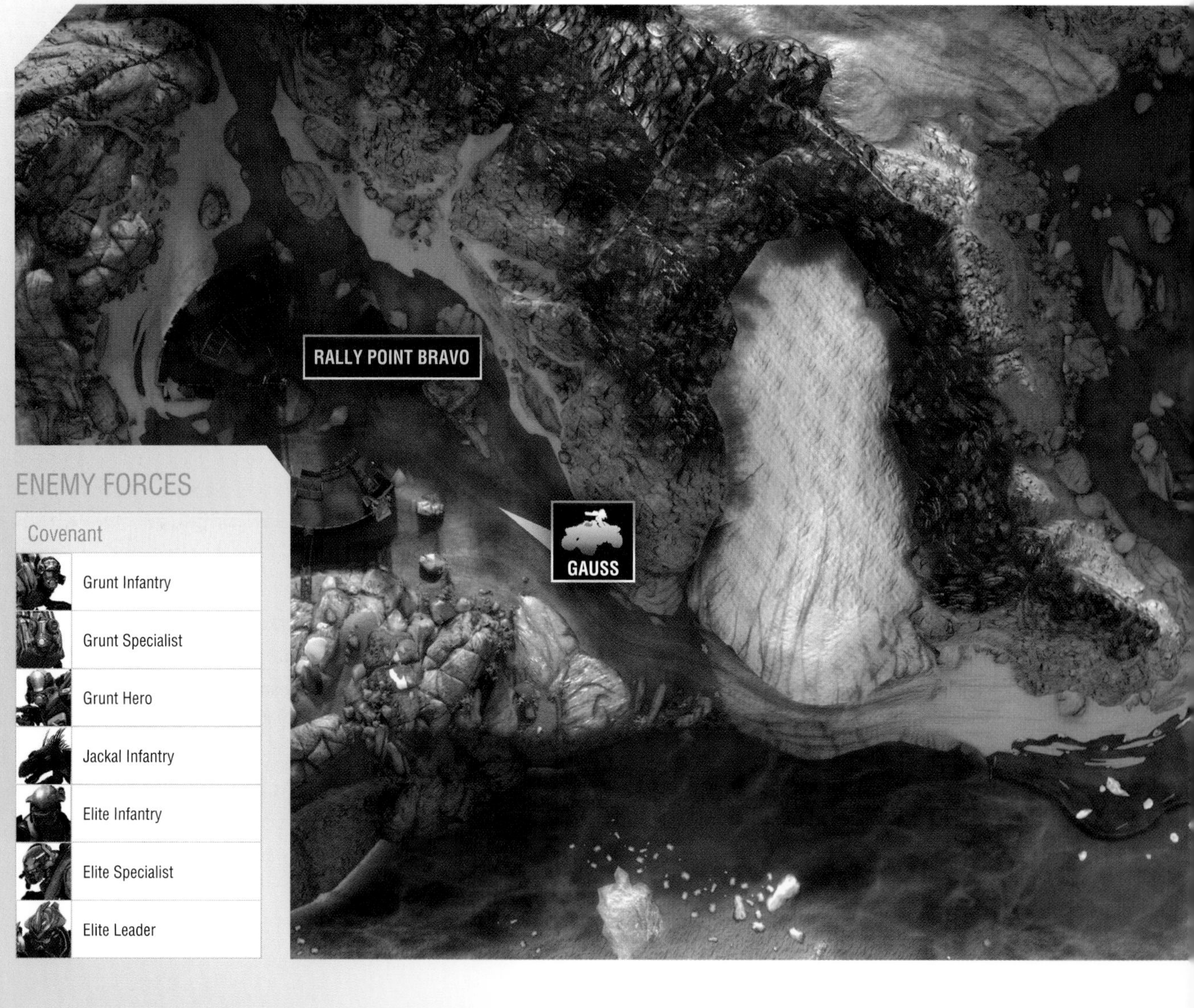

ENEMY FORCES

Covenant
Grunt Infantry
Grunt Specialist
Grunt Hero
Jackal Infantry
Elite Infantry
Elite Specialist
Elite Leader

CAMPAIGN

OBJECTIVE

F: RETURN TO BASE

The Covenant forces have found another route into Sword Base. Return to the base and find the source of the attack.

Another Pelican arrives on the scene to deploy a Warthog mounted with a Gauss Cannon. Unlike the standard machine gun mounted on most Warthogs, the Gauss Cannon emits a devastating energy beam capable of destroying most enemies and light class vehicles with a single blast. The trooper that descended with the Warthog is a crack-shot, so you don't need to worry about manning it yourself. Stay behind the wheel and continue east, around the snout of the glacier and past the ice floe to the Sword Base entrance.

Ascend the hill on the left-hand path, then follow the stream between the rocks to avoid enemy fire and to give your gunner a clean shot at the Revenants.

Open the eastern gate via the controls on the left and drive up to the barriers at the base of the curving road. A number of Covenant troops, including an Elite, are making their way down the road towards your position. Hop out of the driver's seat and use the Gauss Cannon to blast all of the visible Covies on the road. Two additional Elites lurk around the bend in the road atop the hill, so have the DMR ready and try to gather up any Plasma Grenades you can find. Whatever you do, don't use up your Sniper Rifle ammo on the Elites.

ENEMY VEHICLES

Covenant	
	Ghost
	Revenant

A pair of Hunters makes their way into the center of this ground-level entrance, just as you descend the ramp directly ahead. Take cover behind the central pillar (near the gun rack) and open fire with the Sniper Rifle you took from Farragut Station. Grunts generally work their way out of the elevator room in the southwest corner (where you must ultimately go), so watch your motion tracker for additional blips and take them out. Of course, your main concern must be the Hunters. These heavy foes can be defeated with four rounds to the back and one to the neck with the Sniper Rifle.

Take cover near the entrance and use the supply of Frag Grenades and your remaining Sniper Rifle ammo to take out the Hunters heading inside.

Hunters are the most heavily armored of all of the enemies Noble Team encounters. They move slowly and purposefully and make every effort to cover their weak points with heavy plated armor and shields. Even though a Hunter's armor can eventually be blown to pieces if it takes enough damage from explosive or concussive forces, your best bet at damaging the Hunter is to aim at the fleshy skin on its neck and back. The safest way to do this is to keep your distance and target the orange skin of the Hunter's neck with the Sniper Rifle or DMR. Another option is to move in close with the Assault Rifle or Shotgun. Hunters switch to a melee-style attack when confronted at close range, so use Sprint to avoid their powerful strikes and open fire on their blind sides. Since the Hunters always strike with their shield (in their left hand), you can consistently evade their melee attacks by always dodging to the left (as viewed facing them). Whichever technique you employ, it's absolutely vital to stay in cover and avoid the Hunter's green energy blasts, as a single direct hit is enough to kill Noble Six on contact.

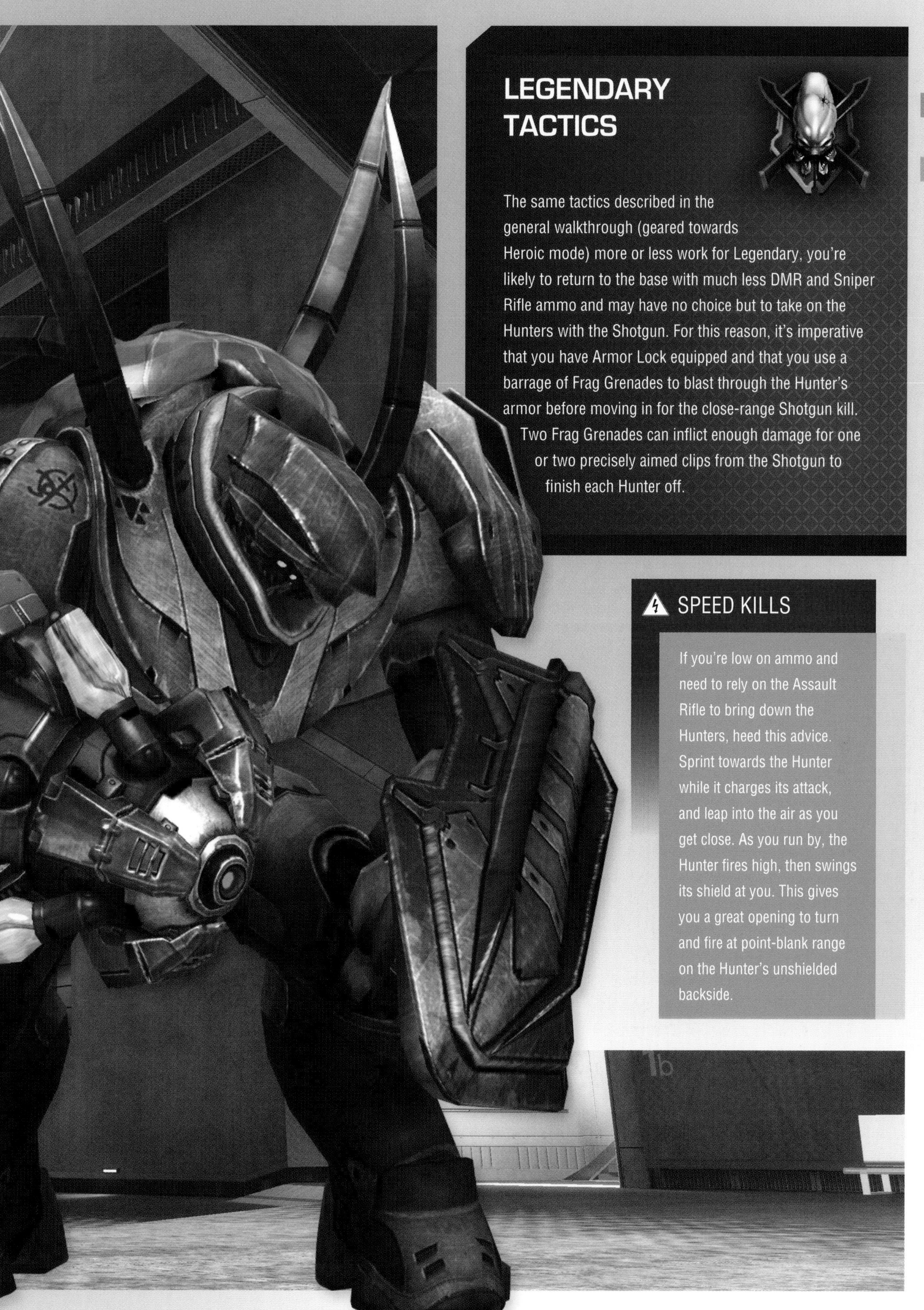

LEGENDARY TACTICS

The same tactics described in the general walkthrough (geared towards Heroic mode) more or less work for Legendary, you're likely to return to the base with much less DMR and Sniper Rifle ammo and may have no choice but to take on the Hunters with the Shotgun. For this reason, it's imperative that you have Armor Lock equipped and that you use a barrage of Frag Grenades to blast through the Hunter's armor before moving in for the close-range Shotgun kill. Two Frag Grenades can inflict enough damage for one or two precisely aimed clips from the Shotgun to finish each Hunter off.

SPEED KILLS

If you're low on ammo and need to rely on the Assault Rifle to bring down the Hunters, heed this advice. Sprint towards the Hunter while it charges its attack, and leap into the air as you get close. As you run by, the Hunter fires high, then swings its shield at you. This gives you a great opening to turn and fire at point-blank range on the Hunter's unshielded backside.

IV OFFICE OF NAVAL INTELLIGENCE

RECOMMENDED EQUIPMENT

ENEMY FORCES

Covenant
Grunt Infantry
Grunt Specialist
Jackal Infantry
Jackal Specialist
Jackal Hero
Skirmisher Infantry
Elite Infantry
Elite Hero
Elite Specialist
Elite Leader

OBJECTIVE

G: FIND TOP FLOOR BREACH

The Covenant troops have blasted a hole in the top of Sword Base and are attacking from above. Get to the top of the base.

Take the elevator to the secure entrance to Sword Base and quickly fight your way past the Grunts and Elite in the lobby to the main atrium, where a number of UNSC Troopers are pinned down. Pick up any dropped grenades on your way out of the lobby, along with a Plasma Pistol if one is available. Fire charged blasts (or multiple shots) from the Plasma Pistol at the Jackals to employ an EMP effect on their shields, then switch to the DMR and take them down. Join Jun and the troopers near the sculpture and assist them in finishing off any other Jackals in the area. Walking past the troopers gets them to serve as your Fireteam. They'll accompany you for the rest of the mission (or until they die) and offer fire support and help with distracting the enemy. You don't have to give them any commands, nor are you penalized if they perish. They simply follow you where you go and provide whatever help they can muster.

Work with the rest of Noble Team and any Fireteam members you have to clear out the Jackals and Elite on the lower level of the Atrium. Don't be afraid to let them take point and soak up some of the attacks.

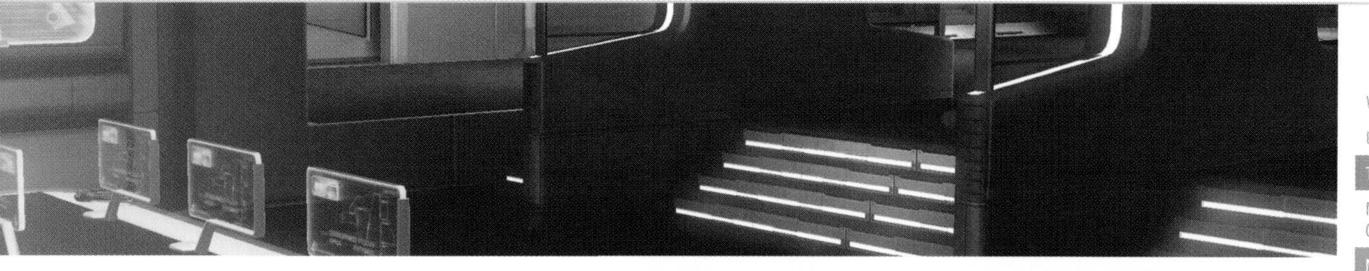

Sword Base is a multi-level facility that spirals upwards around a towering central atrium. Emile is at the top floor trying to clear a squadron of Banshees taking flight from a Corvette, and he needs your assistance. Lead your comrades into the room on the north side of the atrium and begin the long counter-clockwise ascent. Look for opportunities to snipe across the atrium from one side to the other before crossing any of the bridges. This can be done with either the DMR or Needle Rifle, the latter of which should be in high abundance. Don't overlook the gun rack on the second floor of the north side—the DMR ammo comes in handy.

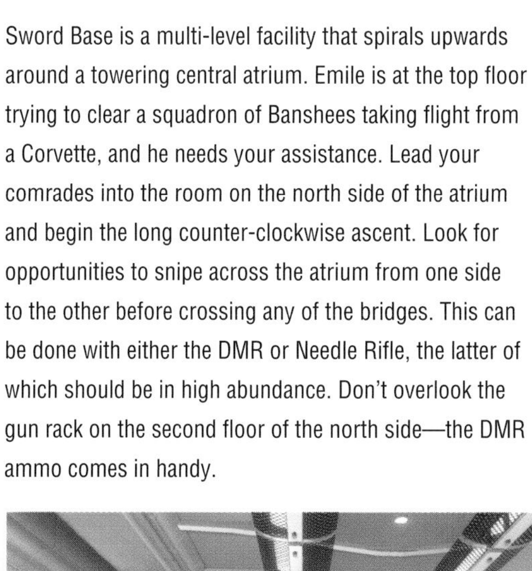

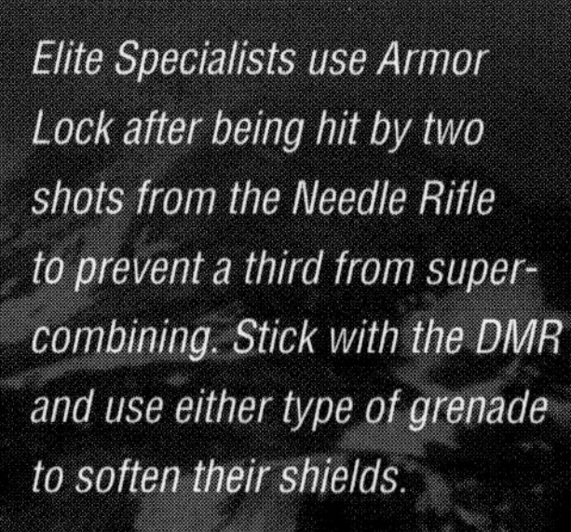

Elite Specialists use Armor Lock after being hit by two shots from the Needle Rifle to prevent a third from super-combining. Stick with the DMR and use either type of grenade to soften their shields.

Use the available cover in the hallways and near the doorways to sweep upwards through Sword Base. Teams of Grunts and Jackals, along with the occasional pair of Elites, try to slow your ascent. Be mindful of the glass-floored balconies and check each corner as you go to ensure no Elite strikes you down from behind. Additionally, be sure to carry enough DMR ammunition; you can restock your ammo supply at the cabinets on each floor.

Cross the final bridge to the uppermost floor on the south side of Sword Base and activate night vision. Lob a grenade down the hall to the left at the squad of Grunt Specialists and Elite in the vicinity. Continue down the darkened hallway to the fallen trooper with the Rocket Launcher. Swap out your secondary weapon for the Rocket Launcher, note the Medkits on the wall, and prepare for battle.

Bring a full Fireteam of troopers with you across the final bridge. The Covenant have reinforced the breach with a number of well-armed enemies, including an Elite with a Fuel Rod Gun.

OBJECTIVE

H: SECURE BREACH AND ELIMINATE AIR FORCES

Emile has his hands full taking out Banshees. Take care of all ground forces so he can clear the sky.

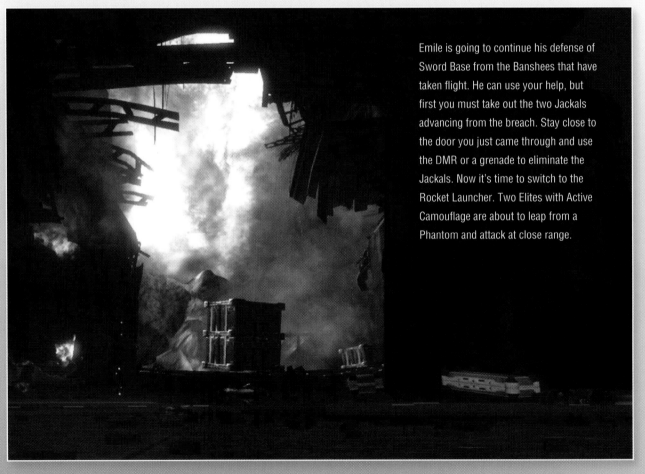

Emile is going to continue his defense of Sword Base from the Banshees that have taken flight. He can use your help, but first you must take out the two Jackals advancing from the breach. Stay close to the door you just came through and use the DMR or a grenade to eliminate the Jackals. Now it's time to switch to the Rocket Launcher. Two Elites with Active Camouflage are about to leap from a Phantom and attack at close range.

LEGENDARY TACTICS

The Elites that leap into the breach from the Phantom on Legendary are quite a bit harder to kill and require a more delicate approach. Instead of rushing straight up the middle of the area in hopes of killing them as they land, it's safer to hang back near the entrance to the left-hand hallway and let them come to you. Watch the hallway for the shimmer of the Elite and open fire with the Rocket Launcher. The confines of the hallway all but guarantee at least some heavy splash damage, even if your aim isn't true. Fire again quickly, then reload and rush back out the door to the room where the Medkits are. Heal up, then return to the room to hunt down the final Elite.

Rush straight up the middle and target the Elite leaping down on the right-hand side first. A second Elite approaches on the left. Watch for that telltale shimmer of Active Camouflage and fire at once with the Rocket Launcher. Quickly back away and fire again. Work quickly, and even a non-fatal rocket may knock the Elite off the edge of the breach—and not even an Elite can survive a fall from that height.

WELCOME
UNSC TRAINING
THE CAMPAIGN
M1: WINTER CONTINGENCY
M2: ONI
M3: NIGHTFALL
M4: TIP OF THE SPEAR
M5: LONG NIGHT OF SOLACE
M6: EXODUS
M7: NEW ALEXANDRIA
M8: THE PACKAGE
M9: THE PILLAR OF AUTUMN
FIREFIGHT
MULTIPLAYER
REFERENCE

Collect the Rocket Launcher ammo from the UNSC corpses and gun cases and take out that Phantom. But not until you've eliminated all three Elites!

Collect the Rocket Launcher ammo from either of the two corpses on this floor (and in the prior hallway near the Medkits) and step out onto the ledge to take aim on the enemy ship. You'll need five rockets to down the Phantom, which requires two or more reloads, depending on your accuracy. Take cover behind the crates to avoid any incoming fire from the Banshees or the Phantom. Wait until achieving target lock-on with the Rocket Launcher before firing.

NIGHTFALL

MOVE IN BEHIND ENEMY LINES AND EVALUATE THE OPPOSITION.

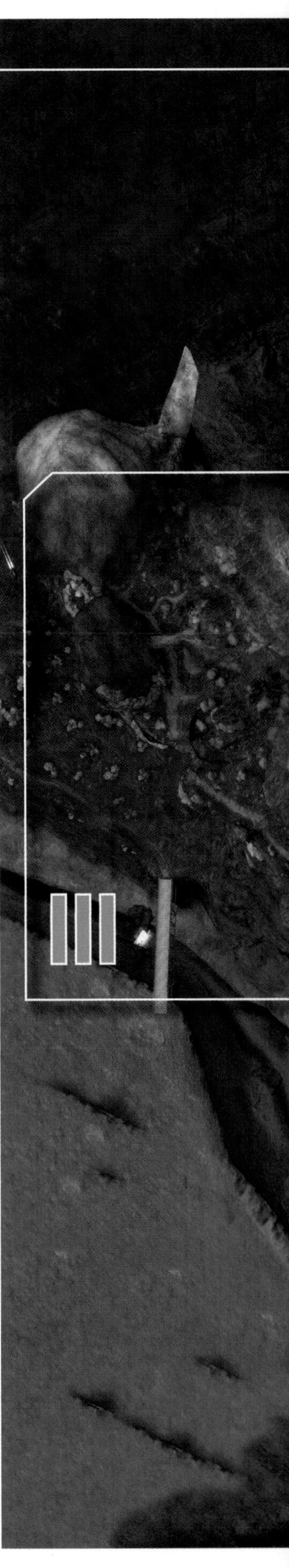

INTELLIGENCE BRIEFING

BASIC TACTICS

I Advance along the cliffs with the Sniper Rifle to infiltrate the dark zone. Jun takes an alternate approach, leaving this route to you. Assassinate the Elite and first few isolated Grunts to conserve ammo and maintain the quiet, then begin sniping each of the dozens of enemies near the settlement. Proceed slowly, stay high, and use the Sniper Rifle to eliminate all high-level foes before they spot you. To conserve ammunition, you may want to switch to the Magnum to take out the Grunts.

II Continue south towards the sound of battle. Pick off the Covenant as they try to "enlist" the giant gúta's service, then slay the beasts before they turn on you too. Continue to the pump station and snipe the Covenant attacking the militia. Eliminate the Covy forces deployed from the three Phantoms that appear by maintaining the high ground and using the DMR, Rocket Launcher, and grenades to slay them as they hit the ground. Accompany the militia through the dry riverbed leading south.

III Follow the path along the cliff and snipe as many of the Covenant troops as you can around the Stealth Pylon before crossing the bridge. Commandeer one of the Plasma Turrets from atop the pylon and eliminate the Skirmishers and other remaining Covies. Grab the Rocket Launcher from the spillway and use it to eliminate the Hunters that are deployed while Jun sets the bombs. Continue beyond the gate towards the dark zone. Focus your fire on those enemies manning the Shade Turrets first, then hug the edge of the canyon and attack from long distance to avoid being surrounded.

MISSION OBJECTIVES

- Recon Covenant combat capabilities.
- Proceed south out of the settlement.
- Protect militia.
- Recon hydro plant via riverbed.
- Neutralize Covenant defense.
- Defend Jun.
- Proceed further into the dark zone.

CHAPTER-SPECIFIC ACHIEVEMENTS

I Need a Weapon: Complete the 4th mission on Normal or harder.

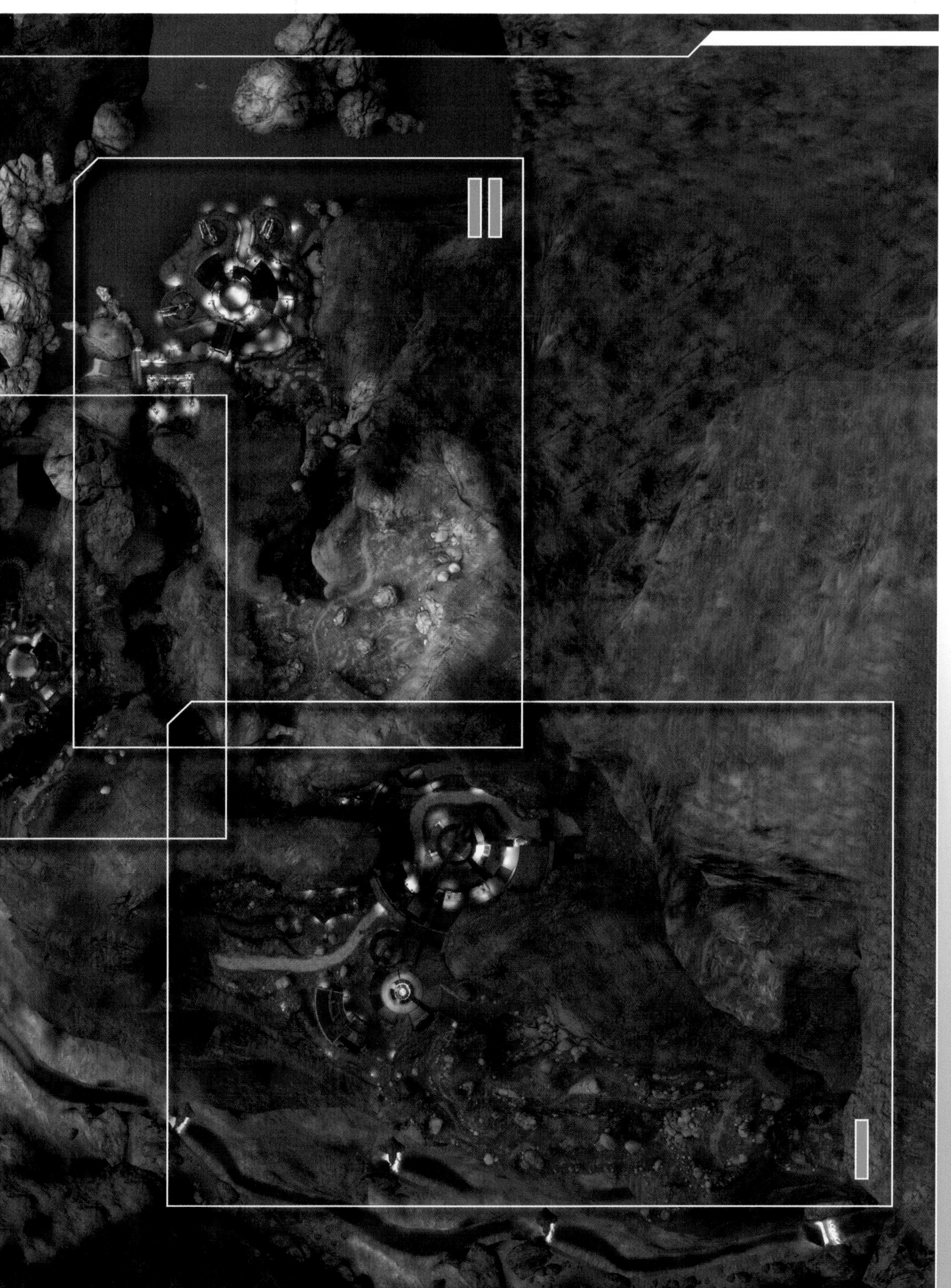

...TOO QUIET

RECOMMENDED EQUIPMENT

OBJECTIVE

A: RECON COVENANT COMBAT CAPABILITIES

Infiltrate the Covenant dark zone and determine the Covenant's combat capabilities.

Noble Six receives an oversized ammo allotment for his Sniper Rifle from Jun just before they split up. Jun is about to negotiate the upper route while Noble Six proceeds along the side of the cliffs. The goal of their recon is to go where electronic surveillance cannot—into the heart of the Covenant camp to see exactly what they're up to.

The time of day and available weaponry should tell you that this is not your typical firefight. You're going to be heavily outnumbered, and it's imperative that you not only stay behind cover and maintain your distance from the enemy, but also that you use your weapons wisely. Save the Sniper Rifle for Elites and Jackals and switch to the Magnum when preparing to gun down any Grunts. Even with 50 rounds for the Sniper Rifle, you'll be surprised how quickly you can run low on sniper rounds during this mission. You can collect plenty of ammo to reload with later on, but you won't be able to exceed the normal clip capacity of 20 rounds with the Sniper Rifle once Jun's loaner clip of special ammo is exhausted.

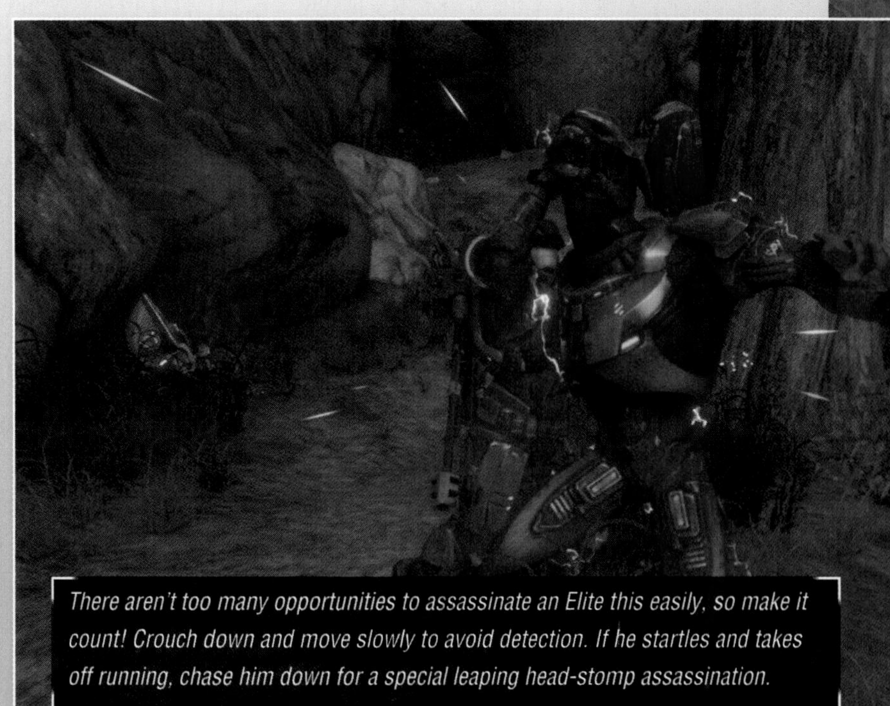

There aren't too many opportunities to assassinate an Elite this easily, so make it count! Crouch down and move slowly to avoid detection. If he startles and takes off running, chase him down for a special leaping head-stomp assassination.

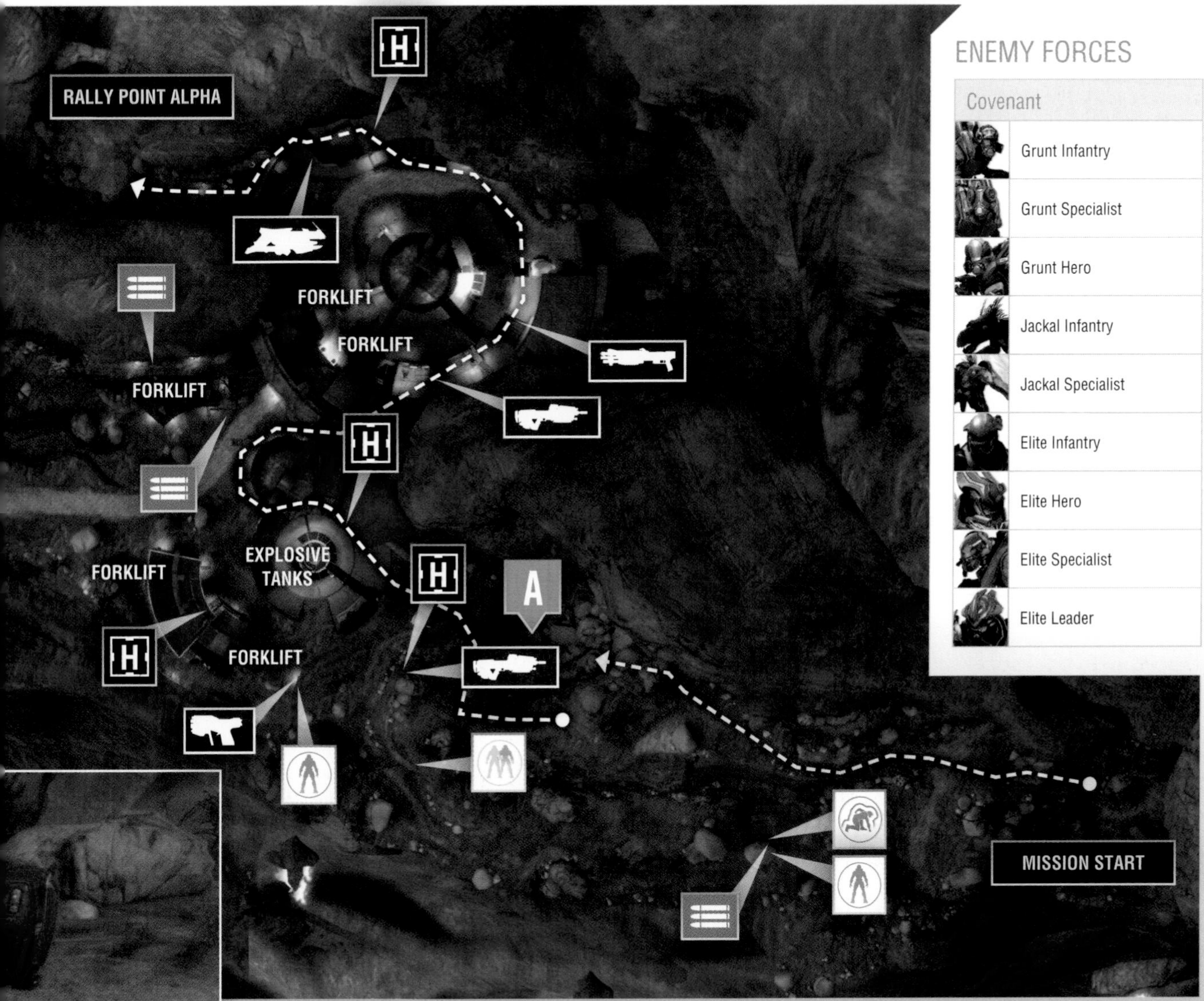

RALLY POINT ALPHA
FORKLIFT
FORKLIFT
FORKLIFT
EXPLOSIVE TANKS
FORKLIFT
FORKLIFT
A
MISSION START

ENEMY FORCES

Covenant
Grunt Infantry
Grunt Specialist
Grunt Hero
Jackal Infantry
Jackal Specialist
Elite Infantry
Elite Hero
Elite Specialist
Elite Leader

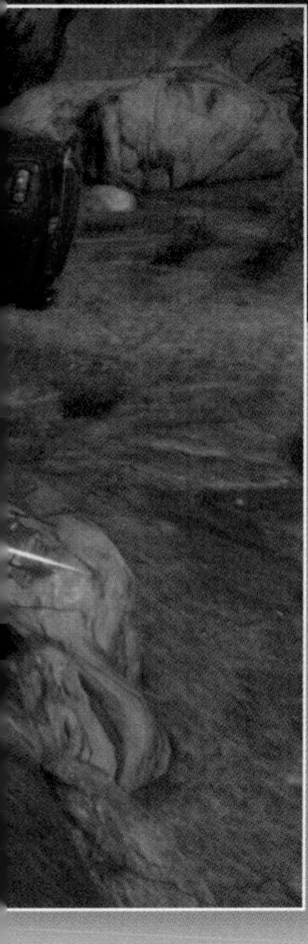

Start up the narrow path leading eastward, along the side of the cliff, and assassinate the Elite up ahead. The position of the Elite varies depending on whether or not you follow the ledge or slip through the cave—walk quietly past the two Grunts to get to the Elite if you go through the cave. Regardless, sneak up behind the Elite and hold the Melee Button down to perform an assassination. Circle around behind the nearby rocks to assassinate the two sleeping Grunts to the right, then peer down at the Grunts and Jackal near the antenna on the ledge below. There's no pretense of being stealthy beyond this point, so go ahead and take out the three Grunts with a single Frag Grenade before sniping the Jackal. Jun rejoins you at the first sound of gunfire.

"When Kat runs an op, direct action is always necessary."

Follow the upper ledge towards the boulders and the first visible confirmation of the settlement to the south. Immediately shoulder the Sniper Rifle and scan the rooftop for the four Elite Specialists to the southeast. Hold up near the large tree and snipe the Specialists and any additional enemies you can spot from this vantage point. Move up to the boulders just beyond the tree and set to sniping the Elites and Jackals that deploy from the Phantom. Watch for Grunts to get close to the fuel tank in the center of the settlement, then detonate it with a round from the Sniper Rifle. Many of the lesser enemies tend to congregate around the two-story structure near the silo. Pay attention to the laser fire from the Focus Rifle and let it direct you to any remaining enemies.

Meet Jun near the green emergency flare by the farmer's corpse and study the motion tracker to spot any enemies encroaching from the east. There are only two routes to this position: through the sloping terrain directly under the ledge to your right and via a narrow path to the left. This makes it very easy to monitor for nearby threats. It's not uncommon to see an Elite and several Grunts attempt to flank your position via the eastern trail. Keep Jun close and use this vantage point to snipe each of the remaining Jackals and Grunts near the center of the farming settlement. Top off your health with the Medkit near the corpse, then descend the slope to the buildings.

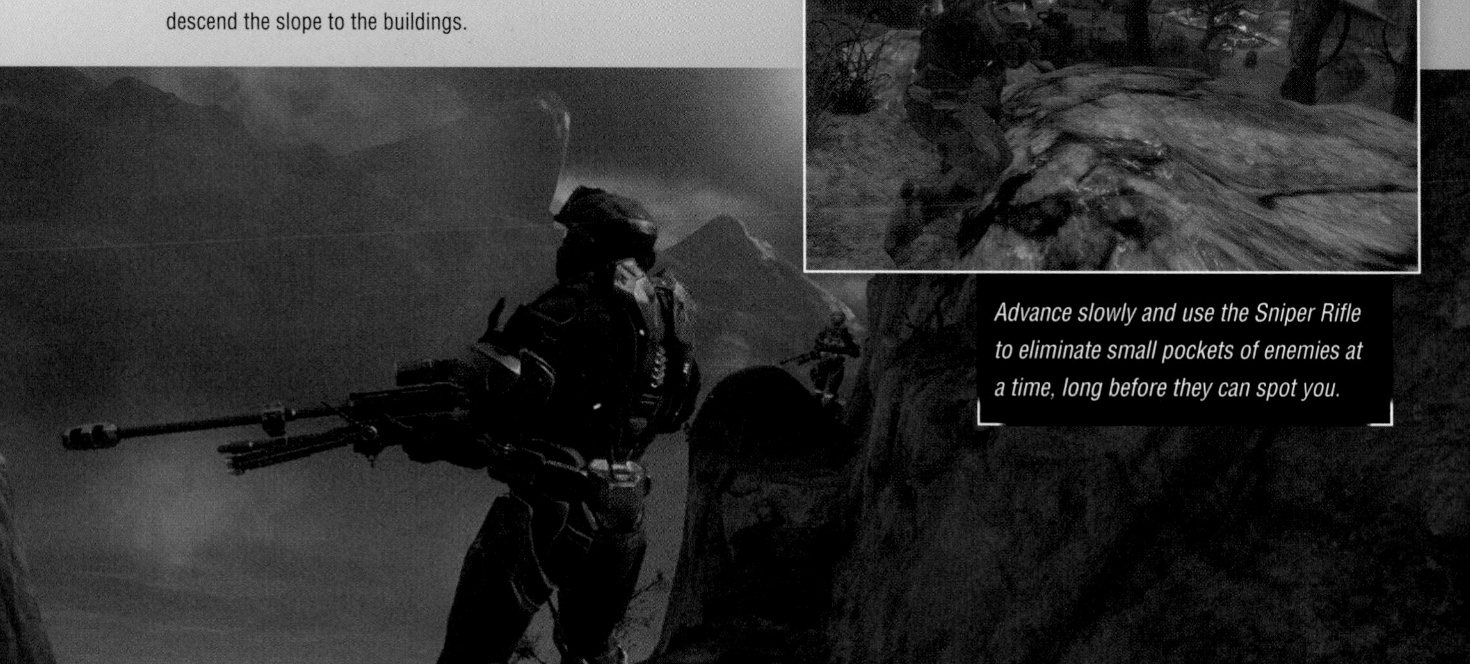

Advance slowly and use the Sniper Rifle to eliminate small pockets of enemies at a time, long before they can spot you.

LEGENDARY TACTICS

It doesn't take long to notice a few distinct changes during this mission on Legendary. For starters, an Elite Leader watches over the group of Grunts that is asleep near the first antenna. There is an Elite sniper here as well (three of them if you are playing co-op). But that's only the beginning. Grunts push up the hill towards your position in greater numbers, along with more aggressive Elites. Other Covies also circle around the base of the hill below the green flare and try to flank your position. Advance very slowly, make use of the Active Camouflage equipment near that first antenna, move laterally from rock to rock to stay in cover, and make sure you snipe every Elite that you can before moving forward. It's also important to use the Magnum for Grunts and any Jackals that get close to ensure that you have enough Sniper Rifle ammo for later on—even if this means passing on the sniper shot and waiting until you're within range for a Magnum shot.

Sweep across the settlement and proceed through the concrete structure in the northwest corner to the next silo area. Circle-strafe along the perimeter in a counter-clockwise direction up the steps to the corpse, where you can pick up a Shotgun. Keep the Sniper Rifle shouldered and aimed skyward—be ready to fire at the Elite on the walkway ringing the silo as soon as it comes into view. A band of Grunts and additional Elites are located on the ground to the right. Continue the slow counter-clockwise perimeter walk past the piles of wood and take them out.

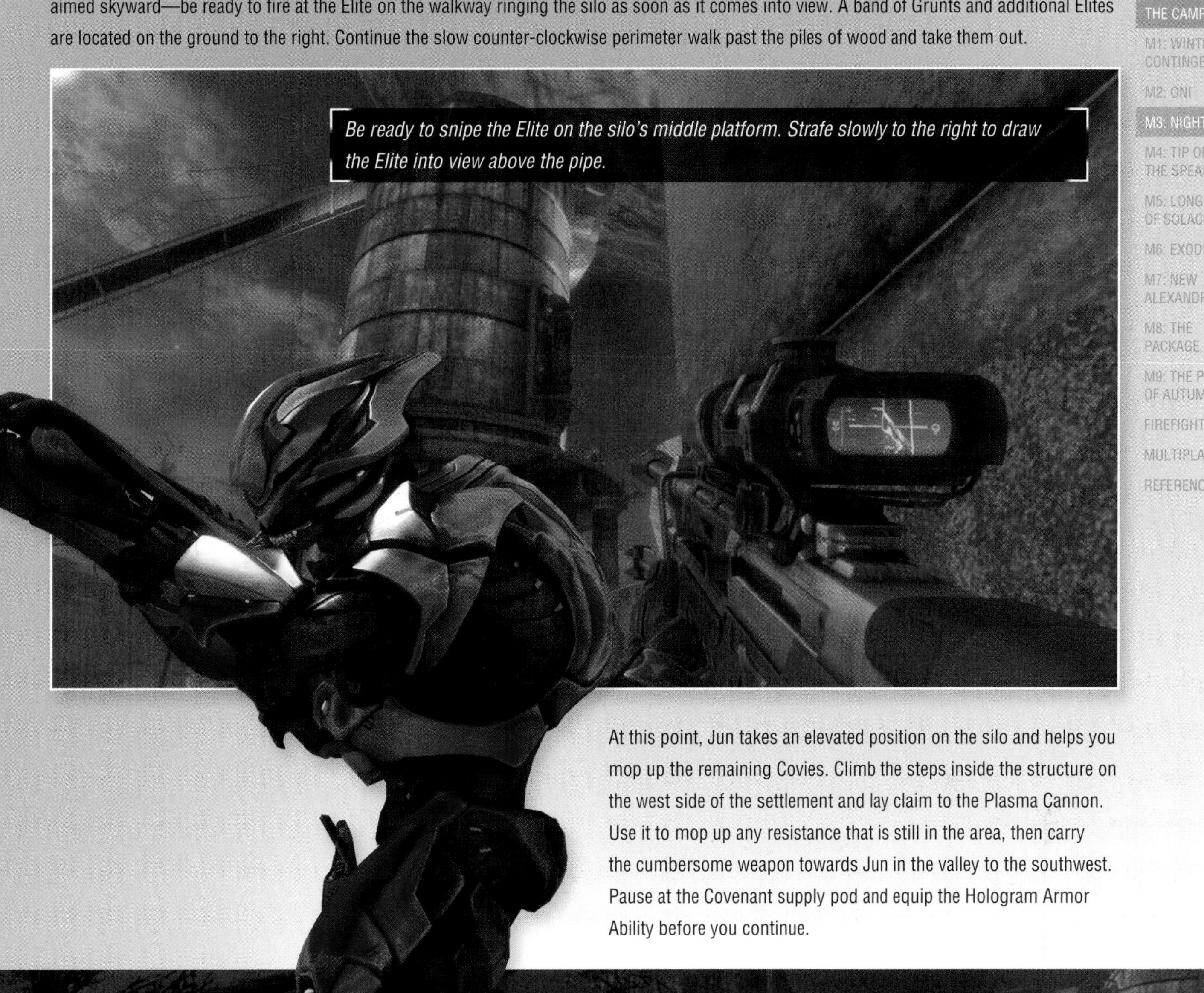

Be ready to snipe the Elite on the silo's middle platform. Strafe slowly to the right to draw the Elite into view above the pipe.

At this point, Jun takes an elevated position on the silo and helps you mop up the remaining Covies. Climb the steps inside the structure on the west side of the settlement and lay claim to the Plasma Cannon. Use it to mop up any resistance that is still in the area, then carry the cumbersome weapon towards Jun in the valley to the southwest. Pause at the Covenant supply pod and equip the Hologram Armor Ability before you continue.

LET SLEEPING DOGS LIE

RECOMMENDED EQUIPMENT

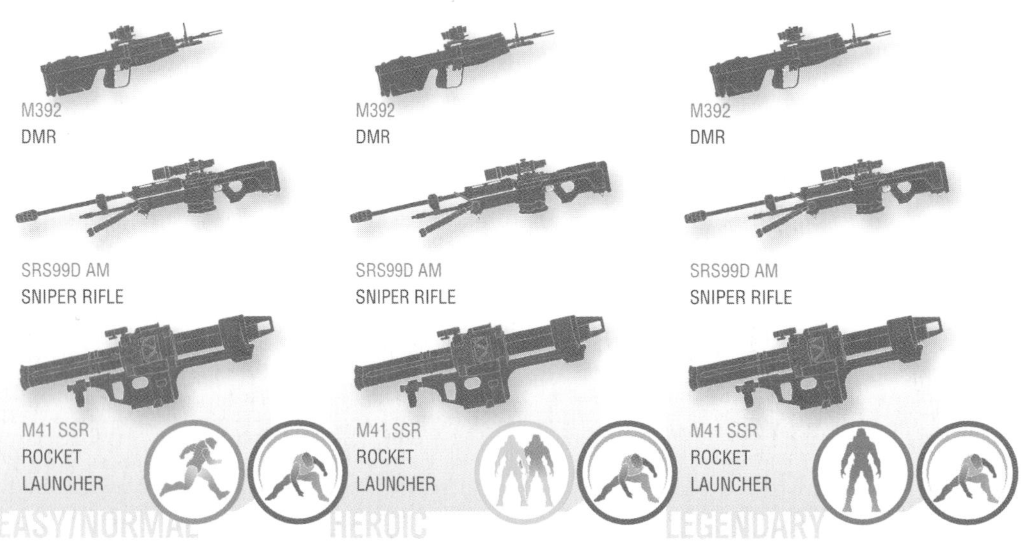

OBJECTIVE

B: PROCEED SOUTH OUT OF THE SETTLEMENT

Move on from the settlement by taking the southern path out of the silo area.

Carry the Plasma Cannon into the valley and climb up onto the pile of boulders to the left. Stand back and watch the gúta lay waste to the Covies in the area. Once the Covenant are dead, the massive beasts turn their attention—and their claws—on you. Open fire with the Plasma Cannon to dispatch them without using up any pistol or sniper rounds—it's important to keep at least a dozen Sniper Rifle bullets for the upcoming battle. Drop the heavy weapon and join Jun at the far end of the valley. Resist the urge to swap out your Magnum or Sniper Rifle for any other weapons unless you're running really low on ammo. If so, ignore the Energy Sword and opt for the Needle Rifle or the Assault Rifle near the corpse along the trail.

The gúta can't get you if you stay on this pile of rocks. Use the Plasma Cannon from the settlement to cut them down so you don't waste any ammo.

Proceed southwest into the valley beneath the crumpled staircase. The path forks just beyond the Moa, where you should begin hearing the sound of munitions fire. Both paths lead to the same general area, but you should consider taking the right-hand path, since it leads to a better initial vantage point. Drop the Plasma Cannon and load the Sniper Rifle.

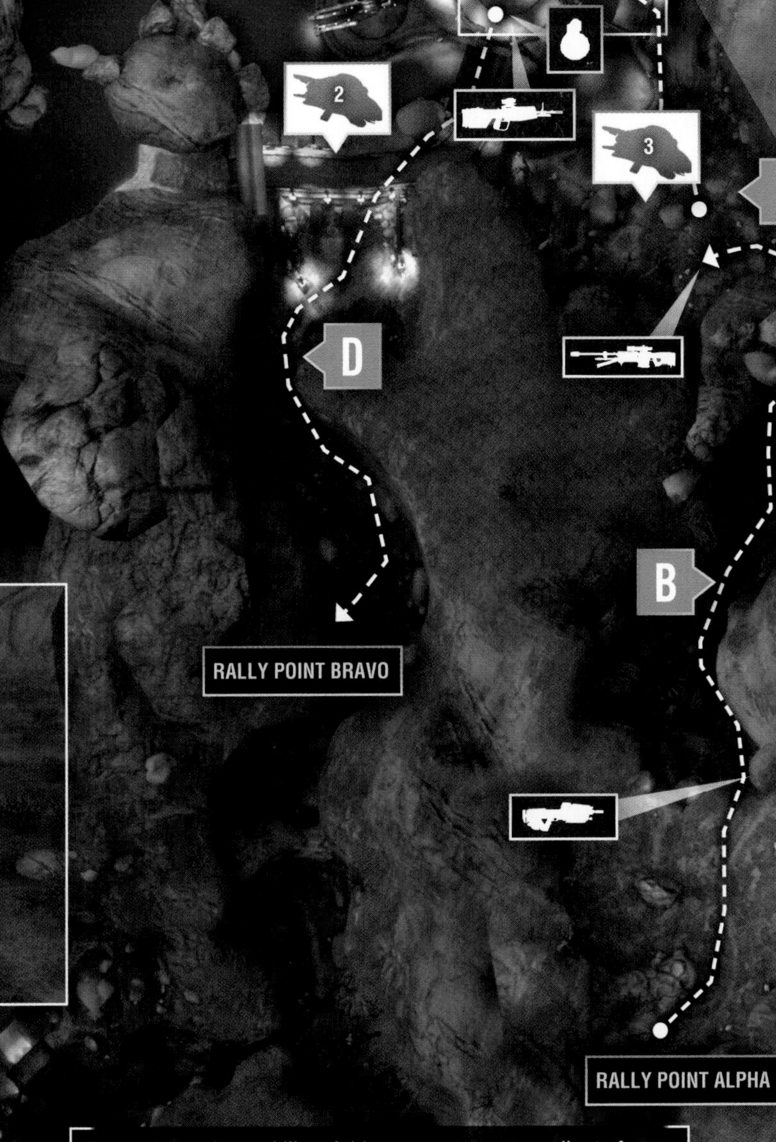

To maximize the usability of this map, extraneous callouts for the Magnum and the Assault Rifle have been removed. These areas have been marked with a *

ENEMY FORCES

Covenant
Grunt Infantry
Grunt Specialist
Grunt Hero
Jackal Infantry
Jackal Specialist
Skirmisher Infantry
Skirmisher Specialist
Elite Infantry
Elite Specialist
Elite Leader
Gúta

OBJECTIVE

C: PROTECT MILITIA

Defend the militia at the pump station.

A militia group is under attack. Work with them to fend off the Covenant and retake the pump station. They will inform you about the ordnance that is stockpiled in the station—one of the items is the Drop Shield Armor Ability. Use the Sniper Rifle to eliminate the Elites first, then focus on the numerous Jackals and Skirmishers near the water and on the bridge in the center. Try to shoot the Plasma Cannon off the Phantom when it deploys reinforcements, and note the location of where it falls (likely near the staircase due south). Take out as many foes as you can before running down to join the militia.

Lend your initial support to the militia from within the cover of the valley. Snipe the Elites and Jackals, then join the militia near the center of the pump station.

The pump station contains a wealth of Medkits and ammunition, not the least of which is inside two gun cases on the center platform. The militia members soon reveal their valuable weapons stash: a couple of DMRs, a Sniper Rifle, and a Rocket Launcher. Go ahead and help yourself. Temporarily swap out your weapons for the DMR and Rocket Launcher and equip the Drop Shield. Move fast, there are multiple Phantoms on their way with an army of additional Covenant forces.

"No. We're just going to steal it back."

The first Phantom deploys a pair of Elites and a number of Jackals in the canal between the two pumps to the southwest. Ascend the stairs to the roof, deploy the Drop Shield for protection, and fire the Rocket Launcher straight into the heart of the Jackals as they touch down. The militia and Jun provide plenty of support from the roof and can take down the Elites on their own. If an Elite does manage to get onto the central platform quickly enough to engage you, simply open fire with the DMR and continue to back away towards the bridge.

Resist the urge to fire the Rocket Launcher at the Phantom, and instead let a rocket fly straight into the crowd of Covies that leaps out of the ships.

I'LL TAKE THAT CANNON IF YOU DON'T MIND!

It's possible to shoot the Plasma Cannon out of a Phantom's passenger bay. Open fire on it with the DMR, Sniper Rifle, or even the Needle Rifle, and continue hitting it as the Covenant disembark from the ship. It takes a few rounds (more depending on the weapon), but the cannon eventually falls to the ground. Make your way over to the fallen weapon and lay claim to it before the second Phantom arrives. You can even pull this off with the very first Phantom—the Plasma Cannon falls in the water, but it's shallow enough that Noble Six can wade out to get it without difficulty.

The second Phantom deposits an Elite Specialist and an army of Grunts on the dam along the east side of the pump station. Move quickly across the bridge to the large boulder near the start of the dam and ready the Rocket Launcher. Fire it at the road surface atop the dam where the mass of Grunts leaps out for a multi-kill. The Grunts exit the Phantom on the closer, left-hand side of the ship, while the Elite exits on the right. Use your remaining rocket, a Plasma Grenade, and the DMR to down the Elite Specialist as quickly as you can. Or, you can give the Rocket Launcher to a militia member to supply him with unlimited, explosive covering fire. You need to get back into cover fast! The Elite may use its Armor Lock to evade grenade blasts, so only throw a grenade if you have some to spare.

Use Hologram to draw the attention of the Grunt manning the Plasma Cannon (or a Drop Shield for protection), then ready the Rocket Launcher for a Killtrocity attack on the Grunts.

LEGENDARY TACTICS

The three Phantoms deposit their passengers in quick succession, making it imperative that you eliminate the first wave (those that land near the water to the southwest) as soon as possible. Rather than post up on one of the rooftops, take the Rocket Launcher and some Frag Grenades and wait for the Phantom from behind the corner of the building. Lob a Frag Grenade at the Elites when they first leap out, then fire the Rocket Launcher at the band of Jackals when they splash down. Move fast to the center of the pump station near the bridge and fire another rocket to score a multi-kill on the Grunts as they descend the dirt slope into the water. Turn north and use any rockets you have left to remove the Jackals and Elites being dropped off in the distance. The Rocket Launcher comes with four rockets—make them count! It's also important to consider your overhead cover during this battle and make frequent use of the Drop Shield. The Phantoms come fast and attack relentlessly. Joining Jun and the militia on the roof is a surefire way to get killed as long as the Phantoms are flying. Crouch behind cover, using buildings or even the flooded tunnel beneath the southwest building.

The third Phantom moves in fast to the north, so work quickly to kill the Elite Specialist, then circle around the boulder to the southwest and up to the rooftop where Jun and the others are waiting. Don't delay taking on the third wave of Covies, or else the militia might be overrun and you'll lose some valuable fire support. Swap out the empty Rocket Launcher for the Sniper Rifle in the gun case (or one dropped by a fallen militia member) and start sniping the Covies that were left off on the north side of the canal. Use the Sniper Rifle and DMR to eliminate the Jackals and Grunts that exit the third Phantom, then hunt down the final Elite before regrouping with the militia in the center. Replenish your supply of health and grenades in the station rooms and load up on long-range ammo.

OBJECTIVE

D: RECON HYDRO PLANT VIA RIVERBED

Take the dry riverbed to the northeast of the pump station. Use it to reach the hydroelectric plant.

Eliminate any remaining Covenant and join up with the militia and Jun on the bridge leading to the dam, but not before equipping the Sniper Rifle and DMR if you haven't already. Collect the DMR ammo from the body on the bridge and descend the path into the dry riverbed. Follow the trail eastward towards the hydro plant.

Follow the green flares through the dry riverbed to the northeast. There aren't any enemies in this area, so enjoy the respite.

I'LL JUST LEAVE THIS HERE...

RECOMMENDED EQUIPMENT

ENEMY FORCES

Covenant
Grunt Infantry
Grunt Specialist
Jackal Infantry
Jackal Specialist
Skirmisher Infantry
Skirmisher Specialist
Elite Infantry
Elite Specialist
Elite Leader
Hunter

OBJECTIVE

E: NEUTRALIZE COVENANT DEFENSE

Neutralize the Covenant defense around the Stealth Pylon.

Listen to the radio communiqué between Kat and Jun to learn about the plan for dealing with the pylon, and hold up where the trail meets the cliff. Jun continues to the left, along the cliff. Before you follow him, use the Sniper Rifle to eliminate the Grunts manning the Plasma Turrets on the pylon, as well as the Jackals and Elites directly across the chasm to the south. Use the rocks on the right for cover and try to eliminate the Elite on the hill to the southwest before joining the others near the bridge.

You're not done sniping yet! Take out the Grunts manning the Plasma Turrets on the Stealth Pylon before even thinking about crossing the bridge towards them.

FUTURE PLANNING

Clear out any nearby grenade-hurling Grunts, then hop aboard the forklift truck and drive it half the distance between the bridge and the Stealth Pylon. Forklift trucks are highly explosive, so parking one in this location makes it that much easier to defend Jun from the Hunters that are deployed later on in this area.

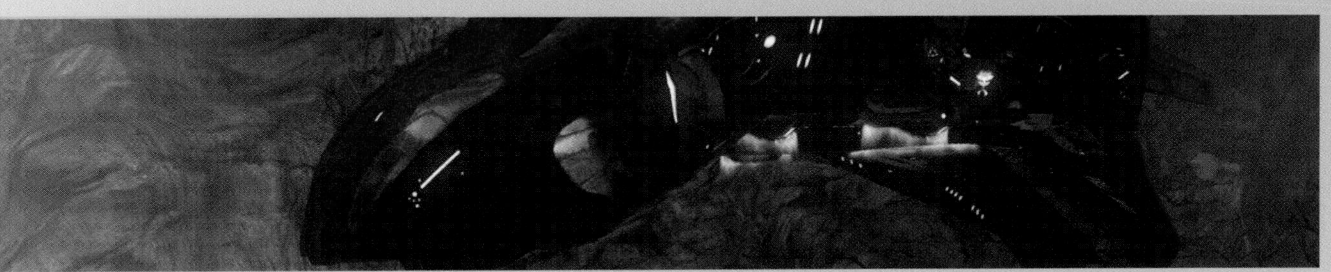

E

RALLY POINT BRAVO

SHADE TURRET

SHADE TURRET

SHADE TURRET

G

FORKLIFT

X3

F

To maximize the usability of this map, extraneous callouts for the Magnum and the Assault Rifle have been removed. These areas have been marked with a *

Cross the bridge towards the pylon, checking for any remaining Elites in the area. Ride the gravity lift (Heroic and lesser difficulties only) onto the pylon to steal one of the Plasma Cannons from its mount and hop down to the east. There are a number of Grunts and Elites still in the area, and each of them must be cleared before Jun can get to work setting the remote-det charges. Sweep through the powerhouse area in a clockwise direction, making sure to stay clear of the circular water-filled area in the middle.

Securing the Plasma Cannon leaves you exposed on the pylon, but it's worth the risk. Just be sure to eliminate all visible enemies before going to get it.

Use the Plasma Cannon to annihilate the Covenant on the hill leading up to the two-story control center, and hunt down the remaining enemies on the catwalk above the spillway. Collect the additional Sniper Rifle ammo from the gun case on the second floor of the circular building in the corner. Step out onto the upper walkway and gun down the Elite Leader roaming the central area. A number of fast-moving but rather weak Skirmishers then make their way across the upper walkways; use any remaining Plasma Cannon ammo or the DMR to gun them down, but save your Sniper Rifle ammo for later.

OBJECTIVE

F: DEFEND JUN

Defend Jun while he plants remote-det charges on the Stealth Pylon.

Listen for Jun's signal that he's going to plant the charges and quickly drop into the narrow spillway radiating off the center pool. Temporarily swap the DMR for the Rocket Launcher. Sprint back up onto the wall of the powerhouse, overlooking the area east of the pylon. This is where a Phantom is about to discharge two Hunters. At the same time another Phantom drops off two cloaked Elites that take positions in front of the powerhouse.

Fire the Rocket Launcher at the ground between the Hunters and the parked forklift truck (see previous tip) to amplify the blast. The rocket detonates the fuel tank of the forklift truck and results in a far larger explosion than the single rocket shell would have caused. Fire the second rocket at the feet of the two Hunters to further damage them. Quickly return to the room near overlooking the pylon and swap the empty Rocket Launcher for the Shotgun. A pair of camouflaged Elites will be closing in on your position any moment. Use the Drop Shield and Shotgun to take them out.

Jun heads to the gate leading east. Take a moment to scour the area for extra ammo; you need as much Sniper Rifle and DMR ammo as you can get your hands on for the final push into the dark zone. Once ready, head to the gate in the eastern end of the clearing and follow the path into the belly of the beast.

The Rocket Launcher only has two shells, so amplify its effectiveness and aim for the ground next to the forklift truck to double the explosion! Or, you can give this weapon to a militia member as long as it has one round so he can give you unlimited covering fire.

OBJECTIVE

G: PROCEED FURTHER INTO THE DARK ZONE

Push into the dark zone and recon large-scale Covenant combat capabilities.

WELCOME
UNSC TRAINING
THE CAMPAIGN
M1: WINTER CONTINGENCY
M2: ONI
M3: NIGHTFALL
M4: TIP OF THE SPEAR
M5: LONG NIGHT OF SOLACE
M6: EXODUS
M7: NEW ALEXANDRIA
M8: THE PACKAGE
M9: THE PILLAR OF AUTUMN
FIREFIGHT
MULTIPLAYER
REFERENCE

FLARES LIGHT THE WAY

The green night-glow flares you've seen scattered throughout this mission not only help light the way for Noble Team, but they sometimes highlight key weapon drops and ammo supplies. The flare just beyond the large gate illuminates a gun case that has some much-needed Sniper Rifle ammo. Remember its location and fall back to collect additional ammo after taking out the first line of Covenant defenses.

Advance only as far as the first Covy antenna and use the Sniper Rifle to take out the Grunt manning the Shade Turret on the hill to the south. Other Grunts approach to fill the empty seat—keep your scope fixed on that position and take them down. If you have enough ammo, go ahead and shoot the Shade Turret five times with the Sniper Rifle to destroy it.

A bulk of Covenant forces are massed on the hills around the corner to the west, including two more Shade Turrets and a number of Elites and Jackals. Let Jun and any surviving militia take the direct approach; it's far more effective for you to hug the edge of the cliff on the left and keep as far from the heavy action as possible.

Once you've cleared the lower portion of the hill of enemies, head up along the left-hand side of the southern slope and cross the rocky bridge to the Medkit on the bluff overlooking the final Shade Turret. Destroy the fixed gun and pan the upper area for any remaining Elites before laying waste to the gaggle of Grunts atop the hill. There is a lot of cover to utilize during this climb up the slope, and alternating back and forth between the DMR and Sniper Rifle gives you all the long-range firepower you need to stay safe from harm. The path leading down the hill to the southeast leads right into the dark zone. Kat and the others can't wait to learn what you see.

Advance slowly along the eastern edge of the area and eliminate the enemies on the south side of the valley before ascending the hill to the Covenant stronghold. Use the Hologram ability to distract the enemy.

Hug the massive retaining wall and continue to the southern edge of the area. Look for Jackals beyond the purple Covenant barricades and a row of Grunts crossing the natural bridge to the west. You'll soon spot another flare-lit ammo stash. Tempting as it looks, it's a bit of a booby trap. Be sure to take out the Grunt in the Shade Turret to the right of the natural bridge before moving in for the DMR ammo and Frag Grenades, otherwise you'll be gunned down faster than you can bend over to pick them up.

Cross the stone bridge back to the northwest and take cover behind the rocks and trees. Snipe the Elites in the distance before making the final push alongside Jun.

"The sun will be up in a few hours, and it's going to be a very busy day."

TIP OF THE SPEAR

TWO MASSIVE ARMIES CLASH! TIME TO GO TO WAR AGAINST THE COVENANT.

INTELLIGENCE BRIEFING

BASIC TACTICS

I Stick close to Kat and use the Grenade Launcher and DMR to clean the hill of Covenant. Pay special attention to the Grunt Specialists manning the Shade Turrets. Drive Kat and your Fireteam companion south towards the Covenant AA gun. Drive the perimeter of AA gun to eliminate all Covenant forces, particularly those in Revenants, Ghosts, and Wraiths. Enter the base of the AA gun and destroy the energy core—exit quickly to avoid being caught in the explosion. Continue to the south with the Warthog over the portable bridge and onward towards the Mining Facility.

II Familiarize yourself with the new Hologram Armor Ability while sweeping the Mining Facility clean of Covenant, including a Zealot-class Elite at the rear of the facility. Utilize (and steer clear of) the explosive fuel tanks to weaken the Elites and other enemies you encounter. Commandeer the Revenant beyond the facility and pilot it to the second AA gun. Resist approaching the AA gun until first destroying the two Wraiths and countless other Covenant surrounding the area. Only then should you take on the two Hunters guarding the entrance to the AA gun. Destroy the energy core in the base of the massive gun and board the Falcon for a lift to the primary target.

III Use the Falcon's mounted Grenade Launcher to clear a path through the canyon. Monitor the motion tracker and rapidly fire grenades at enemy groupings, especially at the Wraiths seen along the canyon rim. Once on foot, use the Jet Pack Armor Ability to move among the rocks and help Jorge advance on the Spire. Fly up onto the elevated bridge on the western side of the Spire and hover across to the gravity lift leading up to the control room. Use the Focus Rifle and grenades to eliminate the Covenant defenses on the top floor and disable the shields.

MISSION OBJECTIVES

- Secure a landing zone.
- Neutralize enemy AA.
- Advance into enemy territory.
- Secure mining facility.
- Neutralize enemy AA.
- Advance to primary objective.
- Access Covenant Spire control room.
- Disable Spire shields.

CHAPTER-SPECIFIC ACHIEVEMENTS

TO WAR: Complete the 5th mission on Normal or harder.

YOUR HERESY WILL STAY YOUR FEET: Kill the Elite Zealot before he can escape during the 5th mission.

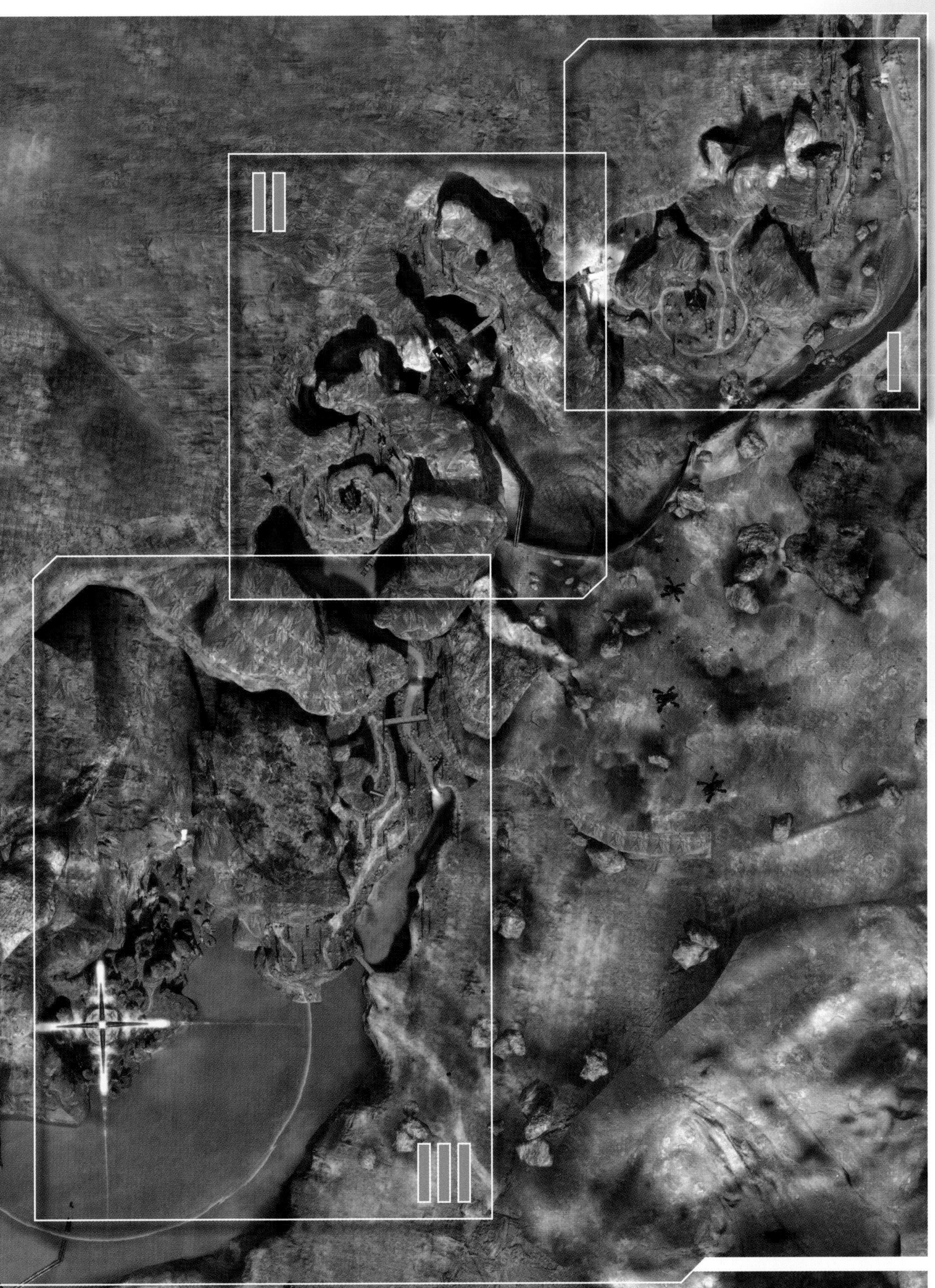

II
I
III

TEMPEST PERIMETER

RECOMMENDED EQUIPMENT

OBJECTIVE

A: SECURE A LANDING ZONE

Push up the hill and secure a landing zone.

Noble Six and Kat are inserted at the base of a hill crawling with far more Covenant forces than ever before seen in one position. Though most are Grunts and Jackals, these lesser units seemingly swarm around an Elite bearing a Concussion Rifle, as if they were any army of bees protecting their queen. Sprint away from the destroyed bridge and take cover behind the rocks to the right. Experiment with the Grenade Launcher's multiple firing modes and clear away the initial rush of enemies.

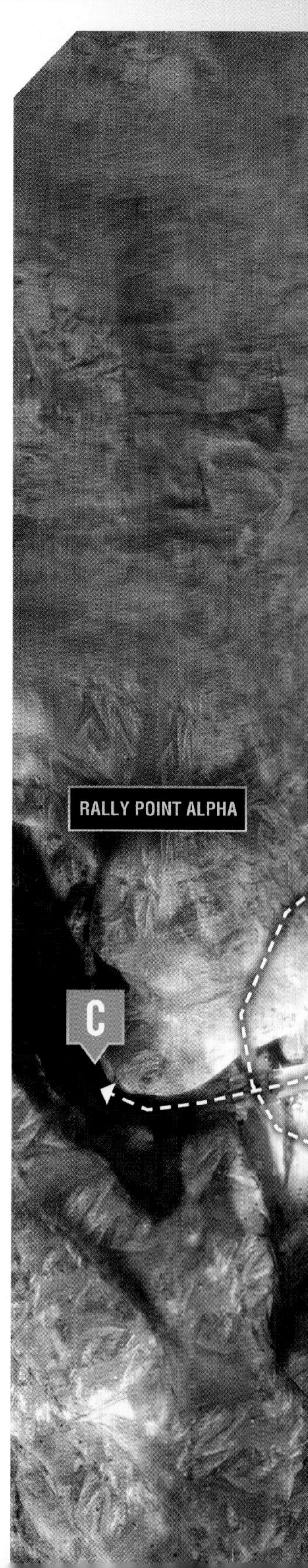

ENEMY FORCES

Covenant
Grunt Infantry
Grunt Specialist
Grunt Hero
Jackal Infantry
Jackal Specialist
Jackal Hero

Covenant
Skirmisher Infantry
Skirmisher Specialist
Elite Infantry
Elite Hero
Elite Leader

ENEMY VEHICLES

Covenant
Ghost
Wraith
Revenant

Grenade Launcher

The Grenade Launcher comes with 15 grenades and has the ability to fire self-detonating grenades or manual detonating grenades that give off an EMP blast. To use the Grenade Launcher in its most basic mode—automatic detonation—all you have to do is aim the weapon and pull the trigger. The grenade detonates upon contact. To employ manual detonation mode, all you must do is press and hold the trigger when firing. The grenade launches from the weapon's barrel and continues bouncing across the landscape off the ground, rocks, or even enemies, and will not detonate until you release the trigger. The grenade may even come to a rest, at which point you basically gain a remote-detonation landmine. It takes some practice to get a feel for knowing when the best time to detonate the grenade is, but the potential is worth the time spent experimenting. Manual detonation's benefit of giving off an EMP blast does come at the expense of explosive damage—if direct damage is what you want, it's best to fire with automatic detonation. Refer to the Ordnance section of the Appendices on page 329 for additional information and statistics about the Grenade Launcher.

Watch for Kat to engage the Elite and assist her from an angle. Use the rocks for protection from the Concussion Rifle's volleys and look for an opening to target the Elite's head with the DMR. Don't advance any further up the hill until you have defeated the Elite. Look for enemies near the mountain on the right, in the center of the hill, and also along the dirt road to the south.

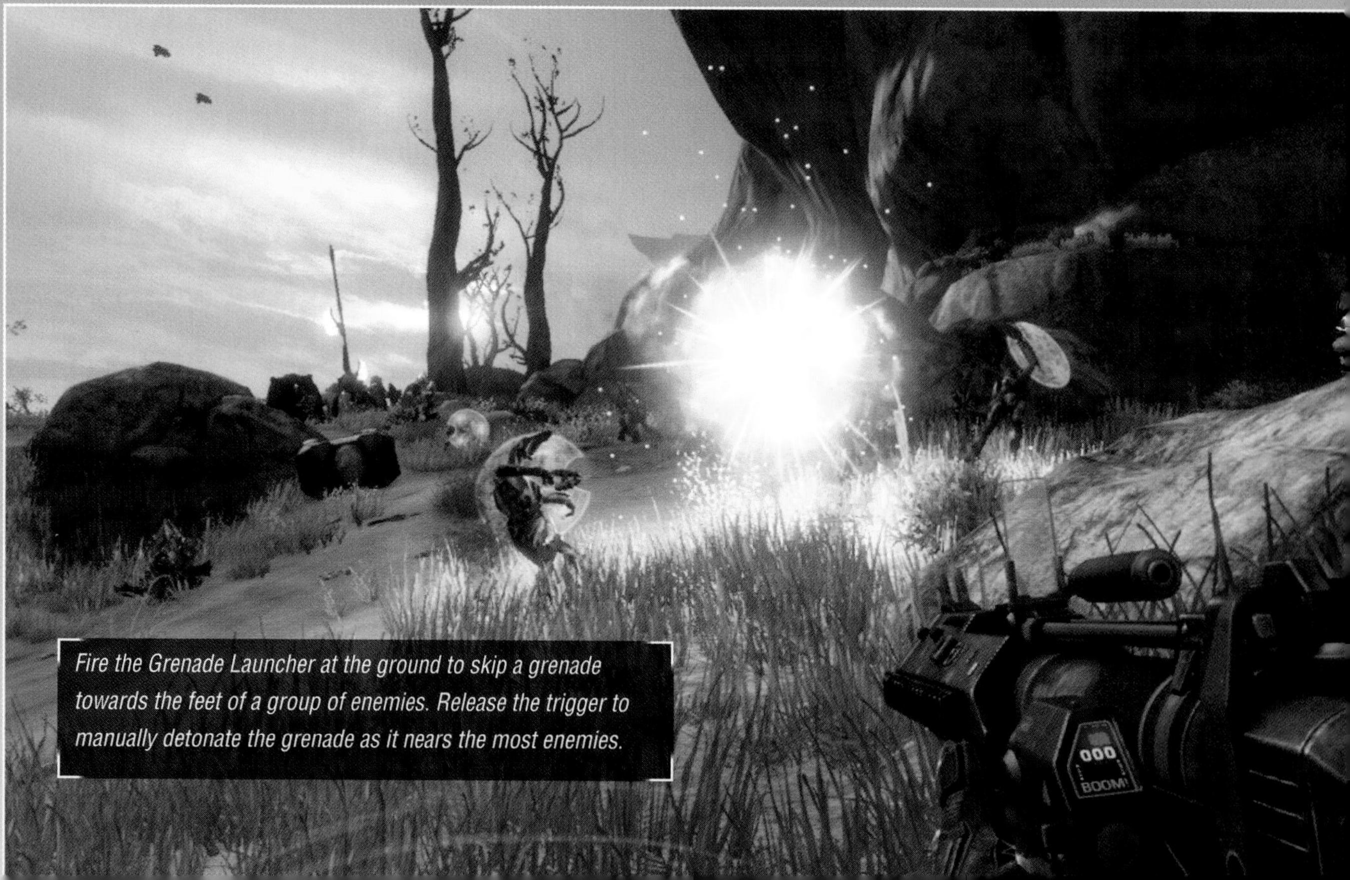

Fire the Grenade Launcher at the ground to skip a grenade towards the feet of a group of enemies. Release the trigger to manually detonate the grenade as it nears the most enemies.

The hillside is further reinforced by a pair of Shade Turrets, one in the center of the hill just beyond the rocks, and another near the road to the left. Use the Grenade Launcher or any Plasma Grenades you find to destroy the first Shade Turret. The approach to the second Shade Turret is a bit more exposed. Take cover behind the boulders near the road and wait for Kat to distract the Grunt manning the Shade Turret. This gives you an excellent opportunity to safely step out and headshot the Grunt with the DMR.

Use the Medkits near the burned-out Warthog and swap out the Grenade Launcher for an Assault Rifle if you are already out of ammunition for it, otherwise continue to hold onto the Grenade Launcher. A Pelican lowers a fresh Warthog for you to drive south along the road to the first of two AA guns. Kat rides shotgun, and a UNSC Trooper mans the multiple Rocket Launcher mounted on the back.

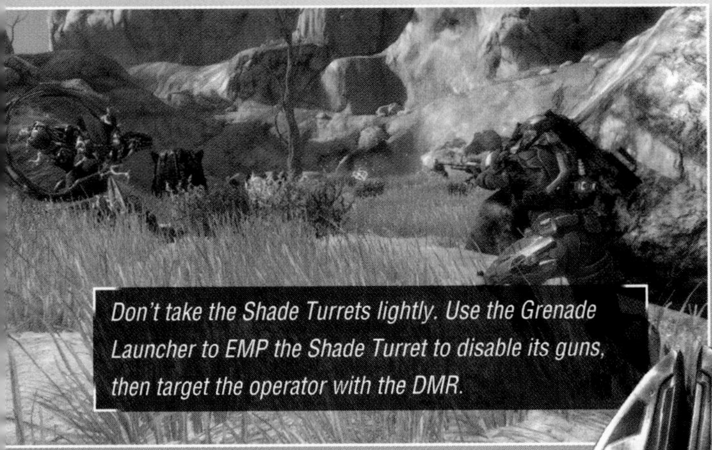

Don't take the Shade Turrets lightly. Use the Grenade Launcher to EMP the Shade Turret to disable its guns, then target the operator with the DMR.

OBJECTIVE

B: NEUTRALIZE ENEMY AA

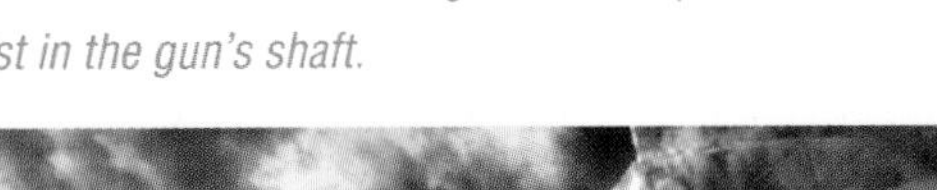

Neutralize the Covenant AA gun. A weak point should exist in the gun's shaft.

"All our birds are stuck out of range unless you can do something about those guns."

Round the corner towards the AA gun and run down the Skirmishers blocking the path. You're going to feel an urge to drive straight for the massive cannon—and Carter implores you to do just that—but don't do it! The area surrounding the AA gun is crawling with Covenant, including many piloting Ghosts and Revenants. The only way you'll survive the getaway is to deal with these perimeter threats first.

CALL FOR A CO-OP ESCORT

You can make this entire mission that much easier while playing co-op with a friend if one of you manages to steal a Ghost or Revenant near the first AA gun from the Covenant. Avoid getting close to the Revenant with the Warthog, since the Rocket Launcher won't leave the Revenant in usable condition. Instead, have one player use the DMR and pick off the Revenant's Covy occupants. With a skilled driver behind the controls, it's possible to continue with this Revenant all the way through the mining facility area and have it for use at the second AA gun location.

Follow the outlying road to the southeast to take on the Ghost and Revenant downhill from the AA gun first. Respect the Revenant's incredible firepower and drive perpendicular to it to give the trooper with you the best chance at scoring a direct hit. Use the handbrake to slide in tight circles around the Ghosts to avoid their front-mounted lasers. Kat chips in with her Grenade Launcher, but you need the Rocket Launcher for most of the heavy lifting.

Use the Warthog to take out the Covenant vehicles before dealing with the AA gun. Drive wide looping circles around the Ghosts, and use the boulders and trees for additional coverage from Revenant attacks.

Additional ground forces are located southeast of the AA gun, near the watchtower. Advance in this direction slowly so the trooper has time to fire the Rocket Launcher at the tower and the enemies nearby. Continue the drive-by massacre in a clockwise direction around the eastern side of the AA gun until you arrive at a fork in the road. Continue up the hill towards the AA gun and the army of Grunts and Jackals stationed in its base. Keep your distance and let the trooper and Kat do as much damage as you can. Watch for enemies to approach the Plasma Battery near the antenna; leap out and shoot the battery for a multi-kill if they get close. If the trooper gets killed, Kat takes control of the Rocket Launcher.

LEGENDARY TACTICS

The final push towards the AA gun is much more difficult on Legendary and requires that you really make the most of your allies. Clear the perimeter of enemies, then park the Warthog close (but not too close) to the AA gun and find a Ghost to drive. This frees Kat up to engage enemies independently, making the most of her unlimited ammunition. Use the Ghost to save ammunition and eliminate each of the Grunts and Skirmishers in the area before getting anywhere near the AA gun on foot. Don't underestimate just how deadly those Needle Rifles can be on Legendary mode—and the Skirmishers seldom miss! The only downside to this strategy is that you may not have a Warthog to drive to the Mining Facility if you leave it too close to the battle.

Exit the vehicle and head into the base of the massive purple cannon. Thick panes of impenetrable glass protect the cannon's energy core on all but one side. Locate the weak panel on the north side of the column, shatter the glass, then open fire on the fueling cell inside. A single grenade from the Grenade Launcher should do the trick. If this ordnance is not available, use whichever weapon you have and continue firing until you hear an alarm sound, then RUN! Exit the structure at once, hop into the Warthog, and get at least 30 feet away from the AA gun as quickly as you can to avoid being caught in the blast.

Clear the immediate vicinity of Covenant and enter the base of the AA gun to cut its fuel supply. Fire on the energy core inside the column until the alarm sounds, then run like hell!

OBJECTIVE

C: ADVANCE INTO ENEMY TERRITORY

Continue to advance towards the primary objective.

Drive the Warthog back to the north for a few moments to ensure that Noble Six and Kat don't wind up as collateral damage when the UNSC frigates initiate their bombing run. Once the dust settles, continue south around the plateau where the AA gun was, and veer left at the fork to pass under the destroyed bridge. A Pelican soon lowers a portable bridge into position over that gap. Spiral up onto the hill, avoid the Wraith guarding the entrance to the bridge, and drive across the gap into the next canyon. You can find a Medkit near the abandoned truck in the canyon, just beyond the drop.

Just because the AA gun has been destroyed doesn't mean there isn't any resistance in the area. Only engage this Wraith if you are going for points, otherwise drive right past it and across the portable bridge.

HAND OVER FIST

RECOMMENDED EQUIPMENT

EASY/NORMAL

M392
DMR

T31 R
NEEDLE RIFLE

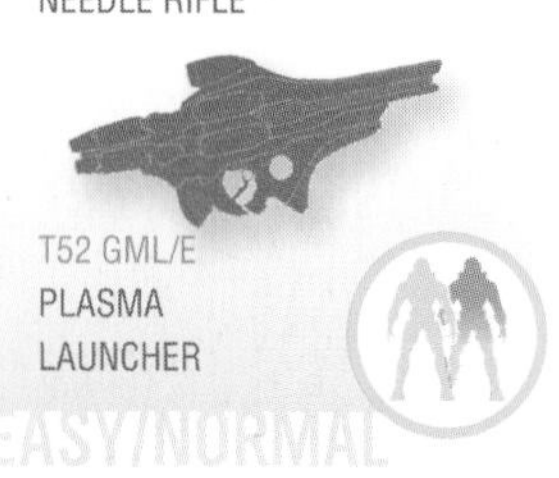
T52 GML/E
PLASMA
LAUNCHER

HEROIC

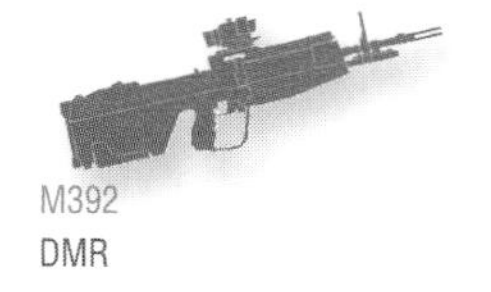
M392
DMR

T31 R
NEEDLE RIFLE

T52 GML/E
PLASMA
LAUNCHER

LEGENDARY

M392
DMR

T31 R
NEEDLE RIFLE

T52 GML/E
PLASMA
LAUNCHER

ENEMY FORCES

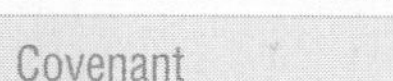

Covenant
Grunt Infantry
Grunt Specialist
Grunt Hero
Jackal Infantry
Jackal Specialist
Skirmisher Infantry
Skirmisher Specialist
Bugger-I
Elite Infantry
Elite Hero
Elite Specialist
Elite Leader
Hunter

OBJECTIVE

D: SECURE MINING FACILITY

Neutralize enemies inside Mining Facility.

Exit the valley near the cliff and drive towards the bridge where the UNSC Troopers are located. A force of Covenant Grunts and Jackals are mounting a formidable defense on the far side of the bridge, near the entrance to the Mining Facility. These troopers can really use your help. Push aside the first two barriers with the front of the Warthog and get close enough so the Rocket Launcher and Kat can target the Shade Turret and other enemies in the area. Hop out of the vehicle and target the Plasma Battery near the antenna and the fuel tank beyond the turret—the explosions should kill any Grunt still alive in the vicinity.

Climb the stairs onto the balcony wrapping around the eastern side of the facility and swap your current Armor Ability for Hologram. When used, Hologram creates a decoy that runs across the battlefield in the direction Noble Six is facing when activated (it runs to where the crosshair intersects the ground). Hologram attracts enemy attention away from you and your Fireteam, but only until you begin firing on the enemy or they realize that the Hologram is merely an artificial entity.

Don't stick your neck out of cover until that Shade Turret is out of commission. Target the Plasma Battery next to it if the Warthog's Rocket Launcher fails to get the job done.

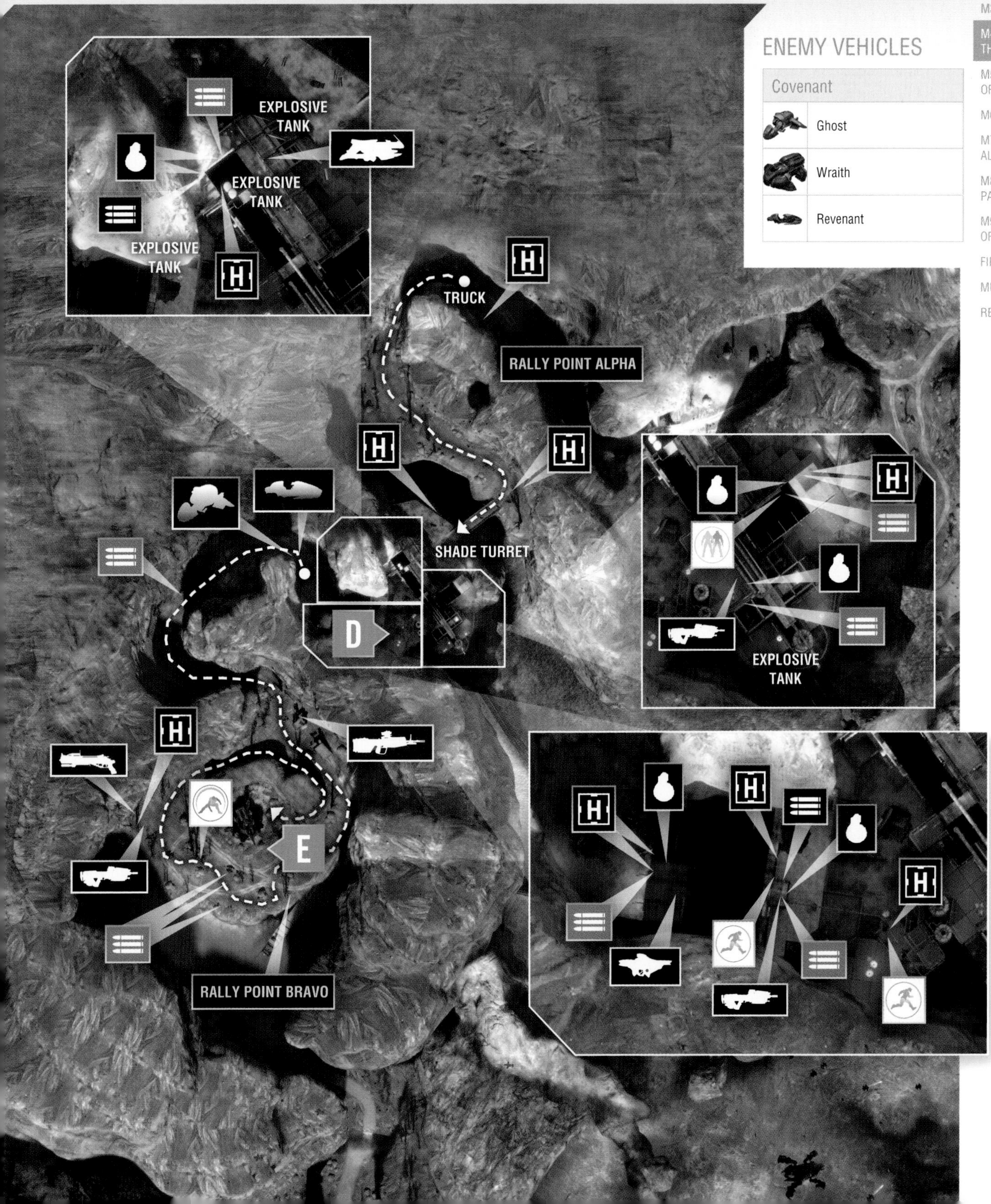

ENEMY VEHICLES

Covenant	
	Ghost
	Wraith
	Revenant

EXPLOSIVE TANK
EXPLOSIVE TANK
EXPLOSIVE TANK
H
TRUCK
H
RALLY POINT ALPHA
H
H
SHADE TURRET
D
H
EXPLOSIVE TANK
H
E
RALLY POINT BRAVO
H
H
H

Down the Skirmishers around the corner from the Covenant supply cases and collect the Needle Rifles they drop. Hopefully, you still have a few rounds left for the DMR, otherwise return to the bridge and swap it out for an Assault Rifle—you to want to have at least one traditional ballistic-style weapon in hand for exploring the Mining Facility. Advance around the corner and look through the metal beams on an angle to spot the fuel tank on the upper platform. Detonate the tank with your UNSC-provided weapon for a quick multi-kill.

Make sure you have an Assault Rifle or DMR on hand to detonate the fuel tanks in this area; a Needle Rifle just isn't enough to pierce the shell.

Continue along the western side of the facility and pause on the stairs near the Covenant supply case to swap Hologram for Armor Lock. The path winds its way around the front of the facility towards an Elite manning a Plasma Cannon around the next corner. Detonate the fuel tank to the left of the turret—it may not kill the Elite, but it should weaken it substantially—and take the heavy weapon with you as you proceed to the center of the structure. Drop off the ledge near the UNSC supply crate and head up the stairs near the Grunts to the south.

YOUR HERESY WILL STAY YOUR FEET

You can find the Elite Zealot that was known to be in the area at the south end of the facility, near the antenna above the stairs. Take out as many of the other enemies as possible from afar, then charge one of the Grunt's Plasma Pistols as you ascend the stairs towards the Zealot. Hit it with a fully charged plasma blast (or Plasma Grenade) to deplete its shields, then quickly switch to another weapon—preferably the DMR or Needle Rifle—and shoot it in the head. Of course, this is all much easier said than done; the Zealot moves with exceptional speed and cunning and is a crack-shot with his Concussion Rifle. Be ready to activate Armor Lock on a moment's notice! He also leaps down the hole and starts running for the vehicles in the distance, likely with Active Camouflage activated. Stay on his tail and keep firing. If you find it too hard to catch up to the Elite Zealot, try again, and this time, swap to the Sprint Armor Ability before climbing the stairs to the target's location.

The Zealot-class Elite won't stick around long enough for you to slug it out with him. Stick close to Kat and use a charged Plasma Pistol blast followed by a quick bullet (or needle) to the head to take him down before he flees.

There's a Medkit and Frag Grenade in the alcove near the USNC supply crate where you fought the Zealot. Gather up some ammo and drop through the hole into the floor near the spools of cable and eliminate the final few Covies in the area. Lay claim to the Plasma Launcher near the Covenant supply case in the next room and put it to use right away on the Grunts trying to flee on the Ghosts outside the facility. Climb aboard the Revenant and head west into the canyon leading towards the second AA gun. Once you take the driver's seat, Kat hops into the Revenant's passenger seat.

Plasma Launcher

The Plasma Launcher is like the Grenade Launcher in that it can be used to fire Plasma Grenades, but that is where the similarity ends. The Plasma Launcher has 2.5x zoom and can be charged to fire between one and four Plasma Grenades at a time. The Plasma Grenades can track any enemy that has been targeted, as long as the reticule achieves lock-on and turns red before the trigger is released. Hold the trigger to charge each Plasma Grenade one by one—four small dots appear on the crosshairs as the Plasma Grenades become active. Though powerful, the Plasma Grenades move quite slowly through the air and can be out-maneuvered if the enemy takes cover. The Plasma Launcher is best used against the slower moving, armor-clad Hunters and vehicles. Refer to the Ordnance section of the Appendices on page 337 for additional information and statistics about the Plasma Launcher.

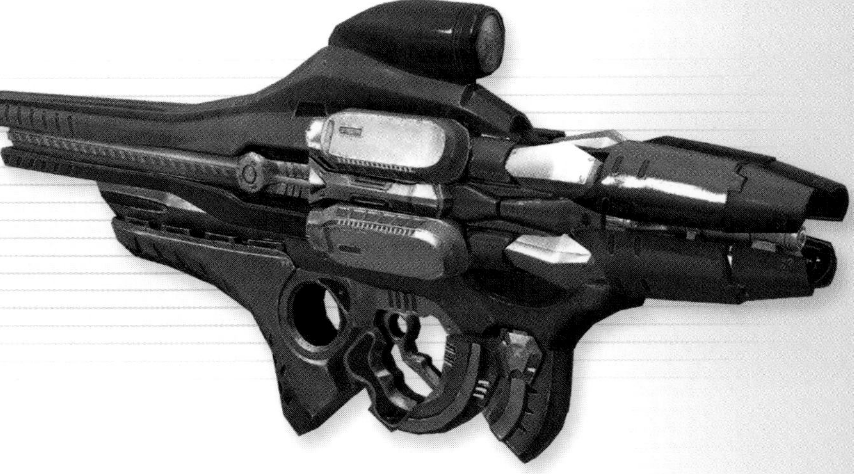

OBJECTIVE

E: NEUTRALIZE ENEMY AA

Neutralize the second Covenant AA gun.

The second AA gun is neutralized in much the same fashion as the first, but this one is far more heavily fortified. The area surrounding the AA gun is home to a number of Wraiths and Ghosts, but in many ways, it's the Covenant foot-soldiers you have to worry about most. Driving ever-tightening laps around the structure works to some extent on the lower difficulty modes, but you should take a much more targeted approach on Heroic and Legendary mode.

A BRIDGE TOO HIGH

The collapsed bridge in this area has a perfectly usable Warthog abandoned on top of it. Though it's best to use the Revenant throughout this objective, those playing co-op with friends can double their vehicular firepower by taking hold of the Warthog. Do so by parking the Revenant against the fractured column north of the bridge. Carefully leap from the Revenant onto the column's lower ledge, then onto the top, and over across the next column and onto the bridge panel where the Warthog rests.

Begin the assault on the AA gun by bringing the Revenant to a halt as soon as you drop off the collapsed road surface and eliminate the pack of Jackals to the right. However, don't proceed down that road to the west. Turn around and head east to begin driving the perimeter road in a clockwise direction towards another group of Jackals led by an Elite. Stay far to the southeast side of the area to avoid the Hunters, Buggers, and Skirmishers guarding the path leading up to the AA gun.

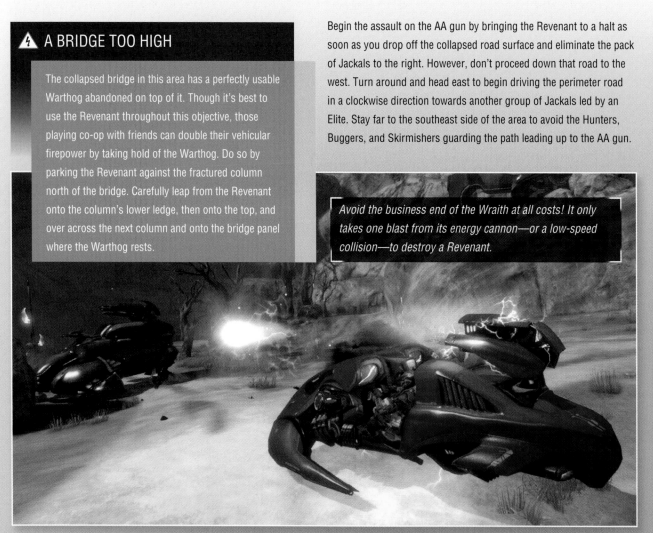

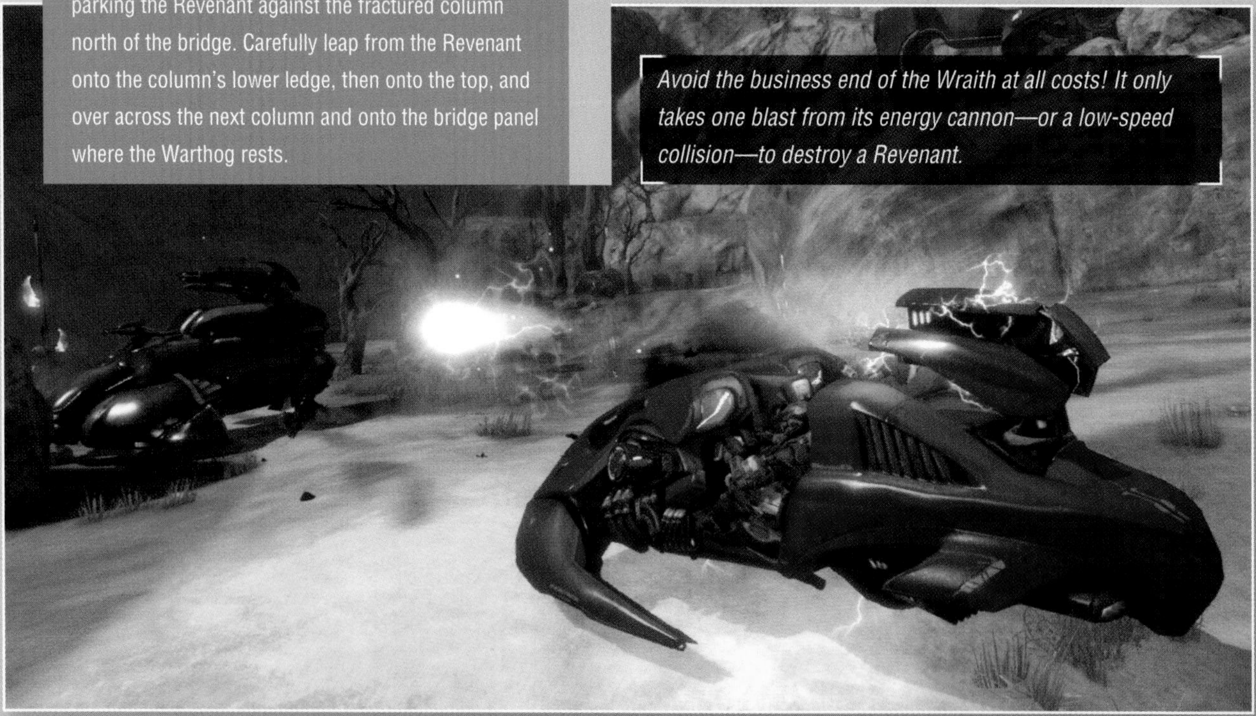

Avoid the business end of the Wraith at all costs! It only takes one blast from its energy cannon—or a low-speed collision—to destroy a Revenant.

ONE CHECKPOINT AT A TIME

This assault on the second AA gun and the enemies surrounding it may very well be the first truly difficult point in the campaign for you. Remember to allow time for the Revenant's shields to replenish between engagements and take on small numbers of enemies at a time. Each small skirmish brings you closer to the next checkpoint (i.e., an autosave) and victory. Checkpoints commonly trigger after you've defeated each Wraith, after you've slain a select band of enemies, and also at time intervals. Don't give up when the odds begin to feel stacked against you; just continue to chip away at the Covenant one foe at a time and let the checkpoints help you accomplish your goal.

Dealing with the Wraiths is sure to be the hardest part of this objective. Maintain a distance of at least 100 feet from the Wraith and strafe side to side in a semi-circular pattern to avoid staying directly in front of it. Use the turbo propulsion to accelerate out of the way if and when it attempts to ram into you. Aim for the energy cannon mounted on top of it and treat it like a bull in a bullfight. Sidestep its rampaging charge and slay it from the side as it rushes past. Ole!

Eliminate the first Wraith (nearest the bridge to nowhere) and quickly head north alongside the base of the plateau to eliminate the Grunts and other Covies before dealing with the second Wraith. This should trigger another checkpoint and also clear out some enemies that would otherwise get the drop on you while you're contending with the Wraith. Destroy the second Wraith using the techniques that you employed against the first, then return to the base of the collapsed road surface where you first exited the canyon.

HAVE FEET, WILL TRAVEL

Having trouble with the Revenant and want to experiment with the Plasma Launcher you picked up at the Mining Facility? It's certainly a viable alternative, but maybe you should at least use the Revenant to drive counter-clockwise around the base of the AA gun's hill to the Covenant supply cases on the far side of the area. You'll not only find some additional ammo for the Plasma Launcher and Needle Rifle there, but also a very helpful Drop Shield ability. Drop Shield allows you to encase Noble Six in a protective bubble. The Drop Shield deflects all projectile-based attacks and has slight healing capabilities. Move in and out of it to attack.

Before you can tackle the Hunters guarding the approach to the AA gun, you should get out of the Revenant and use the DMR or Needle Rifle to pick off the Skirmishers on the promontory north of the AA gun, and also destroy a couple of the Buggers hovering about near the AA gun. With them out of the way, now you can hop back into the Revenant and begin taking out the two Hunters atop the path. Don't ascend much further up the hill than the tree on the left-hand side of the path. Strafe back and forth, making sure to accelerate as soon as either of the Hunters fires their green energy beam. The Revenant's cannon is powerful enough to eventually defeat both Hunters without needing to account for their impressive armor.

Take out the Skirmishers and Buggers on the hills flanking the Hunters to avoid being caught in crossfire. Keep your distance and sweep side to side with the Revenant while firing at the Hunters from beyond the tree.

Drive the Revenant up the hill towards the antenna, and run inside and disable the AA gun just as you had done earlier. Make a quick getaway as soon as the alarm sounds. Drive back down the hill and wait for Jorge and a Falcon to arrive on the scene for your extraction. Feel free to run over any Grunts that show up in the meantime, but just make sure not to run over the troopers that disembark the Pelican.

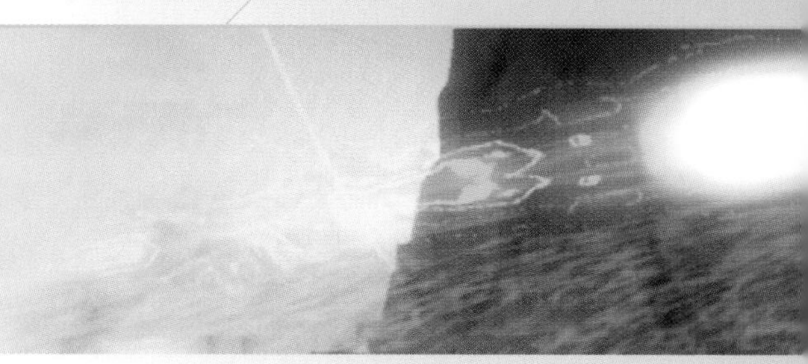

III THE SPIRE

RECOMMENDED EQUIPMENT

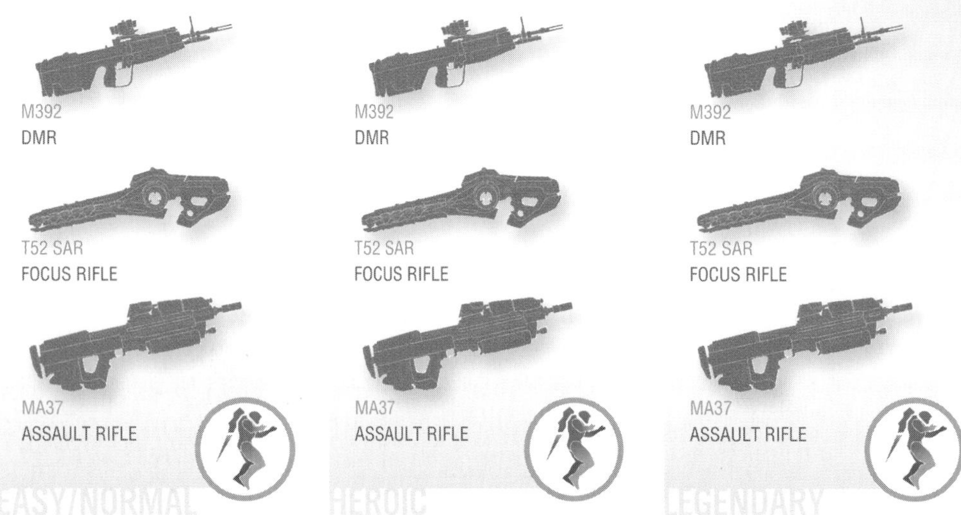

OBJECTIVE

F: ADVANCE TO PRIMARY OBJECTIVE

Ride evac Falcon towards primary objective.

Take a seat on either side of the Falcon (although the best choice is the left-hand side as viewed from tail facing nose) to man the fixed Grenade Launcher. There's no time to nap on this flight, because it's up to you to help keep this bird in the air! The canyon leading to the Covenant Spire is crawling with Covenant forces, including a number of Wraiths that would love nothing more than to shoot a UNSC whirlybird out of the sky. Your job is to make sure that doesn't happen. Fortunately, you've got the right tool for the job. The Falcon's Grenade Launcher works exactly the same as the one you began this mission with, but this one has unlimited ammo and a much faster firing rate thanks to its auto-feed munitions system.

It's best to fire on auto-detonation mode and opt for a rapid-fire assault rather than use precise manual-detonation tactics. After all, an EMP blast isn't going to do you much good—you need to blow those Wraiths and Shade Turrets up! Test the weapon against the four Covies on the bridge, then scan the canyon rim on the side of the Falcon you're sitting on. Individual ground troops don't pose nearly the level of threat as Wraiths or Shade Turrets, so prioritize accordingly. It takes roughly five direct hits with the Grenade Launcher to destroy a Wraith, so fire quickly and make every shot count. Use the Plasma Batteries near antennas to amplify the explosion, and aim between groups of ground troops to score large casualty multi-kills.

Those Wraiths are indeed capable of shooting down the Falcon if you take too long to destroy them. Destroy one Wraith, then quickly scan ahead for the next one.

RALLY POINT BRAVO
F
TRUCK
TRUCK
G
H
SWITCH

ENEMY FORCES

Covenant	
	Grunt Infantry
	Grunt Specialist
	Grunt Hero
	Jackal Infantry
	Jackal Specialist
	Skirmisher Specialist
	Elite Infantry
	Elite Hero
	Elite Specialist
	Elite Leader

OBJECTIVE

G: ACCESS COVENANT SPIRE CONTROL ROOM

Find a way to access the top of the Covenant Spire.

Noble Six and Jorge infiltrate the energy barrier just north of the Covenant Spire. Swap out the Sprint ability in favor of the Jet Pack upgrade on the ground near the Medkits and Frag Grenades. Follow Jorge downstream, deeper into the canyon, but make certain to maintain greater distance from the Covenant lurking in the area. A couple of Skirmishers armed with Focus Rifles fire on you as you leave the wreckage. Take cover and use the DMR to take them out. Jorge needs to get close to put his chaingun to use, but the DMR and Jet Pack afford you the luxury of sniping from atop the rocks on the near side of the creek.

Use the DMR to take out the Grunts working their way down the hill near the pipes, then advance to the east and target the Jackals and Skirmishers hiding amongst the boulders on the side of the hill. The Covies you encounter near the creek don't have the ranged weaponry to contend with the DMR, so post up atop the larger rock piles and pick them off one by one, knowing they offer little threat.

The Elite manning the Plasma Cannon atop the hill is your biggest threat during the approach. Circle around to the left and slip through the gaps in the rocks, and snipe the Plasma Battery next to the Elite to destroy both him and the turret.

Locate the Covenant supply case uphill from where the Elite was with the Plasma Cannon and grab the Focus Rifle lying on the ground. This weapon can help you deal with the Elite manning the Shade Turret on the lower level of the Spire. It also comes in handy with the Elite Specialist in the control room. Make sure to scavenge the area for one or two Plasma Grenades as well—it really makes the final skirmish that much easier.

The control room is located at the very top of the Spire, requiring the use of either of the two gravity lifts extending from the ground all the way up to the uppermost floor. You can access the gravity lift in any of three different ways: via the tunnel below the base of the structure, from the internal corridors leading inside from the ground, or from the vacated platform above the structure's base. It's recommended that you head directly to the roof of the lower base via the elevated pipes on the northern side of the Spire.

Avoid crash landing—and maximize the distance flown—while using the Jet Pack by peppering the propulsion system. Allow Noble Six to periodically fall a short ways to recharge the Jet Pack, then reengage the thrusters to fly even further.

There are a few ways up onto the Spire's upper floor. One way is to use the Jet Pack ability to fly up onto the end of the bridge furthest from the Spire (near the truck) to avoid enemy detection. Use the Focus Rifle to eliminate the Elite in the Shade Turret on the left-hand side of the Spire (as viewed from the conveyor belt bridge), and use the DMR or Needle Rifle to eliminate some of the other Covies running around that lower walkway. Leap off the bridge and fly across to the roof of the Spire's base. From there, you can step into either of the gravity lifts for a risk-free ride up to the control room.

WELCOME
UNSC TRAINING
THE CAMPAIGN
M1: WINTER CONTINGENCY
M2: ONI
M3: NIGHTFALL
M4: TIP OF THE SPEAR
M5: LONG NIGHT OF SOLACE
M6: EXODUS
M7: NEW ALEXANDRIA
M8: THE PACKAGE
M9: THE PILLAR OF AUTUMN
FIREFIGHT
MULTIPLAYER
REFERENCE

STEAL THE BANSHEE

Another way to get to the top of the Spire is to hijack the Banshee flying around the periphery of the area. Use a Plasma Pistol to EMP the Banshee, then fly towards it and press ⊗ to hijack it. Noble Six will toss the pilot out of the craft and slip into the cockpit. Fly all the way to the roof of the Spire, then leap out.

This is a great spot to get a feel for flying the Banshee if you haven't ever piloted one before. Fly up to the Spire and set the craft down on the outer ledge.

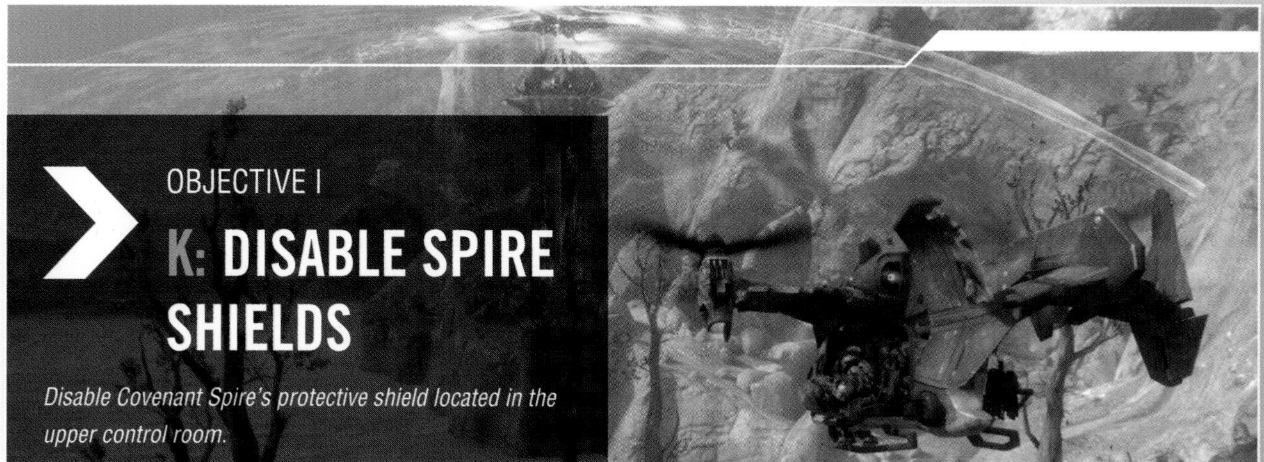

OBJECTIVE I

K: DISABLE SPIRE SHIELDS

Disable Covenant Spire's protective shield located in the upper control room.

The switch controlling the Spire's shields is on the south side of the control room and is heavily guarded by an Elite Specialist and five Grunt Specialists, one of which is certain to have a Fuel Rod Gun. The only approach is via the circular walkway ringing the top of the structure. Enter the center of the Spire and use the Jet Pack to fly near the bulletproof window to scout the opposition in the control room.

Never underestimate the damage that one, well-thrown Plasma Grenade can inflict. Use the Focus Rifle to eliminate the Grunt with the Fuel Rod Gun, then stick the Elite with a Plasma Grenade to clear the room.

Head out into the hallway and advance on the control switch. Move slowly to draw the Grunts towards you one by one to avoid having to take on the whole defense squad simultaneously. The Elite Specialist serving as the last line of defense has an Energy Sword and the will to use it. In tight confines like this, you need to either keep your distance or suffer immediate defeat. Use the Focus Rifle in bursts to avoid overheating, then switch to the Assault Rifle or DMR to finish the job once the Elite's shields are down.

LONG NIGHT OF SOLACE

MOVE UP THE BEACH AND SECURE THE LAUNCH FACILITY. TAKE THE BATTLE TO THE COVENANT SUPER CARRIER.

CHAPTER-SPECIFIC ACHIEVEMENTS

YOU FLEW PRETTY GOOD: Complete the 6th mission on Normal or harder.

WAKE UP, BUTTERCUP: Destroy the Corvette's engines and escort in under 3 minutes in the 6th mission on Heroic or harder.

INTELLIGENCE BRIEFING

BASIC TACTICS

Fight alongside the rest of Noble Team as you make your way up the beach to the top-secret starship facility. Use plasma-based weaponry to deplete enemy shields, then switch to your standard-issue sidearm and finish Elites with a shot to the head. Use the cover of the rocks to flank behind enemies, then cross from the sea to the cliffs to move in behind enemies near the launch facility. Follow Jorge through the flight control room to the launch pad where the Sabre awaits.

MISSION OBJECTIVES

- Proceed to launch facility.
- Proceed to flight control.
- Board Sabre for launch.
- Defend Anchor 9.
- Anchor 9 defenses online.
- Dock with Anchor 9.
- Destroy Corvette fighter escort.
- Corvette engines damaged.
- Board Corvette.
- Clear the hangar for the Pelican.
- Proceed to the bridge.
- Defend the Slipspace Bomb.

WELCOME
UNSC TRAINING
THE CAMPAIGN
M1: WINTER CONTINGENCY
M2: ONI
M3: NIGHTFALL
M4: TIP OF THE SPEAR
M5: LONG NIGHT OF SOLACE
M6: EXODUS
M7: NEW ALEXANDRIA
M8: THE PACKAGE
M9: THE PILLAR OF AUTUMN
FIREFIGHT
MULTIPLAYER
REFERENCE

Zones II and III take place in orbit.

II Familiarize yourself with the Sabre's controls and put its weapons system to use against the Banshees and Seraphs that attack. Use guns to take out the Banshees and Seraph's shields, and use the on-board missile system to destroy the Seraphs. Defeat multiple waves of enemies until Phantoms appear. Fly beyond the Phantoms to get around their impenetrable shields and attack their rear with guns. Don't target the Corvette until the area is cleared of its escort ships, then pull behind it and target its four engines with missiles. Set the Sabre down on the landing deck atop the Corvette.

III Drop through the energy barrier on the deck of the Corvette to enter its interior. Use a Plasma Repeater and Magnum to pick off the enemies in the room below, then advance to the hangar. Use the Hologram ability to distract the numerous Grunts and Elites while you detonate the Plasma Batteries near the enemies in the room. Defeat the multiple waves of enemies and continue alongside your Fireteam towards the bridge, where four high-level Elites await. Move in and out of the cover of the Drop Shield and use the Plasma Repeater and DMR, along with Plasma Grenades, to defeat them. Throw the switch and return to Jorge in the hangar and assist him in defeating the final squad of Covenant.

FIRST FLOOR: BEACHES, ALIENS, TOP SECRET LAUNCH FACILITIES

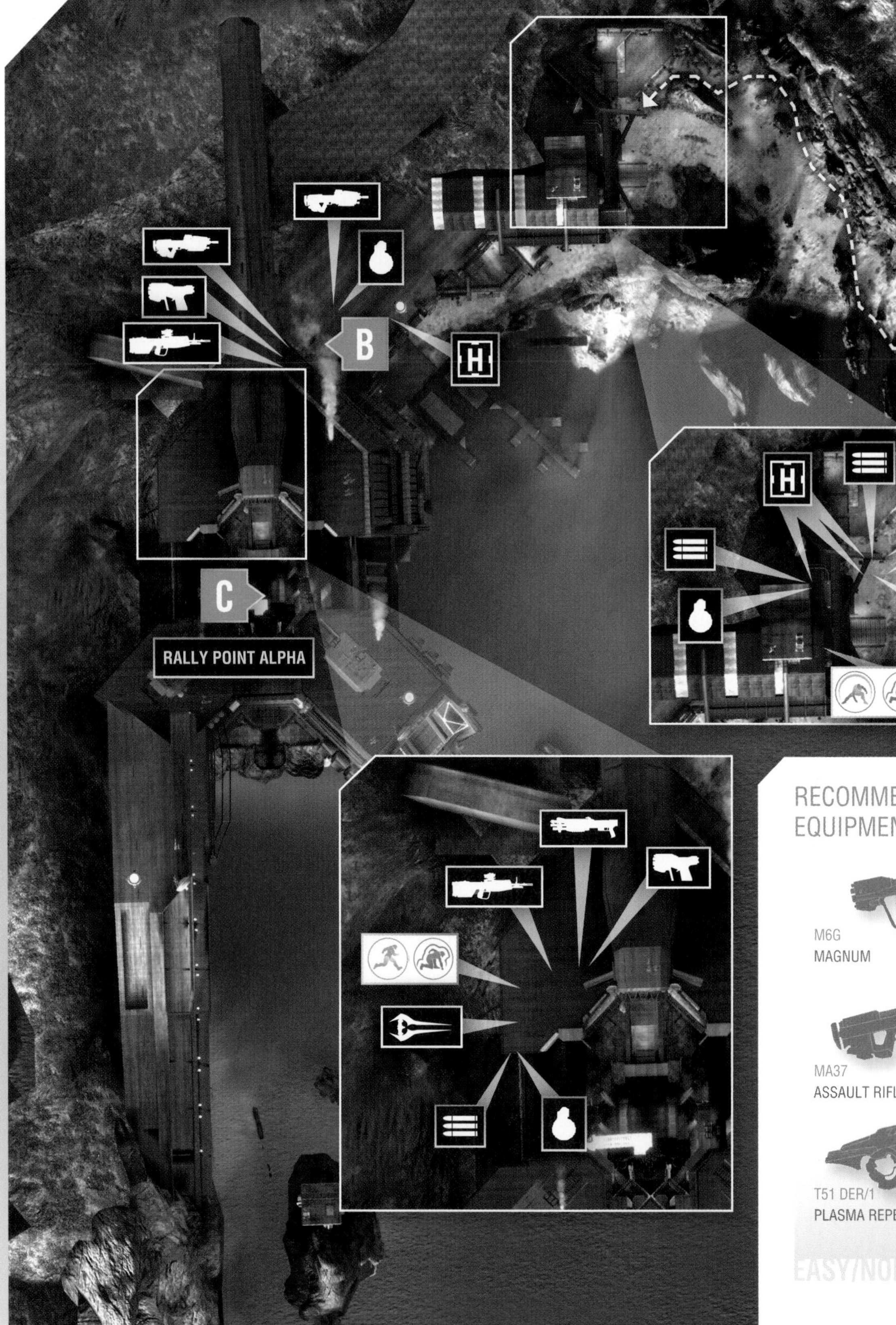

RECOMMENDED EQUIPMENT

M6G
MAGNUM

MA37
ASSAULT RIFLE

T51 DER/1
PLASMA REPEATER

EASY/NORMAL

A

MISSION START

ENEMY FORCES

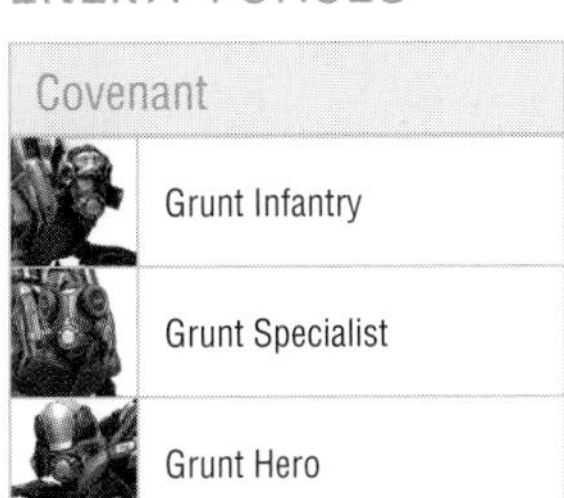

Covenant
Grunt Infantry
Grunt Specialist
Grunt Hero

Covenant
Jackal Specialist
Elite Specialist
Elite Leader

M6G
MAGNUM

T25 DER
PLASMA RIFLE

T51 DER/1
PLASMA REPEATER

HEROIC

M6G
MAGNUM

T25 DER
PLASMA RIFLE

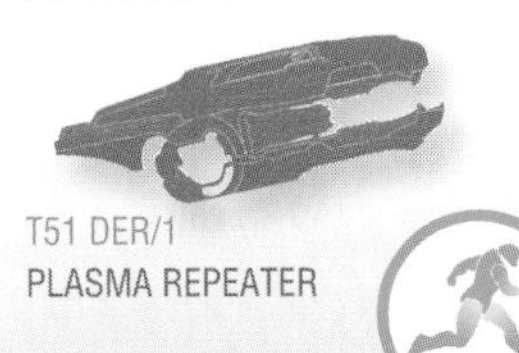

T51 DER/1
PLASMA REPEATER

LEGENDARY

OBJECTIVE

A: PROCEED TO LAUNCH FACILITY

Fight your way to the launch facility entrance.

Noble Team (minus Jun and Emile) is set down on a rocky lakeside beach roughly a mile southwest of the top-secret launch facility. The Covenant knows about the facility and is in the midst of launching a full-scale assault. What they don't know is that Noble Team is coming up the beach behind them! It hasn't been too important up to this point, but you're going to want a plasma-based weapon with you throughout much of this mission. Look to swap the Assault Rifle for either a Plasma Repeater or Plasma Rifle at your first opportunity.

Follow Kat and Carter up the narrow path to where the beach really widens. Small groups of Grunts and Jackals are hiding amongst the rocks here. Advance slowly and use the Magnum to rack up short strings of headshots, but keep your ears open for the sound of a jet pack. Elites soon emerge from inbound drop pods throughout the area. Flank to the left of the rocks on the beach to get a sideways shot on them while Jorge and the others take a more direct approach. Use the Plasma Repeater to deplete their shields and switch to the Magnum to finish them off. The Jackals uphill from this engagement may prove to be quite effective snipers with their Needle Rifles, so be careful not to stray any further up the beach while battling the Elite Specialists.

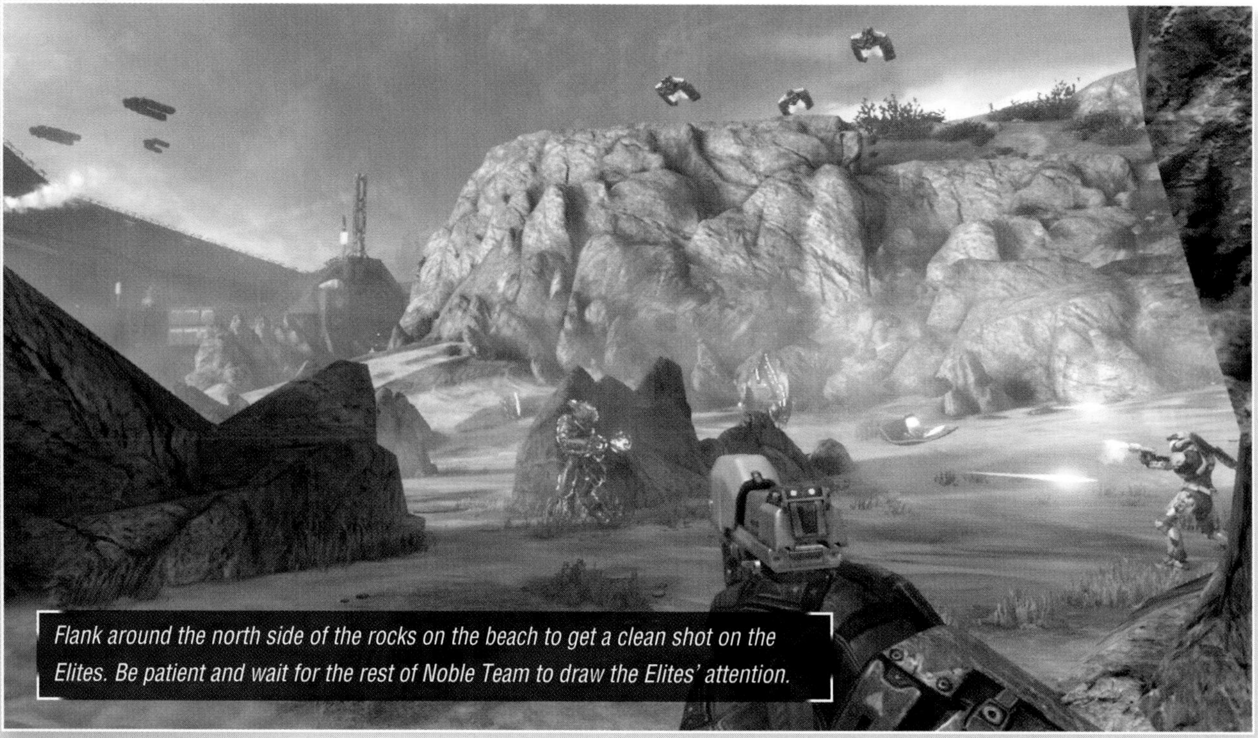

Flank around the north side of the rocks on the beach to get a clean shot on the Elites. Be patient and wait for the rest of Noble Team to draw the Elites' attention.

Advance further up the beach, using the Magnum to take out the lesser foes you see grouped up in the distance. Stick to the left-hand side of the beach as you advance towards the facility, until you reach the massive outcropping of rocks near the UNSC blast shields that have been wheeled into place on the sand. Cut across the face of this defense line to the south and flank the remaining enemies from the base of the cliffs.

Gather up any Plasma Grenades you find and have them ready for the final Elites that drop in from space. Kat and the others typically pick a path that leads straight up the beach, giving you a great opportunity to flank the Elites. Swap out your Magnum for a DMR at the gun rack on the front of the facility's concrete supports and finish off the remaining Covies in the area. Carter lets you know when it's time to go inside. Follow him and the others into the secure area. If you're going for metascore, you can hang out on the beach and help the troopers defend against the Covenant for as long as you like.

However, you will not receive another checkpoint until you go inside the facility past the breach, so you're gambling with your own time. Don't get greedy!

Move in behind the remaining Covenant via the path around the rocks (nearest the cliffs) on the right, and finish them off with one of the DMRs from the gun rack.

OBJECTIVE B: PROCEED TO FLIGHT CONTROL

Meet the flight control officer in the launch facility control room.

NO TRADE-BACKS

The UNSC Troopers won't trade weapons with you if the weapon you're offering is completely out of ammo, but they won't dare refuse a trade if you give them a weapon with at least one or two rounds of ammo left. You won't need any weapons once you get inside the launch facility, but keep this in mind for the future. If you are running low on Magnum ammo, for example, leave one round in the clip and trade it to a trooper with a DMR or other fully loaded weapon that suits your fancy.

Enter the launch facility and proceed through the hallway to the room with the breach in the left-hand wall. A drop ship has set down a Wraith and a number of Covenant on the dock below. The troopers stationed at the facility have the firepower to dispatch the Wraith, so you're free to continue to the flight control room, or you can watch. Of course, if you're trying to earn extra Credits to spend in The Armory, you can take the trooper's Rocket Launcher and take out the Wraith yourself. Another option is to use the DMR to snipe the Covenant foot units, then leap down, board the Wraith, and plant a grenade inside it (make sure you take the trooper's Rocket Launcher first, so he doesn't blow you up). If you opt for this hands-on approach, you'll have to return to the interior of the facility via the path leading back up the slope near the beach.

The trooper can take care of the Wraith if you let him, but you won't earn any Credits that way. Swap him for the Rocket Launcher (or use your grenades) and do it yourself!

Stay close to the rest of Noble Team during the run to the flight control room. An Elite has breached the secured hallways and will attack at close range. Have a plasma weapon ready for him.

OBJECTIVE C: BOARD SABRE FOR LAUNCH

Board the Sabre for launch.

The UNSC Troopers succeeded in holding off the Covenant so far, but it's only a matter of time before the facility is overrun. Follow Jorge to the door at the northeast side of the flight control room and wait for Kat to unlock it. Continue down the hall and up the stairs to the launch pad. The Sabre is mounted atop a set of massive external fuel tanks and rockets. Approach the Sabre with Jorge, look up towards the pilot's cockpit, and climb aboard for blastoff.

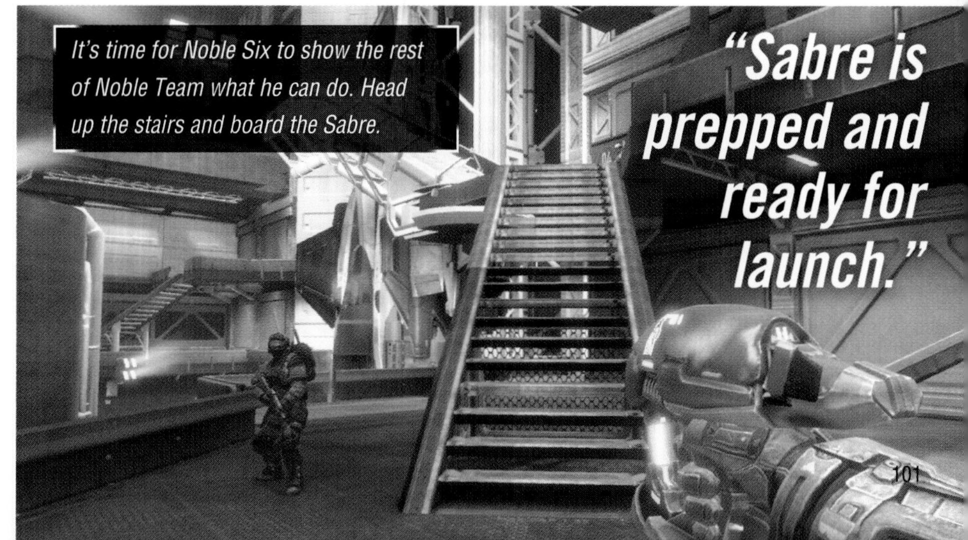

It's time for Noble Six to show the rest of Noble Team what he can do. Head up the stairs and board the Sabre.

"Sabre is prepped and ready for launch."

OPERATION: UPPER CUT

OBJECTIVE

D: DEFEND ANCHOR 9

ENEMY VEHICLES

Covenant	
	Space Banshee
	Seraph
	Phantom

Defend Anchor 9 until the defensive batteries come back online.

The Sabre two-person combat starship is outfitted with machine guns and heat-seeking missiles. Take a minute and follow the on-screen instructions to get a feel for how to pilot the Sabre. The controls (explained in detail in the "UNSC Training" chapter) are quite intuitive, and the Sabre's afterburners and weapons systems are as responsive as you might expect. Fly with confidence, knowing that the most significant risk you face is inadvertently crashing into one of the Anchor 9 space station modules or being caught in a barrage of friendly fire. The former is especially acute when performing evasive maneuvers too close to the station.

Steer clear of Anchor 9's superstructure and use the Sabre's machine guns to blast the Banshees out of the sky.

Anchor 9's defenses are currently offline, and the crew needs you and the rest of the Sabre squadron to defend it from inbound bogies. The first wave of enemies consists of six Banshees. Use the afterburners to speed towards their origination point and open fire with the Sabre's machine guns. Aim the reticule at the Banshees and fire the weapons continuously once the reticule turns red, signaling that you're within range.

The next wave of enemies consists of Seraph ships. Seraphs are larger and slower than the Banshees, but they are equipped with energy shields that neutralize the Sabre's missiles. Destroy their shields with machine gun fire, then switch to missiles, achieve lock-on, and fire. The key to defeating Seraphs effectively lies in throttle control. The Seraphs tend to slow and wobble a bit the moment their shields are disabled. Pull back on the throttle to slow the Sabre down as you get close while machine gunning it to avoid overrunning your target. The Seraph then regains power and speeds off. Activate your thrusters and chase the Seraph at full speed while achieving missile lock. For maximum effectiveness, try to maintain a distance between 200 and 600 meters when targeting the Seraph with missiles.

OBJECTIVE

E: ANCHOR 9 DEFENSES ONLINE

Assist Anchor 9 in repelling the Covenant attack force.

Now that Anchor 9's defenses are online, you're going to have to be careful to avoid inadvertently catching any of the station's bullets. Multiple waves of Banshees and Seraphs attack in relatively quick succession. Clear the area directly between Anchor 9 and the on-screen marker indicating where the Covenant forces will exit slipstream to give the Anchor 9 a clear line of fire. Stick to the periphery and blast the Banshees and Seraphs as they fly past. Focus on picking off any enemy ships that make it above, below, or behind the Anchor 9. It's okay to fly far out in front of Anchor 9, as long as you steer clear of the barrage of yellow machine gun fire.

SHIELDS AND HULL DAMAGE

The HUD displays the damage your Sabre takes to its shields and hull as a percentage basis. The Sabre's shields work just like Noble Six's—they absorb nearly all types of damage until depleted, after which point the hull can take damage. The shields won't protect the Sabre from direct collision with any space debris or other ships (or the Anchor 9), but they will recharge if given enough time. Watch your shield indicator carefully and don't hesitate to fly away from the action if the shields get below 40%. You can fly past debris clusters or behind the station and keep a low profile while the shields recharge, then return to battle.

Assist the other pilots in clearing away the waves of Seraphs and Banshees while paying attention to the radio chatter. The final wave of enemies consists of multiple heavily shielded Phantoms. Unlike the other craft, the Phantoms won't fire on you, and their front-loaded shields cannot be destroyed. Use the Sabre's afterburners to move into position behind the Phantoms and open fire with the machine guns before the Phantoms get within striking range of the Anchor 9.

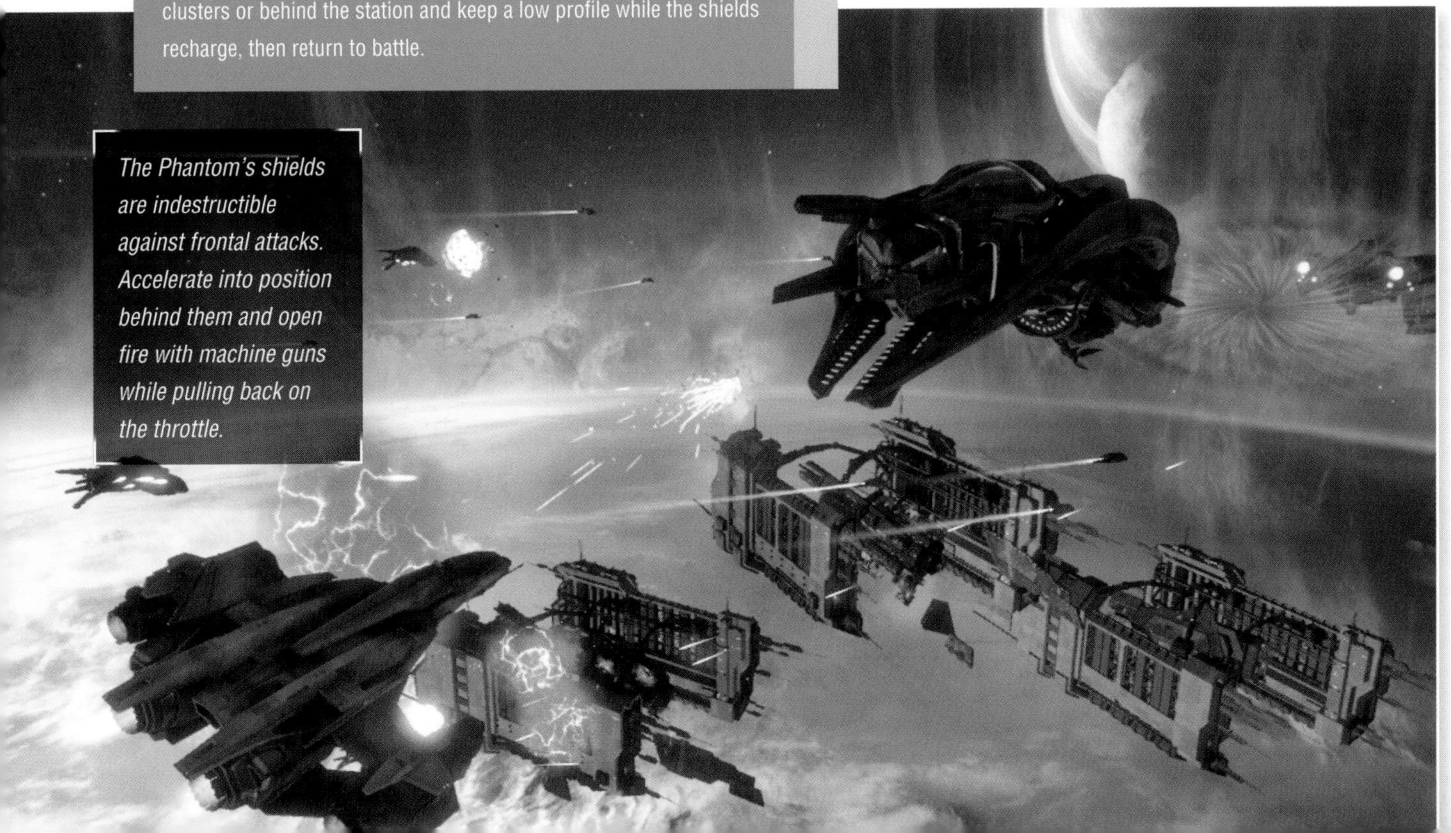

The Phantom's shields are indestructible against frontal attacks. Accelerate into position behind them and open fire with machine guns while pulling back on the throttle.

OBJECTIVE

F: DOCK WITH ANCHOR 9

Dock at Anchor 9 to start Operation: Upper Cut.

With the Covenant strike fleet destroyed, it's safe for you to dock with the Anchor 9 space station. Level the Sabre's trajectory and turn to face the on-screen marker. You'll notice three docking bays on the Anchor 9—fly to the center one to dock with the station.

The Sabre docks automatically once you get within 60 meters of the docking bay. Just line it up and fly straight towards the Anchor 9.

OBJECTIVE

G: CORVETTE ENGINES DAMAGED

Damage the Corvettes main engines to keep it from reaching the Covenant Super Carrier before the Slipspace Bomb is delivered.

Thanks to the communication jamming, the Corvette can't call for help. Take advantage of the situation and destroy the Corvette's four engines. Fly at least 1000 meters beyond the Corvette and slightly below it, then turn around and drift towards the rear of the Corvette. Switch to missiles and use the missiles to lock on to each engine and fire. Pull down on the thruster controls to go as slowly as possible to avoid crashing into the rear of the Corvette while destroying the engines one by one. The Corvette's powerful engines can suck the Sabre into the intake if the Sabre gets too close—be sure to turn away and take another approach once less than 200 meters from the engines.

Speed towards the Corvette and open fire on the Banshees docked beneath the ship. Move fast, and you can cut down the number of escorts you'll eventually have to battle, not to mention you can earn a Killionaire medal! Once the Banshees launch, the belly of the Corvette is a relatively safe place to regain your shields, as is the far side of the Savannah as it orbits the enemy capital ship.

The Corvette's rear hull acts as a shield of sorts to protect the engines. Fly slightly beneath the Corvette to get a clean shot on the engines.

OBJECTIVE

H: DESTROY CORVETTE FIGHTER ESCORT

Eliminate the Corvette's escorts and cover the Savannah as it jams the Corvette's communications.

A number of Covenant squadrons are inbound from patrol. You and the rest of Noble Team must scramble to assist the Savannah in battle. Give the Corvette a wide berth to avoid inadvertently crashing into it while battling the Banshees and Seraphs. Employ the methods used previously to clear the skies of the smaller Covenant craft. You can also take out the smaller AA guns on the Corvette to make your life easier. They're harder to see, but your weapons will lock on them. Look for the tracer fire coming out of the gun ports!

WAKE UP, BUTTERCUP

Those playing on Heroic or Legendary can earn a smooth 25 Gamer Points by defeating the Corvette's escorts and destroying its four engines within three minutes. Increase your chance for success by quickly piloting the Sabre beneath the center of the Corvette, and use your machine guns to eliminate as many of the docked Banshees as you can before they disengage and go on the offensive—this reduces the number of ships you need to fight. Listen to the radio chatter for the cue that it's time to cut the engines. Use the Sabre's afterburners to get far behind the Corvette, then slow the ship down as much as you can and use missiles to take out the engines one by one. The Seraphs will slipstream into the area shortly thereafter. Stay calm and pursue them one by one.

OBJECTIVE

I: BOARD CORVETTE

Land your Sabre on top of the Corvette's comm. center.

The top of the Corvette is suitable for boarding. Pilot the Sabre towards the circular communication center where the blue energy shield is located. As soon as you pilot it close enough, Noble Six automatically sets the Sabre down in a suitable location.

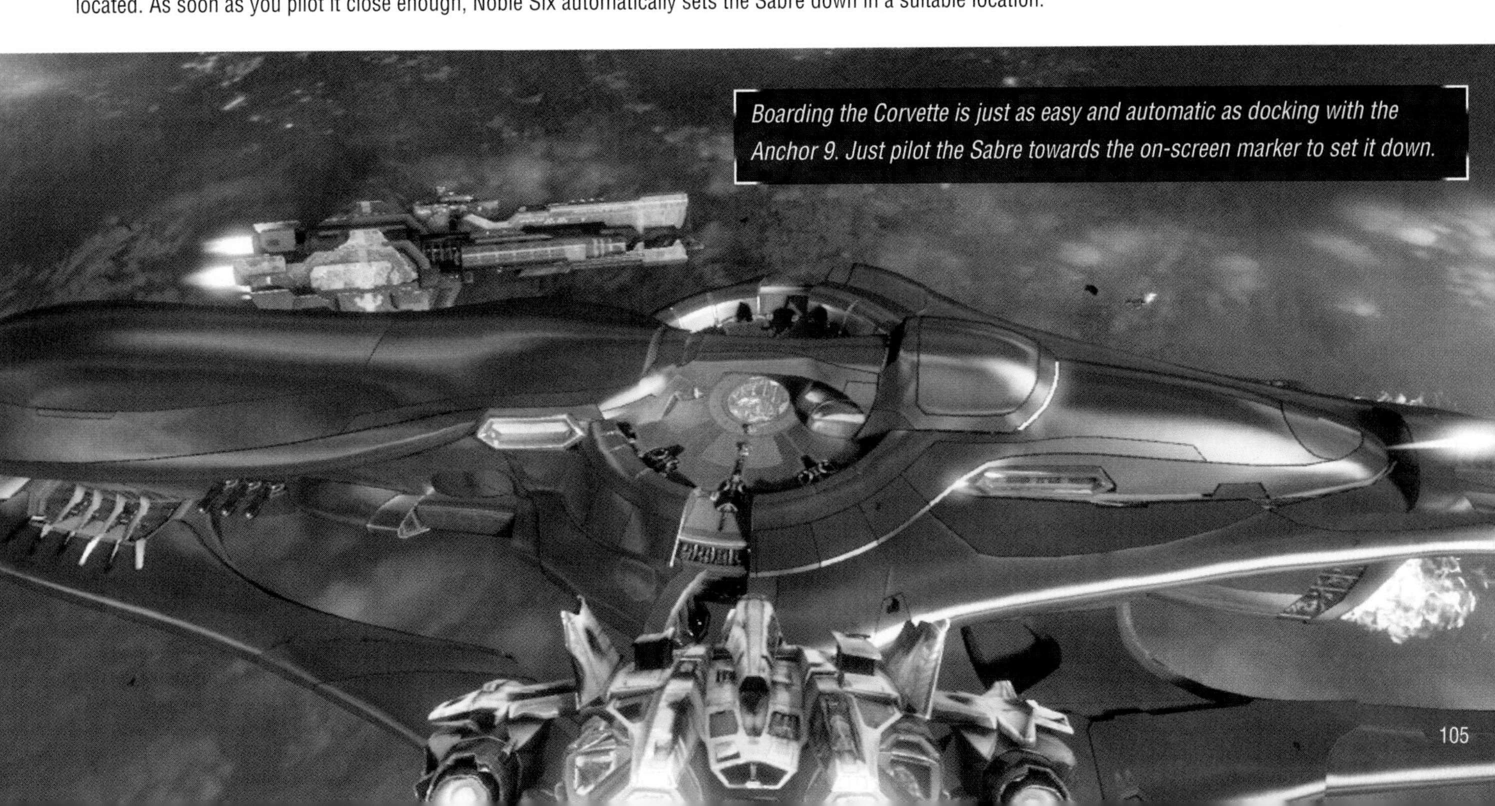

Boarding the Corvette is just as easy and automatic as docking with the Anchor 9. Just pilot the Sabre towards the on-screen marker to set it down.

WELCOME
UNSC TRAINING
THE CAMPAIGN
M1: WINTER CONTINGENCY
M2: ONI
M3: NIGHTFALL
M4: TIP OF THE SPEAR
M5: LONG NIGHT OF SOLACE
M6: EXODUS
M7: NEW ALEXANDRIA
M8: THE PACKAGE
M9: THE PILLAR OF AUTUMN
FIREFIGHT
MULTIPLAYER
REFERENCE

AND THE HORSE YOU FLEW IN ON...

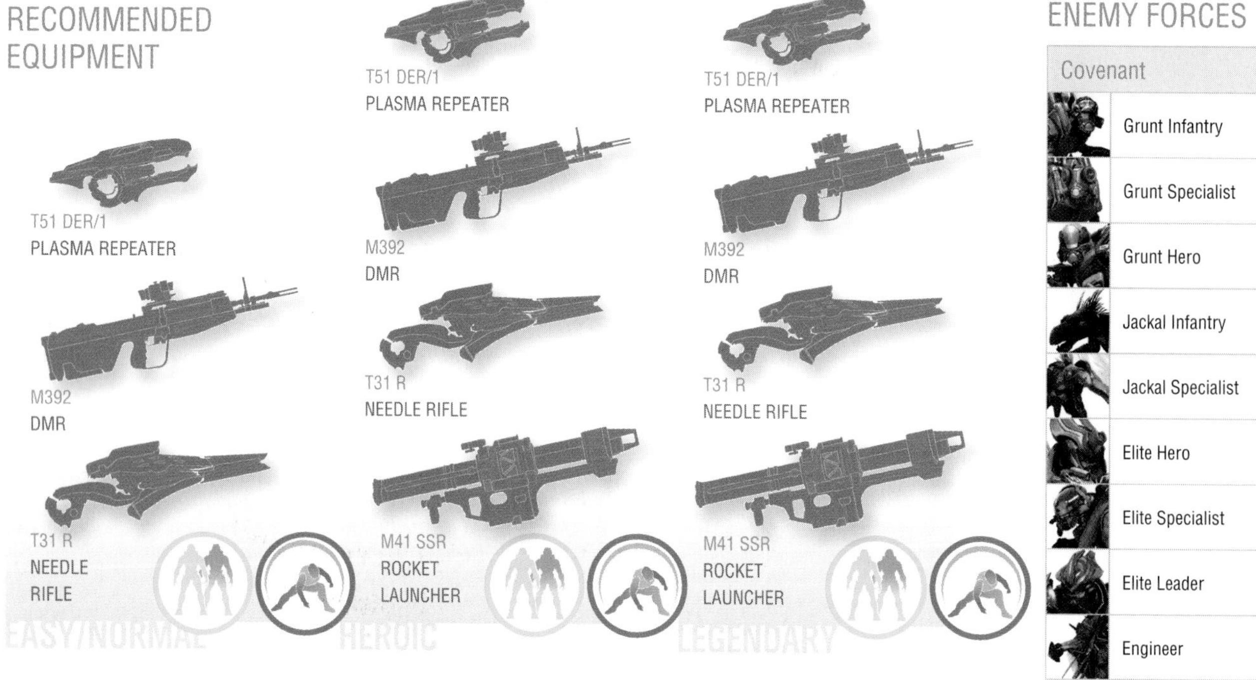

OBJECTIVE

J: KILL CORVETTE COMM. CENTER CREW

Enter the Corvette through the energy shield breach and kill the remaining comm. center crew.

Two Elite Specialists fly out of the energy shield breach and attack on the deck of the Corvette. One appears directly in front of you, while the other is far off to the right. Immediately shoulder the DMR you grabbed on the way into the launch facility and blast away at the flying Elite Specialist to deplete its shields, then pop it with the Magnum to kill it before it even touches down. Take advantage of the decreased gravity and leap to the center of the energy shield breach to land on the uppermost platform within the comm. center below. If you're really feeling confident you can drop through the shield onto one of the space elites manning the terminal and assassinate him.

Avoid falling all the way to the lowermost floor of the comm. center before defeating the Elite Specialists in the area. Use the upper level to your advantage.

Use the elevated position inside the middle of the comm. center to locate and attack the other two Elites in the area. Lob a grenade down at them and use the Plasma Repeater and DMR to finish them off. Locate the loose Armor Abilities on the northern side of the room and swap your Sprint Armor Ability in favor of Hologram. There is a Drop Shield here as well, which is useful if you're in need of health. Covenant ships don't stock up on human health packs so this might come in handy. Look for any plasma weapons with fresher ammo supplies, and proceed towards the corridor on the south side, where you notice multiple enemies running towards the hangar.

WELCOME
UNSC TRAINING
THE CAMPAIGN
M1: WINTER CONTINGENCY
M2: ONI
M3: NIGHTFALL
M4: TIP OF THE SPEAR
M5: LONG NIGHT OF SOLACE
M6: EXODUS
M7: NEW ALEXANDRIA
M8: THE PACKAGE
M9: THE PILLAR OF AUTUMN
FIREFIGHT
MULTIPLAYER
REFERENCE

OBJECTIVE

K: CLEAR THE HANGAR FOR THE PELICAN

Neutralize all enemies in the hangar so Jorge can safely bring the bomb onboard.

Enter the hangar through the door at the end of the hall and turn immediately to the right and ascend to the middle level. Scan the rafters for a large floating creature known as an Engineer (undoubtedly familiar to those who played *Halo: ODST*). Though relatively harmless, Engineers cast a protective shield over nearby Covenant foes and should be destroyed as soon as you arrive on the scene. With the Engineer defeated, use any grenades you have in conjunction with the DMR and the Plasma Batteries in the center of the hangar to lessen the number of Grunts in the center of the room.

In addition to Grunts, the hangar also contains four Elite Specialists, one on each of the southeastern and southwestern platforms and one near each of the energy barriers. The Covenant supply cases in the area are loaded with Needle Rifles that give you the range needed to target the Elites. Remain on the uppermost or middle platform and run the Hologram decoy down towards the Elite near the western side to draw the Elites in closer, where you can target them with the Needle Rifle or DMR. Look for opportunities to detonate Plasma Batteries near the Elites to catch them with an environmental kill and save some ammo.

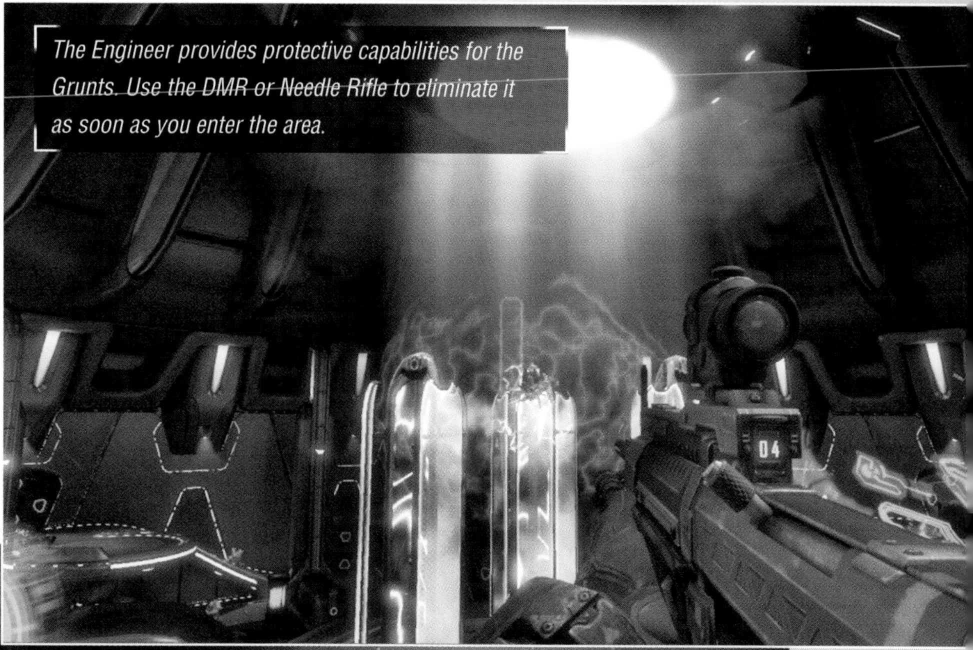

The Engineer provides protective capabilities for the Grunts. Use the DMR or Needle Rifle to eliminate it as soon as you enter the area.

Surprisingly, one of the larger threats in this area comes from the numerous Grunts that make their way up the ramp to your position, often while you're focused on the Elites across the hangar. Watch the motion tracker and periodically strafe over to the ramp to take out any Grunts making their way up towards your position.

The Elites on the upper platforms on the south side of the hangar likely descend to the main floor over the course of the battle. Watch for opportunities to detonate a Plasma Grenade near one of the larger plasma tanks on the far side of the room if the Elites get close. Move up and over the uppermost platform on the north side to get a closer shot on the Elites on the other side of the room, and continue using the Hologram to distract the Elites and create your own clear shots.

Stay on the upper platforms on the northern side of the hangar and send a Hologram towards the Plasma Batteries to set a devastating trap for the Elites.

LEGENDARY TACTICS

The enemies guarding the hangar on Legendary mode form a much stouter line of defense than on other modes. For starters, three Engineers cover the enemies that congregate in the center of the hangar with an extra layer of protection. You must destroy the Engineers before you can really take on the bulk of the enemies in the area. Upon entering the room, climb the ramp on the right to have easy access to the supply of Needle Rifles there, but don't go near the edge overlooking the center of the room. Instead, crouch near the top of the ramp and keep sending your Hologram down the ramp towards the door you entered through to lure Grunts and even an Elite or two into your line of fire. Use Plasma Grenades and the Needle Rifle to eliminate as many of the enemies in this room as you can. There are more Elites in the hangar than on the other modes, so be patient and watch your motion tracker carefully. Return to the supply case for extra Needle Rifle ammo and snipe any Elites you can spot, then drop to the floor and perform a very careful sweep along the perimeter to eliminate the holdouts.

Cross to the southeastern platform and flip the switch on the shield controls, so Jorge can bring the Pelican into the hangar. It becomes safe to do so as soon as you've dispatched the fourth Elite and all of the Grunts,.

OBJECTIVE

L: PROCEED TO THE BRIDGE

Capture the bridge and engage the Corvette's automated refueling system.

The Pelican doesn't only deploy a Fireteam of troopers to assist you, but sends down several gun cases, Armor Abilities, and Medkits as well. Equip a fresh DMR along with a fresh Plasma Rifle or Needle Rifle from one of the Covenant supply cases on the west side of the hangar. Equally important, be sure to swap out the Hologram ability in favor of Drop Shield.

There are three corridors leading south towards the bridge, and a pair of Elites is holed up in the central corridor, just beyond the hangar. Kill the Grunts in the left-hand corridor and collect the Plasma Grenades they drop. Advance down this southeast corridor to the turn and stick either of the Elites with a Plasma Grenade as soon one comes into view. Replenish spent ammo at the gun cases in the hangar and join the troopers further to the south. Sneak up behind the Elite for an easy assasination inside the otherwise vacant room above the Corvette's cannons. Continue through the hallway leading south to the bridge.

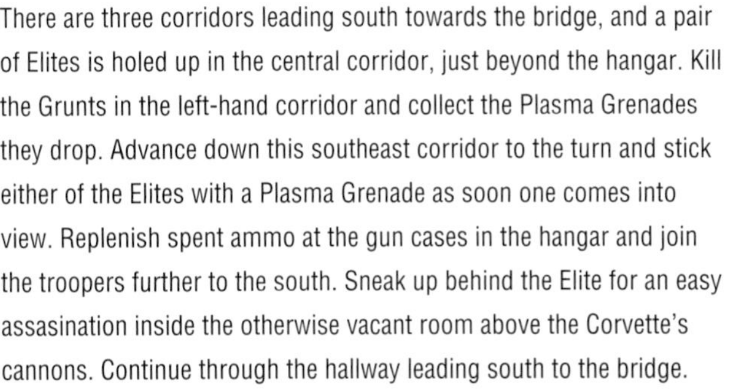

Let the troopers approach the Elites in the hallway leading south from the hangar while you take the left-hand corridor and flank them for an easy grenade-stick

"Noble, you're in deep with no cover!"

A number of Grunts and four Elites guard the bridge. Three of the Elites routinely employ Active Camouflage and wield Plasma Rifles, while the fourth packs a Concussion Rifle. The troopers you're with won't last long against these cloaked Elites, so you're going to have to get this done on your own. Enter the room and immediately deploy a Drop Shield. If the bridge crew is unaware, you can also try sneaking up on a few of the enemies working the terminals for an easy assassination. The marines will hold their fire until you are spotted or you fire your weapon. Move in and out of this Drop Shield while using the DMR to headshot the Grunts while staying safe from the Concussion Rifle attacks made by the Elites. Even though the Grunts don't pose the same threat that the Elites do, they can still hurt you. It's best to quickly reduce the number of guns pointed in your direction, even if it means ignoring the major threats to deal first with numerous minor ones.

Stick to the walkway around the perimeter of the bridge and use the cover of the archways on the western and eastern sides for added cover. Overlap the archway with the Drop Shield to extend the wall of cover and to block all gunfire coming from the south. Watch the motion tracker carefully to get an idea of where the Elites may be—they're not always clearly visible even before they activate their Active Camouflage—and be ready with the Plasma Rifle to deplete their shields. Another option is to simply attack with the DMR—four shots to down their shields, then a headshot to kill them! Once you've cleared the room, flip the switch to initiate the refueling sequence. Don't let your guard down though! Additional Covenant forces are on their way.

Use the Drop Shield for protection from the Concussion Rifle's heavy blasts, then step out and open fire with the DMR. Stick to the perimeter for extra protection and to avoid being surrounded.

SWORDS TO A GUNFIGHT

Another approach to this battle is to grab one of the Energy Swords from the supply case on the right side of the room and use it to slice your way through the Elites. This tactic is quite risky, and tends to work better if you maintain the Sprint ability instead of Drop Shield. With that said, if you've been looking for a chance to use an Energy Sword, here it is. Just remember to use the Melee Button in lieu of the Fire Weapon Button, since it allows you to swing the sword faster and lets you swap weapons and fire a follow-up attack with greater speed than if you had swung the sword with the Fire Weapon Button. Tap the Switch Weapons Button immediately after striking the enemy with a melee attack to instantly switch to a firearm and shoot the enemy while he's stunned from the melee attack.

OBJECTIVE

M: DEFEND THE SLIPSPACE BOMB

Return to the hangar and assist Jorge in defending the bomb.

Load up on ammo before leaving the bridge and gun down the Covies en route to the room overlooking the Corvette's cannons. A small squad of enemies enters from the door opposite the one you enter from; have the DMR or Needle Rifle on hand to dispatch them as quickly as they emerge.

Regroup with the troopers in the hall to the north and follow them to Jorge inside the hangar. Look for a Plasma Launcher on the floor near the entrance and hurry to the Pelican. Jorge has unloaded additional gun cases to the right of the Pelican. Swap out your weapons for the Plasma Launcher and either a fresh DMR or Sniper Rifle. There's also a Medkit on the floor between the cases with the Armor Abilities.

Clear out the enemies in the center of the hangar, then ready yourself for a wave coming in from the southwest platform. Throw a Frag Grenade into the crowd of Covies as they enter the room. The next wave comes in from the north. Snipe the Jackals and Grunts if they get spread out and use the Plasma Launcher against the Elites. The final wave consists of four Elite Specialists, most of which are packing either a Plasma Launcher or Concussion Rifle. Use the DMR and any Plasma Grenades you collect to detonate the Plasma Batteries. Stay on the move and use the Plasma Launcher to stick them while making every effort to avoid the same fate. You can also use the outer area of the hangar to flank the Covenant while Jorge draws their fire from the center. Once the fighting is over, join Jorge near the Slipspace Bomb.

The Drop Shield will deflect the first two Plasma Grenades fired from the Elite Specialists, along with the Concussion Rifle volleys. Don't steal the Corvette without it!

ALL IS NOT LOST. EVACUATE CIVILIANS FROM AN OCCUPIED CITY.

INTELLIGENCE BRIEFING

BASIC TACTICS

I Put the Magnum to use and fight your way through the throngs of suicide Grunts lurking in the maintenance tunnels to reach the concourse of the civic center near Traxus Tower. Head up the stairs near the UNSC Troopers and snipe the Brutes harassing the civilians in the courtyard below. Move into the atrium. Secure the area around the elevator, then defend it from additional Covenant that arrive via Phantom. Use the Machine Gun Turret to eliminate those that deploy in the courtyard, then move to the balconies flanking the elevator lobby to snipe the remaining foes.

II Use the Jet Pack to cross the cargo port to the Covenant-infested platforms on the far side. Use the DMR from within the safety of the red-painted hallways to headhunt the Brutes while remaining safely out of the range of their Spike Rifles. Brutes who have had their helmets knocked off are just one headshot shy of defeat, so aim for the dome! Follow the ODSTs outside to the concourse and use the DMR and Rocket Launcher to rid the area of Jackal snipers and remaining Covenant. Eliminate the Brutes and Shade Turrets at the executive suites to clear a landing pad.

III Load up on ammo and rush for the Warthog up the beach. Stick close to the water's edge and take out the Ghosts and pair of Wraiths. Circle around your vehicular enemies, and never approach a Wraith head-on. Always maintain a position parallel or behind the Wraith. Drive the Warthog to each of the missile batteries to clear them of Brutes and activate each of them. Swap the Jet Pack for the Drop Shield, load up on Rocket Launcher ammo, and push on towards the east complex. Use this combination of equipment to carefully—and slowly—advance up the stairs to the final assembly of Brutes guarding the command console.

CHAPTER-SPECIFIC ACHIEVEMENTS

INTO THE HOWLING DARK: Complete the 7th mission on Normal or harder.

CAMPAIGN

MISSION OBJECTIVES

- Link up with UNSC forces.
- Evacuate civilians from Traxus Tower.
- Advance to atrium elevator.
- Defend position.
- Activate elevator.
- Acquire Jet Pack equipment.
- Traverse cargo port.
- Advance to Traxus Tower.
- Secure landing pad.
- Evacuate civilian transports.
- Arm missile batteries.
- Fire missiles from command console.

THE DEVIL HIS DUE

RECOMMENDED EQUIPMENT

OBJECTIVE

A: LINK UP WITH UNSC FORCES

You've crash-landed near New Alexandria. Link up with UNSC forces defending the city.

The crash has left Noble Six weak and unarmed, save for a Magnum with 25 rounds in it that he found near the crash site. Head up the two flights of stairs directly left of the entry point and go through the doors on the mezzanine to find some additional Magnum ammo near a corpse—it comes in handy soon. Jump down and proceed due west, past the civilian casualties, to the malfunctioning doors to the right of the yellow sign.

Ascend the stairs alongside the fountain and take out the Skirmishers at the top. Tend to Noble Six's injuries with the Medkit near the tables on the left, and slowly approach the door to the civic center. Look for an open doorway behind the reception desk with the help of night vision. Access the supply case containing Armor Lock for added protection against the suicide Grunts.

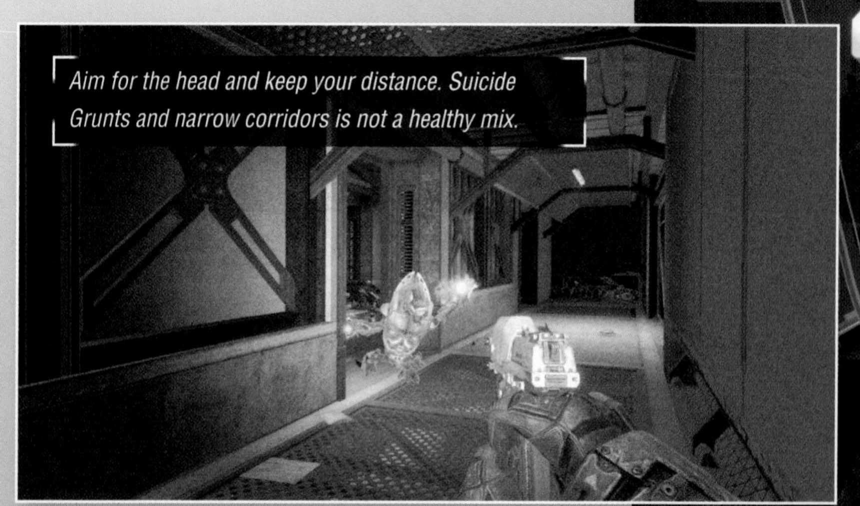

Aim for the head and keep your distance. Suicide Grunts and narrow corridors is not a healthy mix.

ELEVATOR

RALLY POINT ALPHA

D

E

B

A

C

MISSION START

ENEMY FORCES

Covenant
Grunt Infantry
Grunt Specialist
Jackal Infantry
Jackal Specialist
Jackal Hero
Skirmisher Infantry
Skirmisher Specialist
Brute Infantry
Brute Leader

To maximize the usability of this map, extraneous callouts for the Magnum and the Assault Rifle have been removed. These areas have been marked with a *

The maintenance hallways and laundry facility you're about to traverse are crawling with over a dozen suicide Grunts. They'll attempt to swarm you by running towards your position while carrying a Plasma Grenade in each hand. Shooting them makes them drop the explosives, but their forward momentum can put them closer to your feet than you may expect. Watch the motion tracker very carefully, and don't hesitate to lob a Frag Grenade at a larger grouping whenever possible—you only have to take out the front one in order to create a chain reaction. Backpedal while firing on their head and only advance once every Plasma Grenade has detonated. Proceed through the hallways to the northeast, gather additional Magnum ammo from the corpse by the elevator, and continue up the stairs where the last band of suicide Grunts is located.

MAGNUM TRICK SHOT

Precision class weapons such as the Magnum, DMR, and Sniper Rifle are capable of detonating a Plasma Grenade with a single direct hit. This works for those Plasma Grenades being carried by the suicide Grunts. While a bullet to the face works quite well, shooting either of the Plasma Grenades in their hands triggers the detonation on the spot and ensures that the Plasma Grenades won't be tossed your way as the Grunt falls.

Head outside onto the balcony and immediately take cover to the right to avoid fire from the Brutes inside the drop ship. Wait for the craft to depart, then grab the Assault Rifle near the railing and head down the stairs to the south to assist in killing the Brute near the troopers. Incurring civilian casualties by friendly fire will result in mission failure. Check your targets and prevent collateral damage by limiting use of explosive weapons.

OBJECTIVE

B: EVACUATE CIVILIANS FROM TRAXUS TOWER

UNSC forces are evacuating civilians from Traxus Tower. Assist in the evacuation.

Continue due south up the set of stairs beside the UNSC supply case (swap back to the Sprint ability) and hurry over to the troopers near the railing. Grab the Sniper Rifle and move south along this balcony to the corner to get a clear angle on the Brutes down below. The troopers draw the Brutes' attention, giving you a perfect line of sight to their earhole. Give them a sound to remember!

Remain on this balcony near the troopers until you have eliminated all of the Brutes and Skirmishers down below. The Sniper Rifle doesn't have much ammo, so make each shot count!

Snipe each of the Brutes (don't miss the one on the distant balcony, likely torturing a civilian) and watch for the on-screen checkpoint prompt. Fix your sights on the door to the west as soon as you see the checkpoint—your next batch of targets is about to be revealed. A quick shot can take out two Skirmishers with a single bullet. Finish off the others, swap out your empty Sniper Rifle for whichever one you dropped, and leap down.

WELCOME
UNSC TRAINING
THE CAMPAIGN
M1: WINTER CONTINGENCY
M2: ONI
M3: NIGHTFALL
M4: TIP OF THE SPEAR
M5: LONG NIGHT OF SOLACE
M6: EXODUS
M7: NEW ALEXANDRIA
M8: THE PACKAGE
M9: THE PILLAR OF AUTUMN
FIREFIGHT
MULTIPLAYER
REFERENCE

OBJECTIVE

C: ADVANCE TO ATRIUM ELEVATOR

Assist UNSC civilian evacuation from Traxus Tower. Access the tower from an elevator in the atrium.

Enter the atrium and immediately swap the Assault Rifle for the DMR in the alcove to the left of the fountain. Duck into the stairwell to the east and ascend to the second floor to get a better line of sight on the many Covies in this area. Use the cover on the south side of the atrium and snipe each of the Grunts and Brutes in this area with the DMR. It typically takes three headshots with the DMR to knock a Brute's skullcap off, then a fourth to finish the job.

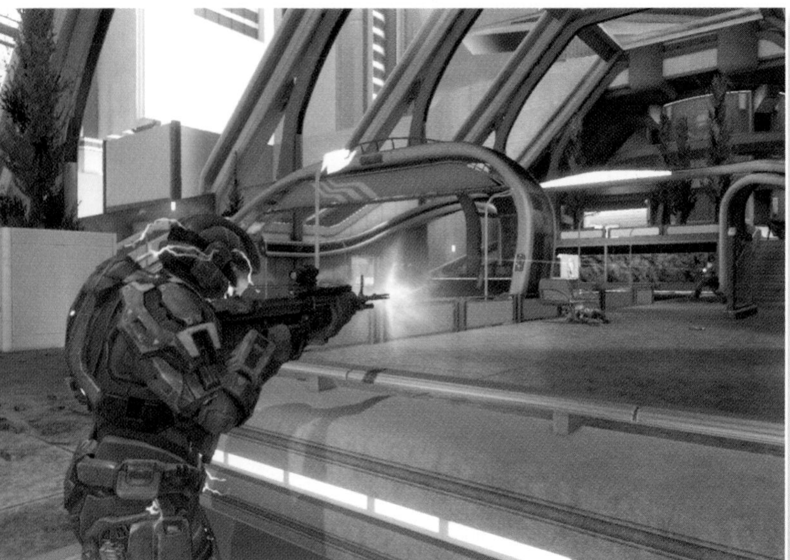

Use the DMR from inside the cover afforded by the planters and stairwells on the south side of the atrium to take out each of the enemies in this area. Start with the Grunts and finish with the Brute Leader above the fountain to the north.

Eliminate each of the Brutes that you can spot before moving on, including the Brute Leader on the second floor balcony to the north. Ascend the stairs on the left-hand side of the atrium and ready a Plasma Grenade for the pair of Brutes behind the planters. Take out the Jackals near the elevator and leap down to the ground floor. Collect any ammo and grenades you can find, then press the elevator button.

OBJECTIVE

D: DEFEND POSITION

Troopers are sending an elevator up to the atrium. Defend your position against the Covenant counterattack until the elevator arrives.

A Phantom is inbound to the courtyard outside the atrium. Hurry through the doors to the east and sprint around the left-hand side of the World Cuisine kiosk near the doors. Detach the Machine Gun Turret from its mount and fall back under cover. The Phantom deploys several Brutes on the side closest to your position—open fire on them the second they touch down! Switch to the DMR to eliminate the Jackals that exit the other Phantom and head back inside. Consider picking up the Gravity Hammer dropped by the Brute Leader if low on ammo.

Lie in wait under the overhang near the food kiosk for the Brutes to exit the Phantom then open fire with the Machine Gun Turret.

The rest of the attacking Covenant forces are working their way from south to north through the atrium. Rush back inside, past the troopers near the elevator you're charged with defending, and up the stairs on the west to where you were minutes ago. Melee the plates of frosted glass to save some ammo, and set to sniping the Skirmishers and other enemies with the DMR. Don't advance any further south than the first planter, so you don't stray from the troopers.

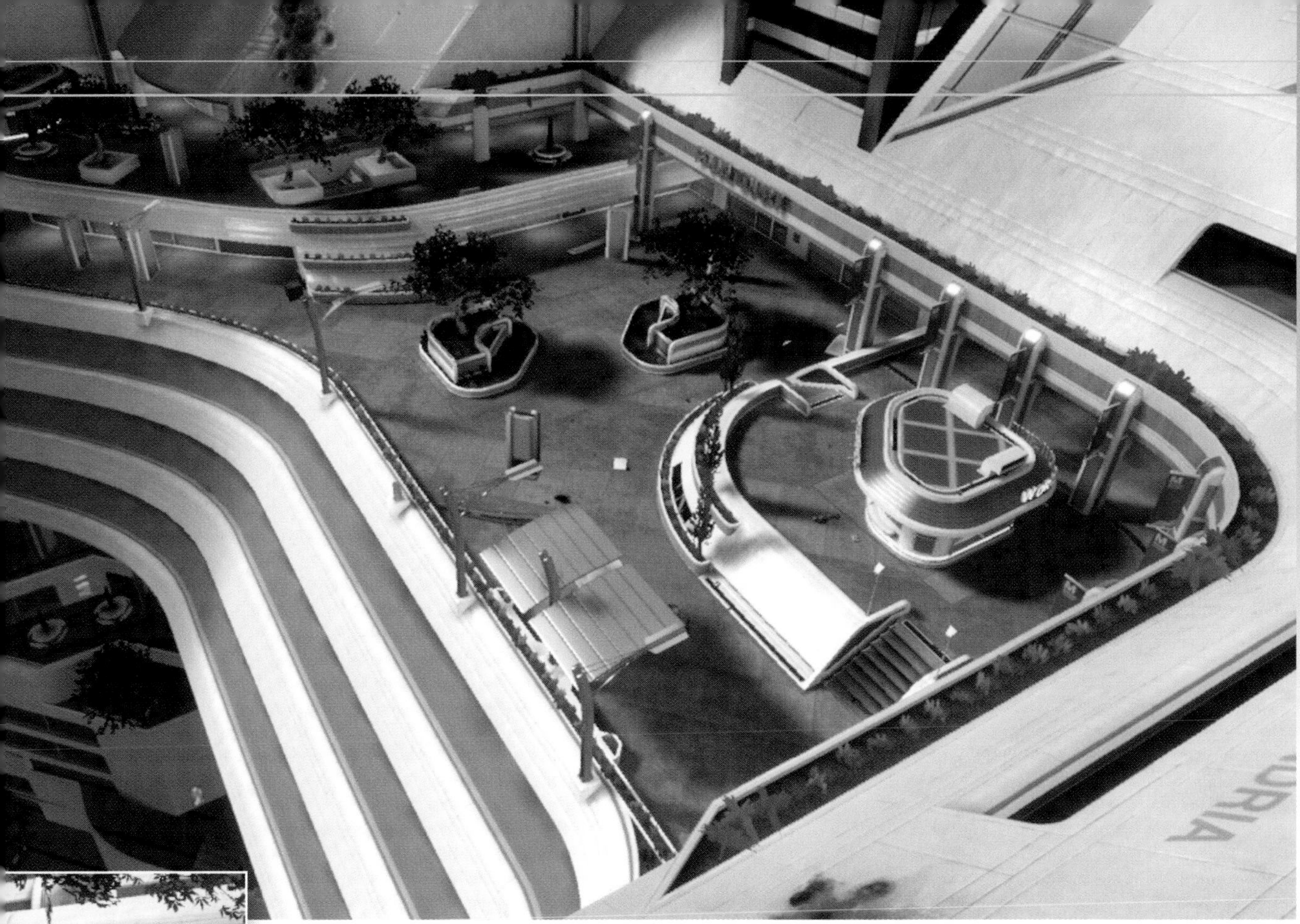

OBJECTIVE

E: ACTIVATE ELEVATOR

Assist UNSC civilian evacuation from Traxus Tower. Take the atrium elevator down to the cargo port to access the tower.

Have a look around the atrium for any fresh ammo or grenades and use the Medkits inside the elevator lobby to top off your health. The going is about to get a bit rough, so prepare now! Ride the elevator downstairs and listen to the Commander's instructions during the ride.

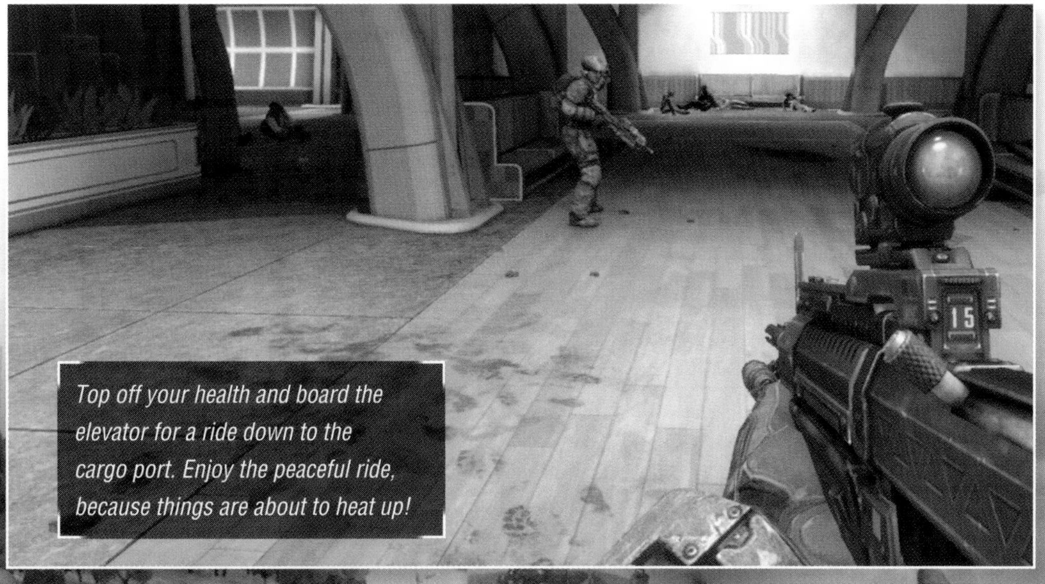

Top off your health and board the elevator for a ride down to the cargo port. Enjoy the peaceful ride, because things are about to heat up!

TOO CLOSE TO THE SUN

RECOMMENDED EQUIPMENT

OBJECTIVE

F: ACQUIRE JET PACK EQUIPMENT

Acquire the Jet Pack Armor Ability and assist ODST squad gearing up to traverse the cargo port.

Cut through the makeshift triage station set up in the lobby and continue outside to the cargo port. Ignore the Banshees drawing fire from the other UNSC Troopers but make sure to swap weapons with the one wielding a Rocket Launcher. Follow the narrow walkway to the ODST squad. Load up on DMR ammo at the cabinet, then go through the gates to swap out your Armor Ability for a Jet Pack.

The Bullfrogs are an ODST squad that accompanies you to the executive flight pad. Try to keep up.

CAMPAIGN

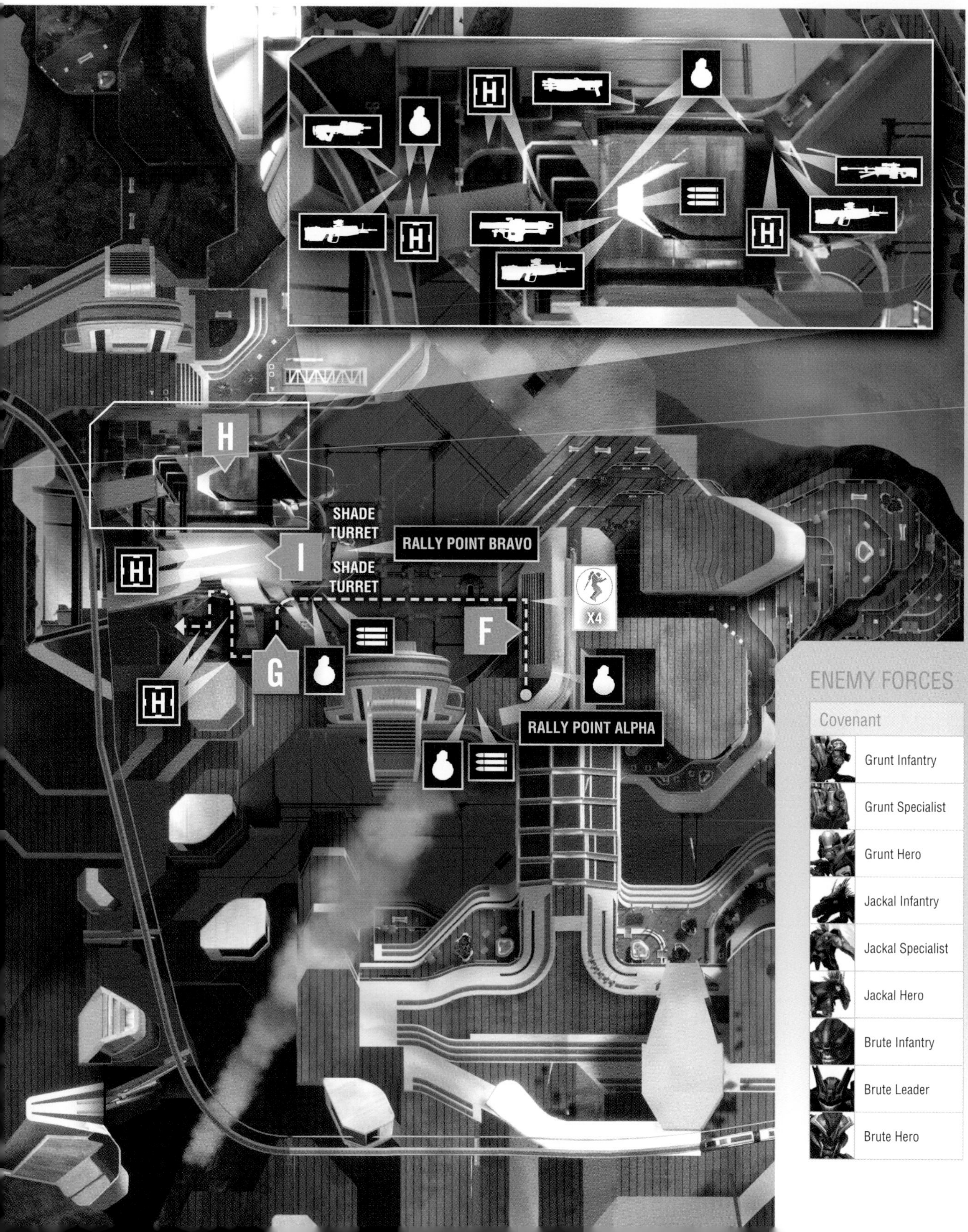

H
SHADE TURRET
RALLY POINT BRAVO
I
SHADE TURRET
H
X4
F
G
H
RALLY POINT ALPHA

ENEMY FORCES

Covenant
Grunt Infantry
Grunt Specialist
Grunt Hero
Jackal Infantry
Jackal Specialist
Jackal Hero
Brute Infantry
Brute Leader
Brute Hero

OBJECTIVE

G: TRAVERSE CARGO PORT

Use the Jet Pack Armor Ability to traverse the cargo port and advance to Traxus Tower.

Leap off the ledge and use the Jet Pack to fly across to the platforms to the west, in the middle of the cargo port. Avoid flying too high, or you may draw the attention of the Banshees in the area. Some of the ODST members veer a bit to the south and attack the Grunts and Jackals directly. Don't follow them. Instead, proceed due west across the port to the lower ledge near the UNSC supply case. You'll have at least two other Bullfrogs with you, so don't worry about getting lonely.

Check your altitude, Spartan! Don't fly too high, or you risk being cut down by the Banshees circling overhead.

LUCKY ME

There are just too many enemies in the cargo port to not try and unlock this Achievement here. Swap weapons with the trooper shouldering the Rocket Launcher as soon as you pass through the triage area. Jet Pack across the cargo port and remain in the covered stairwell near the UNSC supply case until you notice a checkpoint trigger. Now pause and let some of the Grunts on the upper walkway make their way out of hiding. Peer around the corner and look for at least three Covies grouped together. Leap into the air, trigger the Jet Pack, and fire the rocket right at them. Manage to kill three or more Covies with a single attack while jetpacking, and you'll unlock the "Lucky Me" Achievement. This is a perfect spot to do it.

Stay inside the red hallway leading up to the stairs near the crane and pick off as many Brutes and Jackals on the upper walkway as you can, both directly south and to the west. Use the small nearby balcony to get a great angle on the Brutes on the upper path, while enjoying a perch slightly out of range of their Spike Rifles and grenades. Look for opportunities to kill groups of enemies by detonating one of the many green Fusion Cells scattered around the area.

Follow the ODSTs up the stairs to the south and gather up the DMR ammo near any corpses in the area. Circle around the containers and truck to get a clean shot on the Brute Leader on the upper ledge to the west. Use the DMR to drop him before he leaps down and puts the Gravity Hammer to use. Push clockwise around the platform to the stairs leading up to the next level of the port.

WELCOME
UNSC TRAINING
THE CAMPAIGN
M1: WINTER CONTINGENCY
M2: ONI
M3: NIGHTFALL
M4: TIP OF THE SPEAR
M5: LONG NIGHT OF SOLACE
M6: EXODUS
M7: NEW ALEXANDRIA
M8: THE PACKAGE
M9: THE PILLAR OF AUTUMN
FIREFIGHT
MULTIPLAYER
REFERENCE

Patience is the name of the game when crossing the cargo port. Stay inside the cover afforded by the shipping crates and stairwells on either side of the port, and don't come out of cover until you've eliminated every visible enemy.

Ascend the stairs to the red hallway that circles around to the south. Eliminate the Grunts on the metal steps and fly over to the platform in the center of the area to assist the other ODSTs. Use the room atop the stairs for cover while battling the remaining Brutes. Move in and out of cover carefully to avoid the Brute Hero wielding a Concussion Rifle and fire the Rocket Launcher at your first opportunity. Continue up the stairs to the concourse.

OBJECTIVE

H: ADVANCE TO TRAXUS TOWER

Advance towards Traxus Tower and assist ODST assault on Covenant occupation.

Use the Jet Pack to fly to the uppermost floor in the concourse and continue south—out onto the balcony where the ODSTs are waiting. Take the right-hand door to use an interior hallway that will shield you from enemy attacks. Hurry straight for the UNSC supply case and load up on Rocket Launcher ammo. Eliminate the Grunts in the area, and take a moment to survey the situation from the safety of cover.

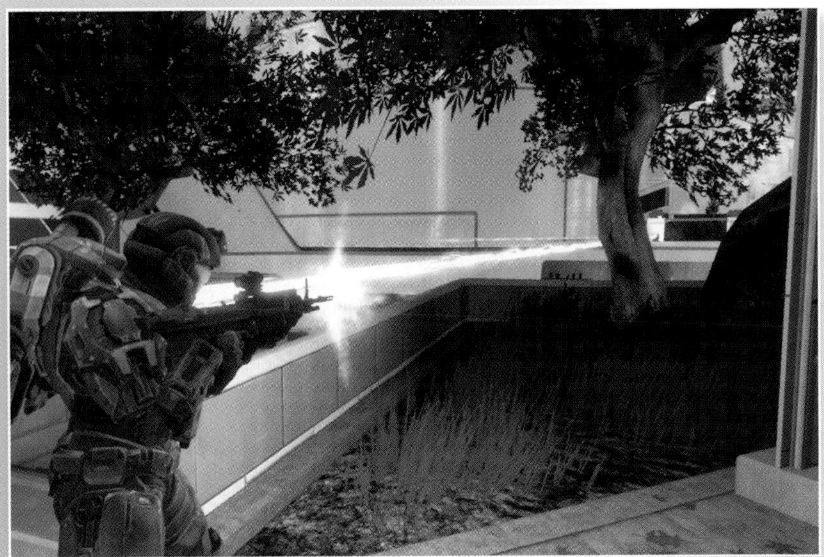

Eliminating the Jackals wielding the Focus Rifles is your top priority in this battle. Fly up to the balcony and immediately start sniping.

Spot the balcony to the northeast, above the New Alexandria sign, and quickly jetpack up to it. The multi-story promenade to the north (your left) is crawling with a number of enemies, but none are more deadly at the moment than the Jackals wielding Focus Rifles. These Jackal snipers target you whenever you poke your head out of cover, so stay crouched and wait for an ODST or two to join you and draw the Jackal's fire, then snipe them with the DMR. The Jackals with the Focus Rifles are located on the northwest end of the tower. They move around a lot, but you'll probably spot one or two near the rocks above the main stairs and a third up higher on the tower.

Advance east along this balcony to the Medkit, DMR, and Sniper Rifle at the far end. Ignore the temptation to fire the Rocket Launcher across the courtyard at the Brutes on the walkway, since they'll just roll out of the way by the time the slow-moving projectile gets there. Instead, put the Sniper Rifle to use and headshot the lot of them. Clear out all visible enemies from this position while giving cover fire for the ODSTs advancing northward. Take the DMR and Rocket Launcher back to ground level and sweep up the stairs towards the civilians.

Move in and out of cover at the far end of the balcony, near the Medkit, to avoid return fire across the concourse. Snipe the Jackals and Brutes before crossing to the north.

Make your way up the stairs one flight a time to root out any remaining Grunts and Brutes in the area. Assist the ODSTs in escorting the civilians across the skywalk to the executive offices to the south. Note the DMR ammo and Medkits on the ground near the planters and be ready with the Rocket Launcher for the battle to come. Some of the Grunts about to exit the door to the south are armed with Fuel Rod Guns. Lob a grenade or two at the first enemies to appear, then fire the Rocket Launcher just a foot or two off the ground to avoid firing it over the Grunts' heads.

OBJECTIVE

I: SECURE LANDING PAD

Assist UNSC civilian evacuation. Eliminate Covenant forces from the landing pad.

There are three ways into the executive office building: the main entrance where the Grunts came out, the stairs to the left of the entrance, and the stairs on the south side of the building. The allure of an elevated position is strong, but there are a number of Brutes on the upper level, and the narrow hallway can make it hard to dodge their Spike Rifle attacks. Move slowly through the main entrance to take out any Grunts milling about, then retreat for cover and try to draw the Brutes out one by one.

LEGENDARY TACTICS

The battle to get to the landing pad is significantly harder on Legendary mode thanks to the incredibly smart A.I. of the Brutes occupying the executive offices. Fortunately, you should be able to scavenge at least one or two Fuel Rod Guns from the Grunts outside. Temporarily swap the Rocket Launcher for the Fuel Rod Gun and head to the front entrance. Take out the first wave of Brutes, then head around the left-hand side of the building and up the stairs to the interior balcony. Stay on the move, use the cover, and flank the higher-ranking Brutes down below. Be careful, as at least one has a Fuel Rod Gun as well. The battle gets much easier once you rid the room of the Brutes with the Gravity Hammer and Fuel Rod Guns. Return to the front, grab your Rocket Launcher, and make the final push towards the landing pad.

A Brute Hero with a Gravity Hammer makes its way across the lobby to your position; have the Rocket Launcher (or Fuel Rod Gun) ready to greet him. Remain on the western end of the lobby (near the entrance) until you have defeated all of the interior Covenant. Gather up any available ammo and swap out the Rocket Launcher for a Fuel Rod Gun if low on ammo.

Don't underestimate the help the Bullfrogs can provide. Draw the Brute Hero towards the entrance, then step back so the ODSTs can lend a hand. Open fire with the Fuel Rod Gun.

The landing pad is straight ahead, but it's heavily fortified with two Shade Turrets, a Brute Leader with a Fuel Rod Gun, and several Grunts and Jackals. Move down either side of the lobby to avoid the direct attack from the Fuel Rod Gun, and clear out the lesser foes with a grenade or two. Ignore the Brute Leader for the time being and focus on the Shade Turrets. Use the DMR to snipe the Grunt occupying the turret's seat—this has the added bonus of destroying the turret. The east end of the lobby is wrapped in protective glass that can't be shot through, so play the angles and shoot through the doorway.

You can't shoot through the windows flanking the exit, so take cover on the side of the column opposite the Shade Turret you're targeting and aim for the gunner's head.

I SHOULD HAVE BECOME A WATCHMAKER

RECOMMENDED EQUIPMENT

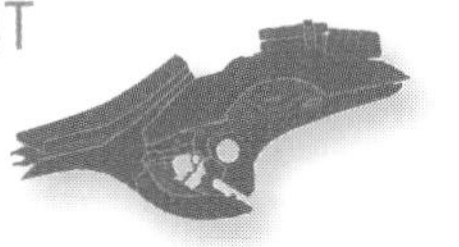
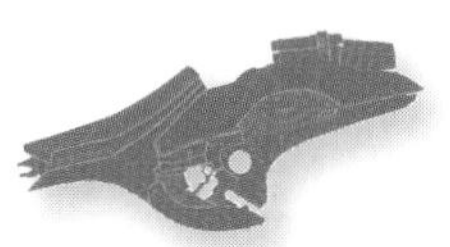

M392
FUEL ROD GUN

M392
FUEL ROD GUN

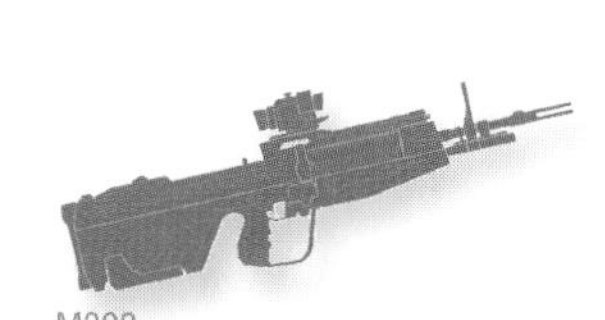

M392
DMR

M392
DMR

M392
DMR

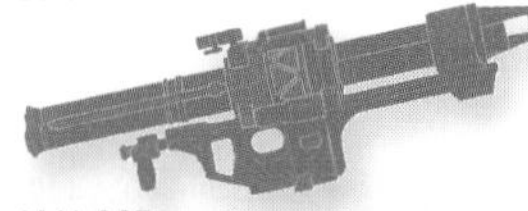
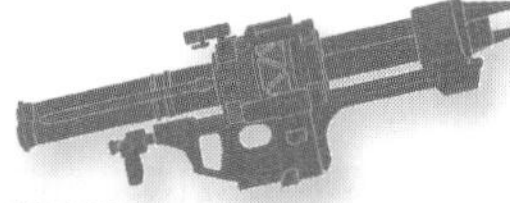

M41 SSR
ROCKET LAUNCHER

M41 SSR
ROCKET LAUNCHER

M41 SSR
ROCKET LAUNCHER

EASY/NORMAL

HEROIC

LEGENDARY

OBJECTIVE

J: EVACUATE CIVILIAN TRANSPORTS

Covenant Corvettes over the city are preventing the evacuation of civilian transport ships. Assist UNSC forces at the Starport.

Clearing the landing pad of those Brutes and Shade Turrets made it possible for a pair of Falcons to land safely. Board the one on the right and take a seat in the gunner's chair. The ODSTs stay behind and help the civilians board the Pelican that moves in to pick them up.

Open fire on the Grunts and Brutes you spot on the balconies or cliffs during the flight to the Starport to pad your score. Banshees and Wraiths are high value targets too!

ENEMY FORCES

Covenant
Grunt Infantry
Grunt Specialist
Jackal Infantry
Jackal Specialist

Covenant
Brute Infantry
Brute Leader
Brute Hero

ENEMY VEHICLES

Covenant
Ghost
Wraith

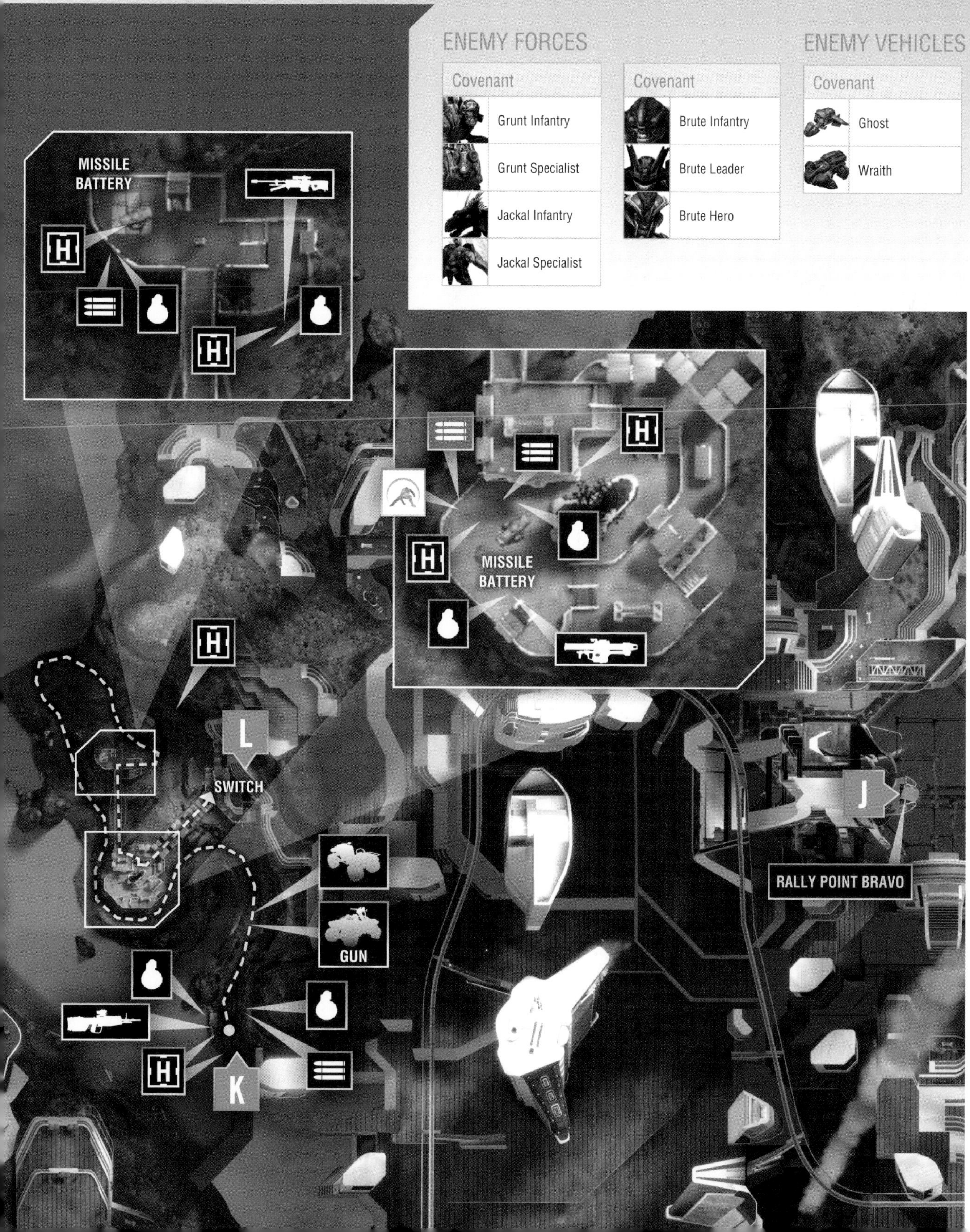

MISSILE BATTERY

MISSILE BATTERY

L

SWITCH

J

RALLY POINT BRAVO

GUN

K

OBJECTIVE

K: ARM MISSILE BATTERIES

Neutralize hostiles and activate missile batteries to assist the evacuation of civilian transport ships.

Use the gun on the Falcon to eliminate the Covies on the south end of the Starport's beach and hop out. Gather up supplies and rush alongside the UNSC Troopers towards the Warthog to the north. Take the wheel of the Warthog, allow a few troopers to climb aboard, then head north, sticking to the coastline.

Take out the Ghost you encounter and circle around to the northwest towards the Wraith beneath the bridge. Drive circles around the Wraith to give your gunner and passenger a clear shot at the Wraith while avoiding its massive energy cannon. Try to maneuver the Warthog behind the Wraith to exploit its weak point. Continue north around the northernmost missile battery, but don't hop out to arm it yet. Loop past it back towards the bridge and gun down the second Wraith that approaches.

Don't exit the Warthog until you've eliminated both Wraiths in the area. Stay parallel to the Wraith to avoid its energy blast and to give your gunner a clear shot at the Covy tank.

Drive the Warthog up the hill towards the northernmost missile battery first, and give the gunner time to eliminate the Brutes and Jackals in the area. It's a tight fit, but you can drive the Warthog between the posts and up onto the bridge. Hop out and activate the missile battery on the north side of the bridge first, then drive up and over the bridge back to the south. Take out the Brutes nearest the bridge and drive down the stairs towards the walkway heading to the East Complex. Leave the vehicle for your Fireteam to use and approach the missile battery on foot.

There's no reason to do without the Warthog's machine gun. Take it between the barriers and over the bridge for added firepower.

Grab the Rocket Launcher near the blast shield and swap out the Jet Pack in favor of the Drop Shield ability. Gather up as much DMR ammo as you can get, then flip the switch to activate the missile battery. Wait to flip the switch until after you've made the equipment changes, since a dropship begins its approach as soon as the second missile battery is activated.

OBJECTIVE

L: FIRE MISSILES FROM COMMAND CONSOLE

Missile batteries are armed and ready to fire on Covenant Corvettes over the Starport. Activate the command console at the UNSC Field Station.

Make your way along the covered walkway leading to the East Complex as quickly as you can with the Rocket Launcher in hand and pointed at the top of the second flight of stairs. Several Jackals come into the picture, but that's not what you're aiming for. Three Brutes leap out of the dropship right atop those stairs. Fire a rocket as soon as they touch down to catch them—and a Jackal or two if you're lucky—in a massive fiery explosion. Three Skirmishers will leap out the side of the dropship nearest your position so have a Drop Shield ready and switch to the DMR.

Don't ascend the stairs until you eliminate all of the Brutes and Skirmishers that deploy from the dropship. Use one rocket on the Brutes, but save the other for later!

Advance on the East Complex carefully, as there are a number of other Brutes and Jackals in the area. The biggest barrier to reaching the command console comes in the form of the final two Brutes guarding the room with a Fuel Rod Gun and Gravity Hammer. Make frequent use of the Drop Shield and step in and out of cover to get a clear shot on the Brutes. Place a Drop Shield on the stairs leading up to the command console and ascend and descend the stairs in and out of the Drop Shield as necessary to draw one of the Brutes away from the other. Use the Rocket Launcher to take out the first, then gather up the fallen weapon and use it against the other. One of the UNSC Troopers in the area is armed with a Spartan Laser; look to swap for it if you run out of rockets or ammo for a Fuel Rod Gun.

The final two Brutes are not to be taken lightly. One has a Fuel Rod Gun and the other a Gravity Hammer. Make good use of the Drop Shield and Rocket Launcher to survive.

NEW ALEXANDRIA

PROVIDE AIR SUPPORT IN A FOREST OF CRUMBLING SKYSCRAPERS.

INTELLIGENCE BRIEFING

BASIC TACTICS

I Follow Kat's directions and pilot the Falcon across the city to three landmark buildings where Covenant forces have installed communications jammers. For each of these buildings, you'll need to land the Falcon on the roof and fight your way through the building's interior to get to the jammer. On Heroic and Legendary, the order of the buildings is random. On Easy and Normal, the hospital is first and the nightclub and Sinoviet buildings are random. Use the Drop Shield found inside the hospital until you get to Sinoviet Tower, at which point you should equip Active Camouflage and the Rocket Launcher for the remainder of the mission. Random emergency objectives are presented in between each of the three major objectives; in three and four player co-op games there will be two simultaneous emergency objectives between each of the major objectives. Follow the HUD and complete the tasks quickly to get back to overloading the three primary jammers.

II Head to the ONI building and assist the Pelican in the evacuation by clearing the surrounding rooftops of the anti-air turrets. Keep your distance to avoid their heavy firepower, and use the Falcon's guns to destroy them all. Follow the on-screen indicators to their locations. As soon as the last of the turrets is destroyed, the Pelican takes off from the ONI building. Kat then extends a helipad directly above where the Pelican took flight. Land the Falcon there to complete the mission.

CHAPTER-SPECIFIC ACHIEVEMENTS

DUST AND ECHOES: Complete the 8th mission on Normal or harder.

I DIDN'T TRAIN TO BE A PILOT: Kill at least 3 anti-aircraft batteries during the 8th mission.

MISSION OBJECTIVES

- Destroy Covenant jammer at the hospital.
- Destroy Covenant jammer at Sinoviet.
- Destroy Covenant jammer at the tower.
- Go to the ONI building.
- Destroy all anti-air turrets.
- Land at ONI.

WELCOME
UNSC TRAINING
THE CAMPAIGN
M1: WINTER CONTINGENCY
M2: ONI
M3: NIGHTFALL
M4: TIP OF THE SPEAR
M5: LONG NIGHT OF SOLACE
M6: EXODUS
M7: NEW ALEXANDRIA
M8: THE PACKAGE
M9: THE PILLAR OF AUTUMN
FIREFIGHT
MULTIPLAYER
REFERENCE

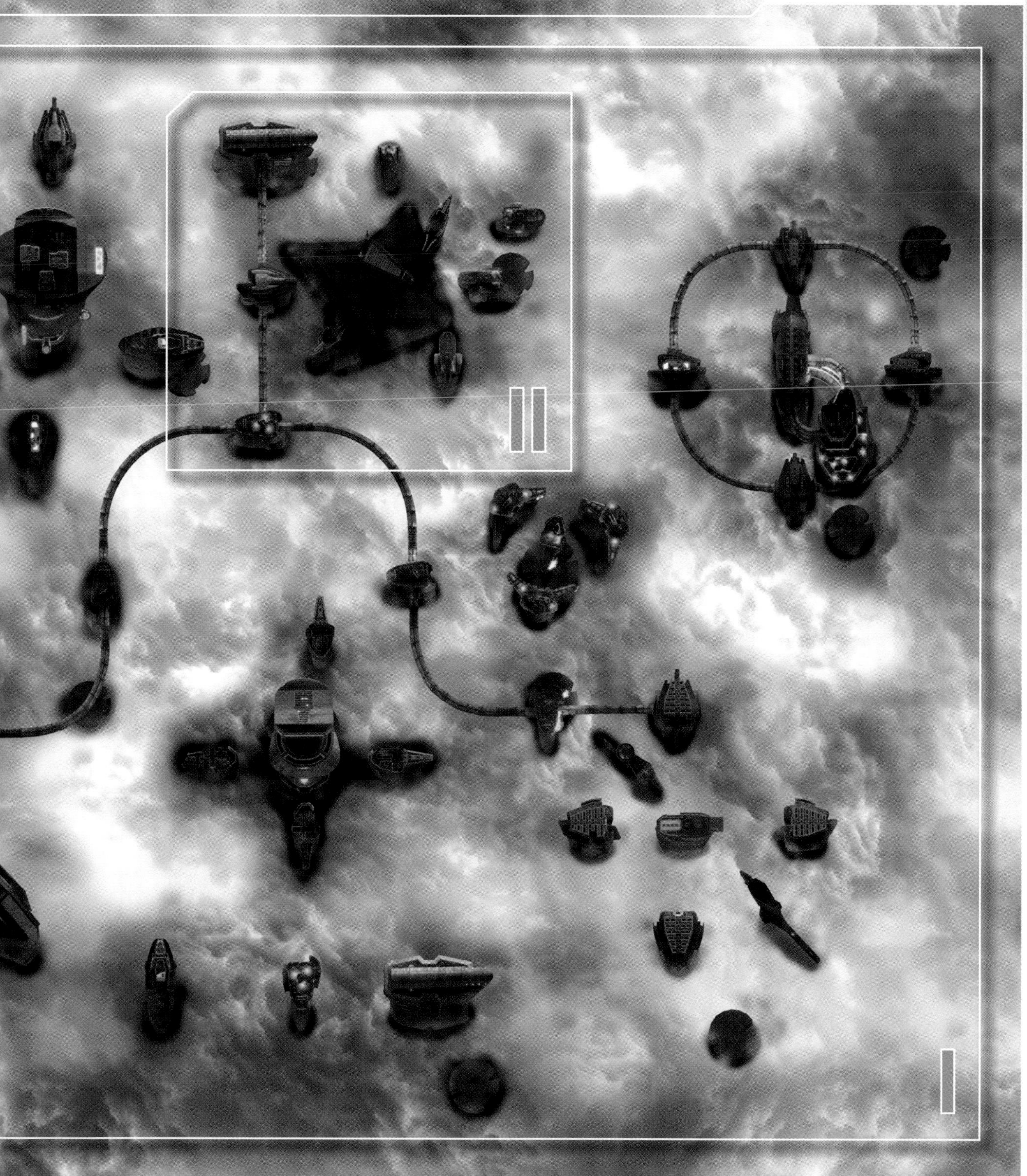

FLY BY NIGHT

RECOMMENDED EQUIPMENT

T25 C
SPIKE RIFLE

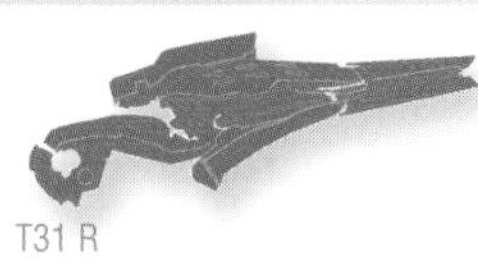

T31 R
NEEDLE RIFLE

M392
DMR

M392
DMR

M392
DMR

M45 TS
SHOTGUN

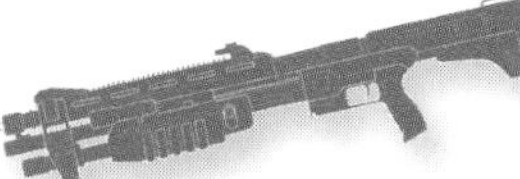

M45 TS
SHOTGUN

M45 TS
SHOTGUN

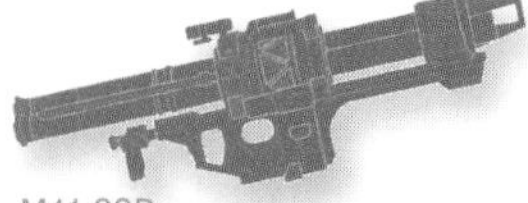

M41 SSR
ROCKET LAUNCHER

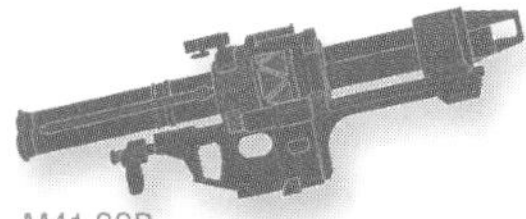

M41 SSR
ROCKET LAUNCHER

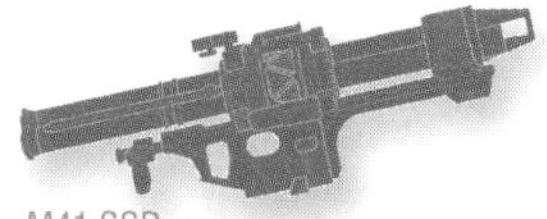

M41 SSR
ROCKET LAUNCHER

EASY/NORMAL

HEROIC

LEGENDARY

OBJECTIVE

A: DESTROY COVENANT JAMMER AT THE HOSPITAL

Destroy the Covenant jammer at the hospital.

Climb into the cockpit of the Falcon and lift off into the night's sky. Kat talks you through a series of seek and destroy operatives across the city to help root out a number of long-range communications jammers the Covenant have stashed around New Alexandria. Once airborne, you'll need to keep an eye out for Banshees—stay above their position and open fire while circling around them—and also watch for anti-aircraft turrets on many of the rooftops.

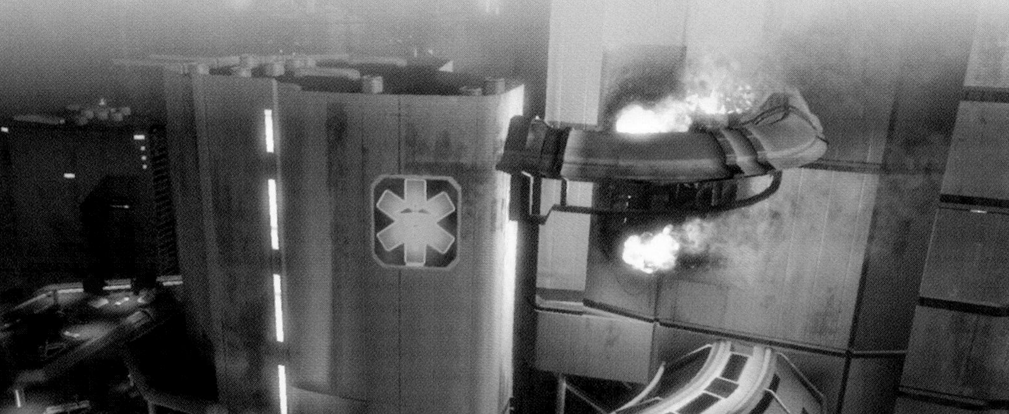

ENEMY VEHICLES

Covenant	
	Banshee
	Phantom

C
E
NIGHTCLUB
F
ONI TOWER
A
HOSPITAL
D
B
SINOVIET INDUSTRIES
MISSION START

ENEMY FORCES

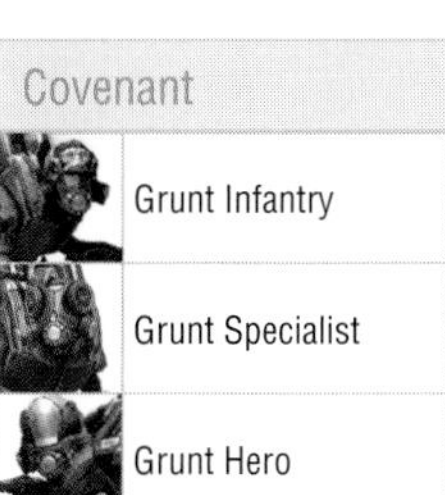

Covenant
Grunt Infantry
Grunt Specialist
Grunt Hero

Covenant
Jackal Infantry
Jackal Specialist
Jackal Hero

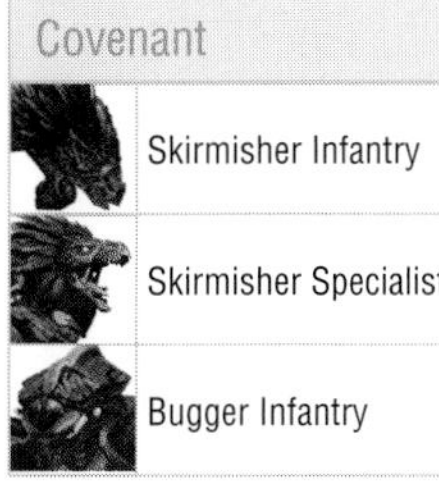

Covenant
Skirmisher Infantry
Skirmisher Specialist
Bugger Infantry

Covenant
Bugger Specialist
Brute Infantry
Brute Leader

Covenant
Elite Specialist
Engineer

Falcon

You've sat in the gunner's seat of a Falcon a number of times before, but now you're the one piloting it. The Falcon is a dual-rotor helicopter with a set of thrusters that helps it travel a bit faster than ordinary helicopters. Control the Falcon's ascent rate using the Left Trigger, and tip the Left Thumbstick to increase/decrease speed. Tap the Right Bumper to toggle the Falcon's altitude lock. This eliminates the need to constantly feather the Left Trigger if you want to maintain a certain altitude. Releasing the Left Trigger while altitude lock is disabled causes the Falcon to descend. Squeeze the Right Trigger to fire the Falcon's heavy machine guns. These guns fire in short bursts and are powerful enough to destroy a Phantom if given enough time. Refer to the Vehicles section of the Appendices on page 343 for additional information and statistics about the Falcon.

In co-op games, a second Falcon will land next to you at the beginning of the level that has two Grenade Launcher side-turrets that you used in 'Tip of the Spear'. This is a more powerful and useful Falcon for cooperative gameplay.

If you lose your Falcon, you can either wait around for an evac prompt (press down on the D-Pad when you see it) or try to board an enemy Banshee!

Fly the Falcon northeast to the hospital. Use the Falcon's guns to defend the craft against any Banshees that approach, and destroy the anti-aircraft turret on the rooftop located just to the southwest of the hospital. Set the Falcon down gently on the rooftop plaza and head inside.

Don't take on a Banshee head-on. Always get above it and circle around to its side to avoid its plasma guns.

A group of four Grunts are standing just inside the hospital entrance. The Engineer floating within the space inside the center of the circular tower protects the Grunts with its special support capabilities; that's why they glow purple. It takes six shots with the DMR to destroy the Engineer, so unless you have a clean shot through the glass barriers near the railing, go ahead and take out the Grunts first. Toss a Frag Grenade at the Grunts to blast through the shielding afforded by the Engineer, then finish them off with the DMR. Move to the glass plates that ring the spiraling walkway and destroy the Engineer through a gap in the plating before continuing on.

The hospital's central tower is a multi-level spiral. Proceed clockwise to reach a UNSC supply case with fresh Armor Abilities and other supplies on each of the top two floors. Head counter-clockwise to reach the staircase curving down to the next level. DMR ammo is pretty limited early on, so use the Assault Rifle (or melee attacks) whenever possible to conserve ammo for the push towards the jamming device. Stop off at the UNSC supply case one floor down from where you enter, and equip the Drop Shield ability. This is a good time to swap the Assault Rifle for the Shotgun lying near the corpse. Descend to the next floor down, take out the Jackals with a grenade, and locate the DMR ammo on the north side of the floor.

The one-two combination of a melee strike followed by a close-range Shotgun blast (or vice-versa) makes quick work of Jackals.

A squad of Grunts and a Brute Leader guard the lower floor of the tower. Use the Drop Shield on the landing above the final stairs and start sniping each of the Grunts. Use Frag Grenades and the DMR to eliminate the Brute Leader while strafing in and out of the Drop Shield to avoid its needle attacks. Gather up more DMR ammo on the north side of the lowermost floor, then head through the doors to the east, proceeding to the hallway that leads north to the jammer.

You'll find the jammer at the far end of the atrium on the east side of the hospital. Take cover behind the planter and inch out into the hallway slowly to avoid detection. While it certainly tests the limits of the DMR's range, use this position to pick off as many of the Brutes as you can before stepping out into the hallway. And even then, make sure to use Drop Shield if there are any Brute Leaders still about. It takes four headshots with the DMR to down a Brute, so line your crosshairs up carefully, then fire quickly.

Eliminate as many Brutes as you can before advancing north, away from the southern end of this atrium.

Advance slowly in a crouched position and target the Engineer hovering just above the jamming device beyond the next wave of Brutes. Eradicate the Brutes just as before, then scour the walkways and balconies for additional DMR ammo before moving in to overload the jammer. If you have a Rocket Launcher from one of the other jammer objectives, pick up some ammo for it on the balcony area mid-way to the jammer.

A small squad of UNSC Troopers joins you at the jammer, but they're not alone. A team of Elite Specialists flies in to intercept you on the return trip. The Elite Specialists fly back and forth around the atrium with their Jet Packs while firing Plasma Repeaters. Stay close to the other troopers, grab a Jet Pack of your own from behind the jammer, and aim for the head. If you can stick one with the Plasma Grenade, do it! Otherwise, keep firing at their heads and be ready to melee at an instant's notice if they fly in close. Swap the Jet Pack for the Drop Shield, once the Elite Specialists have been defeated, and head for the exit. As you return to the stairwell, there will be an Elite Ultra with a concussion rifle on the ground level to offer up a challenge. There will be some Skirmishers up the stairway to also provide cover fire. Return the way you came to the cockpit of the Falcon.

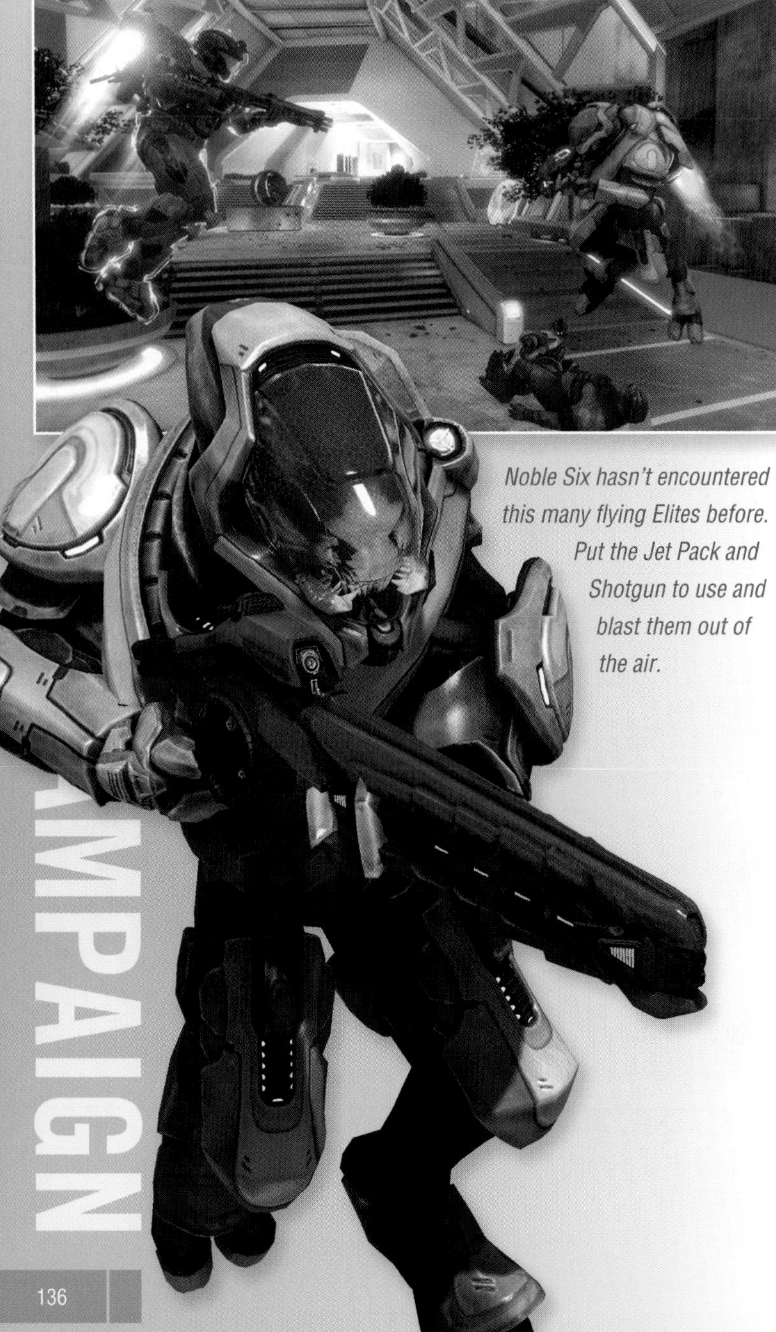

Noble Six hasn't encountered this many flying Elites before. Put the Jet Pack and Shotgun to use and blast them out of the air.

RANDOMIZED EMERGENCY ORDERS

You must contend with three primary communications jammers during this mission, but they are not the only problem facing the people of New Alexandria. The city is on fire, the Covenant are everywhere, and emergency personnel are in serious need of Spartan assistance. Kat instructs you to each of the three main objectives one by one, but randomized emergency assignments often come up between each of these core objectives. These other assignments are short in nature and assigned at random. They typically involve either escorting a UNSC Falcon or Pelican across the city, destroying anti-aircraft turrets, eliminating Covenant infantry on a rooftop, or disabling a hastily placed rooftop jamming device. In a three and four player cooperative game there will be two emergency assignments at once—so split up!

Regardless of which objective you're given, there are a few basic tips that are applicable to each type of emergency. For starters, always circle the target area at a wide radius and eliminate any rooftop turrets or Banshees in the vicinity. Stay high as you approach the target (if a rooftop Covenant force or jammer) and monitor the motion tracker for Banshees. Fire on the targets only after you have defeated all enemy craft. For escort missions, try to fly out in front—and above—the craft you're escorting, and destroy all Banshees and turrets you spot.

OBJECTIVE

B: DESTROY COVENANT JAMMER AT SINOVIET

WELCOME
UNSC TRAINING
THE CAMPAIGN
M1: WINTER CONTINGENCY
M2: ONI
M3: NIGHTFALL
M4: TIP OF THE SPEAR
M5: LONG NIGHT OF SOLACE
M6: EXODUS
M7: NEW ALEXANDRIA
M8: THE PACKAGE
M9: THE PILLAR OF AUTUMN
FIREFIGHT
MULTIPLAYER
REFERENCE

Destroy the Covenant jammer in Sinoviet Industries.

SINOVIET OR CLUB ERRERA?

Orders will come in to send Noble Six to either Club Errera or Sinoviet Industries after visiting the hospital. Though the hospital jammer is always the first objective, the order in which Noble Six takes out the second and third jammers is random. Skip ahead to the next objective if directed to Club Errera first.

Again, on Heroic and Legendary, the order of the buildings is random.

LEGENDARY TACTICS

The major differences between this mission on Heroic and on Legendary involve the intensity of the Banshee pursuit while flying about the city and also the order in which the communication jammers must be taken out. It's common on Legendary mode to have to deal with the jammer at Sinoviet first. This has the benefit of giving you access to Active Camouflage at the very start of the mission, but picking up the Rocket Launcher this early means you need to devote a weapon slot to it for the entirety of the mission in order to have it for the trip across Club Errera's dance floor. And that's exactly what you should do—don't think of using those rockets or not taking them with you. Those rockets are your key to an easy victory.

Fly the Falcon to the Sinoviet Industries tower; it's the one with the large neon green logo on it. Use the Falcon's guns to destroy the twin Shade Turrets stationed near the landing pad, along with any Grunts or other Covenant you spot. Set the Falcon down and look around for a Fuel Rod Gun—if you're lucky, one of the slain Grunts may have dropped one.

Don't bring the Falcon in for a landing until you've first dealt with the Shade Turrets near the landing pad!

A number of Grunts, Jackals, and Brutes guard the entrance to the Sinoviet building. Ascend partially up the left-hand staircase while keeping an eye to the northeast for the Jackal sniper with the Focus Rifle on the balcony in the far corner. Moving up the left-hand stairs gives you enough cover from its attack so you can first deal with the Grunts in the area before worrying about the sniper. Look for opportunities to take out multiple Jackals with a single grenade, and if applicable, use the Fuel Rod Gun to hunt down the Brutes in the area.

Continue north to the middle landing near the fountain and stairs under the elevator Kat mentioned. Additional Brutes patrol this area, as does a Brute Leader on the upper walkway, above the Sinoviet sign. You're probably running low on DMR ammo at this point, so gather up as much Spike Rifle ammo as you can from the slain Brutes. Use the Drop Shield to protect yourself from the Concussion Rifle attack of the Brute Leader near the elevator—remember he always fires four volleys in quick succession—and continue to the elevator.

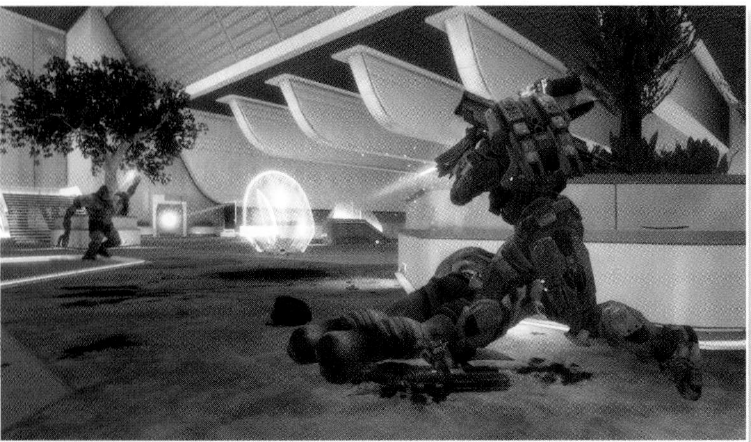

UNSC ammo is pretty scarce inside the lobby of Sinoviet Industries, so be prepared to use whatever Covenant weaponry comes available.

Exit the elevator in the hardwood-lined offices atop Sinoviet Tower. Ignore the branching staircases and stay low to find the UNSC supply case containing the Active Camouflage ability. Equip this at once and take a minute to scavenge the ammo from the many fallen troopers in the area. The jamming device is at the south end of the lowest level of this complex assortment of rooms and hallways, but don't go to it yet. Approach the jammer and turn left to go up a flight of stairs to find a Rocket Launcher (important if you hadn't gone to Club Errera yet). Return to the jammer and collect the additional rockets from the yellow weapons case on the ground. However, do not use the Rocket Launcher now; save it for the next building you'll be flying to!

Overloading the jamming device inside Sinoviet triggers an attack by dozens of Buggers—which explains why there are so many corpses in this area. Use Active Camouflage to make your way back across the area to the elevator without being detected. Active Camouflage will make Noble Six virtually invisible, but only if he moves *very* slowly and doesn't fire any weaponry. Sprinting and firing guns or throwing grenades will cause the Active Camouflage effects to wear off. Buggers by themselves may not be that intimidating, but Buggers are never found alone! Follow the perimeter of the area in a clockwise direction to reach the elevators quickly, without running into too many Buggers. Don't attempt to kill all of the buggers! They will overwhelm you! Get out of the building as soon as possible.

Use Active Camouflage and move very slowly towards the elevator on the return trip or risk being overrun by swarming Buggers.

OBJECTIVE

C: DESTROY THE COVENANT JAMMER AT THE TOWER

Destroy the Covenant jammer at the tower.

I DIDN'T TRAIN TO BE A PILOT

This Achievement unlocks after you've successfully destroyed at least three of anti-aircraft turrets scattered across the city. There are 10 turrets in total, and each of them appears as a small white dome on the roof of a tower. They're not all clearly recognizable from afar, and some are only visible from one side of the building and not the other. Avoid flying in too close to the building, else you'll be within range of the turret. Stay high, circle from a safe distance, and keep blasting until your reticule refuses to turn red. That's when you know it's been destroyed!

Complete the random emergency mission that Kat directs you to, then proceed to the nightclub inside the telecom tower. Eliminate the Banshees in the area, then descend to the landing pad, but keep your distance. The entrance to the nightclub is fortified with a pair of Shade Turrets and multiple Covenant. Use the Falcon's machine guns to destroy the turrets, and gun down any Covies caught out in the open before setting the bird down on the helipad.

Don't go in for a landing until you've dealt with those Shade Turrets and Covenant. You'll probably have to get out of the helicopter in order to target the Skirmishers above the entrance.

The jammer is on the north side of the nightclub, but four Hunters guard it. Two are initially located on the landing near the jammer and two others are downstairs, flanking the giant hologram. Activate the Active Camouflage ability and shoulder the Rocket Launcher you took from Sinoviet Tower (if applicable). It takes three direct hits with a Rocket Launcher to kill a Hunter if you hit it head-on, but you can use the Active Camouflage and the presence of the UNSC Troopers to stealthily flank the Hunters and fire on their unarmored backs. You needn't kill all four Hunters if you don't have the desire, but definitely take out the two on the east side of the club. Drop down, gather up the ammo and Plasma Grenades near the troopers, and head up the northeast steps to the jammer.

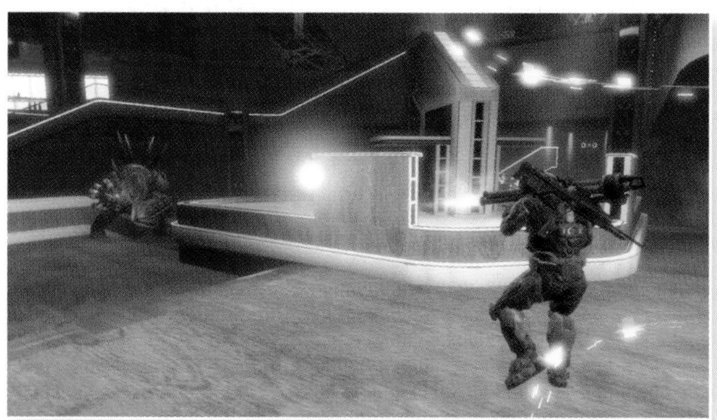

Put the Rocket Launcher to use against the Hunters. Knock their armor off then move in for the kill with the Shotgun if running low on ammo.

If visiting Club Errera before Sinoviet Tower, carefully descend to the bar on the lower floor and equip the Shotgun and Jet Pack. Grab the Rocket Launcher near the hologram, then fall back and open fire. The lower floor of the club contains multiple UNSC supply cases with a bevy of different Armor Abilities, but it doesn't contain the Active Camouflage found at Sinoviet Tower.

You won't need any other weapons or abilities for the remainder of this mission once the third jammer has been dealt with—it's all done in the sky—so don't worry about swapping equipment or looking for a key weapon. Take what you have to Sinoviet or listen for Kat's update. Either way, head back to the Falcon, Spartan.

LAST ONE OUT... TURN OUT THE LIGHTS

OBJECTIVE D: GO TO THE ONI BUILDING

Fly to the ONI building.

Lift off and begin flying towards the ONI building to assist in the evacuation. The battle in the air over the city is really starting to heat up, and the number of Banshees and Phantoms has increased since you've successfully overloaded the three communications jammers.

The Falcon is likely starting to show the damage it's been taking. You've come a long way; don't go needlessly catching plasma bursts now.

OBJECTIVE E: DESTROY ALL ANTI-AIR TURRETS

Destroy the anti-air Shades to evacuate the Pelicans.

You'll be instructed to divert off course temporarily to clear the skies for a Pelican trying to lift off with a belly full of evacuees. Six anti-air turrets need to be destroyed. They're on the buildings surrounding the ONI tower. Some are a bit lower than others, so look for the on-screen indicators to point them out. Kat implores you to take out those turrets as quickly as you can, but don't ignore the Banshees in the process. The Banshees are your true threat, provided you stay far enough away from the turrets.

Follow the red indicators on the HUD to locate the six anti-air turrets Kat needs you to destroy so that the Pelican can evacuate the tower.

OBJECTIVE F: LAND AT ONI

Dock at the ONI hangar.

Kat extends the landing pad at ONI tower. Double-check the skies for hostiles, then limp on over to the landing pad to complete the mission. You flew well tonight, Spartan. Set that Falcon down and head inside.

ENEMY VEHICLES

Covenant	
	Banshee
	Phantom

THE PACKAGE
YOUR ORDERS ARE TO DESTROY SWORD BASE... OR ARE THEY?

INTELLIGENCE BRIEFING

BASIC TACTICS

Eliminate the Grunts in the Shade Turrets and the Jackal sniper (take the Focus Rifle) and cross the water towards the valley to find a Scorpion. Use the Scorpion to defeat the Covenant defenses and destroy the anti-air guns. Move slowly, and don't hesitate to treat each Banshee as your top priority. Continue up the path towards the eastern gate. Be on the lookout for Shade Turrets near the rocks surrounding the valley and for the Revenant hiding behind the boulders in front of the gate.

MISSION OBJECTIVES

- Destroy Covenant anti-air towers.
- Eliminate Covenant gate defense.
- Enter Sword Base.
- Proceed to the coordinates.
- Defend Halsey's Lab.
- Enter Halsey's Lab.

II Ascend the road from the eastern gate to Sword Base, either with a light vehicle or on foot. Use the UNSC truck for cover and assist Noble Team in defeating the Covenant outside Sword Base. Detach one of the Plasma Cannons inside the garage and use it to fight your way up the spiraling walkway to the security entrance leading to the Sword Base atrium. Equip Drop Shield and use the Focus Rifle to eliminate the Elites in the atrium. Carter leads you to the location defined.

III Quickly activate each of the four turrets by sprinting a counter-clockwise lap around the glacier, beginning at Turret C and ending at Turret D. Join Noble Team near the entrance to Halsey's Lab and load up on DMR and Grenade Launcher ammo. Use these weapons, relying on the latter to deal with Brutes and the Active Camouflage ability to fend off the numerous Covenant assault teams. Try to keep Turrets D and C online for as long as you can, or at least until the waves of Elites begin coming. Switch to the Armor Lock and mount your final stand alongside your teammates, under the covered protection from Wraith and Banshee bombardment.

CHAPTER-SPECIFIC ACHIEVEMENTS

THIS IS NOT YOUR GRAVE...: Complete the 9th mission on Normal or harder.

TANK BEATS EVERYTHING: Finish the 9th mission on Legendary with the Scorpion intact.

TORCH AND BURN

RECOMMENDED EQUIPMENT

OBJECTIVE

A: DESTROY COVENANT ANTI-AIR TOWERS

Eliminate the anti-air towers so NOBLE Team can airdrop into Sword Base.

The glassing has melted a major portion of the ice shelf and flooded the coastline east of Sword Base. This includes Farragut Outpost, where you and your Fireteam are set to make your move. A small but potent squad of Covenant guards the beach of the now-submerged outpost. Your chief concerns at the onset of the mission are the Shade Turret and the Jackal sniping from the watchtower above it. Crouch behind the rocks to your right and take out the Grunt in the Shade Turret first, then target the sniper in the tower—these are exceptionally long shots with the rifle, but doable. Maintain this position and eliminate the Grunts in and around the Shade Turret, as well as the one sitting in the Ghost.

Put the DMR's range to the test and take out the Jackal sniper and Shade Turret operator before diving into the water.

ENEMY VEHICLES

Covenant	
	Ghost
	Banshee
	Revenant

ENEMY FORCES

Covenant	
	Grunt Infantry
	Grunt Specialist
	Grunt Hero
	Jackal Infantry

Covenant	
	Jackal Specialist
	Jackal Hero
	Elite Infantry
	Elite Leader

Drop off the rocks into the water and head inside the outpost structure directly ahead. Crouch and ascend the steps inside the doorway slowly to avoid detection by the second Shade Turret. If you are on Easy difficulty, you can find a focus rifle here. Snipe the gunner and any other Grunts waiting to take a turn in the turret and continue across the water and up the eastern bank. Collect the DMR ammo from the gun cabinet inside the building where the generator switch was, and proceed past the Covenant tower and up the road to the southwest.

FOCUS ON THE FUTURE

Swap out the Assault Rifle for the Focus Rifle dropped by the Jackal sniper. You won't need this weapon until you get to Sword Base, but it will be worth its weight in MJOLNIR once you do. If playing on Legendary mode, skip the Focus Rifle and gather up all of the Fuel Rod Gun ammo you can carry from the Grunts in this area.

Eliminate the Grunts in the tower to the left of the Scorpion, then climb into the tank's driver's seat. With any luck, much of your Fireteam comes with you to man the turret and lend some additional support fire. Slowly round the corner and blast the Shade Turret and watchtower into oblivion. The Scorpion's massive cannon is second only to the Target Locator in terms of raw destructive force. Put it to use in clearing out the other Covenant defenses further up the road to the west. Amplify the blast by targeting the Plasma Batteries to avoid individually targeting the Elite and Grunts congregating near the antenna. Put a shell right between the two Ghosts further up the road, and steer the tank across the bridge and up the valley to the beach where the anti-air towers are positioned. If you find yourself without a Scorpion here, you can grab a Revenant near the antenna.

TANK BEATS EVERYTHING

The Scorpion is virtually indestructible on lower difficulty settings, but it can—and will—fall victim to the Covenant on Legendary mode if you're not careful. Increase the Scorpion's chance for survival by moving ahead amongst the rocks where you first find it and snipe as many of the enemies as you can, particularly those in the Shade Turret and by the Plasma Batteries. The more you can thin the enemy's defenses on foot (from a safe distance, mind you), the fewer shots the Scorpion will have to absorb when you start lumbering down the road in it. The other key to ensuring the Scorpion's survival is to advance very slowly and to treat every Ghost and Banshee encounter as top priority. Do not allow enemy vehicles to get close enough to fire! Mind the reload time for the Scorpion and target those Banshees headed directly towards your position first, as they are easier to hit. Keep the Scorpion in one piece all the way to Sword Base, and the Achievement is yours. And if you're still having trouble with this challenge, go ahead and find a friend or two to play cooperatively with you, then instruct your pal(s) to hijack a Ghost and provide an escort.

As powerful as the Scorpion is, it's also a really easy target for the Covenant! Round corners slowly and never expose more of the Scorpion than necessary.

Fire on the group of Jackals near the antenna, then leave the rest of the Covenant ground troops to the trooper manning the Scorpion's turret. Slowly inch your way up the hill towards the antenna to avoid being overrun. Take out the Banshees flying in from the north and scan the area for Ghosts. Bring the Scorpion to a stop atop the hill near the antenna and sweep the reticule across the landscape between the anti-air towers, firing on anything that turns the reticule red.

The Scorpion is the ultimate UNSC vehicle, but it's not indestructible. Take out those Banshees and Ghosts immediately and leave the ground troops for the troopers riding shotgun.

From the position left of the antenna, you can actually fire into the core of the tower with the Scorpion and not have to physically go inside the anti-air tower as you did in the "Tip of the Spear" mission. Continue to fire on it with the Scorpion until it's destroyed, then pull up a little closer to the second tower and look to the skies for more Banshees coming in from the north. Approach the second tower on foot and destroy it from within—shoot the energy barrier with the DMR, then toss a grenade into the core to destroy it. Return to the Scorpion and continue north along the road towards Sword Base. You can also simply destroy the anti-air tower from afar with the Scorpion by aiming it at the back of the turret head.

OBJECTIVE
B: ELIMINATE COVENANT GATE DEFENSE

Clear out the Sword Base gate defense and then regroup with NOBLE Team.

A squadron of Falcons swoops in from the south and lends overhead support for your journey towards the eastern gate. Watch the motion tracker for Banshees inbound from either direction as you make your way north towards Sword Base—the first Banshees to arrive are likely to come from the south, ahead of the Falcons, so get that turret turned around! The Falcons have enough firepower to keep most of the Banshees and Ghosts at bay, but don't let your guard down. Keep the Scorpion moving up the road under the expectation that you need to eliminate all threats by yourself.

The cliffs ringing the road to the eastern gate are home to several Shade Turrets. The Falcons eventually destroy most of them, but the one nearest the gate may require your attention. You'll encounter a number of Ghosts on the way to the gate, as well as a Revenant just in front of the gate. Stay close to the rocks on the left-hand side of the road and either step back or reverse whenever encountering an enemy. Never continue advancing while a known enemy is intact.

Advance towards the eastern gate slowly to allow the Falcons to get out ahead of you and soften up the defenses. Your biggest threats are the Banshees in the sky and the Shade Turrets scattered amongst the cliffs.

JACKING A REVENANT

Do your best to disable the Revenant near the gate without destroying it. The UNSC Trooper manning the Scorpion's turret can sometimes accomplish this task for you, but you may need to move in on foot and hijack it. The battle in the courtyard between the gate and Sword Base is much easier if you have the additional firepower of a Revenant or Ghost.

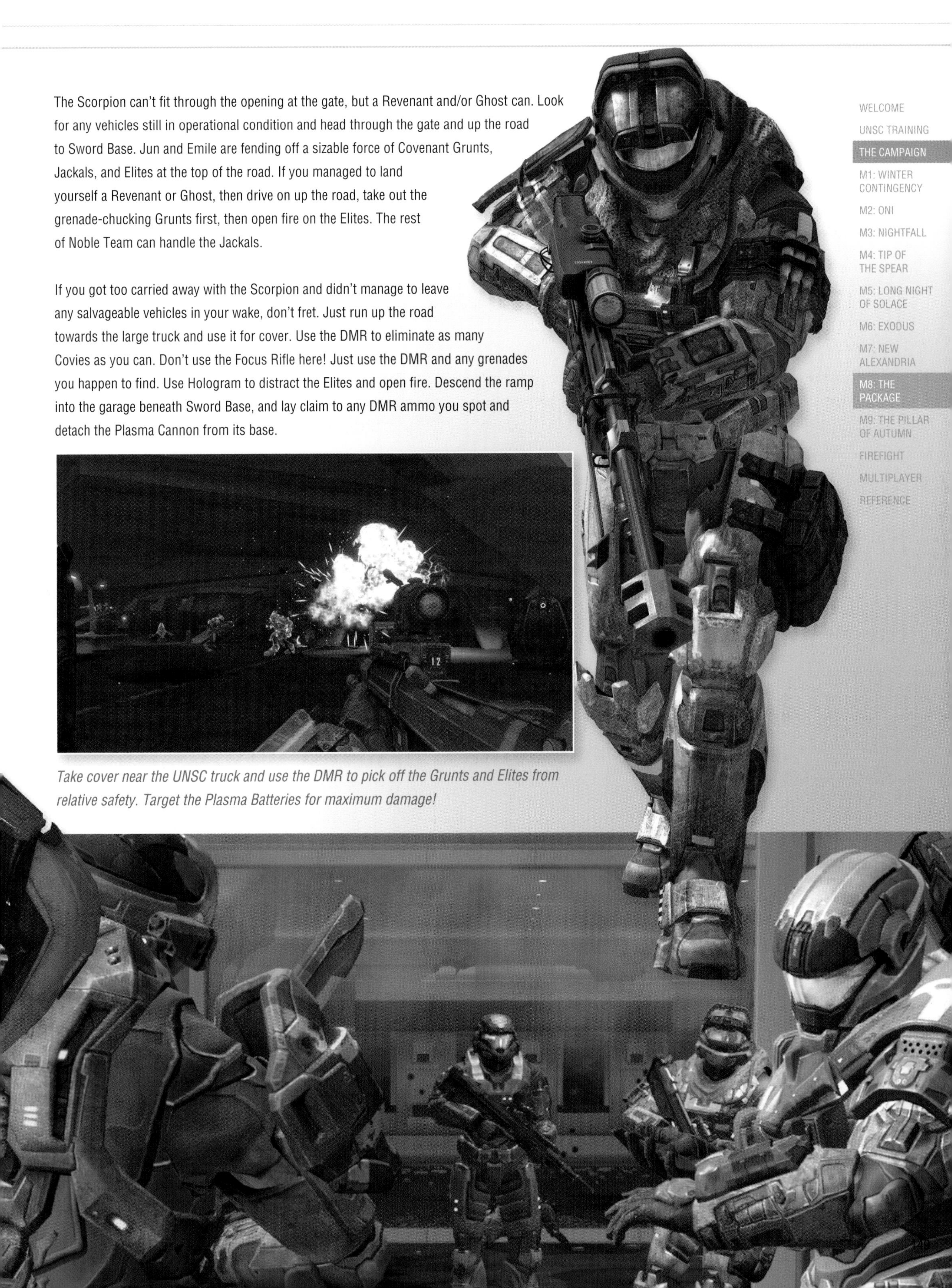

The Scorpion can't fit through the opening at the gate, but a Revenant and/or Ghost can. Look for any vehicles still in operational condition and head through the gate and up the road to Sword Base. Jun and Emile are fending off a sizable force of Covenant Grunts, Jackals, and Elites at the top of the road. If you managed to land yourself a Revenant or Ghost, then drive on up the road, take out the grenade-chucking Grunts first, then open fire on the Elites. The rest of Noble Team can handle the Jackals.

If you got too carried away with the Scorpion and didn't manage to leave any salvageable vehicles in your wake, don't fret. Just run up the road towards the large truck and use it for cover. Use the DMR to eliminate as many Covies as you can. Don't use the Focus Rifle here! Just use the DMR and any grenades you happen to find. Use Hologram to distract the Elites and open fire. Descend the ramp into the garage beneath Sword Base, and lay claim to any DMR ammo you spot and detach the Plasma Cannon from its base.

Take cover near the UNSC truck and use the DMR to pick off the Grunts and Elites from relative safety. Target the Plasma Batteries for maximum damage!

II LATCHKEY

RECOMMENDED EQUIPMENT

EASY/NORMAL	HEROIC	LEGENDARY
M392 DMR	M392 DMR	M392 DMR
T52 SAR FOCUS RIFLE	T52 SAR FOCUS RIFLE	T33 LAAW FUEL ROD GUN

ENEMY FORCES

Covenant
Grunt Infantry
Grunt Specialist
Grunt Hero
Jackal Infantry
Jackal Specialist
Jackal Hero
Elite Specialist
Elite Hero
Elite Leader
Engineer

OBJECTIVE

C: ENTER SWORD BASE

Breach Sword Base with NOBLE Team.

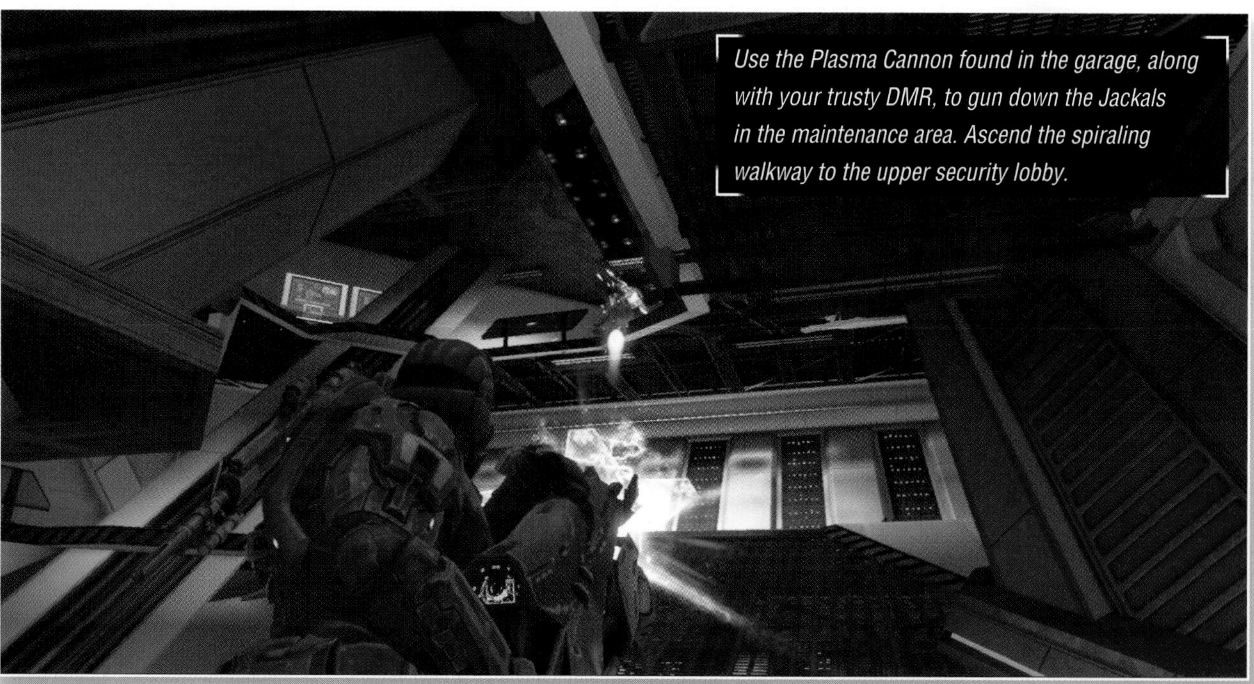

Use the Plasma Cannon found in the garage, along with your trusty DMR, to gun down the Jackals in the maintenance area. Ascend the spiraling walkway to the upper security lobby.

The elevators are offline, so Noble Team must ascend on foot through the maintenance corridors. Carry the Plasma Cannon from the garage into the spiraling maintenance area and use it to blast through the throngs of Jackals in the area—just be sure to drop it in favor of the DMR when you don't have a clean shot. The walkway spirals upwards in a counter-clockwise direction, and multiple Jackals occupy the southern and northern ends of each floor. The final ramp leads up to the security entrance where the elevator let Noble Six and Kat off so long ago.

OBJECTIVE

D: PROCEED TO THE COORDINATES

Proceed to the coordinates and await further instructions.

Gather up whatever ammo you can find in the lobby and equip the Hologram Armor Ability if not already using it. Equip the Focus Rifle you've been carrying and enter Sword Base. Take a few steps to the left and deploy a Hologram to draw enemy fire. There are four Elites in the immediate vicinity, and they're each using Active Camouflage. Hang back near the eastern end of the atrium and look for signs of movement. Open fire on each Elite with the Focus Rifle to burn through its shield, then quickly switch to the DMR and finish it off with a headshot. A fully loaded Focus Rifle can burn completely through the shield and kill the Elite if you aim at the head and you land 100% of the beam, but there's also a very good chance of overheating the weapon. It's safer to switch to the DMR once the shields are fried.

Use Plasma Grenades and the Focus Rifle to finish off the Elites nearest the entrance, then target the Engineer floating above the walkway at the west end of the atrium. The Engineer is lending support to an Elite Leader at the far end of the area, atop the ramp leading up to the second floor. Use the available cover for protection—the Elite Leader has a Concussion Rifle and is not about to go quietly. Follow Carter to the locked door designated by the coordinates Noble has received. Flip the switch on the left to open the door.

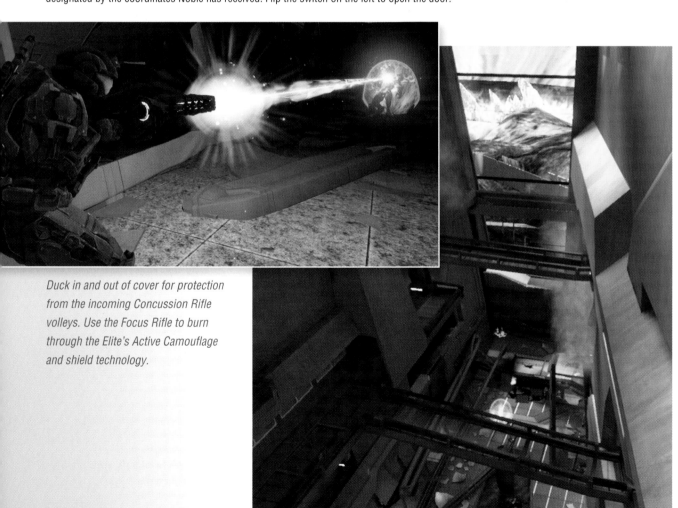

Duck in and out of cover for protection from the incoming Concussion Rifle volleys. Use the Focus Rifle to burn through the Elite's Active Camouflage and shield technology.

THIS CAVE IS NOT A NATURAL FORMATION

RECOMMENDED EQUIPMENT

ENEMY FORCES

Covenant
Grunt Infantry
Grunt Specialist
Grunt Hero
Jackal Infantry
Jackal Specialist
Jackal Hero
Skirmisher Infantry
Skirmisher Specialist
Brute Leader
Elite Infantry
Elite Specialist
Elite Hero
Elite Leader
Engineer

ENEMY VEHICLES

Covenant
Banshee
Phantom
Ghost
Wraith

OBJECTIVE

E: DEFEND HALSEY'S LAB

Defend Halsey's Lab using the defensive systems.

Exit the rail car and descend the series of ramps towards the bottom of the cave. Halsey's lab is to the left, where a wealth of UNSC supply cases has been distributed. You can find all of the Medkits, weaponry, grenades, and Armor Abilities you need. There are also a few Mongooses! This area has also been outfitted with four defense turrets that can automatically detect and fire upon enemy units. The only flaw in this system is that the turrets can only take so much damage before they need to recharge. It's up to you to activate the turrets one by one so they can assist Noble Team in eliminating the encroaching Covenant threat. Listen for cues (and refer to the on-screen indicators) to keep abreast of each turret's status. An ONI officer will announce which turret is online, recharging, or awaiting activation. Consult the HUD and the accompanying map for the whereabouts of each turret.

"Bury any of it and you bury mankind's best chance for survival."

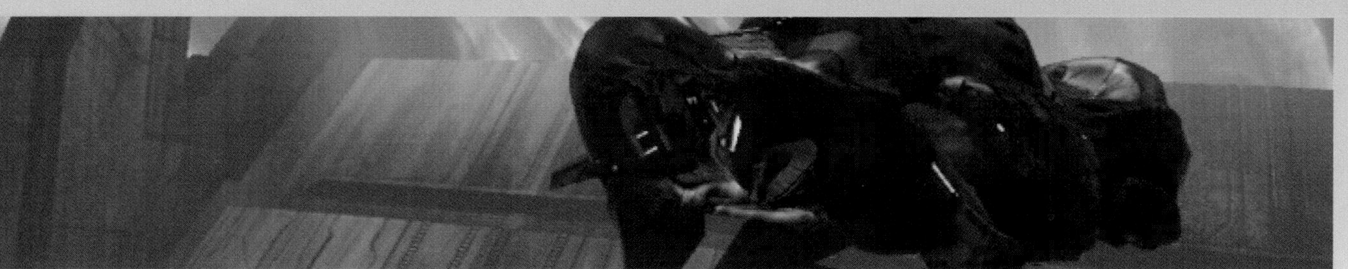

RALLY POINT BRAVO
X4
X4
TURRET-C
TURRET-B
E
F
X3
X2
TURRET-D
TURRET-A

Recommended Route: You'll first approach the glacier from the south, near Turret C. Use the elevated walkway to slip between Turret C and B with minimum exposure to Covenant on the ground below. Turrets D and A, on the north side of the glacier, can be accessed via a narrow gap in the rocks. Sneak behind the northern side of the structure beside the main laboratory entrance and drop down to Turret D. Climb back up to the isolated building by running and jumping up the concrete sloped retaining wall.

WHY RUN WHEN YOU CAN DRIVE?

The twin Mongooses parked near the lab give you a much faster way to make the rounds and activate the turrets, but these are best saved for co-op play or easier difficulty modes only. Though fast, the Mongoose attracts a lot of attention, and using it makes it very hard to move with stealth along the rocks around the periphery of the map, which is important when playing alone. Give the Mongoose a try when playing with three or four players, so you can take on a passenger and even get two Mongooses out there activating the turrets at once.

As soon as you arrive in the area, begin your first counter-clockwise lap to turn on the turrets. Move quickly from turret to turret and turn each of them on in time for the first wave of Covenant attackers. Return to the base where Carter and the others are and load up on DMR ammo, swap out the Assault Rifle for the Grenade Launcher and note the location of the other weapons and equipment.

Monitor the status bars for each turret and note when a turret goes blank. It recharges and becomes available for reactivation in five seconds.

Covenant of all shapes and sizes are ferried to the eastern end of the glacier via Phantoms under the escort of Banshees. The Phantoms begin the assault by forcing their lower level enemies to cross the entire ice sheet from the east all the way to Noble's defenses at the western end, but the Phantoms gradually move further up the glacier and eventually deploy troops directly in front of the lab's entrance. The Phantoms also occasionally deploy a Ghost, and you should also expect to encounter a Wraith on the road beyond Turret A and another Wraith uphill, south of Turret C.

LEGENDARY TACTICS

This is a really tough battle to survive on Legendary mode if you're not playing co-op with one or two others. That said, it is still possible. You just have to be smart and avoid overextending yourself. This means ignoring the turrets on the south side of the glacier. This does indeed limit the amount of support fire you receive, but Turrets C and B are not as easily accessible as are Turrets D and A. Circle around the back of the building to the north of the main lab to reach Turret D without being detected. From there, you can slip through a narrow trail in the rocks to reach Turret A. Turn and jump onto the concrete wall to scale the ledge back towards the base from Turret D to avoid running out in the open.

The other trick to surviving on Legendary is to resist the urge to steal a vehicle, not even a Wraith or Banshee. Vehicles are a magnet for enemy fire and Plasma Grenades, and even the Wraith's massive firepower is not worth the attention it draws. Stay close to Noble Team and put the Grenade Launcher and DMR to work! If things get too hot there, take off to the north and move in behind the enemies near Turret D. Use the alcove beside Turret D, along with Armor Lock, to stay healthy and keep the turret active. The battle is longer on Legendary—and features a couple of Hunters—so take your time, play it safe, and make sure you save some Grenade Launcher or Rocket Launcher ammo for the very end.

The first two waves of enemies consist entirely of Grunts and Jackals, but then things start to heat up. Subsequent waves contain numerous Brutes. The best way to deal with the Brutes is to fire the Grenade Launcher straight at them with the auto-detonation mode employed. A direct hit with the Grenade Launcher is all it takes to kill a Brute. Just make sure you don't aim too low, or the grenade may very well bounce and skip right between the Brute's legs—and ammo for the Grenade Launcher is too rare to go wasting it like that!

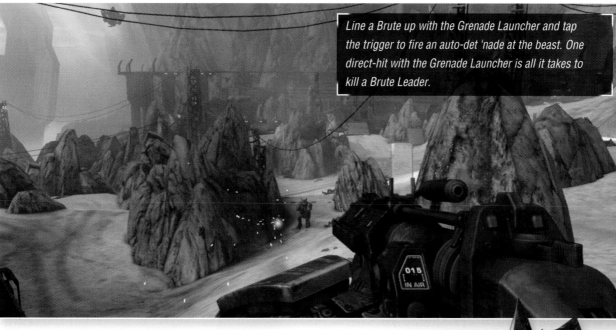

Line a Brute up with the Grenade Launcher and tap the trigger to fire an auto-det 'nade at the beast. One direct-hit with the Grenade Launcher is all it takes to kill a Brute Leader.

BANSHEES, FAST AND LOW

If you've been wondering when another opportunity to unlock this Achievement would come, here it is! Use the Grenade Launcher's manual detonation mode to EMP a Banshee as it flies overhead. The Banshee temporarily loses power and falls to the ground. You have to move fast, but there is a window of opportunity for you to hijack the Banshee before it flies away (you can fly up to meet it if you have Jet Pack equipped). Look for the on-screen prompt and press Ⓧ the moment you see the text appear. Noble Six climbs on and takes control of the Banshee. Hijacking Banshees during this battle doesn't just unlock an Achievement, but it is also a great way to lend aerial support to your team and improve your score. Use its bomb weaponry to blast Covenant as they exit the Phantoms. It's a great weapon against the Wraiths, too!

Focus on keeping at least two or three turrets active throughout the first half of the battle, or the base where the rest of Noble Team is located will surely get overrun. Avoid crossing the glacier out in the open at the eastern end, where the Covenant are being deployed. If you must cross from the north to the south sides to activate the turrets, circle back to the base, where it's much safer.

TO WRAITH, OR NOT TO WRAITH?

The two Wraiths located in the distance to the east and south ends of the map can definitely be nuisances. It's not uncommon for them to rain energy blasts down upon Turrets A and C, respectively. This isn't much of a problem on the lower difficulty settings, but it may be worth eliminating one or both Wraiths on Heroic difficulty. You shouldn't actually drive the Wraith into battle (unless you're curious about how many Plasma Grenades a Wraith can catch), but you should consider destroying at least the one uphill from Turret C. There are two ways to do this. One is to hijack a Banshee, switch to bomb mode, and circle the Wraith overhead while firing plasma bombs at it. Another option is to use the Spartan Laser to take out the gunner (always take out the gunner!), then move in on foot, climb aboard, and either melee it or plant a grenade. It's a risky move, but defeating the Wraiths prolongs the activity of your turrets.

The final waves of enemies are dropped off much closer to the lab, and consist almost entirely of Elites of varying rank and weaponry. They'll also disembark alongside an Engineer. Grab the Rocket Launcher from the rack near the entrance to the lab and move downhill towards Turret D where you can get a clean shot on the Engineer with the DMR, then switch to the Rocket Launcher and take out those Elites! Also, keep an eye on the two Fuel Rod Grunts take them down early if possible! Push back up the glacier behind the Elites to catch them in crossfire. Halsey radios as soon as she has the package ready.

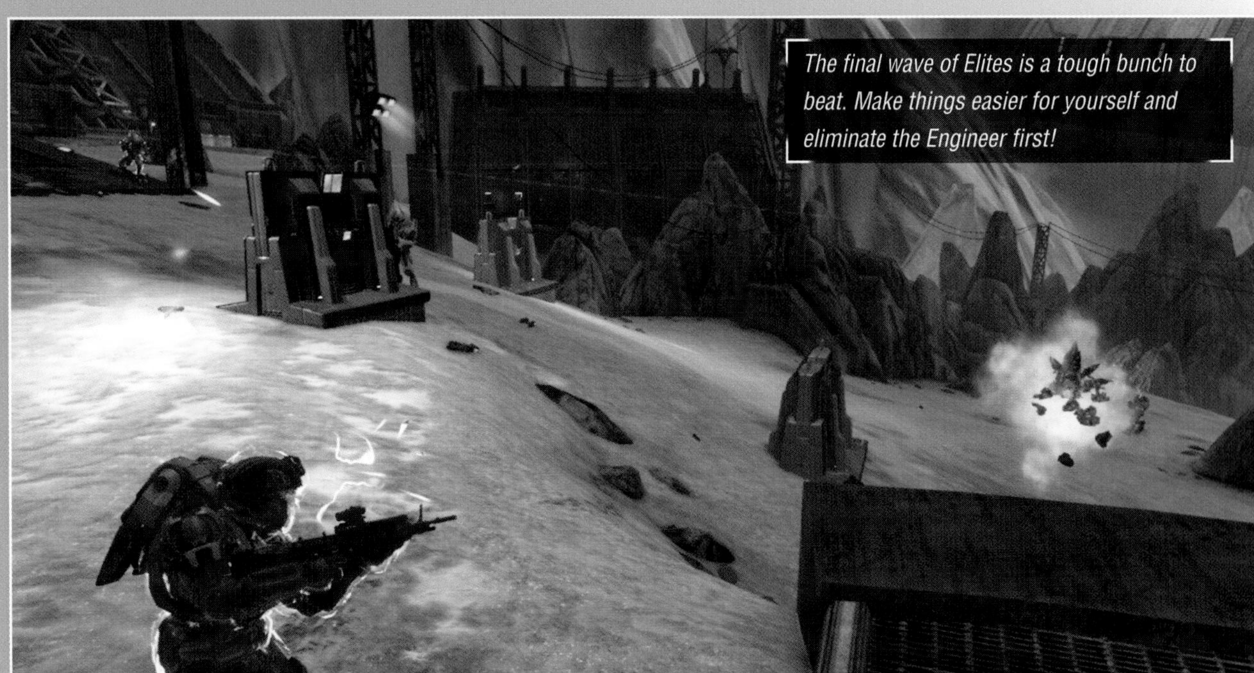

The final wave of Elites is a tough bunch to beat. Make things easier for yourself and eliminate the Engineer first!

CO-OP? IF SO, MAN THOSE TURRETS!

Rolling with a team of three or four? If so, try splitting up and sending one player to each of the four turrets, preferably with Armor Lock equipped for some extra protection. Have each player take cover behind his respective turret and stay there to keep the turret active. Turrets shut down automatically after sustaining too much damage, but they need less than ten seconds to recharge. So long as each player can last those few seconds, the team should be able to keep the turrets going throughout the entire battle. Just hurry back to the lab before the final Phantom makes its deposit outside of the turrets' reach.

OBJECTIVE

F: ENTER HALSEY'S LAB

Meet up with Dr. Halsey.

Return to the lab entrance where Noble Team was stationed (at the west end of the glacier). Open the heavy gate to her laboratory via the switch on the left and head inside. Doctor Halsey has a mission for you.

"UNSC cruiser, Pillar of Autumn, is awaiting your arrival."

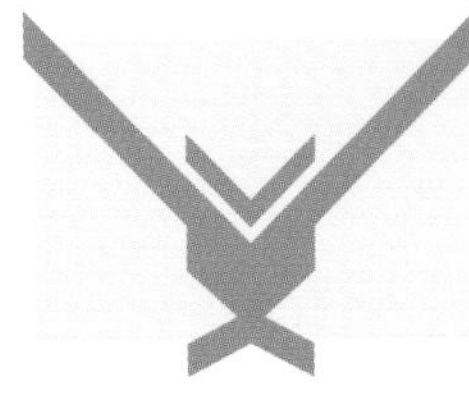

THE PILLAR OF AUTUMN

DELIVER HALSEY'S DATA PACKAGE TO THE PILLAR OF AUTUMN.

INTELLIGENCE BRIEFING

BASIC TACTICS

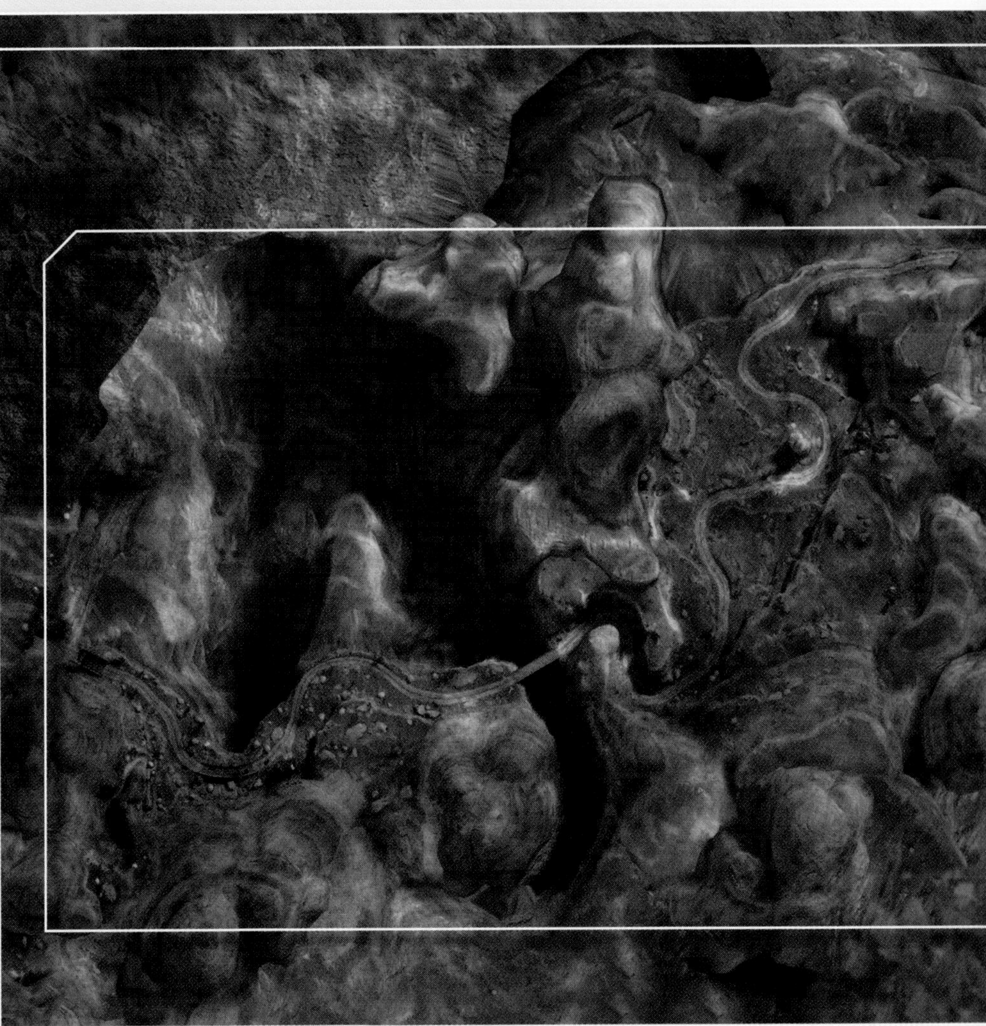

I Stay low and descend the hillside quietly. You do not want to alert the Covenant squads near the bridge. Throw Frag Grenades at any grouped enemies; otherwise, wait for Emile to engage the Covenant. Stay behind the cover of the truck and boulders and focus your firepower on the Elites. Ammo is in short supply, so look for the Shotgun beneath the bridge. Swap your weapons for the DMR and Rocket Launcher inside the outpost, then climb aboard the Mongoose. Lead the way eastward, past the Covenant army, and don't stop until you jump the bridge! To repeat: do not stop for anything!

II Conserve your Rocket Launcher ammo for later, unless given a chance to kill multiple Grunts with a single rocket. Use the DMR and Armor Lock to take down the Jackals in the tower and the Wraith in the distance. Allow Emile to engage the Buggers in the cave and continue to the cliffs overlooking the ship-breaking yard. Use the available power weaponry atop the cliff to reduce the Covenant forces before crossing the first yard on foot. Use the elevated positions inside the first structure you encounter to destroy the Shade Turrets in the second yard and to snipe any Elites in the area. Acquire the Drop Shield equipment and Shotgun to fight past the Hunters to join the UNSC Troopers inside. Make your way outside to the helipad and mass driver cannon.

CHAPTER-SPECIFIC ACHIEVEMENTS

 SEND ME OUT... WITH A BANG: Complete the 10th mission on Normal or harder.

MISSION OBJECTIVES

- Deliver package to Pillar of Autumn.
- Find alternate route through caves.
- Continue towards the Pillar.
- Clear platform for Keyes.
- Reactivate mass driver cannon.
- Destroy Covenant Cruiser.

WELCOME
UNSC TRAINING
THE CAMPAIGN
M1: WINTER CONTINGENCY
M2: ONI
M3: NIGHTFALL
M4: TIP OF THE SPEAR
M5: LONG NIGHT OF SOLACE
M6: EXODUS
M7: NEW ALEXANDRIA
M8: THE PACKAGE
M9: THE PILLAR OF AUTUMN
FIREFIGHT
MULTIPLAYER
REFERENCE

III Leap over the railing and make your way into the room below the crow's nest to lay claim to plenty of Grenade Launcher ammo. Now exit this room and enter the one below it, known in Firefight as the storeroom. Stand back from the two doors and wait for one massive invasion force to funnel through those doors. They won't all come at once—and you may need to exit periodically to lure them into the chokepoint—but the combination of the Grenade Launcher, the Shotgun, and the narrow doorway should see you through this battle. Use the Sniper Rifle in the crow's nest to pick off the Elites guarding the route to the mass driver cannon. Climb the ladder into the cannon's seat and clear the skies of Phantoms and Banshees until the Corvette comes within range. Listen for Colonel Holland's cue, then open fire on the belly of the Corvette.

ONCE MORE UNTO THE BREACH

RECOMMENDED EQUIPMENT

EASY/NORMAL

M6G
MAGNUM

MA37
ASSAULT RIFLE

M45 TS
SHOTGUN

HEROIC

M6G
MAGNUM

MA37
ASSAULT RIFLE

M45 TS
SHOTGUN

LEGENDARY

T25 DEP
PLASMA PISTOL

M6G
MAGNUM

MA37
ASSAULT RIFLE

M45 TS
SHOTGUN

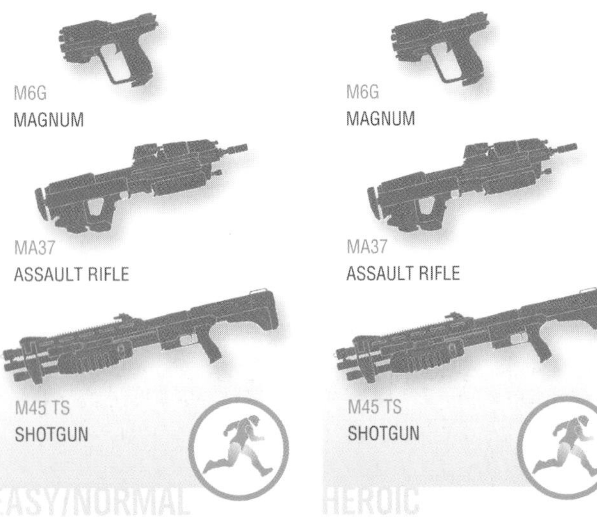

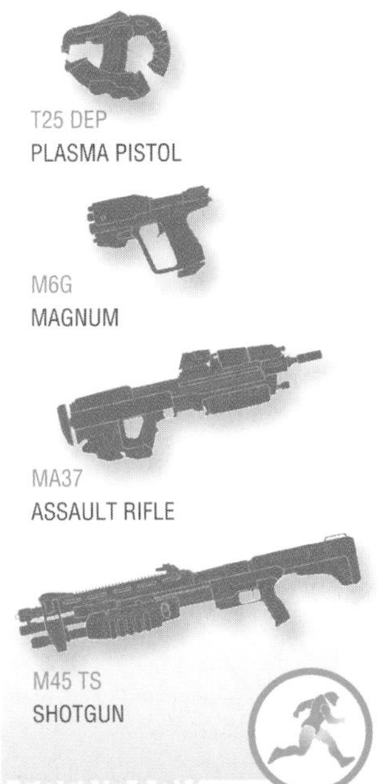

A
H
MISSION START

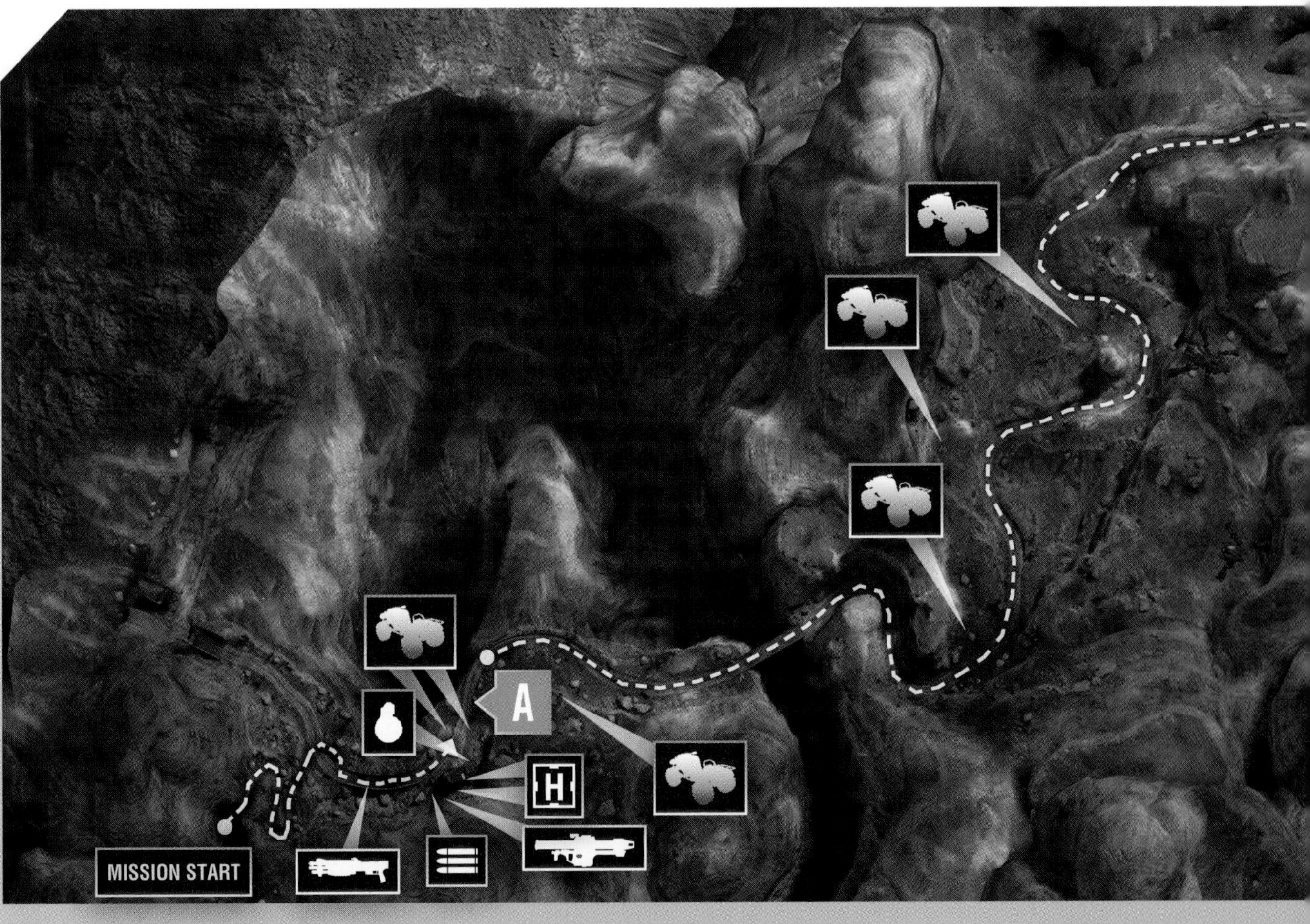

OBJECTIVE

A: DELIVER PACKAGE TO PILLAR OF AUTUMN

Take the package and deliver it to the Pillar of Autumn while Carter covers you from the air. When in doubt, look for the Pillar on the eastern horizon.

Join Emile near the cliffs overlooking the road that leads to the ship-breaking yard and the Pillar of Autumn. Draw your Magnum and descend the hillside to get a closer view of the Covenant below the first switchback. Watch for a group of Grunts near an Elite near the rocks—toss a grenade if you see them, otherwise continue to the left. Emile takes the lead and engages the enemy first. Hug the base of the cliff and strafe left to deal with the enemies near the eighteen-wheeler, while Emile tackles the troops to the right of the bridge. A band of Jackals slowly retreats across the bridge, while the Grunts typically flee beneath it. Take out as many of these lesser foes as you can before engaging the Elites.

"That A.I. chose you. She made the right choice."

IF THEY CAME TO HEAR ME BEG

If you've been wondering where you could possibly take a flying leap and break your fall atop an Elite, this is the place! Meet Emile on the cliff overlooking the road and watch the blue Elite Minor as he paces back and forth. Wait for him to near the grass then take a running leap off the cliff towards him. Hold the Right Bumper down and aim towards him while in the air to land in an Assassination attack. This will likely take a few (dozen) attempts so be patient and stick with it.

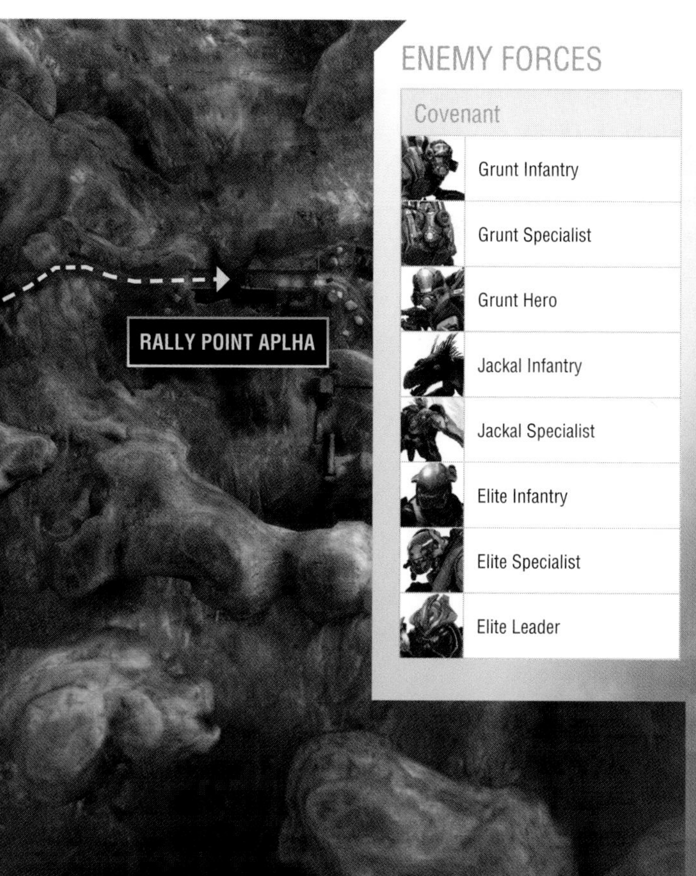

ENEMY FORCES

Covenant
Grunt Infantry
Grunt Specialist
Grunt Hero
Jackal Infantry
Jackal Specialist
Elite Infantry
Elite Specialist
Elite Leader

LEGENDARY TACTICS

The best advice to remember is to listen to Emile—stay low and let him lead the way! Hug the base of the cliffs on the south side of the path and do not engage the enemy until Emile makes his way down the hill. Use the Magnum to pick off a few Grunts, then circle back up and around to the rocks northeast of the eighteen-wheelers. Wait for Emile to engage the Elites there and see if you can lend some additional firepower once their shields are down. You may even look for an opportunity to perform an Assassination. Push across the bridge very slowly. Use a Plasma Pistol or Plasma Rifle to drop the Jackals' shields more quickly.

Straddle one of the Mongooses after collecting the DMR and Rocket Launcher and take off to the east. Drive fast and outpace the Banshees overhead. You must drive as flawless of a route as you can in order to avoid being hit by too many of the Covenant in this area. Keep the throttle fully open until you get beyond the Scarabs, then come to a stop inside the cave to allow the Phantom to clear the area before you jump the bridge.

You begin the mission with limited ammo for the Magnum, so you may have to switch to the Assault Rifle at some point. Alternatively, you can collect the Shotgun lying on the ground beneath the bridge and use it to finish off the Grunts and Jackals in the area.

Don't waste your ammo by attacking enemy forces from the cliffs. Instead, descend the trail and take cover near the big rig before you open fire.

Approach the outpost near the parked Mongooses, then locate the Medkit and Rocket Launcher close to the body near the stairs. Enter the outpost and swap the Assault Rifle for a DMR, and collect some extra rockets. Climb aboard the second Mongoose and start driving down the road to the east. Emile soon follows on the other Mongoose.

If you had any lingering doubts about the severity of the Covenant invasion, they will be laid to rest in the coming moments. The road to the east soon winds around a turn and reveals a massive army of Covenant led by multiple Scarabs. Drop pods rain down like meteors from the sky, each of them depositing another half-dozen Grunts into the area. Heed Emile's voice and do not engage the enemy. You can't win a fight of this order—not even with a Rocket Launcher. Carter offers some covering fire from the air; stay on the throttle and use the handbrake to drift through the turns in the road. Don't stop for anything! Steer the Mongoose straight past the Grunts and other Covies and drive right between the legs of the Scarabs that straddle the road.

WELCOME
UNSC TRAINING
THE CAMPAIGN
M1: WINTER CONTINGENCY
M2: ONI
M3: NIGHTFALL
M4: TIP OF THE SPEAR
M5: LONG NIGHT OF SOLACE
M6: EXODUS
M7: NEW ALEXANDRIA
M8: THE PACKAGE
M9: THE PILLAR OF AUTUMN
FIREFIGHT
MULTIPLAYER
REFERENCE

Listen to Emile! Don't get off the Mongoose even for a second. Stay on the gas and drive as fast as you can towards the Pillar of Autumn.

The bridge up ahead is out. Accelerate towards the centerline and jump the gap in the road to continue east. Enter the structure on the right to find a Medkit, Shotgun, and a number of DMRs. Swap your current Armor Ability in favor of Armor Lock and load up on DMR ammo. You and Emile must proceed the rest of the way on foot.

THIS TOWN ISN'T BIG ENOUGH

RECOMMENDED EQUIPMENT

ENEMY FORCES

Covenant
Grunt Infantry
Grunt Specialist
Grunt Hero
Jackal Infantry
Jackal Specialist
Jackal Hero
Skirmisher Infantry
Skirmisher Specialist
Bugger Infantry
Bugger Specialist
Brute Infantry
Brute Leader
Elite Infantry
Elite Specialist
Elite Leader
Hunter

ENEMY VEHICLES

Covenant
Ghost
Wraith

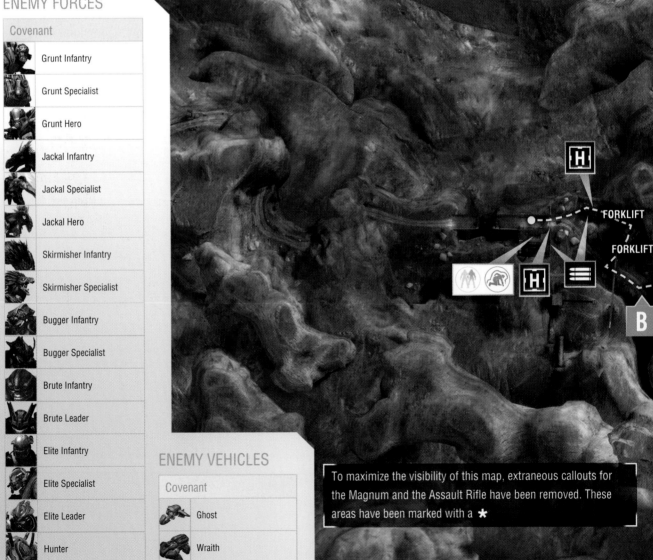

To maximize the visibility of this map, extraneous callouts for the Magnum and the Assault Rifle have been removed. These areas have been marked with a ★

CAMPAIGN

M319 GL
GRENADE LAUNCHER

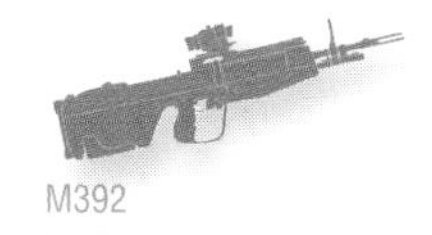

M392
DMR

M6 G/GNR
SPARTAN LASER

M319 GL
GRENADE LAUNCHER

M45 TS
SHOTGUN

M41 SSR
ROCKET LAUNCHER

SSR99D AM
SNIPER RIFLE

M45 TS
SHOTGUN

LEGENDARY

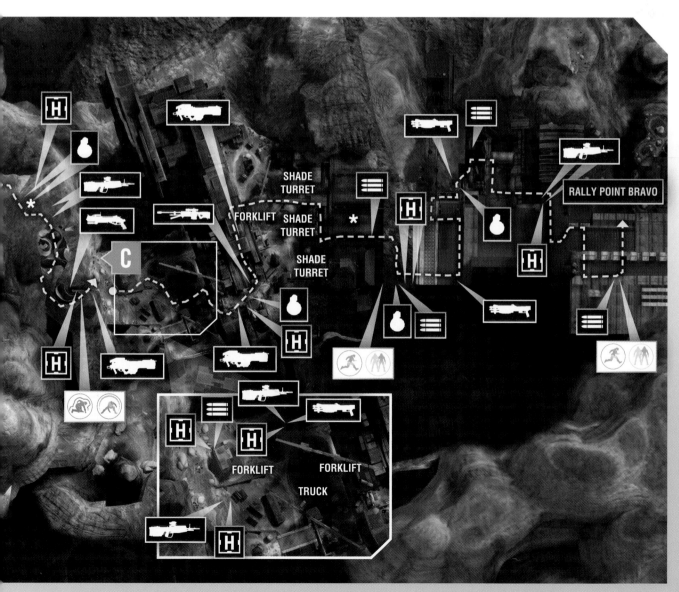

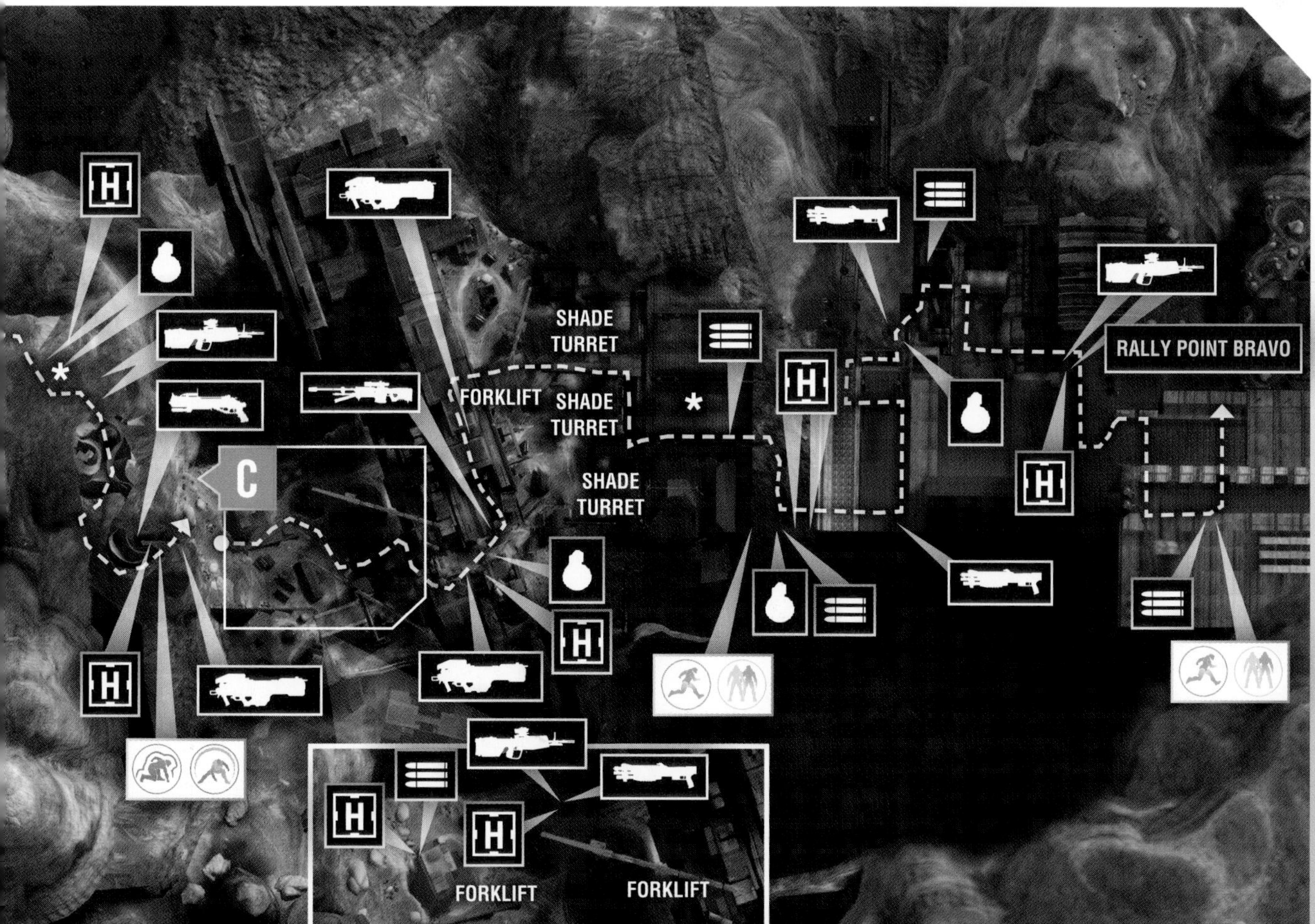

SHADE TURRET
FORKLIFT
SHADE TURRET
SHADE TURRET
C
RALLY POINT BRAVO
FORKLIFT
FORKLIFT
TRUCK

OBJECTIVE

B: FIND ALTERNATE ROUTE THROUGH CAVES

The Covenant forces have blocked the road forward. Find an alternate route through a cave system to the east.

SAVE THE ROCKETS

Don't use more than one of the rockets in this battle (or the subsequent one in the caves) if you can help it. You'll be rewarded for your effort if you manage to carry the Rocket Launcher with you to the ship-breaking yard.

Shoulder the DMR and slip around the left-hand side of the concrete barriers where the road ends. Emile is going to bring the fight directly to the Covenant down the hillside near the entrance to the caves, leaving you to take a more careful approach. Snipe the Jackals on the tower to the right, then drop off the ledge and move through the structure on the northern side of the battlefield. Note the Medkit inside, and use the cover the structure affords to bait the Brutes to the northeast out of hiding. Try to take out the Brutes using only the DMR and grenades, unless three or more appear grouped together. If this happens, switch to the Rocket Launcher and blast them sky-high!

Cut through the first structure on the left and have the Rocket Launcher ready just in case you happen to get a shot at three or more Brute Leaders gathered together.

Eliminate the Wraith's gunner before approaching it on foot. Use Armor Lock to EMP the Wraith at close range, then jump aboard and destroy it by either repeatedly meleeing it or by planting a grenade.

Use the cover of the buildings on the left and the rocks uphill from them to eliminate as many of the ground troops as you can. Circle back around in a counter-clockwise direction to the rock wall on the right and eliminate the Wraith's gunner. Watch Emile's progress and try to converge on the Wraith with him. Dodge its attacks while closing on it to bait it into a ramming charge. Use Armor Lock to EMP the Wraith, then climb aboard and melee it into oblivion.

A number of suicide Grunts and Jackals are hiding behind the rocks and trees near the entrance to the caves. Proceed cautiously to draw them out and open fire on the retreat. Clear the area of Covies, then double back to the building near the edge of the cliffs to restock your supply of DMR ammo. Enter the sandstone canyon to the east and accompany Emile into the cave.

Step quietly past the bodies of the fallen troopers near the cave entrance and hug the wall on the right. Round the corner and open fire on the Buggers that appear. Step in and out of cover to fire a few rounds from the DMR, then back up to avoid being hit. Allow Emile to take point, since this helps you conserve both ammo and health. Also, look for Buggers that have landed on the surface of a wall. These enemies represent the easiest targets to hit. A dozen or so Buggers flutter about the large room around the corner from the bodies, but they won't chase you into the narrow path. Return to the bodies if you need a Medkit or want to collect extra DMR ammo.

The DMR isn't the ideal weapon for blasting Buggers out of the air, but what it lacks in spray-and-pray, it makes up for with accuracy and stopping power.

Proceed to the west, past the next gaggle of Buggers—near the area of the cave with a small pool of water in the bottom. Hang back above the ledge overlooking the water and take out the Buggers from here before moving any further. The cave's exit is up ahead to the east, but a number of Skirmisher Specialists armed with Needle Rifles are guarding it. Resist exposing yourself to their fire until the Buggers have all been defeated.

OBJECTIVE

C: CONTINUE TOWARD THE PILLAR

The Pillar draws closer, and Keyes is awaiting delivery of the package. Keep heading east, no matter what they throw at you.

The cave's exit contains a UNSC supply case. Swap the Armor Lock ability in favor of Drop Shield and note the Grenade Launcher and Spartan Laser on the ground. Temporarily swap out the DMR for the Spartan Laser and approach the edge of the cliffs overlooking the shipyard. The area below is crawling with Jackals and Elites of all kinds, but many of them are too swift to make for an easy target with the Spartan Laser. Instead, fix the weapon on any stationary Elite Specialists you see on the structure across the yard to the east. There should be at least one or two that present a slower target. Those two Elite Specialists eventually leap down into the yard and really complicate things, so take them out now! Use the Spartan Laser and the Rocket Launcher you've been carrying to further reduce the number of enemies in the shipyard. These power weapons can be used to detonate the trucks, eliminate groups of enemies, and even wipe out high-ranking Elites. Use up all of the ammo for both power weapons, then grab the Grenade Launcher and start down the hill.

TOP PRIORITY TARGET

Whether you use the Spartan Laser or Rocket Launcher matters not, but you can do yourself a giant favor and eliminate the Elite Leader with the Fuel Rod Gun before you descend the cliffs. You may need to detonate a truck or two to flush him out of hiding, but track him from atop the cliffs and dispose of him now while it's easier.

The Spartan Laser delivers a one-hit kill to whatever comes in contact with it. Use it to take out the Elite Leader with the Fuel Rod Gun before descending the cliffs.

Descend the southern face of the cliff to the shipyard and lend support to Emile as you cross to the north. A number of troopers are pushing their way across the yard at the northern end, just beyond a supply depot. Cut through the building to find some munitions and another Medkit, and offer whatever fire support you can muster. There's plenty of DMR ammo in the area, so use that weapon as much as you can and conserve the Grenade Launcher ammo for a less wide-open area. Don't take any of the enemies in this area lightly. Use the Drop Shield for protection and avoid moving across open terrain. Move quickly from one piece of cover to the next.

Approach the large structure to the east and ascend the two flights of stairs to the top. Locate the Spartan Laser on the northeast side and use it to destroy each of the Shade Turrets in the yard below. The Spartan Laser can be fired four times at full power, so take out each of the Shade Turrets, then use the final laser blast to destroy either an Elite or a Ghost. Once the Spartan Laser is spent, strafe directly to the right to swap it for a Sniper Rifle. Put a round into the forklift truck in the center of the yard (preferably while a number of Grunts are close by), then set to sniping any Elites you can spot before they run inside the next structure.

The upstairs platform of the first structure in the shipyard contains a Spartan Laser and Sniper Rifle. Use these power weapons to eliminate the Shade Turrets, Ghosts, Elites, and any Grunts you spot wielding Fuel Rod Guns.

Remain on the upper level and approach the north end of the platform to find a bridge leading out to a conveyor belt that is high above the yard. This bridge provides a great chance to fire flanking shots at the remaining enemies in the yard below. Descend the stairs to ground level after the fight to gather up some extra DMR ammo and grenades, then climb the stairs back to the bridge where you were. Continue east, via the defunct conveyor belt, to the next large structure. Exit the conveyor belt on the right, where two of the large screened skylights have been knocked off their mounts. Use the Grenade Launcher and DMR to eliminate the Elites and Grunts inside the room below. These opponents put up a good fight and move around a lot, so use the Grenade Launcher's manual detonation ability to EMP the Elites, then switch to the DMR and achieve headshots on them for kills. If you are out of Grenade Launcher ammo, return to the small office buildings in the prior yard and grab a Shotgun.

Don't enter the second massive structure in the shipyard until you've cleared out the Elites inside. Take advantage of the broken screens on the upper windows and attack from the roof.

FORAGING FOR MUNITIONS

The Grenade Launcher didn't come with much ammo, but there's an entire battlefield of munitions waiting to be collected. Hop aboard one of the abandoned Ghosts and scour the area for any Fuel Rod Guns you can find. It's also worth returning to the small building in the very northwest corner of the shipyard to restock your DMR supply and/or to get a Shotgun.

Proceed down the hallway to the area with several windowed offices. Load up on supplies and continue through the door leading to the room overlooking the foundry. Melee the windows in the room to get a shot on the Covies near the smelting tanks if you have a longer range weapon or want to throw some grenades. Otherwise, exit the room and move along the southern edge of the smelting area. Collect the additional Shotgun ammo in the corner and circle around behind the Elites that exit the Phantom. Rejoin the troopers in the corner of the room beneath the office and use your Drop Shield to regroup.

Circle around the perimeter of the smelting area in a counter-clockwise circle to get the drop on the Elites near the exit.

DROP SHIELD VERSUS HOLOGRAM

The area up ahead contains a pair of Hunters and four Skirmishers. Though it's strongly recommended that you hold onto the Drop Shield for the remainder of the mission, this can make it a bit harder to contend with the Hunters. If the battle against the Hunters proves too difficult, head back to the office inside the foundry and swap it—temporarily—for the Hologram. Just make sure you continue east with Drop Shield.

Exit the foundry area onto the balcony where the mining extraction system is located. Continue east towards the platform where you'll find two Hunters and a number of Skirmishers. Pick up the Shotgun on the ground near the body and immediately put whatever DMR or Assault Rifle ammo you have remaining to use against the Skirmishers while moving in and out of cover near the shipping containers on the left.

The battle against the two Hunters is much easier if you can separate them. Emile helps distract the Hunters so you can isolate one, but you may need to do this on your own (with or without the Hologram). Emile implores you to continue east, but the troopers inside the next area won't open the door as long as those Hunters are alive. Use your grenades to soften up the Hunters and move back and forth between the northern and southern ends to try to separate them. Once one is isolated, switch to the Shotgun and approach close enough to bait it into using melee attacks. Circle-strafe to the left to get a clean shot on its back. Emile has been firing on the Hunters all along, so you won't need to do much to finish them off. Get in behind one, fire two quick blasts from the Shotgun, then deliver what should be a knockout blow with a melee.

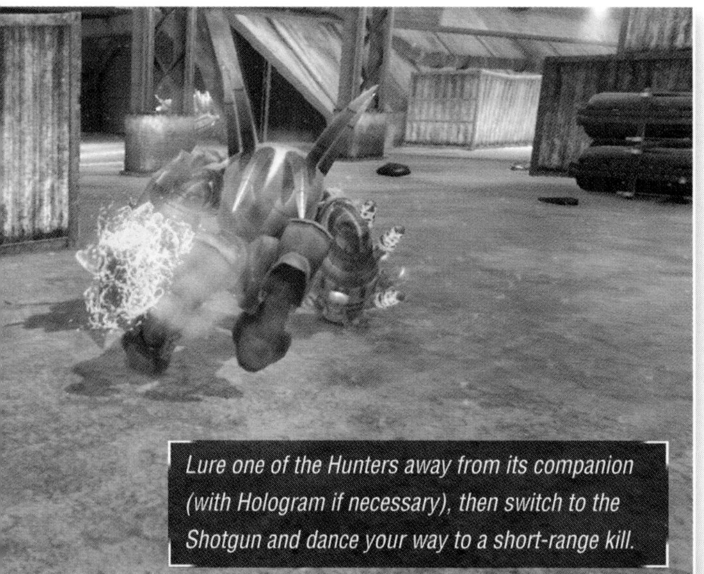

Lure one of the Hunters away from its companion (with Hologram if necessary), then switch to the Shotgun and dance your way to a short-range kill.

Head up the stairs to the southeast to enter the next fabrication area of the shipyard. Sprint on an angle to the right of the Medkit visible on the wall to locate a pair of DMRs. Shoulder the rifle and immediately snipe the Jackals on the walkway to the south. An Elite with an Energy Sword will charge your position as soon as the Jackals on the lower level have been defeated—take out the ones up top so you aren't being sniped while trying to fend off an Elite with a sword. Reward yourself to additional ammo and a Medkit in the office in the southeast corner, then head up the stairs to the catwalk. A number of Elites and Grunts enter via the door to the east. Hang back alongside Emile and take them out. Return downstairs to restock your supply of rounds for the DMR, then head through the door. Continue down the corridors with the UNSC Troopers and swap the Shotgun out for the Grenade Launcher when you reach the next UNSC supply case.

Grab the DMR near the slag pile across from the entrance and eliminate the Jackals upstairs. By the time you ascend the catwalk, Elites and Grunts join the fray, so don't let down your guard.

KEYES

RECOMMENDED EQUIPMENT

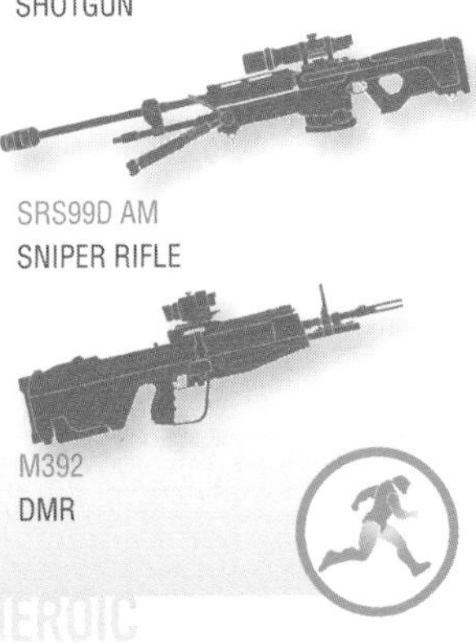

EASY/NORMAL

- M319 GL — GRENADE LAUNCHER
- M45 TS — SHOTGUN
- SRS99D AM — SNIPER RIFLE
- M392 — DMR

HEROIC

- T33 LAAW — FUEL ROD GUN
- M319 GL — GRENADE LAUNCHER
- M45 TS — SHOTGUN
- SRS99D AM — SNIPER RIFLE
- M392 — DMR

LEGENDARY

- M45 TS — SHOTGUN
- SRS99D AM — SNIPER RIFLE
- M392 — DMR
- M319 GL — GRENADE LAUNCHER
- T33 LAAW — FUEL ROD GUN
- M6G — MAGNUM

OBJECTIVE

D: CLEAR PLATFORM FOR KEYES

The Pillar is ready to take off, but not without the package. Defend the platform from incoming enemy forces so Keyes can land for the handoff.

Emile continues on to man the mass driver cannon, leaving you to clear the platform of Covenant troops so Keyes can land. This is undeniably the longest and most difficult battle in the game, but there is hope. And it comes in the form of nearly endless amounts of ammunition for the Grenade Launcher and Shotgun. Enter the room directly beneath the crow's nest and load up on ammo, then exit this room and descend yet one more level to the two-story storeroom below.

THE MURDER CAN WAIT

Don't be lured up to the crow's nest atop the storeroom by the presence of the Sniper Rifle. The reverberations from the mass driver cannon make precision sniping very difficult, not to mention that Brutes and Grunts soon overrun the crow's nest much faster than you may expect.

ENEMY FORCES

Covenant
Grunt Specialist
Grunt Hero
Jackal Specialist
Brute Infantry
Brute Leader
Brute Hero
Elite Specialist
Elite Hero

The T-shaped storeroom is the perfect place from which to mount your defense against the invading Covenant army. There are only two ways into this area, and both can be monitored from the rear of the room. Stand back, above the stairs, and use the Grenade Launcher and DMR to pick off the enemies as they funnel through either door. There is a wealth of additional Grenade Launcher ammo in the room directly above, and the UNSC supply cabinet at the base of the stairs inside the storeroom contains a full complement of Shotgun ammo—switch to the Shotgun once the DMR runs dry or the enemies start getting tougher to kill. This room also contains a number of Medkits, but you should use the Drop Shield to heal as often as possible.

Use the Grenade Launcher and either the DMR or Shotgun to mow down the countless Brutes and Grunts as they funnel through these doors.

Eventually, you may grow tired of waiting for enemies to find you inside the storeroom and crave fresh air. The best place to escape to in order to bring the fight to the Covenant is to go out the storeroom's downstairs door to the L-shaped underground area. Enemies deposited on the helipad and on the cliffs to the north fight their way up to this position. This location gives you complete protection from Phantom attacks and also a clear line of sight in two directions. Best of all, it's close to the Shotgun and Grenade Launcher ammo cabinets. Another option is to use the Shotgun and any Fuel Rod Guns you can find and roam the area between the lowermost floor and the rocky landing to the southeast—just make sure you have the Drop Shield with you!

LEGENDARY TACTICS

There's no getting around the fact that this objective is brutally difficult to survive on your own on Legendary difficulty. It's possible, but certainly not for the faint of heart (or the short-tempered). The basic strategy outlined in this section is still applicable, but you're going to have to conserve your ammo a bit more than normal. You can accomplish this by using the Magnum located in the UNSC cabinet inside the storeroom area. The Magnum allows you to take out the Grunts and Jackals without having to get too close or use the Grenade Launcher. Another tactic to employ, particularly in the latter portion of the battle, is to use the Grenade Launcher to set traps just inside the doorway in the storeroom. Stand back and bounce a grenade from the Grenade Launcher at the door and continue holding the trigger for manual detonation mode. Wait for Brutes (particularly one with a Gravity Hammer) to enter the area, then release the trigger to knock them out. Ultimately, this battle is going to test your skills in ways no other battle in *Halo: Reach* has done. Stick with it, use the storeroom for cover, and put the Shotgun and Grenade Launcher to work! Keyes is depending on you.

Continue to battle the Brutes and Jackals from within the storeroom and the area outside the lowest level until the Brutes with Gravity Hammers arrive. Fall back inside and use grenades and the Shotgun to take them out as they ascend the stairs. Their demise signals the arrival of other tougher, better armed enemies. Gather up additional ammo, then head outside and toward the rocks to the southeast. Eliminate the Jackals and scan the walkways and stairs to the south for a well-armored Brute Chieftain with a Plasma Launcher. This is your top priority. Deploy a Drop Shield outside, near the landing pad and move in and out of it to avoid the Plasma Grenades it fires. Use the Shotgun or a Fuel Rod Gun to take out the Brute Chieftain.

Make your way to the crow's nest as soon as you have eliminated the Brute with the Gravity Hammer. Use the Sniper Rifle to score a headshot on the Brute with the Fuel Rod Gun, then quickly return to the storeroom before the crow's nest is overrun. Leave the Sniper Rifle where you found it until later.

Gather up some additional ammo from the room below the crow's nest and return to the storeroom to mount one final stand. More Brutes are en route, along with a few well-armed Grunts (and some Suicide Grunts, as well). You may need to make quick guerrilla strikes outside of the storeroom, but you shouldn't extend yourself too far, and you should always retreat to the relative safety that the storeroom offers. The external stairs leading up from the storeroom to the crow's nest are a veritable death trap—tread lightly! Finish clearing the helipad and bring the package to Keyes when the Pelican backs in.

OBJECTIVE

E: REACTIVATE MASS DRIVER CANNON

[Redacted] Get to the anti-aircraft gun, defend the Pillar, and [redacted].

Noble Six needs to fight his way past four Zealot-class Elites inside the building beneath the mass driver cannon. This level of enemy doesn't go down lightly, so take a moment to gather up any loose Fuel Rod Guns and/or the Sniper Rifle if you're out of Grenade Launcher ammo. Complement your choice of power weapon with either the DMR or Shotgun, depending on your preferred style of play. Kill the Grunts on the stairs leading up to the building to the south and enter slowly. Stay close to the exit, and isolate the Elite near the small steps straight ahead.

Use the DMR or Sniper Rifle to finish off the Elite nearest the entrance. Don't advance any farther into the building, or you'll draw the fire of the three Elites on the upper walkway.

Don't engage the Elite atop the stairs until you've dealt with the other three. This is the final enemy standing between you and the mass driver cannon; proceed with caution!

Kill the first Elite, then head up the steps to the small workshop on the left. With any luck, you'll be able to collect some Plasma Grenades from the Grunts in this area. Use the objects in this room, along with the walls and pillars, to outwit the second Elite to attack. Collect the Plasma Rifle with the most available ammo before leaving the area.

Besting the final two Elites requires careful planning. One of them is armed with twin Plasma Rifles, while the other wields a Fuel Rod Gun and Energy Sword. In all likelihood, the one with the twin Plasma Rifles descends the stairs and attacks first. Loop in a clockwise direction back past the entrance and over to the south wall. Don't go up the stairs towards the two Elites; instead, enter the room in the southeast corner and load up some additional DMR ammo. Your proximity to the two Elites can draw the one with the Plasma Rifles down into the room. Down his shields with the Plasma Rifle you picked up, then finish him off with the DMR.

The final Elite typically stays on the upper walkway (and may even retreat to the mass driver cannon). Deploy a Drop Shield below the stairs, in case you need to fall back into cover, then inch your way up the stairs slowly and pop his shields with a Plasma Grenade or a series of DMR headshots. The Elite should switch to its Energy Sword as soon as its shields have been depleted. Stay calm and keep firing on its head. It should only take two more headshots with the DMR to finish him off. Climb the ladder to the mass driver cannon.

OBJECTIVE
F: DESTROY COVENANT CRUISER

A Covenant Cruiser is bearing down on your position. Destroy it before it can glass you and the Pillar into oblivion.

The Corvette is currently out of range, but an armada of Phantoms and Banshees is rapidly approaching. Use the mass driver cannon to beat back the Covenant ships until the Corvette moves within range. Depending on the difficulty level you're playing on, this scene can prove to be very tricky. For those playing on Heroic or Legendary, you must essentially destroy every Phantom and Banshee as quickly as possible. It's not enough to shoot them as they get close—you must blast them out of the air the moment they get within range, and in the order in which they appear, or there is a high probability that you will be overrun. This doesn't require pattern memorization (though it helps), but you do have to be efficient and pay close attention to where the incoming fire originates from.

The majority of enemy craft fly in from the left-hand side of the area, beyond the rocky bluff directly ahead. Count your kills, as the sixth and seventh Phantoms attack from far to the right and left, respectively.

The mass driver cannon takes roughly three seconds for its capacitors to reload. You can monitor its reload progress and then follow the weapon's charging either on the HUD or on the back of the weapon itself, via the green lights. The mass driver cannon can insta-kill everything it hits, but it is slow to fire, and it is a very large target for Covenant craft to hit. The Phantoms are your biggest threat and should be treated as top priority targets, but don't ignore the Banshees. Because the Banshees are more numerous, they can buy time for the Phantoms to get in closer. The Banshees commonly fly close enough together that it's possible to eliminate two or three with a single attack. Always take advantage of any opportunities to destroy multiple crafts with a single blast.

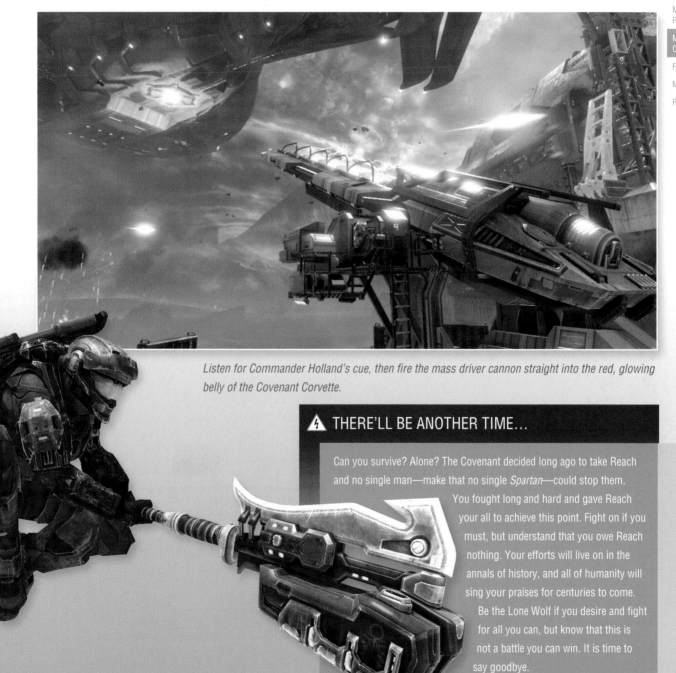

Listen for Commander Holland's cue, then fire the mass driver cannon straight into the red, glowing belly of the Covenant Corvette.

THERE'LL BE ANOTHER TIME...

Can you survive? Alone? The Covenant decided long ago to take Reach and no single man—make that no single *Spartan*—could stop them. You fought long and hard and gave Reach your all to achieve this point. Fight on if you must, but understand that you owe Reach nothing. Your efforts will live on in the annals of history, and all of humanity will sing your praises for centuries to come. Be the Lone Wolf if you desire and fight for all you can, but know that this is not a battle you can win. It is time to say goodbye.

FIREFIGHT BASICS

Firefight is the perfect blend of the Campaign and Multiplayer experiences, giving you the opportunity to battle wave after wave of the Covenant alongside up to three friends over Xbox Live or via system link. Firefight caters to those who long for the good ol' days of high scores lists, endless supplies of enemies, and cooperative teamwork with friends. It's also a great way to earn Credits and increase your Rank, not to mention experiment with Skulls.

FIREFIGHT 101

UNDERSTANDING THE HUD

Firefight introduces several elements to the head's up display (HUD) that you don't normally see during the Campaign or in Multiplayer. Below is a typical scene from a Firefight match with an explanation of the Firefight-specific information conveyed through the on-screen indicators.

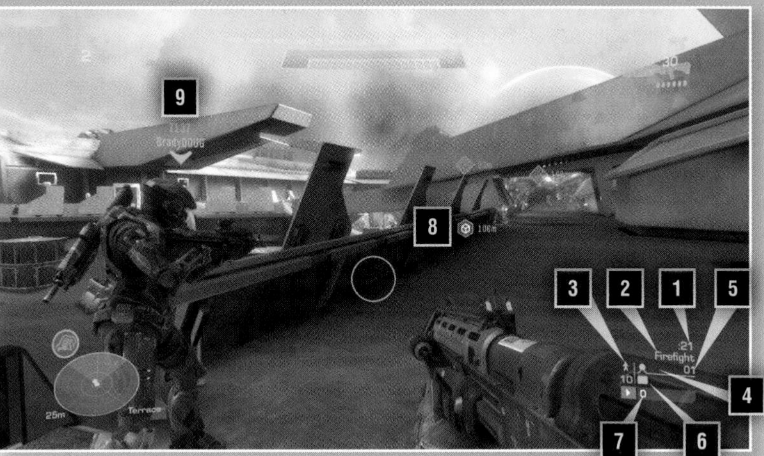

1. **Time Elapsed**: The amount of time that has elapsed since the start of the match. Some modes, such as Versus and Score Attack, have a timer that counts down the time remaining.
2. **Game Type:** The name of the current game type being played. Just in case your friends launch a new game while you were otherwise occupied.
3. **Team Lives:** The number of lives remaining for your team. Remember that this number represents the total for the entire team, not just yourself.
4. **Set:** The number of the current Set. Each Set ends after the completion of three Rounds and a Bonus Round.
5. **Round:** These three dots represent the Round that you are currently playing on. The second and third dots are filled as you progress from Round to Round.
6. **Waves:** These five square blocks represent the five Waves within each Round. Another block is filled in at the start of each Wave, just as the announcer signals that reinforcements have arrived.
7. **Score:** Your team's current point total for this match. Individual player scores are shown in the post-game carnage report, or you may also check your individual score at any time by holding the Back button.
8. **Ordnance:** This green icon guides you to weapon pods that drop from the sky at the start of each Round. Use these weapons sparingly, since there is no way to replenish their ammo until the next Round begins. There are two power weapon drops for teams of three players or less, and three power weapon drops for teams of four players. Ordnance drops are random and do not change per map. You're guaranteed to receive at least one Target Locator on most maps, and the other ordnance drop is randomized between the Spartan Laser, Sniper Rifle, and Rocket Launcher. Some maps may have other weapons in specific positions that respawn at the conclusion of each Round.
9. **Teammates:** These icons help you differentiate your teammates from the enemies. The icon is blue when the teammate is neutral, yellow when attacking an enemy, and grades from orange to red as the teammate takes damage.

SELECTING KIT AND STAYING ALIVE

LOADOUTS

The standard goal of Firefight is to work together with your teammates to survive for as long as you can while scoring as many points as possible (variations on this theme are explained below). The path to longevity begins with the team's selection of loadouts. Players select a loadout both at the start of the game and also each time they die and await a respawn. Some loadouts work better with certain maps and game types than others, but no one loadout is a perfect solution to every situation. Consider your own play style and the degree of teamwork you can expect from your teammates when making your selection. It's worth coordinating with your teammates before starting the game to ensure that you're not all planning to select the same loadout. For example, a team with too many Specters or Operators may find itself lacking the long-distance firepower it needs. Similarly, a team without a Medic could find themselves without defensive capabilities.

SPARTAN LOADOUT CONFIGURATIONS

Loadout	Armor Ability	Primary Weapon	Secondary Weapon
Air Assault	Jet Pack	Assault Rifle	Magnum
Recon	Sprint	DMR	Assault Rifle
Operator	Armor Lock	Shotgun	Magnum
Specter	Active Camouflage	Grenade Launcher	Magnum
Medic	Drop Shield	Assault Rifle	Magnum

ELITE LOADOUT CONFIGURATIONS

Loadout	Armor Ability	Primary Weapon	Secondary Weapon
Ranger	Jet Pack	Plasma Repeater	Plasma Pistol
Royal Zealot	Evade	Needle Rifle	Needler
Gladiator	Hologram	Energy Sword	Plasma Repeater
Champion	Active Camouflage	Concussion Rifle	Plasma Pistol
Sentry	Drop Shield	Needle Rifle	Plasma Pistol

SPECIAL LOADOUTS

The Gruntpocalypse and Rocketfight modes each come with their own unique set of loadouts. You'll have the same selection of loadouts by name, and they'll have the same Armor Abilities as shown in the table above, but every loadout in Gruntpocalypse contains a DMR and Magnum—perfect for popping the heads off of Grunts! Similarly, all loadouts for Rocketfight contain a Rocket Launcher and Magnum.

ELITES? IN FIREFIGHT?

That's right! You can switch teams and play as an Elite in Versus (or turn any other game type into a de facto Versus battle) by switching your team color to Blue in the pre-game lobby. These gameplay modes are addressed in greater detail in the following pages, but it is good to know that this is possible.

EXTRA LIVES

Spartan teams, regardless the number of players, share an initial supply of ten lives (seven in Firefight Classic), and can accumulate as many as 20 lives. This number decreases by one every time a Spartan is killed in battle and is forced to respawn. The game ends once the last Spartan standing dies and there are no lives left. One additional life is awarded at the conclusion of each Round per team member. For example, if your four-player team completes a Round, the team receives four additional lives before the start of the next Round.

Only one team member has to survive the Round in order to respawn the entire team into the next Round. So, if your team runs out of lives on the fifth Wave, and three of the four players perish but one survives, you still receive four extra lives for the next Round. However, you won't see four extra lives appear in the HUD, as three of those lives become used in respawning the deceased teammates. Those playing on the Elite team can enjoy infinite lives and not have to worry about such issues. Covies never say die!

YOUR HOME IS YOUR CASTLE

Standard Firefight matches spawn the Spartan team near what we refer to as a home base (each map calls it something slightly different). The home base typically contains one or two ammunition supply cabinets and a case or two of Frag Grenades. Ammo supply cases contain an unlimited supply of ammo for all standard UNSC weapons issued as part of whatever loadout you chose prior to spawning. Simply run up to an ammo cabinet to replenish your loadout-issued weapons with the maximum capacity of ammo. Ammo supply cabinets do *not* replenish ammo for power weapons obtained from ordnance drops or from weapon pick-ups on the map. Similarly, the supply of Frag Grenades is limited as well and only replenishes after the conclusion of each Round.

Spartans aren't safe from attacks inside the home base area, but these areas are generally well-fortified and offer the enemy few approaches. A team can typically find safety in numbers inside their home base and force the enemy to funnel through one or two narrow entryways. Refer to the following chapter for strategy for each individual map.

Since Elites are technically invading the area in all Firefight matches, they do not have an ammunition supply awaiting them, nor do they have a base they can fall back to. To that extent, Elites cannot replenish the ammo for their loadout weapons without finding similar weapons on the ground from other fallen Covenant. Elites can, however, swap out their weapon in favor of a discarded UNSC weapon and then use the ammo crates inside the Spartan home base to replenish ammo.

Medkits are scattered throughout the home base area and fully replenish lost health if damaged. These Medkits do not respawn until the completion of a Round, so it's imperative that your team use them sparingly and alert one another when one is consumed. Unlike in *Halo: ODST*, Medkits require that the player hold Ⓧ down in order to consume it. This prevents accidentally using a Medkit when you're only partially damaged.

MEDIC!

Increase your team's chances of surviving all five Waves without running out of Medkits by always making sure one of your teammates respawns with the Medic class. Deploying the Drop Shield gives your team an on-demand bubble of relative safety that not only guards against incoming projectiles, but also slowly replenishes lost health.

SETS, ROUNDS, AND WAVES

Firefight pits a team of Spartans against squads of Covenant enemies that comprise what are termed Waves, Rounds, and Sets. Teams must fight through five Waves of enemies in order to clear a Round and receive fresh weapons, additional lives, and Medkits. The break between Sets grows with each Set your team manages to survive.

Set: A Set contains three Rounds and one Bonus Round. You receive a lengthy break to reestablish your defenses and regain all health and shields after completing the Set. As with the conclusion of Rounds, completing a Set earns you fresh ordnance drops, extra lives, and Frag Grenades. There are a total of 15 Waves of Covenant per Set.

Round: A Round contains five Waves of enemies. Complete the Round to receive new weapon drops, extra lives, Frag Grenades, and Medkits. Each Round features five different Squads of Covenant.

Wave: A Wave contains up to six squads of enemies sent to destroy you. There is very little respite between Waves and weapons, and Medkits do not respawn between Waves.

Squad: Squads are the elemental grouping of enemies. The number of enemies in each squad is determined by the squad type, but does not change in proportion to the number of Spartans playing. Multiple squads appear simultaneously.

Bonus Round: Complete three Rounds to earn a chance to win a wealth of extra points before time expires or the entire team is killed. The Iron Skull (Bonus Round only) increases the difficulty by preventing respawning. Extra lives are rewarded for all surviving team members at the conclusion of the Bonus Round. Deceased team members respawn.

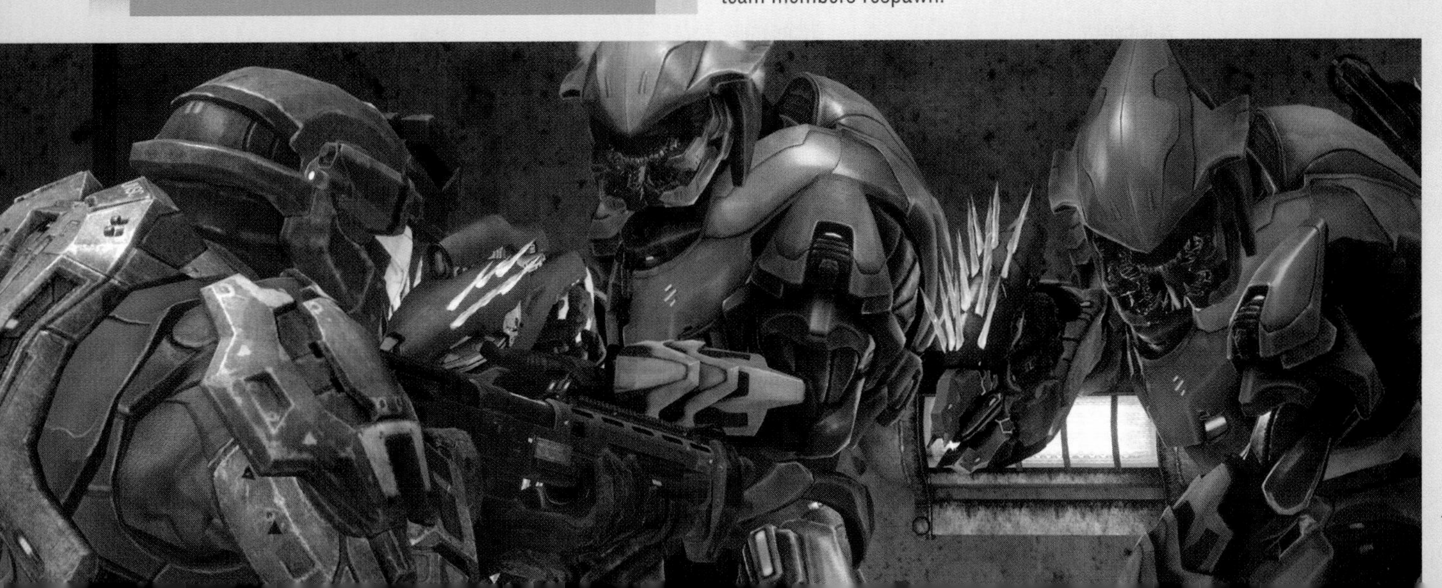

The composition of the squads you encounter in any given Wave can range from mere Grunts to Elites armed with UNSC-sponsored Rocket Launchers and Grenade Launchers. Fortunately, most waves tend to contain a less sadistic mix of Grunts, Jackals, and Elites, with the occasional Hunter thrown in for good fun.

DIFFICULTY AFFECTS ENEMY TYPE

The changes in health, damage, and shield stats across difficulty modes in Firefight are the same as in Campaign, as are the advances in the intelligence of the enemies. The actual class of enemy is upgraded as well. For example, even though you may only face Grunt Infantry and/or Grunt Specialists in Round 1 on Easy or Normal mode, you're just as likely to encounter Grunt Leaders and Grunt Heroes in that same Round on Heroic or Legendary. All classes of a specific enemy type have an equal chance spawning on Heroic or Legendary.

Enemies may arrive on the scene via Phantom, the standard Covenant dropship (which cannot be destroyed even with a Target Locator), or via a random spawn location. Enemies deploying from a Phantom provide a great opportunity for boosting your team score with a Killtrocity (or higher) medal, but it is also the only deployment method that fires back. Don't underestimate the threat posed by a Phantom while it supports with covering fire for the ground troops that have been deployed.

DESTROY THE CANNON

Coordinate with your teammates when the Phantom arrives to focus fire on the Chin Cannon mounted on the underside of the Phantom. Put enough bullets or ordnance into it to knock it off the ship!!

HAZARDS

Enemies deploying onto the battlefield as part of an enemy squad may not be your only concern in Firefight. Depending on whether or not you turn hazards off in the game settings, you may face a randomly generating supply of additional threats. Hazards are map-specific, so consult the data tables for each individual map to learn what to keep an eye out for.

Covy Vehicles: Depending on the map, you may encounter a number of Covenant vehicles during the fight. Even though Wraiths are the most common (and potentially the most beneficial if you can hijack it), Ghosts and Banshees may also appear on some maps. The Spartan Laser is ideal for eliminating any enemy vehicles you do not want to hijack.

FIREFIGHT

Teleportation Drop Pods: These large constructs plummet to the ground—typically not too far from your home base—and grant the Covenant a way to randomly teleport bonus squads into the battle. Hunters are too large to utilize the teleportation drop pod, but all other enemy types can use them. Don't be surprised to suddenly see four Elite Leaders appear at close range!

Snipers: Snipers appear sporadically, outside the boundary of the playable space, and open fire with their Focus Rifles. You won't know they're there until the beam from the Focus Rifle hits you. The Focus Rifle typically can't kill you with its initial jolt, so take cover, then shoulder a DMR or Sniper Rifle and scan the surrounding heights.

Engineers: Engineers only appear on one map (Corvette) and they do not attack directly, but they do offer additional shielding to any nearby Covenant and should be eliminated at once. Depending on difficulty, an Engineer typically requires six direct shots with the DMR to be destroyed.

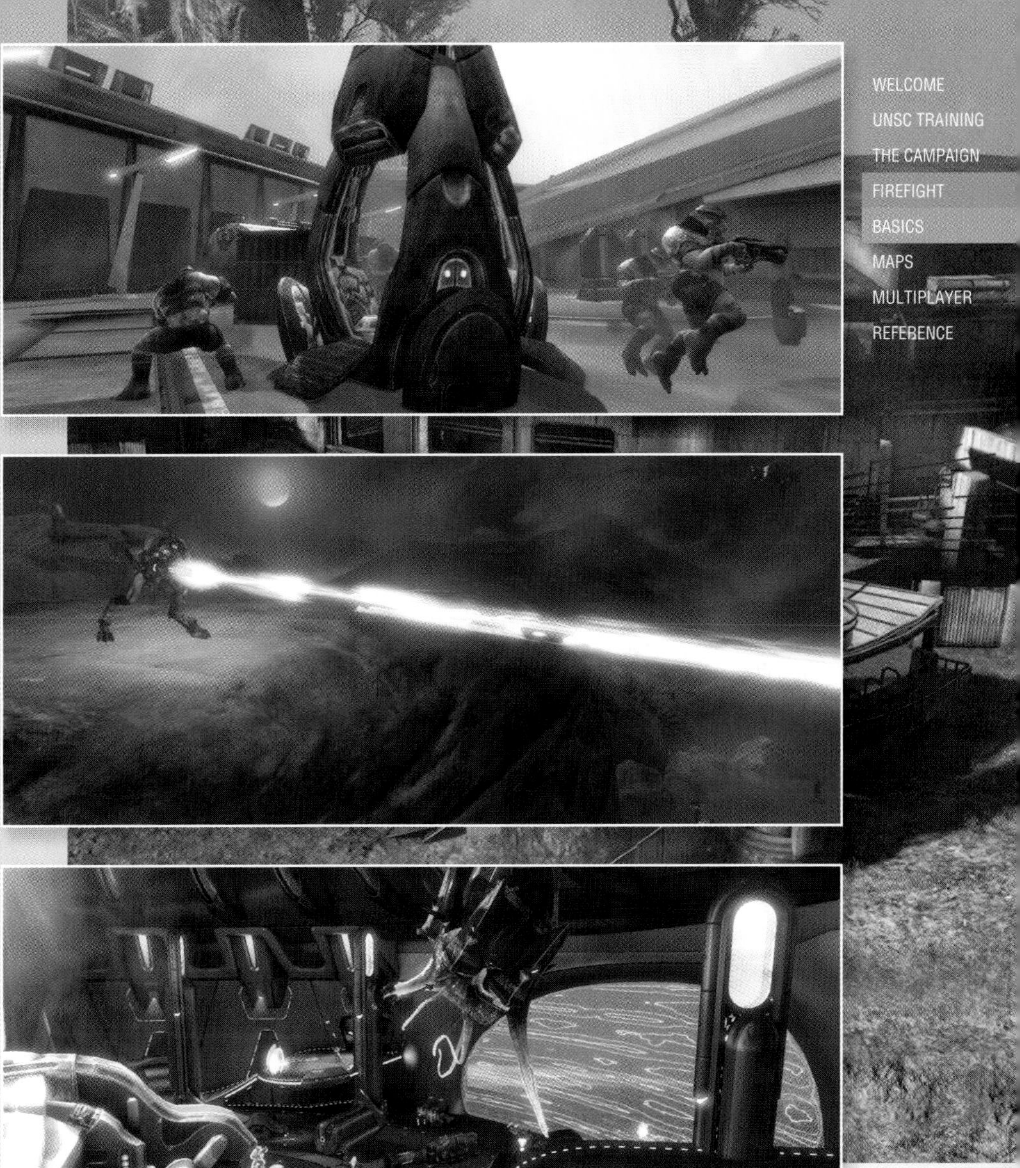

GAME TYPES

Firefight mode in *Halo: Reach* has been expanded in size and scope in ways few gamers could have expected. A number of new game types have been added, including the option for players to join the side of the Covenant and go into battle against other human players. Many of these modes are variations on the core Firefight motif, but as you'll see in the following explanations, there are some very subtle differences. Tables below list the default rules, Skulls, and enemy appearances. The table showing the default enemy structure lists the types of enemy squads that may be chosen to appear in each Wave.

PLAY IT LIKE YOU OWN IT

The following descriptions reflect the default settings for each of the six modes, but customization is king in the land of Firefight. Not only can you modify the settings in countless ways, you can even transform any Firefight match into a Versus mode by simply changing teams before loading the map. Hitting the Left or Right Bumper toggles between the Red (Spartan) and Blue (Elite) teams and gives you the opportunity to battle head-to-head with friends in any of the game types.

FIREFIGHT

FIGHT AGAINST INCREASINGLY DIFFICULT ODDS. ONE SET, AND YOU'RE DONE.

Length: One Set or until all Spartan lives are lost.
Lives: Ten to start, 20 max.
Time Limit: No time limit.
Spartan Team Size: One to four players.

DEFAULT SKULLS

Round	Skulls Active
1	—
2	Tough Luck
3	Tough Luck and Cloud

FIREFIGHT ENEMY STRUCTURE (DEFAULT)

Round	Wave	Possible Squads Appearing
1	1	Jackal Patrol
1	2	Elite Patrol, Skirmisher Patrol, Elite Infantry, Brute Patrol, Hunter Infantry
1	3	Elite Patrol, Skirmisher Patrol, Elite Infantry, Brute Patrol, Hunter Infantry
1	4	Elite Patrol, Skirmisher Patrol, Elite Infantry, Brute Patrol, Hunter Infantry
1	5	Elite Strike Team, Brute Kill Team
2	1	Jackal Patrol
2	2	Elite Infantry, Brute Patrol, Elite Patrol, Brute Infantry, Hunter Kill Team
2	3	Elite Infantry, Brute Patrol, Elite Patrol, Brute Infantry, Hunter Kill Team
2	4	Elite Infantry, Brute Patrol, Elite Patrol, Brute Infantry, Hunter Kill Team
2	5	Elite Strike Team, Brute Kill Team
3	1	Jackal Patrol
3	2	Brute Patrol, Skirmisher Infantry, Elite Patrol, Brute Infantry, Hunter Strike Team
3	3	Brute Patrol, Skirmisher Infantry, Elite Patrol, Brute Infantry, Hunter Strike Team
3	4	Brute Patrol, Skirmisher Infantry, Elite Patrol, Brute Infantry, Hunter Strike Team
3	5	Elite Strike Team, Brute Kill Team

The basic Firefight mode limits the action to one Set of three Rounds and can be played as a team of up to four human players. Extra lives are awarded at the conclusion of each Round. Since this variant limits the action to just one Set, it is a great mode for instances when you don't have a lot of time to dedicate to a longer match, or when you want to either play by yourself or with a smaller group of people. Adjust the difficulty setting to fit your skill and the size of your party. The default assortment of Skulls activates automatically at the start of each new Round.

Firefight matches last one Set and give your team ten lives to start. Push your limits and try the hardest difficulty mode you can handle!

FIREFIGHT

FIREFIGHT CLASSIC

FIGHT AGAINST INCREASINGLY DIFFICULT ODDS. ENDS WHEN ALL LIVES ARE GONE.

Length: Unlimited Sets, ends when all Spartan lives are lost.

Lives: Seven to start, 20 max.

Time Limit: No time limit.

Spartan Team Size: One to four players.

DEFAULT SKULLS

Round	Skulls Active
1	Tough Luck
2	Tough Luck, Catch
3	Tough Luck, Catch, Black Eye

FIREFIGHT CLASSIC ENEMY STRUCTURE (DEFAULT)

Round	Wave	Possible Squads Appearing
1	1	Jackal Patrol
1	2	Elite Patrol, Skirmisher Patrol, Elite Infantry, Brute Patrol, Hunter Infantry
1	3	Elite Patrol, Skirmisher Patrol, Elite Infantry, Brute Patrol, Hunter Infantry
1	4	Elite Patrol, Skirmisher Patrol, Elite Infantry, Brute Patrol, Hunter Infantry
1	5	Elite Strike Team, Brute Kill Team
2	1	Jackal Patrol
2	2	Elite Infantry, Brute Patrol, Elite Patrol, Brute Infantry, Hunter Kill Team
2	3	Elite Infantry, Brute Patrol, Elite Patrol, Brute Infantry, Hunter Kill Team
2	4	Elite Infantry, Brute Patrol, Elite Patrol, Brute Infantry, Hunter Kill Team
2	5	Elite Strike Team, Brute Kill Team
3	1	Jackal Patrol
3	2	Brute Patrol, Skirmisher Infantry, Elite Patrol, Brute Infantry, Hunter Strike Team
3	3	Brute Patrol, Skirmisher Infantry, Elite Patrol, Brute Infantry, Hunter Strike Team
3	4	Brute Patrol, Skirmisher Infantry, Elite Patrol, Brute Infantry, Hunter Strike Team
3	5	Elite Strike Team, Brute Kill Team

The aptly named Firefight Classic mode is Firefight just as fans of Halo: ODST remember it, with the only difference being the ability to play as a team of up to four Spartans. Firefight Classic limits the amount of lives the team starts with to only seven, but skilled players can quickly build a supply of extra lives by clearing multiple Rounds and meeting the scoring requirements in the Bonus Round. Firefight Classic is best saved for teams of at least three skilled players who have the available time to withstand the test of endurance that these matches provide. It is a perfect game mode for those teams striving to score the mythical 1,000,000 points required for the "Heat in the Pipe" Achievement, an Achievement that is certain to go down in Halo lore. The enemy structure for each Set is the same.

Gather up the best Firefight players you know and settle in for the long haul. Firefight Classic is the ultimate test of endurance.

GENERATOR DEFENSE

FIGHT AGAINST INCREASINGLY DIFFICULT ODDS WHILE ALSO DEFENDING THE GENERATORS.

Length: One Set or all Spartan lives are lost or all three generators have been destroyed.

Lives: Ten to start, 20 max.

Time Limit: No time limit.

Spartan Team Size: One to four Spartans.

Elite Team Size: One to three Elites.

DEFAULT SKULLS

Round	Skulls Active
1	—
2	Tough Luck
3	Tough Luck and Cloud

GENERATOR DEFENSE ENEMY STRUCTURE (DEFAULT)

Round	Wave	Possible Squads Appearing
1	1	Jackal Patrol
1	2	Elite Patrol, Skirmisher Patrol, Elite Infantry, Brute Patrol, Hunter Infantry
1	3	Elite Patrol, Skirmisher Patrol, Elite Infantry, Brute Patrol, Hunter Infantry
1	4	Elite Patrol, Skirmisher Patrol, Elite Infantry, Brute Patrol, Hunter Infantry
1	5	Elite Strike Team, Brute Kill Team
2	1	Jackal Patrol
2	2	Elite Infantry, Brute Patrol, Elite Patrol, Brute Infantry, Hunter Kill Team
2	3	Elite Infantry, Brute Patrol, Elite Patrol, Brute Infantry, Hunter Kill Team
2	4	Elite Infantry, Brute Patrol, Elite Patrol, Brute Infantry, Hunter Kill Team
2	5	Elite Strike Team, Brute Kill Team
3	1	Jackal Patrol
3	2	Brute Patrol, Skirmisher Infantry, Elite Patrol, Brute Infantry, Hunter Strike Team
3	3	Brute Patrol, Skirmisher Infantry, Elite Patrol, Brute Infantry, Hunter Strike Team
3	4	Brute Patrol, Skirmisher Infantry, Elite Patrol, Brute Infantry, Hunter Strike Team
3	5	Elite Strike Team, Brute Kill Team

Generator Defense puts an objective-based spin on the standard Firefight mode by tasking the Covenant team to try to destroy three randomly placed generators on the map while Spartans try to defend them. The game ends once all three generators have been destroyed, or when the Spartan team runs out of lives. Spartans can "lock down" each of the generators by approaching the generator and holding down ⊗. This protects the generator from damage for 30 seconds. Generators that are locked down glow orange as the metal heats up. Spartans need not worry about accidentally damaging the generators they're trying to protect—not even with splash damage from a grenade—only Covenant forces can damage the generators.

Generators must cool down for five seconds upon unlocking. Stay close by and re-lock it right away!

GRUNTPOCALYPSE

ALL GRUNTS. ALL THE TIME. AIM FOR THE FACE.

Length: One Round or until all Spartan lives are lost.

Lives: Ten to start.

Time Limit: No time limit.

Spartan Team Size: One to four Spartans.

DEFAULT SKULLS

Round	Skulls Active
1	Catch, Cloud, Grunt Birthday, Cowbell, IWHYBD, Red Skull*
2	N/A
3	N/A

RED SKULL EXPLAINED

Red Skull is a customizable Skull that can be assigned multiple traits that affect the Spartans. In Gruntpocalypse, the Red Skull is set to improve the AI's accuracy, vision, hearing, and luck. They're not just Grunts, they're super-sensory killing machines!

GRUNTPOCALYPSE ENEMY STRUCTURE (DEFAULT)

Round	Wave	Possible Squads Appearing
1	1	Grunts
1	2	Grunts
1	3	Grunts
1	4	Grunts
1	5	Grunts

Gruntpocalypse is the perfect pick-up-and-play game for those craving to send Grunts flying into the great blue yonder on a rocket filled with confetti. This isn't to say Gruntpocalypse is easy—hell no! Depending on the difficulty mode you select, you can find yourself taking on an army of Grunts armed with Plasma Pistols, Needlers, and even Fuel Rod Guns, not to mention a hailstorm of Plasma Grenades. All loadouts in this mode come equipped with a DMR and Magnum, which you'll swap out at your peril. Pop a Grunt's head in a crowd and watch the points roll in.

On Heroic or Legendary the Grunt Ultra shows up which requires two headshots to kill. One to pop his mask, and a second to the dome to finish the job.

ROCKETFIGHT

WHO SAYS YOU CAN'T BRING A ROCKET TO A GUNFIGHT?

Length: One Round or until all Spartan lives are lost.
Lives: Ten to start.
Time Limit: No time limit.
Spartan Team Size: One to four Spartans.

DEFAULT SKULLS

Round	Skulls Active
1	Tough Luck, Catch
2	N/A
3	N/A

ROCKETFIGHT ENEMY STRUCTURE (DEFAULT)

Round	Wave	Possible Squads Appearing
1	1	Jackal Patrol
1	2	Elite Patrol, Brute Infantry, Skirmisher Patrol, Elite Infantry, Hunter Strike Team
1	3	Elite Patrol, Brute Infantry, Skirmisher Patrol, Elite Infantry, Hunter Strike Team
1	4	Elite Patrol, Brute Infantry, Skirmisher Patrol, Elite Infantry, Hunter Strike Team
1	5	Elite Generals, Brute Chieftains

Rocketfight plays similarly to Firefight, except it is limited to just one Round and every player on the Spartan side carries unlimited Rocket Launcher and Magnum ammo. The Rocket Launcher behaves just as you would expect it to—it has to be reloaded after every two rockets fired—but the infinite on-person ammo supply means you never have to head back to base to gather additional ammo. You still don't have unlimited Frag Grenades, but who cares? Wasn't it just mentioned that you have unlimited rockets? And it's a good thing too, since the enemies soon come in fast and furious.

Coordinate your rocket attacks with teammates to keep a steady barrage on the enemy so you're not all reloading at the same time.

SCORE ATTACK

HOW MANY POINTS CAN YOU SCORE IN A ROUND?

Length: One Round or until all Spartan lives are lost.

Lives: Ten to start.

Time Limit: 12 minutes.

Spartan Team Size: One to two Spartans.

DEFAULT SKULLS

Round	Skulls Active
1	Tough Luck, Catch, Cloud
2	N/A
3	N/A

SCORE ATTACK ENEMY STRUCTURE (DEFAULT)

Round	Wave	Enemy Types
1	1	Grunts
1	2	Jackals
1	3	Brutes
1	4	Skirmishers
1	5	Elite Generals

Score Attack is for the competitive solo and duo players who fancy a challenge and want to compare their scores with other teams of players online. Every game of Score Attack features the same composition of enemies, in exactly the same order and number. You must outscore the competition by combining lengthy sprees and killing chains together with headshots and other stylish killing techniques that boost the points awarded from each kill. Of course, the difficulty mode you play on also goes a long way towards increasing your score, as does your completion time. Score Attack can be as serious as you want it. Customize the experience by turning on additional Skulls to boost the multiplier even further—if you dare!

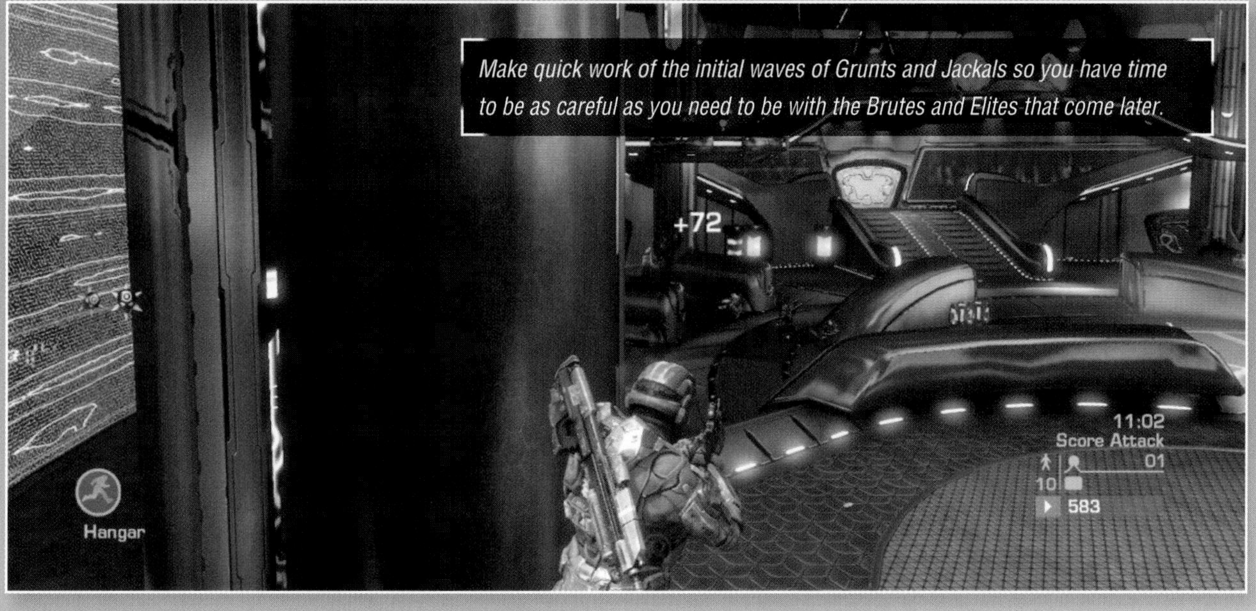

Make quick work of the initial waves of Grunts and Jackals so you have time to be as careful as you need to be with the Brutes and Elites that come later.

VERSUS

TAKE TURNS FIGHTING AS SPARTANS AND ELITES.

Length: Two Rounds total. Switch sides after one Round or when all Spartan lives are lost.

Lives: Ten to start, 20 max for Spartans. Infinite lives for Elites. Spartans receive extra life with each Elite killed.

Time Limit: Ten minutes.

Spartan Team Size: One to three Spartans.

Elite Team Size: One to three Elites.

DEFAULT SKULLS

Round	Skulls Active
1	Catch, Tough Luck
2	N/A
3	N/A

VERSUS MODE ENEMY STRUCTURE (DEFAULT)

Round	Wave	Possible Squads Appearing
1	1	Jackal Patrol
1	2	Brute Patrol, Skirmisher Patrol, Brute Infantry, Brute Tactical, Hunter Infantry
1	3	Brute Patrol, Skirmisher Patrol, Brute Infantry, Brute Tactical, Hunter Infantry
1	4	Brute Patrol, Skirmisher Patrol, Brute Infantry, Brute Tactical, Hunter Infantry
1	5	Elite Generals, Brute Chieftains

Versus mode provides a total of up to four players the chance to divide into teams and compete to see who can outlast and outscore one another. Unlike in Score Attack, teams alternate Rounds playing as Spartans and Elites. Just to make sure the Spartans still feel the pressure, the Elites battle alongside A.I.-controlled Covenant reinforcements. Spartans score points by killing Covenant just as in any other Firefight mode, and it's up to the Elites to limit their total score. Elites have infinite lives, but that doesn't mean they can afford to be reckless—Spartans earn an extra life for each Elite they kill. Teams switch sides after ten minutes, one Round, or when all of the Spartan lives have been used up. The winning team is the one that scores the most points while playing as Spartans.

It's not every day you get to fight as an Elite alongside other Covenant forces. Use your Covy allies to distract the Spartans, then flank them!

FIREFIGHT

CUSTOMIZING THE FIREFIGHT EXPERIENCE

Firefight mode features arguably the largest array of custom settings any game has ever had. By entering the Firefight Settings menu, you can customize the individual game options, Spartan player traits and respawn settings, and Elite player traits and respawn settings, in addition to general options such as friendly fire and betrayal booting. Since there are quite literally over hundreds of options to customize, this section is going to focus on the upper level changes you can make and also point out a few interesting ways to customize. The possibilities are indeed limitless, and every adjustment you make can be saved as a new game type, available for you to play anytime or even upload to File Share.

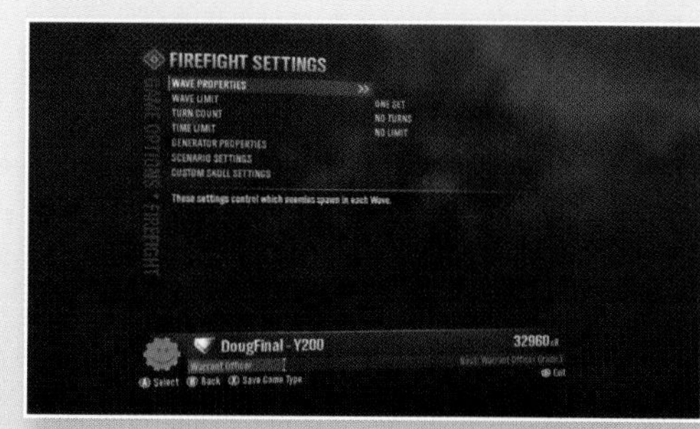

Delve into the settings and build your own custom game types with enemy types and traits just the way you always wanted!

FIREFIGHT SETTINGS

CUSTOMIZE THE FIREFIGHT GAME OPTIONS.

WAVE PROPERTIES

- Round 1 Wave Properties
- Round 2 Wave Properties
- Round 3 Wave Properties
- Bonus Wave Properties

The Wave Properties menu allows you to customize the Skulls that are active for the first Round of each Set and also hand-pick the Squad Types—and the order they appear in—in each Wave. Select the Wave you want to customize, then choose whether or not you want the Squads to use a Dropship and what Squad Type you want to appear. You can specify three Squad Types for Wave 1, five Squad Types for Waves 2, 3, and 4, and three Squad Types for the Boss Wave that concludes each Round.

SQUAD TYPES

Squad Name	Covenant Types	Description
Grunts	Grunts	More Grunts than you can handle. Well…
Jackals	Jackals	Jackal defensive infantry.
Jackal Patrol	Jackals, Grunts	Jackals supported by Grunts.
Jackal Snipers	Jackals	Jackal Snipers, doom of the slow and inattentive.
Skirmishers	Skirmishers	Skirmishers, the deadliest of Jackal troops.
Skirmisher Patrol	Skirmishers, Grunts	Skirmishers and the Grunts they barely tolerate.
Skirmisher Infantry	Skirmishers, Jackals	Skirmishers supported by Jackals.
Brutes	Brutes	Brutes. Even Jackals don't like them.
Brute Patrol	Brutes, Grunts	Brutes accompanied by hapless Grunts.
Brute Infantry	Brutes, Jackals	Brutes supported by Jackals.
Brute Tactical	Brutes, Skirmishers	Brutes supported by Skirmishers.
Brute Chieftains	Brute Chieftains	The Brutes who keep other Brutes in line.
Brute Kill Team	Brute Chieftain, Brutes	A Brute kill team led by a Brute Chieftain.
Elites	Elites	Elites, with nobody to drag them down.
Elite Patrol	Elites, Grunts	Elites accompanied by Grunt cannon fodder.
Elite Infantry	Elites, Jackals	Elites supported by Jackals.
Elite Tactical	Elites, Skirmishers	Elites supported by Skirmishers.
Elite Airborne	Elite Specialists	Elite airborne troops.
Elite Spec Ops	Elite Spec Ops	The most feared Elite ground troops.
Elite Generals	Elite Generals	The Elites that command respect from other Elites.
Elite Strike Team	Elites, Elite General	An Elite strike team led by a general.
Heretics	Elites	Elites experimenting with human weapons.
Heretic Snipers	Elites	Elites experimenting with human ranged weapons.
Heretic Heavy	Elites	Elites who won't turn down a good explosion.
Hunters	Hunters	Hunters, the Covenant's heaviest squad types.
Hunter Patrol	Hunters, Grunts	Hunters, with Grunts underfoot.
Hunter Infantry	Hunters, Jackals	Hunters supported by Jackals.
Hunter Tactical	Hunters, Skirmishers	Hunters supported by Skirmishers.
Hunter Strike Team	Hunters, Elites	Hunters supported by an Elite strike team.
Hunter Kill Team	Hunters, Elites	Hunters supported by an Elite kill team.

WAVE LIMIT

- One Wave to Ten Sets or limitless.

Adjust the number of Waves to determine how long the Spartans must survive in order to win. Set the length of the game to One Wave, One Round, One Set, or any number of Sets up to ten or even a limitless game (e.g., Firefight Classic). This is a great way to set up "time attack" challenges with friends.

TURN COUNT

- No turns to three turns each.

Determine how many turns each team gets when playing a game with both Spartans and Elites. The default setting in Versus isone turn each, but you can increase it to two or three turns each. Just remember that each Round in Versus may last up to ten minutes per side. A three turn game of Versus could last a full hour if both teams consistently go the distance when playing as Spartans.

TIME LIMIT

- One minute to 60 minutes or no limit.

Adjust how long each Round can last. Adjustments can be made in one-minute increments up to ten minutes, then five-minute increments up to a full hour. If you're going to adjust the Turn Count setting higher than one turn each, you probably should adjust the Time Limit down to five or six minutes.

GENERATOR PROPERTIES

- Generator Count
- Spawn Order
- Loss Condition

These settings apply only to games being built on the Generator Defense archetype. Select the number of Generators from one to three and decide whether or not the Generators are placed at random or in pre-set specific positions. You can also adjust the loss condition from the default setting of the game (ending when all three generators are lost) to it ending once the Covenant troops succeed in destroying just one. Adjusting the loss condition down to just a single Generator is great if you are playing with unbalanced teams. Distribute players so the fewer number of players are on the Elite team and set the loss condition to "lose one."

SCENARIO SETTINGS

- Hazards
- Weapon Drops
- Ammo Crates

Adjust the environmental settings to reflect your preference regarding map-specific hazards such as Wraiths or Snipers and whether or not unlimited ammo crates and weapon drops appear on the map. Consult the map-specific information in the following chapter to see which hazards appear on each map to better decide if you wish to turn them off.

CUSTOM SKULL SETTINGS

This is where things really start to get crazy. *Halo: Reach* allows you to customize up to three individual Skulls (Red, Blue, and Yellow) and assign any number of hundreds of modifiers to each Custom Skull. It's possible to adjust your Spartan's health and shielding; whether or not Spartans are immune to headshots and other attacks; the damage weapons inflict; the Spartans' speed and jump height; the behavior and intelligence of each individual Wave of enemy, and much, much more. The only limit to Custom Skull settings is your own willingness to experiment. But if you only use this feature once, make sure it's to create a Skull that gives you invulnerability and infinite ammo, then enter a Firefight Classic mode and unlock those Achievements!

SPARTAN SETTINGS

Lastly, you can adjust nearly every facet of the Spartan experience including respawn time, the available loadouts (and their names), the number of starting and maximum lives, individual weapons in each loadout and much more. It's a dizzying array of options sure to provide countless experiments and adjustments for players. There's no right or wrong way to set up a game to your liking (and giving your team of Spartans 50 lives may be a great way to tackle Legendary mode).

SCORE ATTACK

Bring the fight to them! The final two Waves of enemies in Score Attack can be pretty tough for a one or two person team, but you can't afford to hide inside a room and wait for them to come to you. If your team is gunning for a high score, you must complete the match in a fast time. Work together to hunt down enemies where they spawn and take them out as quickly as you can. Don't stand around waiting for them! This is no time to play it safe!

Pair the DMR with a Grenade Launcher. Since there aren't any power weapons in Score Attack, you have to make the best of what you have. Coordinate with your teammate to have one player select the Recon loadout while the other chooses Specter. The Grenade Launcher can take out multiple low-level enemies for multi-kill bonuses, but can also EMP Elites and soften them up for a DMR kill shot.

Practice often on smaller maps. Achieving a high score in Score Attack doesn't just come from having a lot of skill—it also means picking the right map and memorizing every detail of it, and also trying to predict certain enemy behaviors, including where they commonly spawn. It's a good idea to start out playing Score Attack on Corvette above Courtyard and only then consider moving up to larger maps.

CORE TACTICS

This section covers some basic tactical concepts for each of the various Firefight modes. Ultimately, your team's survival—and score—is going to depend on your familiarity with the map, efficient use of ordnance drops, and your skill at the game. Map-specific strategies are listed in a following chapter, but here are some a few core tactics that lend themselves to team play across all maps for each mode.

GENERAL FIREFIGHT TIPS

Always pay attention to where you die, especially if you are carrying a power weapon. Either return to the spot immediately after spawning to pick up the weapon, or let teammates know where they can retrieve it. Try to avoid exposing yourself to enemy fire when wielding a power weapon.

Don't waste the Target Locator's two strikes. The Target Locator is the most devastating weapon in the Spartan arsenal, but one that should be used with reservation. For starters, don't waste it on the Jackal Patrol squads that appear in the first wave of each Round. Save the Target Locator for those instances when two drop ships are set to deploy Covenant in close proximity to one another. Target the area between the ships for a Killionaire medal! Always alert teammates when you're about to fire the Target Locator.

Coordinate roles and loadouts. The most successful teams are those with designated roles within the team and stick to them. Ask teammates to use just one or two loadouts throughout the battle to make use of their skills and to complement the other players. Successful teams don't randomly choose different loadouts every time someone respawns.

Avoid roaming the map without purpose. Use Sprint or Jet Pack to secure an ordnance drop, then hurry back to an area that offers protection from overhead attacks (Phantoms) and limits the enemy's approach. Your team should stick reasonably close (but not so close as to be eliminated by a single grenade) to one another at all times and hold a position that has just one or two approaches, thereby forcing the enemies through chokepoints.

Manage your ammo. Teams always spawn initially near one of the infinite ammo supply cabinets. Approach the cabinet on your way out of the area to top off the supply of ammunition for each of your loadout weapons. Alert teammates to when you're making a run for ammo or health.

Command the elevated positions. Elevated positions are easier to hold for a number of reasons, not least of which is that they typically can't be reached by enemy grenades. They often offer the greatest visibility across the map as well. The one downside is greater exposure to Phantom attacks. Gather your team inside a Medic's Drop Shield when Phantoms are in the vicinity.

Coach your team. The highest scorers are those who play together well, develop a pre-game plan of attack, and who provide frequent sit-reps (situation reports) during battle. Alert teammates to where enemies are using specific landmarks for reference, when you're in need of a Drop Shield, or where your corpse may be located. Work with teammates to flank enemies, and try to avoid targeting the same enemy.

Hoard available munitions at the end of Rounds. Ordnance drops, power weapons, grenades, and turrets are all replenished at the start of each new Round. Leave the final enemy in the fifth wave alive (the announcer calls out the final five enemies) until after your team has collected all remaining turrets, grenades, and other weapons that haven't been used up.

Understand the scoring system. You and your team can maximize points by killing multiple enemies in quick succession (within 1.5 seconds of each kill), by going on lengthy kill streaks, and by increasing the difficulty or turning on additional Skulls. This means that it's often advantageous to defeat several smaller enemies rapidly than to take out a single, more valuable enemy. Use heavy weapons and grenades to maximum effectiveness by saving them for groups of enemies near drop ships and monster closets.

GRUNTPOCALYPSE

Divide and conquer the enemy spawns. The best opportunity for scoring in Gruntpocalypse arrives in the moment each new squad of Grunts spawns into the map. Line them up and systematically take out the Grunts one by one with your DMR. Make sure your team is dispersed and not all about to fire on the same Grunt. Grunts typically spawn in three or four small groups simultaneously. Have a player monitoring each spawn site, and take them out quickly.

Take cover from the plasma barrage. It's easy to underestimate the danger that Grunts may pose, especially on Normal difficulty—when they're less likely to be wielding Fuel Rod Guns and Plasma Launchers. With that said, Grunts are very adept at throwing Plasma Grenades, and it won't be long before the 'nades are flying in all directions. Be very careful where you roam. Stay high, use the DMR and Magnum to aim for their heads, and only wade out into the open once the wave is cleared.

Stick with the DMR and Magnum. Gruntpocalypse doesn't have any hazards to worry about, so you don't need to worry about gathering up a Spartan Laser or Sniper Rifle. The DMR and Magnum that comes with every loadout in Gruntpocalypse is all you truly need to conquer the Grunts. Since Grunts only appear via random spawn or Monster Closet instead of via a drop ship, you don't really get the opportunity for a massive insta-kill with the Target Locator unless you lure multiple squads to a central area.

ROCKETFIGHT

Big maps are best. Rocketfight is probably best enjoyed on the larger maps, particularly Beachhead, Glacier, and Outpost. Remember that the default setting on Firefight is for friendly fire to be turned on, so unless you plan on changing the game settings, be sure your team watches where they point those things!

Keep your distance. While the rocket's splash damage can kill most of the enemies, bigger enemies like Hunters and Brute Chieftains require more firepower. All the while, they'll be charging towards your position. Never fire the Rocket Launcher at an enemy only a few steps away, since the area-of-effect damage will probably take you down with it. Use Sprint or Jet Pack to get away, then turn and fire.

GENERATOR DEFENSE

Get those Drop Shields ready! A great tactic for defending a generator is to get between the generator and the enemy's most likely attack route and block it with a Drop Shield. Not only does this provide cover for you, but it also blocks enemy attacks from hitting their mark. Stay close to the generator with the Drop Shield and lock it down at every opportunity!

Isolate a single generator as Elites. If you're playing on the Elites side with another human player, you should coordinate attacks against a single generator. Have one player focus on eliminating Spartans in the area while the other damages the generator. Splitting up to tackle multiple generators at once is no way to win.

Know when to cut your losses. It's certainly worth trying to keep all three generators in play for as long as possible, but once your team loses one, depending on how many lives you have left, you should consider abandoning the weaker of the two remaining to form a unified defense of the third. It's better to have your entire team united and defending one generator than divided between two faltering generators.

VERSUS

Have your plasma on the ready. The Spartan team is at a small disadvantage right off the bat when it comes to fighting the Elites, so it's important for Spartans to have a plasma weapon on hand whenever possible. Use a Plasma Pistol, Rifle, or Repeater to down the Elites' shields, then swap to a DMR or other UNSC weapon and aim for the head.

Use the heavy weapons against Elites. The Spartan team gets a free life for every Elite they manage to kill, so save the power weapons for use against the Elites. Coordinate with teammates to finish off a weakened Elite before it regenerates its health. Multi-kills against Elites are rare, but look for an opportunity to kill two at once.

Steal the UNSC weaponry. Elites can pick up and use any weapon that the UNSC drops, including power weapons. Not only does this keep weapons like the Rocket Launcher and Spartan Laser out of UNSC hands, but picking up discarded DMRs or Grenade Launchers grants the Elite access to unlimited ammo in the Spartan base.

SCORE ATTACK

Bring the fight to them! The final two Waves of enemies in Score Attack can be pretty tough for a one or two person team, but you can't afford to hide inside a room and wait for them to come to you. If your team is gunning for a high score, you must complete the match in a fast time. Work together to hunt down enemies where they spawn and take them out as quickly as you can. Don't stand around waiting for them! This is no time to play it safe!

Pair the DMR with a Grenade Launcher. Since there aren't any power weapons in Score Attack, you have to make the best of what you have. Coordinate with your teammate to have one player select the Recon loadout while the other chooses Specter. The Grenade Launcher can take out multiple low-level enemies for multi-kill bonuses, but can also EMP Elites and soften them up for a DMR kill shot.

Practice often on smaller maps. Achieving a high score in Score Attack doesn't just come from having a lot of skill—it also means picking the right map and memorizing every detail of the map, and also trying to predict certain enemy behaviors, including where they commonly spawn. It's a good idea to start out playing Score Attack on Corvette above Courtyard and only then consider moving up to larger maps.

BEACHHEAD

Fight for prime real estate on the shores of New Alexandria.

Beachhead is one of the larger Firefight maps and is best with a full team of four players. The north end of the map contains the New Alexandria annex building featured at the end of the Exodus chapter in Campaign mode. The structure is three stories tall and features numerous staircases and motion-detecting doorways that lead in and out of a central pavilion balcony. A covered walkway extends south to Caracalla Park where a sky bridge extends west to a smaller plaza. The entire area sits on a beach. A ridge runs up from the beach to the covered walkway in the center, making for some bumpy terrain when driving vehicles. The best path for using a Warthog is to use the trail that loops around the south end of the map, near the water.

- Recommended Game Types: Firefight, Firefight Classic, Rocketfight, Generator Defense, Versus.
- Supplies: 6 Medkits, 2 Ammo Cabinets, 2 Grenade Boxes
- Power Weapons: Ordnance drops
- UNSC Vehicles: Rocket Warthog, Mongoose
- Hazards: Wraiths, Ghosts, Drop Pods
- Covenant Delivery: Phantom, Random Spawn
- Par Score: 50,000

MAP TACTICS

CRUISING IN THE 'HOG

Beachhead's size and supply of vehicles makes it conducive to a number of different strategies. But since this is the only map that features a Warthog (one with a Rocket Launcher no less) it's only natural that most players will to want to put it to use. Fortunately, the map is large enough, with enough cover, that the Warthog should be able to survive long enough to make a significant impact. Just make sure a skilled driver—one who really knows the map's topography well—is behind the wheel.

The Warthog is parked in the garage area, on the eastern side of the annex. Exit the spawn location and descend on the left to reach it quickly.

FIREFIGHT

SPARTAN SPAWN
ROOFTOP STRONGHOLD
C
ROCKET
B
H
H
A
H

A good use of the Warthog is to drive laps around the map using the central coastline area to the south. Either circle back near the lagoon to the northeast and beach road to the northwest, or complete the loop by crossing over the walkway. Don't get too speedy when crossing the central walkway because the ridge can really throw a fast-moving Warthog end over end if you are not careful. Remember to continue accelerating if you find yourself doing a nose-wheelie with the Warthog, tapping the brakes will just send the back end up and over but accelerating will give you a chance of pulling out of the near-endo.

The driver should call out enemy locations (e.g. "Elites at 3 o'clock!") to the player manning the turret. Focus on the higher value targets and leave the Grunts, Jackals, and Skirmishers for your teammates to eliminate with their DMRs. The player driving must also anticipate the gunner's actions and avoid steering too close to enemies. The driver should always let the gunner know if he's planning to splatter enemies with the Warthog. Otherwise, the gunner might inadvertently fire a barrage of rockets just as the driver enters the blast radius. Similarly, it's important to communicate with other teammates regarding Covenant vehicles. This map features a number of Ghosts and Wraiths, both of which can be hijacked by Spartans. Don't open fire with the Warthog unless there aren't any Spartans looking to hijack it. Players not in the Warthog should lend fire support from the mezzanine or pavilion levels of the annex.

The driver and gunner should always be in constant communication with one another. The driver should call out enemies and try to drive as smooth a line as possible, without coming too close to enemies.

STEAL THOSE COVIE VEHICLES

There is a definite advantage to stealing a Ghost, especially given how easy it can be to hijack if it's being driven by a Grunt. Ghosts allow you to go on splatter sprees against low level Covenant and offer enough speed, maneuverability, and firepower to even be worth using against high value targets. The downside to using a Ghost is that it can't withstand many attacks and can be easily hijacked by an Elite. Make sure to alert your teammates whenever stealing a Ghost so they don't instinctively open fire on it.

Another good use for a Ghost is to plug up the stairwell leading to the roof area. The roof is perfect for mounting a defense and these stairs are the only way up.

When it comes to stealing a Wraith, the pros don't always outweigh the cons. There's no denying that the Wraith is an absolute beast when it comes to doling out damage and it can withstand quite a bit of punishment as well. Unfortunately, it's also a magnet for Plasma Grenades and, unlike the Ghost and Warthog, doesn't have the speed it takes to avoid being stuck by a well thrown 'nade. Further complicating matters is the fact that the very act of stealing a Wraith requires the Spartans to inflict moderate damage to the craft. Still, the allure of the Wraith is strong.

Take on the Wraith by sniping the gunner then either target the front hood with the DMR or leap onto the front of the vehicle and melee the hood to either melee the Elite inside to kill it (and risk further damage to the Wraith) or hop off and snipe the Elite. You can get in close to the Wraith and use Armor Lock to EMP it. This stops the Wraith in its tracks and also keeps it from firing its energy bomb.

The Wraith's powerful energy attack is hard to resist. Just make sure you have plenty of cover fire from teammates if you decide to take one for a ride.

Once behind the wheel of the Wraith, alert your teammates and invite one of them to hop into the gunner's seat. Be extra careful of Suicide Grunts and remember that Grunts and Elites are very good at throwing Plasma Grenades, especially once the Catch Skull has been activated in Round 2. The focus of your teammates on sniping Grunts and other low-cost enemies is critical to the success of using the Wraith.

THE ROOFTOP STRONGHOLD

As fun as driving around the map firing off strings of unlimited rockets can be, there is always a time in Firefight matches when it pays to hole up in a fortified area. Beachhead's annex building has a number of areas where one can limit enemy approaches, but the roof offers all the amenities of a great stronghold. For starters, Covenant can only enter via a single stairwell—a stairwell easily plugged with a Ghost (see picture on the previous page)—but Spartans can easily leap over the ledge and down to the lower levels for an easy escape if overrun. Secondly, the roof is just a few steps away from a UNSC ammo cabinet and box of grenades. Lastly, skilled snipers can pick off enemies clear across the map from this vantage point while those with a Shotgun or Grenade Launcher can make quick work of those funneling up the stairs.

The roof isn't without its hazards and chief among them is the tendency for a Covenant teleportation pod to land on the mezzanine level of the tower, just below the roof. This means there is always the chance that a squad of Brutes or Grunts with Fuel Rod Guns may be just around the corner or directly below you. Monitor the motion tracker and always have a teammate with a Grenade launcher ready to bounce a grenade down the stairs towards them. The other hazard of being on the roof is that it is just within range of a Wraith's energy bomb. Fortunately, the team can quickly pull back under cover in the east corner of the roof. Send one or two players out to deal with the Wraith (or open fire with the Spartan Laser from the roof) and carry on.

The roof has everything you need to mount a strong defense against the toughest waves of enemies. Use the elevated position to snipe enemies in the distance and to blast away at enemies funneling through the lone stairwell leading up.

CORVETTE

Fight for air superiority inside the belly of the beast.

Corvette is the closest Firefight comes to offering a true arena-like map. The circular hangar is featured in the "Long Night of Solace" mission in Campaign mode and is essentially symmetrical in shape, though the architecture of the ramps and platforms differ on each side. The home base area is on the south side of the map, accessible through two hallways on the main level of the hangar. The south side has two elevated platforms, one in each corner. The north side of the hangar also has two elevated platforms, but they're connected by an even higher walkway that spans the north side of the hangar. The two platforms in the corners on the north side each contain a Plasma Cannon. Drop Ships enter the hangar through the energy barriers on the east and west sides of the room, but Covenant often enter through monster closets spread throughout the perimeter of the map.

- Recommended Game Types: Score Attack, Firefight, Gruntpocalypse, Versus.
- Supplies: 4 Medkits, 2 Ammo Cabinets, 2 Grenade Boxes
- Power Weapons: Ordnance drops, 2 Plasma Cannons
- UNSC Vehicles: N/A
- Hazards: Engineers, Wraiths
- Covenant Delivery: Drop Ship, Monster Closet
- Par Score: 50,000

MAP TACTICS

KNOW YOUR WAY HOME

Corvette may be the smallest of the Firefight maps, but its circular shape and nearly symmetrical layout can make it a bit tough to navigate, especially for first time players. Fortunately, there are a couple of telltale indicators to help you know which side of the map you're on and how to best get back to the home base for extra ammo or Medkits. The easiest way to know where the safe room is to look at the compass on the top of the screen. The home base is on the south side of the hangar, through the doors in the southeast and southwest corner.

The compass doesn't lie. If you're low on health or in need of some ammunition, head south to the safe room.

FIREFIGHT

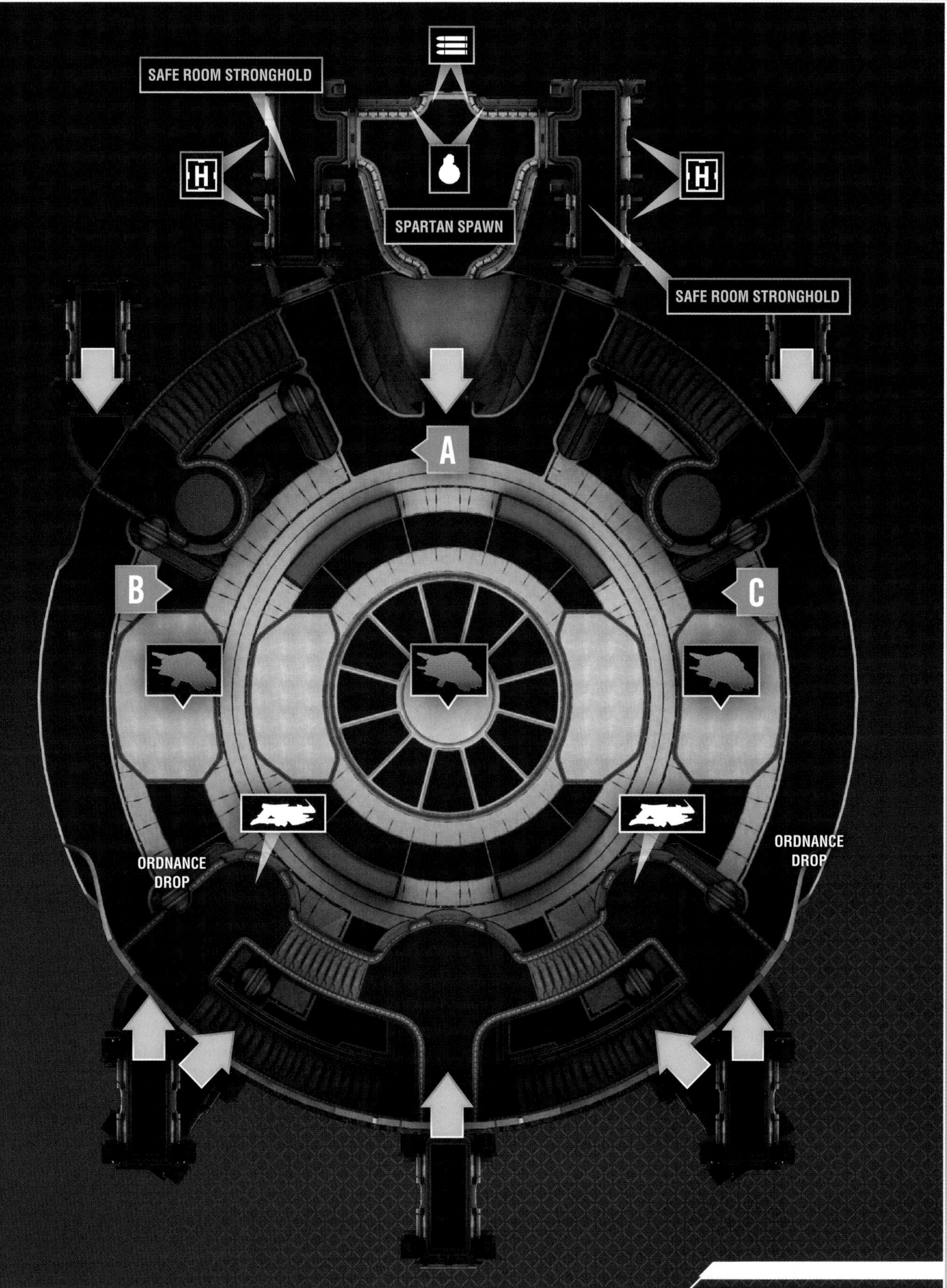
SAFE ROOM STRONGHOLD
SPARTAN SPAWN
SAFE ROOM STRONGHOLD
A
B
C
ORDNANCE DROP
ORDNANCE DROP

The other way to know at all times which side of the map you're on is to understand the differences in the walkways and platforms. The south side of the hangar has two separate ramps leading up to individual platforms, one in each corner. The north side of the room has a large central staircase that forks and leads to two separate platforms connected by an upper bridge. Each of two platforms in the northern corners of the hangar have Plasma Cannons. The Plasma Cannons leave you pretty exposed to enemy attacks, but they are certainly useful against higher value enemies. Be sure to detach the Plasma Cannon before concluding the fifth wave in a round. You can then drop it off in the safe room to stockpile extra Plasma Cannons.

THE GLOW AND RUMBLE OF HAZARDS

You might think this map would be too small to play host to hazards, but you'd be wrong. Though you won't find any snipers or teleportation pods on Corvette, but this map does contain Engineers. Engineers will periodically appear on the map, typically floating high above the floor where you're unlikely to spot them. Though they pose no direct threat to the Spartan team, these support creatures provide an extra layer of shields to Covenant infantry in their vicinity. If you suddenly see Grunts and other Covies cloaked in a pink glow, that means there's an Engineer in the area. Move into cover and look towards the ceiling to spot the floating crystal-like mass. The Engineer can be destroyed with a few rounds from any weapon, so don't waste any valuable ammo on it.

Corvette is the only Firefight map that features Engineers. Don't hesitate to aim your guns skyward as soon as you see Covenant troops glowing pink.

The other hazard to appear on Corvette is the Wraith. Wraiths aren't terribly common, but they will occasionally be ferried in to the hangar by a Drop Ship at the start of a new wave. This map is far too small to even consider hijacking the Wraith—you'd be bombarded with Plasma Grenades in a matter of seconds—so immediately hatch a plan of attack with teammates. Since the Wraith can be seen underneath the Drop Ship as its entering the hangar, it's possible to move into position to hop aboard and plant a grenade the moment it sets down.

It's also worth planning ahead to deal with the Wraith. Since none of the ordnance drops ever contain a Target Locator on this map, you have a very good chance of securing a Spartan Laser. If so, resist using it until a Wraith enters the map, then use the Spartan Laser to destroy the vehicle. Spartan Lasers come with enough ammo to be fired four times. It will likely take two strikes with the weapon to destroy a Wraith. Put the other charges to work against any Hunters that show up.

Whoever gets the Spartan Laser should always save it for use against the occasional Wraith ferried in on the belly of a Drop Ship.

Not only do these corner platforms provide a chance to fire on most enemies from multiple directions, but there is typically only one way of access to each location. The elevated position is also critical in that it allows the team to shoot over and around cover items and hit the Covenant no matter where they stand on the map. These positions also make it rather easy to pick off Grunts and Jackals while they are still on the Drop Ship—wait for the bay doors to open, fix your sight in front of the Drop Ship, and fire as each enemy's head moves into view.

CATCH THEM IN THE CROSSFIRE

The compact design of Corvette makes it possible to essentially split your team up across the four corner platforms and catch the Covenant in crossfire from all directions as they disembark the Drop Ships. Though some of the enemies will enter the battle area from nearby monster closets, teammates can alert one another across the map to enemies sneaking up behind them or, better yet, monster closet doors that are about to open. Spartans can't pass through the energy barriers at the monster closets, but they can throw a Frag Grenade or fire their weapon through the barrier. This is a great way to rack up a lot of kills quickly on Gruntpocalypse, in particular.

Without the help of a Rocket Launcher or timely grenade toss, you won't be able to kill Elites and Hunters (nor most Brutes) before they leap out of the Drop Ship. And some of them move too fast to risk turning your back! Since the team will likely need extra ammo and/or health by the time the fourth or fifth wave comes, it's not a bad idea to return to the safe room area, place two people on each side, and let the enemies come to you. The combined firepower of the team, even when split between two pairs, is substantial enough to hold most enemies at bay as they funnel through the doors to the safe room.

A team of four can do quite well by taking up position on each of the four corner platforms so long as they alert one another to the occasional enemy sneaking up behind them.

Don't hesitate to fall back to the safe room during the fourth and fifth waves of each round. Let the enemies come to you and cut them down as the doors open!

COURTYARD

Fight to secure the fortified ONI plaza.

Courtyard takes place in the depot area outside ONI: Sword Base. The map is rather elongate in design and features lengthy sight-lines, adequate cover, and an interior base area that can be used much like the storeroom on the Holdout map. Courtyard is a mid-sized map that is really conducive for all numbers of players and virtually any gameplay mode. This map favors those who excel at long-range weaponry and offers plenty of opportunity for creativity. Terraces on both the northwest and southeast sides of the map provide elevated vantage points from which to eliminate enemies deploying at either end of the map. A bridge runs across the center of the map outside of the base. Lastly, a curving road winds downhill away from the main battle area in the northeast corner of the map. Enter this area at your own risk.

- Recommended Game Types: Firefight Classic, Rocket Fight, Gruntpocalypse, Generator Defense.
- Supplies: 6 Medkits, 2 Ammo Cabinets, 2 Grenade Boxes
- Power Weapons: Ordnance drops, 1 Machine Gun Turret
- UNSC Vehicles: N/A
- Hazards: Drop Pods
- Covenant Delivery: Phantom, Monster Closet
- Par Score: 50,000

MAP TACTICS

SETTING THE TABLE

One of the best things about Courtyard is the ease at which one can spot inbound Phantoms and tell right away if they are going to deploy their cargo in close proximity to one another. Resist the urge to use the Target Locator on the initial wave in each round unless the two Phantoms pull up alongside one another. Aim the Target Locator at the ground between them and watch the Killionaire Medal pop onto the screen! Nevertheless, it's always worth trying to save one of the Target Locator's strikes for the fourth or fifth wave in a round when the enemies are much harder to defeat.

Only use a Target Locator on the early rounds if both Phantoms are together, thus ensuring a Killionaire level of carnage!

FIREFIGHT

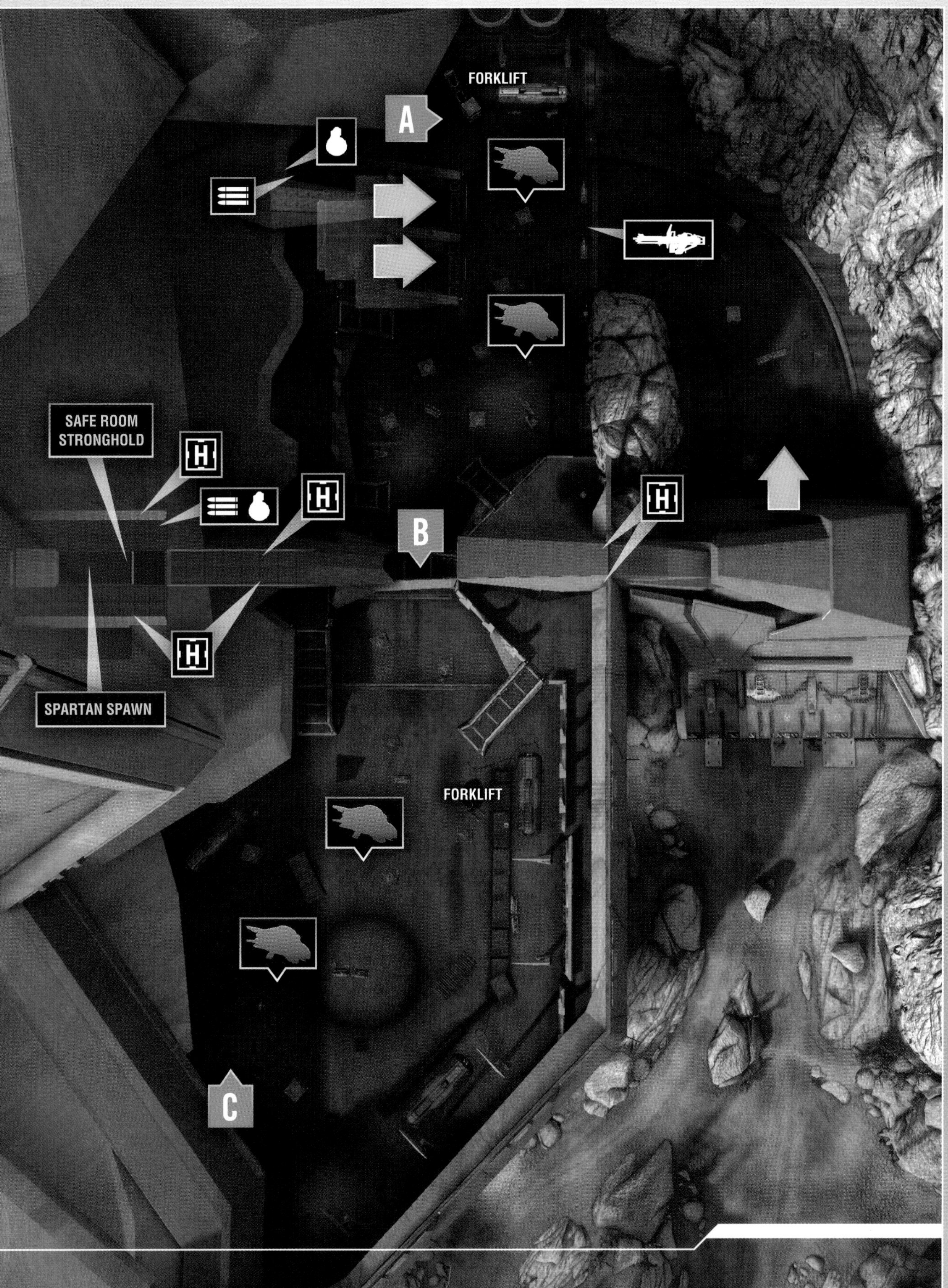
FORKLIFT
A
SAFE ROOM
STRONGHOLD
B
SPARTAN SPAWN
FORKLIFT
C

Fortunately, there is a way to accumulate massive destruction during the start of a wave without using the Target Locator. Courtyard contains two forklift trucks that can be detonated to great effect. One forklift truck is in the northwest corner of the map and the other just south of the ramp leading up to the bridge. Wait for a lull in the action (preferably when you're certain there aren't any grenade-throwing baddies around) and drive the forklift to the central area where the Phantoms tend to deploy their Covenant troops. Now, head up onto the terrace and wait for a Phantom to arrive. Open fire on the forklift truck as soon as a number of Covies get close to it. A single shot from the Sniper Rifle will do the trick, as will a Frag Grenade.

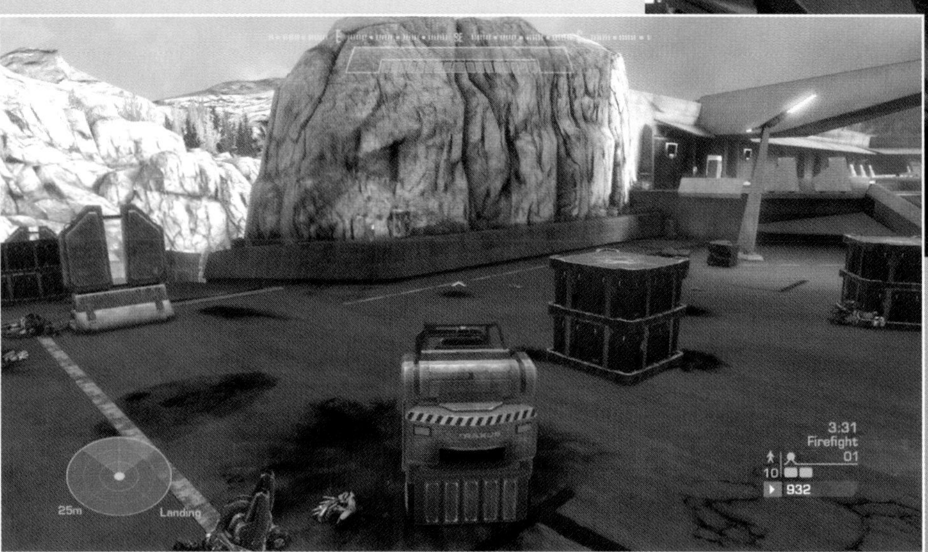

Park the forklift truck out in the open, in the middle of either the northern or southern end of the depot. Scorch marks from prior Target Locator attacks are a good way to tell where to best place it.

ALL ALONG THE WALKWAY

When it comes to positioning your team, Courtyard's northwest terrace is as good a location as there is on any map. Not only does this location provide limited access and plenty of cover, but there is also a UNSC ammo cabinet and box of grenades right there for immediate access. Enemies can reach this location from either of the two ramps flanking the underground garage entrance (monster closet in Firefight mode), or via the far end of the walkway to the south. Make sure your team has at least one player with the Medic loadout who can consistently set up a Drop Shield to deflect attacks originating from the southern half of the walkway.

Enemies are unlikely to ascend the ramp in the northwestern corner of the map, especially if your team is stretched out across the terrace back in the direction of the base. That said, they will consistently approach via the ramp between the garage and the bridge, so be ready. It's important to have your best snipers outfitted with DMRs and/or the Sniper Rifle if it's available. It pays to also have one player equipped with a Shotgun and one with a Grenade Launcher. Lastly, instruct one of your Recon players to sprint for the Machine Gun Turret at the top of the road in the northeast and bring it back to the terrace. It won't have unlimited ammo once removed from its base, but it does very little good where it's located.

A well-coordinated team can spread out along the northern half of the terrace and make quick work of the Covenant forces without significant risk of being overrun.

Even the best of plans can falter if a player misses one too many shots or gets a little careless. That's why it's always good to have a backup plan. In the case of Courtyard, that backup plan is the base area where you spawn. Fall back to that room if left to slug it out with just one or two players against the tougher waves of enemies. The are two Medkits inside this area as well as an ammo cabinet and box of grenades. Stand back, watch the two doors for intruders then open fire. The Grenade Launcher, can be particularly effective in this area, as well as the Shotgun and/or a stolen Concussion Rifle.

STOCKPILING POWER WEAPONS

You can really improve your chances of surviving the final two waves in each round (particularly when playing alone or with just one partner) by stockpiling as many turrets and other heavy weapons as you can, preferably in the base. The Machine Gun Turret at the top of the road often gets destroyed in battle, particularly if you call for an orbital strike anywhere near it. Run and grab it at the start of the round, and bring it to the base where you spawn so as to have it when you need it most. It's highly likely that you'll encounter one or two Brute Chieftains in the final wave that are equipped with Plasma Turrets. Use the Machine Gun Turret to cut them down then pick up their Plasma Turret and continue the fight.

Bring the Machine Gun Turret to the base to use during the fifth wave against the Brutes with Plasma Turrets. Steal their weapons as yours runs low on ammo to continue the fight!

Since the only hazard on Courtyard is the drop pod, you can expect to see quite a few of them. Though normally something to fear, many of the drop pods feature Grunts with Fuel Rod Guns. Try to be there when the drop pod lands and eliminate the enemies quickly to steal as much of their ammo as possible. Leave the guns on the floor until the fourth or fifth wave then gather them up and head to the base.

Retreat to the relative safety of the base to limit enemies to the two doors at the eastern end of the room. Be ready to make a quick escape!

GLACIER

Fight for salvation deep down in the underground caves.

Of all the maps, this may be one where your it pays off best to stick close to the base area. The braided slopes of the namesake glacier provide myriad flanking opportunities for Covenant troops. Combine this with the vision-blocking spires that pierce the ice and you have a recipe for disaster, that is unless you're playing Rocketfight. Advancing too far down the ice without forming a strong line of attack will only get you surrounded. Unlike the other maps, the ordnance drops aren't actually dropped into battle, but located at fixed positions (see map). Securing these weapons, as well as any machine gun turrets you can carry on the return trip, should be a top priority for the start of each round. Deposit the weapons at the base and line up on the rampart for the approaching wave of enemies.

- Recommended Game Types: Firefight Classic, Rocketfight, Generator Defense, and Versus.
- Supplies: 6 Medkits, 2 Ammo Cabinets, 2 Grenade Boxes
- Power Weapons: Fixed Locations (Sniper Rifle, Spartan Laser, and Rocket Launcher), 3 Machine Gun Turrets
- UNSC Vehicles: N/A
- Hazards: Wraiths, Ghosts
- Covenant Delivery: Phantom, Random Spawn
- Par Score: 50,000

MAP TACTICS

SECURE THOSE WEAPONS!

Unlike on the other maps, Glacier has been pre-fortified with three UNSC power weapons located at three distinct locations. The Sniper Rifle is just beyond the ramp leading down onto the ice, to the right. The Spartan Laser is on the left, a slight bit down the glacier and, lastly, the Rocket Launcher lies further to the northwest, halfway down the glacier. Communicate with your team in advance so each player knows which weapon to get. The team's best sniper should hang back and secure the Sniper Rifle while the others fetch the Rocket Launcher, Spartan Laser, and at least one Machine Gun Turret. It's possible to pick up the Rocket Launcher, for example, and still carry the Machine Gun Turret back without having to drop either of the player's other two weapons. Leave the Machine Gun Turrets near the base for use later on.

Make sure your least-capable sniper equips the Recon loadout and sprints for the Rocket Launcher at the start of the round. This is the safest time to retrieve it.

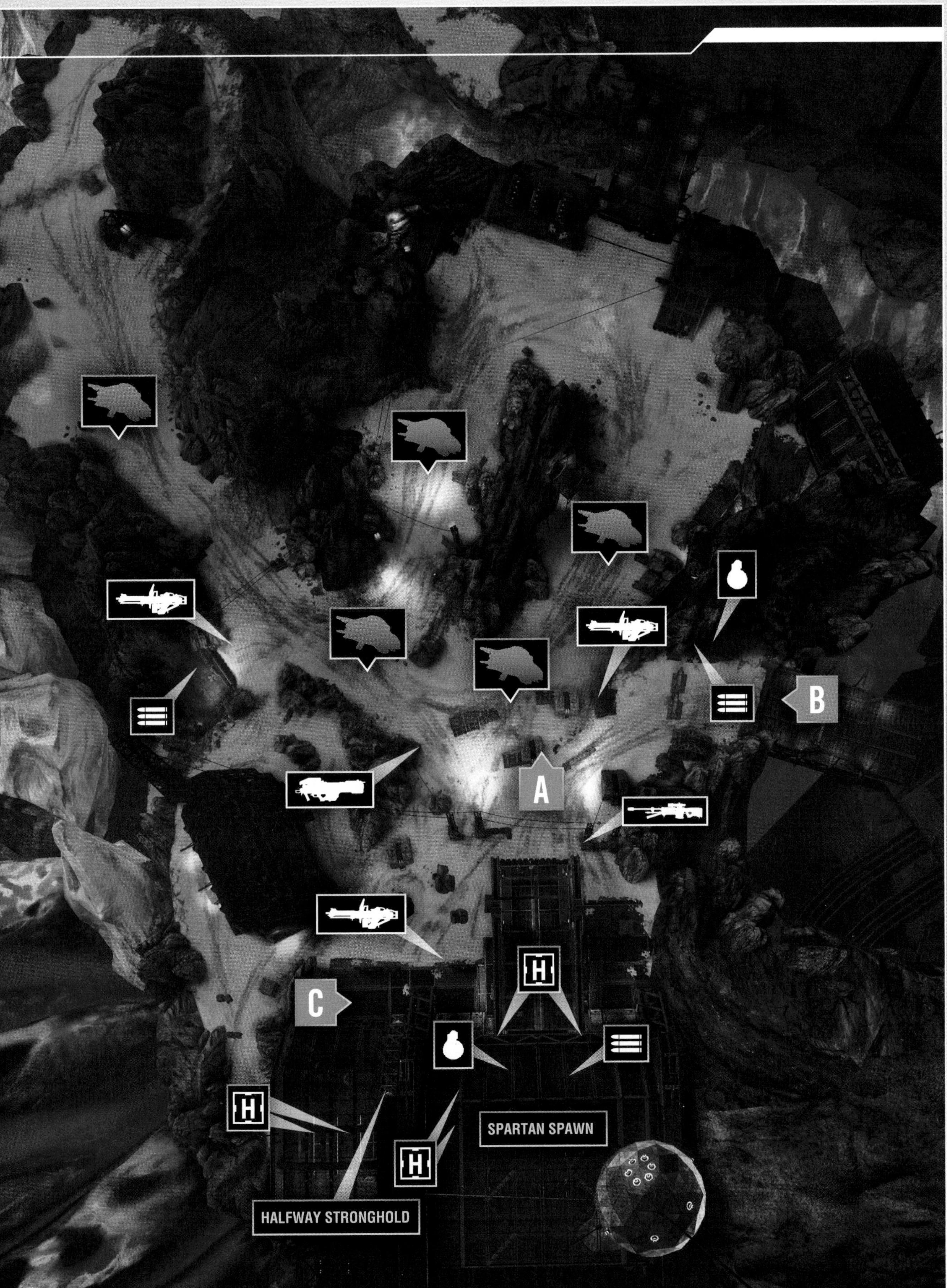
A
B
C
SPARTAN SPAWN
HALFWAY STRONGHOLD

Use the Sniper Rifle eliminate the gunner in the inevitable Wraith that shows up and to also pick off Jackals and Elites from afar. Most Covenant troops will be deployed at least halfway down the glacier, thereby giving a skilled marksman plenty of time to take a few out with long-range headshots. Save the Spartan Laser for use against Ghosts and Wraiths. It's also worth saving the Spartan Laser for use within the base's interior hallway, as it can cut through multiple enemies in a line—fire it as they begin to funnel through the door!

The Sniper Rifle doesn't come with much ammo—just 12 bullets—so make every shot count. Snipe the Wraith's gunner to make it easier for your teammates to plant a grenade.

The Rocket Launcher is a great weapon to hold onto for the fourth and fifth waves in the round, particularly since there is no Target Locator on this map. Use it to eliminate a group of Elites or Brutes bunched together or save it to blast the armor off the back of a Hunter. It can also be used in a pinch to take out a particularly troublesome Ghost, though this should only be done as a last resort.

We don't recommend stealing the Wraith on this map unless you are near the end of a wave and can move it into a safe position before it is bombarded by Plasma Grenades. Also, if you are going to try and use the Wraith, then only melee the Wraith until the cockpit hatch is dislodged. At that time, try to leap off the Wraith, gain some elevation, and shoot the driver with the DMR or Sniper Rifle to avoid doing further damage to the vehicle. It's also possible to leap onto the Wraith (especially with the help of the Jet Pack) and surf the top of it while shooting the driver. Once inside the Wraith, either drive it up onto the rampart near the base, or move it near the east bridge or to the southern end of the glacier—near the power lines. Just make sure to exit the Wraith whenever Phantoms are in the vicinity; climb back aboard once the Phantoms depart.

Coordinate with your sniper so you know when the Wraith's gunner has been eliminated. Jump onto the hood of the Wraith and either repeatedly melee it to kill the driver or plant a grenade.

NEUTRALIZE COVENANT VEHICLES

Phantoms don't just ferry Covenant infantry to the battlefield on Glacier, they also bring in a number of Ghosts and Wraiths as well. Wraiths are clearly the larger threat and should be dealt with as soon as their energy bombs begin to encroach upon your team's position. The most ammo-efficient way to deal with a Wraith is to have your team's sniper eliminate the gunner, then move in on foot. For safety's sake, it's best to EMP the Wraith with either Armor Lock or the Grenade Launcher before trying to board it. Once on board, either plant a grenade or repeatedly melee it until it is either destroyed or until the driver has been killed.

Where the Ghost presents the Covenant with a rather large and easy-to-hit target, stealing a Ghost has much clearer benefits. It's also a lot easier to do. Either snipe the driver off the purple chariot or move into position alongside it and press X when prompted to hijack it. It's as easy as that. Once on board the Ghost, players can mow down low-level Covenant with surprising ease and lend valuable firepower to tougher enemies. The Ghost can still be shot and/or stuck with a Plasma Grenade, and the Spartan driving it is exposed to direct attacks, but it is worth the risk.

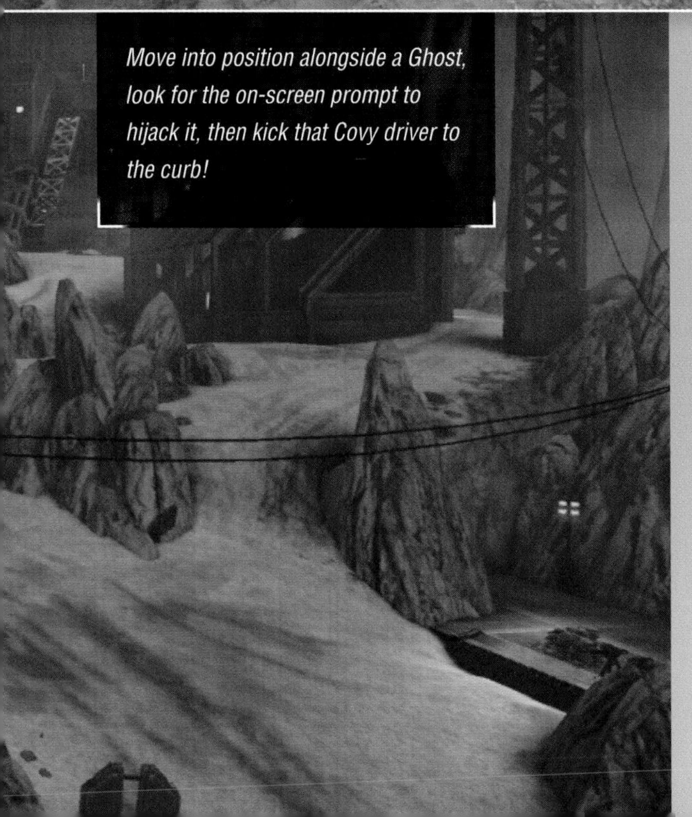

Move into position alongside a Ghost, look for the on-screen prompt to hijack it, then kick that Covy driver to the curb!

THE SAFE ROOM

Those who played "The Package" in Campaign mode will be happy to know that there is a relatively secret hallway within the entrance to the base (aka Halsey's Lab). This corridor leads north from the spawn location to the back door area beside the lab and serves as an excellent place from which to mount a defense. The hallway is quite narrow and therefore forces enemies to essentially line up at the doors on either end in order to get to your team. You could theoretically be trapped between two approaching squads, but this is unlikely. It takes the Covenant a bit of time to reach this position, thus limiting the number of enemies you'll have to deal with simultaneously.

In addition to forcing the enemies through narrow chokepoints, this hallway also has the benefit of being in close proximity to several Medkits, a grenade box, and an ammo cabinet. Prepare your defenses early and stock this area with multiple Machine Gun Turrets during the first wave of each round. The interior entrance to the hallway doesn't have a door, but there is an automatic door in the middle and one at the northern end. Teams of three or more can easily monitor both approaches for enemies, but it's also possible to use the automated doors as an early warning system. Watch the south end of the hallway while standing close enough to the middle door to keep it open. Let the sound of the northern door opening by your cue that enemies are approaching from the back door area.

A couple of Spartans standing back-to-back with Machine Gun Turrets can mow down just about anything that comes through those doors, especially if one can also deploy a Drop Shield.

HOLDOUT

Fight for your life in the UNSC ship graveyard.

Holdout is the most complex of all the Firefight maps in terms of architecture, elevations, and scale. This multi-tiered map takes place in the UNSC ship-breaking yard visited in the "Pillar of Autumn" mission of the Campaign. Built on the side of a cliff, Holdout is a collection of concrete and metal. The map consists of four different levels of interior space, ringed on three sides by rocky ledges and perilous cliffs. Strategically placed Machine Gun Turrets provide Spartans with the firepower needed to cut down the Covenant as they disembark their Phantoms, but at what cost? Contrary to the strategy invoked on most maps, the high ground isn't necessarily the best place to be on Holdout. Stay low under the cover of the deck or, better yet, make your stand in the storeroom or field office.

- Recommended Game Types: Firefight Classic, Gruntpocalypse, Generator Defense, Versus
- Supplies: 6 Medkits, 2 Ammo Cabinets, 2 Grenade Boxes
- Power Weapons: Ordnance Drops, 3 Machine Gun Turrets
- UNSC Vehicles: N/A
- Hazards: Drop Pods, Banshees
- Covenant Delivery: Phantom, Random Spawn
- Par Score: 50,000

Failure to collect the Machine Gun Turrets early in each round could result in them being used against you. Grunts, Brutes, and even Elites are all capable of using the turrets!

MAP TACTICS

MIND THE STORE

If you read along with the walkthrough strategy for the "Pillar of Autumn" mission, then you already know how valuable the storeroom location in this area can be. Located two levels below the crow's nest, the storeroom is a T-shaped, two-story room that has two but two entrances stacked on top of one another. This location is safe from Phantom and Banshee attacks and contains ammo, grenades and two Medkits. In short, it's the perfect place to hole up and let the throngs of enemies come to you.

A
STOREROOM STRONGHOLD
(LOWER FLOOR)
H
H
C
SPARTAN SPAWN
B
H

Take a minute during the first two waves to have one or two teammates collect the three Machine Gun Turrets and carry them into the storeroom for use later on when the action heats up. When it comes time to retreat to the storeroom for safety, set up with two Machine Gun Turrets on the upper level of the room and another behind the stairs on the lower level. A fourth player, if available, can then use the Grenade Launcher or other power weapon to lend additional support fire.

Treat the storeroom like a bunker to retreat to in the face of too many Elites, Hunters, or Brute Chieftains. But stocking it with heavy weapons isn't the only preparation you should make. It's also important to avoid using the grenades or Medkits located in this room until absolutely necessary. The field office directly above the storeroom also contains grenades and three Medkits. Do your resupplying there during the early waves, and save the rations in the storeroom for the end of a round.

Nothing will get through that door in one piece so long as there are Spartans with Machine Gun Turrets inside!

THE UNFRIENDLY SKIES

The presence of Banshees is the skies above Holdout may tempt you into selecting the Air Assault loadout just so you can fly up and hijack one. Sadly, this isn't possible. The ability to hijack a Banshee was disabled in Firefight matches in order to preserve the competitive balance between the Covenant and the overwhelmed Spartans. This is also why it is impossible to use the Jet Pack to fly up on to otherwise unreachable rooftops and ledges. Though you can fly up into the air with a Jet Pack as high as the thrusters will take you, touching down on a ledge or roof will result in a warning that you must return to the battlefield, or suffer immediate death.

Jet Packs can still be used to quickly ascend from one level of the map to another without having to take the stairs, but we caution against their use. Not only do you run the risk of being shot down or knocked out of the sky via a collision with a Banshee, but there are a lot of places where a Jet Packing Spartan could easily fall to his or her death. Jet Packs can be effective on some maps, but there may be too much risk here on Holdout to make their use worthwhile.

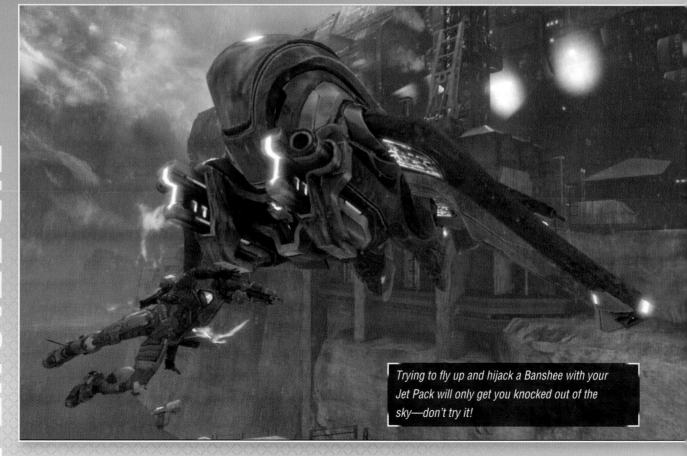

Trying to fly up and hijack a Banshee with your Jet Pack will only get you knocked out of the sky—don't try it!

Though it's not possible to hijack a Banshee during Firefight, you still need to get rid of them. The quickest and easiest way to clear the skies is to use the Grenade Launcher and manually detonate a grenade in the sky next to the Banshee to EMP it. This causes the Banshee to short-circuit and fall from the sky, thus making it an easier target for your Spartan team. Of course, hitting the Banshee with an EMP attack while it's beyond the edge of a cliff will cause it to fall to its death and net you all of the points. It's also possible to EMP the Banshee with the Plasma Pistol or to simply opt for heavier firepower and blast it with the Spartan Laser or Rocket Launcher.

Knock the Banshees out of the sky with the Grenade Launcher. Wait for the Banshee to fly beyond the cliff then manually detonate a grenade in the sky next to it.

You're pretty vulnerable to Phantom attacks inside the crow's nest so be quick! Scan the map and set up a strike with the Target Locator then get behind cover!

BIRD'S EYE VIEW

Conventional wisdom dictates that the best place from which to mount a defense is usually at the highest elevation you can get to. On Holdout, this would be the crow's nest, the small lookout atop the field office. The crow's nest has a number of windows and can be accessed via two sets of stairs, one on each side. Though the windows provide a great view of the rest of the map, they also leave would-be snipers vulnerable to attacks from flying Covenant crafts and other enemies. The best time to head to the crow's nest in traditional Firefight matches is when you have the Target Locator and a new wave is about to begin.

The crow's nest provides a much more strategic purpose in some of the other game modes, particularly Gruntpocalypse. Waves of Grunts spawn in groups of four throughout the map and the crow's nest gives you the perfect vantage point to snipe them as they appear. Use the DMR or Sniper Rifle and aim for the head of the Grunt in the center of the group—the resulting explosion (due to the Grunt Birthday Skull) will frequently eliminate all the other nearby Grunts. The crow's nest is also useful in Generator Defense; Elites can use it to snipe Spartans in defensive positions and Spartans can use this position to fire on and distract the Elites from completing their mission.

OUTPOST

Fight for survival amidst the smoldering ruins.

Set above the shore of a once-frozen lake is an area known as Outpost, a sprawling stretch of land dominated by two massive Covenant anti-air cannons. Noble Six visited this area in Campaign mode, during "The Package" mission and it was his handiwork that left one of the mighty cannons in its current state. The area is strewn with the detritus of war. It would seem that the only thing not at least partially wrecked by battles waged is the central deck, a structure your team of Spartans will get to know very well. The elongated map slopes downhill towards the two anti-air cannons positioned near the cliff. In between those cannons lies the deck. A series of blast shields and a Machine Gun Turret are all the protection you'll have once you go to the roof, but the lone ingress point makes it a desirable position to hold.

- Recommended Game Types: Firefight, Firefight Classic, Rocketfight, Generator Defense, Versus
- Supplies: 6 Medkits, 2 Ammo Cabinets, 1 Grenade Box
- Power Weapons: Ordnance Drops, 1 Machine Gun Turret
- UNSC Vehicles: N/A
- Hazards: Ghosts
- Covenant Delivery: Phantom, Random Spawn
- Par Score: 50,000

MAP TACTICS

GHOSTS ON THE PROWL

Players craving their Sunday Driver medal have come to the right place! Ghosts are the lone hazard on this map and although they appear frequently enough to pose a true threat to the humans—and always with an Elite in the driver's seat—they can be easily hijacked and used to Spartan advantage. Outpost is littered with enough wreckage and rocks to make navigating the bumpy terrain a challenge, but the Ghost is nimble enough to maneuver between the obstacles and run down a number of Covenant on each pass. Ease off the turbo and use the Ghost's weaponry to soften up larger enemies, then slam into them for a fatal blow.

It doesn't take long at all to accumulate a lengthy streak of splatter kills with Ghost. Even Elites and Brutes can be run down with enough speed!

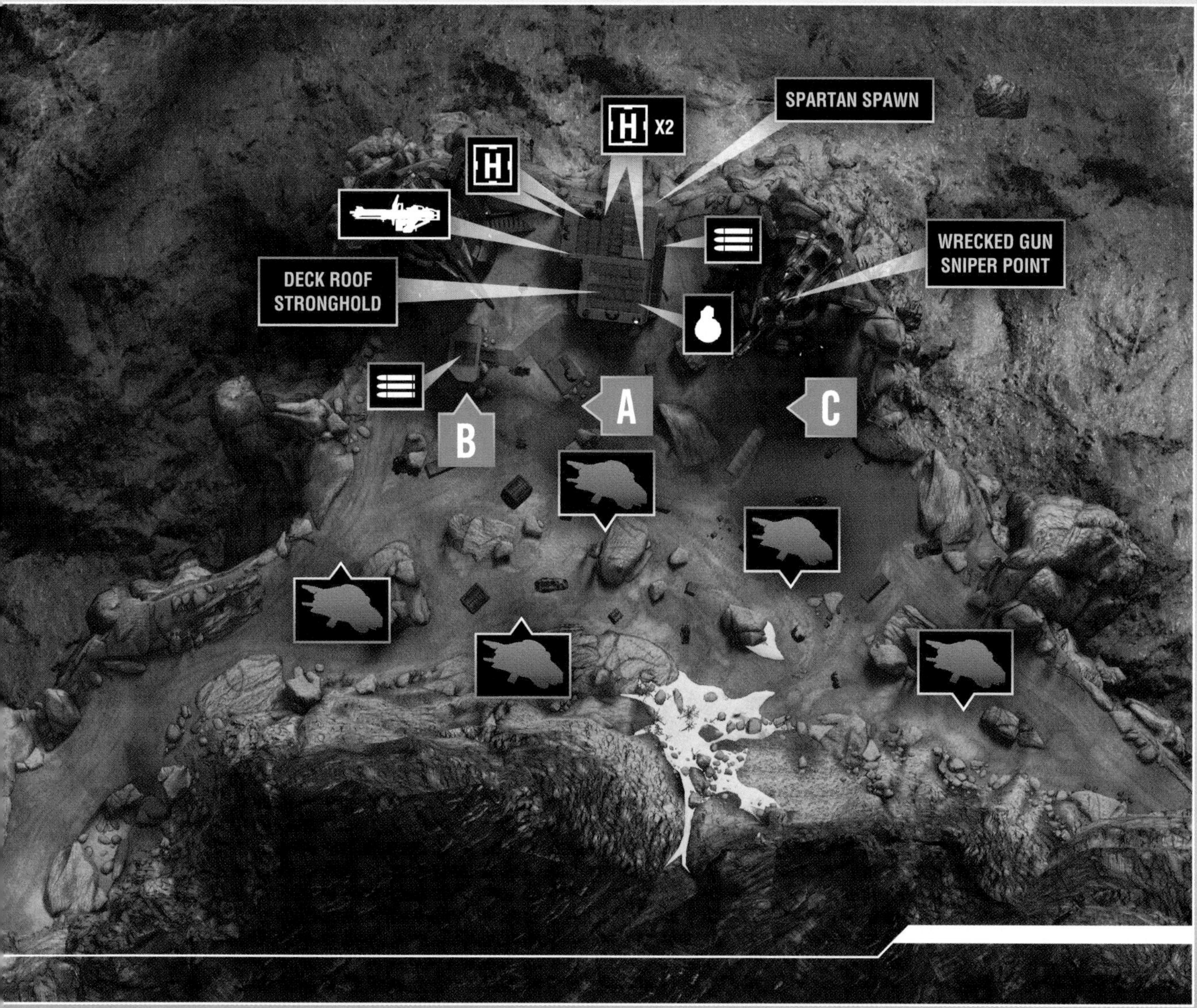

SPARTAN SPAWN
H X2
H
DECK ROOF STRONGHOLD
WRECKED GUN SNIPER POINT
A
B
C

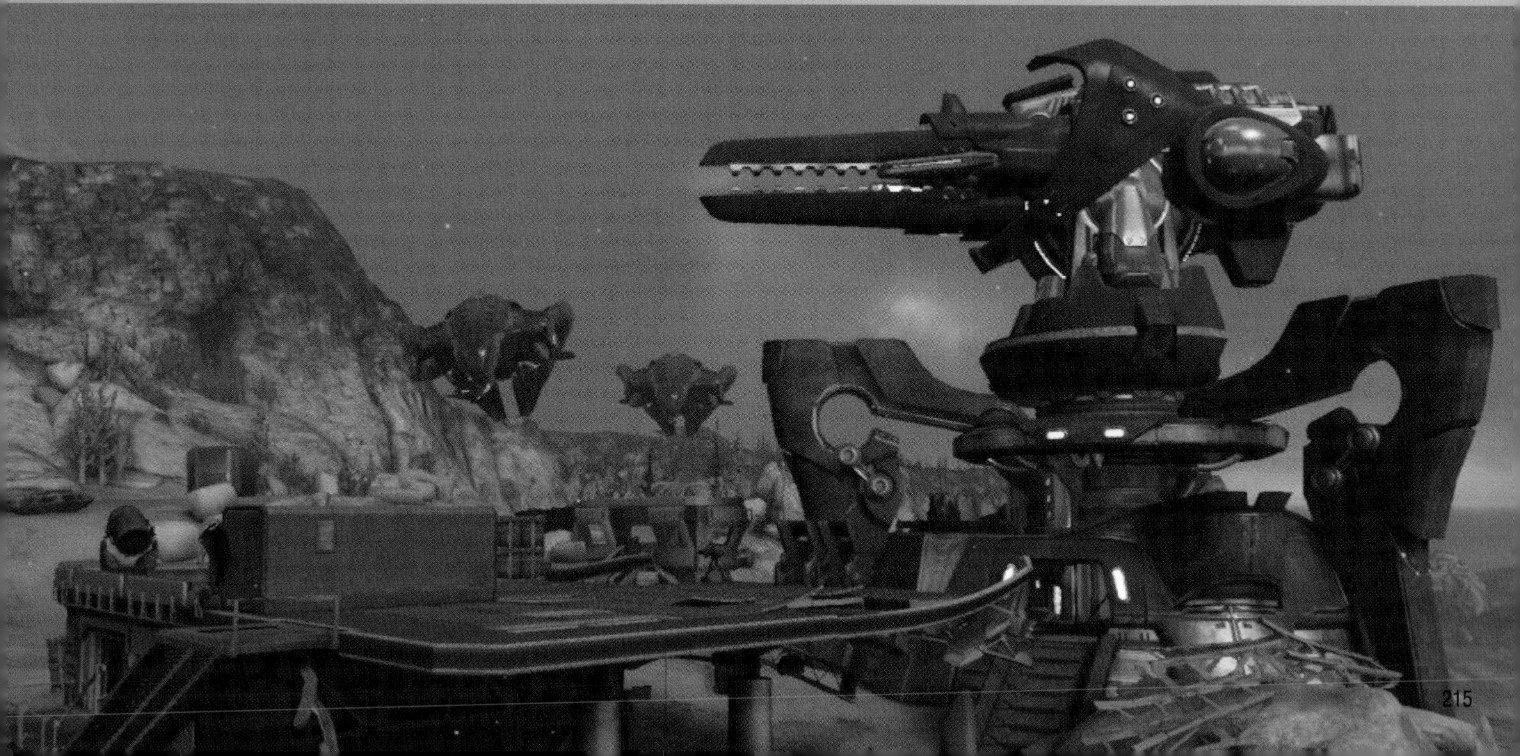

Start on either end of the map, line up your foes, and accelerate towards them. The Ghost can accumulate splatter kills against Grunts and Jackals without much speed, but it usually requires a fair amount of turbo in order to defeat an Elite or Brute with the Ghost. It's even possible to splatter a Hunter, but it' not only ill-advised, it also takes multiple collisions to perform.

The key to being truly effective with the Ghost lies in avoiding the trap. For as fast and nimble as the Ghost is, it can also get lodged against a rock or debris or, worse, flipped upside down. A Ghost stuck in place is a magnet for Covenant attacks, particularly Plasma Grenades and Fuel Rod blasts. Avoid using the turbo for long periods. This will help maintain control and also ensure you have some turbo available if you need to make a speedy getaway. Drive from the cliffs at one end of the map towards those at the other then turn the craft around, assess the spread of enemies, and aim the Ghost for the most amount of Covenant in the most open terrain. Resist the urge to go up against another Ghost. Instead, continue using the one you have until it starts to show some heavy damage then exit your used vehicle and set to hijacking the other one.

Use the Ghost's energy beams to soften up tougher enemies and always, always, use the guns to take down suicide Grunts!

HIT THE DECK

As devastating as a well-driven Ghost can be, there aren't enough of them to go around. Some of your teammates will have to post up and attack the old fashioned way—with UNSC approved boomsticks! The best place to do this is atop the deck along the southern edge of the map. The roof of this guardhouse contains a number of blast shields and a Machine Gun Turret it also offers a relatively unobstructed view of the entire map. The deck lacks aerial cover, making Phantom bombardment a significant threat, but there is only one set of stairs leading to this location.

The interior of the deck (the ground floor) has three Medkits and there is a an ammo cabinet on the ground, just below the southwest corner of the roof. Spartans can easily leap off the south side of the deck to take cover from aerial attacks, to get health and ammo, or to simply flee if the roof gets overrun by Covenant.

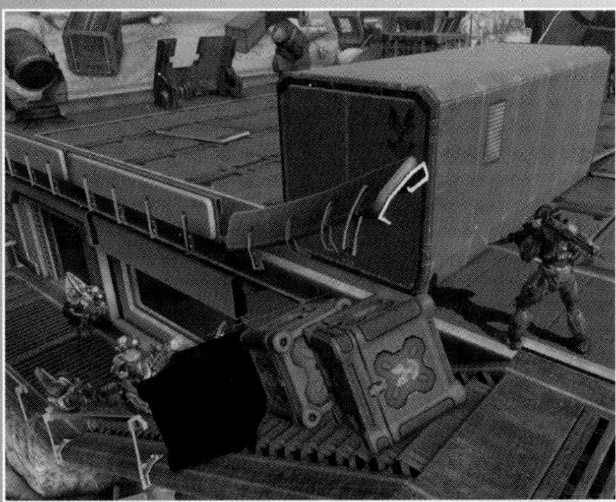

Push the three smaller green crates towards the stairs to block the lone path leading up onto the roof. Elites won't have any trouble knocking the crates aside, but they're enough to stop lesser enemies.

There's no need to put the entire team on the deck, but teams should always have one or two player in this location, preferably armed with the DMR or Sniper Rifle. One player should position himself near the north edge of the deck, overlooking the main battlefield while another stays behind the large container near the stairs.

Using the Machine Gun Turret attracts a lot of attention from the enemies down below. Position a Drop Shield so it protects the gunner while allowing the gun to fire freely beyond the bubble.

The Medic loadout doesn't offer the weaponry best suited for long-range attacks, but the Drop Shield can be used to overlap the roof, thereby causing any thrown Plasma Grenades to bounce or slide off the shield down to the ground below. The Drop Shield also really increases the usability of the Machine Gun Turret in its fixed position. Leave the Machine Gun Turret mounted on its tripod for as long as possible to take advantage of the infinite ammo. Detach it and use it to mow down enemies coming up the stairs during the latter waves.

SNIPER IN THE TOWER

Spartans can further their attempts to divide and conquer on Outpost by sending one of their units—preferably the best sniper in the bunch—up onto either of the massive anti-air cannons. The interior walkway spirals upwards part of the way and it's possible to Jet Pack even higher. This area leaves the player exposed to attacks from inbound Phantoms, but it can't be reached by any of the Covenant.

Of the two anti-air cannons, we recommend climbing onto the "wrecked" one, in the southwest corner. This position gives a wider view of the battlefield without being obscured by the guard tower to the east. Move into position near the top with the Sniper Rifle or DMR and pick off the enemies down below. The Covenant tend to focus their attacks on wherever the nearest threat is, so if you have one Spartan in a Ghost and two on the rooftop of the deck, then the sniper inside the anti-air gun should be relatively safe from harm outside of the Phantom attack.

A sniper in the western anti-air gun can pick off high value enemies otherwise distracted by the rest of the team. This works best with a Spartan in a Ghost and two on the deck.

OVERLOOK

Fight for fertile ground on a deserted farmyard.

Overlook brings you back to the area west of Visegrad Relay, where Noble Team begins the mission "Winter Contingency" during Campaign mode. This sprawling map is much larger than it at first appears, stretching all the way from the two-story barn in the west, down the hill and across the river to the rocky hillside far in the distance. Securing the high ground is critical here, not only for the increased line of sight, but to also avoid being pulled into a confusing gauntlet of rocks, hay bales, and trees. Use the roofs outside the barn, in the yard, to launch your long-distance attack on the lesser enemies as they make their way over the bridge and up the hill, then fall back to the barn's interior to defend against stronger foes. The Covenant snake their way up the hillside along a dozen different paths, including the narrow path to the south of the Machine Gun Turret. Keep your head on a swivel; the enemy can come from anywhere at Overlook!

- Recommended Game Types: Firefight Classic, Rocketfight, Generator Defense, Versus
- Supplies: 6 Medkits, 2 Ammo Cabinets, 2 Grenade Boxes
- Power Weapons: Ordnance Drops, 1 Machine Gun Turret
- UNSC Vehicles: N/A
- Hazards: Wraiths, Drop Pods
- Covenant Delivery: Phantom, Random Spawn
- Par Score: 50,000

MAP TACTICS

SPARTANS ON A HOT TIN ROOF

Overlook is a map where it pays to be patient, maintain the high ground, and resist the urge to hunt the enemy. One of the best places from which to accomplish this is atop the two barns on the north side of the yard, outside the main structure. These rooftops are easily accessed via the hill on the north and it's possible to leap back and forth between the rooftops (something the Covenant cannot do), especially with Sprint equipped. The roofs don't sit too high off the ground, but they are high enough to allow you to fire over the fence along the bluff and snipe enemies on the far side of the river with the DMR. This is also a great spot to head with the Target Locator to ensure a well-placed strike on incoming reinforcements.

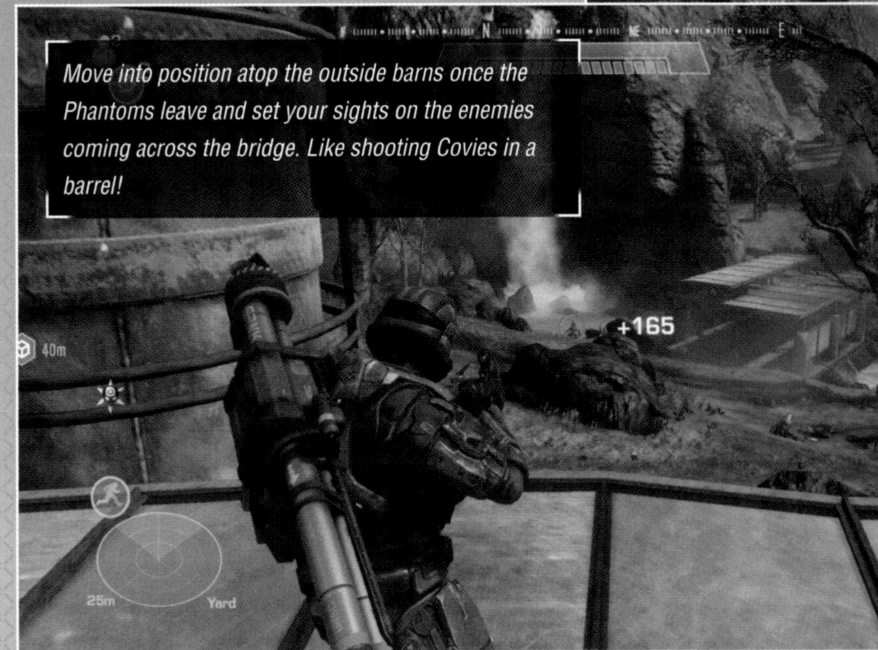

Move into position atop the outside barns once the Phantoms leave and set your sights on the enemies coming across the bridge. Like shooting Covies in a barrel!

FIREFIGHT

A
SPARTAN SPAWN
B
C
FARMHOUSE STRONGHOLD

The Recon loadout is perfect for use on this map, since the DMR has the range to target enemies across the river, as well as on the hill to the north, but having Sprint is also critical for this tactic. It's possible to run and leap back and forth through the nearby window to quickly move between the roof and the second floor of the structure, known as "barn high." This not only allows Spartans to make a speedy run for cover, but there is an ammo cabinet and Medkit inside the building near the window. You don't need Sprint to go from the roof to the interior, but it is necessary to jump high and far enough to leap back through the window onto the roof.

Gather up supplies inside the barn, then Sprint over the rock near the window and leap out the window right back onto the roof to resume sniping.

Being on the roof isn't completely safe, of course. The Covenant can move into very close range, even onto the roof nearest the barn, and have a direct shot on you from almost any side. You have to watch the Motion Tracker carefully and act fast to remove any nearby threats. Being on the roof alone can work, but it's much better to have another teammate on the same roof or on one of the roofs to the south. Make the most out of the buddy system and have one player focus entirely on close-range enemies so the other can snipe the more distant foes.

CAMP THE BARN

It's only a matter of time before things get too dangerous atop the roofs, like when a squad of Elites with Fuel Rod Guns get dropped off at close range! Luckily, there's a two-story barn that you can fall back into. Though there are a number of ways in and out of the barn, it's relatively easy to spread out and keep the Covenant at bay. It also helps to carry the Machine Gun Turret in and leave it in the central area upstairs, near the Medkits and ammo cabinet.

Have one teammate leap onto the storage drums in the northern corner of the barn to monitor activity atop the hill.

There are three entrances to the upper level, a window in the northern corner, a window next to the ammo cabinet, and the door near the stairs on the south side. Position Spartans behind cover near each entrance so that they have a view of any possible Covenant intruders, but aren't exposed to fire. Most Covenant will make their way inside via the basement, either through the basement stairs on the north or the large opening in the center of the basement. This leaves them with no choice but to ascend the stairs on the south side of the barn.

It pays to have a player equipped with the Medic loadout guard the central window (the one near the roofs) since this Spartan can essentially seal it from inbound gunfire with the Drop Shield. This also provides a centrally-located area of respite for the entire team. The other two players, if available, should watch the area near the stairs, preferably with the Machine Gun Turret or Grenade Launcher.

The Machine Gun Turret on Overlook is well-positioned and can't really be used against you by the Covenant, but it can do even more good inside the barn during a defensive stand.

GENERATING TROUBLE

Overlook is particularly conducive to some rather cunning Generator Defense tactics. The location of Generator Bravo inside the barn can work both for and against the Spartan team in charge of protecting it. It's great to have a Generator in an area that is so relatively easy to defend—follow along with the "Camp the Barn" strategy outlined above and you'll surely be able to keep it safe. The problem lies in the fact that the Covenant—particularly humans playing as Elites—know the first thing every Spartan team does is rush out the door for ordnance drops. This provides fast-moving Elites with an opportunity to sneak in and attack Generator Bravo while the Spartans are out collecting weapons.

Drop Shields are great at deflecting attacks aimed at the generators. A well-placed Drop Shield inside the barn can cut off half the attacks aimed at Generator Bravo.

Players on the Elite team shouldn't only go to Generator Bravo if the Spartans are outside, they should always focus first and foremost on attacking this generator. The reason to do this is because the other Covenant are going to automatically attack Generators Alpha and Charlie and the Spartans aren't about to give up completely on those other generators. If they do, then you've succeeded in knocking them down to one generator rather quickly. And if they do head out to defend the others, and you take Bravo, then you've effectively forced them to divide their defenses between two very exposed generators. Generator Bravo is the linchpin—take Bravo and the rest should fall easily.

WATERFRONT

Fight for vital infrastructure that fuels the war effort.

The final map in the list is Waterfront, an area visited by Noble Six during the "Nightfall" mission in Campaign mode. Waterfront takes place at a pumping station near a reservoir. The action centers around a circular platform connected by a bridge that leads to a dam. A large house and a shed occupy much of the central platform and provide both an interior space to occupy, as well as a pair of rooftops that affords an excellent vantage point. Water flows in from the reservoir to a tunnel beneath the house and also beneath the bridge to a stream at the base of the hills. One aspect that really sets Waterfront apart is the presence of Jackal Snipers on the cliffs surrounding the valley. The Jackals stealthily move into position and open fire with their Focus Rifles when you least expect it. Teams must always have a sniper on hand to return fire.

- Recommended Game Types: Firefight, Rocketfight, Generator Defense, Versus
- Supplies: 6 Medkits, 2 Ammo Cabinets, 2 Grenade Boxes
- Power Weapons: Ordnance Drops
- UNSC Vehicles: N/A
- Hazards: Drop Pods, Jackal Snipers
- Covenant Delivery: Phantom, Random Spawn
- Par Score: 50,000

MAP TACTICS

FROM ROOF TO ROOF

The presence of Jackal Snipers and the ubiquitous Phantoms may lead you to think the rooftops on the southwest side of the map would be a bad place to mount your defense, but the benefits greatly outweigh the risks. The spacious rooftops are close enough to leap from one to the other (something Covenant infantry can't do) and provide an excellent view of the map, from the beach to the hillside. One of the best reasons to lead your team onto the roof is because there is only one set of stairs leading onto each roof. It only takes one Spartan at the top of each set of stairs to hold all but the toughest Covy forces at bay.

There's only one way up onto each of the roofs—the stairs! Make sure someone armed with the DMR or Shotgun is guarding against a sneak attack on each roof.

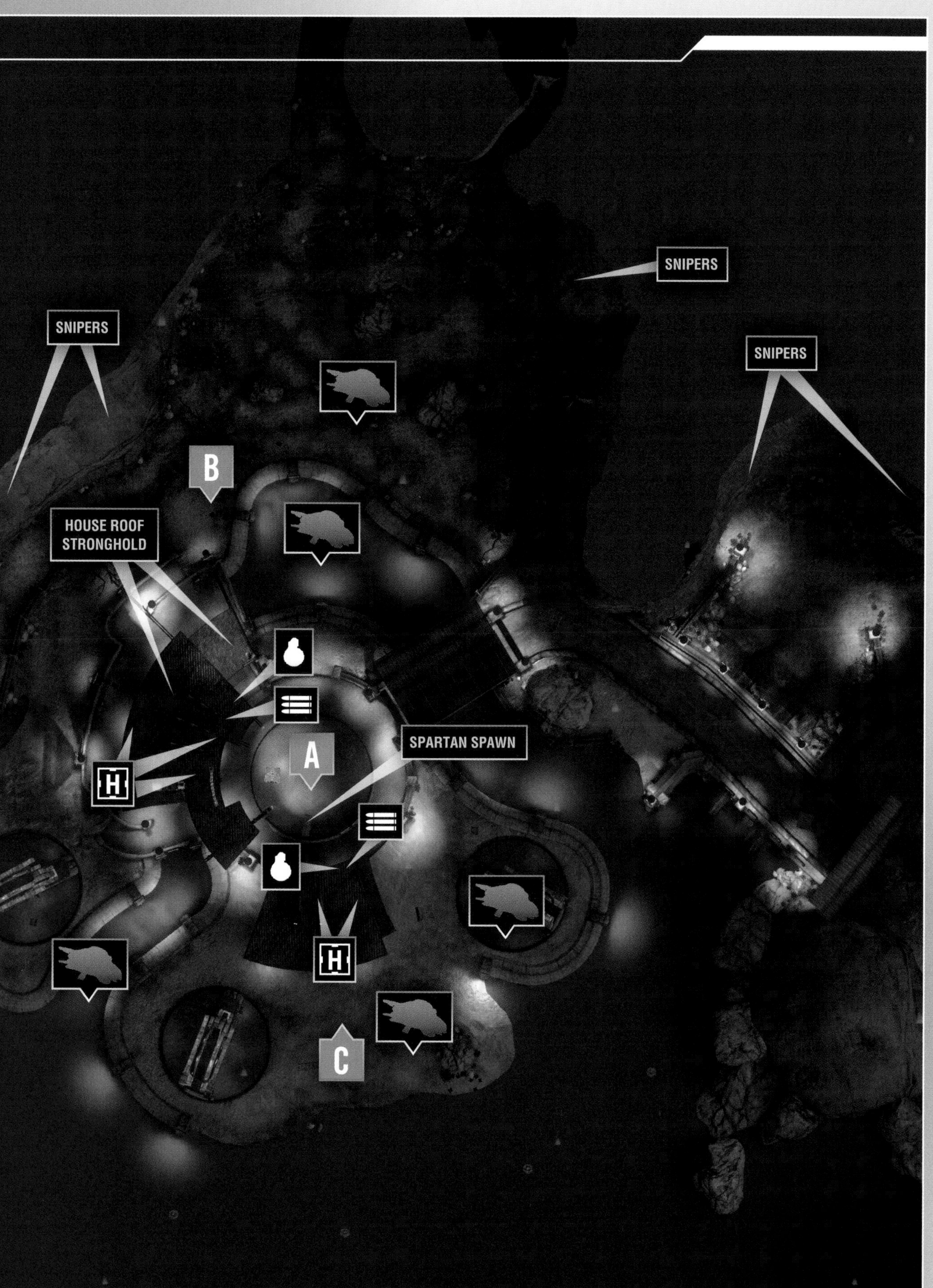
SNIPERS
SNIPERS
SNIPERS
B
HOUSE ROOF STRONGHOLD
A
SPARTAN SPAWN
H
H
C

The benefits to having an elevated position in the center of the map cannot be overstated. Spread your team out across the two rooftops to cover all directions. Most of the action will likely take place near the center of the map, in the water north of the bridge (this is where Drop Pods commonly set down), and between the beach and the house. The DMR is certainly the weapon of choice for those making a long stand on the roof, but the Shotgun and Grenade Launcher will come in handy when needing to defend this position at close-range. The rooftops are only one story off the central platform, but they are quite a bit higher than the beach and nearby water areas. Many enemies will struggle to angle their shots to hit you on the roof, but you'll have no such trouble hitting them.

The roof gives the perfect vantage point to use the Target Locator. Always aim it downward to avoid targeting an area beyond your desired location.

The drawback to being on the roof is the limited amount of cover, particularly from Phantom attacks. Fortunately the skylight eaves are tall enough to crouch down behind for protection from the Phantom's powerful cannons. If things get too crowded on the roof, or the Phantoms have somehow flanked your position, you can always drop off the back side of the roof and enter the house or shed for cover. Take a moment to restock your ammo supplies and use a Medkit before heading back up onto the roof. If things get really bad, consider dropping through the hole in the house's floor to enter the tunnel below.

The northern corner of the roof is the best spot of all to snipe enemies. It's furthest from the stairs and has plenty of cover from Jackal Snipers.

There is one spot on the roof that's a bit better than the others, and that's the lower ledge on the northern corner of the house's roof. This area may be furthest from the beach but it has several fence-like panels that offer nearly full protection from Jackal Snipers and, thanks to the elevation of the roof, offers substantial protection from Phantoms as well. The sight lines aren't quite as great from this location, but the trade off is significant. You can't place your entire team here, but this is a great place to snipe from when Phantoms are around, or when there are a lot of enemies on the southeastern side of the map.

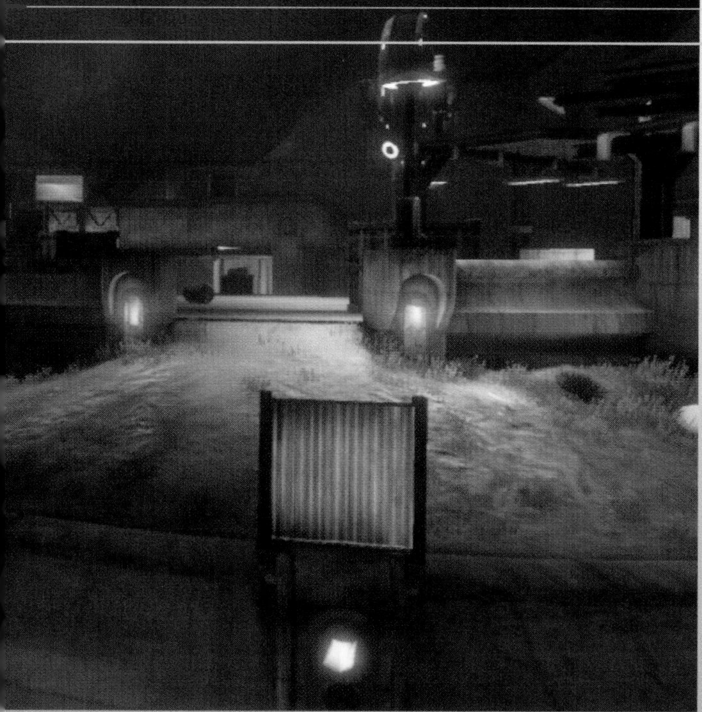

SNIPERS AND DROP PODS

Waterfront is home to a threat the likes of which you haven't seen on the other maps: Jackal Snipers. These wily sharpshooters slither into position high on the cliffs surrounding the map and open fire when you're least expecting it. The blast from their Focus Rifle is sure to startle and the Jackal Snipers can back away under the cloak of darkness just as fast as their attack comes. The Focus Rifle isn't the deadliest of weapons—be thankful they don't have Sniper Rifles!—but it's very hard to continue fighting nearby Covenant while being zapped with a Focus Rifle. Unfortunately, it can be somewhat difficult to spot the distant snipers.

Immediately duck for cover when hit by the Focus Rifle's beam. Reach for the DMR, Magnum, or Sniper Rifle and scan the top of the cliffs in the direction the blast came from. It's not easy to spot the Jackal Sniper—they're very tiny from this distance—but continue to sweep your sights back and forth across the cliffs until they're spotted. One shot to the head is all it takes to quell the threat.

The Jackal Snipers can really prove troublesome if you don't eliminate them immediately. Make sure your team always has a DMR or Sniper Rifle handy to take them out!

Drop Pods are also quite frequent on this map and it's not uncommon to have a squad of Grunts armed with Fuel Rod Guns deployed directly below the roof. Having a Rocket Launcher or Frag Grenade handy makes it much easier to eliminate them quickly. Listen for the sound of the Drop Pod coming in for a landing and move into position on the roof nearest it.

TROUBLED WATERS

It's good to have a place to retreat to, especially one that is safe from Jackal Snipers and Phantoms. On Waterfront, that space is the tunnel beneath the house. Unlike most would-be strongholds, this one has three entrances which does make it harder to defend. We can't recommend making this a permanent part of your strategy, but it gives your team someplace to retreat to when the rooftops inevitably get overrun. Post one man near each of the narrow entrances and two near the wider entrance by the water. Lure the enemies in through the doors and cut them down. Communicate with one another constantly and flee the area (back to the rooftops) as soon as there is a breach on either end of the tunnel. The middle door eliminates the risk of being completely surrounded.

The tunnel beneath the house can be used to lure tougher foes through narrow chokepoints, provided you have enough teammates to guard each entrance.

The dam and bridge are also interesting places to lure enemies away to, so long as there aren't any Phantoms overhead. It's important to have some room to outmaneuver the tougher end-of-wave foes, especially after being reduced to just one or two teammates. There isn't a lot of cover on the eastern side of the map, but the longer sight-lines on the dam and access to the water makes it possible to spot incoming attacks and buy some time to resupply and return to the roof.

MULTIPLAYER BASICS

Welcome back. You hold in your hands a guide to the maps, modes, tactics, weapons, and tools available to you in the multiplayer mode of *Halo: Reach*. This chapter covers the basics of multiplayer, touching on many aspects of the game. For more detail, visit the multiplayer chapters on weapons and vehicles, Forge, multiplayer modes, and multiplayer maps. There is also useful information in the various appendices of this guide, covering the Credit, Armory, and ranking systems.

WELCOME SPARTAN

If you're a returning veteran, you should feel right at home on Reach. The game still plays and feels very similar to past *Halo* titles. There are, however, some significant new additions.

Armor Abilities add new customization to your multiplayer experience, as you can choose (and change) between various Armor Abilities during a match to best suit the map, game mode, and your personal preferences.

Invasion mode is a new "class based" gameplay mode that allows you to battle as Spartans vs Elites in a mix of infantry and vehicle objective combat.

Elites are playable, having slightly faster movement speed, jump height, physical height, and ever so slightly stronger shields that refresh about two seconds faster than Spartan Shields. They also can't use Medkits (but they regenerate slowly over time), and they're only playable in a few gameplay modes.

Halo: Reach also has an almost ridiculous number of gameplay modes, which in combination with the multiplayer maps give you a huge range of possible gameplay types to explore. If that wasn't enough, the newly improved Forge mode and map distribution tools through Bungie.net and Waypoint should allow you to explore new worlds for years to come.

QUICK TIPS

The Motion Tracker is a small display on the bottom left of your HUD that lets you spot any hostile moving targets at a distance. If your Motion Tracker dot is yellow, other players can see you. If there is no dot, you are invisible to the Motion Tracker. By moving slowly, it is possible to conceal yourself.

Critically, you *can* move while crouched and you will not show up on the Motion Tracker—visit the options menu and change crouch to a toggle instead of a hold if you're using crouch on the left analog stick. You can jump out of a crouch, if you need to get moving again quickly.

MULTIPLAYER MATCHMAKING

Any part of *Halo: Reach* can be played with multiplayer, including the Campaign, Firefight, and Forge, but for purposes of organization, when this guide refers to multiplayer, it means online matchmaking in competitive modes, as well as custom games with your friends.

Getting started online in *Halo: Reach* is extremely easy; you can search for a match in any playlist by yourself, or with your party of friends. You can also take your party into a private custom game, or even into Forge together. (In fact, this party functionality is pervasive across all parts of *Halo: Reach*. You can even view recorded games together as a party!)

PLAYLISTS

Inside the Matchmaking for *Halo: Reach*, you will find a set of Playlists that encompass all sorts of mode and map combinations. These combinations can be changed and updated by Bungie as time passes, so expect new map and mode mixes in the future. In general, the list names are self-explanatory: Team Slayer is team-based Slayer with a variety of settings on various maps, and Team Objective tends to focus more on Capture the Flag, Assault, and Territory style games.

SEARCH RESTRICTIONS

You can modify the default search filters of Matchmaking to be a bit more picky about what games and players it will try to match you with.

- Good Connection
- Language
- Skill

Good Connection tries to find other players with good network connectivity to you, Language tries to find players that speak your language, and Skill attempts to match players closer to your skill level.

PSYCHE PROFILE

One interesting new feature of *Halo: Reach* Matchmaking is the ability to set your own "Psyche Profile," essentially just a small questionnaire that lets you tell the Matchmaking system about some of your personal gaming preferences.

- Chattiness: Chatty, Quiet, or No Preference
- Motivation: Winning, Good Time, or No Preference
- Teamwork: Team Player, Lone Wolf, or No Preference
- Tone: Rowdy, Polite, or No Preference

All of the options default to No Preference, but if you *do* have a preference, feel free to change the settings to match your tastes.

CONTROLS

The default controls for *Halo: Reach* are quite comfortable, and will serve you just fine for all of the Campaign and Firefight as well. However, if you spend a lot of time in multiplayer matches, you may wish to look at some of the other configuration options available to you. There are five alternate configurations; each of which moves just a few controls around, but the end result can impact your play significantly. There are also several configuration options you can tinker with.

CONTROL OPTIONS

Several of the control options are simply for adjusting the basic control scheme to your personal tastes, but a few bear special mention for their impact on gameplay.

Look Sensitivity adjusts how fast your reticle moves, as well as you how quickly you can perform a full 360 turn. This is important, as it impacts the speed at which you can respond to a threat on your sides or rear. You can set your sensitivity anywhere from 1 to 10. If you hear a sound behind you with the default sensitivity of 3, you may not be able to turn around in time to respond to the threat. Higher sensitivities allow you to rotate more quickly, and thus scan the battlefield and respond to enemies with greater speed. The downside to a higher sensitivity is a loss of precision—this is most noticeable when attempting to track distant targets with scoped weapons, but it can impact your aim in medium-range firefights as well. It's a good idea to step the sensitivity up to the maximum (generally too fast for normal use), then gradually back it down until you find a level that feels comfortable. Depending on your personal weapon preferences, you may favor a slightly lower or higher sensitivity, since different settings affect each weapon in a slightly different manner. Note that even a sensitivity of 10 is usable if you are gentle with the analog stick—the game does a good job of moderating your aim if you are careful with the stick.

Crouch Behavior seems like a minor setting, as it allows you to toggle between hold to crouch (the default) and toggle crouch (press once to crouch, press again or jump or lunge with a melee weapon to stand up). You should definitely set crouch to toggle—why? Because while crouched, if you move, you are invisible on the Motion Tracker, and holding down the left analog stick while trying to move is awkward at best. It is also possible to adjust your controls specifically for flying vehicles—you can have a separate look inversion set, as well as adjust how the camera tracks you while you are in the air.

CUSTOM CONTROLS

Using a custom control configuration and a non-default sensitivity is *not* necessary for playing *Halo: Reach* well.

If you find yourself playing multiplayer a lot however, you should definitely experiment with the different variations—you may find that a combination of sensitivity and controller configuration simply fits your playstyle better than the default. Please see the manual included with your game or the in game menu for a diagram of the following controller layouts.

DEFAULT CONTROLS

The standard. Comfortable for most FPS veterans, easy to learn for newer players.

SOUTHPAW

A variant for left-handed players.

BOXER

A melee-focused variant, giving you quick access to melee attacks on the left trigger. Enjoy Assassinations? Always fight up close? Give this a try.

GREEN THUMB

Green Thumb swaps the positions of Zoom View and Melee Attack. This is particularly useful if you are fond of scoped weapons—especially the Magnum, DMR, Needle Rifle, and Sniper Rifle. With the new snap-zoom functionality in *Halo: Reach*, you can hold the zoom button to zoom in temporarily, then release it to revert to default zoom. This is most noticeable with the Sniper Rifle, which you can tap once to zoom to 5x, then hold zoom to reach 10x, and then release to revert to 5x. Note that having melee on your right analog stick still works well for regular melee hits, but it can be a bit awkward for jumping melee or Assassinations.

BUMPER JUMPER

Bumper Jumper is a very useful configuration for many situations, because it moves the jump button from Ⓐ (which requires you to remove your thumb from aiming!) to the left bumper, allowing you to jump and aim at the same time. If you use jumping constantly to make yourself a tougher target, or simply bounce around the battlefield often, give Bumper Jumper a shot.

RECON

Recon moves your reload button onto the right bumper, meaning you no longer need to reach over to reload during a fight. The downside is that you lose quick access to melee strikes. Given that melee attacks are used frequently, you may not get a lot of use from this configuration, unless you are a huge fan of weapons that require constant reloading.

WELCOME
UNSC TRAINING
THE CAMPAIGN
FIREFIGHT
MULTIPLAYER
BASICS & TACTICS
ARSENAL
VEHICLES
GAMEPLAY MODES
MAPS
FORGE
REFERENCE

MULTIPLAYER TACTICS

This section covers many of the tactical basics used in virtual combat specific to *Halo: Reach*. Coverage consists of everything from teamwork to sniping, including tips on how to run an offense and how to properly defend an objective or area. The following chapter gives you ideas on how to frustrate your enemy, confuse, distract, and prevail no matter what mode you're playing on or what map is selected. You'll learn how to behave in close quarters combat and what loadouts will provide you with the most advantage. Learn to work together, even with players you don't know, and you'll learn what it feels like to win. Utilizing even the most basic tactics and strategies in *Halo: Reach* can be the deciding factor for your success and your team's success.

TEAMWORK

Playing together with the people on your team is crucial to your survival and victory. Sometimes you'll get on a team with all of your friends and you can all work together, have fun, and win. Sometimes you have to make friends, and quick. Try to establish a leader first. If no one chimes in, take the role yourself. As a leader, you must consider many things including the mode, the map, and terrain, the available enemy resources including weaponry and defenses, and any vehicles or mode–specific actions you may encounter. Enemy player skill also needs to be determined, but you're usually going to have to figure that out on the fly after you are a few rounds in.

Once you've collected all of your intel, start figuring out your roles. Assign players to do whatever they're good at, let them volunteer. Send everyone off to do their part and keep the lines of communication open. Constantly reassess the situation on the battlefield and reallocate troops as necessary. There are going to be occasions that call for sending someone to an area they weren't usually going to go to. Pair players with each other and make them work together toward the team's common goal. Create distractions for teammates when you need to, and sacrifice for the team if the occasion calls for it. Working as a team and giving individual players specific goals will be the key to victory.

Many players choose to do the same thing. If everyone is rushing to get the enemy flag in Capture the Flag, then who's watching YOUR flag? Playing well as a team requires some players to have to do things they wouldn't normally choose to do. If you're going to play any team–based or objective–based modes, you can't all just do what you want. Come up with a duty roster to keep team members focused. You can change it up if you get bored with your position, but as long as everyone does their respective jobs, you and your team can win.

If you're not the leader and no one on your team wants a leader or wants to play as a team, you can still do your part. Pair up with another player and help that person do whatever it is he or she is doing. Usually in team modes, players are willing and want to work together, so you should be able to find at least one player that doesn't mind having you as their wingman.

Be a good team member and volunteer to do the thankless jobs. Stay back to watch your team's flag or bomb. Play a support role such as the medic or a vehicle transport driver or pilot. Showing your team that you're willing to fulfill the roles that no one else wants to fill will earn you their respect and can help strengthen the team overall. Hopefully someone will trade positions with you at some point as well.

Do your best to be part of the team. Sometimes that means leading them, sometimes it means following the other team members, sometimes it's just volunteering to do the things your teammates don't want to do. It depends on how bad you want to win. If you're looking for kills only, go play one of the many free–for–all modes, but you can usually find decent, team-conscious players in objective game types.

Sea Sniper tip

- Melee attacks with the bomb, skull or flag are one-hit kills.

MULTIPLAY

COMMUNICATION

If you've got a mic, use it. Especially in objective–based modes. Getting wrapped up in your game happens to everyone, but keep the lines of communication open. Not only will you succeed in the game, but you might make a few friends along the way. Don't sing or play recordings of movie scenes over the mic. That's the quickest way to make enemies. Relay important information when necessary. Have fun and joke when appropriate, but try to keep the mics clear for your teammates.

In objective–based modes such as Capture the Flag, for instance, you may need to communicate important information to your teammates, such as, "I'm heading back with the flag and I've got two on my back"! Or, if you are defending your team's flag, you may need to let your teammates know that your flag has been stolen and you died. This way, they can fall back to help out. If you find yourself with a nice overview of the map from a high location, you can communicate enemy positions to your teammates. Let them know which areas are being sniped or what routes are open so they can make their approach towards the enemy objective. You can direct traffic from your location by using communication. This isn't really leading the team as much as it is just relaying important information.

If you're driving or piloting a vehicle, you may need intel from your gunners to tell you which way to go, or if you need to stop for a second for your gunner to get a steady shot. You can also help direct your gunner's focus to areas that you might not be able to fire on yourself. Sometimes the communication might be as simple as, "Get out! It's gonna blow up!" You can also devise alternative methods of communication, such as beeping the horn. One beep for enemies ahead, two beeps for enemies on the left, three for enemies on the right. You can use alternative methods of communication when you're not in vehicles as well. You can let your teammates know that when they see the force field go down, that it's time to attack. Experiment with different methods and see what works best for you in different modes or maps. Talk with your team about the most efficient ways to communicate the information you all need.

Plan out your strategies before the game starts. Talk to your teammates and see what players want specific jobs. Have players volunteer for the various positions you require for a specific mode or map. If you know you're playing defense on Assault (on Powerhouse), talk to your team before the round starts to find out who is interested in watching each of the chokepoints. You're going to need to communicate in the heat of battle as well. Do your best to keep the comms short and to the point. Try not to stutter your communication, since mic time is precious. You don't want to try to get your words out while someone else is trying to talk over you. Limit your battle comms to things like "two in the garage" or "sniper on the roof." Try to call out things that will actually help your teammates.

Also, you should concentrate on calling out pertinent information—like the number of enemies and their location. Things like which Armor Abilities you saw enemies use can be helpful, too. For instance, letting your team know that you've got two following you with the flag is good, but letting your teammates know that one of them is running Active Camo helps them even more. Keep it short and sweet. Only communicate what you need to and speak clearly. Pre-plan your attack or defense in the lobby or in a party, and try not to talk over other players. If someone is rambling or misusing the mic, feel free to speak loudly over them to get your information out, but otherwise do your best to wait for the other player to finish, then grab the mic.

Sea Sniper tip

- You can be stopped from completing an Assassination move if someone else attacks you while you're doing it.

OFFENSE

Playing offensively includes team–based modes where one side is specifically set to attack, as well as the multitude of free–for–all style game modes. Being on the offensive side of things doesn't just mean run as fast as you can to the objective and shoot the best you can. You don't always have to rush things. Practice coming up with different techniques and experimenting with options you may never have tried before.

While speed may help you complete your objective on certain maps and in certain modes, it is not the only way to get things done on offense. Situations may require you to be stealthy, strong, smart, or deceptive. You may have to use timing to succeed in your assault, or even provide some defense at the same time. Some modes also require you to play offense and defense at the same time.

For a mode like Assault where your team must acquire and plant the bomb at the enemy's base, you may need to divide your team into parts. Consider putting a good sniper to work if the map layout permits it. While the sniper overlooks your team's path to the enemy plant site, consider what kind of abilities your plant team should have. The bomb carrier will be moving slowly and will become the primary target. Think about having the bomb carrier's squadmates choose abilities such as the Drop Shield and possibly Active Camo. These two abilities can help get your team to the enemy plant site safely and with enough time to plant the bomb. Drop a shield around your carrier if that player is getting pounded, and use your cloaked teammates to sweep around behind enemies trying to melee attack your bomb carrier.

Many times, you may need to set up a multi-tiered offense. This can be done in different ways depending on the mode and the map. Let's say you're playing King of the Hill or a variant of it. You may decide the best offense here is to split your team into two. One team should be designated as the capture team, while the other is on prevention duty. While your capture team goes for the hill, your prevention team should stick together and try to stop the enemy advance before they can disrupt your capture team. Other variations of a multi-tiered offense include sending an initial wave of attackers towards the enemy objective, then following that up with another wave of players. Time your second wave's advance so that as soon as your initial wave is cut in half, you send in the next wave. This can help create a steady flow of attackers streaming toward your objective. If you and your team can be patient and wait until they are supposed to move forward, you can make this tactic work for you.

Sea Sniper tip

- You cannot use any Armor abilities while in possession of an objective such as a flag, bomb, or skull without dropping the objective!

Sometimes, you'll have to split up and move in to objective locations from two different areas and converge simultaneously. This requires good communication and skill to pull off, but can be extremely effective if done correctly. You can even stagger the convergence and have one part of your team move in first, then have the other half move in a few seconds later after the enemy starts to focus on the first team.

However you decide to run your offense, remember that you must complete the objective at hand. Just because you keep getting killed trying to complete your objective doesn't mean you should stop. You just need to reformulate a new plan of attack and come at it from a different perspective.

DEFENSE

Defending can be fun. When you know your team's only objective is to stop the enemy from getting into your base or capturing one of your flags, etc., it doesn't make things necessarily easy, just predictable. When things are predictable, you can have a better plan for what's to come. You'll want to take the map and mode into consideration of course, but don't forget about your Armor Abilities. Some of the best abilities for defending include the Drop Shield, Armor Lock, and Active Camo. The Drop Shield is great to deploy so your teammates can use it to heal or stay protected from long–range enemy fire. The Armor Lock is best for close quarters engagements or if you come across any melee-happy opponents. The Active Camo can be a great tool for defense if used correctly and timed just right. The Hologram isn't usually seen as a tool for defense, but when properly utilized, it can keep enemies at bay and force them to expend ammunition that they were saving for you and your team. When your team has set up camp and is hidden under cover, locate the chokepoints en route to your base, and when enemies start heading your way, fire off your Holograms. Your opponents will assume you are trying to seal the chokepoints, and you may get them to waste their power weapon's ammo on useless targets.

DISTRACTION AND SACRIFICE

Defending isn't all just about camping, campfires, and s'mores. Sometimes defense requires players to actively push forward to defend certain objectives. You may have to stay mobile and continuously relocate to effectively defend your team's objectives. If this is the case, then you may want to select a different Armor Ability such as Sprint or the Jet Pack.

Some defensive situations will include heading out to grab a vehicle and taking it halfway up the map to prevent enemies from crossing the fifty-yard line. You may need to send out infiltrators to the enemy base to be the most effective. It all depends on the map and mode you're playing, so choose your loadouts wisely.

Playing defense requires players to be able to assess the terrain and objectives from both points of view. Locate any and all chokepoints in to your objective's location, and assign players to specific points. This way, there are no avenues of approach that are left unguarded. Too many times you and your team may wonder how someone got in behind you. It was probably because a teammate wasn't watching his/her position or chokepoint. Make sure everyone knows where to watch, and if someone goes down, send in another player to fill in until the original player can get back on the job.

Different objectives may require your team to split up into different groups. In modes such as Invasion, you are tasked with defending two generators at a time. Attackers can succeed by gaining control of either generator location, so they must both be defended. Split your team in half and defend each location to the best of your ability. If you find that one team is getting overrun by the entire other team, send players from the other generator to help out, since you won't need them all at the generator that no one is attacking. Also, keep in mind that once a generator location gets down to a small amount of time left on it, enemies will move for this objective in greater numbers. If you need to add more players to that location to strengthen defense, you should do so.

Just remember to play defense while you're on defense. Too many players want to just run out and get kills when they should be waiting for targets to come to them. Good defense requires patience and communication. Use these tools to your advantage. Since you know that the enemy has to come to you to win, sometimes all you have to do is delay their advance long enough for the timer to run down. Consider all of your options and choose the best defense for all situations.

For the good of the team, you may find yourself as the bait from time to time or to even sacrifice yourself to help complete an objective. Some of these techniques can be employed on offense or defense, and some are side–specific, but all of them can help your team complete the objectives at hand.

Vehicles are one of the biggest distractions in a multiplayer battle. When a Scorpion or a Wraith enters the scene, everyone takes notice. You can use this to your advantage whether on offense or defense. Once you get into a heavy vehicle, head for the area you wish to make a commotion at. Start firing randomly at the direction of the enemy team. While they scramble to see what's going on, let your team know they've been distracted and they can continue to attack, opposite of your location.

If you make enough noise at one location, your team should be able to progress through another. Keep this in mind, and practice with different modes and different contingents of players. You may only need one player to go grab a bomb. Send the rest of your team away from the entrance your potential bomb carrier intends to move in from, and start making noise. Be careful not to expend too much ammo, and try to burst fire your weapons. Ultimately, you want to bring the enemy in to your position and away from the bomb carrier. Once your teammate gets control of the package and starts to retreat, the enemy may catch on to what you're doing and relocate to dispatch the infiltrator.

You can also make this work by reversing the numbers. Try outfitting your team with Active Camo and send one player to distract either the Hologram or the Drop Shield. The Hologram can help virtually add numbers, and the Drop Shield will hopefully draw enemies in close and away from the rest of your team. While this player is keeping the enemy busy, the rest of the team can proceed in force to the objective under the Active Camo ability.

Even though creating distractions can count as a sacrifice, your objective shouldn't be death when you're the one doing the distracting.

Let's create a scenario for a sacrifice in Invasion mode. Your team has the Core. The enemy has just obtained a Scorpion and is heading for your Core carrier. All of your teammates that were escorting the carrier have expended all of their ammunition trying to stop the vehicle. You're piloting a Banshee. There's no time to do another loop to get a good shot on this thing, so what do you do? Head on collision! Ram your Banshee straight into the Scorpion before they can get another shot off on your Core Carrier. This is the kind of thing you'll need to do to sacrifice for the team. All the hard work you put in getting the two sets of generators down and actually getting the Core would be for naught if you didn't sacrifice yourself. Sacrifice can happen at any time, and you have to decide if it's worth it or not to do it. If you manage to grab the Core, and enemies have just respawned and are moving in to engage your carrier, you might need to sacrifice yourself by staying back to fend them off. Sometimes, you need to take yourself out along with your enemies to help your team overall. If an enemy jumps into your vehicle, drive him off a cliff. Try to jump out before you do, but either way, take the foe with you. Maybe you're getting chased by two or more enemies down a hallway and you need to keep them from getting to your objective bearer. If you've got a Rocket Launcher, don't worry about getting hurt, just blast away and go out in a blaze of glory.

SQUADS AND FORMATIONS

The pace of play in *Halo: Reach* isn't always suited for utilizing squad–based movement or specific troop formations. However, in some instances, it can greatly benefit your team if it is employed correctly. Many modes only allow four players per team, but some offer more. Various configurations are described below.

In smaller maps and faster–paced modes, you may be best off moving in two sets of two. Wingman teams can be very effective in *Halo: Reach*, and you should employ them even if your teammate doesn't know you are using these tactics. Setting off by yourself isn't a great idea when you're playing objective–based modes. Grab a buddy and work together to achieve victory. With two teams of two, you can more effectively breach areas that are defended by your opponents. One team can move in from the left while the other moves in from the right. One team can move in first and the other team can move a few seconds later. One team can snipe while the other team hits the ground. There are many options for wingman teams to succeed. You just need to figure out what needs to be done and how best to do it.

For instance, you may need to enforce one team more than another in game modes like Stockpile. Try sending out a team of three to grab flags while you keep just one player back at the base to defend the flags that you've collected. The opposite may need to be done as well, depending on how the enemy team is playing. Of course, you can create many more squad configurations with a larger amount of players on each side. You can try setups such as a four-man offense with a delayed two-man enforcement team. You can run a five-one or a three-three. You can create vehicle teams as well. Use your troops effectively, and you can end up on top.

Squad formations are basically shapes that you mimic with players, kind of like a marching band at a football game spelling out letters. You're not going to be making letter "H's" in *Halo: Reach*, but loose formations can help you on offense. Not so much on defense, since you will be more static than mobile. On offense, you can try to run a chevron formation or basically a triangle. With one player at the top, and one player behind and left, and the other player behind and to the right, you can move as a unit in a triangle formation. This formation is best used when infiltrating enemy bases by showing them a strong united front. If your lead player goes down, the next player in the formation should step up and fill his or her shoes.

Formations also work well with vehicles. You can go about this a few different ways. You can send your smaller scout or anti-personnel vehicles out first and keep your big boys in the back. This lets the little guys take care of the foot traffic, and the big guns take care of the power weapon wielders or other vehicles. You can create air and ground formations as well. If you have your air contingent head out first, your ground vehicles should follow and focus on enemies targeting your air group. If your ground vehicles head out first, your air team can help assist them if they get into trouble. Try spreading out your entire ground team in a line to create an impenetrable barrier. You can also mix and match formations. Use a Scorpion as the tip of the spear. The rest of your team should follow it closely on foot and stay out of sight. When trouble erupts, you can all move out from behind the tank and surprise the enemy with a much larger force than they anticipated. Try utilizing the Hologram Armor Ability here to send out what looks like even more players.

Sea Sniper tip

- Invasion modes will let you spawn on your teammates.

Sea Sniper tip

- The Hologram can use the Gravity Lifts.

SPARTAN/ELITE DIFFERENCES

While Elites are only available for play in a few game modes, there are some differences that are worth noting. On a basic level, Spartans are taller, move slightly faster, jump higher, and have a different physical profile (affecting your aim when going for headshots).

More specifically, Spartan and Elites have different Shield and Health profiles.

Spartan Shields recharge 6 seconds after taking damage. They regenerate fully in 3 seconds.

Spartan Health regenerates in thirds (ie, it will regenerate no more than a 'section' of three health blocks).

Spartan Health regenerates 4 seconds after taking damage, and takes 5 seconds to regenerate. The first third of health will regenerate more quickly than the last two.

Elite Shields recharge 4 seconds after taking damage. They regenerate fully in 4 seconds.

Elite Health regenerates fully, beginning its regeneration quickly, ending slowly.

Elite Health takes 16 seconds to fully regenerate.

MULTIPLAYER

COMBAT STYLES

The two basic combat styles are close quarters combat and open ground fighting. Close quarters combat is more easily described as fighting indoors with minimal engagement distances. Close quarters fighting CAN happen outdoors such as in a forest or canyon. Open ground fighting is just that, fighting out in the open with minimal cover across large areas.

Close quarters combat requires a little patience and a lot of firepower. You'll want to bring weapons like the Shotgun, the Gravity Hammer, or the Energy Sword. The Assault Rifle works well at close range too, and it's also more accurate at shorter distances. Whichever weapons you decide to bring along, think about loading out with the Armor Lock ability for this type of battle. Since you're usually going to either be surprised by an enemy rounding a corner or you'll be the one doing the surprising, the Armor Lock can give you the time to regroup and figure out what your next move should be. It also gives your team more time and an opening to deal with your opponent. If you get the EMP blast to go off and damage the enemy from your Armor Lock, if you're in close enough quarters, the blast may be magnified by the walls, floor, and ceiling.

When you engage in close quarters battles, the object is usually to clear areas like rooms and hallways. When entering a room with a team, designate a player to go in and clear left, and another to clear right. The rest can move in through the middle, but also make sure to check up and down if the room is laid out that way. You'll have to form this up quickly to make it happen, but once you and your team gets used to it, you can use it much more quickly the next time you need to breach and clear a room. There are other ways to make sure a room is clear. Stack your team up outside the entrance to your target and have a couple of players toss grenades inside. Your team should go in after they explode and clear the room as described above. You can also use Rocket Launchers and Grenade Launchers for this job. The Concussion Rifle makes a nice doorknocker too, if it's available.

Close quarters combat requires quick reflexes. You have to be sure to clear any and all areas before you proceed, but you must do it quickly. It's a good idea to get used to peeking through a doorway then backing out to see if an enemy fires on your position. If this happens, you can rethink your plan or move in with this new information in mind. Be ready to shoot every time you round a corner. The first time you aren't ready is the first time someone will shoot you instead.

Open ground battles are the complete opposite. For this style of game play, you're going to want to bring weapons like the Sniper Rifle, the DMR, the Needle Rifle, or even the Focus Rifle. Many of the other weapons will work as well, including the Magnum to a certain point, but it is important to think about your Armor Abilities as well. You should load out with abilities like Sprint, Active Camo, Drop Shield, and sometimes the Hologram, if applicable. Being able to Sprint from cover to cover over large open areas is a great ability to use instantly. The Active Camo can keep you almost invisible to enemy snipers, as long as you limit your movement out in the open. The Drop Shield can be a great asset to your whole team. If you are moving as a single unit across open ground, have your lead player drop a shield when you come under fire. Everyone in the group can tuck in under it, heal up, then scatter once the shield goes down and they've located the threat. Remember that the shield can be taken down and it won't last forever, so locate your enemies quickly and be ready to fire when the shield drops. Sometimes the Hologram can be your best friend, even if you don't treat this false image all that well. Get set up with some scoped weaponry, and wait for your opponents to fire on your loyal Hologram soldiers. Take them out, regroup, and get as far up the map as you can before they respawn. You may have to repeat this process more than once depending on the size of the map and where exactly you need to go.

If you're set up to snipe with your team, you can get good results if you have everyone target the same enemy at the same time. This can take foes down much more quickly. You'll need to have great communication in these types of battles, constantly letting your team know where enemies are hiding and shooting from.

You can, and should, also use vehicles to traverse large open areas, but if you cannot, use the techniques above to thin out your enemy and move up. This kind of war requires you to be accurate, patient, and smart. Put it all together with a good team, and you can succeed here instead of just continuing to run to your death by the hands of snipers.

Sea Sniper tip

- The Armor Lock ability will heavily damage vehicles if they make contact with it at high speed.

RUNNING AND GUNNING

The act of gunning whilst running. You're going to have to do it eventually if you don't do it already. This is less of a tactic and more of a technique. This style of play has players constantly on the move, highly mobile at all times, and loaded to the gills with heavy weaponry. Always looking for a power weapon and always looking for a fight.

Run and gunners are a different breed. They don't stop moving, and they hate to wait for the three–second respawn timer. Run and gunners look for battles, not objectives. They want to kill, not complete the mission. In the various free–for–all game types available in *Halo: Reach*, that's exactly what you NEED to do. In team–based objective modes, it only goes so far.

You'll almost always have one of these guys on your team, so use them to your advantage. If they can get around behind enemy lines, they can disrupt the enemy from the rear, allowing your team easier access through the front. Try to time your assault with theirs, and move in when they start blowing everything apart!

If you're running and gunning, get some practice with the Assault Rifle. While you should always be on the lookout for power weapons, if you're going to be running around a lot, you won't have much time to find a new gun. Aim for the head of your enemies. Aim for the head of your foes with every round you've got, then throw a grenade at them and melee them in the face. If that doesn't finish them off, your teammate can come in and kill them with one shot. Of course, you should choose something like the Scout or Assault class for this style of gameplay, but you should also grab a melee weapon as soon as you can find one. As a mobile unit, you should be fighting your way to and from power weapon locations, not just to acquire them for yourself, but to ensure you get into a fight. The melee weapons are always sought after. Find one of these, and you'll find yourself a fight. If you manage to get one for yourself, use it on as many players as you can before you die. You don't want it to go to waste! The Armor Lock ability combined with running and gunning can be a double threat. You can get into a fight with someone up close, deal some damage, then engage the lock. Let it go, melee your foe, then re-engage lock. End program, begin loop until dead. This ability also fires off an EMP burst right before its cycle is complete. This can be of great use to you if you can throw yourself into a group of enemies in a tight area. The blast can hit them all at the same time. You don't have to run and gun all by yourself all the time either. A team full of these players can be an imposing force. If you find yourself up against such a threat, be patient and wait for them to come to you. They will come. Set traps, go invisible, stock up on grenades. Run and gunners are also unpredictable and they should be. Changing up the attack each time keeps opponents guessing and at a disadvantage.

Sea Sniper tip

- In Capture the Flag, throw the flag ahead of you then pick it back up to move it more quickly.

SNIPING

Long–range rifle work can effectively increase your odds in almost any game mode. Sniping is an art form. Not only do you need to be accurate and quick on the trigger, but you have to be able to get to your weapon and outsmart your enemies. Knowing when and where to relocate will also be a part of the equation in your sniping formula. Sniping isn't necessarily done only with the Sniper Rifle. You can use other weapons such as the DMR, the Needle Rifle, the Focus Rifle, and to a lesser extent, the Magnum. Shooting long distances with the Magnum can be difficult, but it is powerful and can help you pin down an area if you happen to be without a real scoped weapon. This isn't the gun you want for sniping, but it can be used for medium–range engagements if necessary.

The DMR is a good gun to snipe with, and many players will use it quite a bit. It doesn't offer the additional zoom of a Sniper Rifle or the power, but it can get the job done and done well. As a replacement for the actual Sniper Rifle, the DMR surpasses it in rounds per magazine, but again, not in power. It's going to take you a few more shots with the DMR to drop someone's shield and finish that player off. If you've got a Needle Rifle, you may not have the same power as the DMR, but you will get less recoil from firing the weapon. This lets you put more follow up shots on a target more quickly. The minimal to no recoil feature of this gun is countered by its power. It takes a few more shards to drop someone compared to the DMR.

The Sniper Rifle is the obvious choice for sniping duty. It has the zoom capability that you need and the power that you crave. However, it does not have many rounds in the magazine, so you have to make sure you hit your mark. Practice getting the feel of the weapon. Shoot it from close, medium, and great distances to see how it handles.

Once you know how to shoot it, you can practice some sniper techniques. Of course, choose whatever Armor Abilities will benefit you the most in each situation, but choose your location wisely. There are several "spots" that snipers will always move to. Usually these are good spots. The problem is that everyone else will be looking for people to be there, including other snipers. Try to choose a location that you haven't seen other enemies frequent. When you find a good spot, you can hang there for a little while, but once someone gets an eye on you, that's it, you're going to need to relocate. You can look for elevated areas and Sniper Rifle spawn locations to grab additional ammo without having to go too far. Always consider what you look like from an enemy's point of view. You may not realize you're a dark spot on a light wall. Always check your surroundings

Practice sniping without being zoomed in all of the time. Many times you're able to melee snipers because they aren't looking at you. They're looking through their scopes or not watching their back. You need to occasionally watch behind you or put your back to a wall. Try finding targets without being scoped in, then quick zoom in when you spot someone and fire. This allows you a much wider field of view and the ability to acquire more targets more quickly.

WEAPON ACCURACY

The crosshair at the center of the screen gives you useful information about the accuracy profile of any weapon you are using.

The first shot fired by any weapon will always fall within the reticule marker, meaning that first shots are always fully accurate, and each shot fired causes 'bloom' on the reticule, increasing inaccuracy, until you stop firing and the accuracy resets.

Crouching will slightly increase the accuracy profile of a weapon, and zooming increases the accuracy by a factor of the zoom amount[md]meaning that high zoom weapons are very precise, and that scoped shots are *always* more accurate than 'hip fired' shots.

The reticule is also useful as an indicator of a weapon ready (after you switch, pick up, reload, or fire a weapon), which can be useful for perfectly timing Sniper Rifle shots.

The reticule will also turn red within the 'effective' range of a weapon when aimed at another player. This doesn't mean that you can't use the weapon outside the red reticule range, only that it is generally more effective within that range band.

All Sniper class weaponry that can perform headshots will also get a small red dot in the center of the crosshair when you are targeting a 'headshot' area on another player. This doesn't guarantee a hit, it's just another useful piece of HUD information.

CAMPING

Camping doesn't always mean defending. Many times, you'll find yourself out and about but you need to settle down for a moment to rack up kills. Sometimes, you may need to camp a spawn or an objective. This isn't defending, this is camping. Yes, you may have to camp to defend, but not necessarily, and vice versa. It's not a bad thing; you're going to have to do it at some point just to survive. You may have just gotten into a battle that has drained your health and you need to recuperate. You duck under a set of stairs to heal, but enemies continue to pass by you, and you start picking them off with your Shotgun. Is that camping? Yep.

A very effective tactic is if you camp an enemy's spawn points or their flag drop on a mode such as Stockpile. Everything's fair in love and war. Think about running the Active Camo if you plan on occasionally camping. You never know when you're going to be able to get into an area where you can set up shop. The Active Camo can be a great asset in these situations. Try to save it up for the times when you're going to really need it.

Certain maps provide players with good locations to camp. Swordbase, for instance, has many rooms and levels that you and your teammates can commandeer and control. Set up a player to watch each entrance to your locale and fend off enemy through traffic. This isn't really defending in modes like Team Slayer, it's just camping. It can be used very tactically if used tactfully.

You can camp power weapon spawn points, too. Once you figure out where the good weapons are respawning, grab one for yourself and wait for the next poor sap who comes looking for it. You can also set traps here with things like the Grenade Launcher. Fire off a can near the power weapon spawn point and keep the trigger held down. When someone goes to pick it up, let them have it. You can also try camping things like vehicles, since players will always look to acquire them. Make sure you get a weapon that will put the player down in one shot, since you don't want them to get into the vehicle, turn, and waste you. Grab something like the Rocket Launcher for this type of job.

Of course, you can and should camp on defense, but don't always sit in the same places that everyone else does. This is the quickest way to get killed first, then wonder how they knew you were there. They know you're there because everybody goes there! Find a nice out-of-the-way location where players don't normally look for campers, plug in your Active Camo, and wait for the fish to bite.

Sea Sniper tip

- Throw grenades into Gravity Lifts to punish players camping them.

MULTIPLAYER ARSENAL

One of the most crucial steps to learning how to fight effectively online in *Halo: Reach* is learning how to use your arsenal.

This chapter is designed to give you solid instruction on all of the weapons of war available to you, UNSC or Covenant, close ranged or long, all of the lethal tools are covered in detail. In addition, this section covers each of the Armor Abilities that you can equip and gives you advice and ideas for making the most of your newfound powers.

WEAPON BASICS

AMMUNITION

Most *Halo: Reach* weaponry is sharply ammunition limited. With some exceptions (the general, all-purpose weaponry), most weapons in the game have enough ammunition to last only a few firefights before you must either find more ammo or switch to a different weapon. Because of this, any power weapons that you manage to acquire should be quickly utilized, since you don't want to fall in battle and let enemy troops use your remaining heavy ordnance against you! Ammo management is also often a crucial factor *during* a fight because many weapons have limited magazine size or overheating limits that prevent you from firing continuously if you are inaccurate.

RESPAWNING

With few exceptions, weapons in multiplayer maps (*especially* power weapons) will not respawn until they have been used up or discarded. More general purpose weaponry like DMRs, Needle Rifles, Plasma Pistols, and Repeaters often have higher weapon limits, so they may respawn fairly quickly even if several are in player hands, but any stronger weapon is almost always an exclusive (and slow) respawn.

As a result, it is *vital* that you make a beeline for any power weapons on the map, or at least get into a position where you can ambush anyone on the other team who does race for the power weapons.

Securing and locking down power weapons gives your team a marked advantage in any game mode, and holding the power weapons has another advantage—if you know when a weapon was picked up and used up, you know roughly when it will respawn, meaning you can go back to that position to pick it up or intercept anyone else in the area before it actually reappears. Take a look at the weapon respawn times chart (at the end of this chapter) for a quick overview of average weapon times. Remember, weapon respawn times (and the number of instances a given weapon can have on a map at once) are all set per map, individually. As a result, if you want to check the exact times for a given map and mode, start up Forge and go take a look at the weapons!

For the most part, respawn times are exactly what you would expect—

GRENADES

Frag and Plasma Grenades are special purpose tools that every player can take advantage of. Any player can carry up to two Frag and two Plasma Grenades and freely switch between them. In many modes, you begin with one of each, though some modes start you with two Frag or two Plasma 'nades instead.

For both grenade types, be very careful about using them *during* a firefight with another player. The time that it takes to wind up and throw the grenade is easily enough time for someone to kill you and simply move away from the blast. It's almost always a better idea to throw a grenade either just before or after you engage in direct battle, or when you deliberately duck out of sight to reload, using the grenade to cover you.

FRAG GRENADES

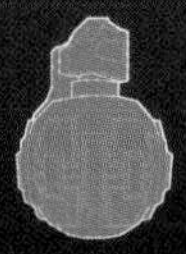

Frag Grenades are generally more common than Plasma Grenades, they inflict slightly less radius damage, and they can be thrown farther. These weapons are ideal for flushing an enemy out of a closed area, defending yourself while you are retreating, or for knocking over lighter vehicles.

A single Frag rarely kills an enemy on its own, but it can be used to effectively soften an enemy or finish them off if they have already been damaged. In short, Frag Grenades inflict more radial damage than Plasma

PLASMA GRENADES

Plasma Grenades have a different throwing arc than Frag Grenades, and cannot be tossed quite as far, nor do they bounce in the same manner. In exchange, Plasma Grenades have two advantages: they inflict significantly more damage, and they can stick to any player or vehicle that they directly impact. Sticking a player guarantees a kill in most situations (though they can be Armor Locked off), and sticking a vehicle deals heavy damage to it.

Otherwise, Plasma Grenades should be used in the same manner as Frags, to flush out an enemy in cover or an enclosed room, cover yourself when you retreat from an undesirable battle, or give you time to reload. Plasma Grenades can also be used to knock vehicles around in the same manner as Frags, but if possible, you should aim for sticks against vehicles, since these attacks deal very heavy damage.

MELEE

All players always have access to a melee strike with any carried weapon. Though there are many animations, all melee strikes have the same properties, with the only exceptions being the actual melee weapons, the Gravity Hammer and Energy Sword. For "normal" melee swings, they always deal the same damage—one hit will crack a target's shields *regardless of how much shield strength was remaining*, and one hit on a shield-less target is fatal. Again, even if a player only has a sliver of shielding left, a melee strike will *not* kill or damage the player. It will only drop his or her shield.

If you hit a player from behind, even if shielded, he or she is killed instantly. It is also possible to perform an Assassination from behind by holding the melee button. However, outside style points (and a medal), Assassinations are *always* riskier than simply performing a quick rear execution on a target. The Assassination animations are lengthy, can be interrupted by enemy teammates, and leave you open to any nearby enemies while you are performing the kill. Of course, if that sniper has really been annoying you and you just snuck up on him...

Using melee in combination with close range weaponry or during a close range firefight is an important skill to master, but you need to develop a feel for the right time to use melee.

When you are just starting out and learning, don't be surprised to either lose or tie many melee battles until you have a good sense for exactly when you will crack your opponent's shields and score a clean one hit kill. Getting into melee range fighting is always a risky proposition. Even when you have the timing down cold, it is still dangerous to get into melee battles—both because of the melee clashing system and because you are likely to come out of a melee range battle with no shields, and possibly some health damage—easy pickings for other enemies.

Typically, the best ways to make use of melee is either a) quick rear insta-kills, or b) when you have ambushed an enemy and can drop their shield and melee kill them before they can break your shield or damage you significantly.

Remember that there is a slight delay after performing a melee strike before you can swing again (even longer when performing a lunge with the Gravity Hammer or Energy Sword), so it is quite possible to be killed by an enemy before you can finish off a player with a second melee swing. Note that charging into melee range against a backpedaling opponent that is firing at you is usually *not* a good idea.

WEAPON COMBINATIONS

You can carry two weapons with you at all times in almost all game modes (a few modes restrict weapon usage, but these modes are special cases). In some game modes, you begin with a primary weapon and a sidearm of some sort, whereas in others you only begin with a primary weapon.

As a result, you should always try to carry around a pair of complementary weapons. This can be a close range and a long range weapon, a power weapon and an all-rounder, a shield breaker and a finisher, or simply two weapons that you are most comfortable using.

Remember that no matter what weapon you start with, you can always pick up and use any weapon, UNSC or Covenant, even in modes where you are playing as a Spartan or an Elite. Want to use a DMR as an Elite? Find one and take it, or take out a Spartan and pick it up!

HUMAN AND COVENANT WEAPONRY

While there are too many differences between individual weapons to give really broad generalizations about UNSC and Covenant weaponry, there are some distinct quirks that do tend to hold true across most of their weapons. First, almost all UNSC weaponry uses magazines and must reload frequently. Second, UNSC weaponry typically deals better health damage and worse shield damage. Covenant weapons, on the other hand, are often powered by plasma batteries, and do not have to be reloaded, though they must often deal with heat management, which can still limit your overall rate of fire. Many Covenant weapons are also ideal for stripping shields, and somewhat less effective at dealing health damage.

WEAPON TAGS

We've given each of the weapons in the game a handful of "tags," so that you can quickly identify the unique properties of each weapon.

INSTANT HIT

Instant Hit weapons impact their target the instant the trigger is pulled. This makes these weapons just as useful at medium or long range as they are up close. Typically, instant hit weaponry is either less useful or completely useless for indirect fire attacks around corners or over cover.

PROJECTILE

Projectile weapons must travel to reach their target, which means they can be dodged and are much less useful as the distance to your target increases. These weapons typically make up for this deficiency by having special tracking abilities or explosive splash damage, giving them the ability to hit targets that instant hit weaponry could not.

EXPLOSIVE

Explosive weapons deal splash damage in a radius—this means that even a near miss can be lethal, and they excel against multiple targets clustered together in an area.

ANTI-VEHICLE

Anti-Vehicle weapons are especially good for fighting vehicles, either because they can outright destroy them with high damage, or they are otherwise disruptive or highly damaging against vehicles.

EMP

EMP weaponry is great for destroying shields, and also has the special ability

SCOPED

Scoped weaponry is particularly useful for fighting enemies at medium to long range; however, a few weapons have scopes that cannot fire while zoomed in.

SNIPER

Sniper is a term devoted to a class of weapons. It refers to more than just the UNSC Sniper Rifle, indicating several traits that are unique to sniper style weapons. Specifically: one unshielded headshot with a sniper weapon is instantly lethal. Sniper style weapons also have the unique ability to detonate grenades on the ground with a direct hit.

SHIELD BREAKER

Shield Breaker weapons deal high damage against player shielding, either destroying it instantly or taking it down exceptionally quickly.

POWER

Power weapons are highly dangerous weapons that you should always prioritize as key targets for collection on any map where they spawn. Power weapons are often lethal in one or two shots, or have other attributes that make them very dangerous in your hands or the hands of an enemy!

AUTOMATIC/SEMI AUTOMATIC

Some weapons can be used in a rapid-fire mode by holding down the trigger, while others require to you to fire each shot manually.

RARE WEAPONRY

The Fuel Rod Gun, Plasma Rifle, Spike Rifle, and Spartan Laser are either exceptionally rare or nonexistent in the shipping maps for *Halo: Reach* multiplayer. However, they are fully accessible in Forge (and of course, in Firefight and the Campaign), and we fully expect to see them show up in future content and custom maps.

Just a heads up in case you're wondering why you can't find a Spike Rifle or Plasma Rifle while running around the maps that launch with the game!

UNSC WEAPONRY

ASSAULT RIFLE

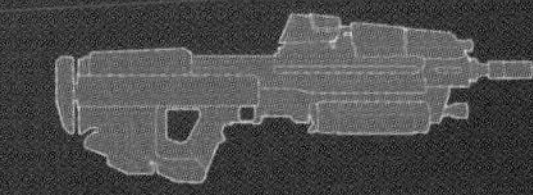

MAGAZINE SIZE: 32
MAXIMUM SPARE AMMO: 288
SHOTS TO KILL: 19
SCOPED, AUTOMATIC
SHOTS TO BREAK SHIELDS: 12
HEALTH DAMAGE PER SHOT: LOW

The default weapon issued in many game modes, the Assault Rifle is a reliable weapon for close to close-medium range fighting. Unfortunately, its severe ammo limitations mean that it is not an ideal weapon for sustained combat against multiple enemies, or for fighting enemies at greater range.

At close range, you can either strip the shields of a target and attempt a melee strike (if you are at very close range), or simply continue firing until they drop.

Because the Assault Rifle is the default weapon, be very wary of engaging in Assault Rifle duels with other players—against a roughly equally skilled player, at *best*, you can expect to come out with your shields stripped and a good chunk of your health gone.

If you manage to get the drop on another freshly spawned player, don't hesitate to unload your Assault Rifle magazine into the back of your opponent's head and finish your foe off with a melee strike (if close) or continuous shots (at a distance).

Keep in mind that it takes about 19 shots to kill an undamaged target, which is roughly two thirds of your full magazine. And that's assuming that every shot hits. In practice, at a distance, it often takes nearly your entire magazine, or, frequently, your entire magazine will leave them with nearly no health and time to duck away from you (or worse, for another player to swoop in for the kill).

This damage deficiency at a distance is exacerbated by the limited ammunition that you spawn with. Typically, you have *one* extra magazine of ammunition on spawn, and even two near-miss encounters can deplete your ammunition.

The end result of this should be for you to seek out a new weapon as quickly as possible after you spawn—ideally without engaging an opponent along the way. This isn't always possible, but you should make it a priority.

If you do find yourself in an Assault Rifle vs Assault Rifle fight, remember that it is fairly easy to back off, get behind some cover, and protect your retreat with a grenade. By the time your opponent can catch up, you should have acquired another weapon.

A few other points: one, the Assault Rifle is fairly accurate at medium range if you burst fire—but the rate of damage output is so poor that your target can very easily seek cover, and two, you can often load up on Assault Rifle ammunition from picking up the leftovers from other freshly spawned duels. This can solve the ammo problem, but not the reloading problem.

The Assault Rifle is useful for one specific task at longer ranges: you can knock a player out of his/her scoped view fairly easily. This is particularly useful if you are being targeted by a sniper and don't have any cover in easy reach. Fire in very short bursts, and if even one bullet connects, you will stop your foe's sniping for at least a moment—often enough time to find cover.

BINARY TRANSLATION

Translate the binary code 01000100011000010111011001100101 in the bottom left of the scope with the Assault Rifle and it reads "Dave," as in Dave Candland, UI designer for Bungie!

DMR

MAGAZINE SIZE: 15
SHOTS TO BREAK SHIELDS: 4
MAXIMUM SPARE AMMO: 60
HEALTH DAMAGE: MODERATE
SHOTS TO KILL: 7
SNIPER, SCOPED, SEMI-AUTOMATIC, INSTANT HIT

An accurate semi-automatic rifle, the Designated Marksman Rifle is ideal for picking off targets at close-medium to medium-long ranges.

With a quick trigger finger and good headhunting aim, you can take down targets at close range reasonably quickly, but you will lose fights against opponents armed with more appropriate close-range weapons. At moderate ranges while scoped, you can hit your target accurately even while firing as quickly as possible, but at longer ranges, you should limit your firing speed to compensate for the increased inaccuracy at a distance.The DMR is a good weapon choice on any map where medium to long range encounters are common. On smaller maps, you may want to consider other options for your primary weapon. Several modes actually focus on the DMR (and other sniper style weapons), so if you want to improve your headshot and long range accuracy, spend some time playing SWAT, Slayer Pro, or Headhunter Pro. The DMR is able to kill a target with a single headshot if your target's shields are down. So, you should always be aiming for your opponent's head when their shields are down, unless you are shooting at such a distance that you might miss the shot entirely.

This also means that you have a few aiming options at closer ranges—you can aim for the head the entire time while you drop your target's shields, and try for an instant follow up headshot, or you can aim for four body shots to crack your target's shields, then aim up for the headshot. Either method works, but the first requires steadier aim to ensure that you don't miss a critical shield hit while firing the first four rounds. Be careful about getting into close-range scraps with the DMR. If you get the jump on your opponent, you may be able to finish your target off before any reprisal, but in an even battle up close, you're looking at an uncertain outcome based on your opponent's weapon.

GRENADE LAUNCHER

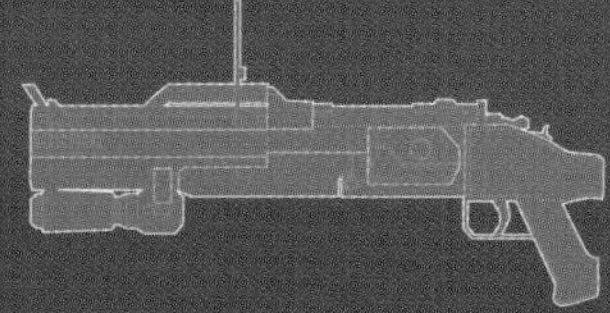

MAGAZINE SIZE: 1
MAXIMUM SPARE AMMO: 15
SHOTS TO KILL: VARIABLE, ONE ON DIRECT HIT
SHOTS TO BREAK SHIELDS: VARIABLE, ONE ON DIRECT HIT
HEALTH DAMAGE: VARIABLE, OFTEN LETHAL
PROJECTILE, EXPLOSIVE, ANTI-VEHICLE, EMP, SHIELD BREAKER, SEMI AUTOMATIC

The Grenade Launcher is a powerful and versatile weapon, but it has a sharply limited ammunition supply and a relatively low effective range.

The Grenade Launcher is a multi-purpose weapon, since it can be fired in two ways—a tap of the trigger launches the grenades in automatic mode, and they will bounce around and detonate on contact with an enemy, vehicle, or after enough time has elapsed.

However, if you hold the trigger, the grenade is launched in manual EMP mode. In this mode, the grenades still detonate if they contact an enemy or vehicle, but otherwise, as long as you hold the trigger, they remain un-detonated.

This has two important implications: the first, and more critical, is that you can airburst the grenades to create an instant EMP. This is ideal for stopping a vehicle or stripping enemy shields (or, if well placed, stripping multiple target's shields).

The second is that you can hold a grenade as an explosive trap—use this to mine a vehicle approach, cover a door or hallway, cover an objective, or set a trap for a pursuer. While holding a charge, you can still throw regular grenades to threaten (or attract) enemies.

Note that the radius of the EMP is *larger* than that of the grenade explosion itself, so against other players, it is a good idea to aim for a near-miss EMP airburst, since you have a good chance of stripping some or all of their shields in one shot, allowing you to switch weapons and finish the job.

However, the Grenade Launcher is *not* ideal for taking out other players—while it is a lethal weapon if it scores a direct hit, doing so against an alert, mobile target is difficult at best. Carry a secondary weapon and use the combination of the two weapons to win your battles. This also has the added benefit of saving your ammunition, which is important when the EMP grenades are one of the more useful anti-vehicle weapons in the game.

Note that the EMP from the grenades will *not* kill a player—in fact, it won't even harm him or her. The grenade explosion itself *will*, but if you're airbursting a lot of grenades near your target and wondering why he or she isn't falling, that's the reason.

Grenade "traps" *can* be detonated by Sniper class weaponry, but you can expect this to be a rare occurrence—an enemy would have to spot you placing the trap, have the right weapon, and have the time and presence of mind to target your grenade. On the other hand, if you are alert to the possibility, you can make a trap harmless, or possibly even cause a very amusing backfire...

MAGNUM

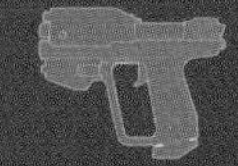

MAGAZINE SIZE: 8
SHOTS TO BREAK SHIELDS: 4
MAXIMUM SPARE AMMO: 40
HEALTH DAMAGE: MODERATE
SHOTS TO KILL: 7
INSTANT HIT, SCOPED, SNIPER, SEMI AUTOMATIC

The Magnum is, in many ways, an excellent close to medium ranged weapon. It has the same overall damage profile as the DMR, but it actually fires *faster*, meaning it has a higher potential damage output—at close ranges. On the downside, the Magnum has much less accuracy after the first shot, has less scope zoom (2x compared to the DMR's 3x), and has a smaller magazine. The Magnum is nevertheless still an excellent secondary weapon, and in a pinch can be used in a close range firefight to finish an opponent quickly.

The Magnum works very well with a shield-stripping Covenant weapon, since you can crack your target's shields and finish him with a single well placed shot to the head or several rapid body shots. If you're going for distance shots, moderate your rate of fire carefully—unlike the DMR or Needle Rifle, even a single shot causes significant accuracy penalties, so carefully lining up each shot is a must. The Magnum takes four shots to break shields, then three to kill, or one headshot.

ROCKET LAUNCHER

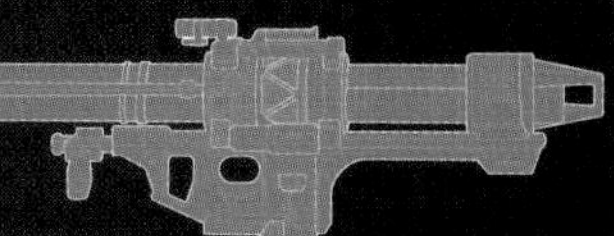

MAGAZINE SIZE: 2
SHOTS TO BREAK SHIELDS: 1
MAXIMUM SPARE AMMO: 6
HEALTH DAMAGE: LETHAL
SHOTS TO KILL: 1
PROJECTILE, EXPLOSIVE, ANTI-VEHICLE, SCOPED, POWER, SEMI AUTOMATIC

The Rocket Launcher is a serious, heavy duty power weapon. One shot anywhere in the vicinity of another player creates a kill, and one clean shot can easily take out smaller vehicles.

The Rocket Launcher has a few (significant) downsides to balance its power: it has sharply limited ammunition, a long respawn time, relatively slow projectile speed at greater distances, and a very large blast radius, making it a dangerous weapon to use in close quarters. If you can catch another player in the open at medium range while armed with a Rocket Launcher, or if you know that a group of players is defending an area, the Rocket Launcher can win the fight almost for free.

On the other hand, if your target is at long distance, or you know you may be forced into a melee range fight, put your Rocket Launcher away—in those situations, it's either a waste of ammunition, or potentially fatal to yourself.

The Rocket Launcher has another perk against vehicles—it locks onto the Banshee and Falcon, and while both can potentially evade your shots, if they don't swiftly maneuver away, you will take them down with ease.

Because the Rocket Launcher is so strong, it's advisable to quickly use up its ammunition supply and grab a different weapon—whenever possible, you don't want to hand your enemies a Rocket Launcher. If there is a specific vehicle that you *must* take down, or a chokepoint or defense that your team is having trouble breaking, bring the Rocket Launcher along, but otherwise, be careful about holding on to it—your insurance policy can easily backfire.

SHOTGUN

MAGAZINE SIZE: 6
MAXIMUM SPARE AMMO: 30
SHOTS TO KILL: 1-3
INSTANT HIT, SEMI AUTOMATIC
SHOTS TO BREAK SHIELDS: 1-3
HEALTH DAMAGE: HIGH

The Shotgun is, as you might expect, a close-range powerhouse. It is also *extremely* range limited—outside of close-range firefights, it is completely ineffective. Consequently, the Shotgun is best used in situations (and on maps) where close quarters fighting is inevitable. If you can force a close-range engagement, even on a larger, more open map, the Shotgun is a very useful tool, but if the majority of the map is open ground, or if your enemies have little incentive to get into close-range fights with you, skip the Shotgun.

Some good methods to force an engagement are to bait a nearby enemy into following you: send a Hologram down a hall behind you to lure your opponent with the motion tracker, carry a Flag or Bomb into a narrow area, or shoot at a player at medium range and then duck behind cover. You can also make good use of the Shotgun if you know that *you* have to get into a close-range fight with your target. Enemies on a Territory, a protected Flag carrier, or simply a smaller map that has a lot of close-range fighting: any of these situations are ripe for Shotgun use.

Keep in mind that the Shotgun is poor at a distance, so if there is any on-approach fighting before you get into lethal range; it's preferable to use almost any other weapon to deal damage, so that the Shotgun can finish the job.

The Shotgun *can* one-hit kill a fully shielded player, but only at near point blank melee range. At the range where your crosshair first turns red, you still only deal about three quarters of their shield in damage. At max red reticle range, you can expect it to take about three shots to kill a player, but if you can strip his or her shields, you can cut that down to one or two shots. Only at point blank distances can you get that one shot kill from the Shotgun.

Soften up your targets with grenades and other weaponry if you're closing in to finish the job with the Shotgun, and save the Shotgun as a primary weapon for situations where you *know* you will be engaging your opponents at ultra-short ranges.

SNIPER RIFLE

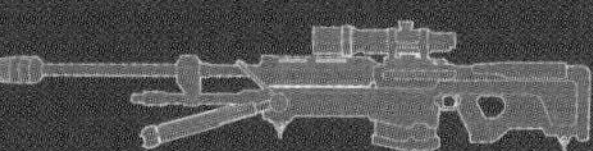

MAGAZINE SIZE: 4
MAXIMUM SPARE AMMO: 20
SHOTS TO KILL: 1 HEADSHOT, 2 BODY SHOTS
INSTANT HIT, SCOPED, SNIPER, POWER, SEMI AUTOMATIC
SHOTS TO BREAK SHIELDS: 1
HEALTH DAMAGE: FULL HEALTH

Another high-powered weapon, the Sniper Rifle is exactly what you'd expect—lethal at long ranges, dangerous at medium, and less effective at close ranges (though still potentially dangerous).

The Sniper Rifle has several powerful attributes—it has a reasonable rate of fire, can kill in a single headshot regardless of shielding levels, strips shields in a single hit, and (depending on your aim) proves effective even at close range. It also has two levels of zoom, making it useful for medium and long range sniping, something that the other sniper class weapons cannot do. It also has a fairly generous ammo supply, given its power, so grabbing this gun should be a high priority on almost any map that it is present on.

When fighting *against* a Sniper Rifle, quickly seeking hard cover should be your first reaction to a shot, hit or miss. If you are shot in the head, there's nothing you can do, but a near miss or a body hit gives you just enough time to get behind nearby cover. Pay attention to the tracer from the sniper shot and the distinctive firing sound, since both can give you the information to identify the location of the shooter.

Remember that a single hit from any weapon disrupts zoom, so if your sniper opponent is at a range where you suspect he or she is scoping to try to hit you, any other sniper class weapon can be used to hit your opponent out of zoom. The DMR, Needle Rifle, or possibly Magnum can be used to distract the sniper long enough to get to a safer position, and then close the distance or escape in one piece.

One other point—even if you don't consider yourself an especially effective sniper, you should still grab this weapon on any map where you can make use of it at long ranges. At greater distances, very few other weapons can retaliate effectively against the Sniper Rifle, which means you can take your time trying to pick off targets—even if you only knock the shields off of several players, you can still influence the behavior of the other team members and potentially assist your teammates fighting near them.

Players hate getting sniped, so they tend to go after a long-range sniper with a vengeance—exploit this behavior whenever possible.

SPARTAN LASER

MAGAZINE SIZE: 100
MAXIMUM SPARE AMMO: 0
SHOTS TO KILL: 1
INSTANT HIT, ANTI-VEHICLE, SCOPED
SHOTS TO BREAK SHIELDS: 1
HEALTH DAMAGE: FULL

The Spartan Laser is a supremely strong anti-vehicle weapon, which, while considerably less effective against infantry, is still dangerous in the right hands.It must be charged before it can be fired, and while charging, it projects a distinctive red laser pointer across the map, pinpointing your location to any enemies and warning them that you are charging a shot. Once it is fully charged, the Spartan Laser unleashes a devastating beam of focused energy, shredding vehicle armor plating or shielding easily. It is even possible to lance multiple players if they happen to be lined up just right. Because the Spartan Laser hits instantly at any distance with such power, it is perfect for taking down dangerous vehicles at range—the Scorpion or Wraith, the Banshee or Falcon, or a key Revenant or Warthog driving away with your flag. Against infantry, this weapon is less effective. Simply because you have a lengthy charge-up period, and a dodging player is a much harder target than a larger, slower vehicle. The shot is is instantly lethal however, so if you have no better option, you can certainly spear a player with the Spartan Laser. The Spartan Laser *does* deal splash damage, but it is an extremely minor amount—if you're aiming for a player, either hit him or her dead on, or don't bother.

COVENANT WEAPONRY

CONCUSSION RIFLE

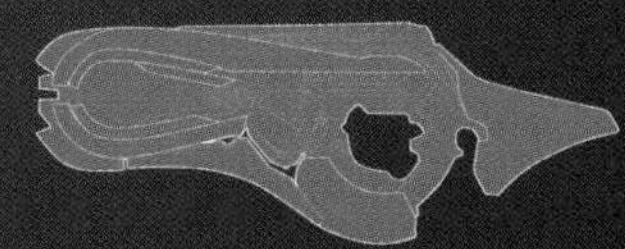

MAGAZINE SIZE: 6
MAXIMUM SPARE AMMO: 24
SHOTS TO KILL: 3
PROJECTILE, EXPLOSIVE, SEMI AUTOMATIC
SHOTS TO BREAK SHIELDS: 2
HEALTH DAMAGE: HIGH

A semi automatic explosive plasma launcher, the Concussion Rifle lives up to its name—you can deliver quite a pounding with this weapon. It deals only moderate splash damage, but because its rate of fire is quite good, you can easily saturate the area around a target and eliminate your opponent without scoring direct hits. The only downside to the weapon is that your ammo supply is sharply limited, and scoring more than two to three total kills with indirect fire is unusual. Direct hits are considerably more lethal, though relatively difficult to land at any distance outside of short range.

The Concussion Rifle works best when you are in an elevated position and your target is below you, with plenty of ground, walls, or other debris nearby to hit with your shots. You can also make good use of the Concussion Rifle in enclosed areas, but you should be wary of self-inflicted damage in these situations—while this gun is safer to use up close than the Rocket Launcher, you can still cause significant damage to yourself if you aren't careful. This weapon is also very powerful for delaying or stopping a runner in any objective mode—a target carrying a Flag or Bomb can be stopped cold by repeated Concussion hits. Any map that has ledges or cliffs is also a good candidate for Concussion usage, since you can knock your target off of said terrain with just a few accurate shots.

Finally, the Concussion Rifle is a decent weapon against the lighter vehicles—not for damage, but rather, for its knockback properties. You can easily send a Ghost, Mongoose, or Warthog severely off course, or occasionally cause an outright flip. Anything much heavier is more difficult to affect, and don't bother wasting your ammo on the heavier vehicles. You can take down another player with the Concussion Rifle in three direct hits, or about five to six indirect fits.

FUEL ROD GUN

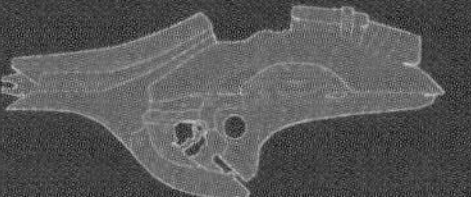

MAGAZINE SIZE: 5
SHOTS TO BREAK SHIELDS: 1
MAXIMUM SPARE AMMO: 25
HEALTH DAMAGE: LETHAL
SHOTS TO KILL: 1
PROJECTILE, EXPLOSIVE, ANTI-VEHICLE, POWER, SEMI AUTOMATIC

The Fuel Rod Gun is a rarely seen Covenant analog to the UNSC Rocket Launcher. While it still fulfills a similar role—high damage explosive projectile delivery, it has several important differences that set it apart.

First, it has a much more generous ammo load. While the Rocket Launcher only has two shots per magazine, the Fuel Rod Gun can fire five times before reloading.

Second, it has a significantly different delivery system. When fired, the luminous green projectile takes a moment to accelerate to full speed, and while it is in this "launch" state, it deflects off surfaces if fired at a shallow enough angle—this allows you to "bounce" the explosive off of floors, walls, or ceilings with practice, useful for indirect fire, a feat that the Rocket Launcher cannot replicate.

Curiously, the Fuel Rod owrdinance does not move as quickly once it has finished its initial launch state, so like the Rocket Launcher, it is a poor weapon against targets at great distances.

Note that it is also more difficult to use the Fuel Rod Gun to kill another player at close-medium range with ground splash damage, since it bounces rather than detonates at short ranges. The Fuel Rod Gun also does not lock onto aerial targets, so you generally have a tougher time taking down a Banshee or Falcon with a skilled pilot.

The explosive power of the plasma projectile is somewhat less than the Rocket Launcher, but it is still enough to easily down an infantry target in one near hit, and while it takes a few more shots against heavy vehicles; it is still a very effective anti-vehicle weapon as well.

As with the Rocket Launcher, you do not want this tool to fall into enemy hands. When you acquire it, use it to its fullest effect, then find a replacement weapon (possibly from the charred and smoking remains of

FOCUS RIFLE

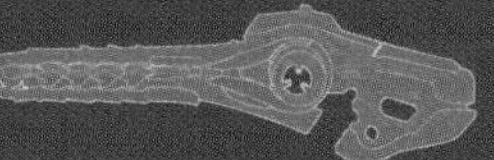

MAGAZINE SIZE: 100
SHOTS TO BREAK SHIELDS: 5
MAXIMUM SPARE AMMO: 0
HEALTH DAMAGE: MODERATE
SHOTS TO KILL: 7
INSTANT HIT, SCOPED, SHIELD BREAKER, AUTOMATIC

A new tool in your arsenal, the Focus Rifle is a powerful Covenant weapon that fires a lethal beam of energy.

Held on a target, it can take down an opponent in a matter of seconds, but accuracy is key, because it heats up quickly and has a lengthy cooldown cycle if you do overheat the weapon.

The Focus Rifle requires a clear line of sight to your target to deal uninterrupted damage, and it is usually best to try to take down your target in two short bursts, rather than a single long burst—a single burst requires near perfect accuracy, and if you are off by a even a small amount, or if you miss-time the firing duration, you overheat the weapon.

Curiously, the Focus Rifle can scope in to a great distance, but it is difficult to score kills at long range with it, because the instant that targets are being hit with the beam, they seek out nearby cover, and the glowing energy beam back to your position makes it very easy for your target and his teammates to locate you.

If you do have targets at a distance in very open terrain, you *can* score kills, but otherwise, try to save the ammunition for medium-range engagements, unless you are trying to keep a sniper's head down.

The Focus Rifle is good against infantry, but don't waste your energy on vehicles—while they are easy to hit with the beam, the damage output is less than impressive. However, for open-topped vehicles, you can certainly attempt to take out the driver and passengers!

It takes roughly 7 to 9 energy to take down a fully healthy target, depending on if you pulse fire or hold the beam on target.

NEEDLER

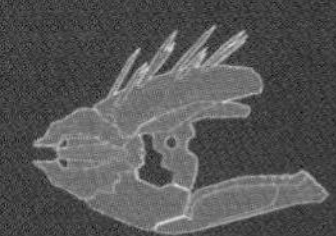

MAGAZINE SIZE: 24
MAXIMUM SPARE AMMO: 96
SHOTS TO KILL: 12
PROJECTILE, AUTOMATIC
SHOTS TO BREAK SHIELDS: 6
HEALTH DAMAGE: VERY LOW

The Needler is extremely strong against single targets in the open. With its slight homing capability, shots aimed anywhere near your target almost always hit, unless your mark evades or finds cover quickly.

Needler shots inflict relatively low individual shield damage and almost no health damage, but they fire quickly, and if six Needler shots hit an unshielded target, they super-combine, detonating with lethal explosive force. However, this weapon has a few significant downsides—it is poor at long range, does not work well against targets with access to hard cover, and drains ammo at a ferocious rate.

While you have it, the Needler is best used as a quick disposable weapon—pick it up, take out a target or two, then ditch it when its ammo is too low to finish off a final target. You can save the Needler for a specific engagement if you know you are moving into a defended area where it can be used to eliminate a key defender, but don't expect it to win against the stronger one-hit kill weapons in a stand up fight—you need time for the Needler to do its explosive work.

It takes six hits for the Needler to strip shields, and a further six hits to super-combine and detonate, killing your target. Individual Needler shots do *very* low health damage, so if you saw a shield crack on your target and he ducked behind cover before the super-combine triggered, expect him to re-enter the battle at full health.

You can conserve ammo with the Needler by trying to fire a little more than a half magazine against a target—with each mag holding 24 shots, 12 to 15 shots is just enough to crack your target's shields and kill him. In general, more shots are a waste, since your target is already dead (due to tracking needles in the air), or he or she has reached safety and more shots are a waste. Needler shots bounce off hard surfaces if fired at a shallow angle, though they do not track targets once they bounce.

NEEDLE RIFLE

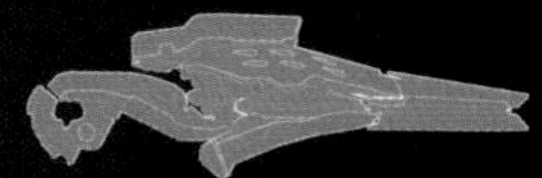

MAGAZINE SIZE: 20
MAXIMUM SPARE AMMO: 84
SHOTS TO KILL: 6
INSTANT HIT, SCOPED, SNIPER, AUTOMATIC
SHOTS TO BREAK SHIELDS: 3
HEALTH DAMAGE: VERY LOW

A Covenant counterpart to the DMR, the Needle Rifle has several unique characteristics that set it apart. First, it is an automatic weapon, has very little recoil, and can fire more sustained shots without losing accuracy. Second, the Needle Rifle, like the Needler, causes a super-combine detonation if three rifle shots impact an unshielded target, dealing lethal damage and area damage to any other hostile targets in the area. Finally, Needle Rifle shots bounces if fired at a slight angle at a hard surface—this is very difficult to utilize in a moving firefight, but you *can* score bank shots in some situations.

The Needle Rifle is distinct from the DMR in that it is slightly more effective at medium to long range than close-medium to medium-long, primarily because it is more accurate with sustained shots and has automatic fire capability. The other reason is the number of hits it takes—while both weapons can kill with one unshielded headshot, the DMR takes four shots to crack a target's shields, while the Needle Rifle requires six.

The upshot here is that while the DMR begins to lose accuracy after two shots, the Needle Rifle is accurate out to three, and it can be fired on automatic for those three shots. Ideally, you want to take down your targets by firing two bursts of three shots with just enough delay to recover your accuracy, then finish with a headshot.

Much like the DMR, the Needle Rifle can also kill in three body shots, but the difference is that the Needle Rifle kills by super-combining, causing instant death. This is important, because if you land two hits after cracking a target's shields, and then your opponent finds cover, the target will have taken *very* little damage.

Just like the Needler, the crystals fired by the Needle Rifle deal very poor health damage. You always need to either land the headshot, or get all three follow up shots to land after breaking your target's shields. At shorter ranges, the Needle Rifle is less effective, due to the number of shots it takes to drop a target's shields, but it does have a larger magazine than the DMR and you can take advantage of that by firing longer bursts at closer ranges, where you are less likely to miss.

THE SUPER-COMBINE

Both the Covenant Needler and the Needle Rifle have the ability to "super-combine" when multiple needles impact an unshielded target. The resulting reaction from the crystals causes a devastating explosion, killing the target and damaging anyone nearby. For the Needler, six hits triggers an explosion, while the Needle Rifle requires three.

Shots from different players *will* combine, but shots from the Needler and Needle Rifle will not (that is, three hits from two players firing a Needler will combine, but two hits from a Needle Rifle and a third hit from a Needler will not).

PLASMA LAUNCHER

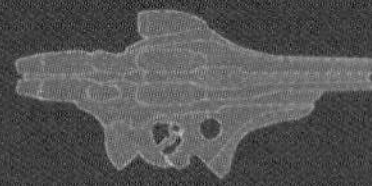

MAGAZINE SIZE: 100
SHOTS TO BREAK SHIELDS: 1
MAXIMUM SPARE AMMO: 0
HEALTH DAMAGE: LETHAL
SHOTS TO KILL: 1
PROJECTILE, EXPLOSIVE,ANTI-VEHICLE, POWER

The Plasma Launcher is a high powered anti-vehicle and area saturation Covenant weapon system, capable of launching homing Plasma Grenades that lock onto players or vehicles and track them to a limited degree.

Charge the Plasma Launcher by holding the fire button, loading up to four grenades at a time that can then be held for a short while longer or discharged at any time after at least one grenade has been loaded. You cannot hold a full load of grenades charged indefinitely; after a few seconds of loading all four, they fire automatically, so be careful in close quarters! If you need to "cancel" a charge, hit your switch weapon button to change weapons, or double tap it to switch back to the Plasma Launcher—either method safely defuses any loaded grenades.

The Plasma Launcher is a good weapon for dealing with most vehicles, since it deals heavy damage and knockback, but the projectiles are relatively slow, so locking on (and hitting) a fast moving target can be difficult. Slower, larger targets are easily dispatched.

Against players, the Plasma Launcher is a bit more difficult to use. Unlike the Rocket Launcher or Fuel Rod Gun, the Plasma Launcher has a "loading" time as you charge up grenades to fire, and even after you launch them, there is a brief delay before they explode. Consequently, this is a poor weapon to use in close quarters fighting, beyond concerns about splash damage.

Ideally, you should seek out targets in mixed terrain at medium range, where you can make good use of either the tracking or indirect fire capabilities of the weapon.

The Plasma Launcher is also good for area suppression and denial. Players tend to scatter when they see a full load of four grenades incoming, and then they have to wait a few seconds for the grenades to actually detonate before the area is safe to return to. This can be useful in territory objective modes, or for key areas on maps that can be blocked for a few seconds—just enough time to stop an enemy carrier, or save a friendly one. It locks on to any target, but its tracking capabilities are not especially strong—this means that trying to use a full load of four grenades against a mobile player that is aware of you is generally a bad idea.

If you have the drop on someone in the open, go for the lock, but otherwise, you may have more success simply sticking the grenades to a nearby surface and letting them detonate naturally. This can also be effective against some lighter vehicles, depending on how they are moving and if they are aware of you.

Firing the Plasma Launcher consumes roughly 8.33 energy, or about enough to fire 12 Plasma Grenades.

PLASMA PISTOL

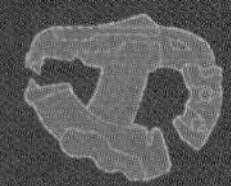

MAGAZINE SIZE: 100
SHOTS TO BREAK SHIELDS: 3
MAXIMUM SPARE AMMO: 0
HEALTH DAMAGE: LOW
SHOTS TO KILL: 7
PROJECTILE, EMP, SHIELD BREAKER, SEMI AUTOMATIC

The Plasma Pistol is back, in all its shield-cracking glory. It is a Covenant sidearm, but it is substantially different from the UNSC Magnum. While the Needle Rifle and the DMR have some parity, the role of the Plasma Pistol is focused in two areas: shield breaking and vehicle disabling.

The Plasma Pistol can either be fired semi-automatic (very quickly), or charged to unleash a single powerful shot with limited tracking capability. While holding a charge, you can still throw regular grenades. The charged shot has EMP capability, and will disable vehicles that it impacts. Players hit by the charged shot have their shields broken instantly. However, using a charge shot against other players is generally overkill, because it only takes three shots to break shields!Because the Plasma Pistol is a projectile weapon, it is relatively poor at hitting targets at long distances. While you can extend its range somewhat with the tracking of the charged shot (especially against vehicles), in most cases, you are best served by using it to break another player's shields at close-medium ranges, then switching to another weapon to finish the job. The reason for this is that while it takes only three normal shots to break a target's shields, it takes *seven* more hits to actually kill them—ten total.

Charged shots aren't much better: a charged hit and five follow up shots will kill, so in either case, you usually have a secondary weapon that is better for finishing off a target (or using melee, at close ranges!). However, the charged Plasma Pistol bolt will EMP to varying degrees, even if it doesn't make direct contact with the target (it'll also EMP the player who fires the shot, if they are too close to the point of impact). There are other issues with the charged shot—while charging, you glow, make an audible noise, and drain ammo continuously. In short, don't use a charged shot if you don't have to—it instantly gives away your location to alert players. Against vehicles, you should absolutely make use of the EMP and tracking, but against other players on foot, you are usually better served by rapidly tapping out several normal shots, then switching weapons, unless you are in a situation where you do not care if other players know you are charging a shot. The charged shot homes in on a targeted player or vehicle, but the tracking is relatively soft—it is definitely enough to be helpful in hitting vehicles at medium ranges, or unaware players. However, alert players who are actively dodging can usually avoid it fairly easily.

PLASMA REPEATER

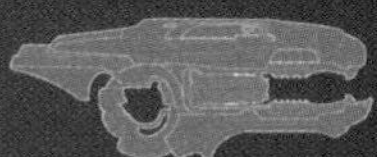

MAGAZINE SIZE: 100
MAXIMUM SPARE AMMO: 0
SHOTS TO KILL: 10
SHOTS TO BREAK SHIELDS: 5
HEALTH DAMAGE: LOW
PROJECTILE, SCOPED, AUTOMATIC

Another new weapon in *Halo: Reach*, the Plasma Repeater is, in some ways, an "assault rifle" for the Covenant forces, though much like the Plasma Pistol, it has very significant differences.

In battlefield utility, the Plasma Repeater is very similar to the Assault Rifle because it is best used at close range, and can down a player at almost the exact speed of an Assault Rifle.

However, since it is an energy-based projectile weapon, it is much less useful at a distance (don't bother trying to de-scope snipers, for example), but does not suffer from the reloading issues if you are careful about your heat management.

The Plasma Repeater is also unique among Covenant weapons that have heat, since it can continue to fire when overheated—albeit at a greatly reduced rate. It is also unique among all weapons, in that when you "reload" by venting heat, you can interrupt the heat discharge by firing, something no other weapon can do while reloading. When fired normally, it is a fully automatic weapon that sprays lightly damaging bolts of plasma. It takes five hits to break a target's shields, and another five to down an unshielded target.

The Plasma Repeater, much like the Assault Rifle, is generally best used only until you can find a more specialized and effective weapon on the battlefield, but you can certainly take players down with this weapon at close to close-medium ranges effectively.

PLASMA RIFLE

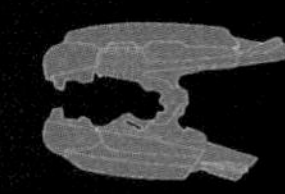

MAGAZINE SIZE: 100
MAXIMUM SPARE AMMO: 0
SHOTS TO KILL: 7
SHOTS TO BREAK SHIELDS: 3
HEALTH DAMAGE: LOW
PROJECTILE, SCOPED, SHIELD BREAKER, AUTOMATIC

The Plasma Rifle is the classic Covenant plasma weapon, firing damaging projectile bolts of at a high rate of fire.

In *Halo: Reach*, the Plasma Rifle falls somewhere between the Plasma Pistol and the Plasma Repeater in terms of damage. It breaks shields very quickly like the Plasma Pistol—just three shots, but it still takes a further five shots to kill, just like the Plasma Repeater.

The Plasma Rifle can be used either to crack shields for a quick melee hit or weapon switch, or used to burn down a target at short ranges. It builds up heat extremely quickly when fired on full auto, but it also vents heat quickly if you do not fire it in extended bursts, so you can easily maintain a good rate of fire without ever overheating if you are mindful of your heat buildup.

Because of its ability to break shields quickly with automatic fire, it is a superior weapon for infantry combat in most instances to the Plasma Pistol, but it lacks the ability to disable vehicles, and suffers from the same difficulty with fighting targets at medium to long-range.

Given the choice, don't hesitate to use a Plasma Rifle over the Pistol or Repeater if you are fighting other infantry at short to medium ranges.

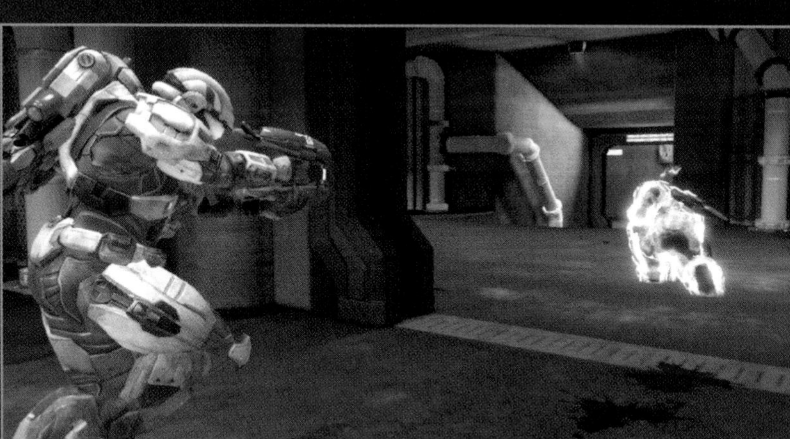

SPIKE RIFLE

MAGAZINE SIZE: 40
MAXIMUM SPARE AMMO: 120
SHOTS TO KILL: 18
SHOTS TO BREAK SHIELDS: 5
HEALTH DAMAGE: VERY LOW
PROJECTILE, AUTOMATIC

The Spike Rifle is a weapon of Brute origin, rarely used by other Covenant troops. Suitably brutish, it is a close-range rapid-fire projectile weapon that launches metal spikes at a high rate of fire.

Unlike the Needler, the only similar weapon in the game, the Spike Rifle does *not* automatically track targets, so you need to be fairly close to take down a target. This weapon does decent shield damage and poor health damage, but it has a good rate of fire, so it can be used to burn down a single target or finish off a wounded target fairly easily.

It takes five hits to crack a player's shields, and another 13 to finish him or her off, and headshots do not help with damage dealt.

The Spike Rifle is generally best used at close-medium range on open terrain. Very uneven terrain or fights against weapons more suited to close or long-range fights at their preferred distances are a bad idea, even more so for the Spike Rifle than most other weapons, since it lacks any real flexibility.

Like the Plasma Rifle, you won't encounter the Spike Rifle on the default *Halo: Reach* maps, so you initially only encounter this weapon when playing

MELEE WEAPONS

There are two special melee weapons in *Halo: Reach*, both Covenant in origin. The massive Brute Gravity Hammer and the Elite Energy Sword are powerful melee weapons, both capable of killing a target in a single hit.

Remember that in *Halo: Reach*, it is now possible to "parry" an incoming melee hit by timing a melee swing. This leaves you severely damaged against a dedicated melee weapon, but damaged is always better than dead!

ENERGY SWORD

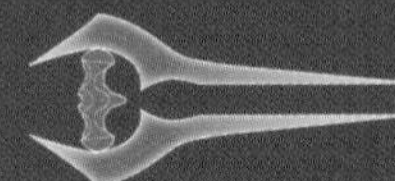

MAGAZINE SIZE: 100
MAXIMUM SPARE AMMO: 0
SHOTS TO KILL: 1
POWER
SHOTS TO BREAK SHIELDS: 1
HEALTH DAMAGE: LETHAL

The Energy Sword is a lethal blade of concentrated plasma, capable of instantly killing another player with a single strike—lunge or regular melee swing.

When you swing with the trigger, you perform a lunge that automatically closes the distance on any player within red reticle range, killing him or her instantly unless he or she gets *very* lucky (in midair falling off a ledge, for example).

A regular melee button press results in a faster swing that does *not* lunge, but has quicker recovery—usually safer if you encounter someone suddenly at point blank range, or close the distance yourself. Note that the lunge works even in midair, so you can use it while jumping, jetpacking, or attacking a target in a vehicle.

The Energy Sword has limited energy, so you can't use it indefinitely, and it is very much worth using and abusing if you can get your hands on it. While using it, you should stick to closed corridors, indoor areas, and constricted routes in outdoor areas to make use of the Energy Sword to its fullest.

One particular Armor Ability bears special notice when using the Energy Sword—when using Cloak, unlike other weapons that have a glow, the normal ambient glow from the Energy Sword is concealed completely. This makes cloaked ambushes with the Energy Sword especially devastating.

It *is* possible to kill a player lunging at you with an Energy Sword (and in fact, you get a medal for doing so), though only a few weapons, such as the Shotgun and Sniper Rifle, have any real chance of doing so in time!

Hitting with an Energy Sword consumes 10 energy.

DEFLECTIONS

A deflection, parry, clash, or however you want to describe it, deals minimal damage to each player *if* the weapons are of equivalent strength.

That is, a normal melee swing or Gravity Hammer regular melee hit deflects dealing light damage to each player. However, a deflection by a normal swing against a Gravity Hammer or Energy Sword full strength hit will leave you with either no shields (for the Gravity Hammer) or no shields and only around 30% health (for the Energy Sword).

Deflecting a hit from a power weapon deals very light damage to the player using the power melee weapon.

GRAVITY HAMMER

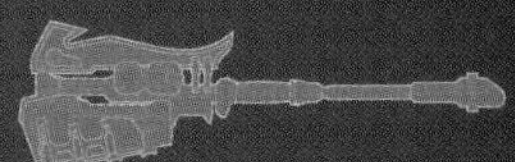

MAGAZINE SIZE: 100
MAXIMUM SPARE AMMO: 0
SHOTS TO KILL: 1
POWER
SHOTS TO BREAK SHIELDS: 1
HEALTH DAMAGE: FULL

The Gravity Hammer is another power melee weapon, only a hair weaker than the Energy Sword, but it has other unique attributes that set it apart.

As with the Energy Sword, performing a trigger attack causes a lunge that moves forward and strikes any target in range, killing him or her instantly. However, the Gravity Hammer has a slightly shorter red reticle range. In exchange, it gains a powerful ground smash that knocks back players *and* vehicles. You can even bounce back a grenade in midair if you time it right…

The Gravity Hammer is surprisingly effective against vehicles. If you move well, you can get into position to knock a Warthog spinning, dislodging its passengers and opening them up for a coup de gracé.

Unlike the Energy Sword, regular melee swings with the Gravity Hammer behave like normal melee swings—that is, they break shields in a single hit, and then kill with a second hit. Keep this in mind if you're trying to go for a faster melee swing and wondering why your target isn't going down!

Hitting with the Gravity Hammer consumes (roughly) 8.33 energy, or 12 swings total before it is used up.

TURRETS

A few maps have mounted turrets placed on them (and more can be placed in Forge on custom maps). Mounted turrets can be used with infinite ammunition while they are mounted; you only need to worry about overheating. Both types of turret can also be ripped off their mounting and carried around. This reduces their available ammunition to what you can carry, but increases their mobility.

Turrets, whether mounted or removed, are very powerful anti-infantry weapons, and decent against vehicles as well, but they reduce your movement

PLASMA CANNON

The Plasma Cannon fires projectiles rapidly, perfect for saturating a hallway or objective point or taking down infantry targets at medium to close-range.

MACHINE GUN

The Machine Gun is slightly more dangerous than the Plasma Cannon simply by virtue of its instant hit bullets, but like the Plasma Cannon, it is less effective at greater distances, where its bullet spread becomes very pronounced. speed while carried.

AVERAGE WEAPON RESPAWN TIMES AND SPARE AMMO

Weapon	Respawn Time	Spare Magazines
Sniper Rifle	120	2
Shotgun	120	2
DMR	45	2
Needler	45	2
Plasma Repeater	30	0
Needle Rifle	45	2
Plasma Launcher	180	0
Rocket Launcher	180	1
Magnum	30	2

Weapon	Respawn Time	Spare Magazines
Plasma Pistol	45	0
Focus Rifle	180	0
Plasma Grenade	30	—
Energy Sword	180	—
Concussion Rifle	90	2
Gravity Hammer	120	—
Focus Rifle	180	—
Frag Grenade	30	—
Grenade Launcher	90	5

WELCOME
UNSC TRAINING
THE CAMPAIGN
FIREFIGHT
MULTIPLAYER
BASICS & TACTICS
ARSENAL
VEHICLES
GAMEPLAY MODES
MAPS
FORGE
REFERENCE

WEAPON RESPAWN TIMES

BOARDWALK

Weapon	Respawn Time
DMR	45
Needler	45
Needle Rifle	45
Plasma Launcher	180
Plasma Pistol	45
Plasma Repeater	30
Rocket Launcher	180
Shotgun	120
Sniper Rifle	120
Medkit	Never
Plasma Grenade	Never

COUNTDOWN

Weapon	Respawn Time
DMR	30
Concussion Rifle	90
Energy Sword	180
Needler	45
Needle Rifle	30
Plasma Pistol	30
Shotgun	180
Medkit	15
Plasma Grenade	30
Frag Grenade	30

BONEYARD

Weapon	Respawn Time
DMR	30
Focus Rifle	180
Needler	60
Needle Rifle	30
Plasma Launcher	180
Plasma Pistol	30
Plasma Repeater	30
Rocket Launcher	180
Sniper Rifle	180
Mounted Machinegun	120
Scorpion	180
Mongoose	30
Ghost	60
Warthog	45
Banshee	180

POWERHOUSE

Weapon	Respawn Time
DMR	60
Focus Rifle	180
Gravity Hammer	120
Grenade Launcher	90
Magnum	30
Needler	30
Needle Rifle	60
Plasma Pistol	30
Plasma Repeater	30
Rocket Launcher	180
Shotgun	180
Frag Grenade	45
Plasma Grenade	45
Medkit	15

REFLECTION

Weapon	Respawn Time
DMR	30
Energy Sword	180
Magnum	30
Needler	45
Needle Rifle	30
Plasma Pistol	30
Plasma Repeater	30
Rocket Launcher	180
Shotgun	180
Sniper Rifle	180
Frag Grenades	45
Plasma Grenades	45
Medkit	Never

SPIRE

Weapon	Respawn Time
Concussion Rifle	60
Focus Rifle	120
Grenade Launcher	60
Needler	30
Needle Rifle	45
Fuel Rod Gun	120
Plasma Pistol	30
Rocket Launcher	120
Sniper Rifle	120
Frag Grenades	45
Plasma Grenades	45
Ghost	45
Warthog	45
Mongoose	30
Falcon	180
Banshee	180
Scorpion	180

SWORD BASE

Weapon	Respawn Time
DMR	60
Energy Sword	120
Magnum	30
Needler	60
Needle Rifle	60
Plasma Pistol	45
Plasma Repeater	60
Frag Grenades	45
Plasma Grenades	45
Medkit	15

ZEALOT

Weapon	Respawn Time
DMR	60
Concussion Rifle	180
Energy Sword	120
Magnum	60
Needler	60
Needle Rifle	60
Plasma Repeater	60
Frag Grenades	45
Plasma Grenades	45
Medkit	15

FORGE WORLD: ASYLUM

Weapon	Respawn Time
DMR	30
Energy Sword	90
Needler	30
Needle Rifle	30
Plasma Pistol	30
Plasma Repeater	Never
Shotgun	90
Sniper Rifle	90
Frag Grenades	45
Plasma Grenades	45
Mounted Machinegun	180
Medkit	15

FORGE WORLD: HEMORRHAGE

Weapon	Respawn Time
DMR	30
Concussion Rifle	60
Magnum	30
Needler	45
Needle Rifle	30
Plasma Launcher	180
Plasma Pistol	30
Plasma Repeater	30
Sniper Rifle	120
Frag Grenades	45
Plasma Grenades	45
Warthog	45
Revenant	180
Scorpion	180
Mongoose	30
Ghost	60
Medkit	15

FORGE WORLD: PARADISO

Weapon	Respawn Time
DMR	45
Concussion Rifle	30
Grenade Launcher	99
Needler	30
Needle Rifle	45
Plasma Pistol	30
Plasma Repeater	30
Sniper Rifle	180
Frag Grenades	45
Plasma Grenades	45
Medkit	No
Ghost	45
Mongoose	30
Warthog	60
Banshee	120
Scorpion	180
Mounted Machinegun	60

FORGE WORLD: PINNACLE

Weapon	Respawn Time
DMR	30
Magnum	30
Needler	30
Plasma Pistol	30
Plasma Repeater	30
Rocket Launcher	180
Shotgun	180
Sniper Rifle	180
Frag Grenades	60
Plasma Grenades	60
Medkits	no

FORGE WORLD: THE CAGE

Weapon	Respawn Time
DMR	30
Needler	30
Needle Rifle	45, Never
Plasma Launcher	99
Plasma Pistol	20
Plasma Repeater	20
Shotgun	60
Sniper Rifle	75
Frag Grenades	Never
Plasma Grenades	45
Medkits	15
Overshield	150

ARMOR ABILITIES

New to *Halo: Reach*, the seven different Armor Abilities added to the game grant new powers to all players in multiplayer arenas.Not all abilities are available in all multiplayer modes, but in most modes, you have your choice of several different abilities. Each ability has different strengths and weaknesses, depending on the mode you are playing as well as your own personal preferences. You can change abilities each time you die, but you *cannot* change your ability for your next spawn, so be sure to remember to swap abilities before the respawn timer elapses! In Invasion mode (and Firefight), Armor Abilities are tied to specific class loadouts that give set weaponry. In all other modes, Armor Abilities do not carry any particular weapon loadout, since they come along with whatever the default weapon is for that mode and map.

Armor Abilities *cannot* be used while carrying a Flag or Bomb, and they cannot be used inside of a Territory. In some cases, temporarily dropping an objective to use your Armor Ability is a worthwhile tactic, depending on which specific Armor Ability you are using.

Armor Abilities draw their energy from a renewable pool, but the method in which they use the energy varies—a single Drop Shield usage drains the tanks, while Sprint or Jetpack can be used continuously in short bursts without needing to recharge fully.

ARMOR ABILITY DATA

Ability	Effect	Duration	Recharge	Minimum Activation Energy	Activation Cost	Notes
Sprint	1.5x Movement Speed	4s	4.2s	1%	None	Possible to Melee or throw grenades while sprinting
Armor Lock	Invulnerability	5s	14s	15%	5%	Shield will regenerate while Locked, Camera can be rotated, Slows and damages players who melee you
Active Camouflage	Invisibility	45s Still, 15s in motion	17 seconds	1%	2%	Motion Tracker interference out to 30M, causes sound suppression in a bubble around player
Hologram	Creates duplicate player	10s	7s	100%	100%	Holograms can be destroyed, will move through objects or vehicles, Holograms do not cast shadows, have player names, red reticules, or make noises
Drop Shield	Creates impenetrable bubble	15s	20s	100%	100%	Drop Shields will heal friendly or hostile players. Drop Shields block grenades (toss one while inside to flush out a player)
Jetpack	Flight	4s	7s	10%	5%	Feather the trigger to stay aloft longer. Jump and then boost to gain more height.
Evade	Quick directional dash	4s	3.5s	50%	50%	Elites evade farther and faster than Spartans. You can melee out of an Evade. Tracking weapons lose lock if you Evade. You can aim your view in any direction while evading

SPRINT

Sprint is the most basic of all the abilities. When activated, it grants the user a boost of forward movement speed. It is simple, straightforward, and very effective.

Sprinting has myriad uses in all game modes:

- ***Reaching a power weapon spawn at the beginning of a match***
- ***Outrunning pursuit***
- ***Chasing down another player with a melee or close-range weapon***
- ***Catching up to a Bomb or Flag carrier***
- ***Dodging incoming fire***
- ***Escaping bad combat situations***
- ***Evading vehicles***
- ***Reaching objective areas more quickly***
- ***Can be used to help jump difficult or normally impossible gaps***
- ***Boosts height from Gravity Lift jumps***

Sprint *does* have a few weaknesses, however. First, you make a *very* distinct panting sound while running. For any alert player with a decent audio setup, he or she *will* hear you coming. Unless you're playing psychological warfare (and you want your opponents to know you're coming), be careful about sprinting around a map unless you simply don't care if your targets know you are en route.

Second, Sprint lowers your weapon while you are running, and it takes a moment to raise it again after you stop sprinting—just long enough to get killed in a straight up firefight against another player. Always stop sprinting *before* you reach your target to get your weapon ready.

With that said, Sprint is a very useful all-around ability. In almost all modes, you should always make sure your team has at least one player with Sprint who is in charge of reaching power weapons before the other team can do so (or at the very least, contesting the weapons while other slower teammates catch up).

Sprint is also very powerful for abusing the Energy Sword or Gravity Hammer because you can use it to close distances very quickly, getting in range of a lock-on lunge far more swiftly than is normally possible.

Be careful about sprinting to use regular melee swings, however: running straight into gunfire is a good way to end up dead. Chasing down a fleeing enemy can also be dangerous, as you are vulnerable to rebounded grenades and baiting.

Sprint works quite well for evading fire at medium and long ranges, because even if a player is good enough to track you and stay on target, you're still exposed for a significantly shorter period of time than if you were simply moving normally—the end result is that you'll survive a sprint across open ground or a gap that you might not otherwise, even if your assailant *is* a good shot!

If you're ever unsure about what Armor Ability to take, Sprint is a good option.

ARMOR LOCK

Armor Lock is a unique ability that freezes you in place while sealing your armor with an impenetrable energy shield. This shield deflects all incoming attacks, reflects some attacks, and, when released, triggers a short range EMP explosion that destroys player shields and can disable vehicles. Armor Lock, while active, prevents you from taking damage from *any* source, including being rammed by a vehicle—in fact, if a vehicle hits you at high speed, it will take serious damage and may even be destroyed!

Some good uses for Armor Lock:

- ***Blocking vehicle ram attempts***
- ***Saving yourself from power weapon attacks***
- ***Blocking doorways***
- ***Resetting Flags***
- ***Reflecting Plasma Launcher, Fuel Rod, and Rocket Launcher shots***
- ***Saving yourself from a stuck Plasma Grenade***
- ***Breaking a Drop Shield***
- ***Locating a sniper***
- ***Saving yourself from a melee weapon***
- ***Draining part of an opponent's magazine***

Armor Lock is a powerful defensive ability, but because it immobilizes you, in most situations it is very important to use it at the last possible moment, for the shortest amount of time. The reason for this is that if you hold an Armor Lock in place, your opponent is given time to back off, reload, and draw a bead on you, as well as timing a grenade toss to detonate when you release the shield.

If you quickly lock and release to block a shot (or shots) and then stand up and resume your attack, you can kill an enemy who burned a chunk of his or her magazine on you or missed a critical power weapon shot and is forced to reload or rearm. This also can save you from melee weapons—if you Armor Lock a lunging Energy Sword or Gravity Hammer, the EMP that you release may well drop your opponent's shield, giving *you* the instant melee kill.

Armor Locking in mid battle against rapid-fire weapons with low magazine capacity is also an effective tactic—Armor Lock the instant your opponent starts firing an Assault Rifle or Needler at you, release the lock, and resume fighting like normal—your opponent is forced to reload before you, often giving you the win.

In addition to its power as a defensive tool, Armor Lock also discharges a short-ranged EMP blast when it is released. The radius of the explosion is dependant upon the length of your Armor Lock hold—though there are almost no situations where holding Armor Lock out in the open for a bigger discharge is a good idea. The EMP has several uses, though—the aforementioned anti-melee EMP can save you from melee power weapons, instantly break an enemy Drop Shield, and get used against vehicles reasonably effectively.

The easiest way to land an EMP is to bait your opponent into trying to it usually stops him or her dead, and when you release the lock, the resulting EMP may freeze the vehicle in place. Even if the EMP misses due to the vehicle bouncing, you are still in a perfect position to hijack the vehicle.

The more difficult method is to get close enough (or onto!) the vehicle and then discharge the EMP. In almost all situations, this is a bad idea, as you'd be better served by hijacking the vehicle, but it is possible to jump on a tank and use EMP to disable it!

In objective game modes, remember that you can block narrow doorways with Armor Lock, potentially allowing your bomb or flag carrier to escape safely, while your frustrated opponents have to wait until your armor energy drains! Also, it is important to remember that any time you are using Armor Lock, you can spin the camera around—this allows you to Armor Lock, get a bead on a player attacking you from behind or a great distance, and attack or evade the enemy as soon as you release the lock. This works both ways, so be careful about trying to wait at close range "behind" players using Armor Lock, as they can and will come out of the lock facing you! And remember if you ever get stuck, you can Armor Lock instantly to save yourself from the resulting blast!

ACTIVE CAMO

Active Camo grants you a form of limited invisibility, as light bends and warps around you while moving, making you very difficult to track at a distance, and still harder to spot up close.

When motionless, or moving very slowly, the effect is increased, making it even more difficult to spot you. If you move at full speed, you become partially visible, and therefore more easy to spot. Any "glowing" weapon except the Energy Sword becomes visible while cloaked—this includes charged Plasma Pistols, Plasma Launchers, the Spartan Laser, and of course, any weapon's fire.

Firing a weapon, throwing a grenade, using a melee attack, or getting hit temporarily disrupts the cloak, so it is best used for getting in to close range, escaping from combat, or using powerful weapons that can kill in a just a few shots. Any time Active Camo is functioning, all external sounds are deadened—this makes it very difficult to hear footsteps or in some cases, even combat at medium-range.

While online, Active Camo disrupts all nearby Motion Trackers—yours included, but not your teammates'. Because of this disruption effect, you should wait to activate Active Camo when moving towards a known enemy position, because the instant an enemy sees that his or her tracker is being scrambled, he or she begins actively hunting for the cloaked player. You can use this to your advantage in some situations, when you're in an enclosed area and you have a close-range weapon—having them hunt for you is the next best thing to a free kill when you're packing a Shotgun or Energy Sword and you're cloaked.

You can also use the Motion Tracker disruption very effectively on vertical maps—get beneath an enemy position and activate your cloak while your teammates move in—you don't even need to join in the fight to help your teammates stage a very effective assault! Because of the sound deadening and Motion Tracker disruption, Active Camo is typically best used in short bursts to engage and kill a key target, get into a critical area, or escape from a bad situation. Active Camo drains energy more quickly while moving, so remaining stationary not only makes you harder to spot, it also allows you to remain cloaked longer.

This cloaking is a very powerful offensive and defensive weapon, as it can be useful for many battlefield tasks:

- ***Making invisible alpha strikes with a Rocket Launcher, Sniper Rifle, or other power weapon***
- ***Abusing the Energy Sword, Gravity Hammer, and Shotgun***
- ***Disrupting enemy Motion Trackers for your team***
- ***Sneaking into or escaping from a key area***
- ***Concealing your approach at long range***
- ***Hiding from pursuit***
- ***Ambushing enemies in confined, multi-level areas***

When fighting *against* a cloak, a rapid-fire weapon is your best friend, since you can disrupt the cloak with a single hit from any weapon. Area effect weaponry or grenades are also effective for causing the shield "flare" when a cloaked player is hit, allowing you to get a bead and finish off the sneaky player.

One final very important point—when moving below the detectable visual speed, or moving while crouched, autoaim (the red reticle "lock on") does NOT function for enemy players. This includes Energy Sword/Gravity Hammer lunges, and *all* forms of autoaim or target detection from other weapons. At very close ranges, this usually doesn't matter (though you are still devilishly hard to spot while crouched near a wall), but at a distance, if you are moving slowly, it is almost impossible for a player to pick you up unless you happen to silhouette yourself against a player looking directly at you.

Active Camo is a very strong piece of gear, but be careful about overusing it—against good players, you won't pull off more than a few "obvious" ambushes, and they'll become increasingly guarded when they spot the Motion Tracker disruption. Try to make use of Active Camo in ways that they cannot fight effectively even if they *are* aware of your usage, such as disrupting their trackers for your team, or abusing close-range weaponry.

CROUCH CLOAK

If you crouch and move at full speed, you will *not* trigger the increased visibility that you suffer while moving at full speed normally. This allows you to creep around while remaining very difficult to spot, which is very useful if you're trying to sneak up on someone.

It *is* possible to move around without triggering the visibility (you can see the effect on your own weapon to some extent), but doing so requires very careful movement control, so it's much easier to simply crouch and move, certain in the knowledge that you are remaining fully cloaked at all times. Just be sure to stand up once you actually get into a fight... Duckwalking Spartans are not a fearsome sight. Remember that you can jump to break a crouch, in addition to simply standing up.

JET PACK

As you might expect, the Jet Pack lets you fly!

This is, needless to say, extremely useful. Much like Sprint, the Jet Pack is a mobility tool. It allows you to get to areas on a map that would be difficult or impossible to reach on foot, and to change vertical levels far more quickly than you would be able to do so normally.

In some cases, you can even reach "soft kill" out of bounds areas that kill you in 10 seconds—just enough time to fire down on your foes without threat of retaliation, because they cannot reach you! The Jet Pack is not without weaknesses, however, since you are a very exposed and an obvious target while you are making use of it in the open.

Be very careful about using the Jet Pack to "hover" or float across open spaces, because every hostile enemy in the area naturally tends to gravitate to an exposed target making a lot of noise. You're also extremely vulnerable to tracking shots like the Plasma Launcher, Pistol, and Needler.

Instead, use the Jet Pack to quickly escape pursuit, chase down a fleeing enemy, reach a higher or lower level quickly or safely, or get to an objective or power weapon more rapidly. In some situations, you can even use the Jet Pack to airjack a Banshee or Falcon!

A few points: EMPs will not disable your Jet Pack, and rockets won't track you, though Gravity Hammer or Energy Sword lunges *will* track you, as do Needler shots or Plasma Launcher locked shots. Traveling via Jet Pack is considerably slower than Sprint in a straight line, but potentially a lot faster vertically.

Consider the level and game mode before taking a Jet Pack and abuse its strengths to the fullest—if you aren't using its mobility to bypass level flow, you aren't getting good use from your Armor Ability!

HOLOGRAM

Another deceptive Armor Ability, Hologram allows you to create mobile Holograms of yourself that runs in a straight line towards a point of your choosing. Holograms do not attack enemies, and can be destroyed with enough weapon fire. Holograms jump over low obstacles to reach the point you targeted, and also make use of any Gravity Lifts in their way. When hit, Holograms distort, giving away their disguise. Holograms also do *not* trigger red reticle autoaim, and Plasma Launchers do not lock on to them, nor will Needlers or charged Plasma Pistol shots track them. Another curious quirk of the Hologram—the viewfinders on both the Sniper Rifle and the Spartan Laser show Holograms as a flashing silhouette. Not the best way to discover a Hologram, but it is an option! However, while Holograms are fairly easy to detect, due to their movement and the other means of uncovering them, they are still extremely useful as tools of misdirection. Holograms *do* trigger the Motion Tracker. In any game mode with the tracker active, you can easily fool an enemy by sending a Hologram ahead of you.

You can also make good use of Holograms by sending them into rooms, onto objectives, around corners, up Gravity Lifts, and out into the open if you suspect a sniper or long-range vehicle is monitoring your position.

While good players can very quickly identify a Hologram as fake, good players also tend to very quickly fire at any target they acquire—this means that, at a minimum, they waste ammunition and give away their location to you. Ideal, if they happen to be lying in wait with an Energy Sword or Rocket Launcher. Another good trick to pull with the Hologram is to move in one direction, then stop moving or crouch and send the Hologram along the same path. By doing this and ducking into a corner, you can easily fool pursuers. Unless they have a visual on you when the Hologram emerges on the Motion Tracker, it looks like you simply continued running in the same direction.

Holograms make perfect scouts because you can use them to discover entrenched snipers, and they are also very useful for fishing out defenders around an objective who aren't in immediate view. It is also possible to occasionally save yourself from a vehicle by running in a straight line in one direction and dispatching the Hologram in another direction. This won't always work, but every now and then, your pursuer may choose the wrong target to squish.

Be careful about overusing Holograms in the open, or against the same players on defense, or in smaller games. If you are careful about when you trigger a Hologram, even the best players will have a hard time guessing correctly, which can give you an edge in battle.

DROP SHIELD

The Drop Shield is a powerful defensive Armor Ability that creates a large spherical shield of energy that repels all incoming weapons fire and grenades, while not impeding player or vehicle movement.

Because of this, the Drop Shield is perfect for protecting yourself from long-range weapon fire, vehicle fire, snipers, and other mid to long-range threats.

It is still useful against close-range threats, *especially* if you have a short range weapon, because you can force a melee range engagement by placing the Drop Shield. Your opponent's options are cut down to either waiting out the shield, destroying it, or moving through it to reach you, putting him or her in striking distance for all the close-range weaponry in the game.

The Drop Shield is also great for guarding objective areas, blocking hallways behind you, or creating cover in otherwise exposed areas.

Even in wide open outdoor spaces, a Drop Shield placed behind you while you are running can block many incoming shots, and the Drop Shield is strong enough to absorb even the most powerful weapon fire, including that of vehicles.

In addition to blocking shots and grenades, the Drop Shield also heals any friendly players inside it—this is perfect for holding the line in a defensive position, or recovering from a near fatal battle if you can't get to a Medkit easily.

Note that the Drop Shield has a brief delay before it deploys. This makes it slightly less effective at blocking incoming heavy weapons fire than the Armor Lock ability, which can be triggered more quickly. However, you can still use a Drop Shield to save yourself from long distance fire, as it almost always comes up before a fatal shot can arrive. It also helps to recover health if you happen to take a few damaging shots!

DESTROYING THE DROP SHIELD

While any weapons fire can eventually take down the Drop Shield, most weapons simply take too long to destroy a Drop Shield when employed alone. If you *must* destroy a Drop Shield without ideal weaponry, talk to your teammates and focus fire—otherwise, destroying a shield with Assault Rifles, DMRs, or similar weaponry is simply too slow.

For quick elimination, use the Rocket Launcher (one shot), Fuel Rod Gun (three shots), Spartan Laser (two shots), two grenades just outside of it, or EMP class weaponry, which also takes two hits (charged Plasma Pistol or Grenade Launcher manual detonation).

Vehicle weaponry also works well, as do any mounted or vehicle turrets. Four Revenant shots or one shot from the Wraith, Scorpion, or Banshee Plasma Cannon can take down a Drop Shield. Finally, the EMP from the Armor Lock instantly destroys a Drop Shield.

WELCOME
UNSC TRAINING
THE CAMPAIGN
FIREFIGHT
MULTIPLAYER
BASICS & TACTICS
ARSENAL
VEHICLES
GAMEPLAY MODES
MAPS
FORGE
REFERENCE

EVADE

The final Armor Ability in *Halo: Reach* is Evade.

Unlike the other Armor Abilities, which are shared by all Spartan and Elites in all game modes, Evade is a rare ability that is only present in multiplayer games in the Invasion mode, where it is exclusive to the Elite forces. Evade is somewhat similar to Sprint because it is a mobility upgrade.

Unlike Sprint, however, Evade provides up to two rapid dashes in any direction, and then takes a short time to recharge, contrasting with Sprint's continuous burst of speed. This makes Evade ideal for rapid movement in close quarters combat, and indeed, you can actually Evade in one direction *while aiming in another* and still firing. This makes Elites skilled with Evade very dangerous to fight at close-range, as they have a serious mobility advantage over any other player.

Evade is less effective for covering ground than Sprint (though it still beats just walking!). However, it is useful for evading incoming sniper fire, as it can break up your movement pattern enough to save you from a quick demise on open ground.

To get the most use out of Evade, seek out weapons that you can use and abuse in combination with the close range dashes, and you can dominate your enemies. Few Armor Ability combinations are scarier than an Elite with a Plasma Sword and Evade.

MULTIPLAYER VEHICLES

Vehicles in *Halo* are an integral part of the experience, and an integral part of the combat. Learning how to both use the vehicles and fight against them is extremely important in many different game modes. They are not present in every game mode or map, nor are all vehicles on every map, but over time, you can expect to see new maps and custom maps that will have different mixes of vehicles present.

RAMMING SPEED

Smashing vehicles into one another is a grand old *Halo* tradition, but you should be aware of a few points.

First, the speed of an impact affects its damage considerably, and second, the weight of the vehicle doing the smashing also has a significant impact on the resulting damage. By and large, the vehicles interact exactly as you'd expect from looking at them—the Mongoose and Ghost can deal similar ramming damage, as can the Revenant and Warthog, the Wraith and Scorpion, or the Banshee and Falcon. Covenant vehicles have the advantage of using boost to propel themselves into enemy vehicles, so be aware of the danger if you're facing an enemy Covenant vehicle.

Generally speaking, a larger vehicle trumps a smaller vehicle in terms of health and survivability, both from incoming damage and from incoming ramming damage. This means it is always a bad idea to ram a larger vehicle with a smaller one, *unless* that larger vehicle is already heavily damaged.

VEHICLE TAGS

We've attached a set of "tags" to each vehicle to give you a quick idea of its capabilities.

OPEN TOP

Open-topped vehicles have the driver (and passengers) exposed to incoming fire. This means that is entirely possible to kill (or be killed) in an open-topped vehicle without the vehicle itself being destroyed. Open-topped vehicles are also particularly vulnerable to sniper class weaponry—a good shot can take down a driver or passenger at long-range.

SECURE

Secure vehicles have the pilot protected by external armor—the pilot cannot be directly attacked, though "bleed through" damage can potentially kill the pilot if he is already damaged.

TURRET

Some vehicles have turrets that can be manned by a passenger, increasing the firepower of the vehicle (and the reward if it is destroyed by an enemy...

WEAK POINT

A few vehicles have a structural weakness that can be exploited—weapon hits on the target area deal increased damage, potentially destroying the vehicle much more quickly than would normally be possible.

TRANSPORT

Transport vehicles have passenger seats or can otherwise accommodate multiple players, particularly important when playing CTF or Assault on a map with vehicles present. Note that there's nothing stopping someone with a Flag jumping *on* a Scorpion...

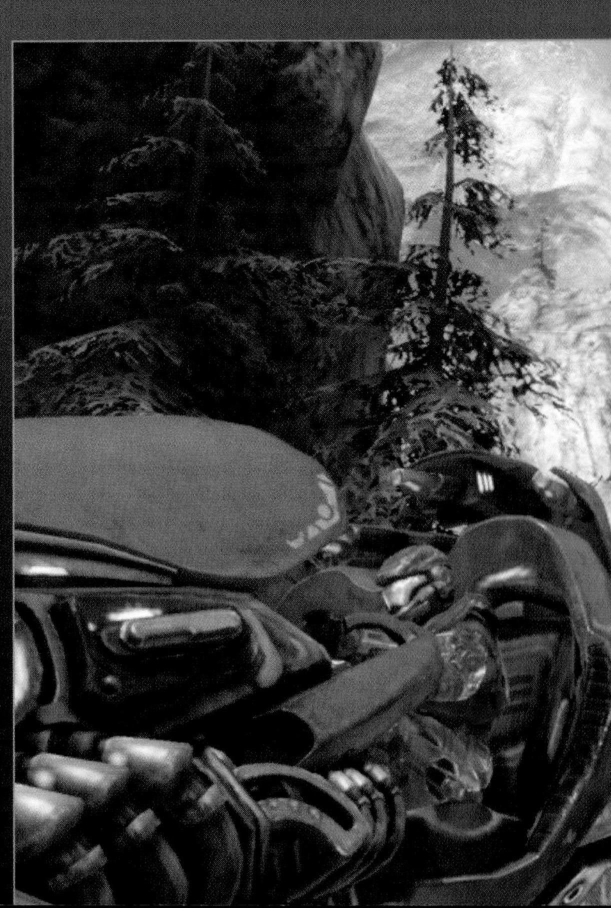

FOUR WHEELING

Both of the four wheeled UNSC vehicles, the Mongoose and Warthog, have similar driving characteristics. Both are quick, have good maneuverability, and are highly vulnerable to being flipped, either by enemy explosions or by poor driving.

A handy tip for staying on your "wheels" when driving either vehicle: steer *into* the wheels if you are launched into the air. That is, if you start to tilt on your two left wheels, steer into those two wheels. Similarly, if you wind up doing a wheelie on the back two, pull back. If you get severely flipped (i.e., outright sent spinning by a high powered explosion), and you land hard but still on your wheels, you can also kill the input completely—let the vehicle settle out, *then* start giving it the gas, or you can try to steer into the wheels that did hit the ground.

Spend some time practicing—it's extremely useful to be able to recover from a bad turn or an explosion.

UNSC VEHICLES

MONGOOSE

OPEN TOP, TRANSPORT

The Mongoose is a four wheeled, two person, fast transport vehicle. It has no weaponry, and riders are highly exposed to incoming fire. The tradeoff is that the Mongoose is very quick, quite maneuverable, and easy to mount or dismount from. Your passenger can also fire from the rear position, though hitting most targets while moving at high speed over uneven terrain is difficult to say the least.

The Mongoose is ideal for fast transit to or from an objective, and it is also useful for quickly reaching a key area on a map—either a useful tactical position, or a power weapon spawn point. When driving the Mongoose, it's important to control your speed and changes of direction—it's very easy to flip the Mongoose if you simply move at full speed over rough terrain.

Some quick tips for the Mongoose:

- If your passenger is skilled, he can make good use of the Rocket Launcher (while moving) or the Sniper Rifle (if you periodically stop to give him a shot)
- Got a Jet Pack? Hit a ramp on the Mongoose and fly off to catch an unsuspecting Banshee or Falcon in midair!
- The Mongoose is great for making Flag runs in CTF game modes

WARTHOG

OPEN TOP, TRANSPORT, TURRET

The Warthog is a four wheeled, three passenger vehicle, with one driver, one passenger, and a turret gunner. This vehicle is great in a few roles: either transportation in objective modes, or as a mobile gunnery platform.

For transit, you can use it to take a flag runner home, or to move a small team into position to stage an assault, or to cover a key piece of terrain. The passenger seat *can* fire, though it is difficult to fight while on the move, and usually a better idea to have the second player on the turret if you only have two people in the Warthog. With a gunner active and a skilled driver, the Warthog can be a serious threat to infantry and a reasonable threat to other vehicles.

The Warthog is an open-topped vehicle, and as such, it is vulnerable to incoming weapons fire for all passengers. Sniper weapons are particularly dangerous, and you need to be aware if you're likely to encounter an actual Sniper Rifle when approaching an enemy position. Explosives are also dangerous, as the Warthog can be flipped fairly easily. In general, you should avoid getting close to infantry on the ground whenever possible, as a single Frag Grenade can ruin your day. If you do get hit by a Frag (or other explosion), steer opposite the direction that the explosion occurred and try to get away as quickly as possible.

When driving the Warthog, maneuvering is similar to the Mongoose, though a bit slower overall. When driving long distances, avoid the temptation to hit every jump in sight—you present a more obvious target when doing so, but more importantly, you lose speed compared to moving over terrain as smoothly as possible. If you are driving with a gunner, you need to be aware of your position relative to the position of your target. If you move in an erratic manner and drive over rough terrain continuously, your gunner won't be able to deal much damage, if any at all. On the other hand, if you are careful about making long arcs around your target of choice, your gunner has plenty of time to line up the shot and keep a stream of fire on the target until it is taken down.

Working with your partner by calling out targets and threats is very useful, both for figuring out where you need to be driving to provide a clear shot, and for setting up the next shot. Avoid getting close to the target, let the gunner have time and the angle needed to deal damage, and you can inflict a lot of damage with a Warthog. It's also important to protect your gunner—if you are taking fire from behind, e-brake and reverse so that the gunner is protected by the front of the Warthog, but can still fire at any enemies in view.

Quick Warthog tips:

- Almost as good as the Mongoose for Flag running
- Can be a powerful mobile gunship with a partner on the turret
- Be careful about carrying two passengers into battle, three players is a very tempting target for the enemy

SCORPION

SECURE, TURRET, WEAK POINT

The Scorpion is the UNSC heavy tank, a lumbering behemoth of a vehicle armed with a massively powerful main cannon and a front mounted turret that can be manned by another player. It is powerful but slow moving, so it is best used at a distance, where its main cannon can keep an enemy team suppressed and destroy any hostile vehicles that come into view. The main cannon on the Scorpion launches a projectile at very high speeds that is even capable of taking down a Banshee in flight. The splash damage on the cannon is also considerable, so a near miss on infantry is usually lethal.

Use and abuse the Scorpion to cover a key area of the map, or protect your objectives. If you work with your teammates, it can be a real nightmare for the enemy team to dispatch the Scorpion, and good usage of it can easily win a match for you if you aren't opposed. When tracking a target and mobile, keep your distance and move in a distant circular arc around your target, or if possible, stay hull down behind cover and use the height of the Scorpion's main

Another player must man the Scorpion's front turret, which adds some useful anti-infantry defense, since it can fire continuously while the main cannon reloads. The turret has a frontal arc of around 270 degrees, so it cannot shoot behind the Scorpion. This weapon isn't a guarantee of protection against infantry, but having another player nearby can be—they can simply hop out of the turret and fight on foot if you are threatened by enemy infantry, potentially giving you time to back up and eliminate the threats with your main cannon while they are distracted.

The Scorpion is vulnerable to a few threats—heavy weapons, other powerful vehicles, and infantry at close range. Of these, infantry getting close is by far the most common way to lose a Scorpion, so it is imperative that you work with the map and your teammates to keep enemy players away. If an enemy does get close, they can kill the Scorpion instantly by mounting it and sticking a grenade, so don't let this happen! If a player happens to mount onto the side or rear and you are aiming towards them with the main cannon, you have a split second to fire at a nearby piece of terrain and kill them with splash damage. This won't always work, but if you are parked near walls or rocks, you can occasionally blast off a player before they have a chance to plant a grenade.

The Scorpion, like the Wraith, has a weak point in its rear armor. The back end of the Scorpion around its rear vent takes roughly double damage from all incoming weapons fire. This is important if you are trying to destroy the Scorpion at a distance—try to get behind it and aim for the vulnerable vent.

Don't waste time going for the weak point shot if you are going to expose yourself to the Scorpion's main cannon, however—better to get in *some* damage than no damage and a free kill for the Scorpion.

Vehicles with turrets or other heavy weapons can also work well against the Scorpion, but you have to expect that attacking it makes you target #1 in most situations. Even this can be useful, if it allows a friendly teammate to sneak up on foot and take it down.

There is one other unique point about the Scorpion—the hatch that covers the pilot can be shot off or destroyed by mounting the Scorpion and meleeing it twice from the left side of the tank. Once destroyed, the pilot is exposed to Sniper class fire, and a few well placed shots can eliminate the pilot while leaving the Scorpion intact. Generally, this is a more difficult method of dealing with the Scorpion, but it has the (significant) advantage of leaving the Scorpion mostly unharmed. If you can coordinate with

FALCON

SECURE, TURRET

The Falcon is a new aerial vehicle, a UNSC troop transport and gunship that can hold one pilot and two passengers, each armed with a side-mounted Machine Gun Turret.

The Falcon is the most unusual of all vehicles in terms of controls, so it's strongly recommended that you spend a bit of time practicing in Forge mode (or in the Campaign) before you hop online, or you may end up with some very annoyed teammates.

Operate the Falcon by holding the "gas" to lift off and gain altitude. Move it forward by tilting forward while holding the accelerator. You can also lock your altitude by tapping the right bumper, which allows you to stabilize your altitude and fly at a consistent height—particularly useful for giving your gunners a stable platform from which to fire.

FALCON MOTION TRACKING

One very unique attribute of the Falcon is that as a special purpose reconnaissance vehicle, it has a greatly extended Motion Tracker range.

It is very possible to spot targets while inside a Falcon on your Motion Tracker that aren't visible, and wouldn't be seen on a normal Motion Tracker at all. Use this advantage to identify threats and call them out to your teammates, particularly when assaulting or defending a specific position. Early warning of enemy movement is often all you need to suppress a threat.

The Falcon is very useful for transporting friendly infantry across the map. Like the Banshee, flying close to the ground and using larger terrain features to stay out of sight is important, but in the Falcon when transporting passengers, it is even more important.

As a gunship, the Falcon can be effective against enemy vehicles and potentially against enemy infantry in the open, but flying slowly and keeping a stable platform for your gunners also puts you at tremendous risk from incoming enemy fire, and because the gunners are exposed, Sniper weapons can kill them fairly easily. Be very careful about using a fully loaded Falcon against enemy forces—with three players onboard, and as a flying vehicle, you are a *very* tempting target. It is often safer to simply transport infantry to a key area on the battlefield and make use of the Falcon's superior sensors to spot enemy forces as they move around the map.

One last point—the cockpit area of the Falcon takes roughly double damage from incoming weapons fire, in much the same way as the rear hatches on the Scorpion and Wraith. While this is rarely an issue due to the small size of the target, you can be hit by Sniper Rifle fire, and a lucky shot from an enemy can take you down more quickly than you might otherwise expect.

COVENANT VEHICLES

COVENANT BOOST

An ability shared by all of the Covenant vehicles, each one has a boost meter that allows you to hold the left trigger to gain a boost of speed for a limited amount of time. The amount of boost (and the speed increase) varies depending on the vehicle, with the lighter, faster Ghost receiving a more noticeable speed increase than the lumbering Wraith.

Boost is useful for ramming other players or vehicles, moving about the map more quickly, evading incoming fire, and occasionally for stabilizing your ride after a hard hit.

GHOST

OPEN TOP, WEAK POINT

The Ghost is a fast Covenant single manned vehicle, much like the Mongoose, but armed with rapid-fire plasma guns. This vehicle also has access to a boost ability that makes it ideal for ramming infantry.

The Ghost is perfect for quick transit across large open maps, and also ideal for harrying larger, slower vehicles with its plasma guns. You can deal with infantry either by saturating them with plasma fire or by trying to run them down. Just be careful with ramming, because if your target jumps at just the right time, they can easily hijack you, and ramming a player with Armor Lock is never a pleasant experience.

The Ghost is considerably more stable than the Mongoose due to its hover technology, but you are still vulnerable to being flipped or knocked around by explosives, so avoid getting close to enemy infantry when possible.

The Ghost also has several weaknesses—first, it is an open- topped vehicle, so you are exposed from the sides and rear to any incoming weapons fire. It is fairly common to be killed while driving a Ghost without the Ghost itself being destroyed. The Ghost is also unusual because it has a very distinct weak point—at the front left foot of the driver is a large energy cell—if this location is targeted by incoming weapons fire, it destroys the Ghost very quickly. A single shot from the Sniper Rifle on this target detonates the Ghost instantly!

Like the other Covenant vehicles, the Ghost has access to a boost that can increase its forward movement speed, perfect for ramming targets or for moving across terrain at great speed. You can even use the boost to knock a Mongoose or Warthog sprawling if you hit it just right. Just be careful about avoiding a head on collision with the Warthog (or anything bigger), since you won't survive the impact. Boosting can also help stabilize your movement if you get knocked askew by an explosion—boost quickly, and the Ghost tends to level out. You can also hold the opposing trigger while boosting with the Ghost to raise the hood of the vehicle to get more air off of jumps and to spear through the enemy that you are attempting to hit.

When boosting at players, many will wait for you to get close, then jump over your Ghost, trying to melee you, hijack, or toss a grenade. To avoid this, fake a boost by charging at a player, stop boosting when they jump, then boost and squish them when they land, while they're unable to adjust their movement in the air.

The Ghost's plasma guns aren't extremely high damage weapons, so you usually need to keep an infantry player in your line of sight for several seconds to take them out. This is also true if you are trying to destroy any larger vehicle. Nevertheless, the ability to move quickly, boost, *and* fight from a single one manned vehicle is quite useful, and the Ghost is a very helpful vehicle on many maps. The one thing it cannot do is transport a flag carrier, as it lacks any space for a passenger.

REVENANT

OPEN TOP, TRANSPORT

The Revenant is a new Covenant vehicle. Like all other Covenant vehicles, it has both hover and boost technology.

The Revenant fills the "midsize" combat role for the Covenant, fitting roughly into the same space as the Warthog for UNSC forces, and falling between the Ghost and the Wraith for the Covenant. It is an armed, two man vehicle that moves at moderate speed, and has moderate size and damage resistance. It is also open-topped, and both passengers are vulnerable to enemy fire.

The Revenant is armed with a plasma launcher that is similar in size and arc to the Wraith's main cannon, but it is both faster and weaker than the Wraith's powerful shot. This shot is surprisingly weak, considering the explosion and impact that it makes, and you might be unpleasantly surprised if you try to take out a player on foot and learn the hard way that they can take a few glancing hits. This also applies to combat against other vehicles—you do NOT want to get into a slugfest with a Wraith or Scorpion, because there is a good chance that you won't come out standing. On the other hand, the explosion from the projectile is very disorienting, and shelling a defensive infantry position while your teammates move in on foot is effective, and it also works quite well for knocking around medium and light vehicles.

The Revenant is also unique because it is a good mix of firepower and speed that can be controlled by one player—the heavier tanks give up mobility, and the Ghost gives up the extra passenger seat. As a result, you can make good use of the Revenant either as a mobile fire support platform for your team or as quick armed transport for teammates or flag runners.

Note that at the time of this writing, the Revenant is only present on one map, but as you can expect to see the Revenant used in custom maps and new maps in the future, it's worth your time to learn to use it effectively.

WRAITH

SECURE, TURRET, WEAK POINT

The Wraith is the powerful Covenant battle tank, similar to the UNSC Scorpion. It is an anti-gravity vehicle, so it is somewhat more maneuverable than the Scorpion. It does have access to the boost feature, even though it can only boost for a very short amount of time.

Like the Scorpion, the Wraith has a forward turret that another player can man, providing some rapid-fire support against infantry or other threats that are not easily dealt with by the Scorpion's main gun.

The Wraith's main cannon is a plasma launcher, very different from the Scorpion's battle cannon. The plasma is launched as a ball of energy in a slow arc that impacts with devastating explosive force. Because of the plasma ball's arc and speed, it is a poor weapon for hitting mobile targets at long range, but it is superior to the Scorpion's cannon in that it can fire at targets indirectly. This means that you can "mortar" an area by lobbing plasma shells at long distance over terrain or buildings and still cause serious problems for your opposition. This is ideal for sieging a defended position or covering an objective or area that your teammates need to run through.

Unfortunately, the Wraith also suffers from a defensive weakness—its rear vent takes increased damage. The Wraith's rear panel is actually *more* vulnerable than the Scorpion's, so it is very important that you do not expose the vehicle's vulnerable rear to enemy attacks. The Wraith's other vulnerabilities are identical to the Scorpion—the pilot cockpit can be shot or knocked off with a melee attack (though curiously, it can be removed from either side with a melee attack, unlike the Scorpion's offset cockpit), and infantry getting close to stick grenades are a serious threat.

Like the Scorpion, if you are quick, you can potentially kill a player who boards you by using the plasma cannon to kill them with splash damage. You also have an additional tool—you can use your boost to slam into a nearby wall, potentially splattering your assailant.

BANSHEE

SECURE

The Banshee is a flying Covenant vehicle. Powerful as both transport and aerial support for your team, the Banshee is a very dangerous vehicle in the right hands. It is relatively simple to pilot—just like the ground based vehicles, point where you want to go, and "steer" in the air.

This vehicle has a few unique quirks, however. First, it is always in motion; normally, you cannot hover. There is a way around this, however—if you stick your nose against a solid bit of terrain, you can stop your forward momentum without taking damage. This is a particularly useful maneuver if you duck behind a large physical obstruction where you still have camera view over the landscape around you. You can use this to hide out and spot for specific targets, then pop out and eliminate any key threats before returning to cover.

As with most other Covenant vehicles, the Banshee has thrusters that can increase its forward movement speed. In the open, if you aren't on an attack run, you should be using these to move quickly from place to place, minimizing your exposure in the open.

The Banshee also has the unique ability to roll—by tapping the shoulder bumper while pressing left, right, or back, you will perform a side or backflip. The flips cause locked on Plasma Launcher or Rocket Launcher shots to temporarily break lock. In the case of the Plasma Launcher, they are extremely unlikely to reacquire you, but Rockets *will*, so make sure you get in cover quickly. If you boost in a long circular arc, you can avoid incoming rockets, but just be aware that the space needed to do this usually leaves you exposed to any other ground based enemies who want you dead. Generally, boosting behind the nearest cover is a better idea than flipping, since the flip takes time and gives your enemies a chance to set up another shot while you are locked in the motion. Backflips are also useful because they do move you backwards slightly, which can be helpful if

The Banshee is *always* a high priority target for the enemy team, and since you are particularly vulnerable to Rocket Launchers, Sniper Rifles, the Spartan Laser, and turrets, it is important that you be aware of where these weapons are on the map, and how likely you are to encounter them while flying around. A keen eyed player in a Scorpion can also knock you out of the sky with a single shot, so watch out if the other team has access to the UNSC tank.When flying around the map, you may also want to try hugging the ground as much as possible—this might seem counter-intuitive as a flying vehicle, but the idea is to conceal yourself from enemy view. If you fly high in the sky, *everyone* will see you, and usually, target you!

The Banshee has two different weapon systems, a rapid-fire plasma gun, and a powerful plasma launcher that locks on to other vehicles. The plasma launcher also deals heavy splash damage against infantry, and a single shot near a player on the ground is almost always fatal. The plasma gun, on the other hand, can be useful for targeting larger vehicles—fire a launcher shot, switch weapons, and continue hammering the vehicle while your launcher reloads. Note that while you can lock on to vehicles with the launcher, you aren't guaranteed a hit—the faster, more maneuverable vehicles can and will escape the shot if there is obstructing terrain in the area.

One other point—it is totally possible to ram players on the ground with the Banshee. Just be very careful about doing this if your target is aware of your attack, you don't want to get airjacked five feet off the ground!

If you do happen to get airjacked while in mid-air, if you're quick, you may be able to flip and ram the player into a nearby surface. You may as well try, even if you fail. If you cause serious damage to the Banshee by ramming it, you make it easier to destroy once it is in enemy hands.

When facing a Banshee, you should do everything in your power to take it out of the sky, whether that means finding a power weapon and shooting it down, landing an impressive EMP grenade shot, or making an awesome

ANTI-VEHICLE TACTICS

As much as using vehicles is important, learning how to fight against them is equally important, as you are forced to fight vehicles while on foot quite often.

HIJACKING

All vehicles in *Halo: Reach* can be hijacked (or airjacked, in the case of the Banshee and Falcon).

Simply approaching a vehicle and holding Ⓧ causes you to board it, and this same functionality lets you board a vehicle even if it is in motion, piloted by an enemy. There is one important point here, however—you can board multiple points on vehicles that can hold passengers, so it's important that you are on the right point on the vehicle you are trying to hijack—there's nothing stopping you from hopping in as a Warthog passenger! This also means that you can hop onto a Warthog's turret and start shooting enemy players while a hostile player drives the Warthog!

It's worth taking a few minutes to run around the various vehicles and see where you can board them. This is fairly straightforward, but there are a few vehicles that require you to be in a specific spot to board and hijack them.

With the Scorpion and Wraith, you can't actually hijack either one, but you can hop on board and destroy them, either by meleeing them repeatedly once onboard, or by sticking a grenade (Frag or Plasma works just fine).

For the Scorpion, it is possible to use a melee attack to knock the pilot's cockpit off, but you must board on the front left of the tank. If you board on the rear or right, you can still melee it, but damage simply destroys the tank. The Wraith is more flexible, and you can destroy the cockpit by boarding on the front left or right, but not the rear.

In the case of the Banshee and Falcon, airjacking them is not the easiest task, but you can reach them if they are foolish enough to get low to the ground, or if you can surprise them by dropping or jumping from a high point on the map, or by making use of the Jet Pack, or even by launching with a vehicle and then dismounting, falling, and airjacking (yes, it's possible). There's nothing stopping you from hopping out of an airborne Banshee or Falcon and attempting an airjack either (be sure to upload the video if you pull that one off…)

WEAPONRY

Naturally, the various weapons in the game can be used against the vehicles. Against open-topped vehicles, any weapon can kill the driver or passengers, though Sniper class weaponry is especially effective for killing the passengers.

Some weapons are notably more powerful in an anti-vehicle role:

- Rocket Launcher
- Plasma Launcher
- Fuel Rod Gun
- Spartan Laser
- Sniper Rifle
- Plasma Pistol
- Grenade Launcher
- Grenades

The Rocket Launcher, Plasma Launcher, Fuel Rod Gun, and Spartan Laser are explicitly powerful anti-vehicle weapons. They can be used to outright destroy even the strongest vehicles with just a few shots. The Sniper Rifle is a bit of a surprise—it is much more powerful against vehicles than you might expect, and is particularly useful for taking down a Banshee at very long range, or for targeting weak points on the Falcon, Wraith, or Scorpion. The Plasma Pistol and Grenade Launcher EMP are both useful for shutting down a vehicle. Note that vehicles with turrets or guns do not have their weapons disabled when they are EMP'd; only their movement is stopped.

EMPing an airborne vehicle is especially effective, since these vehicles drop like stones and can then be easily hijacked or destroyed. EMPing any vehicle can give you the time needed to get close and kill the driver or hijack the vehicle, or for your teammates to destroy the vehicle with other vehicles or powerful weaponry.

Finally, grenades are quite useful against all vehicles. Frag Grenades are only effective against the medium to lightweight vehicles, as they can be used to flip or disorient anything from a Ghost to a Warthog. Plasma Grenades, on the other hand (especially if you land a stick) deal very heavy damage and are useful for destroying even heavy vehicles.

EXPLOSIONS

Any weapon that causes explosions, be it a vehicle weapon, player weapon, or grenade, can be useful against the lighter vehicles.

The Mongoose, Warthog, Ghost, and Revenant are all vulnerable to explosions knocking them around. A well placed hit at the right time can send these vehicles spinning, dislodging all of their passengers.

If you can't find a weapon to destroy the enemy vehicles, go for a weapon that can disrupt them.

- Rocket Launcher
- Plasma Launcher
- Fuel Rod Gun
- Concussion Rifle
- Grenade Launcher
- Gravity Hammer
- Frag Grenade
- Sticky Grenade

DEALING WITH VEHICLES

Use a true anti-vehicle weapon: Rocket Launcher, Plasma Launcher, Spartan Laser, Fuel Rod Gun

- Use a disruptive weapon to bounce the vehicle: Concussion Rifle, Grenade Launcher, Gravity Hammer, Frag Grenades
- EMP the vehicle — Charged Plasma Pistol fire, Manual Grenade Launcher detonation, Armor Lock discharge
- Stick a Plasma Grenade
- Target the driver in open top vehicles, especially with sniper class weapons (DMR, Needle Rifle, Sniper Rifle, Magnum)
- Get close and hijack the vehicle
- Armor Lock, Drop Shield, Jet Pack can all be used to defend against or avoid vehicles, Sprint is somewhat useful
- Vehicle weak spots — Ghost left foot, Wraith rear (more vulnerable than Scorpion), Scorpion rear, the cockpit on Wraith, Scorpion and Falcon
- Use Machine Gun Turrets or Plasma Cannons

WEAPONS TO AVOID

Some weapons simply aren't suited to an anti-vehicle role. If you're using something on this list, it's probably a better idea for you to spend your time finding a better weapon or vehicle, or focusing on an objective. The only exception to this is if you're *trying* to draw the attention of a vehicle to you. Make sure you're coordinating with your team if you're pulling this kind of maneuver—it is risky!

The sniper class weapons on this list can be used against the player in the vehicles in open-topped vehicles, just don't waste your time firing at the vehicle itself!

- Needler and Needle Rifle
- Assault Rifle
- Magnum and DMR
- Plasma Repeater, Rifle, and Pistol (without EMP)
- Shotgun

VEHICLE DENIAL

The last word on vehicle combat is vehicle denial. Destroying or (even better), stealing enemy vehicles before they can be used can be a real coup for your team. A stolen tank will *not* respawn until it is destroyed, so if you can use your own Scorpion or Wraith and steal your enemies as well, the other team will be in a very painful situation.

Try to use fast vehicles and stealth or movement armor abilities to get to the enemy spawn, hide out, and steal or destroy their vehicles before they can be used. Another option is to partially damage strong enemy vehicles. A Banshee or tank that is damaged before it even leaves the base can score your team both a vehicle kill *and* an enemy infantry kill—effectively wasting the opposing team's time.

MULTIPLAYER GAME MODES

What follows are the descriptions of each mode available in the multiplayer portion of *Halo: Reach*. We will explain how to play them, and relay all pertinent intel regarding the intricacies of each mode. Not sure how to play Invasion? We'll brief you in detail on how it works and how you can win no matter what side you're on.

This section will also include in-depth tactical suggestions for how to excel in each mode. These battle-tested tactics are just suggestions and can be tweaked and twisted to suit you and your team's play style. Use them to your advantage and as a building block to create either more advanced or less complex strategies of your own.

MODE DESCRIPTIONS

ASSAULT:

In Assault, offense is tasked with planting their bomb in the enemy's base and defending it until it detonates which takes 10 seconds. Offense starts with the bomb at their base. If the bomb is dropped, it will automatically reset back at the offense's base in thirty seconds. Defenders can manually return the bomb to the offensive base by standing on it for five seconds.

As the bomb carrier you cannot use any Armor Abilities. You cannot sprint, you cannot shoot, all you CAN do is melee with the bomb. Bomb melee's are one-hit kills, however performing an Assassination move while holding the bomb will drop it allowing you to execute your enemy. If you want to hang on to it, melee to the face! If you switch weapons or try to use an Armor Ability with the bomb, you will drop it immediately and it will again light up on the radar.

Not only can the defenders return a dropped bomb, but they can defuse the bomb after it has been planted by standing on or near it for five seconds. You will have to do this quickly as the fuse is only ten seconds long. If you haven't started defusing the bomb by the time the fuse hits five, run away, it's over.

ONE BOMB ASSAULT:

This mode is exactly like the main Assault mode however there is no offense or defense, and the bomb is centrally located. Both teams have the same chance to acquire the bomb and plant it at their enemy's base. Melee while in possession of the bomb is still a one-hit kill.

NEUTRAL BOMB ASSAULT:

This mode variant features a single, centrally located bomb and four teams. Any team can acquire the bomb. What's different in NBA is that you can plant the bomb at any of the enemy team's bases. Armor Abilities are available in Assault modes however only when you do not have possession of the bomb.

GRIFBALL:

Usually played on open, arena-style maps, this assault mode features melee weapons only. The Gravity Hammer and the Energy Sword are your only options here. The bomb is centrally located and can be picked up by either side. One team must plant the bomb in the enemy's base to win.

The bomb carrier gets an Overshield which will recharge over time, and fall away if you drop the bomb. Passing the bomb to teammates will grant them their own Overshield, but once you drop the bomb, your Overshield will disintegrate over time.

While it takes multiple melee attacks to kill someone holding the bomb, it only takes one hit from behind to kill them outright. Sword or Hammer attacks from behind are also one-hit kills.

Make good use of the Gravity Hammer's shock pound to knock enemy players away, or move friendly carriers forward, and to reposition the bomb itself.

CAPTURE THE FLAG:

Each team has a flag at their base which they must prevent the enemy from stealing. Grab the other team's flag and bring it back to your base to gain a point. You cannot return an enemy flag if your flag has been taken. You must return your team's flag before you can return an enemy flag for a point. It takes three captures to win a CTF game.

If a flag is dropped, it will auto-return to its respective base in thirty seconds. You and your team can manually return the flag by standing on it for fifteen seconds.

If you are the flag carrier, the flag is your only weapon. The flag creates a one-hit kill if you are close enough to someone to melee with it. As in all objective based modes, you will move more slowly while in possession of the objective itself such as a flag or a bomb.

Armor abilities are available in Capture the Flag modes but you cannot utilize them when you are in possession of the flag itself. Switching weapons or using an Armor Ability will make you drop the flag immediately.

MULTI FLAG CTF:

This four team variant on Capture the Flag is played exactly the same as standard CTF but with four teams. Each team has a flag that they must defend while trying to acquire any of the other three team's flags and return it to their base. Capture enemy flags to gain points. Three points to win.

Remember that you cannot return an enemy flag if your flag has been taken. Return your flag first, then bring the enemy flag back your base for a point.

NEUTRAL FLAG CTF:

This variation on standard Capture the Flag removes the flags at each team's base and adds a single flag in the middle of the map. Both teams fight to grab the one flag to rule them all and bring it back home to your base. Each capture gets your team one point and it takes three points to win the match.

ONE FLAG CTF:

One flag mode has you and your team either defending or attacking. Defenders start with a flag at their base which they must prevent the enemy from grabbing and returning. The only way to score here is to steal and return a flag.

You will switch sides every time a point is gained by the attacking team, or when the timer hits three minutes. Defense cannot score points. You have four rounds to rack up as many points as you can. Most points after four rounds wins.

HEADHUNTER:

In this free for all mode you collect flaming skulls from enemies and deposit them at a randomly selected drop zones. These zones will change every thirty seconds so try to keep an eye on how long each zone has been active for. It takes twenty five points to win.

Every time you kill someone, they will drop their skull. If they have picked up any skulls from other enemies they've killed, they will drop those as well. Run over them to pick them up, and run into the drop zone to rack up one point for each skull you've got.

The number of skulls you currently have is displayed in your HUD as well as over your head for all to see. If you can collect ten skulls and deposit them all at once, you win even if you haven't reached the twenty five point limit. Armor abilities are available in this mode as well, even if you're holding skulls.

HEADHUNTER PRO:

In the pro version of this mode, players start with a DMR and two Frag Grenades. Your only Armor Ability here is Sprint. The only way to acquire skulls in this variant is to headshot an enemy. Twenty five points will win you the match. You can still kill enemies without headshotting them, but they will not drop their own skull for you to collect. If they happen to have been carrying other skulls they've collected by headshotting other enemies, they WILL drop those skulls and you can collect and deposit them at will.

INFECTION:

This is a free for all mode that can be played with teamwork. Three players are chosen at random to be the infected, or zombies. Everyone else is an uninfected human. Regardless of which side you start on, your main objective is to get as many kills as possible.

Kills equal points and most points wins. As a Spartan, work together with your fellow humans to eliminate the infected. As a zombie, kill as many humans as you can, as quickly as you can. If a human is killed by a zombie, they become part of the infected "team".

Spartans start with only a Shotgun, a Magnum, and the Sprint ability. Zombies are outfitted only with Energy Swords and the Elite Evade ability. The last man standing gets half of an Overshield. The round is over when all Spartans have been infected.

SAFE HAVENS:

While otherwise identical to the standard Infection mode, this variation includes random "safe zones" which Spartans can stand in to be protected from the infected players. Spartans will not take damage in the safe zones. These zones are randomly generated and will remain active in their location until a human stands inside of one.

Zombies cannot activate a safe zone. Once a Spartan enters a zone, a timer starts counting down from fifteen. Once time runs out, a new randomly selected safe zone will appear somewhere on the map. There is no set number of safe zones, they cannot be used up, only relocated.

INVASION:

This massive, objective-based mode pits Spartans against Elites in a three tiered battle across expansive environments. With six on six gameplay, each team is broken up into wingman teams. You can spawn on your wingman or designated spawn locations on the map.

The offensive team must penetrate two tiers of defenses and then capture a Core. In tier one, you must infiltrate the enemy base and capture a territory. You must run the timer down from twenty seconds to zero as quickly as possible. The more players you have in the territory, the faster the counter will tick down.

The defenders can regenerate the territories, but only up to seven seconds. There are two territories to capture but you only need to capture one of them to advance to the next tier. Each round lasts four minutes. If the defense can hold out for that long, they win the round.

If the offense capture one of the tier one territories, the second set opens up. New areas of the map will become accessible and each team will get new loadouts as well as new vehicles. Once tier two is unlocked, the defense must protect the new set of territories.

If the offense manage to capture one of the two tier two territories, more loadouts and vehicles become available. At this point, there are no more territories, only a single Core. The offensive team must steal the core and return it to their pick up point. Players carrying the core will move very slowly and of course cannot use any Armor Abilities.

Note that unlike the Bomb or Flag in Assault or CTF modes, the Core is *not* a melee weapon. If you want (or need) to fight, you must drop it first.

If the Core is dropped, the defensive team can return it by standing near it. A progress bar will appear letting you know how much longer you have until it is returned. The more players you have standing near the dropped core, the faster the progress bar will move.

INVASION SLAYER:

This mode is played on the same maps as standard Invasion however there is no Core, only randomly selected and generated territories which either team can capture. There is no offense or defense here. It remains six on six wingman-based gameplay however in this version, kills amount to points, and first to one hundred points to win.

To capture a territory, stand inside the visible zone for ten seconds. Once you capture it, you will be rewarded with team specific weapon or vehicle drops in that territory's location. You must defend the territory for fifteen seconds for the drop to take place. Remember that capturing territories does NOT get you any points, only vehicle and weapon drops.

Each tier in this version of Invasion unlocks new loadouts. You start with one loadout, then tier two unlocks three, then tier three unlocks five loadouts. Tiers can be unlocked either based on total kills or time. Tier two is unlocked at ten minutes or twenty five kills, tier three is unlocked at fifteen minutes or fifty kills.

JUGGERNAUT:

Kill the guy with the ball. Except in this case, the ball is really a big hammer! One player is randomly selected at the start of the round to be the Juggernaut. Juggernauts can take massive amounts of damage, can move much faster than everyone else, and only have a Gravity Hammer for a weapon. Everyone else gets the Assault Rifle, Mangum, and one Frag Grenade. Your main objective? Kill the Juggernaut! The Juggernaut gets ten points per kill and everyone else only gets five for killing non-Juggernauts. You need one hundred and fifty points to win. Newly spawned Juggernauts get ten seconds of invulnerability when they become the new Juggernaut. Be careful about getting into fights against non-Juggernaut players. If you spend too much time without cooperating, the Juggernaut can rack up an insurmountable lead!

KING OF THE HILL:

The name says it all. Take control of the hill and rack up one hundred and fifty points to win. One ten minute round is all you get, so do your best and be quick about it. Both teams fight to gain control of a single static hill, gaining one point per second that your team controls it. Kills do not get you any points here.

The more players you have inside the hill the faster you will gain control of it. The enemy team can take control from you and put you on the offensive.

Note that you cannot use any Armor Abilities inside the hill, however you can engage a Drop Shield just outside of the hill and have it extend into the hill itself, providing protection to your teammates and healing them simultaneously.

CRAZY KING:

This mode is just like King of the Hill except that the hill is randomly selected and placed somewhere on the map. It still takes one hundred and fifty points to win, but the hill will move every thirty seconds making it more difficult to dominate one location. This is also one ten minute round.

You can only gain a total of thirty points per hill before it relocates. Bear in mind that when there is only five seconds left in the lifetime of the current hill, it will flash so you know it's time to move out.

ODDBALL:

Ball taken! Ball dropped! This mode really IS kill the guy with the ball. This free for all awards players points only for each second they have control of the ball, which is a flaming skull, of course. One hundred and fifty points to win. The ball starts in the center of the map and will nullify any of your Armor Abilities as soon as you pick it up. Trying to use an Armor Ability or a weapon will immediately drop the ball. The only weapon you have IS the ball which is a one-hit, flaming kill. Picking up the ball also puts you on enemy radar, so be ready for the constantly incoming mob.

RACE:

Saddle up your Mongoose and step on it. This three lap race mode pits you against other racers hell bent on beating you, or at least, wrecking you.

As you race you need to hit all of the checkpoints scattered throughout the track. If you miss one, you will stop getting points for any future checkpoints until you go back and hit the one or ones you missed. Landmines dot the track so be wary and drive carefully. Races last ten minutes or three rounds.

RALLY:

This racing mode also features landmines but instead of preset checkpoints, you must locate and drive through a series of randomly selected flags. Fifteen flags to win, one point per flag. There is no track here and it isn't really a race. You only have a Mongoose to drive and can choose to drive through as many flags as you can or just the ones closest to you. Keep an eye on how many flags and points you have compared to the leader.

ROCKET RACE:

Guess what? It's a race, with rockets! Once again you will be dodging landmines and driving through flags like in Rally mode, but now you'll be granted a wingman with a Rocket Launcher. One player drives and one rides on the back of the 'Goose. Drive through as many flags as you can since this is the only way to gain points, and use your rocket buddy to stop the competition.

SLAYER:

Every man for himself. To win, you need to be first to twenty five kills inside of ten minutes. Armor Abilities are available here at any time, and weapon pickups are scattered throughout the maps. The only thing that matters here is how fast you can get twenty five kills. If no one has hit twenty five by the end of ten minutes, whoever has the most kills will win.

SLAYER CLASSIC:

Ah the good ol' days. Slayer Classic mode is your standard free for all however you do not have access to any Armor Abilities at any time. All players start with the Assault Rifle, one Frag Grenade and one Plasma Grenade. There are weapon pickups on the map, but aside from that, everyone here will be on a level playing field.

SLAYER PRO:

This mode plays just like standard Slayer. The difference in Pro mode is all players have limited weapon and ability access. You'll get precision weapons only, with two Frag Grenades and Sprint as your Armor Ability.

ELITE SLAYER:

Just like regular Slayer other than the fact that you're all Elites. All of your loadouts and abilities are Elite based. This mode is still twenty five kills in ten minutes to win the match. Elites are bigger, faster, and can heal on their own slowly over time.

SWAT:

For those of you who want a little more hardcore gameplay, this mode starts all players off with the DMR and the Magnum. The only ability players have here is Sprint. There are no grenades on the maps and no one has shields, but all players have increased base health. Twenty five kills to win and a ten minute time limit. Headshots anyone?

STOCKPILE:

There are several neutral flags located around the map in this mode. Grab flags and return them to your drop off zone. Flags must be defended for sixty seconds before they actually get counted as a point towards your score. The team with the most points after ten minutes wins.

Multiple flags can be dropped in the zone at different times; however, once the first flag is dropped in the zone, the timer will begin to count down. If you have two flags in the zone and there are thirty seconds left, you can drop two more flags in the zone and they only have to be defended for thirty seconds.

You can grab flags that the enemy has waiting in their drop zone to prevent them from scoring points. Just grab them and pull them out of the zone to stop their timer.

TERRITORIES:

THREE PLOT:

Three Plot is a territory control mode. There are three territories on the map which teams will fight to take and keep control of. Your team gets one point per second that you control a territory. Control more points simultaneously to gain more points per second. Holding all three territories will speed your point count. First team to three hundred wins. It takes five seconds to capture a territory at which point it will change color to your team colors letting the enemy know that you've got control of that territory. Armor abilities do not work inside of territory zones.

LAND GRAB:

There are five territories up for grabs here. Both teams fight to gain control of as many territories as they can. Once a territory is taken, it will lock and cannot be retaken by the other team. It will drop a flag in your team's color and you no longer need to worry about it. It takes thirty seconds for your team to actually capture each territory and you get one point per territory

that you've taken. Prevent the other team from capturing any territories while trying to take them all for yourself.

TERRITORIES:

This territorial variation has one team attacking and one team defending. You play each side once, and the most territories captured wins. Territories still take thirty seconds to capture, and will lock once taken. Defense does not gain any points for defending territories, they are just trying to stop the enemy team from getting any points. All points are achieved while on Offense only. Five points to win, or most points after two rounds.

MODE TACTICS

In this briefing, we will offer up detailed strategies and tactics for succeeding in each game mode. While these concepts have been proven in-game, they may not work for you and your team or fit how you play.

Use these ideas as a base for learning new strategic concepts you may not have thought of, and as a solid foundation to build your own tactics upon. What follows are tactical suggestions for ways to win in each of the modes that Halo: Reach has to offer.

ASSAULT:

This is one of the premier objective-based modes available. The inability to utilize any Armor Abilities while in possession of the bomb is a key reminder of how much teamwork you're going to need to get through this mode on top.

Let's talk offense. Putting the bomb carrier out in front of your team to lead the way to the enemy base isn't usually the best idea, however, it gives the assaulting team behind them the ability to pick up the bomb if the initial carrier gets killed. Then they can proceed with their assault. You'll want to have at least a couple of teammates running with the carrier and packing Armor Abilities such as Armor Lock and Drop Shield. If your carrier is under attack, use the Armor Lock to keep yourself alive and make the enemy waste their ammo on you. If you notice your carrier is getting pummeled, activate your Drop Shield and get them inside to heal. This can keep your momentum going and prevent the bomb from having to be reset all the way back at your base. Offense can also try using the Hologram Armor Ability to send out a "scout team" ahead of you. Once you grab the bomb and start heading to the enemy base, have two of the players escorting the carrier fire off their Holograms into enemy territory. Enemies will hopefully fire on the light-based projections and give you a chance to locate them in the map. Then you can follow your Holograms in and dispatch the enemy contingent. Keep your Holograms coming as you move in to plant the bomb making the enemy think you've got more players in the area than you actually do.

While the three of you move in however you choose to plant the bomb, send one player around the outskirts of the map to flank the enemy. If your offense is using Holograms, the opposing force may very well assume your entire team is sticking together and assaulting in force. This will give your flanker time to sneak around behind them and help clear them out from the back. When you've whittled them down far enough, go ahead and plant. Remember that it only takes ten seconds for the bomb to detonate, so just try to get it planted. Most of the time, once a bomb is planted, there will not be enough time for an enemy to defuse it, which takes five seconds.

You can also try splitting your offense into two teams, a carrier team and a scout team. Your carrier team should both run Holograms and fire them off into enemy territory. Even though you will drop the bomb and it will show up on radar, you can pick it back up immediately and move forward while the enemy deals with what they think is your whole team.

Another option is the single file column. Space your teammates fifteen meters behind one another, with your bomb carrier at the tip of the spear. Try to be patient as you all progress in a single file toward the plant site and keep your spacing. If the carrier drops the bomb, the next in line picks it up and continues. Think of this tactic like rushing a football. Keep pushing the ball towards the enemy base. Since it only takes five seconds to plant and ten to detonate, you really just need to get it there. What will happen in this formation is that when the first player goes down, then next

Defenders should always remember to defend! We all know how it goes, you get into a game and just want to kill. Play it smart and do your job Spartan. Think about it this way, if you don't guard the plant site, they'll just storm the plant and the round will be over. Then who are you going to shoot?

Assuming you know the lay of the land on whichever map you're fighting on, designate teammates to defend each chokepoint. You don't always have to just camp the plant site. Many times it is more advantageous to watch the funnels. These are areas that the other team must pass through to get to your base. While defending the chokepoints, some good Armor Abilities are of course Armor Lock which will work especially well if the chokepoint is small, and Active Camo. The Active Camo ability can really give you and your team the extra few seconds needed to get the drop on incoming enemies.

You can make good use of the Hologram as well on defense if you can coordinate it with the rest of your team. If two of your teammates use Active Camo and two of you use Holograms, wait for the enemies to reach the chokepoints and fire off your Holograms to make them look like they are attacking the offense. Once they become engaged you won't have much time before they figure out they are shooting at fakes. That's when your Active Camo team comes in to Assassinate them from behind.

There are lots of concepts for defending. If you feel comfortable enough, try setting up a couple of snipers in a crossfire position overwatching the plant site. Since many players will look for snipers to be looking into the middle of the map, set your snipers up at the chokepoints under cover and aiming back towards the plant site. Let them come in, then take them out before they can plant.

Remember that you must try to stop them before they get close to the plant site since it only takes five seconds to plant the bomb. This is why you should put the two remaining players in a close support position near the bomb plant. They should use Active Camo and camp somewhere close to be able to melee or finish off the attackers. If you eliminate the enemy rush and get them to drop the bomb, fall out and get on top of the bomb. It will reset it in their base in five seconds. Before you do this, decide if you want to use the bomb as bait. While it will return itself in thirty seconds, enemies WILL be trying to get to it. It's up to you if you want to send it back to them quickly or not, but you should do it while you can. If you don't return it right away, an enemy using Sprint or the Jet Pack may be able to get back to it quickly enough and plant it or at least move it a bit closer to the plant site and reset the timer. Your best bet is to continue to send it back as far from your plant site as possible.

You can always send out a player or two to set back the incoming force, but be careful not to get too close to the bomb carrier. Their melee attacks are one-hit wonders, so pick them off with projectiles from distance. If you do send a player out, they can make good use of the Drop Shield ability to stay alive longer and delay the incoming assault. Remember that you just need to stop the offense from planting the bomb, so ticking time off the clock isn't a bad thing.

ONE BOMB ASSAULT:

In this team-based Assault variant, there is no pre-selected offense or defense. Two teams square off against each other with a single bomb located between them. You need to plant it to win, so let's go over some of your options.

You need to gain possession of the bomb if you're going to plant. You're going to need to plant it if you want to gain any points. You're going to need points to win. The first concept we're going to explore is speed.

Half of your team should head for whatever power weapons might be available on the map you're playing. They should be outfitted with the Scout class and Sprint. This will give them a better chance to get to their weapon of choice before the enemy. The rest of your team should also choose the Sprint ability. They will be going after the bomb as quickly as possible. Your power weapon team should be laying waste to the area around the bomb to give your grab team time to get it. As your carrier team continues to make their way to the enemy plant site, your power weapon team should continue to clear the way.

While your bomb carrier is planting, everyone else needs to set up in a perimeter around the plant site. Don't get too far from it, since it only takes five seconds to defuse it. Your Sprint ability should let you get up close and personal in a hurry if an enemy manages to sneak up to the planted package.

Consider that the enemy's plan could be very similar to yours. They may very well be making for the power weapons available on the map. You can use this to your advantage by forgetting about grabbing the power weapons for yourselves and just sprinting in a group to the bomb and to the plant site.

Many times while the enemy is looking for that Sniper Rifle or Rocket Launcher, they are putting aside the objective. Rush your way to the bomb and then to the plant site as fast as you can, lock it down and defend it.

You can run this tactic in different ways, for an example similar to standard Assault tactics above, send a flanker or flank team to distract and engage while your carrier team pushes forward with the bomb. Try different formations and spread yourselves out. Time your assault in steady waves and keep constant pressure on the opposition.

Of course there's always brute force. You don't have to be the fastest if you're the strongest. Let's play this option out with the mindset of a defensive offense. Load your team out with Armor Lock and Drop Shield Armor Abilities and make for some power weapons. Most maps will have at least a few power weapons located near where you spawn so make haste and grab yourselves some heavy guns. Since you're not going to be running, gradually make your way towards the bomb by way of the chokepoints to your base. This will enable you and your team to prevent them from getting in past you.

As your leviathans march to their destination, keep your teammates healthy using the Drop Shield and keep yourselves alive to fight another day by dropping some Armor Lock in battle. Use whatever power weapons you've acquired to force your way to the plant site and set up a perimeter. The defensive offense can also be used as either a preliminary or secondary tactic. Use these techniques to get started or to finish. Swap to a fast loadout or even a distraction loadout such as Holograms or Active Camos. Using the right loadout at the right time can be the key to victory here as well as many other modes.

NEUTRAL BOMB ASSAULT

This mode is identical to One Bomb Assault with the only difference being the addition of two other teams. Four teams scramble for the bomb and can plant it at any other team's base. As if one team to fight wasn't enough, now you've got three enemy teams to consider. This isn't necessarily a bad thing. You can use this to your advantage and get other teams to help you with your own objectives without them even knowing.

The only way to get points in this mode is to actually plant the bomb. Defending doesn't get you any points. It only prevents other teams from getting points from you. So you'll need the bomb.

Get to the bomb as quickly as you can and start moving it towards whichever team's base you think may be the weakest. Keep pushing the bomb as close to their plant site as you can. What this does is brings the fight to a specific enemy base. All other teams are going to have to move to the bomb. Wherever it is, that's where everyone will be. The chances that other teams will try to grab the bomb and run it across the map to another team's base, is slim at best. They're going to plant it at the base it's closest to. Knowing this, you can play it a few different ways from here on out. You can continue to push the bomb into the selected weak team's base and try to plant, or hide and wait for another enemy team to bring it all the way in for you, then finish them off and plant it yourself. Remember to keep eyes on the bomb location at all times. If you are unsure as to where it is, keep a defender back at your base. If you happen to become the defense team and the other teams have pushed the bomb closest to your base, then you'll want a few more than one player defending.

Concentrate on pushing the bomb as far from your base as possible while trying to plant it at any other enemy's base. It doesn't take long to plant, so once it's down, it's pretty much over. Don't put all of your plasma eggs in one basket. You should always try to keep at least one player in the vicinity of your own base, just in case.

GRIFBALL

The main objective here is to plant the bomb. Played on arena-style maps, this mode only gives players melee weapons to get the job done. With the bomb dead in the middle of the map, it's going to be kind of like the start of a dodge ball game.

Since the bomb carrier gets a rechargeable Overshield, they can force their way through to a certain point. Try tossing the bomb to your fellow teammates, kind of like a lateral to give them some Overshield as well. This will give you and your teammates a little more juice to withstand the initial onslaught.

You're going to need to stick close to your bomb carrier in this mode. When they start getting whacked, it's time to step in and beat them away. Try creating a wedge formation with your carrier at the front. Remember that if you melee an enemy with the bomb in hand, it's an instant one-hit kill. Melee enemies from behind for a single shot kill too. Your best bet here is to keep pushing forward and keeping the bulk of your team behind the bomb carrier. This will allow all players behind them to pick up the bomb and continue to push it forward and closer to your objective.

You can hit the bomb with the Gravity Hammer mimicking a polo-style kind of game play. This can help you push the bomb closer to the enemy base and even wound nearby enemies with the force generated from hitting the bomb. You can use this technique to effectively "pass" the bomb to players further up the field.

Grifball is going to end up being a massive blob of players bashing each other up, so be ready for this to happen. Sometimes the best laid plans are laid to waste. Prepare yourself for the ensuing melee combat.

CAPTURE THE FLAG

This mode requires both offense and defense to be played simultaneously. You must capture an enemy flag to gain points and you need three points to win. You cannot capture an enemy flag if your flag has been taken, which is why you must play defense while playing offense.

For this mode we're going to start by splitting your team up in half. You need to create an offense using Armor Abilities such as Sprint and Jet Packs. This will give them good mobility and the chance to get to the enemy flag quickly. Your offense can also make good use of the Hologram and Active Camo abilities. If they choose to run Holograms and Active Camo, this can give them a different advantage than getting to the flag quickly. By firing off a Hologram, you can distract enemy campers into thinking you're coming for their flag while your friend with Active Camo runs in to Assassinate them from behind. You can send your Hologram in to trick the enemy into thinking you're coming for their flag, then follow them in and finish them off.

Steal their flag and head back to base. You can (and should) continue to use your Armor Abilities on your way back to base as long as you're not the carrier. If you're using the Hologram, send one out in front of you or even behind you to distract the enemy. If you're using the Active Camo, trail your flag carrier from a little further back and pick off any of their attackers.

Remember that you can drop the flag at any time while you're carrying it. Switching weapons or trying to use an Armor Ability will immediately drop the flag. You can benefit from this by almost throwing the flag ahead of you then picking it back up. You move very slowly while carrying the flag so this can help you to more quickly return the flag to your base for a capture. Tossing the flag down a slope will cause it to slide faster than you can move with it. While in your possession, the flag is your only weapon. It serves as a single shot melee weapon, so don't hesitate to use it if someone gets in your face.

The flag will return to the enemy base by itself in thirty seconds or if the enemy stands on or near it, it will return in fifteen seconds. This will buy you some time to toss it and retrieve it repeatedly. Just be quick about it. You can also be successful by sending your entire team after the enemy flag, then killing their flag carrier on your way back to your base. Keeping everyone on your team together is a good idea here especially since the flag carrier is quite vulnerable while running the flag. You can utilize several different Armor Abilities, but it might be a good idea to load everyone out with the same kits. If everyone is on the assault and carries the Hologram ability, you can all send in your Holo-team simultaneously and stage a fake attack. While the enemy is focused on your fake friends, you need to follow them in and clean up the mess. Grab their flag and head back to base. As you fall back, turn and fire off another set of Holo-soldiers behind you to make it seem as though you've doubled back to camp their spawn. This should give your carrier enough time to make it back to base.

This mob technique can also be well executed using the Active Camo ability. Stick together and move in as a group. When you reach the first hot spot on the map, engage your camo and split up. Meet back up at the enemy flag and grab it. Your carrier will now be able to be seen so you will need to try to follow them from a distance to support.

Following the enemy too closely will get you noticed, since they will be focused on the flag bearer. Try to follow your carrier along the perimeter of their route back to base and pick off enemies as quickly as you can. If you can acquire a power weapon on your way back, you should. The more quickly you can dispatch the enemies chasing your flag carrier the better.

Take note that flags cannot be thrown into any Gravity Lifts on any maps, they will just sit there. You can use this to your advantage by having a fellow teammate wait at the bottom of a lift to grab a flag you toss down to them. On a similar note, Holograms WILL use a Gravity Lift! Send them in and watch them go for a ride. This is a handy technique and can really trick the enemy into thinking it's a real player, since Holograms just run in a straight line.

ONE FLAG CTF

The mechanics of this mode are very much the same as basic CTF however one team is offense and must capture flags and one team is defense and must defend their flag. You do not get any points on defense here, you just need to prevent the enemy from getting points.

Going in on offense you know the enemy is going to be camping their flag. You only have three minutes so you'll have to get going but you don't necessarily need to run a fast class. Try something tricky like the Active Camo or the Hologram tricks as mentioned in the standard CTF tactical section. Since everyone will be camping the flag, you can try to move everyone on your team to engage enemies around the perimeter while one player hangs back until you are all engaged in combat. Then using Active Camo, they can rush in and steal the flag while everyone is fighting. If you get into a struggle on your way back to base, you can think about someone running Drop Shields to accompany you. When you get into a gun fight, have your Shield buddy drop one around the both of you. This will force the enemy to move in close at which point, the flag carrier can one-hit melee them and you can both proceed. You can switch things up if this isn't working for you, or just keep the enemy on their toes. Try sending a sprint team out to fast attack their flag base. If all of your teammates are moving at the same speed as you are, you should all get to the flag about the same time.

Use your speed to not just get in quickly but to get back quickly. Your flag carrier will be moving much more slowly than you here so they should implement the toss and retrieve technique explained earlier. Toss your flag in front of you by switching weapons or using an Armor Ability, then run after it and pick it back up. This will light up the flag on radar so you're going to have to stay mobile and hope for the best. Hopefully, your team can sprint ahead of you and clear you a path to your base. Try tossing it down embankments and hills to speed it up even more.

Remember that you switch every time a flag is captured or every three minutes. It doesn't give you much time to get the job done, so use the best option based on all available intel. Be prepared for your enemies to pick up on some of the tricks you've shown them while you were on offense as well. Be able to defend against your own tactics. Make good use of any found power weapons here as well. These can help you get in unscathed by eliminating enemy forces before they can do much damage to you and your team. They can also help you escape by clearing a path back to base. Find them first, and grab them often.

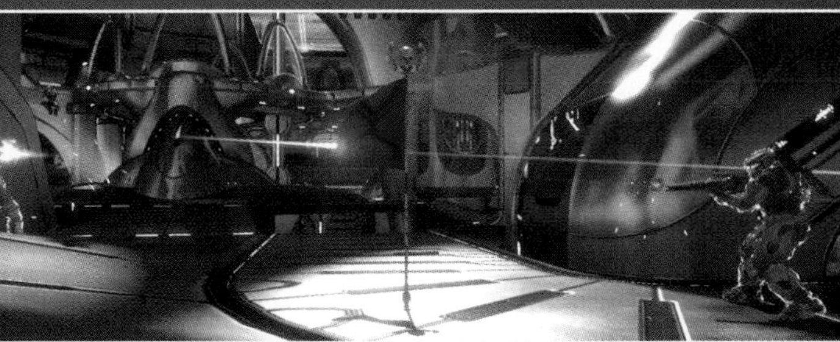

NEUTRAL FLAG CTF

This mode plays very similarly to One Bomb Assault. Replace the bomb with a flag and you've got Neutral Flag CTF. Neither team is on offense or defense here. Both teams have an equal chance to acquire the flag. Sitting back doesn't score you any points, so you need to devise a plan to get the flag.

Gear up with Jet Packs and Sprint and make your way to the closest power weapons available on the map you're playing on. Regroup with your teammates and move in on the flag. The enemy may have already taken it by this time so start firing and suppress them as quickly as you can. Keep the fire on their approach while you grab the flag and start bringing it back towards your base. This is going to be a sort of "tug of war" for the flag, so try some techniques like flag tossing to get the flag back to your base fast. At this point it might be a good idea to have half of your team escort the flag and the other half defend it from incoming attackers.

You need three points to win, so you're going to have to do this more than once. Switch up your plan of attack from time to time from fast and powerful to tricky and sneaky. If your enemy doesn't know what you're going to do, they have less time to react when they see what you actually do. Psychological warfare is a big part of the game. You can always try to push the flag back to base by tossing it and chasing it, just remember enemies can grab it too and you don't want to toss it to an enemy. Use this technique with caution.

MULTI FLAG CTF

This interesting take on Capture the Flag pits four teams against each other in a four flag CTF battle. There are three flags for the taking in this mode and you can go about it many different ways.

Push your entire team fast and strong to the closest enemy flag. Muscle your way in and grab their flag. Start running it back to your base as fast as you can and leave the rest of your team lagging behind you to slow any respawning bees that might be angry you stole the honey from their hive.

When you're able to capture your first flag, switch to the next closest enemy base and move in. Make sure there's a flag still there before you head in. With three other teams, someone might have beaten you to the punch. Switch it up in this manner, rotating or alternating different enemy flags and keep them guessing. You can split your team and assault the two closest enemy bases simultaneously. Send half your team to one and the other half to the other to grab and capture. Hopefully you can get some wanted distraction from the other teams trying to do the same. Don't forget you're not the only one who wants those flags.

If the closest bases or flags to your base are under major contention, move to a less busy thoroughfare. You won't just be fighting off the enemy base defenders, but other attacking teams vying for the same flags as you and your team. Because this inevitably will occur during matches, your best bet is to stick together as a team and only split up from time to time to confuse the enemy into thinking you're going to be doing something different now.

WELCOME
UNSC TRAINING
THE CAMPAIGN
FIREFIGHT
MULTIPLAYER
BASICS & TACTICS
ARSENAL
VEHICLES
GAMEPLAY MODES
MAPS
FORGE
REFERENCE

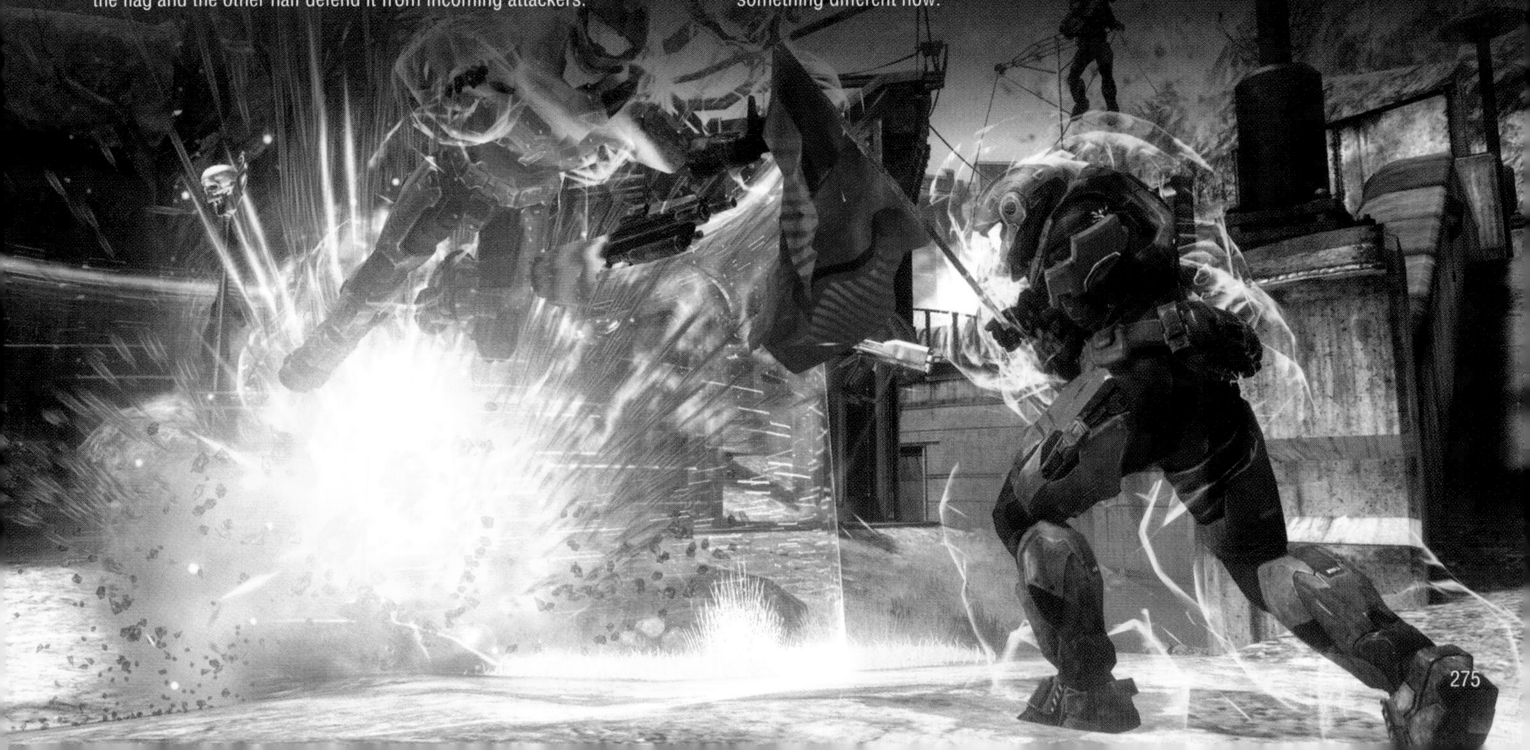

While this is all going on, players will be gunning for your own flag. You're going to have to leave a player behind. This player can benefit from finding a Grenade Launcher and firing off a potato right at your own flag. If you use the Active Camo ability, you can sit back with the trigger held and wait for some poor fool to rush in and nab your flag, then release the trigger and send them flying. Even if you can't get to a Grenade Launcher, someone needs to defend. There are several critical Armor Abilities to use on defense. The first is Armor Lock. Engage your armor during a fight to hold off incoming thieves while communicating to your team that your flag is under attack. This should keep you alive long enough for your team to fall back and help. The next ability is the Drop Shield. Use this in the same manner and fire it off when you come under attack. This is best coupled with a melee weapon such as the Gravity Hammer or the Energy Sword since enemies will have to move in to melee range to damage you while your Drop Shield is engaged. This will also be healing you if you have taken any damage from fire.

You can use most of the abilities on defense however the Sprint ability isn't going to do you much good unless you fail to do your job and have to chase someone who stole your flag. This goes for the Jet Pack as well.

HEADHUNTER

You need to capture twenty five skulls to win or capture ten at one time to end the match. There are a couple of ways to go about approaching this mode, the casual way, the individual way, or the "that's just mean" way.

The casual way is to just head out and start killing enemies free for all style and collect however many skulls you feel comfortable carrying around before dropping them off. This can work well as players won't be able to pin down any kind of style of play from you. Get a couple of kills, steal a couple of heads, and drop them off. Don't get too greedy. When the little number of skulls you have above your head gets to two or more, you become much more of a high-value target. Try to memorize the locations of the random drop zones and mill around those areas whenever you have any skulls, just stay mobile and keep your head on a swivel. Drop 'em if ya got 'em.

The individual approach can be more like long term investing. Try dropping off skulls as soon as you get them, one at a time. This is going to be a much slower process of racking up kills and you won't get able to end the round by dropping off ten at a time by doing this, but you won't be as much of a target since you'll only ever have a "1" above your head. Players tend to go for enemies with two or more skulls at least. This style of play will allow you to kind of fly under the radar a bit and still rack up points. Granted it will be a slower process, but it will be consistent and almost guarantee you a steady flow of points. If you notice your nemesis is getting too far ahead in points based on the time left in the round, you'll need to change up your tactics.

On to the "that's just mean" way of play. Once you learn where the drop zones are spawning, you can make your way there and loiter waiting for enemies to run in and deposit their haul. Make your way to a power weapon before you do this, since players only need to step inside of a zone to accrue points. Pick off enemies as they get all excited about dropping off their pile of skulls to really make them angry. Grab the skulls and drop them off in the zone yourself, you thief! You're not going to make any friends doing this, but you can rack up large amounts of skulls quickly. It IS every man for himself, you know.

If you're going to be mean, you might as well try chasing down players with the highest skull counts, stealing their stash, and dropping them off as your own. This is what you want to avoid when using the individual skull style of play. Remember that if you kill someone with five skulls, they drop their own as well making it one more skull than the number above their heads. If you can find a number "9" and drop them all in the zone, you win and the round will end.

This mode enables the use of Armor Abilities while you are in possession of skulls. You'll want to seriously think about abilities like Sprint and the Jet Pack to get in and get out as fast as you can. The Armor Lock can be a big help here as well if you start to get bombarded. Of course the Active Camo will let you sneak up on those high skull count enemies and steal their loot, while the Drop Shield can be combined with a nice melee weapon to keep enemies off your back. The Hologram ability isn't much good here, so pick one of the abilities that best suits your style of play. Sprint is going to be one of the most useful abilities in this mode. While you'll be tempted to use it more often than you should, try to save it up until you have a handful of skulls and are very close to a drop point. Hit the gas and stream into the drop zone before you die! One of the most frustrating things is to be two feet from a drop zone and have it move to a new location before you can make the drop, then get shot.

HEADHUNTER PRO

The pro variant of Headhunter requires you to get a headshot on an enemy to get their skull to drop. You can still kill enemies without headshots, but they will not drop their skull. If you kill someone without a headshot and they were carrying skulls from other players they did get headshots on, they WILL drop those skulls, just not their own.

You begin with a DMR, two Frag Grenades and just sprint. To start, there won't be many available skulls, so steady your crosshairs and aim for the dome. Try not to kill enemies from to far away. Since this is a free for all mode, there may be other players closer to your kill than you are and they can steal your hard earned skull. Do your best to engage at close range. This way you can shoot their skull off and pick it up almost immediately. You'll see the same kind of scavengers in pro mode as you will in the standard version so be ready for players rushing around like vultures looking for your young.

If you're the vulture type, fly around looking for players with at least two or more skulls and use whatever you need to eliminate them. You don't have to headshot them to gain skulls if they have a number above their head. That number does not include their own skull. If you DO headshot them, you'll get yourself a bonus skull, but don't worry too much about it when playing this way. This style of play requires you to gather as many skulls as you can in a hurry.

INFECTION

Humans vs Zombies. Get the picture? You kill the zombie, the zombie respawns, repeat. The zombie kills you, now you're a zombie too. As a human you only have a Shotgun, a Magnum, and the ability to Sprint. Zombies are chosen at random and only have the Energy Sword and the Elite's Evade ability. They also do not have shields.

Since there are three zombies chosen at random at the start of each round, the need to be capable of doing well as either a zombie or a human. As a zombie, you get to respawn so you'll have a chance to kill more enemies, at least at the beginning.

Use your burst rush to move in fast and melee those puny humans. If you see your fellow zombies hacking at someone, join the party, you might be able to steal the kill. Keep your burst rush until you spot a human. Then fire it off when you're close and insert sword. Zombies don't have shields so you're going to have to get in and out fast. You can heal from a Medkit however. You can't really use any kind of team work as a zombie as it is essentially a free for all mode, but you can use the rest of your zombie team to your advantage by letting them help you locate humans. Check out where they're going and find a faster way there.

Conversely, as a human, you almost need to stick together to stay alive. Try to find a high point on the map or somewhere with limited chokepoints or entrances. Double up the coverage on the entrances and don't worry about having grenades tossed in at you as the zombies only have melee weapons.

Your human contingent will slowly wither down to very few players at which point you may have to just go back to back with the only remaining human just to stay alive. You should try to relocate from time to time to avoid the zombies figuring out ways to kill you from where you're defending from.

As a human, start with your Magnum to put some rounds into zombies that are too far for the Shotgun to be effective. Save that for the up close and personal entanglements. The Magnum fire quickly and is a one-shot kill to the dome since zombies have no shields. If you find yourself out of ammo, you can still melee with whatever weapon you're holding. You can use this to push zombies back from encroaching on your little campground. Use this as a last resort and try to conserve ammo as much as possible. You don't get to respawn as a human. If you die, it's going to be by the hands of a zombie which means,…yep you guessed it, now you're a zombie. The only abilities that players have on either side in this mode is Sprint.

SAFE HAVENS

Played exactly the same as Infection, this mode incorporates a "safe zone" which players can stand inside to remain protected from zombie attacks for fifteen seconds. Once the zone has been entered by a human, the countdown begins. When the zone's timer has run down, a new zone will be selected and another fifteen seconds of safety are available.

If you start out as a zombie, head for the safe zone. This is where most of the humans are going to be. Once they see you coming, they're going to duck into the zone, so try to approach from behind. Sometimes it's ok if they see you. Sometimes you want them to see you. This can force them into the safe area giving your zombie buddies time to surround it. Wait for them to time out and start stabbing!

As a human you want to fight as close to the safe zones as you can. Be careful not to accidentally step inside of one during a fight, triggering its timer and wasting fifteen seconds of safety you didn't need. Wait until your team needs it, then engage it. You'll want to use the Magnum to start inflicting whatever damage you can before they get too close to you to melee you, but once you've depleted your ammo, switch to the Shotgun and let the approaching zombies check the barrel for obstructions.

All humans will only have the Sprint ability here which is a good thing. Use it to bug out from a used up safe zone and head to new ground. Try to learn where the safe zones are so you can at least move to one of those areas in hopes that your location will be randomly chosen as the next Safe Haven. Safe Havens do not stop being generated. Once a zone times out, a new one will appear in a different location. You should move out and restart your fight at the next zone and keep moving from zone to zone. You will be able to stay alive much longer if you can use these correctly, giving the humans more of a chance to rack up kills.

INVASION

This in-depth objective mode pits Spartans (red) versus Elites (blue) in a three tiered six on six battle. Take note that you can respawn on your fellow wingman as long as they are not in enemy territory or in combat. You can also spawn in a couple of different, pre-determined areas.

On offense you will need to infiltrate the enemy base and disable one of their two initial generators. Stand in the zone and the counter will tick down from twenty seconds to zero. More players in the zone will make the timer speed up, so try to stick together at least with your wingmen to get inside and take as much time off the clock as you can.

Once you are in the initial base, you can utilize a couple of strategies. You can have your wingman sit just outside of enemy territory so that you can spawn on him when you die, making the long walk from your spawn to the enemy generator much shorter. This will lessen your firepower, but combined with the rest of your team, it could work well.

If timed correctly, and if everyone does it, you can send three attackers in at a time by way of three offense respawn points. Make sure your mobile respawn points don't get picked off or it's all for naught. If your respawning team of three can stick together, they should move in and concentrate on one generator at a time. This will speed up the clock and keep the timer low for your next attack. The defense can bring the generator timers back up to seven only, so if you can tick it down that far, the next time you make it in, you shouldn't have long to finish it off. Be aware that the defenders will be sending more reinforcements to the generator that has less time on it as it becomes the high-value target.

If the personnel respawn concept isn't working, team up and push one generator as a six man, full team. This will give you more of an imposing force to get yourselves some time to get inside. Once there, stand in the zone to start the countdown. If you can manage to get all of your teammates inside of a single generator zone, the timer will countdown extremely quickly and the enemy will be forced to fall back to defend the next set of generators. At this point more routes will become available by way of deactivated force fields. Know your map and find the fastest way in with the least resistance. While sticking together, don't bunch up. Be patient and keep your spacing as you move towards the next objective.

The second set of generators should be treated the same as the first. Get as many players into the zone at the same time as you can to run the counter down fast. Be aware that the defense may have acquired a nice selection of power weapons at this point and may be able to eliminate a good chunk of your team quickly. If this becomes the case, split your team in half and head to each generator. Try to take them simultaneously so that the defense has to split up their fire. Hopefully you can count the timer down far enough so that you don't have to do much work when you make your way back there if you die.

When you're in a generator zone, you are going to get pounded on. Do what you can to keep enemies off of you such as tossing grenades into the oncoming path of enemies, using Armor Abilities like Active Camo, Hologram, Drop Shield and Armor Lock, and using communication to let your teammates know where the defense is coming from. After you've taken down the final set of shield generators, it's time to head for the core. The core is heavy and makes you move very slowly. You also cannot use any Armor Abilities or melee while in possession of the core. You need to grab it and run it back to your drop point to win.

By now you've unlocked all three tiers of loadouts and vehicle drops. You will need to use the vehicles to get your core carrier back to the drop point. Spawn back wherever the vehicles are being dropped and grab the most devastating vehicle you can. High powered vehicles should be escorted, to allow them to inflict the maximum damage possible.

While you're on core running duty protecting your carrier, think about using a load out like the Hologram or Drop Shield. If you can get enough of your teammates to select this with you, you can fire them off around the carrier to confuse the enemy into shooting your holograms or provide some direct protection and time for your runner.

The Drop Shield will work well here for those that are running close quarters support for the carrier. Engage one around your carrier to hold off any enemy attacks until your team can eliminate them and you can continue. You will have to try to withstand the waves of enemies one wave at a time, and make your run while they're respawning. Keep moving the core towards your drop point. The closer you can get it the better. The defense will be trying to stand near it to return it to their base. Play it like rushing a football. Every yard counts. If you can drop it close but then get killed, your teammates should carry on and pick it up to continue. Keep pushing it no matter if you live or die and you'll eventually push it to the drop point for the win.

As the defenders, you're going to have to split up, at least in the beginning. Halve your team and send three to one generator and three to the other. If you get intel from your teammates stating that the entire enemy team is moving towards one generator, then you should relocate to help enforce the other generator. Otherwise, sit tight as the enemy may have split up as well.

Fend off the offense from the start by sniping or using any long range weaponry you might have available. Check your base spawn area to see if there are any decent power weapon pickups, or at least something better than what you start with. If you can grab a Needle Rifle or a DMR or similar sniper weapon, use them to keep the enemy delayed. You only have to hold them off for four minutes. If they manage to get in, switch to a more close quarters kind of weapon and engage. Use grenades and launchers to continue to keep the enemy pushed back. Try setting mines with the Grenade Launcher at the chokepoints to your base and set them off when enemies round the corner. Pre-toss grenades into areas of approach when you think enemies are near. Anything you can do to delay them from getting into your generators will be good.

Let's say you can't weather the incoming assault and you need to fall back to your second set of generators. Regroup and search for any power weapons that might be available and head back to defend the next set. Try not to sit inside them or in too close proximity to the generators, they will be expecting you to be there. Instead, move out a bit and seal off the entry points to the areas that the generators are located in. You should still retain one player close to the generator just in case. By now you should have gained access to the Active Camo and can remain undetected a bit longer. Any of the defensive Armor Abilities will work here of course, so use them wisely and change them up when necessary. Try to be unpredictable when defending. Players will learn where the good hiding spots are and look for you there first. Hold off the enemy invasion as long as possible, but be prepared to set up a defense to prevent your core from being stolen. Once the second set of generators has been taken down, you should send some players out on vehicle duty. Keep the majority of your team inside watching the core and give your vehicle team to get set up.

You'll want to get into something like the Scorpion or Wraith to be able to take out enemies attackers and keep the area clear if they drop the core so your teammates can defend it. If you stand on the core, a progress bar will appear showing you how much time you have left until the core is returned to your base. Try to get everyone you can to stand on it to send it back more quickly. Hopefully you can dispatch the initial enemy threat and return the core before their next advance.

Make full use of your available abilities now that the third tier has been unlocked. The Hologram can be useful if you send a few out to meet the Elites. It can buy you valuable time to return the core and slow their advance. Remember that all you need to do is take time off the clock. If you can keep them from stealing the core and dropping it off for four minutes, you win.

Make sure to take note of what loadouts and vehicles become available to you and your team as you reach each tier. These upgrades can provide you with step up if you choose the right combination of weapons and abilities based on your current situation. For instance, you won't really need Armor Lock once the core has been stolen. You'll want something like the Jet Pack or Sprint. Choose wisely.

INVASION SLAYER

This mode is still played on the large maps that standard Invasion is played on. The twist here is that there are no generators to bring down and no core to steal. Just territories that you can decide to capture or not. The only thing that really matters in this mode is killing 100 enemies before the other team does. The territories you capture will only get you and your team weapon and vehicle drops.

If you decide to start capturing territories to gather weapons and vehicles, be aware that you'll have to defend them for fifteen seconds after you capture them which takes ten seconds. If you can hold the enemy off long enough, you can get some pretty sweet drops. There are also tiers in this mode. They offer players new sets of loadouts at intervals of ten minutes or twenty five kills, or fifty kills and fifteen minutes. Remember that if you take the territory yourself that you will only get weapons and vehicles native to your team's race. If you're a Spartan you'll get Spartan weapons and vehicles, if you're an

Elite, you'll get Elite weapons and vehicles. If you want enemy gear, you can wait for the enemy to take the territory, then move in and steal their drops. The most important thing to remember is that you only get points for kills. You'll want to capture the territories since you'll be provided with heavier firepower, but concentrate more on eliminating enemy forces. If you can get a decent drop, you can move up towards the enemy advance and pin them down giving your team more time to capture another territory.

Try splitting your team into a prevention team and a gathering team. The prevention team should of course, prevent the enemy from getting to the territories while the gathering team concentrates solely on capturing territories. Once the drop comes in, the prevention team can retrieve any

This tactic is going to be very useful if you can get the cooperation of your team. If everyone does their job, you'll end up with more firepower and more kills than the enemy and win the match. You can eventually acquire a Scorpion or a Wraith and really put the beat down on your enemies. Use your drops wisely and position your heaviest forces where necessary. If you're going to sit back and wait for the enemy to come in and get the drop for you, that's just fine. Be sure to think about what abilities will help you do this based on the map and available terrain. Don't stray too far from the drop zones since it doesn't take much time for a team of hostiles to roll in and capture the point and get the drop started. Time your attack to begin right after they have started the drop countdown.

Move in and kill everyone off and commandeer their goods. At this point you can utilize the concepts above and split off your prevention team. If half of your team can kill the enemy at a distance while the others take the territories, you can stop the enemy from getting kills on half of your team which puts the balance of power in your favor. However you decide to go about playing this mode, remember that kills equal points, and points equal the win. Don't get caught up in trying to "complete the objective" by taking territories when your real objective is racking up kills.

JUGGERNAUT

With limited weaponry and abilities available in this mode, you're going to have to go with volume over power. Someone is going to spawn as the Juggernaut. The only way you get points is by killing him or if you are the Juggernaut, killing everyone else. Don't bother trying to kill anyone else in the game, focus on the big boy.

Since you get ten points per kill as the Juggernaut, you WANT to become it often and for as long as possible. When it's your turn to Jugg it up, try to stay mobile even if you stay in a single area. You can move in a circle keeping your back to a wall so that all of your enemies will be coming at you from the front. You will move faster than everyone else and be invincible for ten seconds when you are chosen to be the Juggernaut.

You only have the Gravity Hammer and you can take one heck of a beating, so get ready, it's clobberin' time. Bash down as many foes as you can in the time you're allotted. You can take a couple of approaches to being the Juggernaut, one being to bring the enemies in to you. By sticking in a certain area you can focus on where the enemies are coming in and meet them as they cross the thresholds. Try to find a place with limited entrances and float back and forth between them so as not to get flanked. You can hold off quite a few enemies by doing this, but they're going to get wise eventually and team up with each other to dig you out of your hole. After you smash a few brains out, relocate to a new campsite and being again.

Another strategy to employ as the Juggernaut is to run laps. If you proceed around the map's perimeter, you can kind of make a train of enemies behind you and be able to turn and take them on one at a time. Turn, kill one, then continue around the perimeter and repeat. Enemies will start to head you off at the pass, but you should be able to get a good chunk of points before someone strikes you down and they become your former self.

You'll need one hundred and fifty points to win and if you're not Mr. Handsome, you'll only get five points per kill instead of ten. All non-Juggs get Sprint an Assault Rifle, the Magnum and one Frag Grenade. Use what you have carefully and give it to the Juggernaut all at once.

KING OF THE HILL

This territorial team-based mode requires players to take and hold a territory for as long as they can. You get one point per second that you hold a hill and you need one hundred and fifty points to win. Both teams are on offense here until one captures the territory, at which point they become the defense.

Getting the hill first should be your top priority so gear up with the Scout and Assault or Jet Pack loadouts. These will help you get to the hill first and start scoring points. As soon as any player enters the hill, it will turn to that players team color and begin accruing one point per second they remain within the hill boundaries. The second they step outside of the hill, its color changes back to white and you stop getting points.

Since you only need one player to be in the hill at a time, there's no need to have your entire team inside of it. More players do not increase the point count speed. Strategically set up your squadmates in a perimeter around the hill and defend the approach from respawning enemies. You can utilize sniping and stealth here, as well as distraction. Now that you're on defense, you need every advantage you can get. Grab a Hologram and while you remain hidden, send it towards the entrance points of the hill area to make it seem like your Hologram is attacking the attackers. The more time you can buy yourself while holding the hill the better. In fact, you don't even need to kill anyone as long as you get to one hundred and fifty points before them.

On defense if you have one player holding the hill, try posting up a couple of guards with Drop Shields. They can fire these off just outside of the hill boundaries and it will expand into the hill itself letting your hill holder regain health and be invulnerable to projectiles. This will increase the time you will be able to hold the hill thus giving your team more points. Remember that if an enemy happens into your hill, your point count will stop and the hill will turn to neutral. Sometimes you can use this as an early warning system if you don't already see them in the hill. Some hills are large and have places to hide within them, so keep an eye on the color of your hill at all times.

Retaking a hill is difficult. Time is of the essence here but quickly try to find any power weapons you can before your assault. Once you and your team regroup at the hill, hit it with everything you have. Be aware that enemies will be lurking outside of the hill itself and possibly even sniping. If you have Holograms, it's a good idea to send them into the hill ahead of you to further deplete your enemy's ammo and distract them while you and your team come in to retake the hill.

If no one has taken control of the hill yet and you find yourself in a secluded location with a devastating power weapon such as the Plasma Launcher or something similar, stay where you are and fire on the hill from a distance. If you can eliminate the other team trying to get control, you can give your team the time they need to get in and take it. Weapons such as the launchers in this mode are better used from afar. Even if you must be in the hill to gain points, you need support and varied loadouts for the team to work as a whole and win the match.

Consider what your personal role will be in the match. Will you be run and gun objective guy? Then you'll want something like the Jet Pack or Sprint and weapons like the Shotgun or melee weapons. If you plan on being the sniper or perimeter support with heavy weapons, think about taking a loadout like Active Camo. Both of these roles can also benefit from the Hologram using it to be your scout. Sending Holograms into the hill before your real teammates is a great way to pick off your enemies

CRAZY KING

Played just like standard King of the Hill, this mode features a randomly selected hill which moves every thirty seconds. This is going to require not only speed and mobility, but playing positions as well.

Know the map. Whichever map you're playing on, learn where the hills are and post up players in and around those areas. If you constantly have all of your players running together in this mode, you're going to end up doing more running than point taking.

Try to stay spread out and near possible hill locations and wait until they appear. Once you've found where the next one is, call it out to your team so they can come and help you defend it. Hopefully they can help from a distance so they don't have to relocate and can remain near where the next hill might appear. If they cannot, then they still need to come and help you defend the hill.

Each hill is only active for thirty seconds, so you must get in and get as many points as you can which means staying alive in that little box for thirty seconds. Thirty seconds in a video game is a long time. The key here will be getting in first and staying put longer than the other team. Remember that the hill itself will flash when there are only five minutes remaining in its lifespan. Start heading out when it starts flashing, but leave one player behind to grab those last five points if they can.

Another option to try is to split up evenly in teams of two for instance and have one player in each team take a Drop Shield and the other take Sprint. When the sprinter gets in the hill, the Drop Shield equipped player can use their shield just outside of the hill to envelope themselves as well as the sprinter in the hill. You can't use Armor Abilities in the hill, so this trick is as close as you can get. Keep them alive the longest by timing when you deploy your shield.

You can keep your team together as a single unit here to defend more effectively if that is where you are failing, but splitting up will be more advantageous in the long run. However if most of you choose the Scout loadout, you may not have an issue getting to and from each new hill. Trial and error will be your friend. If something isn't working, try some of the other options we've suggested and come up with some of your own with your friends. Hopefully some of these concepts give you ideas of your own that you might never have thought of.

ODDBALL

This fast paced free for all features a single "ball" (it's actually a flaming skull) in the center of the map that you must acquire and hold as long as possible. You need one hundred and fifty points to win and you get one point per second you are in possession of the ball.

When you don't have the ball, all you need to do is kill the guy with the ball—so let's go over ball stealing and holding. You may be better off quickly heading for a power weapon here. If you can snag one before everyone gets to the ball in the first place, great. Fire off a barrage of heavy firepower at the ball. If not, wait until you can catch up with the carrier. They will show up on radar as long as they retain the ball.

Once you find where the player with the ball is camping out, try to lob something nasty their way before you get there. There's going to be a mob of players on top of him trying to grab it for themselves. Toss a few grenades into the pile and move in to clean up the mess. You're going to have to be quick about it and be wary how close you get to the carrier. Their only attack is a melee with the ball and it is a one-hit kill. Rocket Launchers, Grenade Launchers, Plasma Launchers are all great weapons to have here. As for Armor Abilities, you need to seriously consider the Active Camo and the Armor Lock.

So now you've got the ball. You can approach this a few ways. First, you can move to a small defensible area and put your back up against a wall. You cannot use any Armor Abilities with the ball in hand and your only attack is a one-hit kill melee with the ball. If you try to switch weapons or use an Armor Ability, you will drop the ball immediately and stop getting points. You will move very slowly with the ball in hand and you also light up on everyone's radar. Good luck! Try to align yourself near or next to a Medkit in case you take a bit of damage. Do your best to kill as many enemies as you can, then relocate. Hiding doesn't work here due to the radar, but you can lock yourself in somewhere and fight them off. You can think about choosing the Armor Lock ability and engage it if you see an incoming rocket or grenade, but you will drop the ball, so make sure you pick it up immediately after the incoming projectile has detonated. Try taking the ball and hanging out near a Gravity Lift. If you start taking too much damage, just jump in and head upstairs. Your enemies will of course follow you up, so as soon as you exit the lift, turn and be ready to face bash your foes. You can also position yourself as high as you can and near drop offs. Try to find a drop off that won't kill you if you jump off of it so that when your enemies start dealing too much damage to you, you can just base jump off the ledge and relocate. Stay alive as long as you can here to gather as many points as quickly as you can. Getting possession of the ball again isn't going to be easy.

If you're not the hidey hole kind of player, you can risk keeping mobile. The problem is that everyone else is going to be faster than you. Whether it's via Jet Pack or Sprint or even just a Spartans normal speed, they're going to catch you, so you cannot outrun them. The only benefit to moving is that you might be able to fight less enemies at a time and a bit more spaced out. Practice your melee timing with the ball based on the speed you move with it. If you don't have possession of the ball, you need to go get it, so camping and sniping aren't an option here.

RACE

Hope you're good at driving the Mongoose. Your objective here is to complete three laps while hitting all of the checkpoints. Sounds easy enough, but with the rest of the racers and landmines all over the course, maybe easy isn't the right word to describe this free for all mode.

You have ten minutes to complete the course, but whoever hits all of the checkpoints and finishes three laps first wins. If you miss a checkpoint you have to go back for it otherwise your points for future checkpoints will not count.

The mode is called Race for a reason. While you can force other racers into landmines or off the course, or away from checkpoints, you should concentrate most on actually driving and trying to win the race. Cut people off, avoid landmines, and hit all of your checkpoints to win. You don't want to spend time trying to force other racers off course. That will only slow you down. There aren't any points for blowing up other players vehicles or shooting them if you get off your ride, so there really isn't any reason to do anything other than race, unless you're just mean and want to try to wreck as many players as you can. You can 'Goose-jack other players if you want to, but by the time you do, you'll have already lost the race. Get the feel of your vehicle in a custom game before you think about trying to win one of these races. The Mongoose is difficult to drive with no practice, so set up a custom match on a map you know is used in Race mode. Practice quick turning and readjusting for the terrain as you will have to be quick to avoid not just other racers, but the landmines as well. Don't be afraid to use the brake. Sometimes even just letting off the gas will give you enough time to make the turn you need to or avoid wrecking your ride.

Once you feel comfortable with your wheels, go ahead and try your hand against other racers. Practice taking the inside of corners, and get good at the cop-tap technique where you push the back end of another player's vehicle out to one side forcing them to spin out. If you can keep your speed up and still perform this maneuver, you can win the race by the

Slight adjustments and tapping or rubbing enemy drivers can help you force them either into landmines or out of checkpoints. Either way they will be delayed enough that they probably won't be able to catch up with you again. As long as you don't wreck yourself. Since other players are going to be trying to do the same to you, do your best to steer clear of them during the race.

RALLY

This race variant has randomly generated flags that you must hit to gain points. Fifteen points will win you the race. It's not really a race however in the traditional sense of the word or how standard Race mode is played. You still have landmines to contend with and other racers too. You get one point per flag you hit and once someone hits a flag, it disappears.

Assuming you have some semblance of driving skill, try to speed your way to each flag. You won't know where they're going to show up, so you shouldn't bother racing towards any flags in the distance if you see someone ahead of you. All this is going to do is put you farther away from the next randomly selected flag.

Picking and choosing your flags is tough to do since you won't want to stop driving and just sit around waiting for the next flag to appear. Train your brain and wait for it. Don't forget that you cannot take flags while on foot, only while on board the Mongoose.

If you can only see one player in front of you on the way to one of the distant flags and you think you can catch up to them, go for it and ram them into a mine or at least away from the flag. Offensive driving here has its place, but use it wisely. This isn't really the mode to try to destroy other players. You'll achieve more wins by actually racing and not wasting time on flags you can't get to.

Rubbing with opponents is fine but it could send you flying as well, or instead of them. The flags do not have a large capture radius, so sometimes just a little love tap can be enough to push your enemy out of the capture area to take it yourself. Be precise when you're about to hit a flag and make sure no one is around you to bump you off of it.

ROCKET RACE

This mode is set up exactly like Rally mode with the addition of... yes you guessed it, rockets! You and your buddy have ten minutes to hit fifteen points. One of you drives, the other sports the Rocket Launcher.

Use the same techniques described above for Rally mode, but this time, you can use your rocket man to keep opponents away from any flags you're trying to capture. Speed towards the randomly generated flag and let your buddy do all the work. Try not to flip the 'Goose while racing to the point and hold her steady so your wingman can get a more accurate shot off on your enemies.

The driver should concentrate exclusively on driving towards all flags. You don't have to sit and wait for a closer flag in this mode all the time since you have rockets to keep other driving teams off of the flag you want. Take the verbal cues from your buddy as to where to go, if you need to slow down or stop for them to get a better shot, etc..

Your rocketeer should keep you informed of where they think the next point might be showing up, or if you should just forget the one you're headed to. While on the back of the Mongoose, they should focus on flipping enemy vehicles by shooting at the base of them and slightly ahead of their projected path. Lead opponents with your rockets and keep them off your flags.
You can try to use the rockets to guide enemy drivers into landmines or obstacles. Fire off a rocket either to the left of right of a driver so that when they try to avoid it, they end up either missing a flag, or hitting a landmine or other obstacle on the map. This mode is extremely fun so don't take it too seriously.

SLAYER

In this mode, if it moves, you can shoot it. This true free for all takes twenty five points to win. The only way to get points here is to eliminate as many other players as you can in ten minutes. Players that know the lay of the land here will beat you every time. Learn each map and the locations of all of the key elements within it. Know where the power weapons are, the Medkits, Gravity Lifts, grenades and vehicles if available.

Players will head for the power weapons right off the bat and you should do the same. Think about the Jet Pack or the Scout class to get there in a hurry, then switch it up to your loadout of choice later. If you can make it safely to a nice power weapon like the Rocket Launcher, grab it and start doing laps.

While some players like to "camp" in Slayer, it isn't necessarily the best way to get the most kills the fastest. Take your new found launcher and proceed to loop around the map's perimeter. Keep your back to the walls or the outsides of the map, and put your crosshairs toward the middle of the map.

If you have any grenades left from trying to get to your Rocket Launcher, toss a few into your path to clear out possible enemies, and send one or two into the middle of the map or into places you know to be enemy or camper hotspots. Every once in a while, you might want to check your back or toss one behind you or into buildings you came through.

Players love to sneak up on other players. Switch up your lap rotation from clockwise to counterclockwise from time to time to change things up and keep the enemy guessing. Cut through the map somewhere in the middle using cover to make your change or do it after a respawn. If you manage to find yourself in a nice location with a single chokepoint or just a couple close together, you could benefit from staying for a couple of kills. Set up so you can see all of the chokepoints at the same time if you can, grab your weapon of choice and ready some grenades. Wait for any impatient opponents and hose them down accordingly. When you find the locations of the Medkits on the level you're playing on, it's also not a bad idea to hang out near them in case you lose too much health. You can quickly replenish your system and get back in the fight.

Try to work around the Medkits. Once you find where they all are, choose one that you think you can do loops around. Loop around and shoot anything that moves. If anyone gives you any trouble, duck inside and heal away. This is only necessary if you do not want to use a Drop Shield.

Many maps feature Gravity Lifts that you can use to reach higher elevations. Just like the Medkits, you can use these to rally around and fight near. If the competition gets too heated, scoot over into the lift and away we go! When you reach the top, you can bet little Jimmy is going to follow you. Turn around quickly and be ready to melee. You can rack up a few kills by sitting at the exit of Grav Lifts, but enemies can toss grenades up as well, so be wary.

In general you'll want to stay mobile most of the time other than the few instances where you can sit down for a while and shoot squirrels from your front porch. Keep on the lookout for the power weapons, even if you don't prefer them for whatever reason, it's better that you have them than your enemies.

SLAYER PRO

This pro variant of Slayer offers players only two loadout options containing single shot weapons, plus two Frag Grenades and the ability to Sprint. You won't find any pickups in this mode other than previously stated.

This mode is played very much like standard Slayer games but without the ability to quickly drop enemy's shields, you really need to be accurate and relentless. Make sure you put enough rounds into someone to drop their shields, then finish them off with a headshot or a melee strike. While you may be more tempted to hang back and camp, that isn't the best way to get the most kills. You should continue to stay mobile and practice aiming for the head of your opponents. Remember that you can shoot enemies anywhere on their body to disintegrate their shields. Then pop them in the brain for the quick elimination. Melee attacks should be on your mind here. While you need to try to steer clear of close quarters engagements with your opponents, when possible, you should attempt to get in behind enemies for a quick melee to the back. Don't go for the Assassination here, since it takes too long for the animation to complete and enemies can stop you from finishing the job mid-way.

You won't have to worry about looking for Holograms, so shoot anything that moves. Just focus on dropping enemy shields, and popping heads. Since you won't have many rounds in your weapons, get used to saving your Sprint for finishing the job. Drop their shields and Sprint up to kill with melee.

SLAYER CLASSIC

All players start with the Assault Rifle, one Frag Grenade and one Plasma Grenade. No Armor Abilities are available here. There are weapon pickups scattered around the map, so make your way to something nasty to gain a quick advantage over your opponents.

The lack of Armor Abilities in this mode can give you a bit of a break from the frustration of beating a player down only for them to Armor Lock while their buddy Assassinates you from behind.

Play this mode variation like Slayer Pro but with the addition of weapon pickups around the map. Look for the Plasma Pistol to drop an enemy's shields, then switch to a Shotgun or a DMR and send them to respawn. Stay mobile in these matches to gather the most kills.

ELITE SLAYER

You always wanted to be a little taller right? This mode pits Elites against each other in a free for all battle. All of your loadouts here are Elite based. This means starting with weapons like the Needle Rifle. Nice.

The only real Armor Ability difference here is the Elite burst rush which you can use to roll up on enemies for melee kills. Since you get such a fast burst of speed with this ability, think about looking for a nice melee weapon and wait for someone to engage you. Burst on the scene for a little stab and smash. Elites can also heal themselves over time so consider this before wasting your time trying to get to a Medkit. Hanging out in a dark corner to restore your health may be a better option. You can use Medkits, but don't make yourself a target by using one if you don't have to.

Make good use of the Elite specific weapons in this mode. For instance, if you see someone using the Needler and you have one of your own, you can add fuel to the fire and combine shots to make the target explode in hail of crystal shards and pink mist.

SWAT

This is as hardcore as it gets in *Halo: Reach*. Players can only use a DMR, a Magnum, and Sprint being your only ability—no grenades or shields. This means you're going to have to actually aim at your enemies and not just hope for the best.

Headshots are the key to success, so practice with the zoom on your weapons. Steady your hand and once you get your elevation set, sidestep to align the shot where you want it. While you're on the move, keep your pistol or rifle set about head level. This way, when enemies round the corners, you're already going to be pretty close to the head and you can just sidestep and shoot.

Sniping in this mode is hugely beneficial. If you can find yourself a nice corner with limited chokepoints and visibility, sit tight for a while. If you practice your headshots, you can really rack up a good amount of kills doing this. Enemies will find you. Once you've worn out your welcome in your hiding spot, relocate to your next nest. Sniping is an art form. Not only will you need to be skilled with your weapon, you'll need to know when and when not to shoot. Taking a random shot at someone who is about to round a corner and go out of sight, may only alert enemies to your location if you miss. You don't have to wait for the perfect shot, just make every one count. Good sniping roosts are few and far between, so do your best to

MULTIPLAYER

STOCKPILE

You've got ten minutes to gather as many flags and return them to your base as possible. You'll need to guard them for a minute before they can be counted as points towards your team. This team-based mode can be very tactically played, so let's go over some of possible tactics.

Of course you can just send your entire team out to fetch flags and bring 'em back, but you risk having the enemy team snatch them out of your drop zone and take them for themselves. Consider splitting your team up into two divisions, a Scout team and a Defense team.

Your Scout team should head out with the Scout loadout or the Assault loadout with the Jet Pack. This will enable them to get to the flags before the enemy team. Know that you cannot use your abilities while actually carrying flags, but these loadouts will get you to the flags fast.

Your Defense team should outfit themselves with Armor Lock, Active Camo, or Drop Shields. These abilities can substantially affect your team's ability to retain the flags that you capture. Use the Armor Lock if you're getting pummeled by incoming enemies up close. Go with the Drop Shield if they are trying to pick you off from a distance. Try the Active Camo ability to hide near your drop point and make the enemy team think the coast is clear. Then drop a couple of 'nades at their feet, plunge the sword into their chest, and get your flags back.

While the Scout team heads out to maintain a steady stream of flags coming in to your drop point, your Defense team should be there to make sure they get counted. Flags have to sit tight for at least sixty seconds, however flags that are added to the zone after the one minute countdown has begun, only have to wait as long as the initial timer has left on it. You can use this to make sure your flags get counted quickly. Drop a single flag into your zone and start the timer. Have your defense make sure no one steals it out of the zone. Calculate roughly how much time you need to return a flag based on where you're going to grab it from. Flags are located at five different locations throughout the maps. Once you figure out how much time it will take to get a flag back to base, let's say fifteen seconds, have your defense tell you where there is roughly fifteen seconds left on the initial flag timer.

Your Scout team should hang around the flags and prevent any enemies from taking them. Once you get the go ahead from your Defense team, grab the flags and bring them back to base. If you've timed it right and don't encounter any resistance, you'll be able to drop off the new flags and get them counted immediately or at least with just a few seconds left. This assures that your flags will be counted towards your team's score.

This technique allows you to divide your team up with more players out grabbing flags and less players on defense. The enemy team won't worry so much about trying to steal one flag that's all the way back at your base when they can grab one that is located centrally. Use the single flag to get the timer started, then dump three flags in at the end of the timer and pow—four flags at once!

Let's discuss something a little more complex. With four players on your team, keep one back to defend your base. Send two players out to grab flags, and the remaining player should be tasked with preventing the enemy team from capturing any of the flags they've brought back to their drop point. Offense, defense, and prevent.

While your offense is grabbing flags, your defense is keeping them in the drop zone. While they're both doing their jobs, the prevention player should be skulking around the enemy drop point getting ready to steal flags out of their zone. This player should run the Active Camo ability and hide in view of the enemy drop zone. They should let the enemy continue to bring flags to their base. Wait until the timer is about to run down and count their flags, then sneak in and toss them out of the zone. Man, that is mean! It's a very effective technique to employ regardless of how despicable it might seem. Remember when in prevention mode, you can toss flags into Gravity Lifts since they are not affected by them and they will sink right to the bottom. You can toss flags off of high elevations and even better, to a waiting teammate below.

By preventing enemies from capping flags of their own, grabbing flags and bringing them back to your base, and defending the flags you've gathered, you can become a triple threat. Make sure to assign players to positions they're going to be good at. Don't put your best run and gunner on defense duty.

Another option is to run a single defenseman and the remaining players on flag duty. As the majority of your team brings back flags, they should stay and help defend until all of the flags have been counted, then start the process again. This kind of doubles your offense and your defense. It may take a bit longer to get multiple flags, but you will be gaining a steady stream of points.

You can try to remain under the radar of the other team. If you find that the enemy is continually trying to steal flags from your base that you've collected, that you might be in need of a stronger defense. In this situation, just send one player out to grab one flag at a time. The rest of your team should play defense. Use combinations of the Drop Shield, Armor Lock and Active Camo to keep the enemy from stealing your flags.

WELCOME
UNSC TRAINING
THE CAMPAIGN
FIREFIGHT
MULTIPLAYER
BASICS & TACTICS
ARSENAL
VEHICLES
GAMEPLAY MODES
MAPS
FORGE
REFERENCE

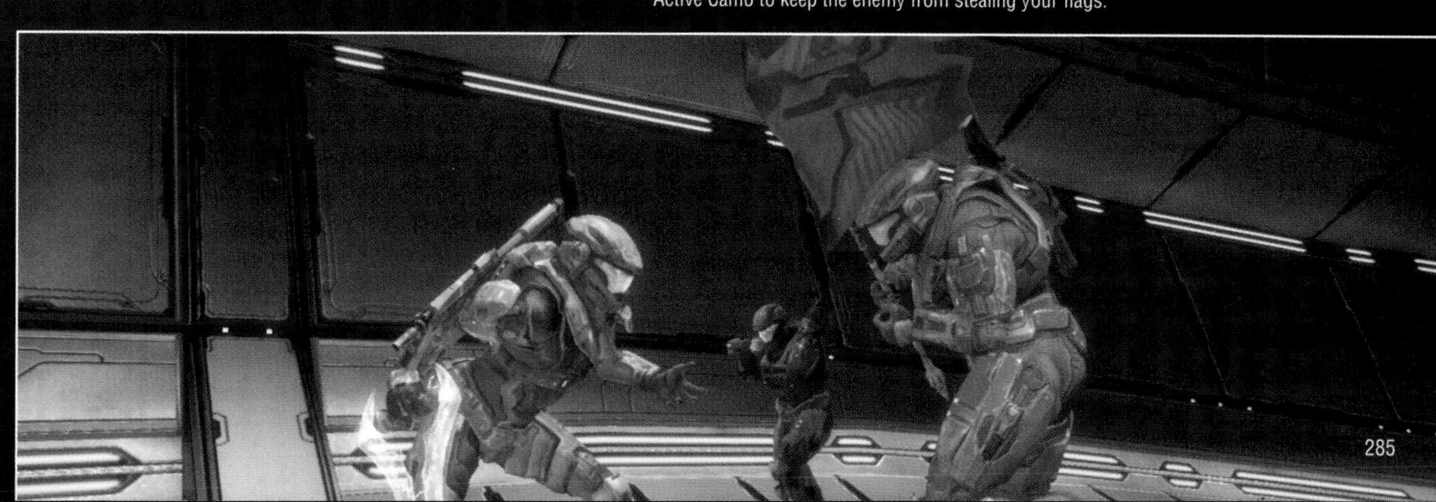

Eventually they're going to tire of wasting time trying to grab flags from your base, since there will only be one flag at a time in the zone and your defense is near impenetrable. Concentrate on just securing one flag at a time and letting your defense prevent it from being taken. This tactic offers some great tactical possibilities if you can coordinate with your team well enough to pull them off. Work on new ideas and concepts and build off of what we've discussed here to dominate one of the most entertaining modes in the game.

TERRITORIES

This team-based objective mode has teams trying to capture and defend five different territories. You switch sides in this mode playing both offense and defense. First to five wins or most points after two rounds. We're going to discuss offense first.

There are several ways to go about taking territories but we're going to work on sticking together to start. All players should grab the Scout ability and run it to the closest territory. Territories take thirty seconds to capture, so keep that in mind—as well as the fact that the closest territory to your team is probably the furthest away from the enemy. Continue taking territories as a group—once a territory is taken, it becomes locked so you no longer have to worry about it. Move on to the next one and as you move from territory to territory, try to notice if any are more heavily guarded than the others and go for the weak points. You need to get as many as you can on offense because you do not get any points on defense. This is your only chance. You can explore this method of zone capture and tweak it by changing up your Armor Abilities. Grab some Holograms and use them to send into hotly contested territories to pull enemies out of hiding and waste their ammo on paper targets. Try the Active Camo to slip past camping defenders and Assassinate enemies from behind who are looking for visible targets. Fire off a Drop Shield just outside of a territory to encompass your teammates inside the zone. There are lots of options and variations you can try just within the group dynamic. Experiment.

Some other divisional variations you can try are every man for himself, and the lone wolf. Using the every man for himself concept, send all players out individually to take different territories simultaneously. This can confuse and divide the enemy contingent. These players should equip Armor Lock in case they get into trouble. This style of play can let you get many territories at the same time to dishearten the enemy.

The lone wolf strategy puts the majority of your team together in a group as described before, but leaves one player off by themselves to grab territories that become abandoned. While the majority of your team heads off to jointly capture a territory, your lone wolf should be running Active Camo to slide into a different territory unseen. The enemy will assume that when they see three of your players in one place, that all of your players are in one place. This will leave several territories unguarded or at least, lightly guarded allowing your wolf to infiltrate and capture.

Try rotating through all of these concepts during your stint on offense to confuse the enemy and keep them guessing. Doing the same thing in a row too many times will leave your enemy prepared well enough to withstand your attacks the next time. By rotating through these different tactics, the enemy will never know what you're going to do and this gives you a major advantage.

You have a few options on defense for this mode and the first one you should consider is sending everyone out to a different territory. Splitting everyone up isn't going to give you a strong defense any any one territo

Once the time runs out and the round is over, the offense has to go to defense and they will no longer be able to gain any points. This is what this tactic is designed for. By putting someone on each point, you can at least delay the enemy from controlling a territory. If that player goes down and calls out to their teammates that their particular territory was being overrun by the entire team, your team can make a choice, reinforce, or double up somewhere else. Go out and defend the territories that are closest to your spawn. Consider using abilities such as Armor Lock, Drop Shield, and Active Camo. You can use the Hologram towards incoming enemies to buy yourself some time as well. Don't worry about gearing up with Sprint or the Jet Pack. They will help you get to the territories more quickly, but you will benefit more from the previously suggested abilities.

If you find that the enemy is pushing their entire team to each territory, then you may need to reevaluate your stance on defense. Consider running a rolling defense. While a bit risky, this could be the force you need to stop the enemy team from capturing more territories than you. Now you should gear up with Sprint and Jet Packs, since you will be relocating often and need to get there quickly. Territories only take thirty seconds to capture.

When you notice a territory being taken, rush your entire team to engage. Toss in some Frags to push enemies out of the zone and begin blasting away with whatever power weapons you've collected. You need to keep them from getting control of the territory. Another way to do this is to get inside of the territory yourself. Enemies cannot capture a territory while an enemy is inside of the zone. When you get into trouble fending off a zone, just get inside and delay them from taking it as long as you can while you fight. This might even give your teammates the time they need to get back into the fight and help you out. If you can keep at least one player inside the zone at a time, you can force the enemy to regroup and maybe choose to go for another territory.

If you have a good sniper on your defensive squad, put them to good use. Get them set up in nice little spot overlooking one or more of the territories if possible. All they need to do is to fire off a couple of rounds at a player trying to capture a territory, and the enemy should bug out. They will eventually figure out your hiding spot and send rockets your way, but until they do, hold them off for as long as possible. This is a great way to have one player defend multiple territories at the same time.

LAND GRAB

This mode is played just like Territories mode, however there is no offense or defense. Both teams can acquire territories and the first to five wins. You get one point per territory and they lock once taken. They become marked with a flag in your team's color. Since both teams can capture territories at the same time, try to take your team to territories that the enemy isn't trying to take as well. If you use speed to your advantage here, you can just run around and get more points than the enemy. Grab Sprint or a Jet Pack and get moving.

You may encounter a good bit of time where you don't engage any enemies at all. If they're going for one territory and you're going for another, there's no need to engage. You will eventually bang into each other, probably at the most central territory since most teams will be heading towards the territories that are closest to their spawns. Since this could very possibly be the most contested territory, you might want to think about heading to the central one first. Send two players out together to grab the central territory while the other two players on your team split off to take two other points by themselves. They should go for the ones closest to their spawn. The two players heading for the central zone should try their best to grab any power weapons on their way, but not at the expense of getting to the zone late. If you can get in the zone quickly enough, use grenades to splash some damage out in a perimeter from the territory you're taking.

Another way to approach this mode is to take the fight to the enemy. Head out to see which territory they are taking and move in to disrupt the timer and take the zone for yourself. Follow the enemy around and continue to prevent them from capturing zones then take them for your own.

Think about using Holograms and Drop Shields in this mode as well. The Holograms can be best used by launching them off to a territory you don't plan on taking. This is a great distraction. Hopefully you can even get the enemy to call out to their team that they've got incoming at a territory that you're not really incoming to.

The Drop Shield is very useful in all zone capture modes. Since you cannot use the shield in a territory, you can activate it just outside the zone and have it extend into the territory itself. This way you can just head inside and remain protected from incoming projectiles while continuing to capture the territory. Remember that once you capture a territory, it becomes locked and cannot be retaken by the enemy team. You do not have to worry about these points once you've taken and locked them. Move along to the next zone.

3 PLOT TERRITORIES

This mode also does not put teams on offense or defense. Everything is up for grabs for either team. You need three hundred points to win and you get one point for every second you hold a territory. There are three static territories to capture which takes five seconds, and they will change to your team color when you are in control of them.

Since you only need to get to three hundred points before the enemy does, you really only need to worry about taking and holding two of the three territories. This will increase your forces at each point you're holding and not thin your team out too much. Holding just the two territories will get you two points per second while the enemy will only get one per second. This will get you to three hundred twice as fast as the enemy.

Send two players to each of two territories, get at least one player inside the zone while the other sits back a little bit. Try running that player with Active Camo and the other with a Drop Shield. Drop the shield just outside of the zone and duck inside. You will only be vulnerable to melee attacks, but we wary of plasma charges and Armor Lock discharges which will take down your shield. Do the same at the other territory near your base, and think about a melee weapon for the player actually standing IN the territory. You'll usually want to take the territory closest to your spawn to start, then move for the central one. Instead, try moving around the enemy and going for their base territory. It could very well be unguarded since the fight usually takes place for the central point. Sneak around back and steal their home base. This will effectively pin them in the middle of the map. You should be able to fend off intruders with two players on each of the two territories and get double the points!

You and your team can also decide to roam as a group taking territories as you progress throughout the map. This method is the most popular, so be ready to defend against it in public. Ready your team first before you just all pick Scout and rush for the territories. Varying your kits can be a big help to the team. Have a player designated to be the Scout with Sprint to gain the territories quickly. The next player should run Active Camo to hide and defend the zone while your Scout is inside. Bring a heavy for defense with Armor Lock and a power weapon if possible, one player can also use the Hologram to play tricks. The Hologram player can activate the ability to send it out from the territory while defending or send them ahead as virtual scouts.

If you're sticking together as a group, you can also go with a mobile team. Gear up with Sprint and Jet Packs and run from point to point as quickly as you can to start getting points before the enemy. This can be a crucial element in your offense. Many times the first team to start getting points is the team that wins. You're going to have to either keep mobile and move to each zone quickly and continue to loop, or if enemies are in close proximity, set your team down and defend—if only for a short time. Don't forget that sitting and camping a single territory won't necessarily be the best way to get the most points. You need to control at least two territories to rack up points faster than your opponents.

While it may seem like a frenzy of chaos, this mode can be played quite tactically. If you and your team play it together and communicate well and plan ahead, you're going to have much more fun. Always take the map into consideration when you're choosing what loadouts to select. They can play a big part in your decision making and they should. You don't want to be without a Jet Pack on Sword Base, for instance. Gear up accordingly and have fun.

MULTIPLAYER MAPS

In this briefing we will provide you with all of the necessary satellite imagery containing detailed locations of all high-value items and objectives. This will include any and all Spartan and Elite weaponry, vehicles, and mission critical objectives. We will also brief you on location specific details critical to your survival. This includes surroundings and terrain, engagement locations, campgrounds, and even terrain specific suggestions for Armor abilities, weapon usage and various other options which can help you carry out your duties.

MAP OBJECTIVES

For each multiplayer map in Halo: Reach, we have marked all possible objectives that can be present in any game mode. Depending on the specific game mode you are playing, you will only see a fraction of the possible objectives (no Flags in Assault, no Bombs in King of the Hill!).

Flags are used in Capture the Flag and Stockpile game modes. Bombs are used in Assault and Oddball game modes. Neutral Flags and Bombs are used for certain sub-game types under Capture the Flag, Assault, and for Oddball. Hill Markers are used for most other game modes, including King of the Hill, Territories, Race, Headhunter, Invasion Slayer, and Infection Save Havens.

LEGEND

ICON	NAME	OBJECT	USED IN MODES
	TEAM FLAG	FLAG	CAPTURE THE FLAG, STOCKPILE
	NEUTRAL FLAG		
	TEAM BOMB	BOMB	ASSAULT, ODDBALL
	NEUTRAL BOMB		
	BOMB TARGET SITE		
	KING OF THE HILL	HILL MARKER	KING OF THE HILL, TERRITORIES, RACE, HEADHUNTER, INVASION SLAYER, INFECTION SAVE HAVENS
	(TIER 1 OR 2)	INVASION	INVASION
	DATA CORE	DATA CORE	INVASION
	CORE DROP	CORE DROP	INVASION

BOARDWALK

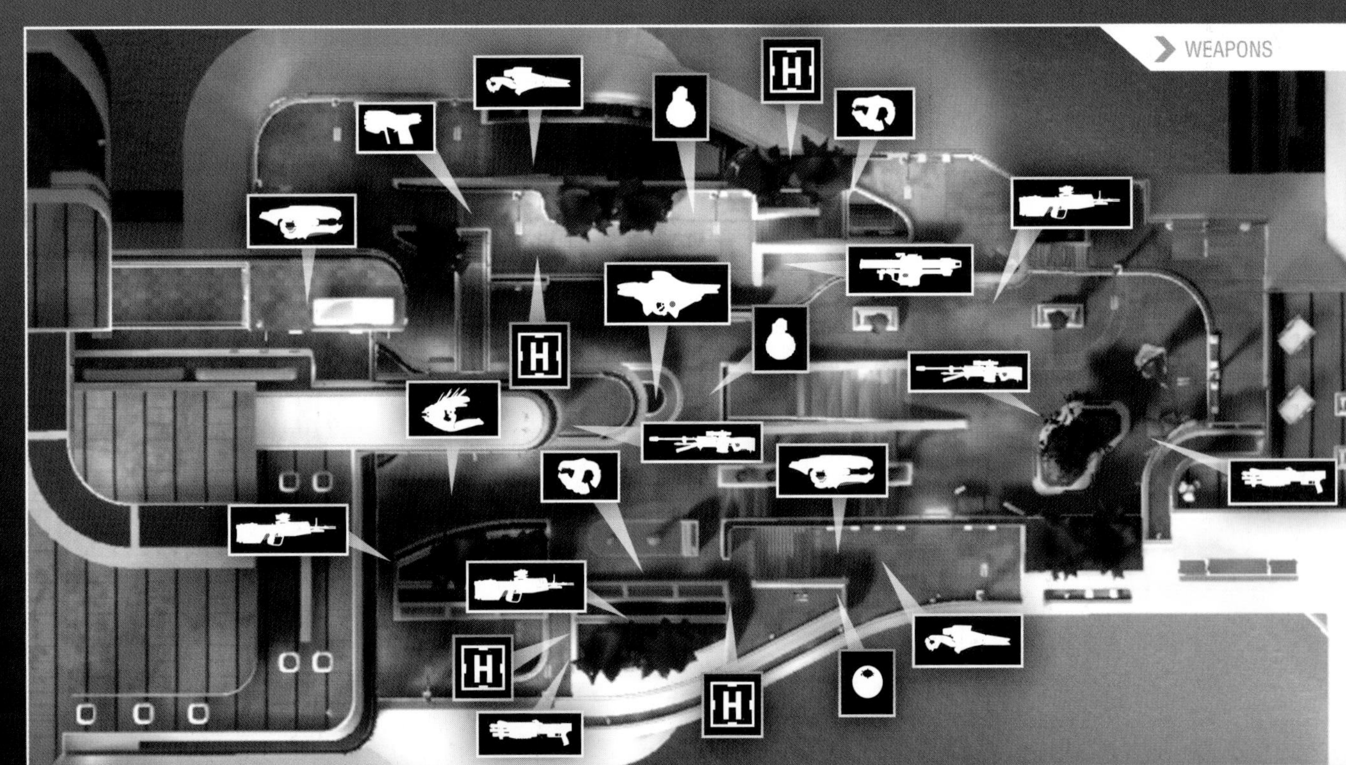

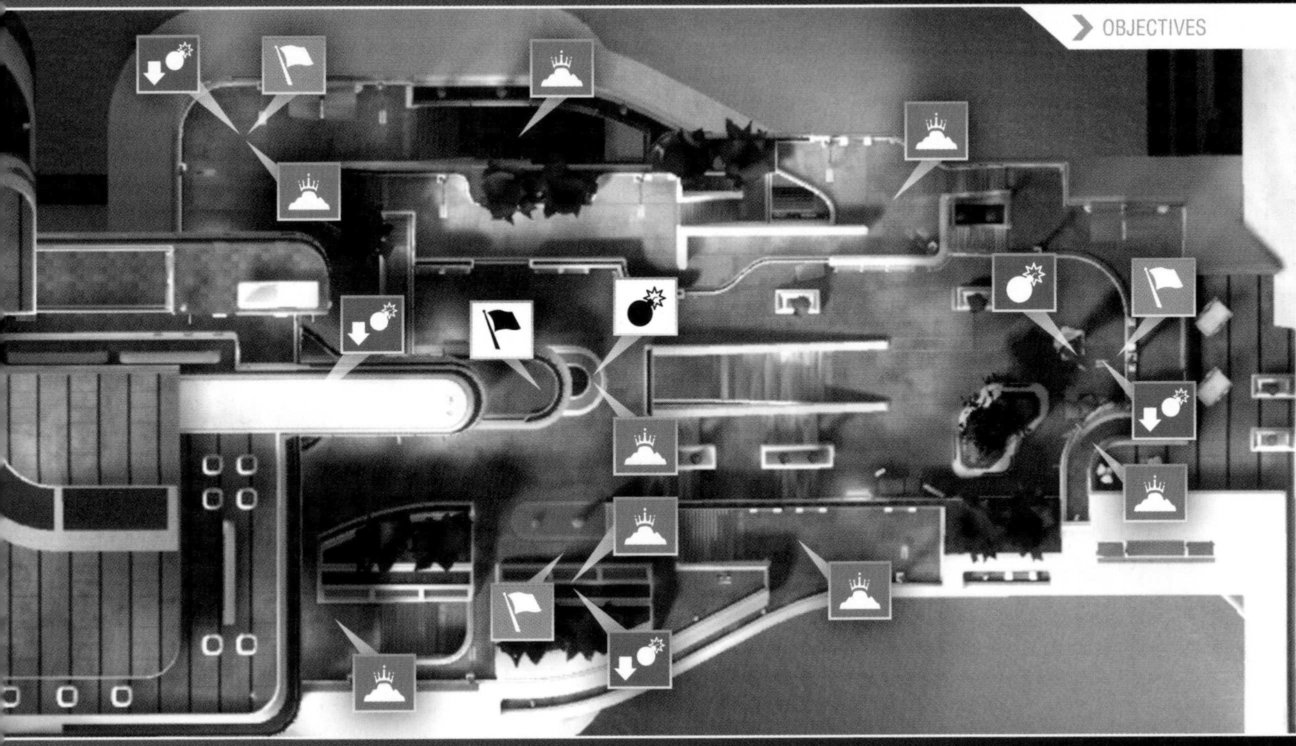

This medium size, multi-level building complex offers cover in the way of scattered foliage such as trees and rocks located in various planters mixed with some boulders. This map's layout features a long open central area which snipers will be covering almost all of the time. If you need to maneuver from end to end, use the sides of the map and the lower level to remain out of sniper crosshairs.

The lower level contains the two power weapons available, the Rocket Launcher and the Plasma Launcher. These are going to become two of the hottest zones on the map. The Plasma Launcher is under the waterfall and the Rocket Launcher is near the stairs on the high side of the map. Grab them if you can or consider defending their spawn location while players continually stream towards them.

Use the sides of the map to flank your enemies and the underground level as well. You can loop around from underneath to either side of the map or the center. You can also use elevation here to gain the high ground on your enemies. There are several trees that you can climb into for great cover and vantage points. And, you can use other players to gain higher access by getting on their backs and jumping to higher points.

Try crouching in and under the trees and rocks on the map and wait for enemies to rush past. Remember that while you are crouched, you do not show up on enemy radar—moving or not. This is going to be very useful here to get from one end to the other, since there are half walls that will block you from enemy view.Think about choosing the Hologram loadout and activate them to run out into the center of the map from time to time. This will get enemy snipers to fire off a locating round that you can trace back to their location and find a way around them or finish them off with a power weapon.

There are several elevation changes here that you can use to fight near and escape quickly out of enemy range if you get into trouble. Jump down when your shields go down but be careful not to end your own life from the impact. Stick to low light areas while maneuvering around the map and stick close to walls to minimize your silhouette.Try setting traps and using your Hologram as bait. If you have made your way to a power weapon, this could be a great trick to use. Fire off a Hologram and wait for an enemy to take the bait. Lock on to them with the Plasma Launcher or splash them with explosions from the Rocket Launcher. You don't need a power weapon for this, but it will make short work of any opponents.

With the open layout of this map, you can also make good use of the Active Camo. Sometimes you may need to use the center of the map to move to your desired location and this can help you do it. Continue to stick to the inside walls of the middle area while cloaked since enemy snipers will be watching for movement and you will be semi-noticeable. Try to move slowly and from cover to cover.

This map also offers some decent cover to use in conjunction with the Hologram. If an enemy sees you duck behind cover and begins firing on you, you can quickly fire off a Hologram while you stay put. Send it out in the same direction you were moving in and trick the enemy into thinking you just stopped for a second, then continued. While they train their weapons on the fake "you", pop up and pick them off. Done correctly and timed right, this technique can infuriate your enemies and keep you alive at the same time.

This map will be slow paced on top and out in the open, but fast paced down below offering close quarters combat and splash damage from explosions off of the walls and floors.

BONEYARD

This map is enormous. With two major outdoor areas separated by a decommissioned Spartan ship running down the middle of the map and a refinery at one end, you will need to make use of the vehicles supplied here. The terrain outdoor is rugged desert littered with cranes and multiple small support buildings—some of which can be accessed by players. The ship features several half levels which can be useful for cover, and the refinery has three levels plus roof access.

While outside, be aware of the many sightlines the enemy may be able to spot you from. Look high, low, and far away. Snipers can prove to be deadly here if they are fast and accurate at distance. Try to make good use of the cranes, bridges and buildings to move from one area to the next. Change up your approach elevation moving from high to medium to low ground and rotate.

Try to use any available vehicles to get where you need to go in a hurry and do your best to load up vehicles with other players as well to increase your numbers at your final destination. Some vehicles can be used not just for transportation but for offense and defense as well. Even if your opponents happen to have acquired a heavy weapon, the Wraith or Scorpion can obliterate pedestrian foes quickly and easily.

The refinery offers a couple of mounted machine guns that players can access via building roofs. You can dismount these weapons and carry them with you. Bear in mind that you will move extremely slowly while wielding these guns, so choose to use them wisely.

If you can manage to get up on one of the cranes or other high points on the map and remain undetected, you can use them to call out enemy locations to your team. Sometimes being a team player doesn't mean you have to shoot everything that moves. Try using the Active Camo ability here to further minimize your visibility from enemies.

There are no underground areas here to sneak through and while much of the fighting that takes place here is long distance, the decommissioned ship and the refinery will provide the close quarters combat that you know and love. The Jet Pack can work wonders here and allow players to access small alcoves and roosts to either snipe from or get the drop on enemy players.

The sheer size of this map means that vehicles will play a large part here. Don't fear respawning way back in your main base since this is where most of the vehicles will appear. Many players will become impatient and continue to spawn in and around where the fighting is taking place. You do not have to succumb to this theory. Spawn back at your base and grab a Scorpion or a Wraith and lay waste to the impatient!

Be careful entering the ship and the refinery. These structures have limited chokepoints and they are not very wide open. The splash damage from grenades or heavy weapons can be increased due to the tight layout of the building interiors. Toss a couple of grenades inside before entering to help clear the way. Alternatively, you can make great use of the Hologram to breach through chokepoints. Just send one through and follow it in.

MULTIPLAYER

SEA SNIPERS

SEA SNIPER TIP

- You do not show up on radar while you are crouched, moving or not.

OBJECTIVES AND VEHICLES
GUN
GUN
TIER 2
TIER 1
TIER 2
GUN
GUN
GUN
H

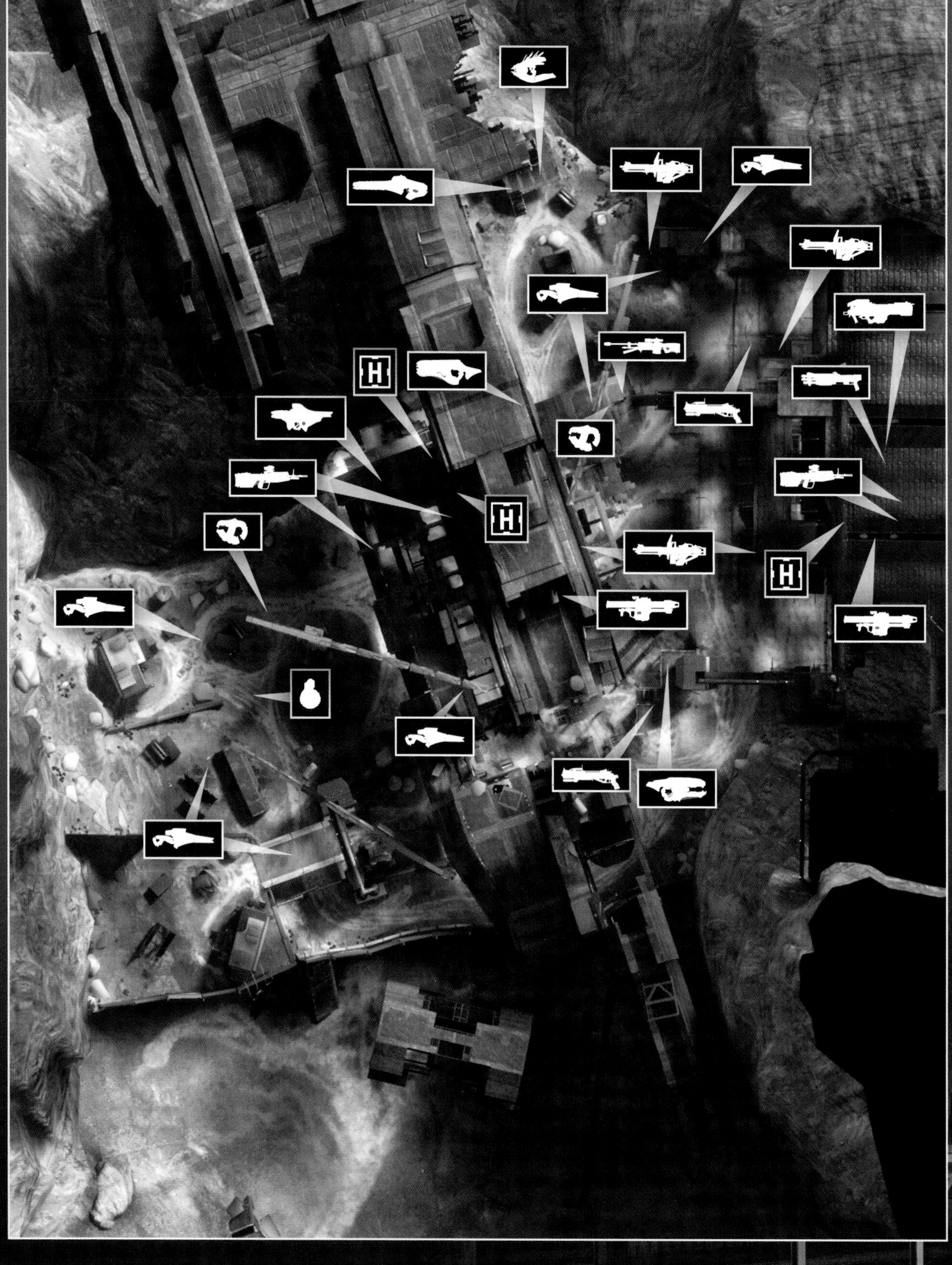

MULTIPLAYER

When moving your team throughout this map, try to split up initially and regroup later to become a more imposing force. Starting off going in as a group can be detrimental to your numbers. Try using a vehicle convoy to infiltrate more safely. If you can be patient enough to get all of your teammates into several vehicles at once and follow each other to your destination, you can seriously put the enemy on their heels.

You may find yourself getting pinned down from your start point from time to time. If this happens, think again about using the Active Camo, but also the Scout loadout. Being able to sprint in short bursts from cover to cover can get you out of enemy sight forcing them to focus in on another, slower moving target. The Armor Lock can also provide some protection here on your way to engagement areas such as the central ship. If you happen to see an enemy vehicle coming toward you at breakneck speed, don't move. Just fire off the Armor Lock at the last second and make them explode!

While inside any structures, try to use the Drop Shield in locations that need to be defended. This can help keep your team healthy and waste enemy ammunition. The Drop Shield can be passed through but not shot through so be wary of enemy melee attacks when utilizing this ability. The Drop Shield is also vulnerable to plasma and EMP attacks, so don't trust it completely.

With so many open areas, nooks and crannies, keep your head on a swivel and the advantage on your side. Use your vehicles, use stealth and use speed to achieve victory in any mode on this map.

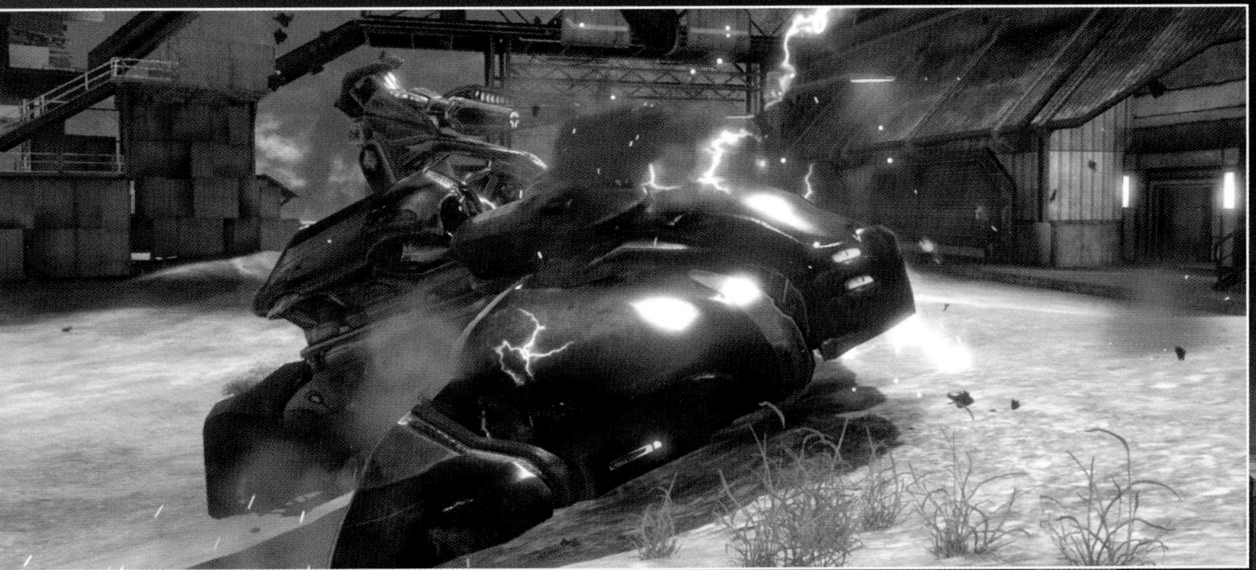

COUNTDOWN

This spacecraft launch station is circular in shape with three main levels. A fourth level is accessible via Jet Pack, but only for ten seconds at which point you will be prompted to return to the map. Countdown is a small map with only three power weapons available here, the Energy Sword, the Concussion Rifle, and the Shotgun. These weapon's locations will be highly contested areas.

Jet Packs are a great choice here. The stacked, multi-level structure almost requires you to use one. Get to upper and middle tiers before enemies and without having to use the Gravity Lifts where enemies might be waiting for you. The Hologram is a good tool on this map as well. Firing one off into the center of the map will always attract attention cluing you in to enemy locations.

The circular layout creates a constant flow of play—keeping players moving throughout it at a fast pace. Use the Gravity Lifts to quickly change elevation and evade enemies. Under the ship are three Gravity Lifts you can duck into during a battle if you need to recover some health. There are also two lifts located in the inside corners of the central portion of the level.

Be aware of enemies camping the Gravity Lifts just waiting for you to pop up so they can stab you. Toss a grenade or two up the lift if you can before you jump in. If you are so equipped, try sending your Hologram up the lift, then while the enemy is busy with it, toss a grenade up and finish them off. Camping the Gravity Lifts is a little cheap, but can get you some quick, easy kills if you are in need. Use the Energy Sword or the Shotgun for best results.

Most of your engagements here will be close quarters so prepare for that kind of battle. Think about Armor Lock as your Armor Ability, and don't forget to melee. Don't worry too much about trying to Assassinate players here since while the layout is stacked vertically, it is very open, similar to a stadium. Performing an Assassination that everyone will see will attract attention and focus all eyes on you, possibly resulting in someone stopping you mid-assassination. Everybody loves power weapons right?

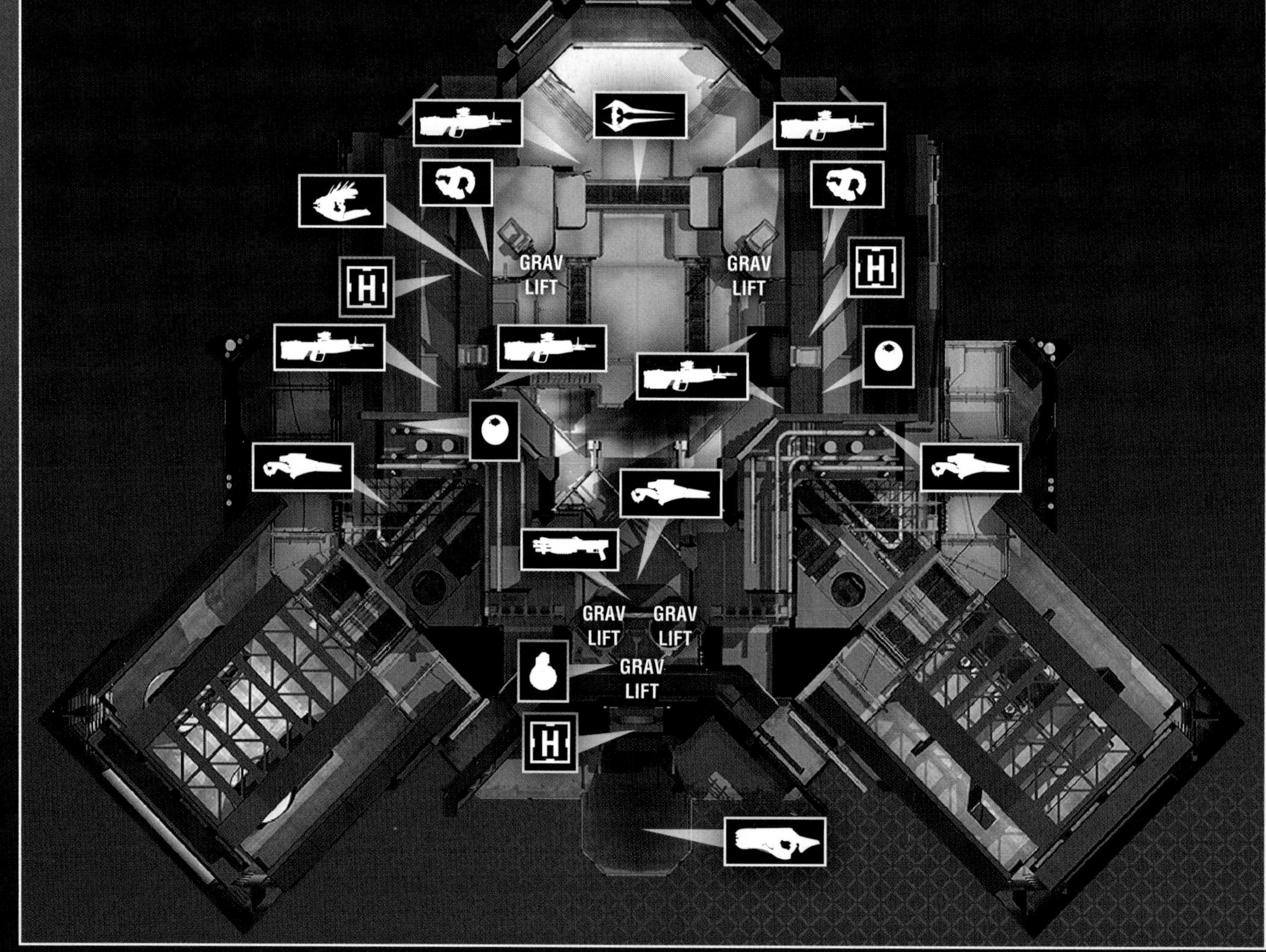

MULTIPLAYER

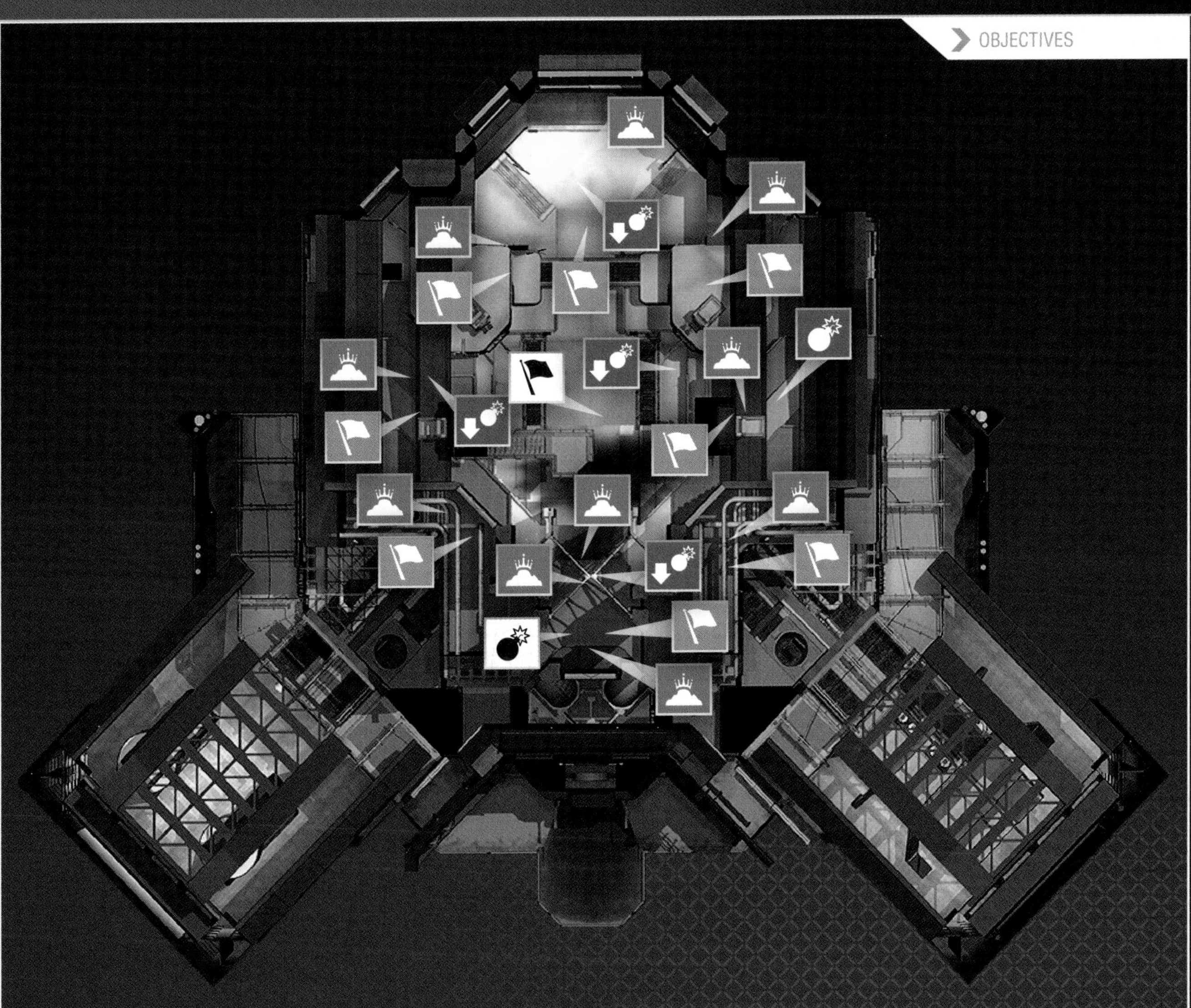

Since this small map only offers three of them you can bet they are going to be fought over fiercely. The Concussion Rifle is outside on the third level, the Shotgun is underneath the ship by the Gravity Lifts, and the Energy Sword is standing up like a birthday candle on the third floor bridge.

A nice place to sit and snipe enemies is under the ship near the Gravity Lifts. You can see the middle ramp to the second level from there, and since it is a fairly heavily trafficked area, you can squeeze off a couple of kills. If anyone catches on to your secret hideaway, just fall back into one of the lifts and relocate. It's good practice to turn quickly after exiting a Gravity Lift to make sure you haven't been followed, whether it be by a person or a grenade.

You'll want to steer clear of the central "arena" part of this map because you'll just become fodder for grenades and other various weaponry. Use that area for Hologram fights. What you should be doing is keeping on the move. Sitting still for too long is just asking for someone who's doing laps to melee you from behind. If you do need to stop for a while, try to do it near a drop off to the level beneath you. This way you can just step off the ledge if you're about to get a beatdown.

You can also use the upper levels to drop down on your enemies. Wait for unsuspecting players to pass underneath you then drop down or use the Jet Pack to fly down and stab them in the back! The high ground is a great advantage on this map allowing you to toss grenades down with more precision, as well as remaining much more hidden. Being up higher than your enemy gives you more options to deal with them than they have coming up from underneath of you.While the Active Camo and Drop Shield are always useful, they aren't as much of a benefit or advantage over Sprint, Jet Packs, Armor Lock and Holograms here. These four loadouts will help your cause on this map more so than the Camo and Shield. Being able to sprint away or Jet Pack out of sight is not just good for you, but frustrating for your enemy.

This map is tons of fun for modes like Headhunter, Oddball, Capture the Flag and of course Slayer. While its footprint is small, the map plays a little bigger than it actually is, making it fun for the modes listed above. Try this map in a custom game with Rocket Launchers only for a little Rocket Arena.

Remember to keep looking up if you're down low, and keep looking down if you're up high. Keep moving and working towards grabbing a power weapon if you can. Trick you enemies with the Hologram, and relocate with the Jet Pack. Watch the Gravity Lifts for exit campers and try exit camping the Gravity Lifts!

POWERHOUSE

The cliff-side hilltop setting for this powerhouse structure is considered a medium sized map with minimal foliage and rocky, dry terrain. The circular structure in the center gives players access above and below as well as some decent cover; however, it also acts as a kind of arena where the spillway empties into. There are lots of elevation changes on this map so make sure you look high and low for possible threats.

The power weapons that are available here include the Rocket Launcher, the Gravity Hammer, the Shotgun, and the Focus Rifle. The Rocket Launcher and Gravity Hammer will be the weapons of choice for most players and you should work to get to them as quickly as you can. The Rocket Launcher in the spillway under the powerhouse bridges will more than likely be the first weapon players go for. Try to get a couple of grenades off in its direction before you get there to deter enemies.

The Gravity Hammer works great especially in some of the closed in areas scattered throughout this level. Hunker down in an enclosed area and bash away.

The Shotgun isn't the best choice here unless you plan on staying inside. Consider using it only indoors or for hard defensive situations. There are also a couple of Needlers on this map which can prove to be quite effective due to the open nature of most of the map. Combine Needler shards with a teammate to decrease the number of shots each of you has to fire at an enemy before they explode.

Sprint and the Jet Pack will be your best friends on this map. Getting to the power weapons here will be a big advantage for you and your team, and these abilities will help you get them first. The Jet Pack will also allow you to quickly change elevations and relocate or drop off of high areas without taking damage.

Armor Lock and Drop Shields can be quite useful here on defense. The Armor Lock works best in close quarters since it will fire off a burst at the end of its cycle dropping enemy shields. The Drop Shield works better in open areas when you may be getting sniped.

If you're looking to rent a nice piece of real estate in Powerhouse, the main facility is a great place to spend the night. With only four entrances, this structure can be fairly easily defensible with as few as two players. Setting up shop in the upper level may require another player since there are going to be three entrances to that level if you include the stairs from the bottom.

You can defend from the lower level a little more easily since you can see enemy players' feet as they come down from the stairs before they can see you. Either level is possible to defend effectively with the right loadouts and weaponry.The lockers located in the bi-level building attached to the center of the spillway can be a great place to either abuse the Gravity Hammer and infuriate players trying to dig you out, or a great place to snipe from. The top level here offers a long window and a dark environment to shoot from. You can catch players crossing the concrete walkway around the central spillway, and see most of that side of the map.

Well timed jumps and Jet Packs can get you to some unique and seldom observed locations. There is a small piece of a pipe which the water flows from into the spillway just above where the Rocket Launcher is located. Use the Jet Pack or jump to it from above. You can see enemies crossing the powerhouse bridges and of course anyone trying to get to the Rocket Launcher.

As will all maps, use your knowledge of your surroundings to enhance your game play. Knowing how to get from one place to the next can be a vital bit of information allowing you to not only evade enemies, but to come at them from areas they weren't expecting. Use the various levels of elevation here to gain the advantage and change up your play style to match up well against enemy players.

REFLECTION

Reflection is a tranquil Japanese-style indoor playing field with three main levels, multiple half-levels; and corridors aplenty. Many of the hallways and catwalks have glass railings which you should not mistake for cover. They can be broken just by touching them.

The four available power weapons here are the Sniper Rifle, Energy Sword, Shotgun and Rocket Launcher. The sword and the launcher are located quite close to each other in the center of the map and on the lower level. These weapons are going to create the arena style play in the middle of this map as they will be most fought over.

The Sniper Rifle is a good choice if you're good with it. There are lots of places to tuck in to and remain concealed. The Energy Sword is always extremely effective when used to camp Gravity Lift exits of which there are four on this level.

The Rocket Launcher can be used just about anywhere, just aim for the feet and watch enemies bounce around to their death. The Shotgun can be your bread and butter here if you can keep it long enough. Stay mobile and show the business end of it to your enemies to see what they think.

Sprint and Armor Lock are good choices here due to the multitude of corridors and corners. Use sprint to quickly gain access to the various levels and to escape through the Gravity Lifts. You can also benefit from the Scout class to attain the power weapons faster than your enemies here, just be careful not to Sprint and jump off of ledges that might deal you damage from falling too far.

Make good use of the Active Camo and Holograms here. The cloaking abilities of the Active Camo can help you "predator" into areas the enemy won't expect you. Use it to gain access to higher levels of the map.

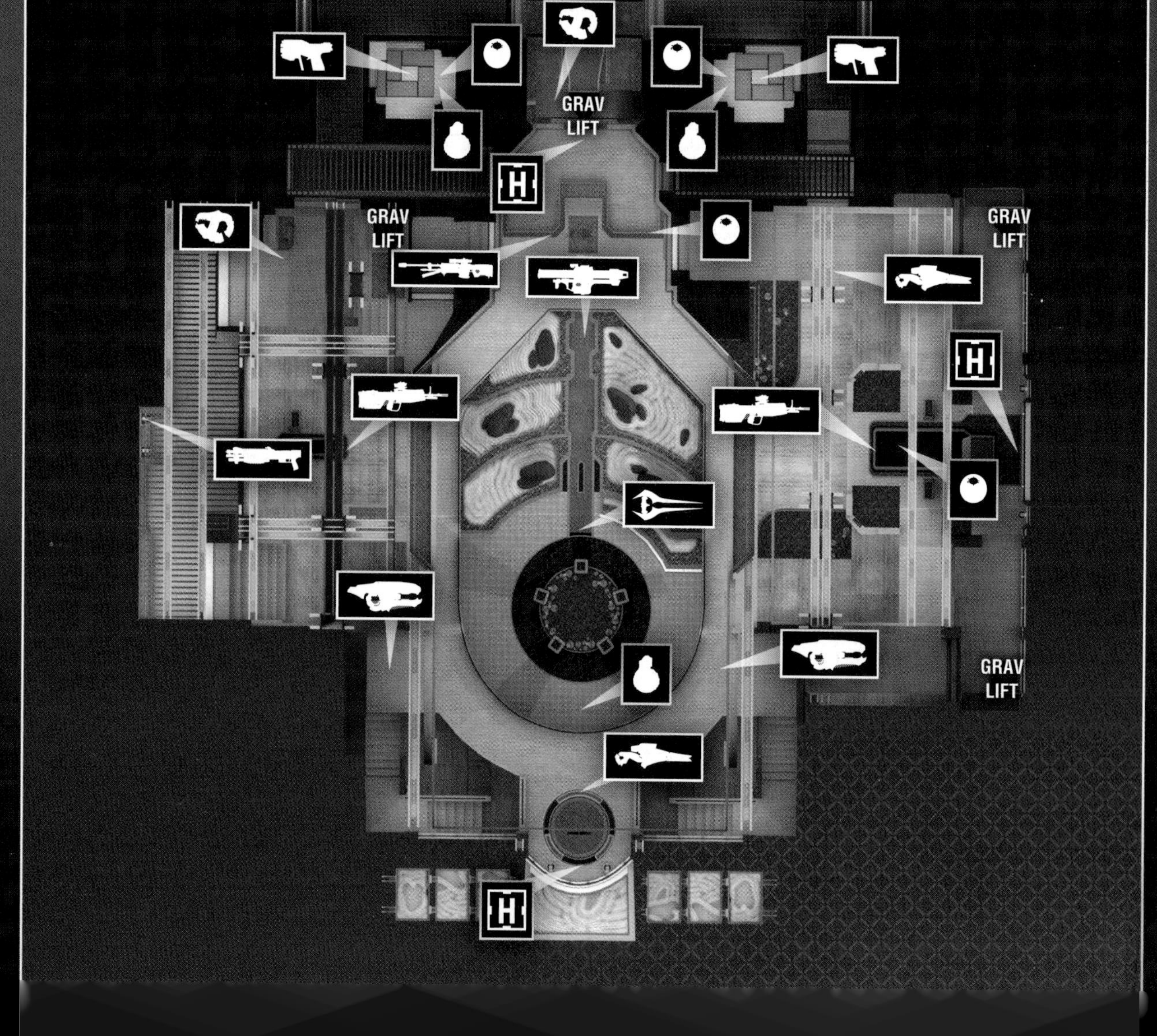

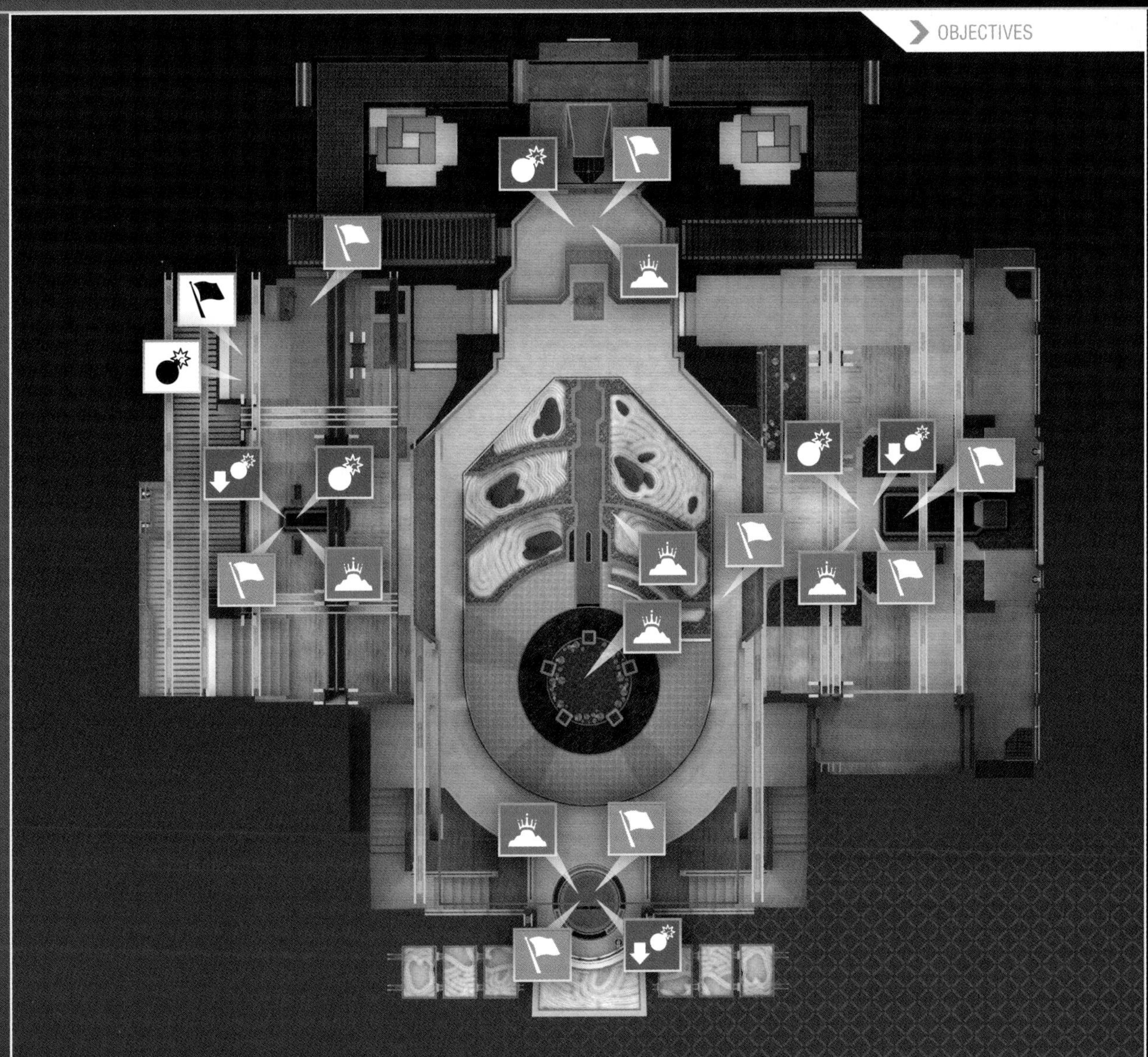

WELCOME
UNSC TRAINING
THE CAMPAIGN
FIREFIGHT
MULTIPLAYER
BASICS & TACTICS
ARSENAL
VEHICLES
GAMEPLAY MODES
MAPS
FORGE
REFERENCE

Use the Hologram wisely and you can draw out enemy locations. Since there are multiple levels, you may have a hard time actually finding enemies. Use the Hologram to draw them out and get them to fire on your hologram. Pinpoint their location by backtracking their tracers.

A good use of this ability here is to bait an enemy into tracking you from across the map. When you pass behind a barrier or wall, send your hologram out in the same direction you were running, then peek out and snipe them to death.There are some great locations to be sneaky here. Just above the Energy Sword and Rocket Launcher locations are a series of open slots in the floor where you can shoot through or more deadly, lob grenades through. Enemies will be trying to go for these two weapons and you can almost always get a kill or two from this spot.

Another key spot is only accessible by Jet Pack. In the middle of the map at one end is a golden Japanese symbol or character. Jet Pack up to one of the pillars that line the middle of the map, then jet over on top of the character. Players won't always look up this high for enemies and this can give you the time you need to eliminate you opponents without them ever seeing where you shot them from. Eventually someone's going to spot you and return for revenge. Bounce out of there and Jet Pack over to one of the other pillars or the ledges or moldings to relocate and maintain your height advantage.

There are a handful of beams you can access with the Jet Pack and some by jumping. Not all of them have decent visibility, but they can be used as a hiding spot to jump down on players and Assassinate them from behind.

As always, learn where the Gravity Lifts are and use them to your advantage by either fighting near them so you can jump into them in case you start taking too much damage, or even send a Hologram up them to confuse the other team. If you plan on maneuvering via the lifts, it's always a good idea to toss a grenade up as a scout first.

This map offers the possibility of playing it many different ways from close quarters combat to sniping and tactical team based movement. Try to get your team to switch up their techniques and play styles to fit what's going on at any given moment. Being able to adapt on the fly is key in *Halo: Reach* and very much so on this particular map. While it seems a little convoluted, the map is only medium sized and stacked vertically. You'll be able to learn the layout fairly quickly with just a game or two.

SPIRE

Spire is one of the largest maps in the game. The rocky outdoor terrain features hills and elevations, a small stream, a Cliffside and lots of boulders. There are only two major structures on the map that are accessible to players, the Spire itself, and the BFG. The Spire is a two level, circular building with the roof accessible via Gravity Lifts. The BFG is a much smaller version of it also with two levels and a Gravity Lift.

All around the main spire are several Gravity Lifts however they are not intended to get you to a higher level. They are meant to cushion your fall from the roof if you happen to be without a Jet Pack. You can use them to get up and away from a fight if you need to, but they will not give you access to the spire without the aid of a Jet Pack.

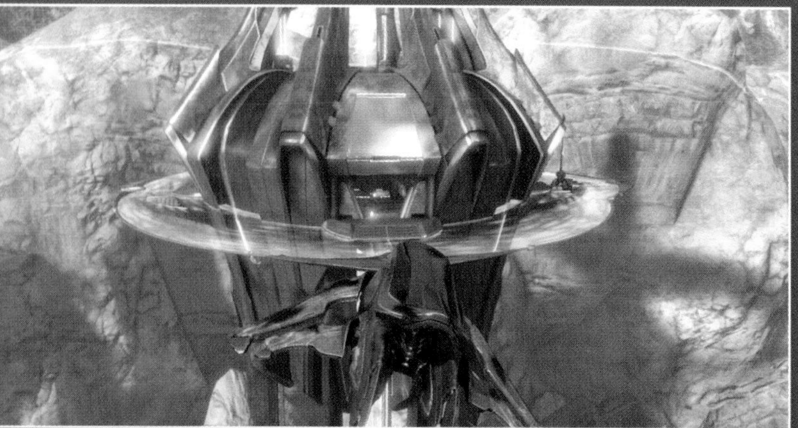

There are lots of power weapons available here as well as several other very useful weapons in the non-power category. Don't forget about the Plasma Cannons located on opposite parallel roads. Use them to decimate incoming vehicle convoys.

The Rocket Launcher is of course present, but try to limit its use to vehicles which will be in play on this map. The Concussion Rifle is also available here and works very well against vehicles too. It's best used to flip vehicles over while in motion.

There is a Focus Rifle and a Sniper Rifle here and they are both good for long range engagements and this map is huge. There's also a Grenade Launcher tucked away near the overhanging ducts. Considering the size of this map, you might want to carry either the Scout class with sprint or the Assault class with the Jet Pack. Many times you'll be killed and forced to respawn quite far from the action. Use these classes to get you back in the fight fast. The Jet Pack can also help you gain high ground here by getting atop the various boulders that dot the landscape.

The other four loadouts can of course be useful here, but not much at the beginning of the round. You can make good use of these other loadouts, specifically the Drop Shield and Armor Lock later in the round. Since one team starts down low with the enemy firing down from above them, you can engage a Drop Shield to protect you and your team from all angles of fire while healing at the same time.

Since vehicles are going to be in play, the Armor Lock ability can be a life saver. If you're about to get run down by an enemy vehicle, engage your ability and watch the vehicle explode while you remain unharmed. You can also use the Jet Pack to fly out of the way, but by using the Armor Lock you can kill two birds with one stone.

There are lots of places to set up an ambush or get around to flank enemies here. The spire offers decent elevation at the second level and roof to take on approaching enemies. Use the lifts around it the break your fall if you need to get down without a Jet Pack. There are lots of scoped weapons here and you should make use of them.

There are several rocky outcroppings and enormous boulders you can access sometimes just by jumping but mostly my Jet Pack. These rocks will make your opponents wonder "how did they get up there?". Bounce from rock to rock to avoid any incoming grenades but try to keep the high ground. Add a power weapon and you're a god! You can use these boulder groupings to mask your approach as well. They create multiple paths for your team to use to split up then regroup. Use them to confuse the enemy in conjunction with the Hologram ability. When you all head to the rocks, send your holograms out to the right and you continue up left making the enemy feel pinned in.

There will be lots of vehicle fighting here. The Falcon, Scorpion, Banshee and the rest are going to make it difficult to survive without either a power weapon or a vehicle of your own. Grab them whenever you can and use them for as long as you can to even the odds. If you find yourself without a vehicle or maybe just don't want one, use the perimeter of the map to get from one point to the other and avoid detection.

The Falcon is a great transport ship but be careful, it can be EMP-ed with Plasma Pistol charges and drop out of the sky. Falcon pilots should use their Jet Packs as makeshift or replacement parachutes just in case! One the best vehicles to have is the Banshee, since you can drop bombs and fire plasma charges from the air. Good pilots can keep enemy teams at bay for quite some time with these vehicles, so commandeer them whenever possible.

Fighting in the Spire is all close quarters. It can get hectic inside so use the elevation it offers to your advantage. Use the Gravity Lifts when you can to change levels, and try using the boulders around the outside of the spire to gain access to the second level. There are no Medkits anywhere on this map, so think about choosing the Drop Shield and becoming a makeshift medic for your team.

WELCOME
UNSC TRAINING
THE CAMPAIGN
FIREFIGHT
MULTIPLAYER
BASICS & TACTICS
ARSENAL
VEHICLES
GAMEPLAY MODES
MAPS
FORGE
REFERENCE

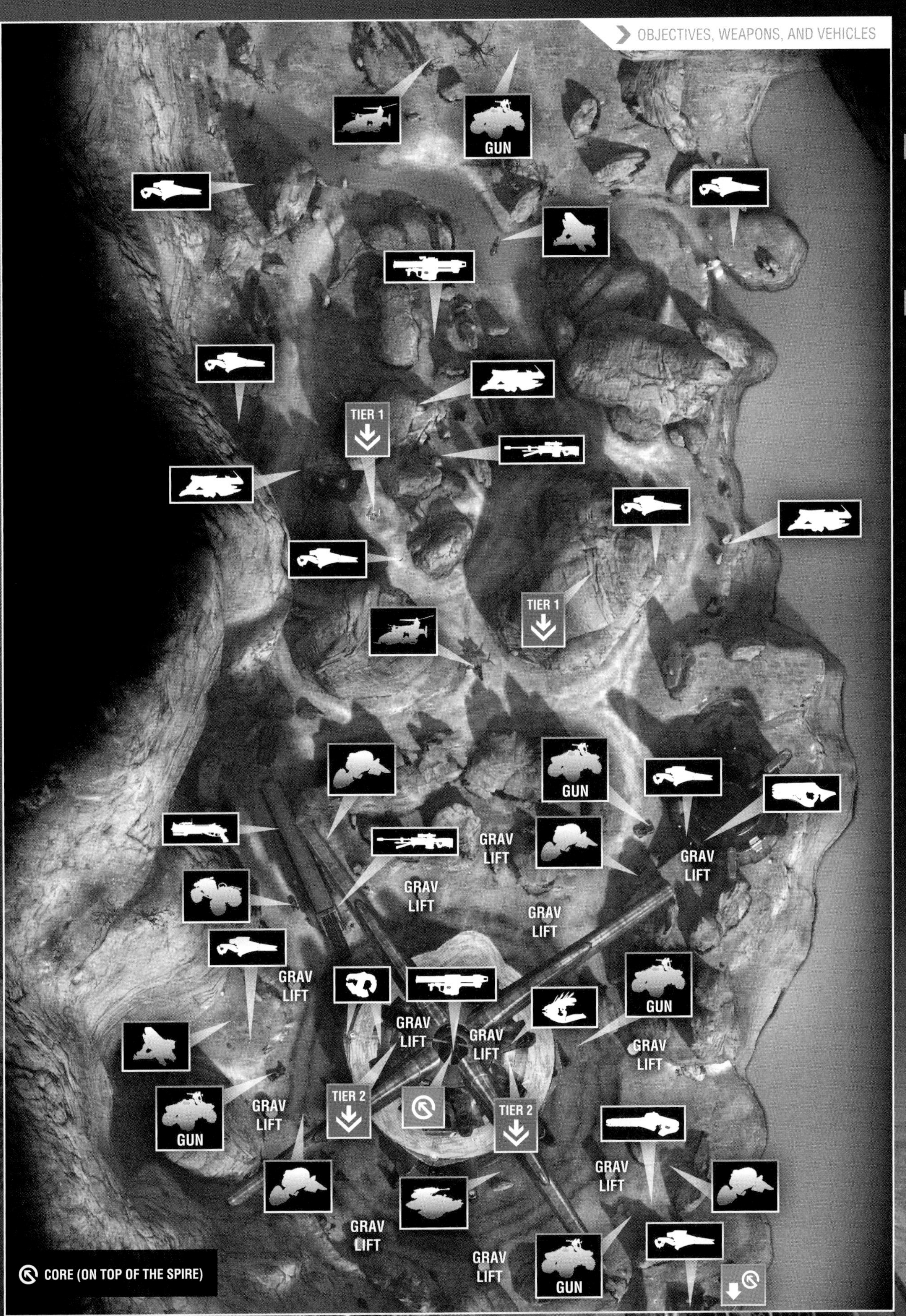

SWORD BASE

This six level vertically oriented map features two almost identical buildings facing each other. Three Gravity Lifts provide access to the higher levels, one in each building and one in the center of the map. Four glass bridges connect the two buildings as well as a few glass ledges which are all heavily travelled. There are various ledges to Jet Pack to and from, and a sniper roost accessible only by a single ramp.

The most hotly contested weapons here are going to be the Shotgun, the Concussion Rifle and the Energy Sword. If you can manage to get to one of these weapons quickly, find a place or a technique that makes the most of them. The Shotgun of course is going to work very well indoors so try not to venture outside once you've acquired it.

The Concussion Rifle is a great weapon when used from above on this map. Since there are many places to get up to and fire down from, use one of the Gravity Lifts or a Jet Pack to get up to where you want to be and lob plasma balls at enemies below.

As mentioned earlier, the Jet Pack is going to be your best friend here. Since this map is so vertically oriented, you're going to need it to get back into the action as quickly as possible and to gain access to some great sniping spots. You can and should also use it when you need to jump off of any of the upper levels to escape certain death. Fire up the Jet Pack just before you hit the ground to soften your landing.

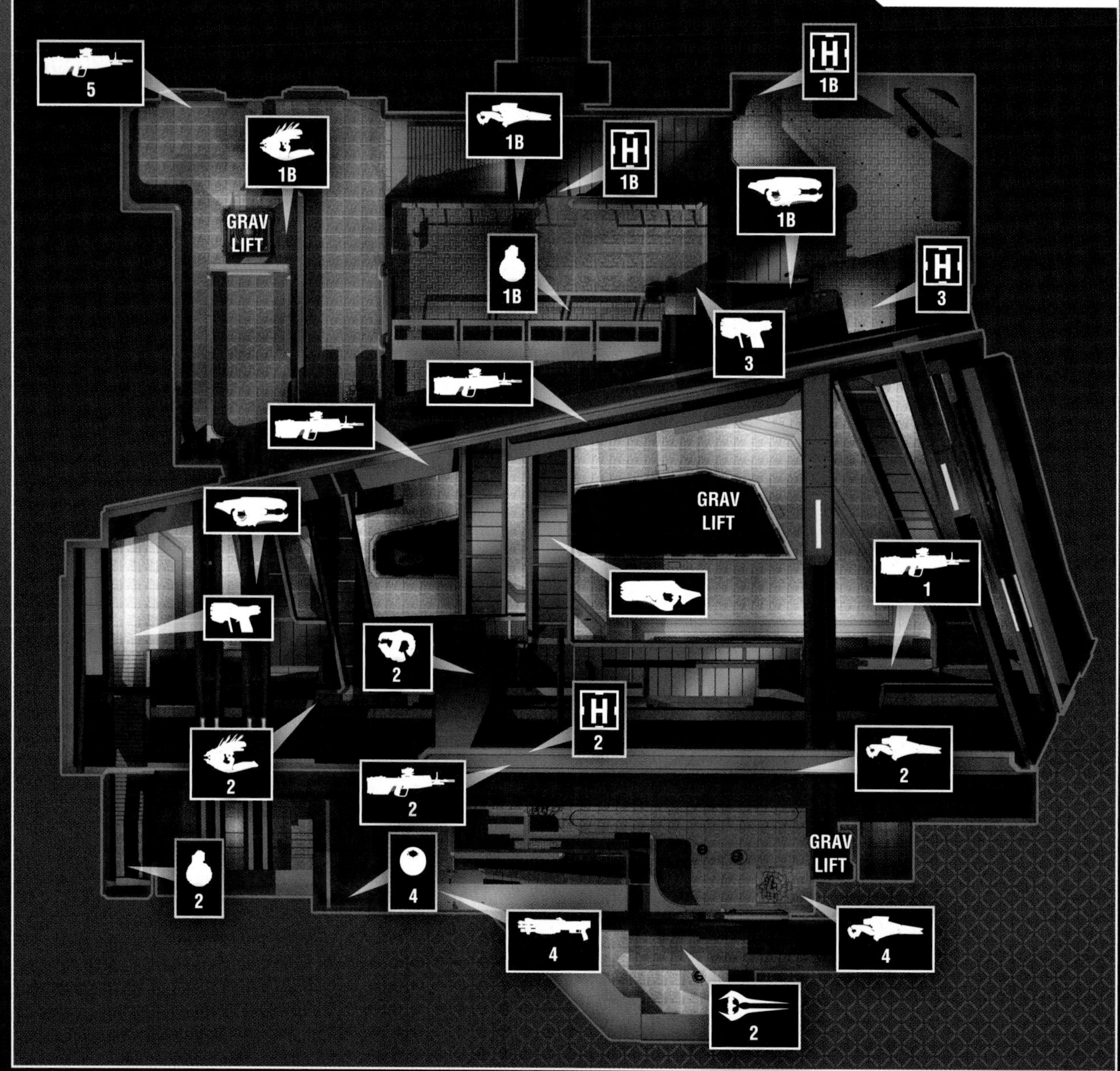

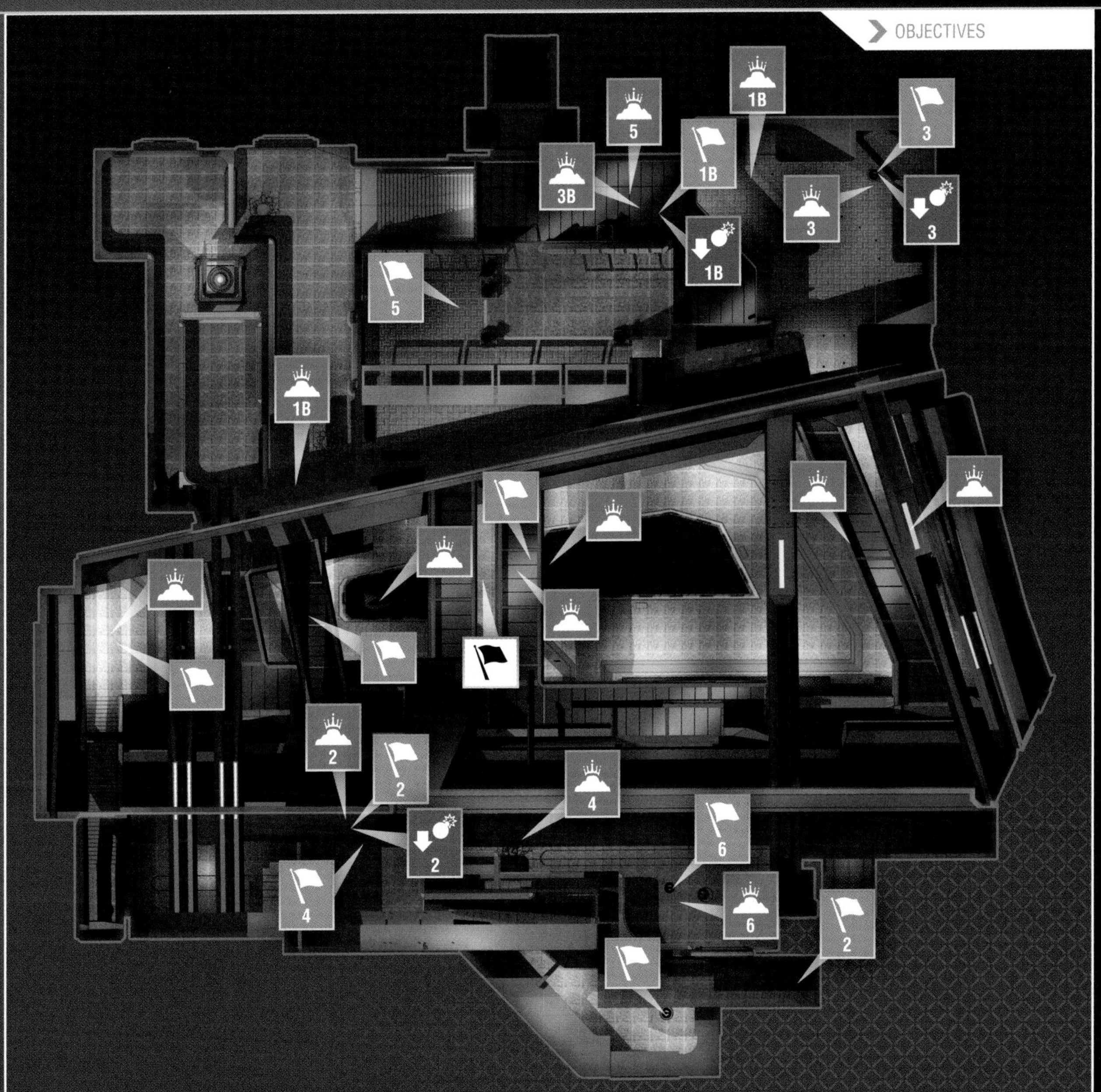

WELCOME
UNSC TRAINING
THE CAMPAIGN
FIREFIGHT
MULTIPLAYER
BASICS & TACTICS
ARSENAL
VEHICLES
GAMEPLAY MODES
MAPS
FORGE
REFERENCE

Armor Lock can be very useful in close quarters situations since it gives off a final burst of energy when it has been used up. The Drop Shield is a decent choice too if you and your team plan on defending a particular area of the map. Fire one off as often as you can in the middle of your team so they can duck in whenever necessary.

The three Gravity Lifts on Swordbase are heavily used. The one located on

Many of the entrances to the bridges will have snipers at the ends. Be wary and try to lead your approach with grenades or even Holograms. Holograms can help you expend enemy ammunition letting you advance with a full mag ready for your opponent. The rooms attached to these bridges also usually contain the Medkits you'll need to stay alive longer. Make a note of where they are located so you can heal up if necessary.

ZEALOT

The layout of this map is very symmetrical and circular in nature with three levels plus a fourth accessible via Gravity Lift. Gravity Lifts allow players to access the various levels here. Each half of the map is colored either red or blue. Use this color coded design to orient yourself during game play.

There are only two power weapons available here, the Energy Sword and the Concussion Rifle. The rifle is on the top level and is the only projectile based power weapon available. The Energy Sword is located at the point where the red and blue sections of the map meet. The close quarters nature of the fighting here will create a tug of war for the sword immediately.

The Energy Sword can be extremely useful tool when combined with the Active Camo ability. Use them to tuck into a cubby hole and wait for enemies to pass you by, then stab them.

This map gives players the option of using almost any of the available Armor abilities successfully. Sprint of course is useful here since the map is laid out in a circle and with multiple levels. You can also use it to rush up behind enemies for a quick Assassination especially if you happen to have won the sword.

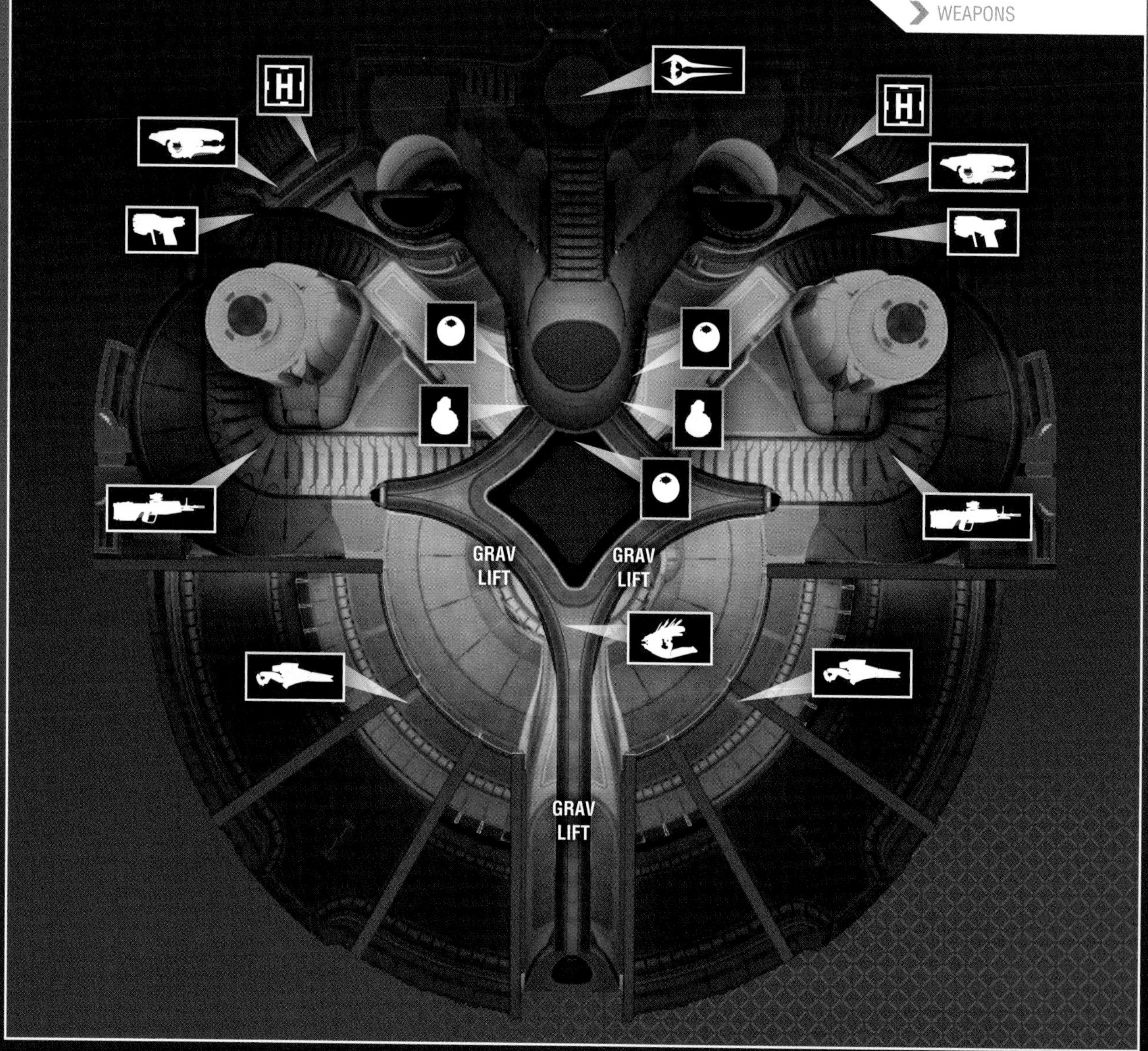

From the highest level you can see down on the rest of the map but you cannot fire through the shield. You can only drop back down through the shield. Enemies cannot fire at you through the shield either. This is a good place to exit camp with an Energy Sword, just be careful heading back down, since enemies can see you from below.

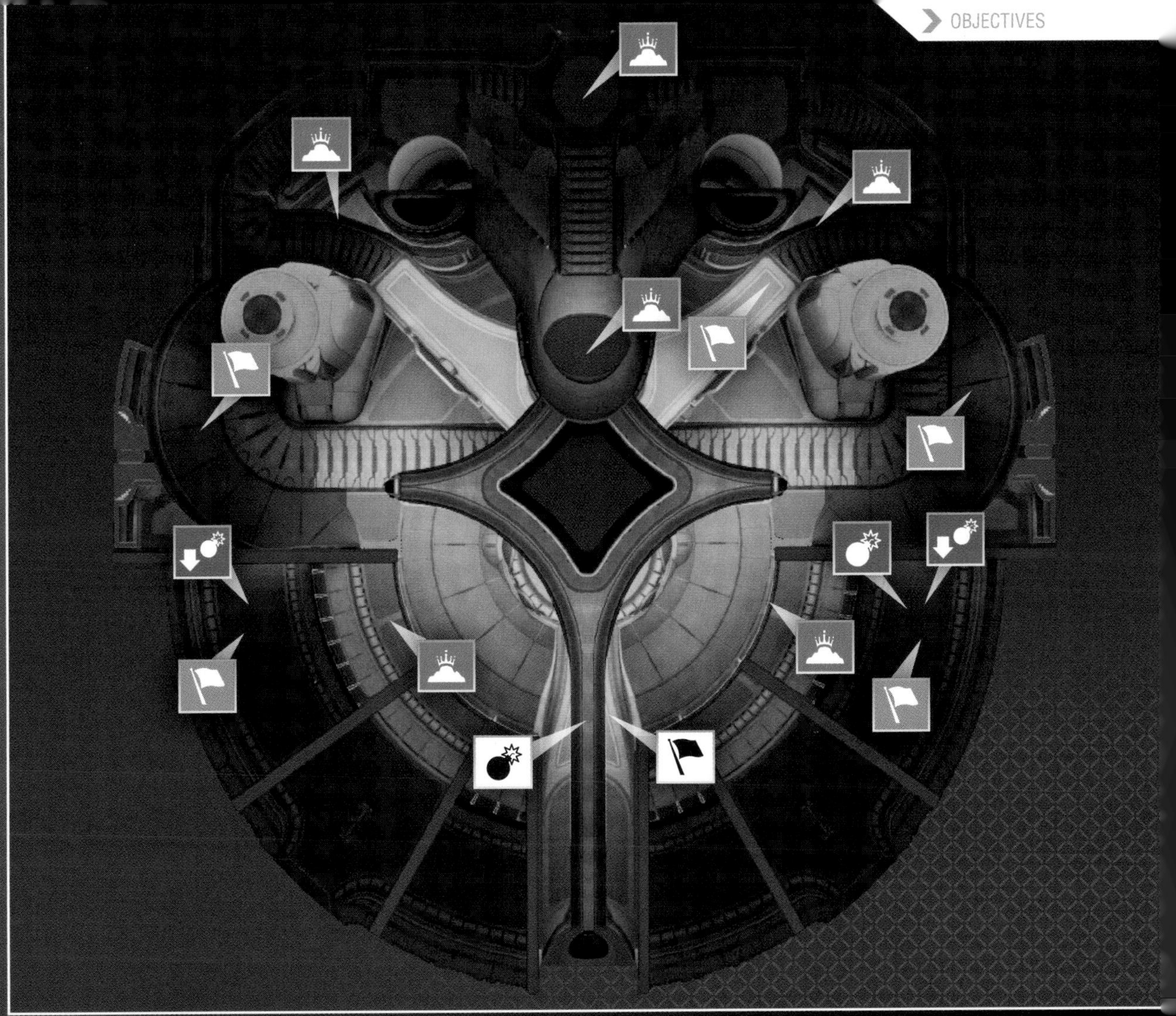

You can make use of the Jet Pack here but you have to get used to bursting it to control your height. Use it to quickly get off of the first level and up to the second or third quickly. You'll have to control your thrust to be able to squeeze through some of the openings that will get you out of harm's way so practice controlling your ascent and decent with the Jet Pack.

The tight construction of this Covenant ship allows players to seriously benefit from using the Armor Lock ability. You can attract enemies with the Energy Sword (since everyone will want it) and bring them in close. Fire off the Armor Lock and try to burst any enemies who get too close. If they back off right before your lock bursts, run up and melee them.

The Drop Shield can of course be used anywhere here but can be especially useful if you find yourself getting pummeled by something like the Concussion Rifle from above. Practice using the shield around corners, so you can heal and then pop out from protection without the enemy knowing or being able to anticipate you shooting back at them. Set up a medic station for your teammates.

The Active Camo ability gives players the ability to get from level to level without being seen. It can help you escape certain death if you can use it correctly. Engage it immediately after turning a corner and go hide and wait for your attacker to follow, then take them out. Try using the Holograms here as bait. Bait your enemies into certain areas by getting them to chase your hologram into areas where you can ambush them. Remember that you can send holograms up the Gravity Lifts too. This can really trick your enemies into thinking they are an actual player since holograms usually just run straight and do not interact with anything on the maps.

Use the catwalks and ledges as overlooks to see what's going on below. Don't hang out on them for too long as you will be visible to enemies doing laps around the map including snipers. They will offer a good place to drop holograms from as well as grenades or let you jump down on top of enemies for a quick melee kill.

Keep moving on this map and use the available environment to occasionally hide and wait for passing enemies. Many players will just continually make loops or do laps around the map. You will need to do this too if you want to stay alive and get more kills than your opponents. Just remember to try to keep changing your elevation and direction as often as you can, to not just clear out enemies, but avoid anyone who might have been chasing you.

THE CAGE

This metallic floating prison complex comes complete with open catwalks and connecting platforms and no place to hide. Floating over an open ocean, this precarious map requires players to have steady footing since one wrong step can send you over the edge to your death. This map forces a fast pace of play due to its open nature and circular layout. There are only three power weapons on this map. The Plasma Launcher, the Shotgun and the Sniper Rifle. Of course they are going to be the weapons of choice for all players here, so try to grab some for yourself if only to keep them from killing you. There are several other weapons that will come in handy here including the Needler which works well in this open level to ensure lock-ons without someone ducking into a building. There are also a couple of Needle Rifles for some faux sniping. Look for grenade pickups all around here but be precise when you throw them so you don't waste them over the edge.

The Plasma Launcher can best be used from slightly higher points in the map like the small, multi-level corner near the Shotgun. Get a good overview of the map, find some poor loner, lock on and fire away. Try to resist the temptation of firing all four Plasma charges into him, it's just one kill!

The Sniper Rifle works well from this position also, but try setting up crouched at the end of one of the long walkways, wait for enemies to turn the corner and head straight at you. You can get slightly higher in the center area off of the main platform. Head up there and take a look around. You should be able to get a great look toward the Gravity Lift, but remember that you cannot shoot through the windows here. Check to see which window areas actually have glass. You cannot shoot through the glassed-in windows.

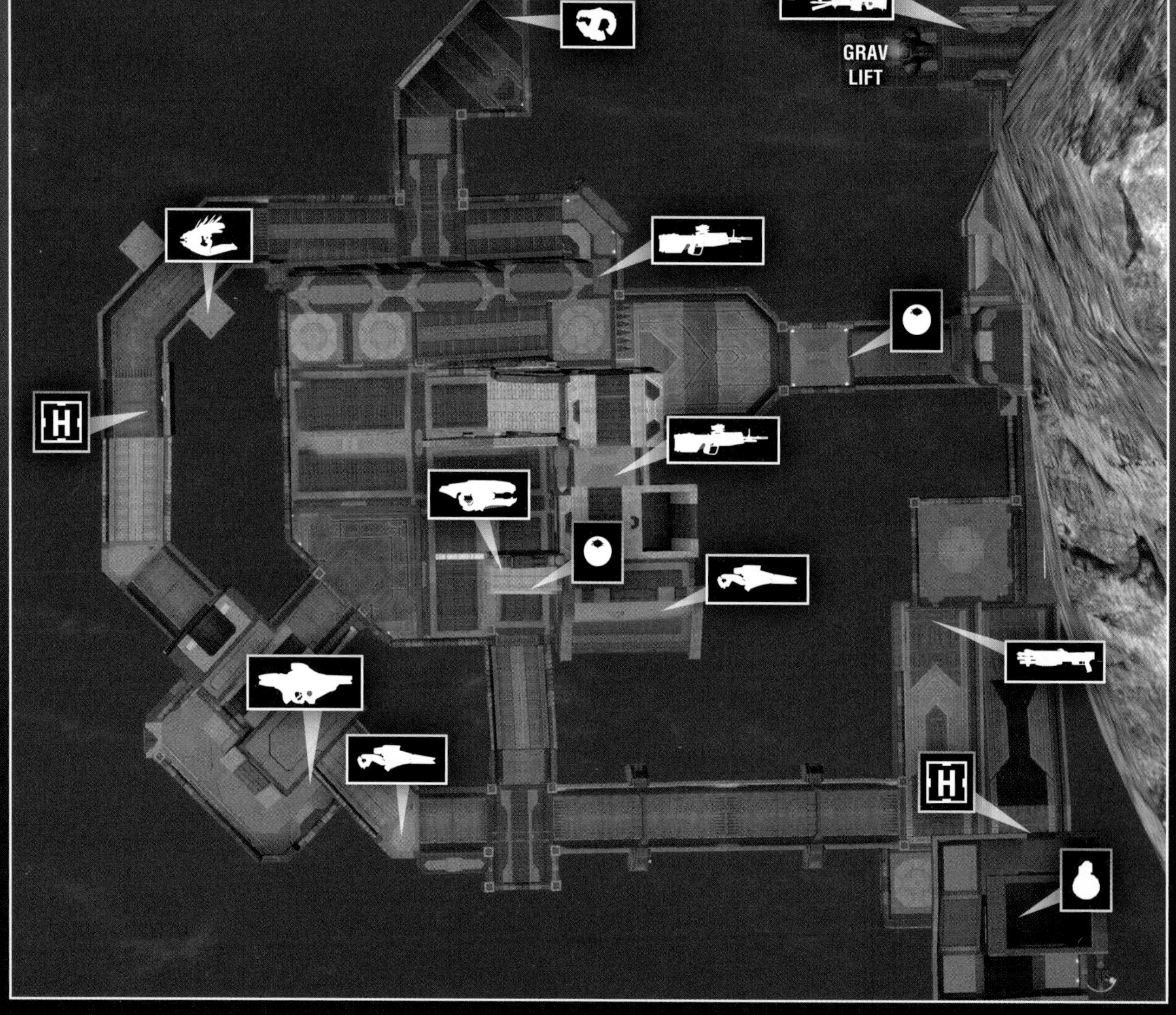

The Shotgun here can be deadly if you use it in conjunction with your map knowledge. Running around with a Shotgun isn't the best idea. You're going to want to stick and move. There are a handful of small outcroppings and corners you can hang out and wait for passersby, just make sure no one saw you duck in. Otherwise, someone's going to serve you a platefull of Plasma. Slide into a corner, wait for someone to rush past, pick them off then move along.

All of the available Armor abilities are going to be useful here. Sprint of course will always be a useful ability to pack, allowing you to speed out of harm's way when you need to, but the Jet Pack here can be a boon. It gives you the ability to relocate from catwalk to catwalk quickly and gives you the advantage of high ground over your enemies. Drop down on top of them from an opposing catwalk, or get yourself to a higher location to snipe from.

The Armor Lock works well on The Cage too, especially in the central platform or if you get into a pickle on a catwalk. Place a Drop Shield if you're getting sniped from across the map and get enemies to find a new target instead of waiting for your shield to die off. The Active Camo can help you get to positions such as the power weapons or higher elevations, but the Hologram can be one of the most useful tools for players on this map.

Firing off a Hologram down one of the catwalks will almost always draw enemy fire letting you focus in on their locations and flank them for an assassination. You can also use them as you run around the walks by activating one as soon as you enter a covered area of the catwalk. Players will see you go in and see a Hologram come out. When they start firing on your Hologram, head back out the way you came in to take them out.

The Cage offers only one Gravity Lift located by the Sniper Rifle. This is not a standard Gravity Lift, it's more of a jump jet. It propels you across the water to a small platform with very little room for error. If you're going to use this lift to escape from enemy fire, make sure you concentrate and make the jump or you'll find yourself at the bottom of the ocean.

The central platform and the small building where the Plasma Launcher is located are going to see the highest traffic. Players are going to continue to head for the Plasma Launcher. This small building connected to the center platform has three entrances to it and doesn't provide much protection from melee combat, but it can be used as cover for short periods of time. This is not a place to set up camp, however.

Try to hover around the middle of the map then spread out as necessary. Keep moving and use a variety of Armor abilities when they are most effective for you. Keep moving around the perimeter of the map and stay on the hunt for the power weapons whenever they are accessible.

PINNACLE

A remake of the classic map Ascension (sans banshee), Pinnacle is a largely open map taking place on top of a large rock spire—one misstep and you will be plummeting to your doom in the waters far below.

There is a huge 'radar' dish in the center of the map that acts as the center point for travel (and conflict), consequently, it is also the least safe area to travel through. Platforms and a few structures that can barely be classified as 'buildings' cling to the edges of the mountaintop, and they provide transit around the edges of the level. Because of the open nature of the level (only the lower platforms on the Rocket Launcher and Sniper Rifle sides of the map are out of sight), Sniper class weapons are highly effective, and any Armor Abilities that can shield or defend against long range weapons fire are quite useful.

If we treat the DMR structure as northwest, there is an open platform on the southwest, a sniper perch in the east, and on a lower level, the Rocket Launcher platform to the 'south'.

You can also walk north to reach the Needler, or down the northeast through a very small structure that houses the Shotgun and an teleporter exit.

The southern platform holding the Rocket Launcher has both a machine gun and a teleporter as egress, because both are static, forced exit routes, it pays to monitor their exit locations if you know someone has just gone for the rockets.

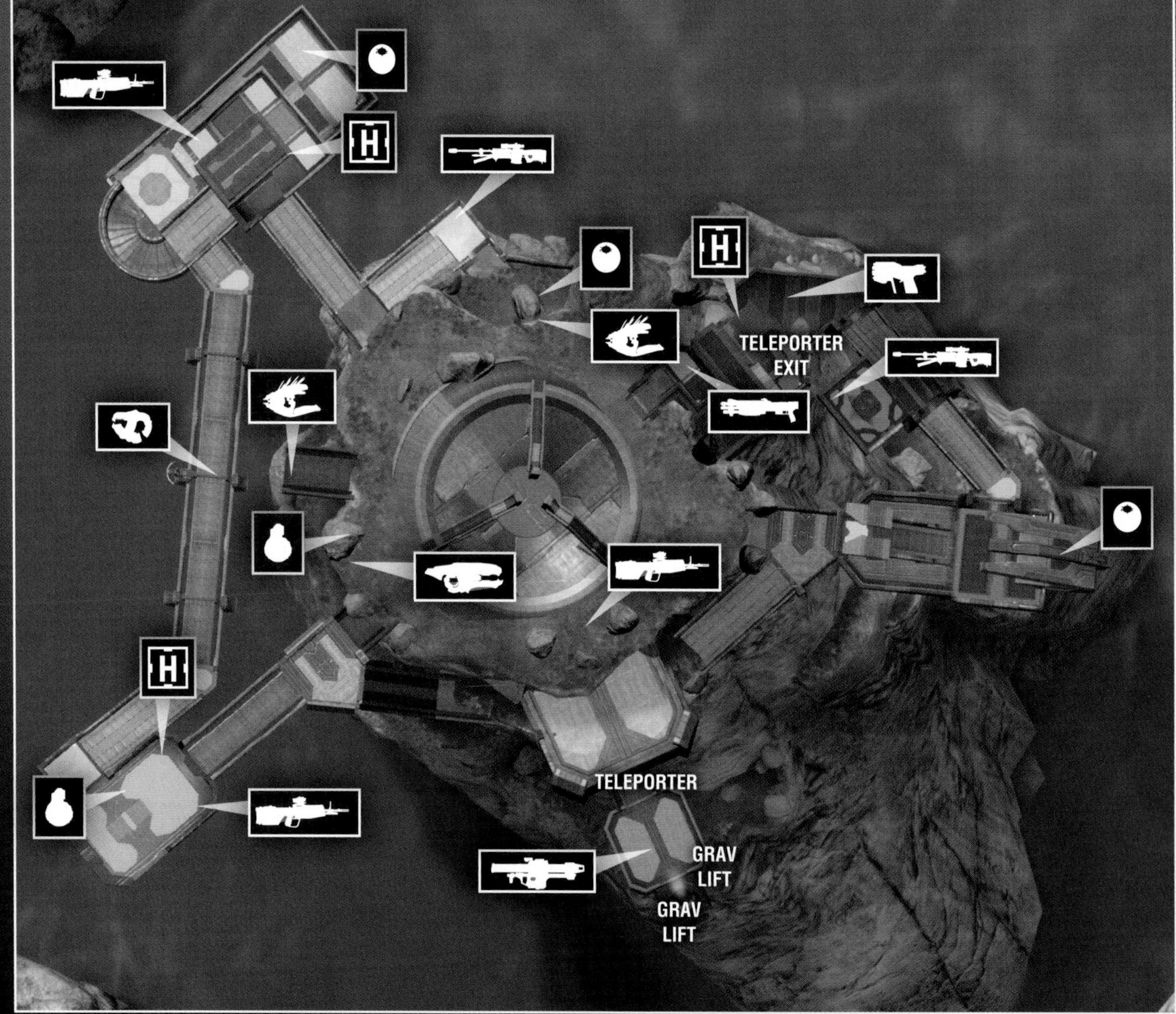

There are are two Sniper Rifles present on this map, both on the north side of the level, both also conveniently located with nearby access to either of the two sniper perches on the northwest or east sides of the level. You need to be constantly vigilant for snipers making use of those perches, as they command a clear view of most of the map, and they will rack up a substantial frag lead if you let them.

Other weapons (and medkits) are distributed roughly evenly around the map, but we recommend you avoid the pathway between the western platform and the northwestern DMR structure, as you are very exposed on it, and there are no significant key weapons anywhere along the pathway. If you can't get your hands on one of the Sniper Rifles, you can secure a DMR from the northwest or west structures, or on the ground to the south of the center platform. Keeping your distance and picking off targets with the DMR is quite effective, given the open layout of the level.

The Needlers and Shotgun have varying effectiveness. Burn off Needler ammo on targets in the open center, and if you take the Shotgun, try to confine your fighting to the lower northeastern platforms, or the structure to the northwest, both areas where you can force a close range engagement.

Grenades are useful for flushing targets out of the eastern or northeastern structures, but don't try to do an open approach simply to throw grenades—just make use of them once you're actually in range.

Sprint is helpful here for moving around quickly, though because all parts of the map are connected to the central section, it isn't absolutely vital for reaching Power weapons quickly. Jetpack is downright dangerous here, you're hugely exposed almost anywhere on the map, and there are very few vertical areas that need to be accessed quickly.

The 'finesse' Armor Abilities are all quite useful here. Active Camo, Hologram, Armor Lock and Drop Shield can all be put to good use. Drop Shield is a bit more useful than Armor Lock for saving yourself from snipers, while camo or Holograms can be used for tricky shenanigans anywhere on the level.

HEMORRHAGE

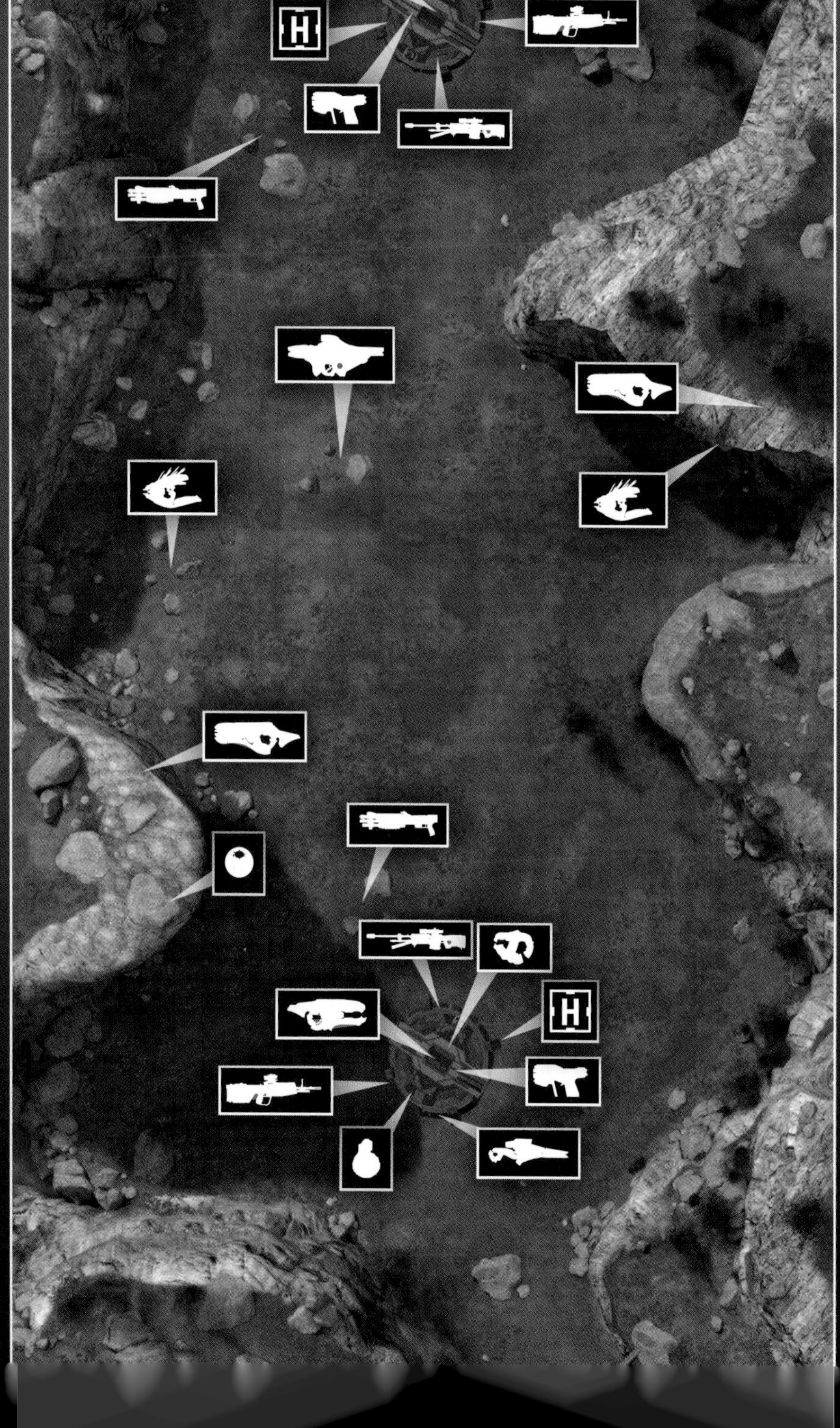

Another remake, any *Halo* fan will recognize this map instantly: it's a remake of Blood Gulch!

Again taking place on Forge World, this recreation has the red and blue bases at each end of the valley. There are pathways along the canyon walls on both sides, a small cave near the center on one edge, and a lone Plasma Launcher (not Rocket Launcher) located amongst some rocks near the center of the map.

The bases in this remake are the simple versions, not the more complex bases that have been used in past remakes. You can get in, get the Flag, and get out quickly.

Both bases are equipped with long range weaponry—a Sniper Rifle, DMR, and Needle Rifle are all present, with Plasma Repeaters and Plasma Pistols downstairs.

If you need to deal with the vehicles, you can use the charged Plasma Pistol, seek out the Plasma Launcher at map center, or track down a Concussion Rifle on the ledges at either side of the map. The Sniper Rifle also works reasonably well for dealing damage, and any of the Sniper class weapons work just fine against drivers or passengers in the open topped vehicles.

Both bases have a Ghost, two Mongooses, two Warthogs, a Revenant and a Scorpion.

The Scorpion and Revenant should be the first manned vehicles, as they can easily lay waste to any lighter vehicles that make their way across the map.

Once the opposing heavy weapon vehicles have been dealt with, you can make good use of a Warthog with a gunner, or the Ghost.

Warthogs, Mongooses, and the Revenant can all be used as effective flag transport once the enemy heavy vehicles have been dispatched.

The terrain across the valley floor isn't completely flat, so take advantage of this when moving around, you can avoid exposing yourself to sniper or vehicle fire by staying behind hillsides.

The side ledges, except for a few small cave tunnel passageways are completely exposed, but near the center of the map, they delve into the side of the mountain a bit, so they aren't easily visible directly from either base.

There are teleporters in each base that lead to the center of the map, so be sure to monitor those positions if you are trying to control the midfield, either with sniper covering fire, or with an armed vehicle.

Hemorrhage is a very straightforward map, almost all of the fighting will be with long range weaponry and vehicles. Do your best to always have one or the other in your possession!

SEA SNIPER TIP

- Dropping the bomb will make it show up on radar.

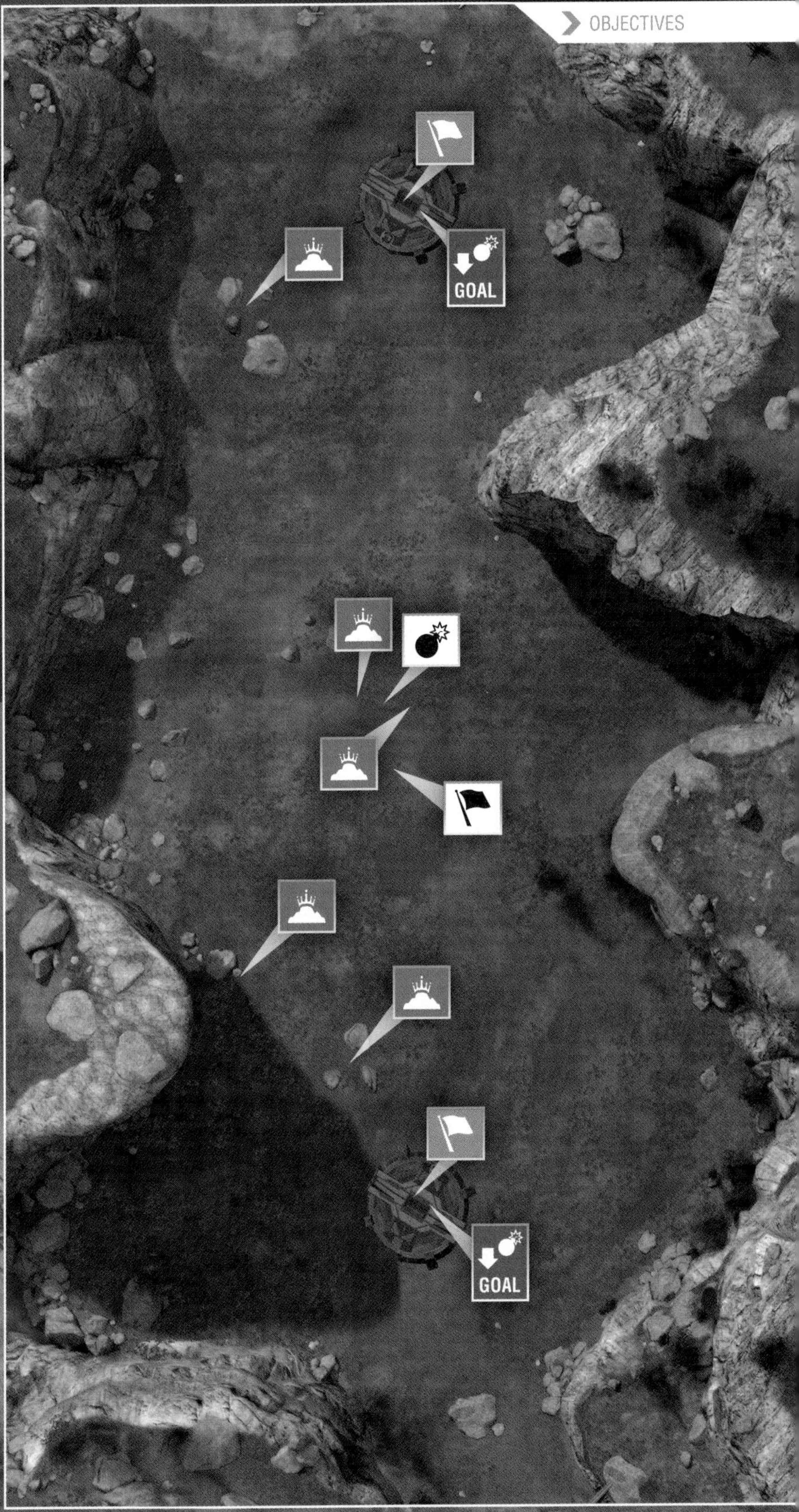

OBJECTIVES

GOAL

GOAL

PARADISO

Paradiso has a large mountain in the center, and three bases—two symmetrical bases on the 'east' and 'west' of the island, and one central base on the 'north' edge of the island. The 'south' has a short bridge connecting the two sides, and just north of that bridge, a short tunnel passes under the mountain. There are pathways up around the edges of the mountain, and a series of walkways that wrap around the sides towards the north, where a mancannon will take you to the northern base if you wish.

To the north of the 'east/west' bases, there is a small structure that holds a Concussion Rifle and a teleport that takes you instantly to the north center base, use these if you need to reach the base to intercept a friendly or enemy player and you don't have a vehicle handy.

Weapons are located in the bases, and near the edges of the mountain on the east and west sides. You can find DMRs and Needle Rifles in the bases, Sniper Rifles and Needlers near the mountain side, and a Spartan Laser in the north base and a Grenade Launcher in the mountain tunnel help to deal with vehicles. Combat on this map tends to take place at medium to long range, so arm yourself appropriately.

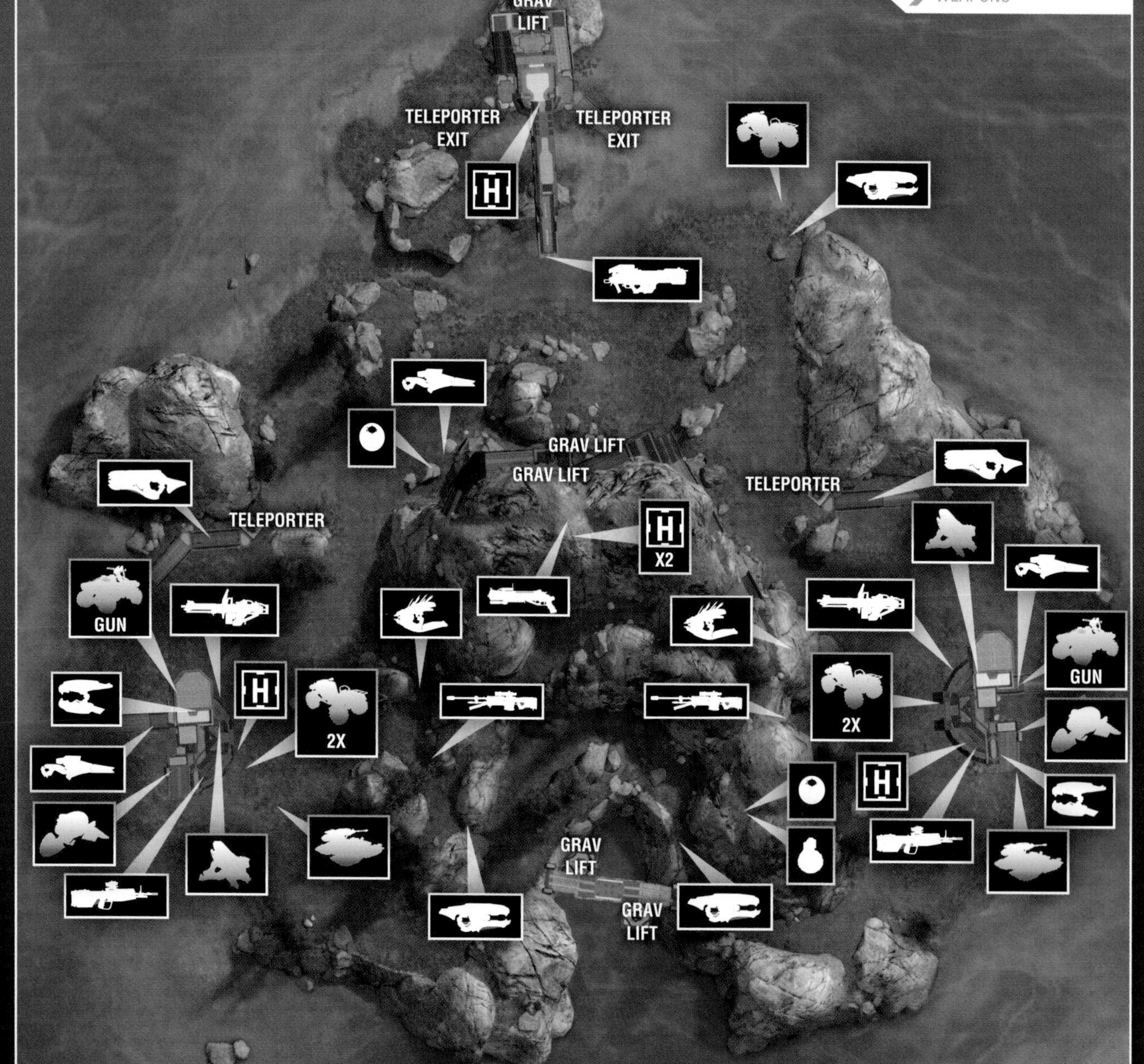

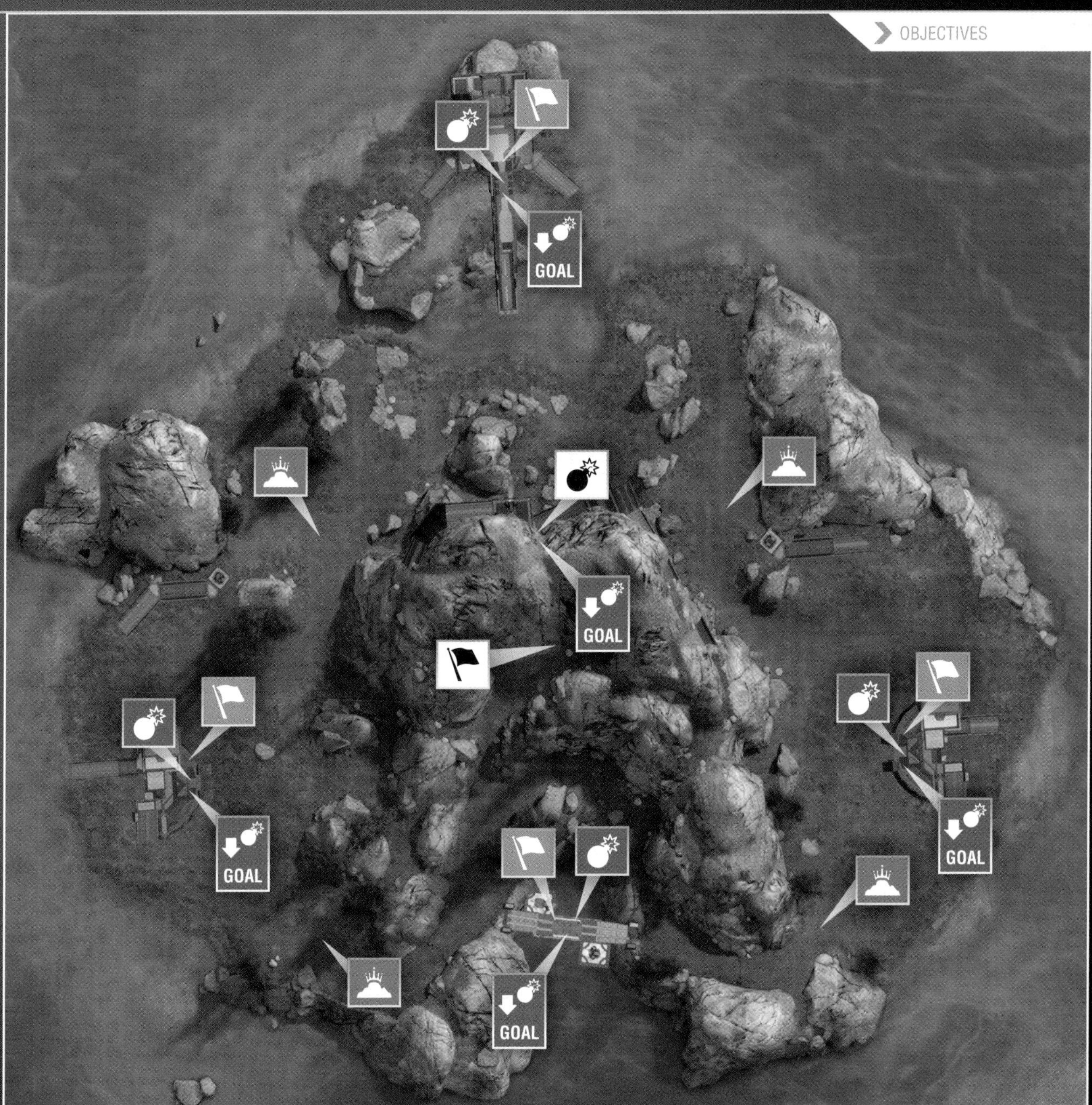

Vehicle combat is mostly restricted to the fields around the bases, and the northern shore near the north base, a very rocky area with plenty of cover and elevation changes, perfect for evading incoming fire. Each base has a Scorpion, Ghost, Banshee, Warthog, and Mongoose, so you have a full range of vehicles available. The power of the Scorpion is moderated somewhat by the terrain here, but you can still cause a lot of damage by locking down the north shore, or driving over to the enemy base and staying at a distance, bombarding the other team.

The Banshee is very important on this level as well, so be prepared to take it down, either with the Spartan Laser, Sniper Rifle fire, your own Banshee, or the Warthog or Scorpion weaponry.

It is entirely possible to get all the way up on top of the mountain, so watch out for snipers hanging out up there. You can also use the altitude granted to bomb enemy vehicles with the Grenade Launcher, just be wary of an enemy Banshee, as you have little cover from a flying enemy.

Combat on the south side of the mountain, near the bridge, tends to be fairly close range, as there are narrow pathways between the rocks, and a fair amount of cover. You can make better use of grenades and shorter ranged weaponry here, and this is also a good area to use if you want to approach the enemy base on foot, rather than taking the long way around, a track often exposed to enemy vehicles.

The north base is important to control for the Spartan Laser—if your team can lock down the north base, you can prevent enemy vehicles from leaving their base area and projecting any power towards yours, but remember that enemy troops can teleport into the base on the first floor at any time, so watch your back!

All Armor Abilities are useful on this map, though you may want to give some weight to Sprint, Drop Shield, and Armor Lock, all of which are useful for either getting around the map quickly, or protecting yourself from the heavy vehicle firepower.

ASYLUM

Asylum is another classic remake, this time of Sanctuary.

Asylum is a very simple, symmetrical deathmatch style map—two small 'bases' face each other across a small grassy field, with a large central circular arena structure in the center blocking line of sight between the two base areas. The center structure and bases are connected by walkways, and both bases have open grassy areas in front of them with plenty of rocks for cover. You can find an Energy Sword with a pair of Needlers in the center circular structure, along with Sniper Rifles and Shotguns on the outer buildings.

The 'bases' each have a DMR, and there are Needle Rifles on the walkways leading up to the center structure. Both bases also have a turret that can be torn off and used to good effect against enemies in the open (though be wary of entering the central arena, you are at risk from too many directions).

Most combat on this map is short to medium ranged, but if you can keep your distance, you can make good use of the Sniper Rifle. Killing a distant target with the DMR or Needle Rifle is more difficult, since there is a lot of cover to duck behind if you start firing at a distant player.

Be very careful about traveling through the central ring, unless you're timing an Energy Sword pickup. The ring gets the most traffic on the level in most cases, and you are very exposed when passing through it.

You may wish to patrol the outskirts of the map, picking off players at a distance. If you want to hang back, go for a Sniper Rifle, if you want to get stuck in up close, pick up a Shotgun and use the cover available for closing the distance.

Hologram, Active Camo, and Drop Shield can all serve you well, either for mixing up players to get the jump on them, or for protecting yourself from long range snipers. Armor Lock can help at a distance, but it does little to protect you from followup Sniper Rifle shots that can be potentially instantly lethal.

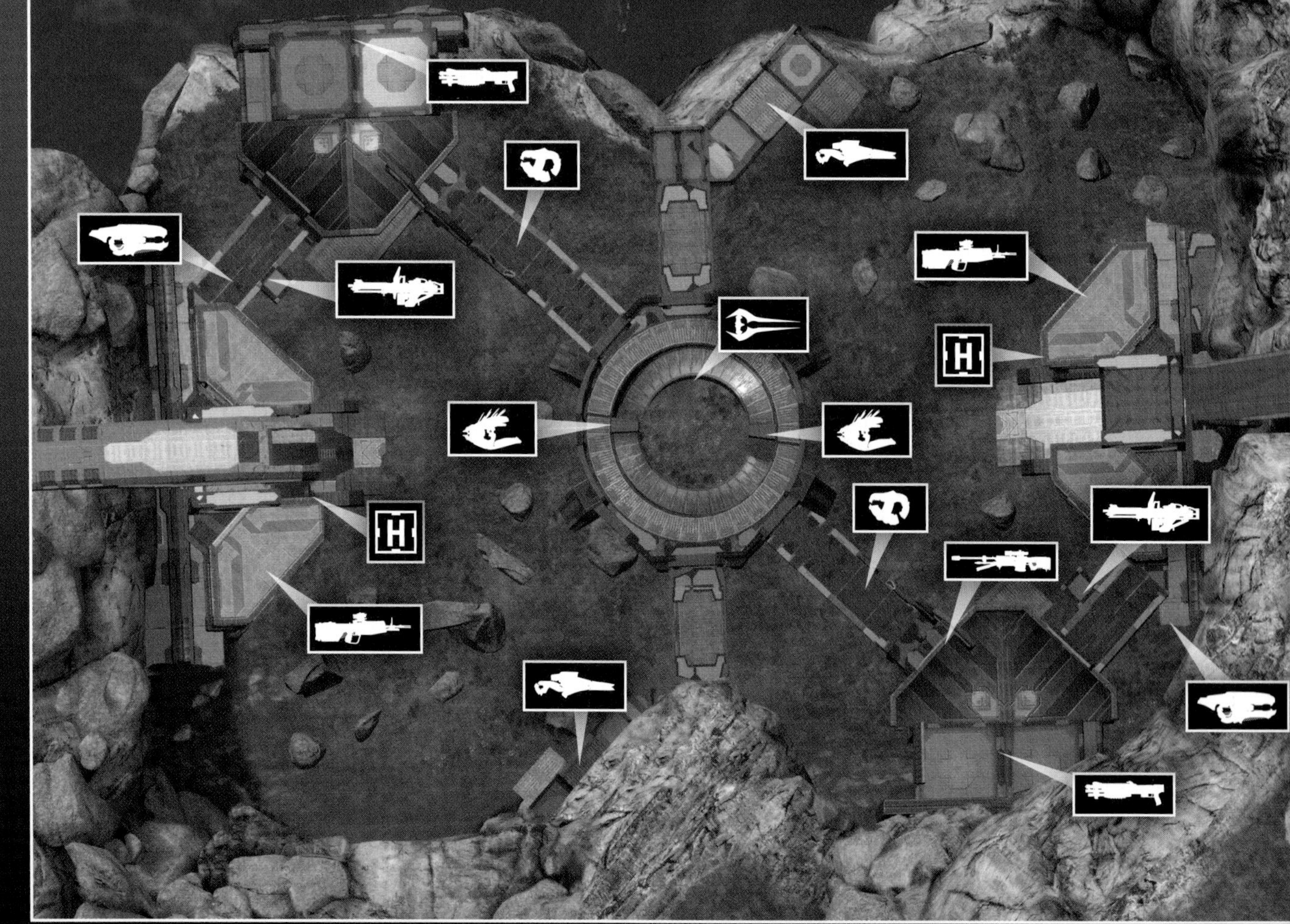

MULTIPLAYER

OBJECTIVES

Sprint is quite useful on here, simply for getting around the map, though Jetpack is somewhat less so, becasue you're very exposed to all parts of the map while in the air.

Asylum is a very straightforward map, stick to combat fundamentals and you can do well on here. If you're looking for a balanced small scale battleground, this is it!

FORGE MODE

WHAT IS FORGE?

The Forge is a powerful content creation and map editing tool introduced to the *Halo* series in *Halo 3*, expanded through DLC packs, and now revitalized for Halo: Reach, with the addition of powerful new features that will aid both veteran and green users of the Forge. It is also a playground that you and your friends can hop in and create together in private multiplayer games. Ever wanted to have tank fights, infinite ammunition, and more weapons than you could ever use? Forge is the place for you. The Forge is a very powerful tool, so powerful it can be used to create entirely new levels, for almost any game mode. It is also very easy to use, and even after a few minutes experimentation, you can begin creating your own custom content for *Halo: Reach.* Maps created with Forge can be saved locally on your system, or uploaded to your personal Bungie.net filespace. Files shared in this manner can then be downloaded by your friends, or other players!

It is also possible to use the Forge to modify existing Bungie maps—both those included in the game, and any new maps released in the future. Your variations of these maps can also be saved and uploaded—don't like the placement of certain weapons on Sword Base? No problem, change them. Want to move the flags or bomb points around? The work of a few minutes. Forge also allows you to tinker with the properties of any object on a map—you can make a grenade cache that respawns instantly, a Spartan Laser that takes three minutes to respawn, or a Scorpion that does not appear until two minutes have elapsed.

We've designed this chapter to introduce you the basic features and functionality of the Forge, and to get you to a level of comfort where you can begin to learn and develop more advanced techniques on your own. The Forge community for *Halo 3* created some truly impressive projects (even more impressive when you realize how difficult it was to use the tools they had at the time), and you can expect an explosion of new content in even the first few weeks of *Halo: Reach's* release. Keep an eye on Bungie.net for community highlights, and guides for new techniques and tricks as Forge development progresses.

FORGE WORLD

The Forge tool can be used to edit any map in *Halo: Reach*, but Bungie has created a map known as Forge World (that is located *on* a *Halo*), specifically for content creation in Forge mode.

It is a *huge* level, far bigger than any other map in the game, with numerous large open spaces to place your creations (including a remake of the Blood Gulch valley).

Due to the immense size of Forge World, you will usually only want to use one small section of the map for your own map creation, and there are tools in Forge that will allow you to block off areas that are 'out of bounds', to prevent players from getting lost in the wilderness.

There is nothing stopping you from allowing flying vehicles and creating an aerial race track, or a small level in one section of the map that has a teleport to an entirely different level elsewhere on the map.

WORKING WITH FORGE: BASICS

To begin using Forge, enter Forge from the Main Menu. You and your party can enter together, or you can go in alone.

Once inside, set the Game Type and pick a Map to begin editing. You can choose any existing Bungie created map, or use Forge World as a 'blank slate' for your own creations. Game Options can be set for Forge in the same way they can for any Custom Game—this is particularly useful for coming up with custom rule settings for 'honor rules' games that require players to keep track of specific winning conditions that Halo: Reach won't track for you (Grifball came directly from a player created variant, and is now on the official playlists!).

CONTROLLING THE MONITOR: EDIT MODE

Once inside any map in Forge mode, you can then enter Edit Mode by pressing up on the D-Pad. Doing so transforms you into a Monitor (of Guilty Spark or Penitent Tangent fame). You can revert to Spartan (or Elite) form at any time by pressing up on the D-Pad again. Just be careful that you aren't too high in the air...

While in Edit (or 'Monitor Mode'), you can fly freely around the map, delete, modify or move any existing object on a map, and place, modify or move new objects. You are limited in your placement of new objects on a map by two factors: your Budget, a 'cash' allowance that is expended as you place new items on a map (each of which has a 'cost'), and a maximum item limit for specific objects (eg, you cannot place more than four Scorpions on a map). There is no limit to your ability to modify objects (or delete them) once they are placed.

MONITOR CONTROLS

While in Edit Mode as a Monitor, you have a slightly different set of controls than on foot.

- RT + : Rotate held object
- LT + : While holding an object, Up or down to Zoom in or out on the object, Left or Right to rotate the object.
- LT: While not holding an object
- RB: Fly Up
- LB: Fly Down
- A: Drop a held object or pick up a targeted object
- B: Access Tools (access tools specific to an object while holding an object)
- X: Place a new object or Examine Options for the targeted OR held object
- Y: Delete a held or targeted object (be careful with this one!)

PLACING A NEW OBJECT

Creating a new weapon, vehicle, spawn point, teleporter, wall, rock, or any other object is extremely simple with Forge.

Aim at any area not occupied by another object and press X. This pops up the Place Object menu, with several categories:

- Weapons, Human
- Weapons, Covenant
- Armor Abilities
- Vehicles
- Gadgets
- Spawning
- Objectives
- Structure

Each category has a number of objects beneath it, some more than others. For casual map editing, Weapons, Armor Abilities, Vehicles, and possibly Spawning or Objectives will be your most visited sections. Gadgets include objects such as explosives, health and powerups, grav lifts and man cannons, teleporters, and a few other goodies.

The final menu, Structures, has all the parts for actually creating a new level (or heavily modifying an existing one).

It is entirely possible to make use of (and have fun with) Forge without ever placing new Structures, but take your time experimenting with the various items you can drop on a map. You can't break anything, so feel free to drop four Scorpions and place a bunch of respawn points nearby, just to see how they work.

WELCOME
UNSC TRAINING
THE CAMPAIGN
FIREFIGHT
MULTIPLAYER
BASICS & TACTICS
ARSENAL
VEHICLES
GAMEPLAY MODES
MAPS
FORGE
REFERENCE

QUICK MONITOR MOVEMENT

Normally holding the Left Trigger while moving is sufficient to zip around a map, but Forge World is so huge this may not be sufficient for you.

If you find yourself moving around the level a lot, try holding Left Trigger and then also pushing Left or Right Bumper at the same time—the extra movement actually increases your forward travel speed.

Another option is to place several teleporters around the map, save that map as your 'base' Forge World, and simply make use of the teleports while traveling around the level, then erase them later so your players can't use them.

UNUSUAL OBJECTS

Most objects, such as weapons, vehicles, and even initial/respawn points are straightforward, but there are a few that aren't quite so obvious.

CUSTOM POWERUP

In addition to the Camo and Overshield powerups, you can also place a *custom* powerup. This has NO special effect initially; to modify it, you need to visit the Custom Game settings menu and adjust exactly what the Custom Powerup does. You can make it give extra shielding, or less, make the player tougher or weaker, faster or slower, jump higher or lower, or any combination of properties. This is particularly useful for creating a powerup (or powerdown) that will be used in a custom game of your own creation.

TELEPORTERS

Teleporters are easy to set up, but there are a few quirks worth mentioning. First, there are two types of teleporter: One way and two way. One way teleporters consist of a Receiver and a Sender node. Place a Sender node anywhere on a map, then place a Receiver node elsewhere. If a player steps on a Sender node, he'll end up at the Receiver node, and cannot return through it. Two Way teleporters link up the same way, but you can enter either end and emerge on the other side. Now the quirks: To link up multiple sets of teleporters on a map, you need to visit the Properties for the Teleporter and set its *Teleporter Channel*. This defaults to Alpha, and can be set to Bravo, Charlie, etc, all the way to Zulu. Any teleporters set to the same channel are linked, and this is how you set up three sets of one way teleporters. Place three Sender nodes, three Receiver nodes, and set each pair to a different channel: Alpha, Bravo, and Charlie in this case. You link up two way teleporters the same way, place two, set them to the same Teleporter Channel.

You can actually create 'random' teleporters by placing more than two two-way teleporter pads and setting them all to the same channel. A player who steps on such a pad will end up at a random exit point on the same channel if there is more than one exit.

ALL THINGS RESPAWN

Initial Spawns and Respawn Points are exactly what you'd expect: They set the initial spawn points for players on a map, and provide all the respawn points where they can respawn after death. If you set them to a specific team color, only players of that team will spawn there. Remember to place *enough* respawn points on a map to provide unpredictability (and to prevent good players from learning the spawn points easily).

There are a few special tools you can use to tinker with spawn point behavior, these are known as Respawn Zones. Respawn Zones are placed and controlled just like a Territory objective—drop one down, then give it a shape of a Cylinder or Box, and set its Team. Any respawn points within that area then belong to that team.

What's even more useful is that you can set the Respawn Zone to only apply to a specific game mode, so if you want to make separate Red and Blue respawn areas for CTF, you can do so without having to place a ton of Red and Blue respawn points by hand. Just cover a batch of your normal, neutral respawn points with a Red or Blue Respawn Zone, and the game will take care of the rest.

There are two special types of Respawn Zones: Weak and Anti.

Weak Respawn Zones function just like a normal Respawn Zone, the only difference is that their effect is *weaker* (hence the name). That is, a 'Weak' Red or Blue respawn zone will *usually* cause Red or Blue players to respawn inside the zone, but not always.

Anti Respawn Zones are simply 'reversed' Respawn Zones. Instead of trying to spawn players of a certain team (or in a certain game mode), they will try to make players NOT spawn inside the area.

This can be useful, because you could, for example, set a Blue Respawn Zone that is tagged to apply only if the Flag is away (or home). You could do the same thing to a Red Anti Respawn Zone, to force Red players to spawn closer to (or farther away from) the Blue players route home. Using these respawn zone tools, you can quickly and easily modify how the default respawn point behavior works in any game mode on the same map. Remember that the core respawning behavior is controlled by the internal multiplayer settings, which generally try to avoid spawning you right in the face of a hostile enemy player with a Rocket Launcher, but careful placement of respawn points and respawn zones can heavily influence spawning behavior.

BOUNDARIES

Boundaries are a few special objects that can be used to keep players in (or out) of certain parts of the map. You can make killboxes that kill players when they enter them, or you can make safeboxes that kill players if they *leave* them.

Safe Area Boundaries come in two types, regular and 'Soft'. This is also true of Kill Area Boundaries. The 'Soft' versions will give the player a 10 second warning to return to the player before killing them.

Generally, you should place the boundaries in such a way that an obvious fall or death (plummeting off the edge of the level into a cliff or into the ocean) results in an instant death, but if they player is simply trying to walk 'too far', place a Soft boundary so they have time to move back into bounds. You can emphasize a dangerous area by placing mines or other rubble in the restricted area, or attempt to block off most access routes to it (so that it is clear to the players that it is not intended to be a playable area).

OBJECTIVES

Perhaps the most important category for creating custom game modes, Objectives include only three objects: Flag Stands, Capture Plates, and Hill Markers, but between the three, you can create a great many different game modes.

Flag Stands can be used to place objectives for Capture the Flag (all types) as well as Stockpile.

Capture Plates can be used for all types of Capture the Flag, as well as all types of Assault, and Oddball.

Hill Markers can be used for all types of Territories, King of the Hill, Headhunter, and Races.

Configuring the various Objectives requires that you start up Forge in the proper game mode, and then adjust the Game Type Label to an appropriate setting (eg, to place a Bomb for Assault, set a Capture Plate's label to Assault_Bomb, to place a target point, set a Capture Plate's label to Assault_Goal). The same applies for settings flags for Capture the Flag—make sure they're set to the right team colors (typically Red and Blue), then configure the Game Type Labels on the objects. If you're at loss for how to set up any given mode, the fastest and easiest way to check is simply open up an existing Bungie map in Forge, take a look at how the objects are configured, then replicate the settings on your own level.

SPECIAL TOOLS

If you press Ⓑ without an object selected, you only get one option (but it is a useful one!): Constrain Rotation. This setting allows you to set the number of degrees that an object will rotate when you hold the Right Trigger and press the Right Analog stick in any direction. This is especially useful when placing structures in the world; set to 90 or 45 degrees it allows you to place objects in an orderly manner, very useful when stringing together hallways, platforms, and other areas that demand precision.

You can set the degree of constraint to 90, 45, 30, 15, 5, or turn it off entirely.

Generally, when designing 'organic' landscapes and building placements, having the constraint off is fine, but when you are trying to build UNSC or Covenant structures, some degree of order is advisable (not to mention that trying to line up objects for custom construction is *much* easier when they are al lined up properly).

DELETE ALL

When holding an object, you gain a few extra extra commands, the most basic of which is "Delete All of These", which does exactly what it says. This is handy if you decide you want to clear all of one weapon type from a map, or if you're cleaning up someone elses map of objectives that you no longer want present.

EDIT COORDINATES AND RESET ORIENTATION

Finally, if you pick up a structural object, you gain the ability to reset its orientation to default, and the ability to edit its world coordinates directly.

There are six commands in the Edit Coordinates sub menu, you can Nudge the object on the X, Y, or Z axes (Width, Depth, and Height), and you can Rotate the object on the X, Y, or Z Axes (Pitch, Yaw, and Roll). This is particularly useful for getting small platform pieces to line up perfectly.

Place an object in the world normally, then use Edit Coordinates to gently nudge a structural piece onto the same coordinate plane as another adjacent object. This is slow, meticulous work, but if you are trying to create a perfectly lined up series of platforms, walls, or structures, this is the only way to do it.

YOUR FIRST STEPS: MODIFYING A MAP

The easiest way to get started is by tinkering with an existing map. Open up one of your favorites, doesn't matter which one. Now enter Edit Mode and fly around the map to get a feel for the lay of the land. Don't panic at all the strange symbols and icons visible in the Forge—most don't need to be modified. All you're going to do for now is change some object placement. Look around for a weapon and delete it by approaching the weapon, then facing it and pressing Ⓨ. Now find another weapon and press Ⓐ to pick it up. You can now move around freely to drop it in a new position by pressing Ⓐ again. You can do the same thing with a Flag stand, an Assault bomb location, or even a Territories (or King of the Hill) capture zone. Now save the map, load it up in the appropriate game mode, and take a look at the changes you've made. Even a few minutes work in Forge can have drastic gameplay consequences, so be careful with what you decide to move (or remove).

Obviously, a CTF map where one team has access to a stockpile of power weapons isn't going to be very fun for the other team—though there are other ways you could make that scenario more interesting, such as by giving one team many vehicles, and the other more weapons. Even this basic level of modification can give you hours of refreshed gameplay, as you can tinker with the feel and flow of a map by adjusting weaponry and objectives to your liking.

WORKING WITH FORGE: ADVANCED

VIEWING OBJECT PROPERTIES

Approach any existing object on a map and press Ⓧ to view its Object Properties menu. You can also press Ⓧ while *holding* an object to view its properties, but it isn't necessary to pick up an object to modify it (generally you modify a 'held' item when you first create it, before you place it).

PHASED, FIXED, AND NORMAL OBJECTS

Any object in the world can be set to behave with the physics engine in one of thre ways: Normal, Fixed, or Phased.

Normal objects interact with the world normally—if you drop a 'wall' in midair, it will fall to the ground. A grenade will nudge it around, a gravity lift will send it flying.

A fixed object is just what it sounds like—it's fixed in place. Think of it as part of the level itself, rather than an object in the level. Once an object is fixed in place, nothing a player can do will move it.

A key new improvement in the Forge for *Halo: Reach* is the addition of a new type of object tag: Phased.

A Phased object behaves like a Fixed object, that is, it will remain exactly where you place it once you drop the object, but unlike a Fixed object, a Phased object can actually intersect with another object! This means that you can easily stick different building blocks together to create a structure, sink a pillar partway into a floor, and otherwise place level geometry together however you like.

Object Properties allow you to tinker with the way that specific object behaves. Want a DMR that respawns very quickly? Slowly? No problem. Want to change when an object spawns, or if a wall can float in midair or be knocked down? Easily done.

OBJECT PROPERTIES

The properties menu varies slightly depending on what object you are modifying, but here are some of the categories you may see:

- Team
- Red, Blue, Green, Orange, Purple, Yellow, Brown, Pink

Team settings are useful for setting Spawn Points, and in a few cases, can be used on other objects (notably for setting up objectives).

- Physics
- Normal, Fixed, Phased

Explained above, lets you set how an object interacts with the world around it.

- Spawn Time
- 1-180

This is simply a spawn timer for the object. This is how long it takes to spawn, and if destroyed, how long before it will reappear.

- Advanced
- Spawn Sequence
- -100 – 100

Spawn Sequence lets you control the order in which an object will spawn into the world—lower numbers spawn first. This setting is also used for setting the order of flags in Race modes.

- Place at Start
- True/False

Simply sets whether the object in question appears when the map is loaded, or if it only appears after its respawn timer has elapsed.

- Game-Specific
- False/True

This sets whether an object will appear in all modes, or only in modes with a matching Game Type Label (eg, you might want a Warthog or Mongoose to appear in CTF on your map, but not in Slayer or Infection).

For Objective objects, you *must* set Game-Specific to True to have the objective function properly (CTF flags, Assault bombs, Territories, etc).

- Symmetry

- Invasion – Invasion, Invasion_Weapon, Invasion_Vehicle, Invasion_Gates, Invasion_Mancannon, Invasion_Objective, Invasion_Objective_Flag, Invasion_Respawn_Phase_1, Invasion_Respawn_Phase_2, Invasion_Respawn_Phase_3, Invasion_Respawn_Zone, Invasion_Platform, Invasion_Cinematic
- Invasion capture points: Set Spawn Sequence to 1-2-3, set gametype label to Invasion_Objective, Blue Team
- Invasion bomb: Set Spawn Sequence to 1-2-3, Invasion_Objective_Flag
- Invasion bomb target location: Spawn Sequence to 1-2-3, Invasion_Objective, Red Team

There's no problem with creating an entire map in 'general editing' mode in Forge and then saving, exiting, and reloading the map in CTF. That works just fine, for any map and any game mode.

- Min Count
- Varies

Allows you to set the minimum number of this object you want spawned at all times.

- Max Count
- Varies

Allows you to set the maximum number of this object you want spawned at all times. If you set this to four for a Rocket Launcher, up to four players could pick up the same Rocket Launcher spawn—normally a weapon or vehicle will only have one instance present on a map at a time, and must be destroyed or used up before another will spawn.

- Shape

Shape controls don't affect most objects, but they are important for Hill Markers (to set the shape of a territory), and for Safe, Kill, and Respawn Zones (to set how large of an area is covered by the Safe, Kill, or Respawn boundary).

- Cylinder
- Radius 0-100.9, Top 0-100.9, Bottom 0-100.9
- Box Width all 0-100.9, Top, Bottom, Length
- Object Color

Lets you set if an object will assume the colors of the team of the player who picks it up, or always have the color of a specific team. Only some objects have team colors.

- Team Color or specific team color
- Spare Clips

Spare Clips simply lets you set how much extra ammunition a weapon will have when picked up. Use this to moderate the strength of a power weapon, or make a weaker weapon a bit stronger.

CREATING A NEW MAP

The most complicated and daunting task that you can accomplish with Forge is that of creating an entirely new map. We don't recommend that you set out to make a new map as your first goal in Forge—instead, spend time modifying existing maps and tinkering with Forge to learn your way around. Simply by doing so, you will gradually become comfortable with all of the Forge features, and from that experience, you can move on to creating your first new map.

NEW FROM OLD

As with learning Forge, we recommend that when you set out to make a new map, you do so by first modifying an existing map more heavily—instead of only adjusting weapons, vehicles, and objectives, you add in new structures, walls, windows, gravity lifts, and so on. Block off an area of the map, add a new floating platform with an objective or power weapon on it, create new cover. The idea here is to stretch your creative muscles in new directions before you go straining yourself trying to build a whole new map from scratch.

SCRATCH BUILT

Forge World is ideally suited for holding completely new, Forge-built levels. Almost anywhere on the map has enough space to hold a full level, and by dropping a Grid down in midair, you can even create a totally isolated level that doesn't even make use of the terrain.

A few pointers for building a new level from scratch:

- Start small—it's easier to complete a smaller map than a larger one, where you can run out of steam easily. The digital landscape is littered with the unfinished ruins of many, many maps. Don't add to the mess!
- Do some basic planning. You don't need to have the entire level mapped out on paper before you begin (though it helps!), but at least have a rough idea of what type of map you're creating; CTF, Slayer, Oddball, how large it will be, if it will have vehicles, etc.
- Save often. A single push of the delete button can erase a half hour of work, so be sure to save after you place or create each new major element on your level.
- Save multiple versions. It's a good idea to make 'checkpoint' saves with a new map name every hour or so, that way if you take your map in a direction you dislike, you can revert without losing much time.
- Playtest. Even once your map is mostly put together, until you actually play it with some friends, you're not going to know if it feels right. Often, ideas that you had when you started will prove to be unusable, but new ones will arise as you playtest. This is a natural part of the creation process.

BUILDING BLOCKS

When scratch building a map, the Structures menu is your friend. Inside, the objects you can find are *set by the map you are modifying*, and Forge World has the most building blocks of any level. The normal maps do not have as many structure objects that can be placed (though there are plenty, and they can be used to modify a most maps quite extensively), so building a new level on Forge World is recommended.

When putting together a new level, the easiest way to build a full 'floor' is to place a 'Grid' object on the map, large enough to cover the 'ground' area of your level, and then place new structures, cover, and objects on top of the new 'floor'. If you want to use the existing terrain on Forge World, pick a small area; down in the valley, up on one of the cliffs, within the cavern, out on one of the islands, or inside the Forerunner structure. Any of these work fine for a map of considerable size, though adding vehicles typically demands a larger play area.

When possible, try to avoid linking together structure pieces in a manner that demands extremely precise placement—the only way to line up two structure objects perfectly is to place each one, then pick one up and edit its coordinates directly from the Special Tools menu (found by picking an object up with Ⓐ, then pressing Ⓑ to access the menu).

This isn't impossible by any means, but it is time consuming, and its usually more fun to focus on broad strokes and then polish the details than it is to spend 15 minutes trying to get two platforms to line up perfectly.

CREATING GAME MODES

While the three Objective objects are simple, using them to create the numerous modes that fill Halo: Reach's multiplayer is not. This section is designed to provide you with a quick and simple reference for building any game mode you wish to create. For ALL game modes, you can place the Objectives inside a Forge session, but to configure them correctly, you need to quit the map, select the Game Type you want to create, and then re-enter the map. This allows you to set the proper Game Type Labels on the Objective objects (ie, you need Capture the Flag labels to make Capture the Flag games, and Assault labels to make Assault games).

ASSAULT

Assault has four variant modes; Assault, Grifball, Neutral Bomb Assault, and One Bomb Assault.

Assault: One Capture Plate for each team, one Hill Marker Bomb Spawn for each team

Neutral Bomb Assault: One Capture Plate for each team, One Neutral Bomb Spawn

One Bomb Assault: Same as Assault

Grifball: Same as Neutral Bomb Assault

CAPTURE PLATE GOAL SETTINGS

- Team: Red, Blue, Green, Orange
- Game-Specific: True
- Game Type Label: AS_GOAL
- Shape: Controls area where Bomb can be armed or disarmed

HILL MARKER BOMB SPAWN SETTINGS

- Team: Red, Blue, Green, Orange or Neutral
- Game-Specific: True
- Game Type Label: AS_BOMB

CAPTURE THE FLAG

Capture the Flag has four variant modes; Capture the Flag, Multi Flag CTF, Neutral Flag CTF, One Flag CTF All modes: One Flag Stand for each team.

Neutral Flag CTF: One Flag Stand for each team and one Neutral Flag Stand.

FLAG STAND SETTINGS

- Team: Red, Blue, Green, Orange, Neutral
- Game-Specific: True
- Game Type Label: CTF_FLAG_RETURN

HEADHUNTER

Headhunter has two variant modes; Headhunter and Headhunter Pro.

All modes: One Hill Marker for each 'Head capture zone'. Two zones are chosen randomly, and periodically cycle to new zones.

HILL MARKER SETTINGS

- Team: Neutral
- Game-Specific: True
- Game Type Label: HH_DROP_POINT
- Shape: Determines area in which Heads can be dropped off

INFECTION

Infection has two variant modes; Infection and Safe Havens.

Safe Havens only: One Hill Marker for each 'Safe Zone'. One zone is chosen randomly and periodically cycles.

HILL MARKER SETTINGS

- Team: Neutral
- Game-Specific: True
- Game Type Label: INF_HAVEN
- Shape: Determines area in which Human players can hide.

KING OF THE HILL

King of the Hill has two variant modes; King of the Hill and Crazy King.

Crazy King cycles through Hill Markers periodically, King of the Hill uses only one Hill Marker.

HILL MARKER SETTINGS

- Team: Neutral
- Game-Specific: True
- Game Type Label: KOTH_HILL
- Shape: Determines area in which players can accumulate points.

ODDBALL

Oddball is a single mode gametype. Oddball requires only a single Neutral Bomb to work properly.

HILL MARKER SETTINGS

- Team: Neutral
- Game-Specific: True
- Game Type Label: ODDBALL_BALL

RACE

Race has three gameplay variants; Race, Rally, and Rocket Race.

Race: One Hill Marker for each 'flag', with a Spawn Sequence number set to determine the order of the flags.

Rally and Rocket Race: Hill Markers are randomly chosen as goals.

RACE HILL MARKER SETTINGS

- Team: Neutral
- Spawn Sequence: 1, 2, 3, etc
- Game-Specific: True
- Game Type Label: RACE_FLAG

RALLY AND ROCKET RACE HILL MARKER SETTINGS

- Team: Neutral
- Game-Specific: True
- Game Type Label: RALLY_FLAG

STOCKPILE

Stockpile consists of only one gameplay mode.

Stockpile requires one Hill Marker goal zone for each team, and as many Neutral Flag Stand flags as you want to place. Three or four Flag Stands are chosen randomly to have Flags on them each cycle.

HILL MARKER SETTINGS

- Team: Red, Blue, Green, Orange
- Game-Specific: True
- Game Type Label: STP_Goal
- Shape: Determines area flags can be dropped in.

FLAG STAND SETTINGS

- Team: Neutral
- Game-Specific: True
- Game Type Label: STP_FLAG

TERRITORIES

Territories has three gameplay modes; 3-Plot Territories, Land Grab, and Territories. Remember that 3-Plot uses the *first* three Flag Stands set in order (1, 2, and 3), so be sure they are placed in a balanced manner.

3-Plot: Three Flag Stands, with Spawn Sequence set to 1, 2, and 3.

Land Grab and Territories: Up to five Flag Stands with Spawn Sequence set in order (1, 2, 3, 4, 5).

FLAG STAND SETTINGS

- Team: Neutral
- Spawn Sequence: 1, 2, 3, etc.
- Game-Specific: True
- Game Type Label: TERR_OBJECT
- Shape: Determines area the Territory can be contested or controlled.

CUSTOM MODES

One last thought before we punch out. Forge allows you to accomplish a lot with very little effort; modifying an existing level and placing or removing new weapons or vehicles is extremely simple. Even moving around spawns or objective locations is also quite simple, and just those changes alone can make for hours of fun with your friends, because you can fix anything you don't like about the way the default maps handle certain modes. Forge can also be used to create entirely new levels. It takes a *lot* of time and effort to scratch build a new map, but the option is there, and you can expect to see a lot of new custom content online from avid fans.

There is one other 'trick' that Forge can help you to pull off, and that is the creation of entirely new gameplay modes. Grifball is in the game as a custom mode purely because of fans who enjoyed playing the variant, and there's nothing stopping you from coming up with your own little mutant gameplay variation.

You could, for example, create a custom map on Forge World that begins on the beach at one end of the valley, and ends at inside the Forerunner structure far up the cliff over the island in the distance.

You begin with two teams, and each team has a Banshee on the beach. The remaining players on foot then hop into nearby teleporters—teleporters that take them to 'mini' levels up on the cliffs or on the ground in the way of the Banshee's flight path. Each level has more teleports that take you to more mini levels located farther along the 'racetrack' Scatter around anti-air power weapons, and whoever manages to get their Banshee into the 'hangar' safely wins. You now have a mix of a race gameplay mode and a straightforward Slayer gametype, as each team struggles to control the mini deathmatch levels and the airspace around them. You can use killboxes to control the flight of the Banshees (or even place large structures up in the air to force them into very constricted terrain that must be flown through), making it impossible for the Banshees to simply fly around the anti-air levels below.

Many such custom modes require the cooperation of players in the game to work, but some can be subverted from existing gameplay modes. Experiment! Have fun with your creations, Forge is a powerful tool to greatly extend the gameplay of *Halo: Reach*.

ORDNANCE

This chapter contains an overview of each of the weapons found in the Campaign and Firefight gameplay modes. The goal of this chapter is to provide a qualitative and tactical synopsis of each weapon, as it pertains to battle against A.I. enemies. The "Multiplayer Arsenal" section of this book provides a more quantitative look at each weapon for use in Matchmaking. There is some overlap between these two sections and some of the tips can carry over, but this section is based solely on experience in combat with the Covenant. All weapons are discussed in terms of how they perform against the Covenant, even the Covy weaponry.

UNSC WEAPONRY

UNSC weapons are based on centuries of ballistics engineering conducted on Earth. Humans continued to refine their projectile-based weapons as they colonized distant worlds, but the roots of their weaponry can be traced back to the twentieth century. UNSC weapons primarily fire lead-based projectiles that deliver impact and explosive damage. The majority of UNSC arms are designed to be hand-held, but some require a shoulder or turret mount.

MA37 ASSAULT RIFLE

MAGAZINE SIZE: 32 ROUNDS
MAXIMUM RESERVE: 288 ROUNDS

PRIMARY PURPOSE: Suppression fire, close to medium range, non-shielded enemies.

PRIMARY TARGETS: Grunts, Brutes, and Buggers.

COMBAT USAGE

The Assault Rifle's versatility has earned it high commendation from the UNSC and is included as standard-issue for infantry forces. Sadly, fallen Marines represent the best source of additional munitions for this weapon in Campaign mode. The Assault Rifle's effectiveness at close range, combined with its high rate of fire and ability to stun lesser Covenant species, has earned it high praise throughout the Spartan ranks. The weapon is not without its flaws, however. Despite being capable of fully-automatic fire, short bursts are required to compensate for its limited accuracy. Additionally, the 7.62 mm rounds used in the Assault Rifle can be viewed as inadequate against shielded enemies.

- Fire in short bursts while closing the distance on an un-shielded enemy, provided the foe isn't wielding a melee weapon or shotgun. Strike the foe with the butt of the rifle to finish it off.
- Accuracy drops substantially at longer distances, as well as during prolonged automatic fire. Pair the Assault Rifle with the DMR or other long-distance weapon when engaging distant enemies and switch to the Assault Rifle only after gaining a closer vantage point.
- Replenish munitions by scavenging the weapons of fallen Marines or by swapping your weapon with one from a nearby ally.
- Gain an advantage over shielded enemies by first depleting their shields with a grenade, a charged blast from the Plasma Pistol, or rapid shots from a plasma based weapon then switch to the Assault Rifle to finish them off.

M392 DESIGNATED MARKSMAN RIFLE

MAGAZINE SIZE: 15 ROUNDS
MAXIMUM RESERVE: 60 ROUNDS

PRIMARY PURPOSE: Marksman firing, medium to long range, non-shielded enemies.

PRIMARY TARGETS: Grunts, Jackals, Skirmishers, Buggers, Brutes, and Elites.

COMBAT USAGE

The DMR is the newest and most coveted weapon in the UNSC arsenal. The 3x zoom, moderate magazine size, and rate of fire combine to fill the gap in the UNSC's armory between the Assault Rifle and Sniper Rifle. The DMR gives users of all skill levels the power and accuracy needed to target enemies where the damage could be most severe—in the head. The DMR is most effective against delicate material and less so against heavily armored or shielded foes. Though the DMR's 15 round magazine capacity is sufficient for individual encounters, the user must remember to reload after every encounter. The other drawback to using the DMR is the limited amount of ammunition found on the battlefield. The majority of UNSC Troopers currently rely on the Assault Rifle, thus scavenging ammo for the DMR is less reliable. UNSC weapon racks are the most reliable source of ammo.

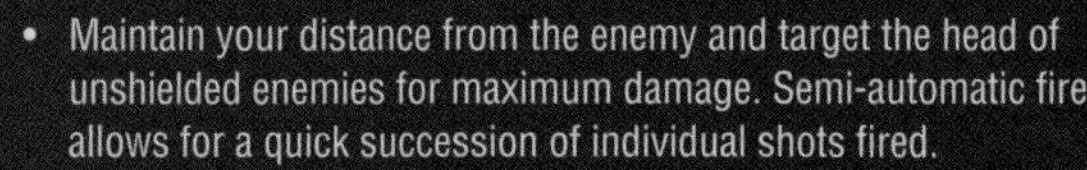

- Maintain your distance from the enemy and target the head of unshielded enemies for maximum damage. Semi-automatic fire allows for a quick succession of individual shots fired.
- The DMR's 3x zoom is excellent at medium to long range, but mustn't be used at close range. The DMR can be fired "from the hip" at close range, but this is not advised.
- Best used in conjunction with a plasma-based weapon against higher ranking Elites and Brute Chieftains, but very effective against lesser Elites and Brutes. Deplete their energy shield with four and two shots, respectively, then fire a final shot to the head to kill them.
- DMR ammo isn't overly abundant so aim carefully. Grunts, Jackals, and Buggers can be killed with a single shot. Shoot a Jackal's exposed hand to jolt its head out from behind its shield, then fire the weapon to kill.

M6G MAGNUM

MAGAZINE SIZE: 8 ROUNDS
MAXIMUM RESERVE: 48 ROUNDS

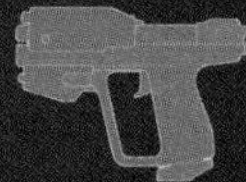

PRIMARY PURPOSE: Support fire, marksman fire, short to long range

PRIMARY TARGETS: Grunts, Jackals, Skirmishers, and Brutes

COMBAT USAGE

The Magnum is an exceptional sharpshooter's pistol that mimics the DMR in most ways, although in a scaled-down package. The 2x zoom makes headshots a breeze at medium range and one-shot kills are possible at longer range against many unshielded foes. The Magnum has a moderate rate of fire and packs enough punch to deliver the fatal blow to Elites and Brutes, provided their shields have been depleted. Ammunition for the Magnum can be found at most UNSC ammo cabinets and throughout the battlefield, near UNSC corpses. The Magnum can be used effectively as a primary UNSC weapon in conjunction with a Plasma Pistol or Plasma Repeater. It can also be effective in combination with a Sniper Rifle or other heavy weapon—use it to take out weaker enemies and conserve more precious ammo for higher priority targets.

- The 2x zoom makes the Magnum a perfect substitute to the DMR or Sniper Rifle for the elimination of Grunts, Jackals, and Skirmishers. Even though this gun is weaker than the two rifles, the Magnum packs enough punch to kill each of these foes with a single bullet to the head.
- The Magnum's accuracy is high across all ranges, but particularly so at medium range. Move closer to target distant enemies and try to switch to a Shotgun or Assault Rifle when encountering enemies at extremely close range.
- Pair the Magnum with a Plasma Pistol or other plasma weapon to defend against shielded enemies. Most Elites and Brutes can be killed with a single headshot from the Magnum once their shields have been depleted.
- The Magnum may feel like a handheld DMR, but its magazine capacity is only half that of the rifle. Reload often and don't waste ammo shooting shielded or heavily-armored targets. The Magnum is best against soft tissue.

SRS99 SNIPER RIFLE

MAGAZINE SIZE: 4 ROUNDS

MAXIMUM RESERVE: 20 ROUNDS

PRIMARY PURPOSE: Sniping, long range, non-shielded or shielded enemies

PRIMARY TARGETS: Elites, Brutes, Brute Chieftains, and Hunters

COMBAT USAGE

The Sniper Rifle offers the ultimate combination of range, power, and accuracy even if it comes at a significant cost to rate of fire. The size of the magazine and scarcity of ammunition mandate that you do not waste this weapon on Grunts, Buggers, or Jackals unless all higher priority targets have been eliminated. The Sniper Rifle comes with a two-stage scope that offers both 5x and 10x zoom. It should not be used at close range except in emergency situations and by those skilled in the art of the "no-scope headshot." The Sniper Rifle is powerful enough to make carrying a plasma-based weapon unnecessary. It can kill most shielded enemies with a single headshot on lower difficulty settings. And only two to three headshots are required to drop even the toughest foes on Legendary. The Sniper Rifle is also the only rifle worth using to attack the weak point on the Hunter's neck.

- Take your time to target the enemy's head, preferably from cover and without alerting the enemy to your whereabouts. The Sniper Rifle's bullets carve tracer-like contrails through the air so line your shot up and don't miss, otherwise the enemy will know exactly where you are.
- The reloading process with the Sniper Rifle is quite time-intensive so always consider your location, the number of enemies, and their ability to target you before unloading the clip. Consider switching to an alternate weapon instead of reloading.
- The Sniper Rifle isn't very common during Campaign, so don't carry it in hopes of finding additional ammo for it. Swap it for another weapon once the ammo has been used up, otherwise you're only limiting yourself.
- Use the 5x zoom to scan the battlefield for enemies or to target enemies on the move. Save the 10x zoom for enemies that are really far away and stationary, or it could be too much zoom to handle.

M45 TS SHOTGUN

MAGAZINE SIZE: 6 ROUNDS

MAXIMUM RESERVE: 30 ROUNDS

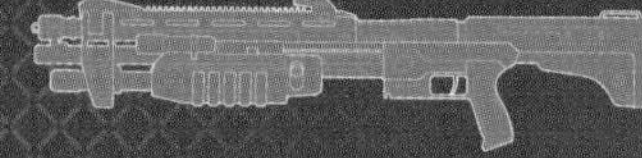

PRIMARY PURPOSE: Close range defense, shielded or unshielded enemies.

PRIMARY TARGETS: Jackals, Brutes, and Hunters.

COMBAT USAGE

The Shotgun is a specialty weapon, best saved for enemies at extremely close range. It has a small ammo capacity as well as a slow reload time, which makes relying entirely on this weapon quite risky. It can kill smaller creatures with a single blast at close range, but it shouldn't be wasted on Grunts—melee them instead for the same result. Using the Shotgun in conjunction with a melee attack is an excellent way to rid Reach of Jackals and Brutes. Similarly, a single Shotgun blast to an Elite is often enough to deplete its energy shield and create an opening to slip around behind it for an Assassination attack. The Shotgun's range does extend beyond that of melee range, but the number and force of its pellets that hit their mark deteriorates at medium range.

- The Shotgun is quite lethal at very close ranges, even against heavily armored or shielded enemies. It seldom takes more than two or three blasts at close range to kill even the toughest of Elites and Brutes.
- Circle-strafe around the left of a Hunter to avoid its overhead shield-slam attack then open fire with the Shotgun on its back. This is an extremely effective way of defeating a Hunter when heavier ordnance is not available.
- The Shotgun has a very slow reload time. Use its five shells cautiously and slip into cover or switch to another weapon when needing to reload. The reloading animation can be interrupted once the first shell has been loaded.
- The Shotgun should be used in conjunction with melee attacks to conserve ammo and create firing opportunities. Melee a Grunt to kill it or a Jackal to knock its shield askew. Stun shielded enemies and slip behind them for an Assassination.

M319 GL GRENADE LAUNCHER

MAGAZINE SIZE: 1 ROUNDS
MAXIMUM RESERVE: 15 ROUNDS

WELCOME
UNSC TRAINING
THE CAMPAIGN
FIREFIGHT
MULTIPLAYER
REFERENCE
ORDNANCE
VEHICLES
ENEMY FORCES
CREDIT SYSTEM
THE ARMORY
SKULLS
ACHIEVEMENTS
DATA PADS

PRIMARY PURPOSE: Support, area of effect, shielded and non-shielded enemies.

PRIMARY TARGETS: Grunts, Brutes, Elites, and Vehicles

COMBAT USAGE

The Grenade Launcher is an incredibly versatile weapon that can provide support in almost any situation. The Grenade Launcher has two firing modes which effectively alter the way the grenades behave when fired. Tap the trigger to fire a grenade that will automatically detonate on contact. This attack method yields a larger explosion and can kill a Brute with a single attack. The actual projectile collision can even kill weaker enemies without detonating. Holding the trigger activates manual detonation mode. When manual detonation is used, the grenade will continue to bounce around and eventually come to a stop if the trigger remains held. Releasing the trigger detonates the grenade with an electromagnetic pulse (EMP) which can deactivate enemy shields and temporarily disable vehicles. The Grenade Launcher can only fire one grenade between reloads and has a slow rate of fire, but is effective over medium to long range thanks to its 2x zoom.

- Aim for the body of the enemy, so as to not bounce the grenade between their legs or send it sailing over their head. Unless targeting an individual Brute or Elite, always focus on groups of enemies where the area of effect damage can be greatest.
- Hold the trigger and allow the grenade to bounce around until coming to a stop, preferably near a chokepoint such as doorway. This effectively gives you a remote-detonation landmine that you can spring on unsuspecting enemies as they draw near.
- Use in conjunction with the Magnum or DMR to take on Elites and Brute Chieftains. Detonate an EMP grenade near an enemy to disable its shields then switch weapons and shoot it in the head.
- Use manual detonation mode to fire in the vicinity of—but not directly at—vehicles to disable them with an EMP. This makes it easier to either snipe the driver or run over and hijack the vehicle. Avoid hitting the vehicle directly to minimize the damage you inflict.

M41SSR MAV/AW ROCKET LAUNCHER

MAGAZINE SIZE: 2 ROUNDS
MAXIMUM RESERVE: 6 ROUNDS

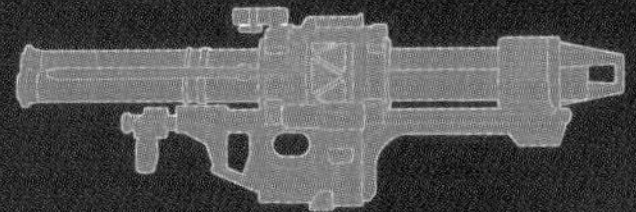

PRIMARY PURPOSE: Support, area of effect damage, terminating of high priority targets

PRIMARY TARGETS: Elites, Brutes, Brute Chieftains, Hunters, and Vehicles

COMBAT USAGE

The Rocket Launcher offers the best combination of power and ease-of-use among all UNSC weapons. It can destroy any Covenant target—living or vehicular—with a single shell (excluding the Phantom). The Rocket Launcher can be loaded with two shells and fired in relatively quick succession; however, the scarcity of ammunition necessitates being conservative with how you use each shell. The Rocket Launcher features a 1.8x zoom and is best over medium to long range—firing it at close range poses too great a risk of being damaged by the blast radius. One of the Rocket Launcher's key features is its ability to track the heat signature of flying vehicles. Wait to achieve lock-on before firing when targeting a Banshee or Phantom.

- The Rocket Launcher is devastating against bands of tightly-grouped enemies. Move into position when a Drop Ship or Phantom is overhead and fire it at the ground when enemies deploy.
- Individual rockets travel relatively slowly. Acrobatic enemies can dodge the incoming rocket and escape damage, particularly when the Tough Luck skull is active. Fire on a downward angle to detonate the shell near your target's feet so the rocket doesn't sail past when they dodge.
- One of the best sources for rockets is the UNSC Troopers you encounter. Swap weapons with them to take their Rocket Launcher if you're continuing on foot. Always give an A.I. ally the Rocket Launcher if they're going to be a passenger in your vehicle—their unlimited ammo will certainly come in handy.
- The Rocket Launcher is a very powerful weapon and is often found only where it could be truly needed. Don't waste it by firing it at lesser enemies, since there may be much more deserving enemy just around the corner. Try to conserve a couple of rockets for Hunters, Wraiths, Revenants, and Brute Chieftains.

M6 G/GNR SPARTAN LASER

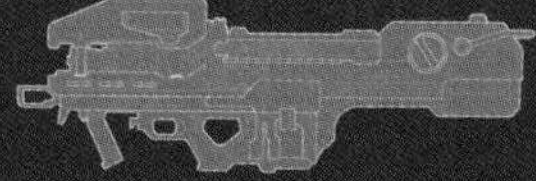

MAGAZINE SIZE: 100 BATTERY UNITS

MAXIMUM RESERVE: 100 BATTERY UNITS

PRIMARY PURPOSE: Support, anti-vehicle, anti-turret, long-range targeting of high value targets.

PRIMARY TARGETS: Brute Chieftains, Elites, Hunters, Shade Turrets, and Vehicles.

COMBAT USAGE

The Spartan Laser is a devastating weapon, but it is very difficult to achieve proficiency with it. The weapon takes 2.5 seconds to charge-up, at which time it emits a powerful laser that destroys anything in its path with the exception of a Phantom. Its 2.5x zoom grants the user pinpoint accuracy, but the slow charge-up period limits the Spartan Laser to targets that are either very large or stationary. It is possible to destroy multiple enemies if they happen to be lined up just right, but this is a very tricky thing to accomplish. The Spartan Laser's 100 battery units are enough to fire it four times—be sure to release the trigger during the charge-up phase if your target moves behind cover or you no longer have a clear line of sight. The Spartan Laser inflicts no area of effect damage, but does not need to be aimed at an enemy's head to inflict instant death.

- Stay in cover and use the Spartan Laser against distant, stationary targets before they can target you. Move between attacks since the laser gives away your location to other enemies.
- Look for a UNSC Trooper to give the Spartan Laser to since he'll be able to use the weapon without running out of ammo. You, on the other hand, only get four shots with it before it runs out of battery power.
- This is a very rare weapon. Use it where you find it and swap it out for another weapon, because you will never encounter extra ammunition for the Spartan Laser nearby.
- The Spartan Laser is best saved for vehicles and other large, slow moving targets. Immediately swap to another weapon if engaged at close range. Never use the Spartan Laser at close range!

H-165 FOM TARGET LOCATOR

MAGAZINE SIZE: 2

MAXIMUM RESERVE: 2

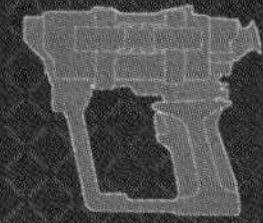

PRIMARY PURPOSE: Support, orbital strike, massive area of effect damage.

PRIMARY TARGETS: Elites, Hunters, Brutes, and Wraiths

COMBAT USAGE

The Target Locator is the UNSC's latest development, and also their prized possession. This targeting system allows the user to designate an area on the battlefield to receive an orbital strike. Once the area has been targeted, a red ring of lasers appears on the ground, delineating the target area. A half dozen bombs will rain down across the area from the sky, instantly vaporizing anything and everything caught within the blast circle. The Target Locator features both 2x and 4x zoom, but also a very low rate of fire. It takes nearly ten seconds after one strike for the weapon to be ready to call in a second strike. The orbital strike affects a wide area and it is not uncommon for the blasts to spread beyond the area outlined by the red ring—make sure you are clear of the target area or you are sure to be counted amongst the casualties.

- There are two main purposes for the Target Locator—to destroy Wraiths and to eliminate huge numbers of Covenant troops as they exit a Phantom or Drop Ship. To use the Target Locator any other time is simply wasting it.
- The Target Locator can be used to target an individual enemy or to target an area on the ground. If the latter, make sure to aim on a downward angle, else you may inadvertently target an area far beyond that which you intended.
- The Target Locator is far more common in Firefight matches (only once in Campaign mode). Use it to target the area between Phantoms to rack up the kills and lay claim to the Killionaire medal!

M247H HMG MACHINE GUN TURRET

MAGAZINE SIZE: UNLIMITED (MOUNTED), 200 (DETACHED)

MAXIMUM RESERVE: N/A

WELCOME
UNSC TRAINING
THE CAMPAIGN
FIREFIGHT
MULTIPLAYER
REFERENCE
ORDNANCE
VEHICLES
ENEMY FORCES
CREDIT SYSTEM
THE ARMORY
SKULLS
ACHIEVEMENTS
DATA PADS

PRIMARY PURPOSE: Support, close and medium range targets, high value targets.

PRIMARY TARGETS: Grunts, Skirmishers, Elites, Brutes, Brute Chieftains, and Hunters

COMBAT USAGE

The Machine Gun Turret can be used in place or detached, as a handheld third weapon. The weapon's capacity, rate of fire, and large-caliber rounds more than make up for its shoddy accuracy. The Machine Gun Turret benefits from unlimited ammo when mounted, but only 250 rounds once detached. The drawbacks to using the Machine Gun Turret in multiplayer matches are reduced in Campaign and Firefight, but the reduced speed of movement and inability to throw a grenade or use an Armor Ability without dropping the weapon do leave you somewhat vulnerable to attacks. A good strategy is to lure enemies to a chokepoint where you can cut them down with the turret before they realize you have it.

- The Machine Gun is capable of cutting down any enemy up to and including shielded Brute Chieftains and Hunters, but you may not always have enough time. Watch for enemies flanking your position with grenades!
- Draw enemies towards a narrow chokepoint, such as a doorway or narrow cave. In Firefight matches, carry the Machine Gun Turret to a chokepoint during the easier waves so it will be there when you need it.
- Use the Machine Gun Turret while it is attached whenever you can in order to conserve ammo. This will leave you locked in place and exposed—two things that will get you killed on Legendary difficulty or in Matchmaking mode—but this isn't always a problem on lesser difficulties or in Firefight.

M9 HE/DP FRAG GRENADE

MAGAZINE SIZE: 1

MAXIMUM RESERVE: 2

PRIMARY PURPOSE: Explosive, area of effect, medium range targets.

PRIMARY TARGETS: Grunts, Jackals, Elites, and Hunters.

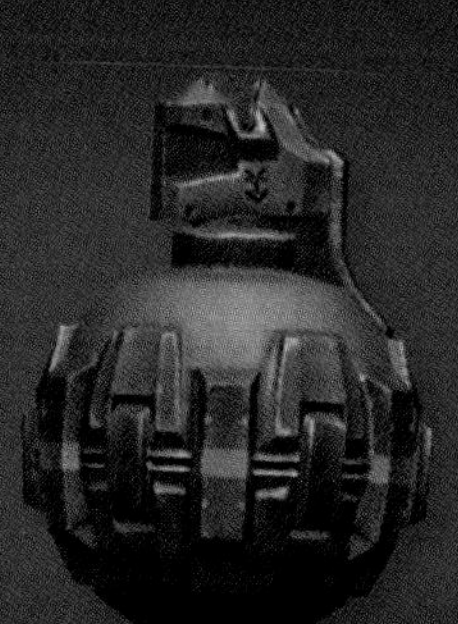

COMBAT USAGE

Spartans are outfitted with a pair of Frag Grenades whenever they head into battle and most ammo cabinets have extra grenades nearby. Frag Grenades lack the explosive force of the Plasma Grenade, and their tendency to bounce and skip along the surface makes using them a less-than-exact science. Nevertheless, Frag Grenades pack a powerful punch and deliver enough area of effect damage to take out entire packs of huddled enemies, provided they're not shielded. Jackals, Elites, and Brutes are capable of dodging Frag Grenade attacks on higher difficulty settings; throw them when the enemies are pinned against an obstacle and are forced to only dive in one direction and toss the grenade to that side. Frag Grenades may not kill higher ranking Elites or Brute Chieftains with a single attack, but can damage them severely.

- Frag Grenades can eliminate numerous unshielded enemies if huddled together. Toss the grenade at the ground in front of the enemies to bounce it towards them.
- Use walls and other objects to ricochet a Frag Grenade around a corner to attack an enemy waiting behind cover. Only use Frag Grenades to flush enemies out of cover when there are abundant Frag Grenades in the area, or when a round of Firefight is about to end and a fresh supply is imminent.
- Frag Grenades will bounce off Jackal's shields so don't throw them directly at a Jackal. Try to skip the Frag Grenade towards these foes at a low trajectory.

COVENANT WEAPONRY

Covenant weaponry is unlike anything ever devised by humans. Whereas UNSC weapons rely on physical projectiles crafted from minerals mined from the ground, the Covenant have turned to plasma and other forms of energy. Many of the Covenant's weapons are designed to rapidly take down energy shields, while others pack a more volatile punch or super-combine to result in a deadly explosion. Higher ranking Covenant troops often carry melee weapons which are each capable of one-strike kills. The Covenant do not have many weapons that compare favorably to the DMR, Sniper Rifle, or Rocket Launcher, but their collection is more numerous and more varied.

T25 DEP PLASMA PISTOL

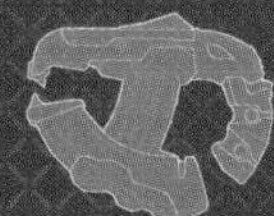

MAGAZINE SIZE: 100 BATTERY UNITS

MAXIMUM RESERVE: N/A

PRIMARY PURPOSE: Disabling of shields, close to medium range enemies, disable vehicles.

PRIMARY TARGETS: Jackals, Brutes, Elites, and Vehicles.

COMBAT USAGE

The Plasma Pistol can be deadly in the right hands, with a fast enough trigger finger, but its primary function is to strip away shields and disable vehicles. Hold the trigger to ready a charged shot then release it to disable an enemy's shields. Pair this weapon with a projectile-based weapon such as the Magnum, DMR, or even a Needle Rifle to perform a one-two knockout blow. Strip your enemy's shields with the charged Plasma Pistol then switch weapons and deliver the knockout blow with a headshot. The Plasma Pistol is also an excellent weapon to use against vehicles you wish to hijack—fire an overcharged shot to EMP the vehicle then move in for the steal. Charging the Plasma Pistol gradually decreases its number of battery units; holding down the trigger for too long will cause the weapon to overheat.

- Fire an overcharged shot to strip away an Elite or Brute Chieftain's shields, then switch to a DMR or Magnum and go for the headshot. Plasma Pistol shots can also disable a Jackal's shield.
- The Plasma Pistol's uncharged volleys can be effective against some enemies if fired at a high rate. It can defeat lesser enemies with relative ease, but you may want to attempt a melee kill or switch weapons once an Elite's shields have been destroyed. Using the Plasma Pistol against a Hunter is utterly inadvisable.
- Use overcharged shots to disable Wraiths and other vehicles to stop them in their tracks, disabling their weapons, and making them that much easier to board.
- The Plasma Pistol's battery units deplete one unit for every five shots fired. Overcharging consumes 10 battery units and an additional three units for every second the overcharge is maintained.

T25 DER PLASMA RIFLE

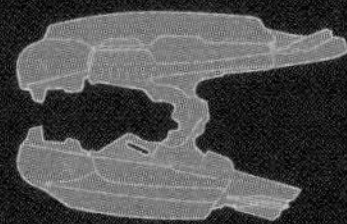

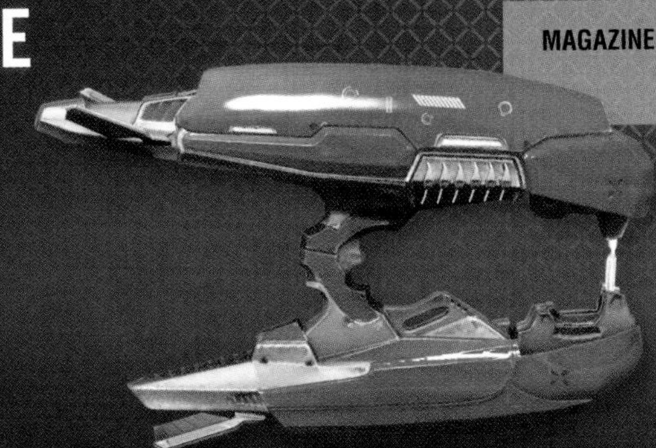

MAGAZINE SIZE: 100 BATTERY UNITS

MAXIMUM RESERVE: N/A

PRIMARY PURPOSE: Disabling of shields, close to medium range enemies.

PRIMARY TARGETS: Jackals, Brutes, Elites, and Hunters.

COMBAT USAGE

The Plasma Rifle is similar to the Plasma Pistol in that it can strip away shields, but this weapon's fully automatic firing mode replaces the latter's ability to fire a charged shot. The Plasma Rifle fires a continuous barrage of plasma blasts for as long as the trigger is held, right until the gun overheats and burns the player. This requires a somewhat lengthy cool down period before it can be used again, so it's best to fire in short bursts. The Plasma Rifle has a very fast rate of fire and can deplete an Elite or Brute Chieftain's shields nearly as fast as a charged Plasma Pistol shot. The Plasma Rifle cannot EMP vehicles and isn't very deadly against unshielded enemies, but it can be used to burn through the armor plating on a Hunter's back.

- The Plasma Rifle can take down an enemy's shields before overheating. Fire in short bursts when using against unshielded foes to avoid overheating.
- The high rate of fire doesn't necessarily make up for the Plasma Rifle's low amount of damage against vehicles and unshielded enemies. Switch to a traditional projectile-based weapon (or Needle Rifle) once the enemy's shields have been stripped away.
- The Plasma Rifle's attacks are not as powerful as an overcharged Plasma Pistol's, but more so than the Plasma Repeater. The ammo (battery units) from one weapon isn't transferrable to another. Swap for a fresh Plasma Rifle whenever prompted to pick one up on the battlefield, as that's a sign that the one on the ground has more juice left than the one you're carrying.
- Firing the Plasma Rifle consumes one battery unit for every three shots fired. It cannot be overcharged.

T51 DER/1 PLASMA REPEATER

MAGAZINE SIZE: 100 BATTERY UNITS

MAXIMUM RESERVE: N/A

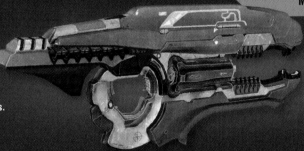

PRIMARY PURPOSE: Disabling of shields, close to medium range enemies.

PRIMARY TARGETS: Jackals, Brutes, Elites, and Hunters.

COMBAT USAGE

The Plasma Repeater is very similar to the Plasma Rifle with one key difference: the Plasma Repeater will never fully overheat. Holding the trigger down for a long period will never result in a scorched hand thanks to the Plasma Repeater's built-in cooling system that automatically slows the weapon's rate of fire as it begins to heat up. The Plasma Repeater has a very fast initial rate of fire, but this slows to a trickle of plasma projectiles as the weapon warms up. Hold X to vent the weapon and increase the firing rate. Venting the weapon can be interrupted either by resumed firing or by switching weapons to attack with another weapon. The Plasma Repeater is best used for stripping shields and shouldn't be relied upon heavily in combat.

- Fire the Plasma Repeater in short bursts to maintain maximum rate of fire. Vent the weapon to ensure it stays cool after prolonged use.
- The Plasma Repeater consumes one battery unit for every shot fired, much like the Plasma Turret. The weapon is powerful enough to strip shields very quickly, but shouldn't be used against unshielded enemies.
- The battery packs that power the Plasma Repeater cannot be combined or recharged. Keep your eyes peeled for a weapon with greater battery life and swap it when the one you're using runs low.

T25 C SPIKE RIFLE

MAGAZINE SIZE: 40

MAXIMUM RESERVE: 80

PRIMARY PURPOSE: Close-quarters defense, melee.

PRIMARY TARGETS: Grunts, Brutes, and Buggers.

COMBAT USAGE

The Spike Rifle is a fast-firing pistol with a very large magazine and near-instantaneous reload time. The Spike Rifle is only used by Brute Minors and Brute Captains and the only way to possess it is by scavenging it from the corpse of a Brute. Despite their impressive rate of fire, the gun's individual projectiles tend to travel slowly and can be avoided, particularly at medium to long range where the Spike Rifle's usefulness declines. The Spike Rifle can be quite intimidating at close range thanks to the large blades that have been affixed to the weapon's underside—the Spike Rifle can inflict significant melee damage!

- The Spike Rifle is a fully-automatic handheld rifle that has a very fast rate of fire and can be reloaded very quickly. Individual projectiles travel slowly and lose accuracy at range.
- Only use the Spike Rifle when trying to conserve ammo for another weapon and no alternatives are present. You can scavenge additional Spike Rifle ammo from the bodies of Brutes in the area, as this is the most common weapon of Brute Minors.
- The Spike Rifle is most effective in close quarters and where enemies are forced into narrow chokepoints. Rush their position while firing then melee any still standing when you get close enough to connect with a hit.

T33 GML NEEDLER

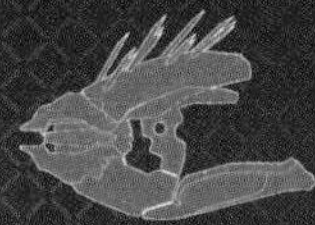

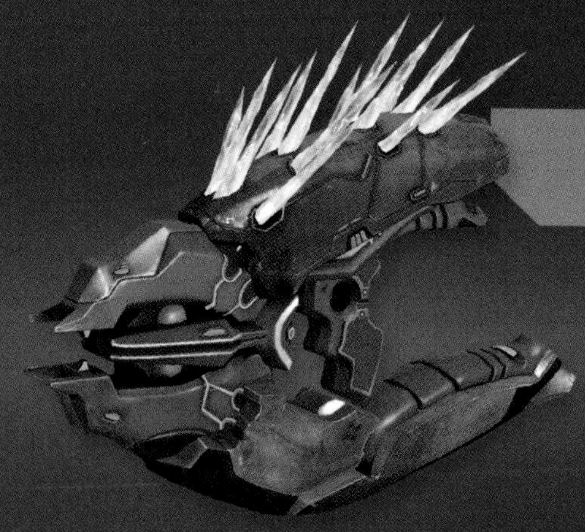

MAGAZINE SIZE: 24

MAXIMUM RESERVE: 96

PRIMARY PURPOSE: Super-combine explosion, tracking, close to medium range, unshielded foes.

PRIMARY TARGETS: Grunts, Skirmishers, Brutes, and Buggers.

COMBAT USAGE

The Needler is a truly unique weapon that fires elongated semi-guided needles that stick into their target like the stinger of an insect. When six of these needles impale the same target, they super-combine to form a deadly explosion. The Needler's projectiles are fired at a very fast rate, but they travel slowly and can be easily avoided at medium to long range. The Needler is much more effective at close range, provided you're not close enough to be caught in the resulting super-combine explosion. The Needler's needles will deflect off a Jackal's shield, as well as off Engineers, Brute Chieftains, and the Hunter's armor. Needlers are not capable of piercing an explosive tank or plasma battery and even though the super-combine explosion is powerful enough to kill, and has some area of effect damage, it cannot kill a shielded enemy with a single attack.

- Only use the Needler at close to medium range and against enemies that are unshielded. Count the projectiles as you fire the weapon and release the trigger once six needles have left the chamber—firing additional needles is a waste if the first six are on target.
- Needlers are commonly used by Grunts, Jackals, and Skirmishers. Though plentiful, the ammo for the Needler can be used up very quickly so choose your targets wisely.
- Though weak, targeting a Grunt with the Needler can sometimes catch other enemies in the super-combine explosion. This is a great way to deplete the shield of a nearby Elite or even defeat nearby Jackals whose shields would have blocked the needles.

T31 R NEEDLE RIFLE

MAGAZINE SIZE: 21

MAXIMUM RESERVE: 84

WELCOME
UNSC TRAINING
THE CAMPAIGN
FIREFIGHT
MULTIPLAYER
REFERENCE
ORDNANCE
VEHICLES
ENEMY FORCES
CREDIT SYSTEM
THE ARMORY
SKULLS
ACHIEVEMENTS
DATA PADS

PRIMARY PURPOSE: Sniping, super-combine explosion, unshielded foes.

PRIMARY TARGETS: Grunts, Skirmishers, Elites, Brutes, and Hunters.

COMBAT USAGE

The Needle Rifle is the Covenant's answer to the DMR. The Needle Rifle provides its user with 2x zoom and arrow-straight projectiles impale any non-shielded enemy they hit. The Needle Rifle's larger projectiles only require three individual needles to stick in order to super-combine in a deadly explosion of pink mist and crystalline shrapnel. Like the Needler, the Needle Rifle's projectiles benefit from some self-guided tracking, which helps make up for their relatively slower flight speed. The Needle Rifle's projectiles will bounce off a Jackal's shield, metallic tanks, and other plated surfaces such as an Engineer or Hunter's armor, but the weapon's precision makes up for this. It is entirely possible to target the exposed weak point on a Hunter with the Needle Rifle and super-combine three needles to deliver significant damage.

- Zoom in and fire the Needle Rifle three times quickly to target an enemy for a super-combine attack. Super-combine attacks are lethal and have some area of effect damage.
- The Needle Rifle is capable of delivering one-shot kills, provided you target a lower level enemy in the head. Grunts, Jackals, and Skirmishers can all be killed with a single headshot.
- Target an Elite with three needles to blast away its shields with the super-combine explosion, then repeat with another three needles to kill it. Note that enemies with Armor Lock—some Elites and Brutes—will activate Armor Lock after being struck with two needles to protect against the super-combine attack.

T50 DER/H CONCUSSION RIFLE

MAGAZINE SIZE: 6

MAXIMUM RESERVE: 24

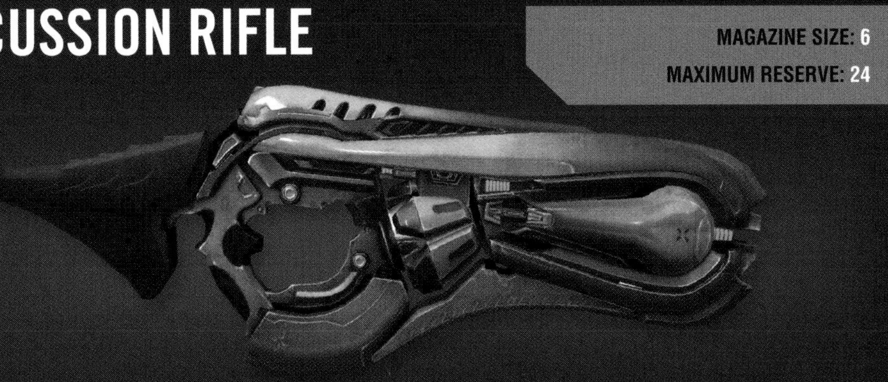

PRIMARY PURPOSE: Are of effect damage, close to medium range, suppression.

PRIMARY TARGETS: Jackals, Elites, Brutes, and Vehicles.

COMBAT USAGE

The Concussion Rifle fires an explosive blast of energy that delivers area of effect damage across a small zone and is perfectly suited to beating back an encroaching horde of enemies. The Concussion Rifle can be fired with surprising speed and can quickly beat enemies into submission with its knockback force. The Concussion Rifle isn't the most accurate weapon and shots can sail wide or overhead of your target if you're not careful—there is very limited ammo for this weapon, so don't waste it! Aim for the enemy's torso at close range or angle the shot at their feet at medium distance. The Concussion Rifle is typically used by Elites and can be found on the battlefield wherever Elites were common. The Concussion Rifle has no zoom.

- Fire two to three blasts at a time in quick succession for maximum effectiveness. This weapon is excellent against individual Elites or Brutes, but can also be used to defeat small groups of lesser enemies.
- Use the Concussion Rifle to blast an approaching Ghost or Wraith. It only takes two shots with the Concussion Rifle to destroy light craft such as these.
- The Concussion Rifle's individual volleys are quite slow and can be dodged at long range. It is best to use this weapon against close-range targets and it is important to be mindful of the weapon's slow reload time. Switch to another weapon until you can safely reload.
- Players skilled in exploring the beaten path will likely find the Concussion Rifle to be an excellent tool for "rocket jumping." Run, leap, and fire the Concussion Rifle downward to receive an extra boost skyward!

T33 LAAW FUEL ROD GUN

MAGAZINE SIZE: 5

MAXIMUM RESERVE: 15

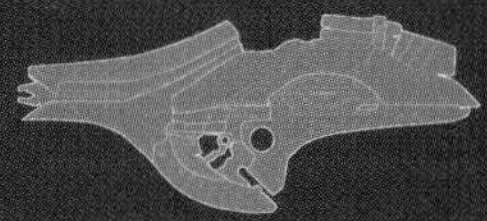

PRIMARY PURPOSE: Heavy explosive, support, medium to long range, high value targets.

PRIMARY TARGETS: Brutes, Elites, Hunters, and Vehicles.

COMBAT USAGE

The Fuel Rod Gun is one of the Covenant's most deadly weapons and is universally feared by all UNSC combatants. This weapon is most commonly wielded by Elite Generals, Brute Chieftains and Spec-Op Grunts. The Fuel Rod Gun fires an unmistakable and highly explosive green gaseous projectile that explodes on contact with massive area of effect damage. The Fuel Rod Gun is best used against groups of enemies, larger high-priority targets, and against vehicles such as the Wraith and Revenant. The weapon's 2.5x zoom makes it possible to fire the Fuel Rod Gun with surprising accuracy over medium to long distances, but the ability to bounce a projectile at close range makes it possible to perform trick shots around corners and over obstacles.

- The Fuel Rod Gun has limited ammo capacity and a slow reload time. It can be fired in moderately fast succession, but do not waste the ammo. Save the Fuel Rod Gun for large groups of enemies or high priority targets.
- The weapon's area of effect damage is quite high, so the projectile does not require a direct hit to be fatal—aim for the ground around enemies if you are worried about missing them with the slow-moving projectile. This same area of effect damage also mandates that you don't fire it at close range unless bouncing a projectile around a corner.
- This weapon is very common in Firefight matches, particularly on maps that feature Covenant Drop Pods. It's not uncommon to encounter four Spec Op Grunts all wielding Fuel Rod Guns. Lob a grenade at them as they exit the pod, then scoop up the weapons for yourself!

T52 SAR FOCUS RIFLE

MAGAZINE SIZE: 100 BATTERY UNITS

MAXIMUM RESERVE: N/A

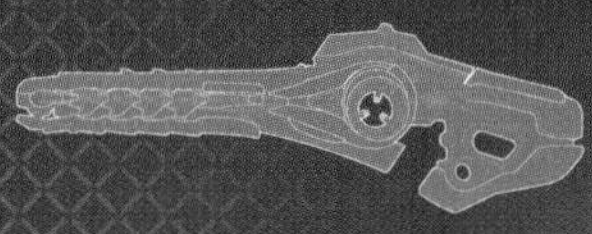

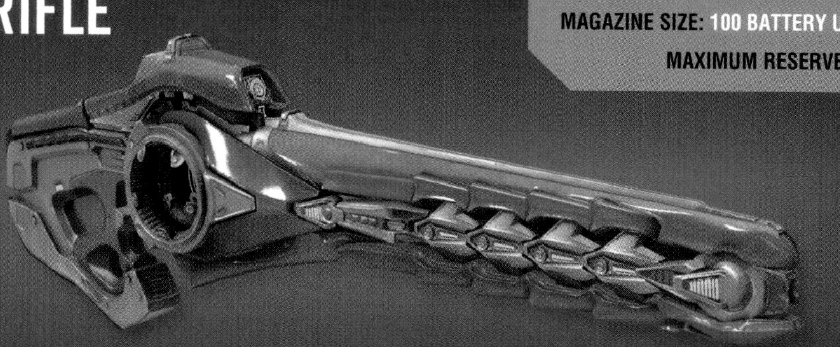

PRIMARY PURPOSE: Sniping, long-range targeting.

PRIMARY TARGETS: Jackals, Brutes, and Elites.

COMBAT USAGE

The Focus Rifle is the Covenant's primary long-range sniping weapon (the Needle Rifle being the other) and fires a continuous beam of plasma energy that gradually burns through the targeted enemy. The Focus Rifle isn't without its drawbacks, however. For starters, it can take a considerable amount of time to defeat a shielded enemy with the Focus Rifle and it may very well overheat by the time the fatal blow is delivered. Though the Focus Rifle is equipped with 3.5x and 9.5x zoom, the trail of energy is visible across the battlefield and betrays your position every time the trigger is squeezed. You can overcome this deficiency by firing in shorter bursts and changing positions between bursts, but this isn't always possible.

- Focus Rifle provides long-range sniping with plasma-based energy. Can burn through shields and deliver fatal damage to Elites and Brute Chieftains but may overheat before delivering fatal blast.
- Can fire two to three short bursts of energy per battery unit. Holding the trigger for a continuous beam depletes four battery units per second.
- Very precise at long range and easier to fire from the hip than other precision weapons. Can be effective at medium range against Elites.
- The Focus Rifle's beam of energy leads enemy attackers directly to your position when fired. Fire in short bursts from a covered position and relocate frequently if trying to be stealthy.

T52 GML/E PLASMA LAUNCHER

MAGAZINE SIZE: 100 BATTERY UNITS

MAXIMUM RESERVE: N/A

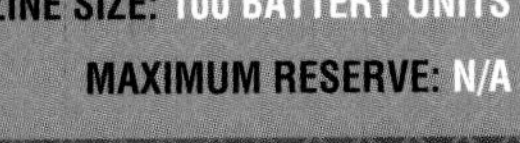

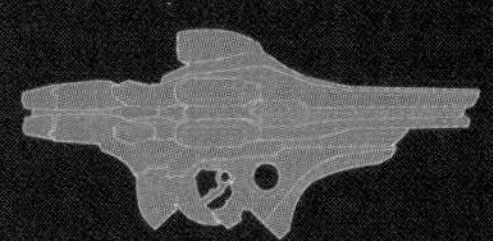

PRIMARY PURPOSE: Support, medium to long range, tracking.

PRIMARY TARGETS: Elites, Brute Chieftains, Hunters, and Vehicles.

COMBAT USAGE

The Plasma Launcher fires up to four independent Plasma Grenades that can track a foe mid-flight and stick to the target on contact. This is a devastating weapon with few drawbacks. Hold the trigger to charge up a Plasma Grenade while targeting an enemy. A small red circle will gradually fill in on-screen for each of the Plasma Grenades to be fired. The projectiles are then launched through the air and home in on the target. Their sticky nature adheres to the targeted enemy or vehicle and explodes with massive area of effect and shield-draining damage. Fire one Plasma Grenade at a group of unshielded enemies; two Plasma Grenades at shielded Elites and Brutes, and three or four projectiles at Hunters and Wraiths. The Plasma Launcher has 2.5x zoom and can is most effective at medium to long range.

- Plasma Launcher is devastating against shielded enemies and can defeat groups of enemies with just one or two Plasma Grenades thanks to its massive area of effect damage.
- Individual projectiles track locked-on targets. This makes the Plasma Launcher exceptionally useful against Revenants, Wraiths, and Banshees. The Plasma Launcher's projectiles do not travel fast enough to catch up to a Ghost at full speed.
- Hold the trigger to charge up to four individual Plasma Grenades. Don't use more than two against any individual enemy unless targeting a Hunter, in which case you should use three.

T52 DESW PLASMA CANNON

MAGAZINE SIZE: UNLIMITED (MOUNTED), 200 BATTERY UNITS (DETACHED)

MAXIMUM RESERVE: N/A

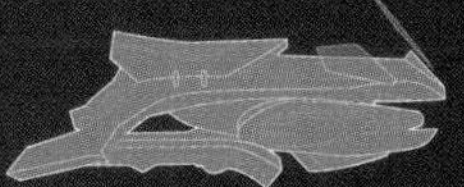

PRIMARY PURPOSE: Support, close to medium range, high priority targets, shielded enemies.

PRIMARY TARGETS: Jackals, Brutes, Elites, Hunters, and Vehicles.

COMBAT USAGE

Much like the Machine Gun Turret, the Plasma Cannon has unlimited ammo when it is mounted on a turret, but only 200 battery units once detached. Each projectile consumes one battery unit and those 200 units can be used up quickly if you don't periodically ease off the trigger. The Plasma Cannon doesn't overheat and can be fired nonstop at its maximum rate of fire. The Plasma Cannon is tremendously effective at cutting through enemies, particularly shielded foes such as Elites and Brute Chieftains. Using the Plasma Cannon in a mounted position opens you up to enemy fire, particularly from snipers, and is not recommended. Detach the weapon and carry it towards a choke point, or near the area where high-priority targets are deploying for maximum effectiveness.

- The Plasma Cannon is very effective against shielded enemies and can fire all 200 rounds nonstop without overheating. The weapon can be carried in addition to your two equipped weapons.
- Movement while carrying the Plasma Cannon is slowed. Drop the weapon if you are overrun by smaller, nimbler creatures and pick it back up after dispatching the immediate threat through other means. Don't waste the 200 battery units on low-priority enemies.
- The most plentiful source of Plasma Cannons is the bay doors on the sides of the Phantoms. Target the Plasma Cannon with a heavy weapon or Sniper Rifle to knock it out of the Phantom then pick it up and carry it into battle.

T1 EW/S ENERGY SWORD

MAGAZINE SIZE: 100 BATTERY UNITS
MAXIMUM RESERVE: N/A

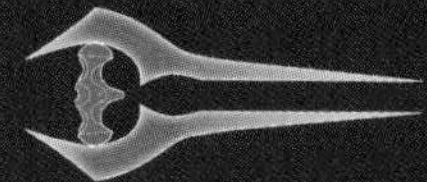

PRIMARY PURPOSE: Melee weapon, close range, defense.

PRIMARY TARGETS: Elites, Brutes, and Hunters.

COMBAT USAGE

The Energy Sword is one of two melee weapons used by Covenant and is exclusive to Elites. The Energy Sword is capable of one-hit kills against shielded and unshielded foes alike, but only from extremely close range. Swing the Energy Sword by pressing either the Right Trigger or Right Bumper. Use the Right Trigger when the reticule is red to perform a lunging attack against enemies several steps away. Ten battery units are consumed every time the Energy Sword makes contact with an enemy, so save it for tougher foes as finding another Energy Sword isn't likely.

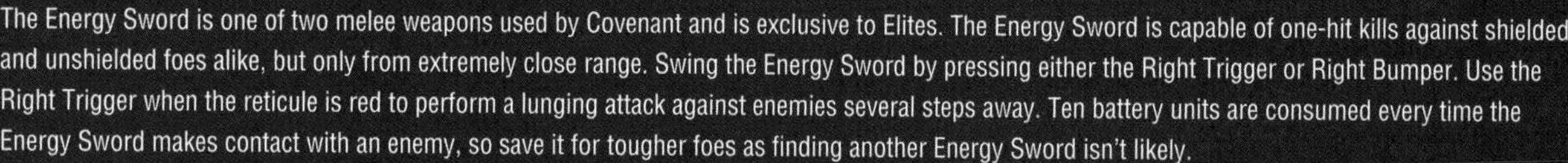

- Enemies can see the Energy Sword and know you have to move in close to them to be effective. Keep it as a secondary weapon to bait foes into getting close, then switch weapons and slice them in two!
- It's possible to parry Energy Sword attacks with a well-timed melee swing of your own. Make a point of swinging with the melee attack (Right Bumper) when engaging an enemy with an Energy Sword, since follow-up attacks are faster after this type of swing.
- Energy Swords aren't as common in Campaign and Firefight as they are in Matchmaking. Refer to the Multiplayer Armory chapter of this guide for even more tips on using this deadly weapon.

T2 EW/H GRAVITY HAMMER

MAGAZINE SIZE: 100 BATTERY UNITS
MAXIMUM RESERVE: N/A

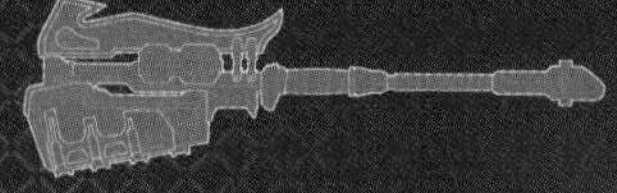

PRIMARY PURPOSE: Melee weapon, close range, defense.

PRIMARY TARGETS: Jackals, Elites, Brutes, and Hunters.

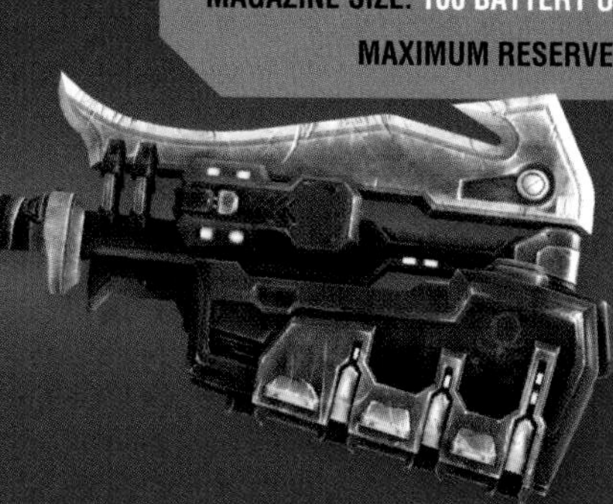

COMBAT USAGE

The Gravity Hammer is one of the deadliest weapons in the *Halo* universe. This long-handled melee weapon offers surprising reach and incredible area of effect damage. It is capable of defeating virtually any enemy type with a single attack—Brute Chieftains and Hunters on higher difficulty settings may require two swings. The Gravity Hammer can be swung with the Right Trigger in a massive overhead swing that delivers ground-shaking damage to entire groups of enemies. Leap down upon a group of enemies with the Gravity Hammer to rack up a handful of kills with a single attack. Better still, using the Gravity Hammer's handle to jab and strike enemies (via the Right Bumper) doesn't consume any of the weapon's energy reserves. Using the Right Trigger to swing the weapon overhead consumes five battery units even if the swing does no damage.

- Deal death to groups of lower ranking enemies with a single swing of the Gravity Hammer. The weapon's area of effect damage can kill enemies without making direct contact. Overhead swings will knock enemies into the air—use this to your advantage near cliffs and other precipices.
- Brute Chieftains are the only source of Gravity Hammers in both Campaign and Firefight. Keep your distance and attack with heavy weapons or Plasma Grenades to defeat them. Pick up the Gravity Hammer once the coast is clear—never let one go to waste.
- Gravity Hammer ammo is a precious commodity. Use melee swings to defeat unshielded enemies and lower-ranking Elites and Brutes to conserve the Gravity Hammer for tougher foes or large groups.

T1 APG PLASMA GRENADE

MAGAZINE SIZE: 1
MAXIMUM RESERVE: 2

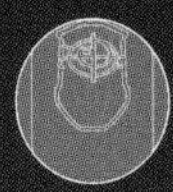

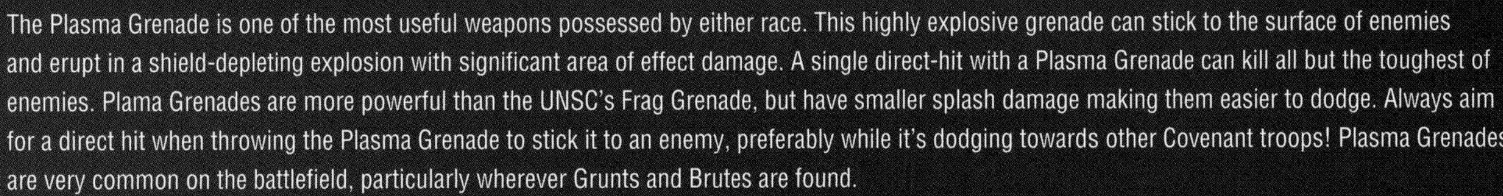

PRIMARY PURPOSE: Explosive, area of effect, medium range targets, shielded foes.

PRIMARY TARGETS: Grunts, Elites, Brutes, Hunters, and Vehicles.

COMBAT USAGE

The Plasma Grenade is one of the most useful weapons possessed by either race. This highly explosive grenade can stick to the surface of enemies and erupt in a shield-depleting explosion with significant area of effect damage. A single direct-hit with a Plasma Grenade can kill all but the toughest of enemies. Plama Grenades are more powerful than the UNSC's Frag Grenade, but have smaller splash damage making them easier to dodge. Always aim for a direct hit when throwing the Plasma Grenade to stick it to an enemy, preferably while it's dodging towards other Covenant troops! Plasma Grenades are very common on the battlefield, particularly wherever Grunts and Brutes are found.

- Can stick to enemies (except Jackal's shield) and deliver devastating damage that only Hunters, Elite Generals, and Brute Chieftains can survive. No enemy can survive successive Plasma Grenade sticky attacks.
- Beware Grunts on a suicide mission—they'll charge your position with two handheld Plasma Grenades primed and ready to explode. Shoot Grunts as soon as you see them to harvest a reliable supply of Plasma Grenades.
- Plasma Grenades lying on the ground can be detonated remotely with precision-class weapons. Target the Plasma Grenade with a DMR, Magnum, or Sniper Rifle to detonate it. Additionally, Plasma Grenades can be detonated in a chain-reaction by other nearby Plasma Grenades.
- Plasma Grenades are very effective against all manner of vehicles. Don't throw a Plasma Grenade at any vehicle you wish to commandeer.

VEHICLES

It wouldn't be a *Halo* game without a fleet of vehicles on hand to carry you across the battlefield in style. This section covers each of the vehicles that you can actively pilot or serve as a gunner on during the Campaign and Firefight modes. There are five such UNSC vehicles and four Covenant craft. Information concerning additional non-playable vehicles is classified!

UNSC VEHICLES

M274 ULATV "MONGOOSE"

UNARMORED VEHICLE USED PRIMARILY BY COURIERS.

Crew: ***1 driver, 1 passenger***

Armament: ***None***

Missions: ***Exodus, The Package, Pillar of Autumn***

Firefight: ***Beachhead***

The Mongoose provides fast transportation for up to two players (or Noble Six and one ally), but offers no offensive capabilities and little protection. The driver is fully exposed to enemy fire from the sides and back. The front of the Mongoose obstructs the view of the driver from the front, leaving the driver's chest and head fully exposed. The Mongoose cannot withstand any significant attacks.

The Mongoose can be fun for running down Grunts, or if you have an ally riding on the back. However, it's best utilized for escaping a sticky situation.

Driving the Mongoose requires a delicate touch. Although it doesn't have as high a top speed as the Warthog, but its narrow body and lighter weight make it highly susceptible to rolling over. Take every precaution to avoid hitting obstacles at an angle, since any significant bump can send the Mongoose careening out of control. The good news is that the Mongoose often lands right-side up, but the direction and proximity to enemy troops may be less than ideal.

Passengers riding on the back of a Mongoose stand on the rear rack and hang onto the driver's shoulders. This position enables the passenger to fire a weapon over the driver's head—a Rocket Launcher is the ideal weapon—and also protects the passenger from frontal attacks. The passenger is fully exposed to attacks from the side and behind, and as with the driver, is offered no armor protection by the vehicle.

M12 FAV "WARTHOG"

LIGHTLY ARMORED FORCE APPLICATION VEHICLE; HIGHLY MANEUVERABLE, EXTREMELY VERSATILE PLATFORM.

Crew: ***1 driver, 1 passenger, 1 gunner***

Armament: ***Vulcan Machinegun or Gauss Cannon or Rocket Launcher***

Missions: ***ONI: Sword Base, Tip of the Spear, Exodus***

Firefight: ***Beachhead***

The Warthog is the quintessential UNSC vehicle. Its proprietary four-wheel steering and independent suspension system allow it to cross virtually any terrain. The Warthog is also extremely fast and surprisingly nimble for its size. It's heavy enough to avoid rolling over as easily as the Mongoose, but faster than any other UNSC ground-based vehicle.

Vulcan Machine Gun

Driving a Warthog with skill takes practice and a devotion to your gunner's needs. Drive smooth, arcing loops around high-value targets and avoid unnecessary jumps and bumps.

Troop Carrier

Rocket

Gauss Cannon

The Warthog offers moderate protection to the driver from the front, rear, and right-hand side. The lack of doors makes the driver somewhat vulnerable to attacks from the left. The Warthog's armor can withstand small arms fire and multiple collisions. The reinforced front-end can withstand splatter attacks against Covenant infantry, but collisions with anything larger than a Ghost should be avoided.

Allies in the passenger seat can use their hand-held weaponry to fire on nearby enemies. They enjoy much of the same protection from attacks as the driver, but their position in the vehicle while firing their weapon leaves them more exposed to enemy attacks. Always try to arm any UNSC Troopers riding shotgun with a Sniper Rifle, Rocket Launcher, or Spartan Laser.

The Warthog comes in three variations, depending on the weaponry mounted to its rear. The most common version is outfitted with the LRV: M41 12.mm LAAG, otherwise known as the Vulcan Machinegun. The Vulcan Machinegun has a very high rate of fire and moderate accuracy against short to medium-range targets. Another version is the LAAV-R: M79 65mm MLRS Rocket Launcher. The twin Rocket Launcher bores on the turret fire a barrage of six rockets with each squeeze of the trigger. Firing rate suffers, as does accuracy, but the firepower is devastating at medium to long-range. Close-range firing of the Rocket Launcher is not advised. Finally, the third version of the Warthog comes equipped with the LAAV-G: M68 25mm ALIM Gauss Cannon. This laser-like weapons system fires a devastating beam of energy with pinpoint accuracy. Its rate of fire is delayed while the system recharges, but the combination of range, accuracy, and destructive force is without match in the UNSC fleet.

M808 MBT "SCORPION"

PRIMARY ARMORED FIGHTING VEHICLE OF THE UNSC; REQUIRES SUPPORT ON TODAY'S HIGH-SPEED BATTLEFIELD.

Crew: *1 commander, 1 machinegunner, and up to 4 passengers*

Armament: *Smooth-Bore High-Velocity Cannon and Medium Machinegun*

Missions: *The Package*

Firefight: *N/A*

The Scorpion is the UNSC's answer to traditional tanks. This tread-based vehicle is heavily armored and resistant to virtually all small arms fire. The driver, also known as the commander, is fully protected within the enclosed cockpit from the majority of infantry attacks, but Plasma Grenades, Fuel Rod Guns, and the high-energy attacks from the Revenant, Wraith, and Banshee are major concerns. The Scorpion gradually takes damage as enemy attacks bombard it—this is your cue that, as a driver, you may soon need to exit the vehicle. The tread covers on the sides get knocked off first, after which the Scorpion begins to smoke and flame before finally exploding.

The commander has full control over the direction and speed of travel and the aiming and firing of the Scorpion's primary cannon. The M512 90mm SBHV Cannon has a very slow rate of fire, but it is extremely accurate over long range and is capable of destroying small vehicles, Shade Turrets, and Covenant watchtowers with a single shell. Each shell also delivers a wide area-of-effect blast of splash damage capable of killing numerous Covenant. The Scorpion's cannon can kill all lower level enemies with a single attack, but Brute Chieftains and Hunters require multiple attacks, especially on Legendary mode.

The gunner position on the Scorpion offers a second player or ally nearly full protection from damage while wielding a M247T 7.62mm Medium Machinegun. The gun doesn't pack the punch of the 12.7mm gun on the back of the Warthog, but it is a sizable improvement over the standard Assault Rifle and is perfect for keeping infantry units at bay. The gunner sits primarily inside the Scorpion, beneath the cannon, but is not fully protected from attacks. In fact, enemy snipers can target the gunner's head.

Up to four additional players can ride along the sides of the Scorpion by sitting on the tread covers. Allies essentially sit on top of the tank, with no protection from enemy fire. They can offer additional small arms fire and assist the gunner, but they are also the first to perish when the Scorpion gets attacked. The tread covers are the first to get blown off, thus stripping away the Scorpion's ability to transport additional units.

The Scorpion's slow speed makes it vulnerable to attacks from Covenant vehicles and Shade Turrets. Target high-value targets with the cannon and leave infantry to the gunner.

UH-144 "FALCON"

PRIMARY GROUND SUPPORT AND TERRESTRIAL TROOP TRANSPORT VTOL OF THE UNSC.

Crew: *1 pilot, 2 gunners, and up to 3 passengers*

Armament: *20mm Auto-Cannon and either 2x Grenade Launchers or 2x 12.7 mm Auto-Cannons*

Missions: *Tip of the Spear, Exodus, and New Alexandria*

Firefight: *N/A*

The Falcon is the primary aerial transport vehicle used by Noble Team and can carry a total of six players, including the pilot and two gunners. The Falcon can withstand a heavy amount of small arms fire but is vulnerable to heavy weaponry attacks, particularly from the Banshee and Shade Turrets. The driver is fully enclosed within a glass cockpit, but there are no side doors on the Falcon, meaning passengers are partially exposed to side attacks. Those manning the gunners' seats on the Falcon sit between the passenger bay and skids, which offers little in the way of protection.

The Falcon offers excellent ground support to troops in the field thanks to its twin gunners' seats. The auto-feed of the Falcon's mounted Grenade Launcher is a marked improvement over the handheld version.

The Falcon's altitude is controlled via the left trigger—pull the left trigger to climb and release it to descend. Tap the right bumper to toggle on/off altitude lock. The pilot is also in control of the Falcon's primary forward-mounted weapon, the UH-144A: M638 20mm Auto-Cannon. This high-caliber machinegun boasts a very high rate of fire and above-average accuracy at medium range. It is capable of destroying enemy turrets and Banshees, and it can even take down a Covenant Phantom if given enough time.

The Falcon comes in two varieties, differentiated only by the weaponry mounted on its sides. One version is equipped with twin M460 40mm AGL Grenade Launchers, while the other is outfitted with two M247H 12.7 HMG Machineguns. The Falcon's Grenade Launchers operate the same way as the handheld version seen in the field, but they are modified with an auto-loading system that significantly increases the rate of fire. Gunners can choose either to manually detonate a grenade or use the launcher's auto-detonation feature. The machinegun variant loses a little in raw firepower, but the heavy machineguns offer an extremely high rate of fire, along with enough stopping power to take down any Covenant infantry unit or light vehicle.

YSS-1000 "SABRE"

PRIMARY PLANETARY DEFENSE FIGHTER FOR THE INNER COLONIES.

Crew: *1 pilot, 1 radar intercept officer*

Armament: *2x 30mm Machinegun and 2x Missile Pods*

Missions: *Long Night of Solace*

Firefight: *N/A*

The Sabre is a top-secret space fighter used for protecting colonies and space stations. The Sabre is highly maneuverable, capable of barrel rolls in either direction and both downward and upward 180-degree turns. The Sabre's pilot is in control of steering, throttle, and weapons aiming and firing, thereby leaving the navigator to call out enemy locations and objectives.

The Sabre offers full protection to its occupants and contains its own energy shields to absorb attacks that would otherwise damage the hull. Although the pilot and navigator cannot be targeted directly, fatal damage to the Sabre results in immediate death to those onboard. The Sabre's shields cannot absorb damage caused by making contact with stationary objects; collisions with any part of a frigate or space station results in immediate destruction to the Sabre.

The pilot can switch between firing the Sabre's machineguns and missiles on the fly with a tap of the Y Button. Use the machineguns to destroy unshielded Space Banshees, or to strip away the shields on Seraphs. Switch to the missiles to finish off Seraphs once they've lost their shields.

Be extra careful when performing evasive maneuvers with the Sabre, as the slightest collision with the Anchor 9 can have disastrous consequences!

COVENANT VEHICLES

WELCOME
UNSC TRAINING
THE CAMPAIGN
FIREFIGHT
MULTIPLAYER
REFERENCE
ORDNANCE
VEHICLES
ENEMY FORCES
CREDIT SYSTEM
THE ARMORY
SKULLS
ACHIEVEMENTS
DATA PADS

T-32 RAV "GHOST"

PRIMARY RECONNAISSANCE AND RAPID ATTACK VEHICLE OF THE COVENANT; VERY LITTLE PROTECTION AFFORDED TO PILOT.

Crew: *1 pilot*

Armament: *2x Plasma Cannons*

Missions: *ONI: Sword Base, Tip of the Spear, Exodus, The Package*

Firefight: *Beachhead, Glacier, Outpost*

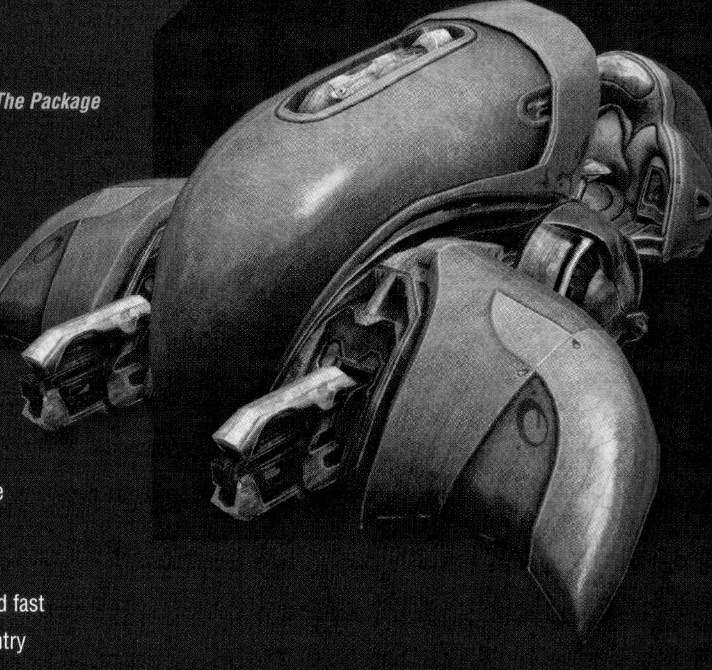

The Ghost may be designed for reconnaissance, but in Spartan hands, it can become a lethal, high-speed battering ram used to devastating effect against infantry units. The Ghost can splatter most enemies with a single collision when the boosters are engaged, but higher ranking Elites, Hunters, and Brutes may require multiple collisions before falling prey to the Ghost's blunt force.

The twin Plasma Cannons offer the pilot an accurate and fast ranged attack. These cannons are effective against infantry and also other light vehicles, particularly other Ghosts. The Ghost's biggest asset is speed, which makes having to battle larger vehicles completely unnecessary. Flee to escape significant threats and hide the craft in cover, then speed out to attack when the coast is clear.

Piloting the Ghost is a relatively risky proposition. Although the Ghost's front shroud and wing-like extensions provide ample coverage from frontal attacks, the pilot is completely exposed on the sides and rear. It's also easy to hijack the Ghost. Despite the obvious risks, the Ghost is still tempting to use. Its narrow size and maneuverability make it possible to drive the Ghost through interior spaces where few other vehicles can access. Sometimes this requires a little modification—melee either of the wings to tighten up the Ghost's width so it can get through narrower doorways! Melee a wing twice to halve its size; the second wing can be halved with a

T-48 LAGC "REVENANT"

LIGHTLY ARMORED MOBILE ARTILLERY; OPEN VEHICLE AFFORDS VERY LITTLE PROTECTION TO CREW.

Crew: *1 pilot, 1 passenger*

Armament: *Plasma Mortar*

Missions: *ONI: Sword Base, Tip of the Spear, The Package*

Firefight: *N/A*

The Revenant blends the firepower of the Wraith with the speed and maneuverability of the Ghost into an impressive do-anything vehicle. The Revenant can strafe and employ boosters for increased speed just like the Ghost (but a bit slower), but its Plasma Mortar attacks are only slightly less powerful than that of the Wraith. The Revenant can't outrun the other enemies quite as well as the Ghost, but it can hold its own against most vehicles by strafing in and out of cover and using its Plasma Mortar to bombard the enemy.

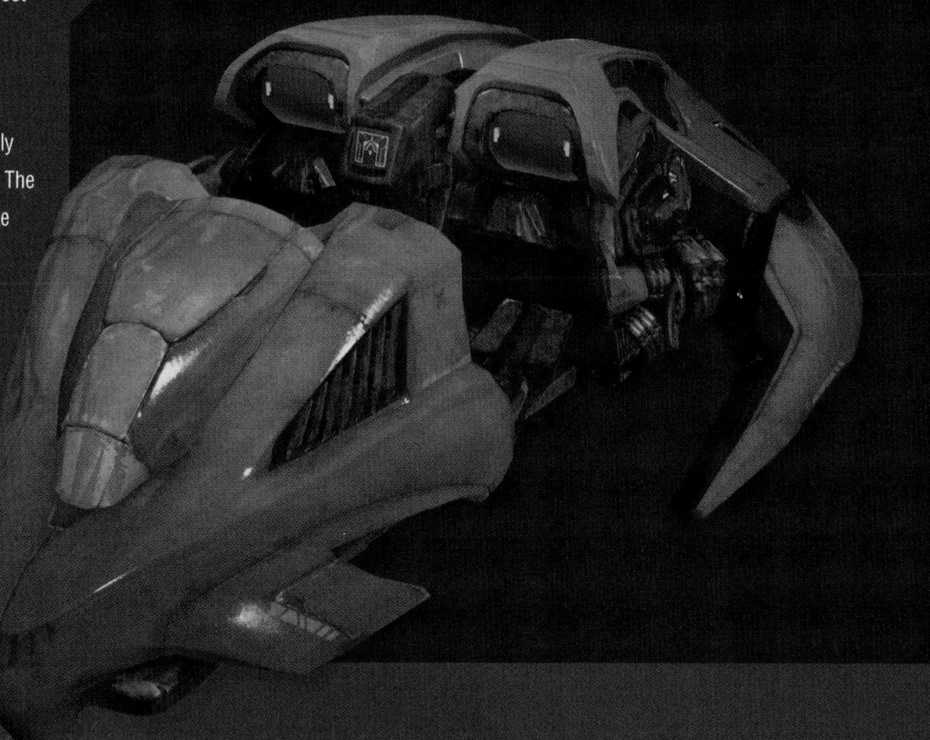

The Revenant can be used to splatter infantry units, but its slower speed makes it more susceptible to hijacking. It's better to use the Revenant's Plasma Mortar to target groups of enemies and rely on the splash damage to inflict the most harm. Passengers should use their handheld weaponry to target light infantry as it approaches the Revenant.

Strafe from side to side with the Revenant to avoid powerful attacks and fire back with the Plasma Mortar!

The only drawback to using the Revenant is the lack of protection it provides its driver and occupant. Although the front of the Revenant is rather bulbous, but the driver and passenger are exposed to attacks from the side and moderately susceptible to rear attacks. The passenger is particularly vulnerable, as he partially stands in the seat and leans out the side for a clearer line of sight. Passengers are essentially fully exposed to enemy fire.

T-26 AGC "WRAITH"

PRIMARY ARMORED FIGHTING VEHICLE OF THE COVENANT GROUND FORCES; BLIND SPOT/RELATIVELY WEAK ARMOR TO REAR.

Crew: *1 pilot, 1 plasma cannon gunner*

Armament: *Heavy Plasma Mortar, Plasma Cannon*

Missions: *ONI: Sword Base, Tip of the Spear, Exodus*

Firefight: *Beachhead, Corvette, Glacier, and Overlook*

The Wraith is the Covenant's answer to the Scorpion. This armored, tank-like vehicle offers full protection for the driver and above-average protection for the gunner. The Wraith's armor isn't quite as resilient as the Scorpion's, and the Wraith's susceptibility to rear attacks is a significant liability. The vehicle has a very flimsy cover that can be shot or knocked off to expose vital engine components. A few shots to the turbine will destroy the vehicle.

Despite structural weaknesses, the Wraith can deflect most small arms fire, provided it's not aimed directly at the front hood of the Wraith. Shots to the front hood eventually knock it off, thereby exposing the pilot's head to attacks—it only takes one very well-aimed shot from a sniper to kill the driver and render the Wraith powerless. The gunner is afforded no cowl and can be easily sniped at any time. Would-be hijackers should always target the gunner before getting anywhere near a Wraith.

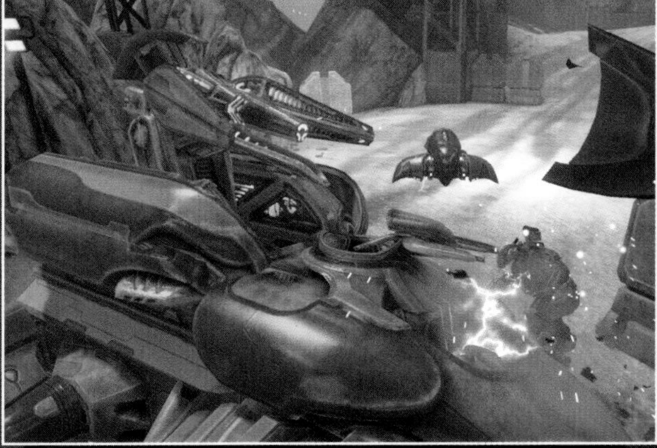

The Covenant don't leave unattended Wraiths lying around—the only way to drive one is to hijack one while it's in use! Hop on the roof and melee through it to reach the driver.

The Wraith's slow speed and limited booster energy make it highly vulnerable to Plasma Grenades and heavy weapon attacks that would typically be too slow to hit a vehicle. Fortunately, the Wraith packs plenty of weaponry of its own. The heavy Plasma Mortar can lob incredibly powerful plasma bombs a considerable distance. Although these bombs move very slowly through the air, they deliver lethal damage to a wide area. The Wraith can destroy any UNSC vehicle except the Scorpion with a single shot, and it only takes two shots to kill that. The heavy Plasma Mortar is the primary weapon, but having a skilled gunner man the Plasma Cannon is every bit as important. The Plasma Cannon keeps attackers at bay and can shoot potential hijackers before they get close enough to do any harm.

T-26 GSA "BANSHEE"

PRIMARY GROUND SUPPORT AIRCRAFT OF THE COVENANT; LIGHTLY ARMORED, BUT EXTREMELY MANEUVERABLE.

Crew: *1 pilot*

Armament: *2x Heavy Plasma Cannon, Fuel Rod Bomb*

Missions: *Tip of the Spear, The Package*

Firefight: *Holdout*

The Banshee is an ultra-nimble, lightweight flying vehicle designed to offer support to ground troops engaged in combat. Its designers compensated for its lack of significant armor by giving the Banshee incredible speed and the ability to perform barrel rolls and 180-degree turns. The pilot's horizontal position within the craft further enhances the feeling that the Banshee is an extension of the pilot.

The Banshee automatically maintains some forward momentum whenever a pilot is on board. While this means that it's impossible to sit motionless behind cover, the benefit is that the Banshee can be flown at low altitude (and low speed) without the use of its boosters. Use the boosters to gain speed and altitude, then ease off the boosters to perform evasive maneuvers or to fire the Banshee's weapons. Additionally, it is possible to melee the Banshee's wings to cut them in half and gain access to inner hallways and spaces where the Banshee is not intended to be flown. This serves more of a comical purpose than strategic advantage, but it is possible.

The Banshee's weapons and boosters cannot be used concurrently. Fortunately, the Banshee can maintain forward momentum without losing too much altitude devoid of the boosters.

The Banshee is outfitted with twin Plasma Cannons that deliver more of a punch than their counterparts on the Ghost, but they can only be fired when boosters are not in use. These Plasma Cannons are useful against other Banshees and some infantry units. Tap Ⓨ to toggle the weapons system over to the far more potent Fuel Rod Bombs. Although slow in rate of fire and relatively difficult to aim at long range, the Fuel Rod Bomb is an excellent weapon against enemy vehicles and also delivers enough splash damage to be useful against groups of enemies on the ground.

ENEMY FORCES

WELCOME
UNSC TRAINING
THE CAMPAIGN
FIREFIGHT
MULTIPLAYER
REFERENCE
ORDNANCE
VEHICLES
ENEMY FORCES
CREDIT SYSTEM
THE ARMORY
SKULLS
ACHIEVEMENTS
DATA PADS

It wouldn't be *Halo* without the Covenant. The following pages cover each of the Covenant varieties you can expect to encounter while playing Campaign and Firefight modes. The amount of damage each enemy can absorb depends upon its rank and also the difficulty mode you're playing on. Unless noted otherwise, all attack plans and mentions of shots required reflect typical conditions on Heroic difficulty.

WEAPON USAGE TABLES

The Weapon Usage Tables outlined in this section for each species reflect general tendencies, but they are not hard and fast rules. Some enemy classes may appear with different weapons depending on the mission or mode you are playing.

Grunt Major

GRUNTS

(UNGGOY)

- HEIGHT: 5'2"

What they lack in brains and discipline, they make up for in viciousness and numbers. They are the first to panic when the local leadership is neutralized.

WEAPON USAGE BY RANK

Standard Weapon	Grunt Minor	Grunt Major	Grunt Ultra	Grunt Heavy	Grunt Spec Op
Plasma Pistol	X	X	X	X	X
Needler	X	X	—	—	—
Fuel Rod Gun	—	—	—	X	X

Grunts are the most plentiful of Covenant species, but they're also the easiest to kill. Grunts, regardless of their rank, can be defeated with a single shot to the head from any precision-class weapon such as the Magnum, DMR, Needle Rifle, or Sniper Rifle. They can also be defeated with a single melee or Assassination attack, plus they are extremely susceptible to grenades.

A lone Grunt rarely poses a significant threat, but their tendency to travel in packs mandates that you take them seriously. Always aim for the head, since their armor-clad torso and backpacks are capable of absorbing a surprising amount of damage. Stand back and line their faces up with the DMR or Magnum and string a quick kill streak together; however, don't hit the portion of their backpack that extends above their head, or else you'll waste ammo and drop your streak.

ON A ROCKET FULL OF STINK

A well-aimed bullet into the vent on either side of the Grunt's backpack ruptures the methane tank encased within. Piercing the Grunt's supply of methane not only instantly suffocates the Grunt, but the leaking gas also propels him skyward to great comical effect. Of course, with all this methane being released, Noble Six may well be the one needing a gas mask before long.

Most Grunts attack primarily with Plasma Pistols and Plasma Grenades—and boy, do they love to throw those Plasma Grenades! Always keep your distance when confronting more than one or two Grunts. Listen carefully for the hissing noise of a charged Plasma Pistol and quickly put a bullet in the dome of the Grunt winding up to throw it. The Plasma Grenade still detonates after falling to the ground, but at least it won't be stuck to your armor when it does so. Try to defeat the Grunts before they throw their Plasma Grenades so you can snatch them up after they harmlessly drop to the ground.

Other Grunts wield the more dangerous Needler, while others lug around the devastating Fuel Rod Gun. Always target the Grunt with the biggest weapon first. The darker colored Grunt Spec Ops are most likely to carry Fuel Rod Guns and only on Legendary mode in Campaign and during Firefight mode, particularly stepping out of a Drop Pod. Don't hesitate to use heavier weaponry, such as a Rocket Launcher or Frag Grenade, agains those carrying Fuel Rod Guns.

SUICIDAL TENDENCIES

Grunts are emotional creatures and become unstable when a higher-ranking Covenant creature has been defeated. It's not uncommon for some Grunts to flee the scene, but others might grab hold of two Plasma Grenades and charge forward on a suicide run. These "Suicide Grunts" are the most dangerous ones of all. Listen for their telltale cry of anguish and the hiss of their charged Plasma Grenades and quickly shoot them in the head to stop their progress. The grenades then fall to the ground and erupt, likely causing a chain reaction of explosions with other Plasma Grenades in the area. A skilled—and patient—player can snipe either of the Plasma Grenades in the Grunt's hand to detonate it mid stride, but this is a risky proposition.

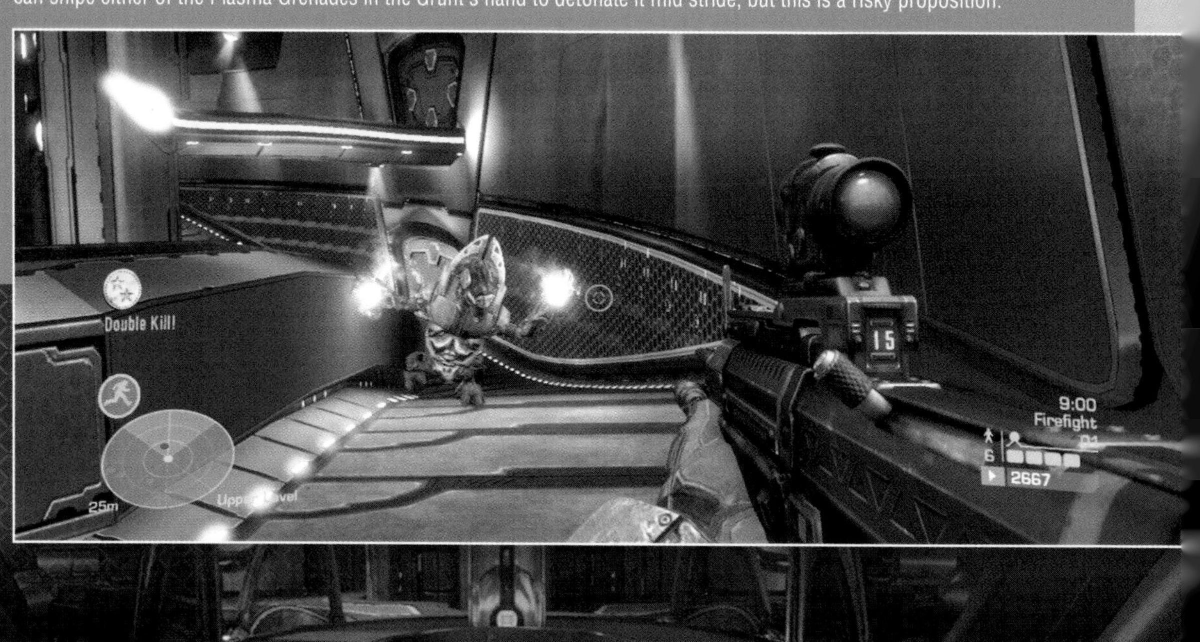

JACKALS

(KIG-YAR)

- HEIGHT: 6'8"

The Jackal Shield is considerably stronger than any other personal shield system, but that is only possible because of its linear configuration.

Jackal Major

WEAPON USAGE BY RANK

Standard Weapon	Jackal Minor	Jackal Major	Jackal Sniper
Plasma Pistol	X	X	—
Dual Wield Plasma Pistol w/Shield	X	X	—
Needle Rifle	—	—	X
Focus Rifle	—	—	X
Dual Wield Needler w/Shield	X	X	—

Jackals aren't any stronger than Grunts—a single shot to the head from precision weapons can kill them—but they are far more cunning than their pint-sized companions. Jackals, which often attack in groups of three, come in two distinct varieties: those with shields and those with long-range weapons, otherwise known as Jackal Snipers. Although some Jackals approach with just a Plasma Pistol or Needler, most dual-wield with a shield. All can be dispatched with a lone headshot, but targeting around the shield can be tricky if the Jackal is facing you head-on.

The Jackal's oversized energy shield can deflect most UNSC munitions, especially bullets from an Assault Rifle. Since the Jackal often crouches down behind the shield to protect its head, your best option is to target any exposed extremity. Use the DMR, Sniper Rifle, Magnum, or Needle Rifle to target the Jackal's foot or gun hand (exposed as it attempts to shoot through the curved embrasure on the side). The impact isn't lethal, but the Jackal will recoil in pain when hit and involuntarily lower its guard. Target its head for the kill.

SHOOT THE HAND TO EXPOSE THE HEAD

Jackals excel at taking cover behind their energy shields and seldom expose their head to enemy fire. Get around this by using the DMR or Magnum to target either their foot or their gun-hand, usually visible in the shield's small cut-out known as an embrasure. Shooting either of these extremities causes the Jackal to recoil in pain; shoot it in the head when it lowers its shield.

This "double-tap" strategy requires pinpoint aim and consumes twice the ammo necessary to kill an ordinary unshielded Jackal. Fortunately, there are other ways to take down these shielded Jackals. If possible, complement your DMR or Magnum with a plasma-based weapon. A single charged blast from the Plasma Pistol can cancel the shield and avail the Jackal's torso and head for traditional UNSC weapons attacks. The Plasma Repeater and Plasma Rifle can also be used in lieu of the Plasma Pistol. A Plasma Grenade can also cancel a Jackal's shield, but more likely it will just cause the Jackal to dive to the ground—both of which expose the Jackal's head to fire. Another option is to use a melee attack on the shield, then quickly blast the Jackal with the Shotgun at close range. Depending on your angle of attack and the shield's strength, one melee attack should knock the Jackal back and create an opening to attack. If not, melee a second time to create the opening.

While the size and color of the Jackal's shields typically reveal their location long before they are in firing range, the Jackal Snipers have no such handicap. These units forego the shield in favor of the two-handed Needle Rifle or Focus Rifle. It's not uncommon to suddenly be shot by a Jackal Sniper you weren't even aware of. This is especially true when playing Firefight mode on the Waterfront map, where Jackal Snipers line the distant cliffs and serve as an environmental hazard. Although dangerous, Jackal Snipers can be easily sniped with any of the precision-class weapons mentioned previously. Duck behind cover to escape their follow-up fire and carefully line up your crosshairs with their head to eliminate the threat.

Jackal Sniper

SNIPE THE SNIPERS FIRST

Never mind the fact that there are multiple enemies marching towards you; you must take out the Jackal Sniper first! A Jackal Sniper, particularly one with the Focus Rifle, can be very disruptive. Take it out before its attacks turn from a nuisance to lethal!

SKIRMISHERS

(KIG-YAR)

- HEIGHT: 6'9"

Although they are of the same species as the Jackals, and are deployed in much the same manner, these foes are much quicker and more agile than their smaller cousins.

Skirmisher Minor

WEAPON USAGE BY RANK

Standard Weapon	Skirmisher Minor	Skirmisher Major	Skirmisher Murmillones	Skirmisher Commando	Skirmisher Champion
Plasma Pistol	X	X	X	—	—
Dual Wield Plasma Pistol w/Shield	—	—	X	—	—
Needler	X	X	X	—	—
Needle Rifle	X	X	—	X	X
Focus Rifle	—	—	—	X	X

Skirmishers, a close relative to the Jackal, are noted for their incredible speed and leaping ability. They forgo the cumbersome energy shields and instead rely on their extreme athleticism to keep them safe from harm. Skirmishers move erratically—and swiftly—and are just as likely to attack from afar as they are to pounce towards their prey and strike their enemy directly.

MANY WAYS TO SKIN A SKIRMISHER

Skirmishers are much easier to eliminate before they go on the move—a single headshot from the DMR is all it takes. You'll need to adapt your approach once the Skirmishers start leaping. Draw them in close for a Shotgun kill, use the Needler's tracking ability to kill them with a supercombine attack, or even anticipate their landing and blast them with a heavy weapon.

Skirmishers pose a significant threat to Noble Team and should be targeted at once, especially if there are larger enemies in the area. As with their defensive-minded cousins, Skirmishers can be defeated with a single shot to the head from the DMR, Magnum, Sniper Rifle, or Needle Rifle. That is, if you can target them before they catch your scent and go on the prowl! The DMR is still a fine weapon to use against Skirmishers, even if they are running and leaping towards you, but the Shotgun and Assault Rifle work well in a pinch. Lure them around corners and blast them at close range with the Shotgun or open fire on their chest with the Assault Rifle. This isn't as clean and fast a kill as a headshot with the DMR, but it does work.

Skirmisher Champions have small energy shields strapped to their arms that they use to protect their heads and body while on the run. Plasma-based weaponry can deplete these shields, but it's seldom necessary. These Skirmishers wield long-range weapons and are more apt to maintain their distance. Stay in cover and wait for them to lower their guard. Use the DMR or other precision weapon and aim for their head.

Skirmisher Murmillones

DRONES

(YANME'E)

- HEIGHT: UNKNOWN

Essentially, these creatures are giant flying insects with guns. Keep your head on a swivel and remember that where you see one, there are bound to be more.

Drone Minor

WELCOME
UNSC TRAINING
THE CAMPAIGN
FIREFIGHT
MULTIPLAYER
REFERENCE
ORDNANCE
VEHICLES
ENEMY FORCES
CREDIT SYSTEM
THE ARMORY
SKULLS
ACHIEVEMENTS
DATA PADS

WEAPON USAGE BY RANK

Standard Weapon	Drone Minor	Drone Major	Drone Ultra
Plasma Pistol	X	X	X

Drones, also known as Buggers, possess the rare combination of traits that make them far more terrifying than their fragile frames should allow. When fighting a lone Bugger, it only takes a single blast to the head from a DMR or Needle Rifle to take it down and even less if the enemy is perched on the side of a wall or ceiling. However, the real problem lies in the fact that Buggers are rarely alone.

True to their insect form, Buggers swarm throughout their territory in an effort to protect their hive. They only appear in three instances during the Campaign mode and never in Firefight, but they leave a lasting imprint. Sadly, you can never scout the entrance to their hive or exterminate the Buggers with heavy ordnance before they disperse. Once airborne, Buggers fly in erratic patterns while blasting away with the Plasma Pistols they clutch in their tiny hands. Some charge the Plasma Pistol for a shield-depleting energy attack, while others opt for a more rapid-fire attack.

WAITING ON TIRED WINGS

Buggers won't fly around indefinitely, which is really too bad for them. Wait behind cover for one to land on the floor or wall, then step out and shoot it in the back. It only takes a single shot to the body from the DMR to kill a Bugger resting its wings. This is a great way to save ammo and it requires far less accuracy than shooting them out of the air. This is not a strategy to employ for anyone trying to sprint through the mission.

Drone Major

ENGINEERS

(HURAGOK)

- HEIGHT: UNKNOWN

They seem to be non-combatant, support "personnel," but they still represent a significant threat to the UNSC and should be dealt with appropriately.

WEAPON USAGE BY RANK

Support Ability	Engineer Minor
Overshields	X

Engineers are a rarely seen support creatures that float above the battlefield, lending support to the Covenant ground troops. Engineers emit a pulsing pink energy field that provides Overshielding to Covenant in the immediate vicinity. Engineers do not attack Spartans, but their effects on the Covenant make them a top priority target.

You can be sure an Engineer is in the area whenever you encounter a group of Covenant pulsating with a pinkish glow. Look for the passive creature with the crystalline top and long, tongue-like appendage floating above the Covenant. Engineers possess no weaponry and are without offensive capability, so there's no need to take cover; instead, open fire with your weapon of choice. A charged blast from the Plasma Pistol is ideal, as is the Plasma Cannon and Machine Gun Turret, but the DMR, Sniper Rifle, and Needle Rifle are also worth using if that's what you have. Fuel Rod Guns and Rocket Launchers certainly get the job done, but that level of ordnance is highly unnecessary.

A PINKISH HUE

Engineers are easy to overlook given the fact that they hover overhead and don't fire any weapons. Turn your attention skyward as soon as you spot Covenant basking in a pinkish glow. This is your cue that an Engineer is in the area! Scan the air roughly 20 feet off the ground to pinpoint its location—the enemies will all have Overshields (2x shielding) until you do!

ELITES

(SANGHEILI)

- HEIGHT: 7'10"

These creatures represent the leadership in any given group. In most cases, neutralizing the Elites makes the rest of the unit lose cohesion.

Elite Minor

WEAPON USAGE BY RANK

Standard Weapon	Elite Minor (blue)	Elite Officer (red)	Elite Ultra (white)	Elite Ranger (gray)	Elite Spec Op (black)	Elite General (gold)	Elite Zealot (Story Character)
Plasma Pistol	X	X	—	—	—	—	—
Dual Wield Plasma Rifle	—	X	X	X	X	—	X
Dual Wield Plasma Rifle w/Energy Sword	—	—	X	—	X	X	—
Needler	X	—	—	—	—	—	—
Plasma Repeater	—	X	X	X	—	—	—
Concussion Rifle	X	X	X	—	—	X	X
Needle Rifle	—	—	—	X	—	—	X
Focus Rifle	—	—	—	X	—	—	—
Plasma Turret (handheld)	—	—	—	—	—	X	—
Fuel Rod Gun	—	—	—	—	—	X	—
Plasma Launcher	—	—	—	—	—	X	—
Energy Sword	—	—	—	—	X	X	X

Elites are the most common of the tougher, heavily armed members of the Covenant army and represent, with few exceptions, the number one threat in any given encounter. The Elite species is comprised of six different ranks, ranging from the blue Elite Minors to the gold Elite Generals. The higher-ranking Elites not only tend to wield superior weaponry, but are also more resistant to damage, possess more advance battle instincts, and are more likely to use Armor Lock or Active Camouflage (shoot the Elite to disable its Active Camouflage effect). The more advanced Elites seldom appear on the lower difficulty settings, but are relatively common on Legendary mode and when playing co-op Campaign.

As the previous table illustrates, Elites are capable of wielding a variety of weapons. Of these, the Plasma Repeater (or Plasma Rifle) and Concussion Rifle are the most common. How you approach an Elite depends on the type of weapon he is carrying and also the difficulty mode on which you're playing. You can afford to take bigger chances on lower settings. It's typically best to keep your distance and use cover when engaging an Elite with Covenant small arms weapons (particularly the Concussion Rifle). On the other hand, it often pays to move in close and use a short-range weapon (or Plasma Grenades) against Elites wielding a Fuel Rod Gun or Plasma Launcher, as the Elites are too smart to fire a weapon with that amount of force at point-blank range. Elites are also skilled at lobbing Plasma Grenades, so always listen for the sound of a charging grenade.

Elite Ultra

Elite Officer

Elite Ranger

Elite General

There are as many ways to kill an Elite as there are weapons, but several tactics have proven useful above all others. For starters, it's important to understand that Elites have a shielding system much like Noble Six's and the shields must be depleted before the Elite will suffer any damage. Depending on the rank of the Elite and the difficulty mode, the Sniper Rifle is powerful enough to drop lower-ranking Elites with a single headshot. Higher-ranking Elites require two Sniper Rifle bullets: one to deplete the shields and a second to make the kill. The standard number of shots using the less-powerful DMR and Magnum is four shots to the body to deplete the shields, then one to the head to deliver the kill. Elites throw their arms in the air and roar in anger after losing their shields—wait a moment for this reaction to end before shooting.

Elite Spec Op

PLASMA TO THE BODY, BULLETS TO THE HEAD

The ultimate one-two punch for dealing with Elites is to use a charged Plasma Pistol to quickly drain the shields, then switch to the DMR or Magnum and shoot the Elite right in the head. Once the Elite's shields have been depleted, it only takes a single round to the head to kill it with a precision weapon or a blast to the body with the Shotgun. The Assault Rifle can get the job done too, but it still requires half a clip to accomplish the task.

UNSC weapons, like the DMR, aren't well suited against shielded enemies, so it pays to have the Plasma Pistol, Plasma Repeater, or Plasma Rifle on hand to complement the traditional human weaponry. These plasma-based weapons can rapidly deplete an Elite's shielding (the Plasma Pistol can accomplish the feat with a single charged shot) and save time and ammo. Drain the shield with the Covenant weapon, then switch to the Magnum or DMR and shoot the Elite in the head to kill it. Lower level Elites can also be killed with a single grenade attack, or direct hit from the Grenade Launcher. Rocket Launchers also inflict fatal damage.

One of the challenges in fighting Elites is their tremendous athleticism. They not only run fast and are skilled at dodging attacks, but they can use martial arts attacks to deliver melee damage. They can even sneak up from behind and Assassinate you. Tracking weapons, such as the Needler and Plasma Launcher, are helpful against the acrobatic Elites and eliminate your need for precision aiming, but higher ranking Elites can and do use Armor Lock to avoid being stuck with Plasma Grenades and Needles. They'll even trigger Armor Lock in between the second and third shots from a Needle Rifle, thus eliminating any chance of hitting them with a super-combine attack.

BASH, STRAFE, KILL

One of the most efficient ways of killing Elites is to drain the Elite's shields with a melee strike, then quickly strafe around to the back of the Elite and Assassinate it. This works particularly well when playing Campaign on Heroic mode and during Firefight missions. A single melee strike depletes the shield, and you can use the time during which the Elite is roaring to move around behind it and deliver the fatal attack.

BRUTES

Brute Minor

(JIRALHANAE)

- HEIGHT: UNKNOWN

Aggressive and prone to shocking acts of violence, these creatures are easily provoked into foolhardy acts of bravado. Whether or not this is advisable is another matter.

WEAPON USAGE BY RANK

Standard Weapon	Brute Minor	Brute Captain	Brute Chieftain Armor	Brute Chieftain Weapon
Spike Rifle	X	X	—	—
Gravity Hammer	—	X	X	—
Fuel Rod Gun	—	—	—	X
Plasma Turret (handheld)	—	—	—	X
Plasma Repeater	X	X	—	—
Elite Shot	—	X	—	—
Plasma Launcher	—	—	—	X

Brutes are another proud species of Covenant that also boasts a structured hierarchy and serves as leaders to the weaker species. As such, Brutes are often seen as being in competition with the Elites and, as such, are never encountered together. Brutes are larger, hulking creatures that move with surprising speed and are considered to be the most aggressive of the Covenant species. Added to this is the fact that they seldom attack alone; Brutes are commonly found in groups of three to five and often led by a Brute Captain or Brute Chieftain.

TAKE YOUR HAT OFF, BRUTE!

Continue to shoot a Brute in the head with the DMR, Magnum, or Needle Rifle until its hat falls off. This is your cue that it only takes one more signal that he's ready to go. Pop one more round in his cap to finish the job. Use this technique to help track which enemy is closest to dying when there are numerous Brutes in the area.

Brutes are very well armored, so don't take them lightly. Even those Brutes wielding just a Plasma Repeater or Spike Rifle are also capable of using Armor Lock and throwing Plasma Grenades. Brutes also favor close-range combat and gradually advance towards your position throughout the fight in hopes of performing a melee attack at close range. This is particularly true of those wielding the bladed Spike Rifle weapons.

Every variety of Brute can withstand an inordinate amount of body damage, even the relatively unarmored Brute Minors. Going up against one of these foes with an Assault Rifle is a surefire way to run out of ammo. Shotguns are an effective way to kill Brutes, but there is a safer way. Stay out of range of their melee attack and use the DMR or another precision weapon to target their head. They'll often stumble backwards or even turn 90 degrees upon being shot (depending on the angle at which they were shot), so don't fire a follow-up shot too quickly. The Brute's helmet falls once it is ready to go—shoot it one more time in the head to finish it off. Brute Minors can be taken down with three DMR headshots, while Brute Captains require four (on Heroic difficulty). The Needler and Needle Rifle are also good to use against Brutes, particularly the former, thanks to its tracking ability.

Brute Major

WELCOME
UNSC TRAINING
THE CAMPAIGN
FIREFIGHT
MULTIPLAYER
REFERENCE
ORDNANCE
VEHICLES
ENEMY FORCES
CREDIT SYSTEM
THE ARMORY
SKULLS
ACHIEVEMENTS
DATA PADS

BRUTE CHIEFTAINS

Brute Chieftains are among the most intimidating of all enemies and deserve special mention, as they share little in common with Brute Minors and Captains. Brute Chieftains carry only the most impressive Covenant weapons and charge into battle unlike any other species. Make no mistake, these Brutes will hunt you down with a reckless ferocity no other species can match.

Brute Chieftan

The armor-clad Brute Chieftains possess an impressive power armor that can absorb lost of damage, even to the head from the DMR. For example, it takes eight headshots with the DMR to deplete a Brute Chieftain's power armor on Heroic mode, and an additional five headshots to kill it. Similarly, it takes two full magazines from the Assault Rifle to kill a Brute Chieftain. Clearly, there has to be a better way...

BEWARE THE GRAVITY HAMMER

Brute Chieftains wielding Gravity Hammers will stop at nothing to get close enough to attack. Not only is the reach of the Gravity Hammer far greater than expected, but the area of effect damage is also considerable. The Needler is the only small arms weapon that you can use to quickly down the beast. Unless you have one handy, you must turn to heavy weapons or a pair of well-thrown Plasma Grenades. Of course, once you down one of these beasts, you can always use the Gravity Hammer it drops!

The Needler is effective against Brute Chieftains, provided you have enough ammo to super-combine on the enemy twice. The same applies to using Plasma Grenades—one for the shields, another to kill. Heavier weapons such as the Fuel Rod Gun, Grenade Launcher, and Rocket Launcher are also effective. Brute Chieftains require three direct hits with the Grenade Launcher on auto-det mode to be killed, but it's possible to manually detonate a grenade near it to EMP the beast, then move in for the Assassination or for a point-blank Shotgun kill. The Rocket Launcher is the only weapon that can kill a Brute Chieftain with a single attack, as even the Spartan Laser can't deplete the shields and kill the Brute Chieftain with a single strike.

HUNTERS

(LEKGOLO)

- HEIGHT: UNKNOWN

The most heavily armed and armored of the Covenant infantry, these aliens are always deployed in pairs. This tends to compensate for their relative lack of speed and maneuverability.

WEAPON USAGE BY RANK

Standard Weapon	Hunter Minor
Fuel Rod Gun (shot)	X
Focus Rifle (shot)	X

Hunters are unlike any other creature in that they are so heavily armored that they sustain very little damage unless you target their two weak points. These lumbering beasts are armored head to toe (and carry a massive shield), save for a small patch on their neck and their lower back. Expert marksmen can use the Sniper Rifle or DMR (or even the Needle Rifle to supercombine) and target either of these pink patches of telepathic eels that comprise the beast's skin. Hunters are hyper aware of their vulnerabilities and tend to turn and use their shield to prevent anyone from targeting their exposed flesh. They'll increase the difficulty of defeating them at range by repeatedly attacking with their massive arm-cannons.

You can create a much larger target by blasting away the armor on their back. This can be done with a Rocket Launcher or by throwing/firing Frag Grenades or Plasma Grenades at the Hunter's back. Use a Hologram to distract the Hunter and then target its back. You'll find it much easier to defeat the Hunter from afar once the entirety of its back has been exposed.

A LITTLE OFF THE BACK

The patch of telepathic eels that comprises the Hunter's skin can be pretty tough to hit once the Hunter knows your whereabouts. If sniping is proving too problematic, move in closer and lob some grenades at the beast's back to knock its armor off. This gives you a much cleaner shot at its weakest point.

There is still another method of dealing with the Hunters, particularly for those armed with just a Shotgun or Assault Rifle. Run and jump towards the Hunter to bait it into attacking with melee strikes instead of its weapons. The Hunter values the weapon on its right arm and will always lunge attack by swinging the heavy shield in its left hand. Strafe left to avoid the shield as it crashes down, then move in behind the Hunter and open fire. The Shotgun can knock the Hunter's armor off with just one or two blasts, and it should only take one or two more to deliver the fatal blow, depending on the difficulty.

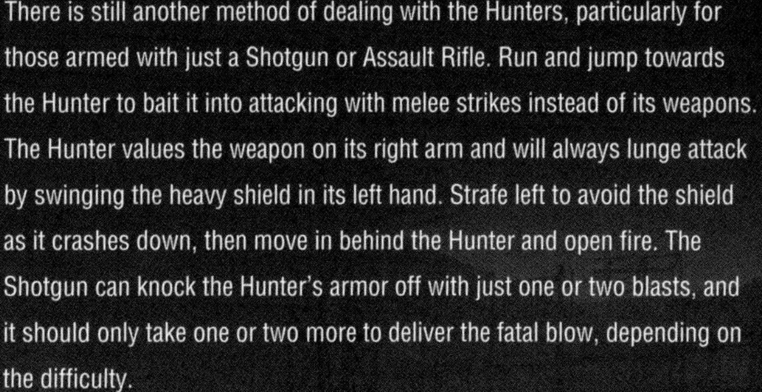

WELCOME
UNSC TRAINING
THE CAMPAIGN
FIREFIGHT
MULTIPLAYER
REFERENCE
ORDNANCE
VEHICLES
ENEMY FORCES
CREDIT SYSTEM
THE ARMORY
SKULLS
ACHIEVEMENTS
DATA PADS

CREDITS, COMMENDATIONS, AND MEDALS

Halo: Reach contains a multi-faceted player reward and incentive system that is guaranteed to keep any fan playing for a long, long time. The following pages detail all the ways you can earn Credits, Rank promotions, Medals, and Commendations.

CREDIT SYSTEM

Just about every action you make throughout your time on Reach is tracked behind the scenes, as a way of measuring your performance and advancing you towards a promotion. There are roughly 15 different ways in each of the Campaign, Firefight, and Multiplayer Matchmaking modes that can earn you what are known as Credits (cR). Credits are different than points and share no relation to the score you may obtain in Firefight or in a Campaign mission with scoring turned on. And, even though many of the actions that trigger Medals also earn Credits, you can also earn many Medals that yield no benefit to your Credit total, and vice-versa. Credits are a measure of your excellence in combat and accumulate across all gameplay modes. They continue to grow for as long as you play *Halo: Reach* (provided you don't start a separate Gamer Profile). In effect, you earn Credits every time you turn the game on, provided you stick around to see the post-game carnage report.

Earning a pile of Credits after a match tends to even make the sour taste of defeat a little bit sweeter.

You'll learn why Credits are important as you read on, but first, you should be familiar with each of the ways that you can earn Credits. The following tables detail each of the actions that earn you Credits for each gameplay mode. You can see in the tables that Credits are awarded for actions ranging from something as minor as killing an Infantry class enemy (2 cR) to much more difficult actions like clearing a Campaign mission without dying on Heroic difficulty (150 cR). In effect, there are only two ways you can play *Halo: Reach* and not earn any Credits: one is by quitting before the game ends (in which case you deserve the full wrath of an unmerciful Banhammer!), and the other is by cowering in a corner refusing to fight. The amount of Credits you earn varies greatly based on skill and gameplay preferences, but you'll earn more Credits the more you play. The better you get at playing, the more your actions will compound to yield greater and greater numbers of Credits.

CAMPAIGN MODE: EARNING CREDITS

Action	Credits per Incident
Earn a headshot.	3
Earn any multikill.	6
Earn any spree.	6
Earn an assist.	5
Kill a foe with an automatic weapon.	2
Kill a foe with a small arms weapon.	2
Kill a foe with an ordnance weapon.	2
Kill a foe with a vehicle.	2
Kill a foe with grenades.	2
Clear a mission.	50
Clear a mission without dying (Heroic or Legendary).	150
Kill a Leader unit.	5
Kill an Infantry unit.	2
Kill a Specialist unit.	3
Destroy an enemy vehicle.	4
Kill a foe with a precision weapon.	2

FIREFIGHT MODE: EARNING CREDITS

Action	Credits per Incident
Earn a headshot.	3
Earn any multikill.	5
Earn any spree.	5
Earn an assist.	4
Kill a foe with an automatic weapon.	2
Kill a foe with a small arms weapon.	2
Kill a foe with an ordnance weapon.	2
Kill a foe with a vehicle.	2
Kill a foe with grenades.	2
Clear a Round without dying.	10
Kill a Leader unit.	4
Kill an Infantry unit.	2
Kill a Specialist unit.	3
Destroy an enemy vehicle.	8
Kill a foe with a precision weapon.	2

MULTIPLAYER MODE: EARNING CREDITS

Action	Credits per Incident
Earn a headshot.	7
Earn any multikill.	10
Earn any spree.	10
Earn an assist.	6
Drive a vehicle while passengers kill opponents.	6
Kill an opponent with an automatic weapon.	4
Kill an opponent with a small arms weapon.	4
Kill an opponent with an ordnance weapon.	4
Kill an opponent with a vehicle.	4
Kill an opponent with grenades.	4
Kill an opponent with a precision weapon.	4
Assassinate an opponent with an elaborate kill.	8
Perform any specialty kill: Bulltrue, Revenge, Hijack, Skyjack, Killjoy, Kill from the Grave, First Strike, Close Call, Sprinting Kill, Pull Kill, Extermination, Showstopper, EMP Assist, Yoink, Avenger, or Protector.	7
Perform a close quarters kill: Bulltrue, Melee Kill, Assassination, Hammer Kill, Sword Kill, or Shotgun Kill.	6

PLAYER RANKS AND INSIGNIA

Now that you understand what Credits are, it's time to tell you what they're used for. Credits do two things: 1) they earn you Rank promotions, and 2) they are used as currency to purchase customization items in The Armory. You can find a full listing of the myriad ways you can customize your Spartan armor in the Reference chapter titled "The Armory," but first, let's discuss Player Ranks. In short, your Player Rank is a quick-glance indicator that reflects how much skill you have, and more importantly, how much time you've played *Halo: Reach*. This may not matter to you on a personal level, but it's useful when playing in Matchmaking, since it gives a general indication of your abilities to other players, and vice-versa. Though the Matchmaking system does an outstanding job of pairing players based on their TruSkill rating (which goes up and down with performance), the rank insignia that accompanies a player's Gamertag and Service Tag in the Lobby helps players know right away the general experience level of those they're playing with.

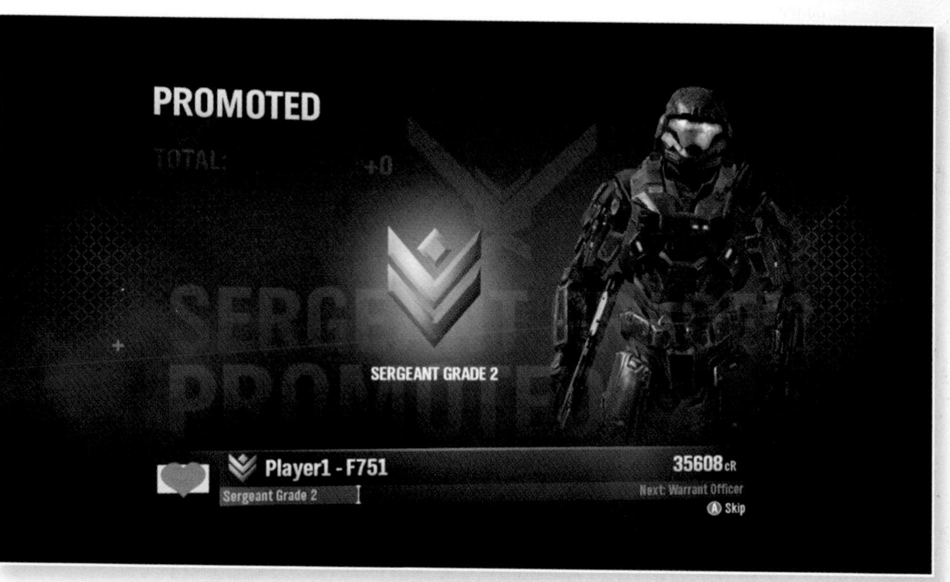

Don't keep your new promotion to yourself. Always be sure to thank everyone who spent the previous match catching your bullets!

Everyone who signs on with a Gamer Profile automatically receives 5000 cR and a promotion from Recruit to Private. Exciting as it is, don't get used to it—you won't get another promotion that quickly again. In fact, the further you climb up the Ranks, the longer and longer it takes to achieve your subsequent promotion. For example, the amount of Credits required for a promotion from Commander Grade 3 to Colonel is more than the total number of Credits for your first eight promotions. And that's just the tip of the iceberg! Only the most dedicated players can ever ascend beyond the ranks of General, but do know that with every Covenant you kill on the battlefield, you take one step closer to your next promotion.

PLAYER RANK PROGRESSION

Insignia	Player Rank	Grade	Credit Milestone (cumulative)	Credits to Next Promotion
	Recruit	-	0	-
	Private	-	5000	5000 (automatic)
	Corporal	-	7500	2500
	Corporal	1	10,000	2500
	Sergeant	-	15,000	5000
	Sergeant	1	20,000	5000
	Sergeant	2	26,250	6250
	Warrant Officer	-	32,500	6250
	Warrant Officer	1	45,000	12,500
	Warrant Officer	2	78,000	33,000
	Warrant Officer	3	111,000	33,000
	Captain	-	210,000	99,000
	Captain	1	233,000	23,000
	Captain	2	256,000	23,000
	Captain	3	279,000	23,000
	Major	-	325,000	46,000
	Major	1	350,000	25,000
	Major	2	375,000	25,000
	Major	3	400,000	25,000
	Lt. Colonel	-	450,000	50,000
	Lt. Colonel	1	480,000	30,000
	Lt. Colonel	2	510,000	30,000
	Lt. Colonel	3	540,000	30,000

COMMENDATIONS

Commendations work hand-in-hand with Credits and the actions that earn them. Every action that earns Credits is linked to a specific Commendation in each of the Campaign, Firefight, and Multiplayer modes. Performing actions not only earns Credits on the spot, but every incident is tracked, and bonus Credits are awarded for reaching various grades of Commendation (Steel, Bronze, Silver, Gold, and Onyx). Commendations not only dish out Credit bonuses, but their varied requirements are designed to reward players who spend time in any gameplay type. Each type of action has a maximum number of incidents that can be accumulated in any one gameplay mode, after which point you stop receiving Credits for that action.

For example, although players receive Credits for a headshot in all three gameplay modes, each of these is tracked separately. Headshots in the Campaign, Firefight, and Multiplayer modes are tracked by the Pinpoint, Dome Inspector, and One Shot Commendations, respectively. You can earn Credits for completing a total of 60,000 headshots, but only 20,000 in each of the three modes. A player who manages to accumulate 20,000 headshots in Firefight, for example, can no longer receive Credits for headshots in that mode, but may still earn headshot Credits in Campaign and Multiplayer.

Commendations unlock in real-time as you're playing the game and appear as a notification on-screen when the next level has been reached. Look for a health Credit bonus after the match.

CAMPAIGN COMMENDATION REQUIREMENTS

CAMPAIGN COMMENDATION REQUIREMENTS

Name	Steel	Steel Bonus	Bronze	Bronze Bonus	Silver	Silver Bonus	Gold	Gold Bonus	Onyx	Onyx Bonus	Max
Pinpoint	50	100 cR	250	750 cR	500	1000 cR	4000	2000 cR	8000	2000 cR	20,000
Walking Tank	25	200 cR	175	700 cR	500	1500 cR	2000	2000 cR	5000	2000 cR	9000
Super Soldier	25	200 cR	175	700 cR	500	1500 cR	2000	2000 cR	5000	2000 cR	9000
Support Role	100	200 cR	375	500 cR	750	1000 cR	1500	1500 cR	3000	1500 cR	6000
Standard Issue	250	500 cR	750	750 cR	3000	1000 cR	6000	3000 cR	10,000	3000 cR	15,000
Small Arms	250	250 cR	750	375 cR	3000	750 cR	6000	1250 cR	10,000	1250 cR	16,000
Splash Damage	100	200 cR	375	750 cR	750	1500 cR	1500	2000 cR	3000	2000 cR	6000
War Machine	200	250 cR	500	700 cR	800	1400 cR	3200	2000 cR	6400	2000 cR	14,000
Nice Arm	50	200 cR	250	750 cR	500	1000 cR	4000	2000 cR	8000	2000 cR	13,000
Demon	9	400 cR	18	400 cR	81	400 cR	135	400 cR	270	400 cR	540
Flawless Cowboy	5	450 cR	10	450 cR	25	900 cR	50	1500 cR	150	2000 cR	300
Leadership Element	100	400 cR	375	750 cR	750	1250 cR	3000	2500 cR	6000	2500 cR	10,000

Name	Steel	Steel Bonus	Bronze	Bronze Bonus	Silver	Silver Bonus	Gold	Gold Bonus	Onyx	Onyx Bonus	Max
Cannon Fodder	250	200 cR	750	600 cR	3000	1200 cR	7000	2400 cR	12,000	2400 cR	20,000
Specialist Kill	175	200 cR	525	600 cR	2100	1200 cR	6000	2400 cR	10,000	2400 cR	14,000
Right of Way	50	250 cR	200	400 cR	1000	800 cR	2400	1600 cR	4800	1600 cR	7200
Precisely	250	500 cR	750	750 cR	4000	1000 cR	10,000	3000 cR	20,000	3000 cR	32,000

- **Pinpoint:** Kill an enemy with a headshot. Must use a headshot weapon (Magnum, DMR, Needle Rifle, or Sniper Rifle), and the headshot must be the killing shot. *3 cR per incident.*
- **Walking Tank:** This Commendation increases with any multikill event, irrelevant of which kill in the multikill chain, weapon used, etc. If a player gets a Killtacular (5x kills), he or she should get 4 increments in his or her multikill Commendation. To get a multikill, you must kill opponents within 1.5 seconds of each other. *6 cR per incident.*
- **Super Soldier:** This Commendation increases with any spree event, which includes all generic kill sprees and also weapon-specific sprees (Hammer Spree, Sword Spree, etc.) and event sprees (Assist Spree). To get a spree, the player must stay alive and rack up consecutive kills. *6 cR per incident.*
- **Support Role:** To get an assist, the player must directly take off at least 40% of the target's shields/health, and the target player must die before the shields recharge. If the shields recharge or if the attacker takes off <40%, then the player will not be awarded the assist, and the Commendation will not be increased. *5 cR per incident.*
- **Standard Issue:** Player must kill enemies using weapons that are classified as automatic weapons (Assault Rifle, Needler, Plasma Repeater, Plasma Rifle, and Sniper Rifle). The weapon must be used to deliver the killing blow to increment this Commendation. *2 cR per incident.*
- **Small Arms:** Player must kill enemies using weapons that are classified as small arms (Magnum or Plasma Pistol). Weapons must be used to deliver the killing blow to increment this Commendation. *2 cR per incident.*
- **Ordnance:** Player must kill enemies using weapons classified as ordnance (Rocket Launcher, Grenade Launcher, Spartan Laser, Plasma Launcher, Fuel Rod Gun, and Target Locator). Weapon must be used to deliver the killing blow to increment this Commendation. *2 cR per incident.*
- **War Machine:** Kill a foe with vehicle velocity (splatter) or a vehicle-mounted weapon. Players who get kills with standard weapons in passenger seats do not get credit for this Commendation. *2 cR per incident.*
- **Nice Arm:** Kill a foe with grenades. Both Plasma Sticks and area-of-effect damage count for this Commendation. *2 cR per incident.*
- **Demon:** Player clears a mission on any difficulty except Easy. *50 cR per incident.*
- **Flawless Cowboy:** Player clears a mission on Heroic or Legendary mode without dying. *150 cR per incident.*
- **Leadership Element:** Kill a Leader class enemy (e.g., Elite Leader). 5 *cR per incident.*
- **Cannon Fodder:** Kill an Infantry class enemy (e.g., Grunt Infantry). 2 *cR per incident.*
- **Specialist Kill:** Kill a Specialist class enemy (e.g., Elite Specialist). 3 *cR per incident.*
- **Right of Way:** Destroy an enemy vehicle that is currently occupied by active enemy A.I. Standard breakable turrets count for this Commendation (e.g., Wraiths). 4 *cR per incident.*
- **Precisely:** Player must kill enemies using weapons that are classified as precision class (DMR, Needle Rifle, and Sniper Rifle). Weapon must be used to deliver the killing blow to increment this Commendation. 2 *cR per incident.*

FIREFIGHT COMMENDATION REQUIREMENTS

FIREFIGHT COMMENDATION REQUIREMENTS

Name	Steel	Steel Bonus	Bronze	Bronze Bonus	Silver	Silver Bonus	Gold	Gold Bonus	Onyx	Onyx Bonus	Max
Dome Inspector	50	150 cR	250	425 cR	500	1000 cR	4000	2400 cR	8000	2400 cR	20,000
Numbers Game	25	200 cR	175	700 cR	500	1500 cR	2500	2000 cR	2500	2000 cR	15,000
Methodical	25	200 cR	175	700 cR	500	1500 cR	2500	2000 cR	5000	2000 cR	10,000
Backup	50	300 cR	250	750 cR	750	1500 cR	1500	2400 cR	3000	2400 cR	8000
Riflin' Through	250	500 cR	750	750 cR	3000	1000 cR	10,000	2000 cR	20,000	2000 cR	32,000
Trigger Happy	250	500 cR	750	750 cR	3000	1500 cR	6000	2000 cR	10,000	2000 cR	16,000
Get Loud	100	200 cR	375	750 cR	750	1500 cR	2000	2000 cR	4000	2000 cR	8000
Vehicular	200	250 cR	500	700 cR	800	1400 cR	3200	2000 cR	6400	2000 cR	14,000
Pull the Pin	50	200 cR	250	750 cR	500	1000 cR	3000	2000 cR	5000	2000 cR	9000
Perfectionist	50	250 cR	250	1250 cR	500	2000 cR	2000	2000 cR	5000	2000 cR	8000
In Command	75	200 cR	375	750 cR	750	1250 cR	3000	2500 cR	6000	2500 cR	10,000
Target Practice	250	200 cR	750	600 cR	3000	2000 cR	7000	2400 cR	12,000	2400 cR	20,000
Specialized	175	200 cR	525	600 cR	2000	1200 cR	6000	2400 cR	10,000	2400 cR	14,000
Grounded	50	250 cR	200	400 cR	400	800 cR	2500	1600 cR	6000	1600 cR	12,000
Longshot	250	500 cR	750	750 cR	4000	1000 cR	10,000	3000 cR	20,000	3000 cR	32,000

- **Dome Inspector:** Kill an enemy with a headshot. Must use a headshot weapon (Magnum, DMR, Needle Rifle, or Sniper Rifle), and the headshot must be the killing shot. *3 cR per incident.*
- **Numbers Game:** This Commendation increases with any multikill event, irrelevant of which kill in the multikill chain, weapon used, etc. If a player gets a Killtacular (5x kills), he or she should get 4 increments in his or her multikill Commendation. To get a multikill, you must kill opponents within 1.5 seconds of each other. *5 cR per incident.*
- **Methodical:** This Commendation increases with any spree event, which includes all generic kill sprees and also weapon-specific sprees (Hammer Spree, Sword Spree, etc.) and event sprees (Assist Spree). To get a spree, the player must stay alive and rack up consecutive kills. *5 cR per incident.*
- **Backup**: To get an assist, the player must directly take off at least 40% of the target's shields/health, and the target player must die before the shields recharge. If the shields recharge or if the attacker takes off <40%, then the player will not be awarded the assist, and the Commendation will not be increased. *4 cR per incident.*
- **Riflin' Through:** Player must kill enemies using weapons that are classified as automatic weapons (Assault Rifle, Needler, Plasma Repeater, Plasma Rifle, and Sniper Rifle). The weapon must be used to deliver the killing blow to increment this Commendation. *2 cR per incident.*
- **Trigger Happy:** Player must kill enemies using weapons that are classified as small arms (Magnum or Plasma Pistol). Weapons must be used to deliver the killing blow to increment this Commendation. *2 cR per incident.*
- **Get Loud:** Player must kill enemies using weapons classified as ordnance (Rocket Launcher, Grenade Launcher, Spartan Laser, Plasma Launcher, Fuel Rod Gun, and Target Locator). Weapon must be used to deliver the killing blow to increment this Commendation. *2 cR per incident.*
- **Vehicular:** Kill a foe with vehicle velocity (splatter) or a vehicle-mounted weapon. Players who get kills with standard weapons in passenger seats do not get credit for this Commendation. *2 cR per incident.*
- **Pull the Pin:** Kill a foe with grenades. Both Plasma Sticks and area-of-effect damage count for this Commendation. *2 cR per incident.*
- **Perfectionist:** Player clears a round of Firefight on any difficulty without dying. *10 cR per incident.*
- **In Command:** Kill a Leader class enemy (e.g., Elite Leader). 4 *cR per incident.*
- **Target Practice:** Kill an Infantry class enemy (e.g., Grunt Infantry). 2 *cR per incident.*
- **Specialized:** Kill a Specialist class enemy (e.g., Elite Specialist). 3 *cR per incident.*
- **Grounded:** Destroy an enemy vehicle that is currently occupied by active enemy A.I. Standard breakable turrets count for this Commendation (e.g., Wraiths). 8 *cR per incident.*
- **Longshot:** Player must kill enemies using weapons that are classified as precision class (DMR, Needle Rifle, and Sniper Rifle). Weapon must be used to deliver the killing blow to increment this Commendation. 2 *cR per incident.*

MULTIPLAYER COMMENDATIONS

MULTIPLAYER COMMENDATION REQUIREMENTS

Name	Steel	Steel Bonus	Bronze	Bronze Bonus	Silver	Silver Bonus	Gold	Gold Bonus	Onyx	Onyx Bonus	Max
One Shot	50	150 cR	250	425 cR	1000	1200 cR	4000	2400 cR	8000	2400 cR	20,000
Multikill	10	250 cR	125	450 cR	500	875 cR	2500	1400 cR	5000	1400 cR	15,000
Any Spree	5	250 cR	50	750 cR	250	1500 cR	1000	2000 cR	4000	2000 cR	10,000
Assistant	50	150 cR	250	425 cR	1000	1200 cR	4000	2400 cR	8000	2400 cR	20,000
Designated Driver	5	100 cR	50	250 cR	750	875 cR	4000	1200 cR	8000	1200 cR	20,000
Trigger Man	100	300 cR	500	1000 cR	4000	2000 cR	10,000	3000 cR	20,000	3000 cR	32,000
Trigger Happy	50	100 cR	250	200 cR	1000	500 cR	4000	750 cR	8000	750 cR	16,000
Sidearm	25	100 cR	150	200 cR	750	500 cR	3000	750 cR	7000	750 cR	14,000
Mobile Asset	25	100 cR	125	200 cR	500	500 cR	4000	750 cR	8000	750 cR	14,000
Grenadier	25	100 cR	125	200 cR	500	500 cR	4000	750 cR	8000	750 cR	14,000
Crack Shot	100	300 cR	500	1000 cR	4000	2000 cR	10,000	3000 cR	20,000	3000 cR	32,000
Rear Admiral	5	300 cR	25	500 cR	100	750 cR	1000	1000 cR	4000	1000 cR	8000
Of All Trades	50	150 cR	125	375 cR	400	1000 cR	1600	1600 cR	4800	1600 cR	9600
Close Quarters	50	150 cR	125	375 cR	400	1200 cR	1600	2400 cR	4000	2400 cR	8000

- **One Shot:** Kill an enemy with a headshot. Must use a headshot weapon (Magnum, DMR, Needle Rifle, or Sniper Rifle), and the headshot must be the killing shot. *7 cR per incident.*
- **Multikill:** This Commendation increases with any multikill event, irrelevant of which kill in the multikill chain, weapon used, etc. If a player gets a Killtacular (5x kills), he or she should get 4 increments in his or her multikill Commendation. To get a multikill, you must kill opponents within 1.5 seconds of each other. *10 cR per incident.*
- **Any Spree:** This Commendation increases with any spree event, which includes all generic kill sprees and also weapon-specific sprees (Hammer Spree, Sword Spree, etc.) and event sprees (Assist Spree). To get a spree, the player must stay alive and rack up consecutive kills. *10 cR per incident.*
- **Assistant**: To get an assist, the player must directly take off at least 40% of the target's shields/health, and the target player must die before the shields recharge. If the shields recharge or if the attacker takes off <40%, then the player will not be awarded the assist, and the Commendation will not be increased. *6 cR per incident.*
- **Designated Driver:** The player must be the driver of any vehicle that has a turret that can be controlled by another player. Only vehicle weapons kills count for this Commendation. Players killing enemies via personal weapons or throwing grenades from the passenger seat does not count towards this Commendation. *6 cR per incident.*
- **Trigger Man:** Player must kill opponents using weapons that are classified as automatic weapons (Assault Rifle, Needler, Plasma Repeater, and Plasma Rifle). The weapon must be used to deliver the killing blow to increment this Commendation. *4 cR per incident.*
- **Sidearm:** Player must kill enemies using weapons that are classified as small arms (Magnum or Plasma Pistol). Weapons must be used to deliver the killing blow to increment this Commendation. *4 cR per incident.*
- **Heavy Weapon:** Player must kill opponents using weapons classified as ordnance (Rocket Launcher, Grenade Launcher, Spartan Laser, Plasma Launcher, Fuel Rod Gun, and Target Locator). Weapon must be used to deliver the killing blow to increment this Commendation. *4 cR per incident.*
- **Mobile Asset:** Kill an opponent with vehicle velocity (splatter) or a vehicle-mounted weapon. Players who get kills with standard weapons in passenger seats do not get credit for this Commendation. *4 cR per incident.*
- **Grenadier:** Kill a foe with grenades. Both Plasma Sticks and area-of-effect damage count for this Commendation. *4 cR per incident.*
- **Crack Shot:** Player must kill opponents using weapons that are classified as precision class (DMR, Needle Rifle, and Sniper Rifle). Weapon must be used to deliver the killing blow to increment this Commendation. 4 *cR per incident.*
- **Rear Admiral:** Kill an opponent with an Assassination move. Player must complete the third-person animated finishing move to increment this Commendation. *10 cR per incident.*
- **Of All Trades:** For the true multiplayer heroes… Trigger the following actions or specialty skills to increment this Commendation: Bulltrue, Revenge, Highjack, Skyjack, Killjoy, Kill from the Grave, First Blood, Close Call, Opportunist, Sprinting Kill, Pull Kill, Extermination, Showstopper, EMP Assist, Yoink, Second Wind, Avenger, or Life Saver. Consult the table of Medals in this chapter for details. *7 cR per incident.*
- **Close Quarters:** Get a kill that is classified as close quarters (Bulltrue, Melee Kill, Assassination, Finishing Move, Hammer Kill, Sword Kill, or Shotgun Kill). Consult the table of Medals in this chapter for details. 6 *cR per incident.*

WELCOME
UNSC TRAINING
THE CAMPAIGN
FIREFIGHT
MULTIPLAYER
REFERENCE
ORDNANCE
VEHICLES
ENEMY FORCES
CREDITS
THE ARMORY
SKULLS
ACHIEVEMENTS
DATA PADS

MEDALS

Medals are the instant-gratification element of the player reward system. They appear on the screen immediately (in Campaign, only if scoring is turned on), and if the feat is impressive, the announcer also acknowledges your greatness. Medals by themselves don't impact your Credit total, your Rank, or help earn you any Commendations. You can view all of the Medals you earned in the post-game carnage report and even track your collection online at Bungie.net, but they are primarily used for bragging rights... but not entirely.

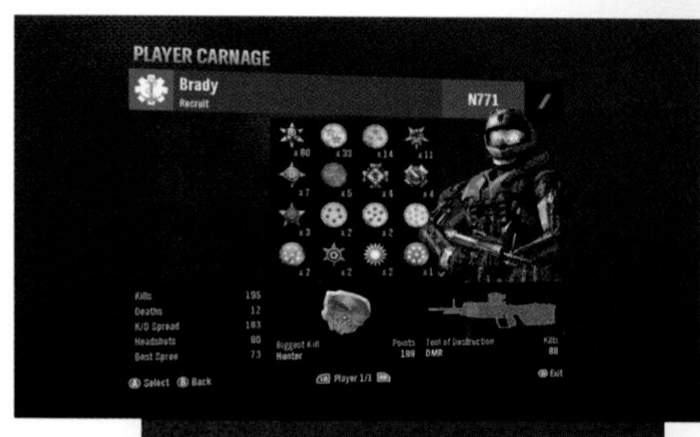

View all of the Medals you earned after a match by selecting your Service Tag in the post-game carnage report.

Many of the Medals share the very same requirements that go towards earning you Credits and incrementing your Commendations. So, while the Medal itself doesn't earn you Credits or impact your score, many of the actions that earn you Medals also earn you Credits. Also, there are style multipliers for many of the actions and sprees in Campaign and Firefight that do boost the score you earn for each kill quite substantially. These multipliers are shown in the right-hand column in each of the applicable tables below. Consult the "Skulls and Scoring" Reference chapter for full details on the point scoring system for Firefight and Campaign.

STYLE MEDALS: DON'T JUST KILL YOUR OPPONENT—DO IT WITH STYLE!

Icon	Medal Name	Description	Style Multiplier (Campaign and Firefight)
	Headshot	Kill an opponent with a headshot.	1.1
	Headcase	Kill a sprinting opponent with a headshot.	1.1
	Assist	Do 40% damage to a player that another player kills.	1.0
	Pummel	Hit and kill an opponent with a melee attack.	1.1
	Beat Down	Hit and kill an opponent with a melee attack from behind.	1.1
	Assassinate	Kill an opponent with a fancy Assassination.	1.1
	Grenade Stick	Kill an opponent by sticking him with a Plasma Grenade.	1.1
	Needle Kill	Kill an opponent with a Super-Combine from the Needler or Needle Rifle.	1.1
	Laser Kill	Kill an opponent while using the Spartan Laser.	1.0
	Sniper Kill	Get a headshot with a precision weapon (Sniper Rifle, DMR, Magnum, or Needle Rifle).	-
	Bulltrue	Kill an opponent that is in the act of a sword lunge.	-
	Splatter	Hit and kill an opponent with your vehicle.	1.1
	Wheelman	Be the driver of a vehicle when a passenger kills an opponent.	-
	Protector	Kill an opponent who had inflicted a significant portion of damage to teammate's health, but had not killed him. Awarded when saved teammate's shields come back.	-
	EMP Assist	Remove an opponent's shield with an EMP blast.	-

Icon	Medal Name	Description	Style Multiplier (Campaign and Firefight)
	Hijack	Board a land-based vehicle by forcibly removing the opponent in it.	-
	Skyjack	Board an aircraft by forcibly removing the opponent in it.	-
	Killjoy	End an opponent's killing spree.	-
	Kill from the Grave	Kill an opponent after you have died.	-
	Revenge	Your first kill upon respawning is against the opponent who killed you.	-
	Avenger	Kill the opponent who recently killed your teammate.	-
	Showstopper	Kill an opponent while he is performing an Assassination.	1.1
	Yoink	Kill an enemy player while he or she is being assassinated (also known as steal-killing and not likely to win you many friends).	-
	Reload This	Kill an opponent who is in the act of reloading.	-
	Close Call	Kill an opponent at close range while you are vulnerable.	-
	First Strike	Earn the first kill of the match.	1.1
	Pull!	Kill a Jetpacking opponent.	-
	Rejection	Activate Armor Lock and survive massive damage.	-
	Firebird	Kill an opponent while you're Jetpacking.	-

MULTIKILL MEDALS: CHAIN TOGETHER A STRING OF KILLS WITHIN 1.5 SECONDS OF ONE ANOTHER.

Icon	Medal Name	Kill Chain (all modes)	Style Multiplier (Campaign and Firefight)
	Double Kill	2	1.2
	Triple Kill	3	1.3
	Overkill	4	1.4
	Killtacular	5	1.5
	Killtrocity	6	1.6
	Killamanjaro	7	1.7
	Killtastrophe	8	1.8
	Killpocalypse	9	1.9
	Killionaire	10	2.0

KILLING SPREE MEDALS: GO ON A KILLING STREAK WITHOUT DYING.

Icon	Medal Name	Kill Spree (Multiplayer)	Kill Spree (Campaign and Firefight)	Style Multiplier (Campaign and Firefight)
	Killing Spree	5	10	1.1
	Killing Frenzy	10	20	1.2
	Running Riot	15	30	1.3
	Rampage	20	40	1.4
	Untouchable	25	50	1.5
	Invincible	30	100	1.6
	Inconceivable	35	500	1.7
	Unfrigginbelievable	40	1000	1.8

WELCOME
UNSC TRAINING
THE CAMPAIGN
FIREFIGHT
MULTIPLAYER
REFERENCE
ORDNANCE
VEHICLES
ENEMY FORCES
CREDITS
THE ARMORY
SKULLS
ACHIEVEMENTS
DATA PADS

ROLE SPREE MEDALS: GO ON A KILLING STREAK WITH THE SPECIFIED WEAPON.

Icon	Medal Name	Weapon/Action Required	Kill Chain (all modes)	Style Multiplier (Campaign and Firefight)
	Sniper Spree!	Sniper Rifle	5	1.1
	Sharpshooter!	Sniper Rifle	10	1.2
	Be the Bullet!	Sniper Rifle	15	1.3
	Shotgun Spree!	Shotgun	5	1.1
	Open Season!	Shotgun	10	1.2
	Buck Wild!	Shotgun	15	1.3
	Sword Spree!	Energy Sword	5	1.1
	Slice 'n Dice!	Energy Sword	10	1.2
	Cutting Crew!	Energy Sword	15	1.3
	Hammer Spree!	Gravity Hammer	5	1.1
	Dreamcrusher!	Gravity Hammer	10	1.2
	Wrecking Crew!	Gravity Hammer	15	1.3
	Laser Spree!	Spartan Laser	5	1.1
	Red Menace!	Spartan Laser	10	1.2
	Sunburst!	Spartan Laser	15	1.3
	Sticky Spree!	Plasma Grenade Stick	5	1.1
	Sticky Fingers!	Plasma Grenade Stick	10	1.2
	Corrected!	Plasma Grenade Stick	15	1.3
	Splatter Spree!	Vehicle Splatter	5	1.1
	Vehicular Manslaughter!	Vehicle Splatter	10	1.2
	Sunday Driver!	Vehicle Splatter	15	1.3
	Wheelman Spree!	Drive a vehicle while passengers rack up kills.	5	1.1
	Road Hog	Drive a vehicle while passengers rack up kills.	10	1.2
	Road Rage	Drive a vehicle while passengers rack up kills.	15	1.3
	Assist Spree	Assist players in killing enemies without dying.	5	1.1
	Assist Spree	Assist players in killing enemies without dying.	10	1.2
	Second Gunman	Assist players in killing enemies without dying.	15	1.3

MULTIPLAYER OBJECTIVE AND SPREE MEDALS: COMPLETE GAME OBJECTIVES AND GO ON KILLING SPREES IN SPECIFIC GAME TYPES.

Icon	Medal Name	MP Game Type	Description
	Perfection	Slayer	Win a Slayer game without dying and at least 15 kills.
	Extermination	All Team-Based Game Types	Wipe out an enemy team with at least one Overkill.
	Oddball Kill	Oddball	Get a melee kill while swinging the oddball.
	Skullamanjaro	Headhunter	Score 10 skulls at once in Headhunter.
	Bomb Planted	Assault	Plant the bomb in an Assault game.
	Killed Bomb Carrier	Assault	Kill an opponent bomb carrier in an Assault game.
	Flag Kill	Capture the Flag or Stockpile	Kill an opponent with a melee attack using a flag.
	Killed Flag Carrier	Capture the Flag	Kill an opponent flag carrier during a CTF game.
	Flag Score	Capture the Flag	Complete a scoring flag capture during a CTF game.
	Killed Juggernaut	Juggernaut	Kill the Juggernaut.
	Juggernaut Spree!	Juggernaut	Kill 5 opponents as the Juggernaut.
	Immovable Object!	Juggernaut	Kill 10 opponents as the Juggernaut.
	Unstoppable Force	Juggernaut	Kill 15 opponents as the Juggernaut.
	Infection Spree!	Infection	Kill 5 Humans as the Zombie without dying.
	Mmmm Brains!	Infection	Kill 10 Humans as the Zombie without dying.
	Thriller!	Infection	Kill 15 Humans as the Zombie without dying.
	Zombie Killing Spree!	Infection	Kill 5 Zombies as the Human without dying.
	Hell's Janitor!	Infection	Kill 10 Zombies as the Human without dying.
	Hell's Jerome!	Infection	Kill 15 Zombies as the Human without dying.
	Last Man Standing	Infection	Be the last Human in an Infection game.
	Hail to the King	King of the Hill	Kill 5 opponents from inside the hill without dying.
	Spawn Spree	Invasion	Spawn a teammate into the game 5 times without dying.
	Wingman	Invasion	Spawn a teammate into the game 10 times without dying.
	Broseidon	Invasion	Spawn a teammate into the game 15 times without dying.

THE ARMORY

Wondering where you go to spend all those thousands—or millions—of Credits (cR) you've earned? The Armory contains over 100 various armor pieces, accessories, special effects, and voices. This appendix details the requirements for unlocking each and every one of them. This section also details the requirements for unlocking each of the Elite armor sets for use in Multiplayer and Firefight.

SPARTAN CUSTOMIZATION

Press the Start Button to access the Player Menu, and select Armory to get started customizing your Spartan's appearance (no effect on actual defensive capabilities or attributes). The choices you make here not only affect the looks of your Spartan in Multiplayer and Firefight mode, but Campaign too—even in the cinematics! You won't see all of the available items right away, since many only become visible after you've been promoted to a certain Rank. You'll be granted 5000 cR at the start of the game. Go ahead and purchase some helmet accessories or some new shoulder pieces to unlock the "Make it Drizzle" Achievement. Your subsequent purchases won't come so easily, however; start saving those Credits now!

RANK HAS ITS PRIVILEGES

Customizing your Spartan isn't done simply through hoarding Credits and spending them on the best piece of equipment you can afford. You first must be promoted to the requisite Rank in order to be able to wear that equipment. Each piece of equipment and accessory in the tables below has a "Rank to see" and a "Rank to buy." The former lists the Rank you must reach before the item shows up in The Armory (only a small sample of the catalog is visible early on), while the latter details the Rank you must reach in order to purchase it. RHIP, Spartan!

HELMETS

Helmets provide the most noticeable change in a Spartan's appearance, and are the most effective way of showing off your Rank and Credit-earning prowess on the battlefield. Helmets come in many styles, and each helmet has two series-specific accessories that can be attached to it. You must purchase the base helmet in a series of equipment in order to buy the accessories in that line. Some of the helmets can only be obtained through *Halo: Waypoint* on Xbox Live, and one item is limited to those with a special pre-order code. Lastly, the Haunted item is only unlocked after you've managed to purchase every other item in the helmet grouping (Waypoint and pre-order excluded), and even then you still must reach the Rank of Reclaimer to buy it—not going anywhere for a while?

MARK V [B]

UA

UA/HUL

The Mk. V [B] helmet is one of several 'privatized' variants of previously classified war material.

Item Name	Credits	Rank to See	Rank to Buy	Prerequisites	Notes
Mark V Base	0	Private	Private	-	Default Noble Six helmet.
UA	1500	Private	Private	Mark V Base	-
UA/HUL	5000	Private	Corporal	Mark V Base	-

CQC

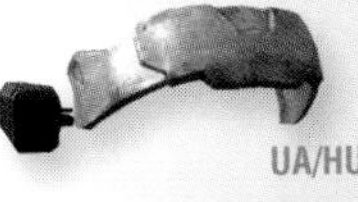

CQC: Predecessor to the current MJOLNIR/C variant; less rigid design allows for field upgrades.

Item Name	Credits	Rank to See	Rank to Buy	Prerequisites	Notes
CQC Base	0	Private	Private	-	Default alternative for Noble Six.
CBRN	1500	Private	Private	CQC Base	-
UA/HUL	5000	Private	Corporal	CQC Base	-

ODST

UA/CNM CBRN/HUL

ODST: The ODST is one of the most recognizable faces in the UNSC's special forces.

Item Name	Credits	Rank to See	Rank to Buy	Prerequisites	Notes
ODST Base	2500	Private	Private	-	Initial purchase option.
UA/CNM	2000	Private	Corporal	ODST Base	-
CBRN/HUL	1800	Private	Sergeant	ODST Base	-

HAZOP

HAZOP: Some operations are considered hazardous even for a fully armored Spartan.

Item Name	Credits	Rank to See	Rank to Buy	Prerequisites	Notes
HAZOP Base	14000	Private	Private	-	Alternative initial purchase option.
CBRN/HUL	10000	Private	Sergeant	HAZOP Base	-
CNM-I	7000	Private	Captain	HAZOP Base	-

EOD

Developed at Damascus Materials Testing Facility on X Ceti; entered service in 2531.

Item Name	Credits	Rank to See	Rank to Buy	Prerequisites	Notes
EOD Base	25000	Private	Sergeant	-	-

OPERATOR

Developed exclusively for the ONI's Beta-5 Asymmetrical Action Group.

Item Name	Credits	Rank to See	Rank to Buy	Prerequisites	Notes
Operator Base	15000	Private	Sergeant	-	-

GRENADIER

The Mk. IV [G] variant is an up-armored prototype based on the basic Mk. IV helmet.

Item Name	Credits	Rank to See	Rank to Buy	Prerequisites	Notes
Grenadier Base	30000	Private	Warrant Officer	-	-

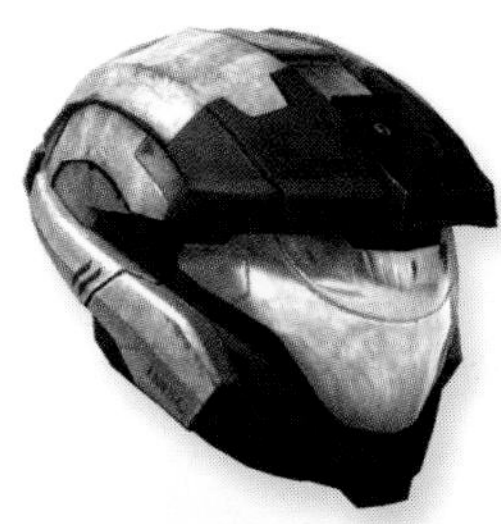

AIR ASSAULT

The MJOLNIR/AA variant was developed as an improvement of the venerable ODST helmet.

Item Name	Credits	Rank to See	Rank to Buy	Prerequisites	Notes
Air Assault Base	20000	Private	Warrant Officer	-	-

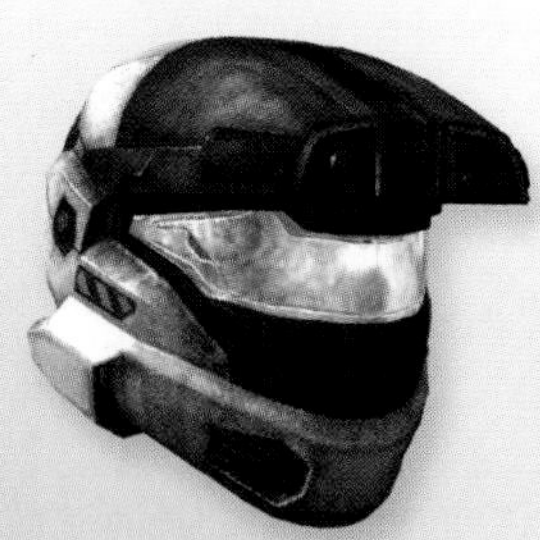

SCOUT

The MJOLNIR VI/S variant was developed and tested at ONI's Ordnance Testing Facility.

Item Name	Credits	Rank to See	Rank to Buy	Prerequisites	Notes
Scout Base	40000	Private	Captain	-	-

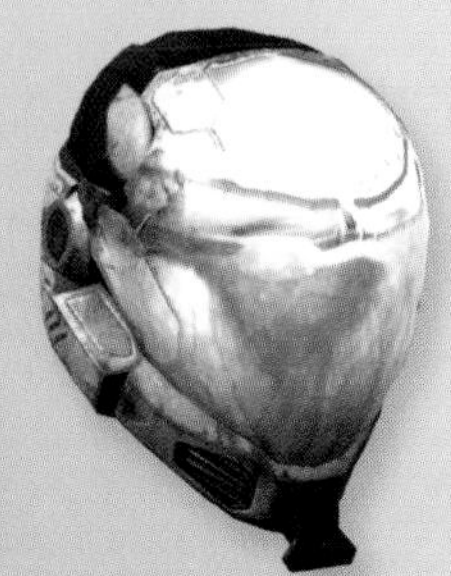

EVA

The MJOLNIR V/V variant was developed and tested at the UNSC facilities in Lister, Aigburth, Ganymede.

Item Name	Credits	Rank to See	Rank to Buy	Prerequisites	Notes
EVA Base	30000	Private	Major	-	-

MILITARY POLICE

The Mk. V [MP] is a shared asset with Beta-5 security; as such, sensor upgrades are many and varied.

Item Name	Credits	Rank to See	Rank to Buy	Prerequisites	Notes
Military Police Base	-	Private	Private	-	Waypoint Award: Waypoint Milestone 15, complete *Halo: Reach* Achievement: "The Soldier We needed you to Be".
CBRN/HU/RS	-	Private	Private	Military Police Base	Waypoint Award: Waypoint Milestone 20, Unlock "Pink and Deadly" Achievement in *Halo: ODST*.
HU/RS/CNM	75000	Private	Private	Military Police Base	Waypoint Award: Waypoint Milestone 25, Unlock "A Spoonful of Blamite" Achievement in *Halo: Reach* and the "Fear the Pink Mist" Achievement in *Halo 3*.

CQB

The MJOLNIR C variant was developed and tested at the UNSC facilities in Essen and Songnam, respectively.

Item Name	Credits	Rank to See	Rank to Buy	Prerequisites	Notes
CQB Base	-	Private	Private	-	Waypoint Award: Waypoint Milestone 20, complete *Halo: Reach* Achievement: "Folks Need Heroes...".
HCNM	-	Private	Private	CQB Base	Waypoint Award: Waypoint Milestone 25, complete *Halo: ODST* campaign on Heroic or harder.
UA/HUL	-	Private	Private	CQB Base	Waypoint Award: Waypoint Milestone 30, complete *Halo: Reach* Achievement: "Gods Must Be Strong" and complete *Halo 3* on Legendary.

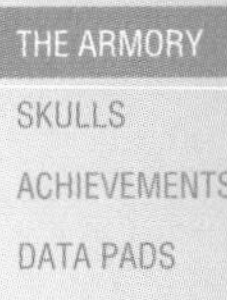

SHOULDER ARMOR

Another effective way to alter your Spartan's appearance and make him or her your own is to buy new left and right shoulder pieces. These pieces of armor are purchased individually, and you can mix and match left and right shoulder pieces from various styles. Go ahead and affix that Jump Jet left shoulder piece with a Recon right shoulder. Nobody will mind.

MARK V [B]

CREDITS	RANK TO SEE	RANK TO BUY
0	Private	Private

UA/MULTI-THREAT

CREDITS	RANK TO SEE	RANK TO BUY
6000	Private	Corporal

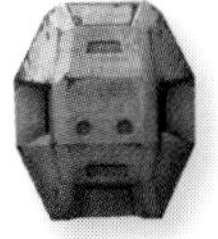

FJ/PARA

CREDITS	RANK TO SEE	RANK TO BUY
1000	Private	Private

HAZOP

CREDITS	RANK TO SEE	RANK TO BUY
500	Private	Private

RECON

CREDITS	RANK TO SEE	RANK TO BUY
4000	Private	Corporal

JFO

CREDITS	RANK TO SEE	RANK TO BUY
1000	Private	Private

CHEST PIECES

Swapping out the default chest piece in favor of one of the available alternatives is yet another great way to personalize your Spartan. Many of these chest pieces become available (or at least visible) as you continue to gain Rank, but some of these can only be acquired via *Halo: Waypoint* on Xbox Live. There are also three additional chest pieces that are upgraded models of other pieces bearing the same name. These only become available after buying the earlier model and continuing to be promoted.

MARK V [B]

CREDITS	RANK TO SEE	RANK TO BUY
0	Private	Private

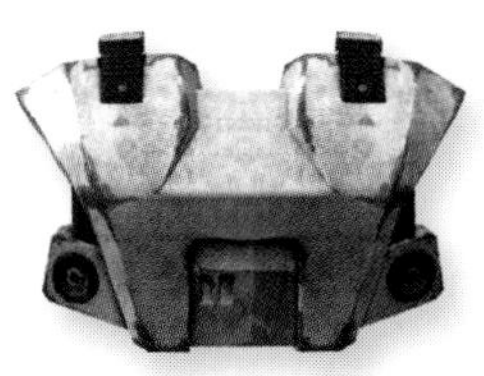

UA/BASE SECURITY

CREDITS	RANK TO SEE	RANK TO BUY
400	Private	Private

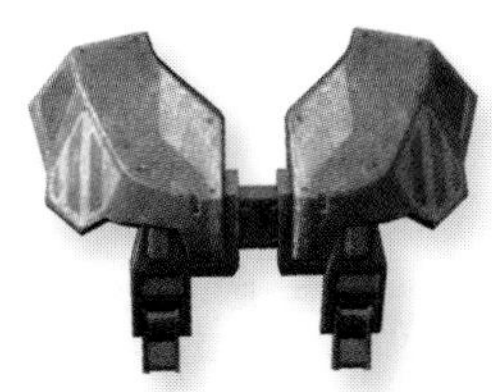

HP/HALO

CREDITS	RANK TO SEE	RANK TO BUY
600	Private	Corporal

UA/COUNTER ASSAULT

CREDITS	RANK TO SEE	RANK TO BUY
600	Private	Corporal

ACCESSORIES

The following tables detail the more subtle customizations that you can add to your Spartan. Wrist pieces and knee guards adorn the Spartan exactly as you would expect. Utility pieces attach to the Spartan's left thigh. Lastly, visor colors give your helmet's glass visor a different color. It doesn't affect your vision on the battlefield, only how your Spartan appears to others.

WRIST PIECES

Item Name	Credits	Rank to See	Rank to Buy
UA/Buckler	5000	Private	Sergeant
UA/Bracer	10000	Sergeant	Warrant Officer
Tactical/TACPAD	50000	Captain	Major

VISOR COLORS

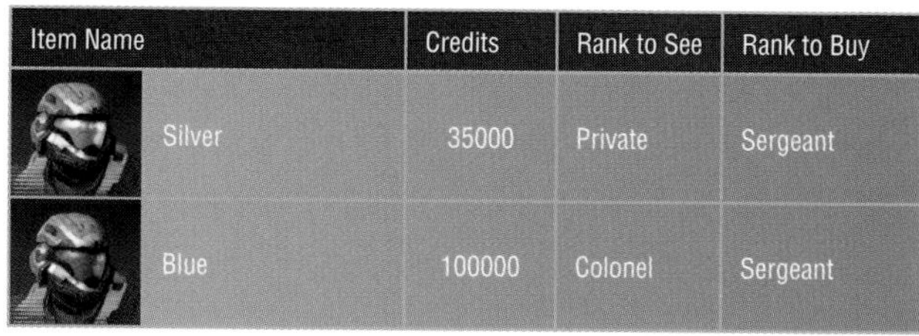

Item Name	Credits	Rank to See	Rank to Buy
Silver	35000	Private	Sergeant
Blue	100000	Colonel	Sergeant

UTILITY PIECES

Item Name	Credits	Rank to See	Rank to Buy	Notes
UA/NxRA	40000	Captain	Major	Hidden until Tactical/Hard Case purchased.
Tactical/Hard Case	40000	Private	Warrant Officer	-

KNEE ARMOR

Item Name	Credits	Rank to See	Rank to Buy
FJ/Para	40000	Colonel	Sergeant
GUNGNIR	50000	Warrant Officer	Captain
Grenadier	75000	Major	Lt. Colonel

ARMOR EFFECTS AND VOICES

This is where you get into the really unique stuff within The Armory. Purchase various armor effects to give your Spartan a flaming helmet, or perhaps make him explode in a bouquet of hearts upon termination. There are a number of amusing options that will not only spice up the battlefield with some festive cheer, but will further show off how many Credits you've earned. The Firefight voices that are available for purchase change your character's voice during Firefight mode. You won't hear these changes in Multiplayer mode—only the announcer speaks during Matchmaking games—but it certainly brings a new voice to Firefight games.

ARMOR EFFECTS

Item Name	Credits	Rank to See	Rank to Buy	Notes
Heart Attack	2000000	Private	Private	-
Inclement Weather	2000000	Private	Private	-
Pestilence	2000000	Private	Private	-
Halo Birthday Party	2000000	Private	Private	-

FIREFIGHT VOICES

Item Name	Credits	Rank to See	Rank to Buy
Noble Six	-	Private	Private
Auntie Dot [A.I.]	15000	Private	Private
Cortana [A.I.]	100000	Private	Private
John S-117	150000	Private	Private
GYSGT Buck	15000	Private	Private
SGTMAJ Johnson	100000	Private	Private
GYSGT Stacker	5000	Private	Private
Carter S-259	10000	Private	Private
Kat S-320	10000	Private	Private
Jun S-266	10000	Private	Private
Emile S-239	10000	Private	Private
Jorge S-052	10000	Private	Private

WELCOME
UNSC TRAINING
THE CAMPAIGN
FIREFIGHT
MULTIPLAYER
REFERENCE
ORDNANCE
VEHICLES
ENEMY FORCES
CREDITS
THE ARMORY
SKULLS
ACHIEVEMENTS
DATA PADS

ELITE ARMOR

Press the Start Button to access the Menu, then select Player from the list of options. Here, you can select which Elite armor class you'd like to use when playing a game of Firefight or Multiplayer in which you play on the Covenant team. Unlike everything else in The Armory, Elite Armor is not purchased with Credits, but simply unlocked one by one as you Rank up through promotions.

ELITE ARMOR

Style	Armor	Rank Unlocked	Notes
Minor	Minor	-	Default Elite available.
Spec-Ops	Spec-Ops	Corporal	-
Ranger	Ranger	Sergeant	-
Ultra	Ultra	Warrant Officer	-
Zealot	Zealot	Captain	-
General	General	Major	-
Field Master	Field Master	Lt. Colonel	-

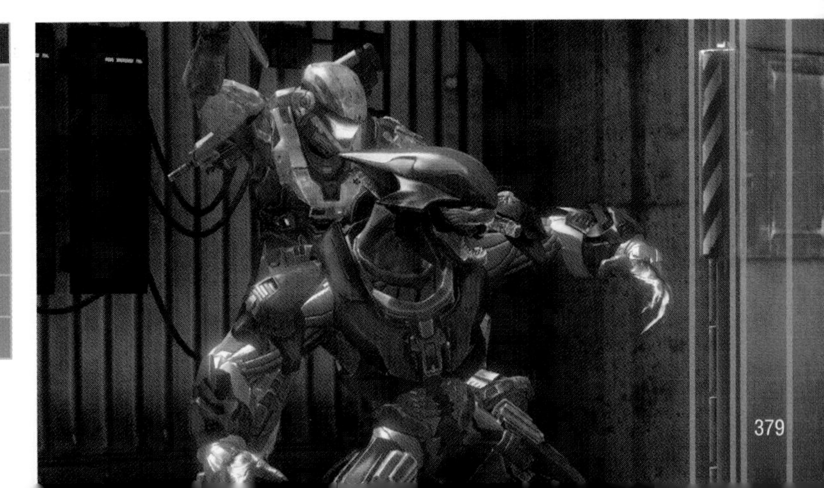

SKULLS AND SCORING

Players looking for a little added challenge can try their hand at besting any of the par scores assigned to each Campaign mission and Firefight map. Par scores are a benchmark score the developers have included to give advanced players a goal to shoot for. It's also a great excuse for experimenting with different combinations of Skulls (difficulty modifiers of a most-sadistic nature). The following pages contain a list of all of the par scores, a breakdown of the scoring system, and tips for besting the Par Score. Note that none of the multipliers and scoring information contained in this section is relevant to the Matchmaking mode; this is for Campaign and Firefight only.

SKULLS

Halo: Reach includes over a dozen Skulls that can be activated in any combination (whenever you want) through the Campaign or Firefight menus. Unlike in previous *Halo* games, you don't need to find the Skulls in *Halo: Reach*—they're automatically available from the start in the settings screens (those who enjoy searching for hidden items can look to the Data Pads appendix at the rear of the book). Skulls alter the rules of the game, turning what is already a stiff challenge into something that is sure to push your abilities to the limit. Turning on Skulls increases the points multiplier and makes it easier to best the par scores. Secondary Skulls do not increase the multiplier.

The Skulls screen contains nine Skulls that impact the multiplier and four secondary Skulls that add a little spice to the experience.

SKULL POINTS MULTIPLIERS

Skull	Multiplier
Iron	1.2
Black Eye	1.1
Tough Luck	1.1
Catch	1.1
Famine	1.2
Thunderstorm	1.2
Tilt	1.2
Mythic	1.2
Cloud	1.1

IRON

CO-OP REVERTS TO PREVIOUS CHECKPOINT ON PLAYER DEATH. PLAYER 1 RESTARTS MISSION.

- Having Iron active during solo Campaign sessions sends the player back to the start of the mission (or most recent rally point) whenever the player falls in battle. Checkpoints are disabled when Iron is activated so there's no chance to game the system and quickly reload a previous checkpoint.
- When Iron is active during Co-op Campaign sessions, the death of one player will cause the entire team to return to the previous checkpoint.
- Iron is automatically activated during Bonus Rounds in Firefight, but its effects there are somewhat different. Players cannot respawn during the Bonus Round, and bonus lives are only awarded for each of those players who are alive during the end of the Bonus Round.

BLACK EYE

SHIELDS DON'T RECHARGE EXCEPT FROM MELEE ATTACKING ENEMIES.

- Black Eye removes the recharging nature of the player's shield energy. The player must melee an enemy in order to initiate shield recharging. The shield will continue to recharge until 100% recharged or the player suffers damage.
- Using primary attacks (trigger button) with the Energy Sword and Gravity Hammer counts as a melee strike and will initiate recharging. You can also perform standard melee strikes with these weapons to satisfy the Black Eye requirement, and have the added benefit of a quicker strike. Hijacking a vehicle also counts as a melee and will initiate shield recharging.
- Black Eye has the same effect in both Campaign solo and co-op, as well as in Firefight missions. It's not recommended on lengthy vehicle missions or for those times when you're primary activity will be long-range sniping. Players who excel at close-range combat and who frequently deliver melee attacks and Assassinations will feel right at home with this Skull on.

CATCH

ENEMIES ARE GRENADE HAPPY—2X AS OFTEN AND 2X AS FAST.

- Catch increases the frequency at which Grunts and Brutes throw Plasma Grenades... to an almost comical level. And, even though it also increases the number of grenades dropped by slain enemies, this only serves to boost the danger and size of the resulting chain reactions.
- Catch is a common Skull in Firefight, particularly in Gruntpocalypse. Depending on the difficulty setting, Catch can make a relatively easy battle much, much harder. Keep your distance and aim for your enemy's head. Don't be afraid to bring out the heavy artillery if you are suddenly swarmed by a number of Grunts and Brutes—saving ammo for the Rocket Launcher won't do you any good once you're dead.
- One of the benefits to activating Catch is that it makes the rest of Noble Team throw more grenades as well and, since they have unlimited ammo just like the Covenant, this can really come in handy. Remember that friendly fire can kill so give your allies a wide berth when they start tossing the pineapples.

TOUGH LUCK

ENEMIES ALWAYS MAKE EVERY SAVING THROW, ALWAYS BERSERK, ALWAYS DIVE, NEVER FLEE...

- Tough Luck makes it much harder to connect with a grenade toss or Rocket Launcher attack. The Covenant's agility and reflexes are markedly improved and they are more successful at dodging slower-moving projectiles including charged Plasma Pistol volleys and Needler attacks. Enemies can still be hit with all attacks—their won't avoid *every* attack—it's just going to require some anticipatory aiming on your part.
- Tough Luck is a staple in Firefight matches, thus reducing the effectiveness of Frag Grenades on many of the maps. Tough Luck will not significantly alter the difficulty on those Campaign missions that take place in tighter quarters, such as "Long Night of Solace" and "New Alexandria."
- Not every enemy will suddenly become a leaping, somersaulting acrobat. No amount of Tough Luck will make a Hunter able to suddenly dodge an inbound Rocket Launcher attack. Still others, like many Brutes, are just as likely to use Armor Lock to absorb the attack than bother rolling out of the way.

CLOUD

MOTION SENSOR DISABLED WITH THIS SETTING.

- Activating Cloud disables the Motion Tracker, thereby giving you no indication of where nearby enemies are in relation to your position. This can increase the difficulty substantially, particularly if you're playing on Heroic or Legendary or if you don't know the enemy locations well. It also makes Firefight much more difficult.
- Reduce the difficulty of Cloud by first playing through the mission a couple of times to learn the locations and tendencies of your enemies. Try to commit the locations of the opposing forces to memory, particularly Elites and Brutes.
- Pay extra attention to the sounds of footfalls, enemy voices, and weapon fire. You're going to have to rely heavily on your ears to know when any enemies are behind, above, or below you. Keep your back to the wall and try to use the rest of Noble Team (or co-op partners) to watch your back.

FAMINE

WEAPONS DROP 50% LESS AMMO.

- Famine reduces the amount of ammunition and battery energy found in weapons dropped by enemies or swapped with allies. This impacts key weapons found on the ground, those in gun racks, weapon swaps with allies, and also those dropped by defeated enemies.
- Playing with Famine activated makes it very hard to plan ahead and "save" a weapon for a key situation later on. Even though this is still possible, you will probably run out of ammo for your primary weapon and be forced to improvise with whatever weaponry happens to drop. This may not be too problematic if you're a good shot and there are plenty of Skirmishers dropping Needle Rifles in the area, but Needlers, Plasma Pistols, and Assault Rifles go through ammo very quickly.
- Playing with Famine also significantly makes games of Campaign co-op much more difficult. The presence of multiple weapons in the weapon rack lessens the strain of using Famine in a solo game, but your entire team will need to rely on those same gun racks to resupply. Instead of limiting the entire team's ammo supply, consider having two players collect the maximum amount while the others rely on weapons found in battle.

TILT

DAMAGE TABLES ARE MODIFIED.

- Tilt forces you into a rock-paper-scissors way of thinking, as each Covenant species' natural resistances to energy and projectile-based weaponry is increased. Essentially, shielded Covenant units become much more resistant to UNSC weaponry but also more resistant to energy-based weapons once those shields have been stripped away. Players must carry complimentary weapons and use energy-based Plasma Pistols, Plasma Rifle, and Plasma Repeaters to strip away the enemy's shielding (Elites and Brutes, specifically), then switch to their traditional UNSC weaponry to inflict the fatal shot.
- Melee attacks can still be used to effectively drain an Elite's shield, single rounds from the Sniper Rifle will no longer get the job done. It's important to always have a plasma weapon with an abundant supply of battery life in it to deal with shielded foes. Pair one such weapon with the Magnum or DMR (or even the Needle Rifle in a pinch) to deliver a fatal headshot once the shields are down.
- The Grenade Launcher can be used to great success while playing with Tilt active since its manual detonation mode delivers a shield-draining EMP blast. It's not the fastest weapon to fire, but its multiple methods of detonation make it almost as effective as wielding two separate styles of weapon.

THUNDERSTORM

MAJOR UPGRADE TO ALL ENEMIES.

- Thunderstorm increases the difficulty of whatever mode you're playing on, not by increasing the health of the enemy, but by promoting them to a higher rank. For example, blue Elite Infantry may be replaced by their gold counterparts. This happens across all species of Covenant.
- Thunderstorm is best reserved for missions that don't involve too many Brutes, since multiplying the number of Brute Leaders or Brute Chieftains you have to deal with can really increase the difficulty. It's also worth noting that the Covenant assigned to drive the many enemy vehicles in later missions will also receive a rank promotion, making them much harder to defeat. Circumvent this whenever you can by aiming to hijack Ghosts and Revenants instead of shooting their driver.
- Skilled players may find that this Skull helps provide the points multiplier they need to achieve par scores on Heroic mode, while not making the game as tough as it would be on Legendary. Most players should only experiment with Thunderstorm during Campaign co-op matches. Combining Thunderstorm and Famine is *not* recommended!

MYTHIC

DOUBLE ENEMY HEALTH.

- Mythic is for those players who want the ultimate *Halo: Reach* challenge. Mythic doesn't adjust the Covenant's A.I. or weaponry, but it doubles their health, thereby making each enemy even tougher than it appears on Legendary mode.
- Mythic is not recommended for solo Campaign play unless you can complete the game on Legendary difficulty without trouble. And if so, our hat is off to you. For most people, however, Mythic is a Skull to only activate when playing in co-op mode with a team of equally skilled players. Make no mistake about it, Mythic makes the game very, very hard.
- As hard as Campaign mode can be with Mythic activated, playing Firefight with Mythic enabled may even be harder. Players must work together to take down larger foes with a joint effort and conserve ammo whenever possible by using melee attacks, grenades, and headshots.

SECONDARY SKULLS

BLIND

HUD AND FIRST PERSON ARMS AND WEAPON ARE HIDDEN.

- This incredible challenge not only hides your ammo and weapon indicators, but also removes the part of the HUD that players rely on the most—the reticule! Help yourself out and put a small piece of tape or sticky note on the screen where the reticule is, then activate the Skull and give it a try.

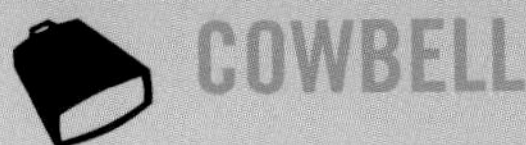

COWBELL

ACCELERATION SCALE FROM EXPLOSIONS 3X.

- Cowbell amplifies explosions of grenades, rockets, and all other things that go boom. Though this sounds like it could make the game easier, it also amplifies the explosions of enemy attacks as well, particularly those of Plasma Grenades, Concussion Rifles, and the Hunter's cannons. If you're careful, Cowbell can be used to increase the size of kill streaks, but using it comes with a price.

GRUNT BIRTHDAY

GRUNTS EXPLODE AS IF THEY WERE PLASMA GRENADES WHEN THEY ARE KILLED WITH A HEADSHOT.

- Grunt Birthday is an incredibly entertaining Skull to activate. Target Grunts that are closest to other enemies and watch them explode in a shower of confetti when hit with a headshot. Using Grunt Birthday in conjunction with Cowbell really increases the damage a single headshot can do. Seek out Grunts in close proximity to Elites and other enemies and shoot them in the head to deliver shield damage to the adjacent enemies.

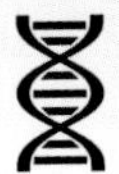

IWHBYD

COMMON COMBAT DIALOGUE BECOMES LESS COMMON, AND VICE VERSA.

- This Skull is purely for entertainment purposes only and doesn't affect the gameplay at all. Some of the Noble Team dialogue is far less common and this shines a light on it. Enjoy!

SCORING

The scoring system used in Firefight can be activated for Campaign mode as well. This provides players with a chance to measure themselves against the par scores that were assigned to each mission and each Firefight map. Scoring can be left disabled for Campaign mode (Off), tracked for the entire team as a whole (Team), or tracked for individual players (Free For All) via the options in the Campaign Menu screen.

Points are awarded for every kill based on a number of factors including the enemy's base score, the difficulty mode being played, specific medal bonuses (aka "style modifiers"), and also any time and Skull multipliers that are applicable. The score for each kill is shown above the enemy with each fatal attack and a running total is shown in the lower right-hand corner of the screen. Points awarded on the spot take into account style, difficulty, and any Skull multipliers. The multiplier shown in the corner of the screen reflects the current time bonus multiplier, as a function of the difficulty mode being played, and will be factored in at the end of the mission.

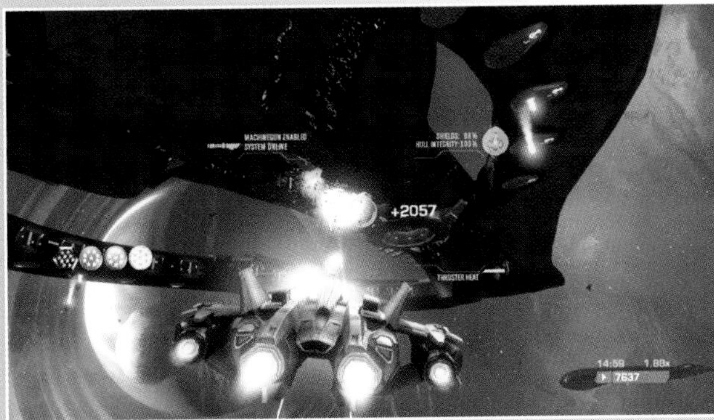

The 2057 points in this shot reflect the value of the Space Banshees, the difficulty being played, and the accumulation of the spree bonuses (no Skulls active). The time multiplier will be applied to entire mission score in the post-game carnage report.

SAMPLE SCORE CALCULATION

Situation: The player destroys a Ghost on Legendary difficulty using a Target Locator (airstrike kill), but it's the 9th kill in a row, and the 50th enemy killed without dying. The player has the Mythic Skull activated.

- Ghost = 150 base value
- Style Multiplier = Airstrike (0.6x) x Killpocalypse (1.9x) x Untouchable (1.5x) = 1.71x
- Legendary mode = 1.5x
- Mythic Skull = 1.2x

Calculation: (150 x 1.71) x (1.5 + 1.2) = 693 points

ENEMY POINT VALUES

Each enemy has an associated base score. Every rank of enemies within a specific race has a different point value, reflecting the increased difficulty in killing them. The following tables show the base point value for each enemy variety and vehicle, per difficulty mode.

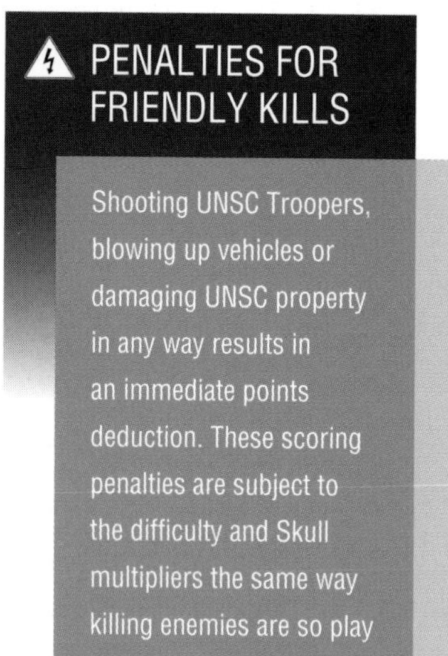

PENALTIES FOR FRIENDLY KILLS

Shooting UNSC Troopers, blowing up vehicles or damaging UNSC property in any way results in an immediate points deduction. These scoring penalties are subject to the difficulty and Skull multipliers the same way killing enemies are so play it clean, Spartan!

COVENANT ENEMIES

Unit Type	Easy (0.75x)	Normal (1.00x)	Heroic (1.25x)	Legendary (1.50x)
Brute Minor	19	25	31	38
Brute Captain	38	50	63	75
Brute Chieftain Armor	113	150	188	225
Brute Chieftain Weapon	113	150	188	225
Drone Minor (Bugger)	8	10	13	15
Drone Major (Bugger)	11	15	19	23
Drone Ultra (Bugger)	38	50	63	75
Elite Minor	38	50	63	75
Elite Officer	75	100	125	150
Elite Ultra	94	125	156	188
Elite Ranger	56	75	94	113
Elite Ranger (grounded)	38	50	63	75
Elite Spec Op	56	75	94	113
Elite General	113	150	188	225
Elite Zealot (story character)	113	150	188	225
Daily Challenge Elite	150	200	250	300
Engineer Minor	56	75	94	113
Grunt Minor	8	10	13	15
Grunt Heavy	11	15	19	23
Grunt Major	11	15	19	23
Grunt Spec Op	11	15	19	23
Grunt Ultra	19	25	31	38
Hunter Minor	113	150	188	225
Jackal Minor	15	20	25	30
Jackal Major	23	30	38	45
Jackal Sniper	34	45	56	68
Gúta	150	200	250	300
Skirmisher Minor	23	30	38	45
Skirmisher Champion	56	75	94	113
Skirmisher Commando	34	45	56	68
Skirmisher Major	34	45	56	68
Skirmisher Murmillones	41	55	69	83

COVENANT VEHICLES & ARMAMENT

Unit Type	Easy (0.75x)	Normal (1.00x)	Heroic (1.25x)	Legendary (1.50x)
Banshee	113	150	188	225
Banshee (Space)	113	150	188	225
Ghost	113	150	188	225
Phantom	750	1000	1250	1500
Phantom (Space)	750	1000	1250	1500
Plasma Turret (Mounted)	23	30	38	45
Revenant	188	250	313	375
Seraph	188	250	313	375
Seraph Bomber	75	100	125	150
Shade Turret	38	50	63	75
Wraith	263	350	438	525

STYLE MULTIPLIERS

The most efficient way to increase your score is to improve your overall technique and perform any of the dozens of style, streak, or spree skills to earn their corresponding one-off multipliers. The multiplier is applied instantly and reflected in the score that appears over the enemy's head when killed. Each of these style multipliers correspond to a particular Medal, but not every medal increases the score, hence the discrepancy between the tables below and those in the Medals section of the appendices. It is entirely possible to earn multiple style multipliers for a single kill. These bonuses will be multiplied together and instantly applied to the kill.

UNIQUE KILL MULTIPLIERS

Unique Kill	Description	Style Multiplier
Headshot	Kill a opponent with a headshot.	1.1
Headcase	Kill a sprinting opponent with a headshot.	1.1
Pummel	Hit and kill an opponent with a melee attack.	1.1
Beat Down	Hit and kill an opponent with a melee attack from behind.	1.1
Assassinate	Kill an opponent with a fancy assassination.	1.1
Grenade Stick	Kill an opponent by sticking them with a Plasma Grenade.	1.1
Needle Kill	Kill an opponent with a Super-Combine from the Needler or Needle Rifle.	1.1
Splatter	Hit and kill an opponent with your vehicle.	1.1
Showstopper	Kill an opponent while they are performing an Assassination.	1.1
First Strike	Earn the first kill of the match.	1.1
Air Strike	Kills earned with the Target Locator.	0.6

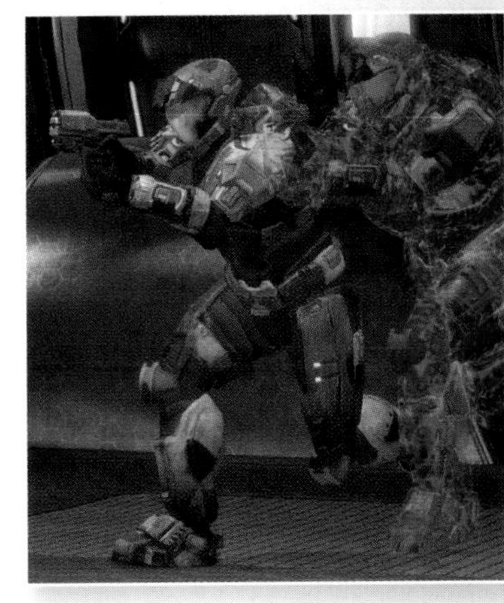

KILL STREAK MULTIPLIERS

Kill Streak	Kill Chain	Style Multiplier
Double Kill	2	1.2
Triple Kill	3	1.3
Overkill	4	1.4
Killtacular	5	1.5
Killtrocity	6	1.6
Killamanjaro	7	1.7
Killtastrophe	8	1.8
Killpocalypse	9	1.9
Killionaire	10	2.0

KILLING SPREE MULTIPLIERS

Kill Spree	Kill Spree	Style Multiplier
Killing Spree	10	1.1
Killing Frenzy	20	1.2
Running Riot	30	1.3
Rampage	40	1.4
Untouchable	50	1.5
Invincible	100	1.6
Inconceivable	500	1.7
Unfrigginbelievable	1000	1.8

ROLE SPREE MULTIPLIERS

Role Spree	Weapon/Action Required	Kill Spree	Style Multiplier
Sniper Spree!	Sniper Rifle	5	1.1
Sharpshooter!	Sniper Rifle	10	1.2
Be the Bullet!	Sniper Rifle	15	1.3
Shotgun Spree!	Shotgun	5	1.1
Open Season!	Shotgun	10	1.2
Buck Wild!	Shotgun	15	1.3
Sword Spree!	Energy Sword	5	1.1
Slice 'n Dice!	Energy Sword	10	1.2
Cutting Crew!	Energy Sword	15	1.3
Hammer Spree!	Gravity Hammer	5	1.1
Dreamcrusher!	Gravity Hammer	10	1.2
Wrecking Crew!	Gravity Hammer	15	1.3
Laser Spree!	Spartan Laser	5	1.1
Red Menace!	Spartan Laser	10	1.2
Sunburst!	Spartan Laser	15	1.3
Sticky Spree!	Plasma Grenade Stick	5	1.1

Role Spree	Weapon/Action Required	Kill Spree	Style Multiplier
Sticky Fingers!	Plasma Grenade Stick	10	1.2
Corrected!	Plasma Grenade Stick	15	1.3
Splatter Spree!	Vehicle Splatter	5	1.1
Vehicular Manslaughter!	Vehicle Splatter	10	1.2
Sunday Driver!	Vehicle Splatter	15	1.3
Wheelman Spree!	Drive a vehicle while passengers rack up kills.	5	1.1
Road Hog	Drive a vehicle while passengers rack up kills.	10	1.2
Road Rage	Drive a vehicle while passengers rack up kills.	15	1.3
Assist Spree	Assist players in killing enemies without dying.	5	1.1
Assist Spree	Assist players in killing enemies without dying.	10	1.2
Second Gunman	Assist players in killing enemies without dying.	15	1.3

SKULL MULTIPLIERS

As mentioned previously, activating primary Skulls will increase the multiplier applied to each enemy kill. Skull Multipliers stack accordingly, so activating two Skulls that are individually worth just 1.1x on their own suddenly increases the multiplier to 2.2x. Using two or more Skulls simultaneously can increase the difficulty tremendously, but also makes for a much higher score. If you have the skill, you may want to turn on as many Skulls as you can stand—your position on the Bungie.net Leaderboards will be that much more impressive.

SKULL MULTIPLIERS

Skull	Multiplier
Iron	1.2
Black Eye	1.1
Tough Luck	1.1
Catch	1.1
Famine	1.2
Thunderstorm	1.2
Tilt	1.2
Mythic	1.2
Cloud	1.1

TIME BONUS MULTIPLIERS

A special time bonus multiplier is applied to your total score upon completion of the mission (Campaign only). Every mission has the same time bonus structure, but some missions are much more difficult to race through than others. If you're looking at these time bonuses and wondering how you can possibly complete some of these missions in under ten minutes, don't fret. The answer lies in co-op! You'd be amazed how fast a team of four skilled players can cruise through some of these missions on the lower difficulty settings, especially once everyone knows the mission well.

COMPLETION TIME MULTIPLIERS

Mission Completion Time	Multiplier
0:00 to 9:59	2.0x
10:00 to 14:59	1.5x
15:00 to 19:59	1.2x
> 20:00	1.0x

PAR SCORES

Each of the missions save for Noble Actual (cinematic only) has been assigned a par score designed to give advanced players a goal to shoot for. Exceeding a par score doesn't earn you any Achievements or Awards, but it certainly serves as a measure of your *Halo* expertise. Beating each of the par scores listed in the table below is nothing to sneeze at; only the best players will beat them all without the help of friends in a co-op match.

Just as completing a mission on Heroic or Legendary requires a certain approach, beating any of the par scores also requires a strategy. Ultimately, your success against the par score will be determined by the following factors: 1) the difficulty you select, 2) the Skulls you activate, and 3) the mission completion time. As a general rule of thumb, it is recommended that you play on the Heroic difficulty setting and increase the multiplier by turning on multiple Skulls instead of playing on Legendary and activating one or fewer Skulls. Some players may even wish to play on Normal difficulty and activate a greater number of Skulls to create an even larger multiplier. Depending on the Skulls selected, this may also help increase the chance of finishing quickly. A very fast completion time, specifically one below 14:59, can have a much greater effect on your final score than anything else.

Mission	Par Score
Winter Contingency	10,000
ONI: Sword Base	40,000
Nightfall	10,000
Tip of the Spear	15,000
Long Night of Solace	20,000
Exodus	10,000
New Alexandria	10,000
The Package	15,000
Pillar of Autumn	20,000
Lone Wolf	50,000

FIREFIGHT PAR SCORES

Every map in Firefight has been assigned a par score of 50,000 points. Since many of the modes only last a single Set or Round, runs at the par score should be done on Firefight Classic. The truly masochistic are welcome to play on Legendary, but since the mode is endless, the masses will likely encounter better luck on Normal or Heroic, with maybe one or two additional Skulls active. Play defensively and don't take any risks. No matter which difficulty and Skull combination you choose, you've got to be in it for the long haul to get those points!

SCORING TIPS

Regardless the difficulty you select and the Skulls you activate, there are a few general tips that you need to keep in mind when trying to get a high score. The following section includes a few general purpose tips, as well as Skull recommendations for each individual mission.

- **Do Your Research:** Play through the mission once or twice while following along with the walkthrough portion of this book to commit the mission to memory. It's important to know ahead of time where the enemies are located, which portions of the mission you can save time on, and how to use the available weaponry and equipment. Make sure you can complete the mission on Legendary in preparation for activating Skulls.
- **Move Fast:** There are few instances where you must defeat every single enemy or where you are forced to wait for Noble Team. Know where you can save time by continuing to progress through the mission. You don't get points for awarding battle but occasionally bypassing a few lesser enemies can result in a very big time bonus multiplier later on.
- **Destroy the Vehicles:** It may take extra time to accomplish, but don't pass up an opportunity to destroy a Wraith or a Phantom. Enemy vehicles are worth a lot more points than individual enemies and can even outweigh any potential time bonus. Sometimes it's worth ignoring an active objective if you have the opportunity to knock a few extra vehicles off the planet.
- **Go Streaking:** Conventional wisdom when facing off against a group of enemies is to quickly eliminate the lesser foes since their cumulative attacks over time may do more damage than the single, tougher foe can deliver while you eliminate his smaller comrades. You need to throw this line of thinking out the window when focusing on score. Lesser enemies can be dealt with quickly, often with a single shot. That means you should start a kill streak with the death of the bigger foe, then carry it across the smaller enemies. Ideally you'd have the streak multiplier applied to the bigger enemy, but you're unlikely to kill it within the 1.5 second window needed to keep the streak alive. Best to leave the lesser foes for last.

WINTER CONTINGENCY

PAR SCORE: 10,000 POINTS.

Iron: Winter Contingency is the easiest of the missions in terms of both enemy type and quantity. Much of the combat in this mission can be done at long-range with the exception of the battle leading from the bridge to the east valley. Be extra careful when battling the Elites before reaching the first truck.

Tough Luck: Grenades don't play too much of a role in this mission, aside from the basement of the farmhouse, and there aren't any Rocket Launchers or other explosive-based weapons that the Covenant can avoid. Activating Tough Luck won't impact the gameplay significantly on this mission.

Catch: Rely heavily on the Magnum, Needle Rifle and DMR to keep the enemies at a safe distance. There is very little close-range combat in this mission if you play it safe and follow the strategy outlined in the walkthrough of this guide. With any luck, you won't even come within grenade range.

Cloud: This may be the only mission where using Cloud doesn't affect the gameplay too much. The structure of the mission leads to most of the enemies being in front of you and clearly visible. It also helps that other members of Noble Team are often by your side and calling out enemy locations.

ONI: SWORD BASE

PAR SCORE: 40,000 POINTS.

Tough Luck: Much of this mission takes place either with a power weapon in your hand or with you behind the wheel of a Warthog. By the time you get to Sword Base, the tight confines of the hallway will limit the Covenant's ability to dodge your grenades no matter how evasive they try to be.

Catch: Use the available long-range weaponry to keep clear of the Grunts in the area and be extra careful once inside Sword Base. It can be tricky dodging the Grunts' grenades on the climb up to the breach, but most of the enemies located here don't throw them so it could be a lot worse.

Thunderstorm: The presence of the Sniper Rifle, Target Locator, and Rocket Launcher make dealing with even higher-ranking enemies a breeze. You're going to have to face down these enemies in later missions with lesser weaponry, so you might as well take advantage of the higher-powered weapons found here. The final push to the top of Sword Base will be tough, so try to stay close to Jorge and use Armor Lock frequently.

NIGHTFALL

PAR SCORE: 10,000 POINTS.

Black Eye: Though the focus of this mission is on sniping, it's often only the enemies that manage to sneak up on you that ever inflict any damage. Turn around and melee them in order to recharge your shields before shooting them.

Tough Luck: You won't be relying much at all on grenades in this mission and the only Rocket Launcher attacks you deliver will be against the sluggish Hunters. Enabling this Skull may well go unnoticed.

Catch: You'll have more Sniper Rifle and DMR ammo on this mission than any other. Most of the mission focuses on long-range combat so staying clear of grenades shouldn't be too hard. Just be careful when protecting the militia at the dam and while protecting Jun at the stealth pylon.

TIP OF THE SPEAR

PAR SCORE: 15,000 POINTS.

Tough Luck: Activating Tough Luck will certainly make the opening push up the hillside more difficult, since the enemies will be able to dodge your Grenade Launcher attacks, but you shouldn't experience too much added difficulty throughout the remainder of the mission.

Famine: This will certainly make things tougher, but so much of this mission takes place in vehicles (limitless ammo) or in areas where there are either multiple Plasma Cannons to detach or plenty of weapons to pick up, so running out of ammo shouldn't be too big of a concern.

LONG NIGHT OF SOLACE

PAR SCORE: 20,000 POINTS.

Tough Luck: There are very few sections of this mission where you'll be relying on grenade tosses, particularly during the beach and space battle sections. The final portion of the mission, on board the Corvette, will be tougher also, but the tight confines of the craft should limit the evasiveness of the enemies.

Famine: You won't have much trouble with ammunition on this mission. Allow Noble Team to do much of the early damage on the beach. Ammo won't be an issue while on board the Sabre, given its unlimited machine gun fire and missiles. Lastly, most of the rooms on board the Corvette are stocked with Covenant supply cases.

Tilt: Make frequent use of Plasma Repeaters and Plasma Rifles on the push up the beach to drain Elite shields, then switch to the Magnum to finish them off. Follow the same tactic on the Corvette where plasma-based weaponry is abundant—just make sure to conserve that DMR ammo until the shields are down. The rest of the mission takes place in space and though the battles may take longer given the Seraph's extra shielding, the Sabre's unlimited ammo won't notice.

BELLY OF THE BEAST

Rack up the points by quickly attacking the ten docked Banshees under the Corvette after leaving Anchor 9. It's possible to rack up a Killionaire medal and more than 2000 points in moments if you move before the Banshees disembark the mother ship.

EXODUS

PAR SCORE: 10,000 POINTS

Black Eye: You won't want to get to close to the Brute Chieftains with the Gravity Hammers or the suicide Grunts, but you should have little trouble being close enough to deliver enough melee attacks to keep your shields recharged during this mission.

Tough Luck: Brutes don't dodge grenades all that well and you'll be relying on heavier firepower for much of this mission anyway. Keep this in mind when you visit the larger exteriors of Traxus Tower. You'll have to be more careful with the Rocket Launcher as well.

NEW ALEXANDRIA

PAR SCORE: 10,000 POINTS.

Tough Luck: You'll be battling a lot of different enemies types of enemies during this mission, but not too many that you'll be throwing grenades at. Hunters can't dodge a Rocket Launcher attack even with Tough Luck activated so you don't need to worry about the beasts in the nightclub.

Famine: Most of the action during this mission takes place on board the Falcon, with you in the pilot's seat. Those segments that take place on-foot aren't that long and there is usually plenty of ammo to collect from the defeated. Make your shots count, and use Covenant weaponry and melee and assassination attacks to conserve your DMR supply.

AIR TO AIR COMBAT

It's entirely possible to beat the par score set for this mission without using any Skulls, provided you go out of your way to blast as many Banshees and Phantoms out of the atmosphere as possible. Destroying just three Phantoms on Heroic mode will go a long way towards beating the par score.

THE PACKAGE

PAR SCORE: 15,000 POINTS.

Tough Luck: Much of this mission takes place either in a Scorpion, at long-range, or with heavy weaponry and a hijacked Ghost or Banshee. The enemies will evade some of your attacks, but with firepower like this, you shouldn't worry too much.

Cloud: It's rather simple to commit the enemy locations to memory through the first two-thirds of the mission, but things will certainly turn difficult out on the glacier. Make it easier—steal a Banshee and use the increased visibility and heavy weapons instead of trying to rely on the Motion Tracker.

PILLAR OF AUTUMN

PAR SCORE: 20,000 POINTS.

Tough Luck: There aren't any Skulls that are easily accounted for in this mission, but Tough Luck offers as gentle a difficulty spike as you can hope for. It will make using the Grenade Launcher in the final battles a bit tougher (particularly outside the storeroom area). The truth is that it's entirely possible to exceed the par score on Heroic mode without using any Skulls, so long as you take advantage of style bonuses.

LONE WOLF

PAR SCORE: 50,000 POINTS.

Iron: Might as well take the multiplier value for Iron since there's no chance of respawning anyway. It's a free 20% points bonus—you can't survive the mission anyway so why turn down free points?

ACHIEVEMENTS AND AVATAR AWARDS

This appendix covers all of the Achievements and Avatar Awards included in *Halo: Reach*. There are 49 total Achievements and 5 Avatar Awards. The majority of these bonuses will be quite accessible to most players. Some are harder than others, of course, but with enough practice, most players can unlock many (if not all) of these Achievements and Avatar Awards.

ACHIEVEMENTS

CAMPAIGN OR FIREFIGHT

6 ACHIEVEMENTS WORTH 55 GAMERSCORE.

You can quickly earn these first six Achievements in Campaign, the very first time you play. You'll almost certainly get 10 kills with the Magnum and DMR in the very first mission, and you will probably use a Medkit as well. Follow the strategy in the walkthrough to find an opportunity to put the Needle Rifle to use in the first mission, and look for a chance to perform an Assassination. You can also swap weapons with one of the UNSC troopers you encounter in the first mission to complete this small subset of Achievements.

Icon	Achievement Name	Gamer Points	Description
	Doctor, Doctor	5	Use a Medkit to recover life after taking body damage.
	That's a Knife	10	Perform an Assassination on an enemy.
	I See You Favor a .45	10	Kill 10 enemies in a Firefight or Campaign session with the M6G Magnum.
	An Elegant Weapon...	10	Kill 10 enemies in a Firefight or Campaign session with the DMR.
	Swap Meet	10	Trade weapons with an ally in Firefight or Campaign.
	A Spoonful of Blamite	10	Kill 10 enemies in Firefight or Campaign with the Needler or Needle Rifle.

CAMPAIGN ONLY

23 ACHIEVEMENTS WORTH 655 GAMERSCORE.

The vast majority of the Achievements in *Halo: Reach* are linked to the Campaign, which should make a lot of fans happy. The requirement for each of these 23 Achievements is self-explanatory, but that doesn't mean they're going to be easy to unlock. Most of these Achievements are linked to completing each of the individual Campaign missions and for completing the game on various difficulties, but each mission also has one or two mission-specific Achievements that are a little trickier. We've provided tips to help you unlock each of the less obvious of these situational Achievements.

It is important to keep two things in mind with respect to Campaign Achievements. For starters, understand that all of these Achievements except "A Monument to All Your Sins" can be unlocked while playing cooperatively with a friend. Secondly, unlike *Halo 3*, there are no Achievements awarded for exceeding the par score for each mission, just a boost to your self-esteem and bragging rights amongst your friends.

Icon	Achievement Name	Gamer Points	Description
	KEEP IT CLEAN	5	Kill seven Moa during the second mission of the Campaign. (Winter Contingency)
	We're Just Getting Started	10	Complete the second mission on Normal or harder. (Winter Contingency)
	Protocol Dictates Action	10	Complete the third mission on Normal or harder. (ONI: Sword Base)
	I Need a Weapon	10	Complete the fourth mission on Normal or harder. (Nightfall)
	To War	10	Complete the fifth mission on Normal or harder. (Tip of the Spear)
	You Flew Pretty Good	10	Complete the sixth mission on Normal or harder. (Long Night of Solace)
	Into the Howling Dark	10	Complete the seventh mission on Normal or harder. (Exodus)
	Dust and Echoes	10	Complete the eighth mission on Normal or harder. (New Alexandria)
	This is Not Your Grave...	10	Complete the ninth mission on Normal or harder. (The Package)
	Send Me Out...with a Bang	10	Complete the tenth mission on Normal or harder. (The Pillar of Autumn)
	I Didn't Train to Be a Pilot	10	Kill all of the anti-aircraft batteries during the eighth mission. (New Alexandria)
	The Soldier We Needed You To Be	25	Complete the Campaign on Normal or harder difficulty.
	They've Always Been Faster	25	Clear the second mission without setting foot in a vehicle. (Winter Contingency)
	Two Corpses in One Grave	25	Kill two vehicles at once with the Target Locator in the third mission. (ONI: Sword Base)
	Banshees, Fast and Low	25	Hijack a Banshee during the Reach Campaign.
	Your Heresy Will Stay Your Feet	25	Kill the Elite Zealot before he can escape during the fourth mission. (Nightfall)

REFERENCE

Icon	Achievement Name	Gamer Points	Description
	If They Came to Hear Me Beg	25	Perform an Assassination against an Elite to survive a fall that would've been fatal.
	Wake Up, Buttercup	25	Destroy the Corvette's engines and escort in under three minutes in the sixth mission on Heroic or harder. (Long Night of Solace)
	Tank Beats Everything	25	Finish the seventh mission on Legendary with the Scorpion intact. (Exodus)
	Lucky Me	25	Earn a Triple Kill while Jetpacking in Campaign, Firefight, or Matchmaking.
	Folks Need Heroes...	50	Complete the Campaign on Heroic or harder difficulty.
	Gods Must Be Strong	125	Complete the Campaign on Legendary difficulty.
	A Monument to All Your Sins	150	Complete each Campaign Mission on Legendary — alone.

Two Corpses in One Grave

Unlocked during ONI: Sword Base.

It's possible to unlock this Achievement right outside the eastern gate when the two Wraiths start making their way up the hill on Normal mode. It's risky because it takes awhile for them to get close enough to one another, but it is possible. Make sure you have Armor Lock equipped to withstand the bombardment from the Wraiths as you lure them towards one another. Another opportunity to unlock this Achievement—and one with a higher success rate on tougher difficulty settings—comes on the drive back to the eastern gate during the "Minimum Safe Distance" portion of the mission. Save one strike with the Target Locator for the drive back from Farragut Station and hop out of the Warthog as soon as you spot the three Revenants. Achieve lock-on with the middle Revenant and hope it stays close to one of the others. You may even get lucky and take out three vehicles with a single strike!

Your Heresy Will Stay Your Feet

Unlocked during Tip of the Spear.

You can find the Elite Zealot that was known to be in the area at the south end of the facility, near the antenna above the stairs. Take out as many of the other enemies as possible from afar, then charge one of the Grunt's Plasma Pistols as you ascend the stairs towards the Zealot. Hit it with a fully charged plasma blast (or Plasma Grenade) to deplete its shields, then quickly switch to another weapon—preferably the DMR or Needle Rifle—and shoot it in the head. Of course, this is all much easier said than done; the Zealot moves with exceptional speed and cunning and is a crack-shot with his Concussion Rifle. Be ready to activate Armor Lock on a moment's notice! He also leaps down the hole and starts running for the vehicles in the distance, likely with Active Camouflage activated. Stay on his tail and keep firing. If you find it too hard to catch up to the Elite Zealot, try again, and this time, swap to the Sprint Armor Ability before climbing the stairs to the target's location.

Wake Up, Buttercup

Unlocked during Long Night of Solace.

Those playing on Heroic or Legendary can earn a smooth 25 Gamer Points by defeating the Corvette's escorts and destroying its four engines within three minutes. Increase your chance for success by quickly piloting the Sabre beneath the center of the Corvette, and use your machine guns to eliminate as many of the docked Banshees as you can before they disengage and go on the offensive—this reduces the number of ships you need to fight. Listen to the radio chatter for the cue that it's time to cut the engines. Use the Sabre's afterburners to get far behind the Corvette, then slow the ship down as much as you can and use missiles to take out the engines one by one. The Seraphs will slipstream into the area shortly thereafter. Stay calm and pursue them one by one.

Lucky Me

Unlocked during Exodus.

There are just too many enemies in the cargo port to not try and unlock this Achievement here. Swap weapons with the trooper shouldering the Rocket Launcher as soon as you pass through the triage area. Jet Pack across the cargo port and remain in the covered stairwell near the UNSC supply case until you notice a checkpoint trigger. Now pause and let some of the Grunts on the upper walkway make their way out of hiding. Peer around the corner and look for at least three Covies grouped together. Leap into the air, trigger the Jet Pack, and fire the rocket right at them. Manage to kill three or more Covies with a single attack while jetpacking, and you'll unlock the "Lucky Me" Achievement. This is a perfect spot to do it.

Tank Beats Everything

Unlocked during The Package.

The Scorpion is virtually indestructible on lower difficulty settings, but it can—and will—fall victim to the Covenant on Legendary mode if you're not careful. Increase the Scorpion's chance for survival by moving amongst the rocks where you first find it. Also, snipe as many of the enemies as you can, particularly those in the Shade Turret and by the Plasma Batteries. The more you can thin the enemy's defenses on foot (from a safe distance, mind you), the fewer shots the Scorpion will have to absorb when you start lumbering down the road in it. The other key to ensuring the Scorpion's survival is to advance very slowly and to treat every Ghost and Banshee encounter as top priority. Do not allow enemy vehicles to get close enough to fire! Mind the reload time for the Scorpion and target those Banshees headed directly towards your position first, as they are easier to hit. Keep the Scorpion in one piece all the way to Sword Base, and the Achievement is yours. And if you're still having trouble with this challenge, go ahead and find a friend or two to play cooperatively with you, then instruct your pal(s) to hijack a Ghost and provide an escort.

Banshees, Fast and Low

Unlocked during The Package.

If you've been wondering when another opportunity to unlock this Achievement would come, it's on the glacier outside Halsey's lab! Use the Grenade Launcher's manual detonation mode to EMP a Banshee as it flies overhead. The Banshee temporarily loses power and falls to the ground. You have to move fast, but there is a window of opportunity for you to hijack the Banshee before it flies away (you can fly up to meet it if you have Jet Pack equipped). Look for the on-screen prompt and press ⊗ the moment you see the text appear. Noble Six climbs on, tosses the Elite piloting it to the ground, and takes control of the Banshee. Hijacking Banshees during this battle doesn't just unlock an Achievement, but it is also a great way to lend aerial support to your team and improve your score. Use its bomb weaponry to blast Covenant as they exit the Phantoms. It's a great weapon against the Wraiths, too!

If They Came to Hear me Beg

Unlocked during Pillar of Autumn.

Aside from throwing yourself out of the Falcon or a Banshee and hoping for a miracle, the only place to unlock this Achievement is at the beginning of Pillar of Autumn, on the cliffs where Emile points out the mission's titular ship. Meet Emile on the cliff overlooking the road and watch the blue Elite Minor as he paces back and forth. Wait for him to near the grass then take a running leap off the cliff towards him. Hold the Right Bumper down and aim towards him while in the air to land in an Assassination. This will likely take a few (dozen) attempts, so be patient and stick with it.

FIREFIGHT ONLY

7 ACHIEVEMENTS WORTH 160 GAMERSCORE.

Unlike Campaign, unlocking many of these Firefight Achievements depends not only on your skill, but on the skills of your fellow players as well. You earn several of these Achievements through applying basic Firefight tactics, such as knowing when to use the Target Locator for maximum effectiveness to earn the "Crowd Control" Achievement, and also through your ability to play as an Elite in Generator or Versus modes.

As for the scoring-based Achievements and the seemingly impossible "Game, Set, Match" Achievement, you can earn these all in due time with a little help from Custom Skulls. Enter the Game Options screen and adjust Custom Skulls. Select the Red Skull option, then select Spartan Traits and Shields and Health. Now you can alter the Damage Resistance, Shield Multiplier, and various immunities and recharge rates however you see fit. It's entirely possible to set Damage Resistance to "Invulnerable" and play a never-ending game of Firefight Classic. We're not going to judge you, and we certainly will understand if you decide to take the high road and try to accomplish the feat on the default settings. That said, it's best that you at least know about this rather easy shortcut.

Icon	Achievement Name	Gamer Points	Description
	Crowd Control	10	Earn a Killionaire medal in Firefight.
5	Knife to a Gunfight	5	Kill five Spartan players in Firefight Matchmaking.
15k	Score Attack	10	Score 20,000 points in Score Attack Firefight Matchmaking.
50k	Firestarter	10	Score 40,000 points in Firefight on any map.
200k	Blaze of Glory	25	Score 120,000 points in Firefight on any map.
1m	Heat in the Pipe	75	Score 2,000,000 points in Firefight on any map.
	Game, Set, Match	25	Complete a Firefight set on Legendary without dying.

MULTIPLAYER ONLY

4 ACHIEVEMENTS WORTH 30 GAMERSCORE.

The Achievements for Multiplayer are quite straightforward, and rather than require you to become an expert in the game mode, they simply reward you for diving in there and experimenting, particularly with Invasion. Play the Invasion mode enough, and you'll eventually win as a Spartan team in the first phase, and you'll certainly have a teammate spawn onto your position at least five times. You can earn the other Achievements by being aggressive out of the gate. In short, even novices who spend any amount of time in multiplayer Matchmaking should have no problem earning all four of these Achievements sooner rather than later.

Icon	Achievement Name	Gamer Points	Description
	Be My Wingman, Anytime	5	Let a teammate spawn on you five times in an Invasion Matchmaking game.
	Yes, Sensei	10	Earn a First Strike Medal in a Matchmaking game.
	Skunked!	10	Win a game of Invasion in the first phase.
	What's a Killing Spree?	5	Earn a Killing Spree in multiplayer Matchmaking.

PLAYER EXPERIENCE

9 ACHIEVEMENTS WORTH 100 GAMERSCORE.

This group of Achievements rewards you for spending time with *Halo: Reach* in any mode, and for exploring the various peripheral modes, such as The Armory, Theater, and the File Share system. Certain Achievements, such as "A New Challenger" and "One Down, 51 to Go," definitely require some skill depending on what the Challenges are, but others are unlocked simply by continued play in any of the main modes of the game. Remember that you earn Credits in every mode of the game, so even though the promotion to Captain may seem as if it would take an eternity to receive, almost everything you do earns you Credits. Keep chipping away at it, focus on advancing your Commendations, and it won't be long before you too are sporting the Captain's insignia.

Icon	Achievement Name	Gamer Points	Description
	Make it Drizzle	10	Purchase any item from the Armory.
	Make It Rain	10	Purchase an item from the Armory that requires the rank of Lt. Colonel.
	The Start of Something	15	Reach the rank of Corporal in the UNSC.
	An Honor Serving	25	Reach the rank of Captain in the UNSC.
	A Storage Solution	5	Upload a file to your File Share using the File Browser.
	A New Challenger	10	Complete all of the Daily Challenges in a given day.
	Cool File, Bro	5	Recommend a file to someone.
	Lemme Upgrade Ya	10	Advance any Commendation to its Silver state.
	One Down, 51 to Go	10	Complete a Weekly Challenge.

AVATAR AWARDS

MEET THESE MILESTONES WHILE PLAYING *HALO: REACH* TO UNLOCK NEW ACCESSORIES FOR YOUR XBOX AVATAR.

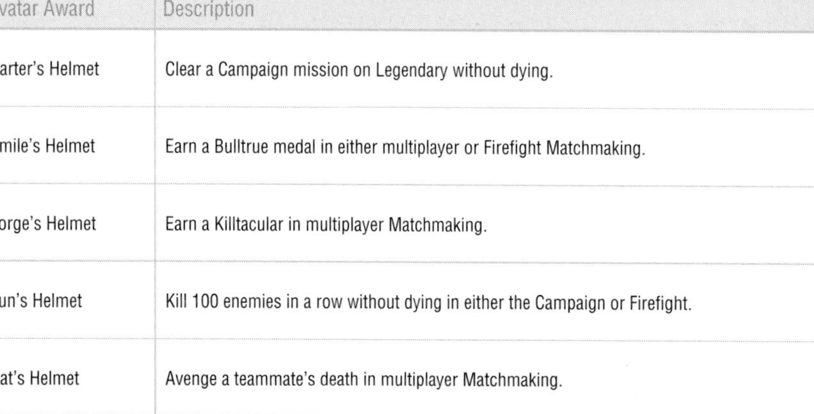

Avatar Award	Description
Carter's Helmet	Clear a Campaign mission on Legendary without dying.
Emile's Helmet	Earn a Bulltrue medal in either multiplayer or Firefight Matchmaking.
Jorge's Helmet	Earn a Killtacular in multiplayer Matchmaking.
Jun's Helmet	Kill 100 enemies in a row without dying in either the Campaign or Firefight.
Kat's Helmet	Avenge a teammate's death in multiplayer Matchmaking.

DATA PADS

Intel confirms that 19 Data Pads have been scattered across Reach in hope that a Spartan of sufficient skill and devotion would one day find them. Locating them all is an exercise for the few—their exact coordinates have never been tracked. Success earns no Achievements or Credits, nor does it confer any special items in the Armory. You take on this challenge for the thrill of the hunt—and for the knowledge that each Data Pad brings.

SOME CLUES TO HELP YOU...

Nearly every mission in the campaign has two Data Pads, one that can be found while playing on Easy, Normal, or Heroic difficulty and one that can only be found while playing Legendary mode. Data Pads are off the beaten path, tucked away in corners where your eyes typically don't wander—and those are the obvious ones! Others require a much more thorough inspection of the landscape, often combined with some expert grenade-jumping or Jet Pack flight.

DATA PAD HINTS

Mission	Difficulty	Hint
Winter Contingency	Easy/Normal/Heroic	Is it nap time already? A nice place to live if you don't mind the Covies.
Winter Contingency	Legendary	It's a Data Pad backpack! And it's getting away!
ONI: Sword Base	Easy/Normal/Heroic	Under the stairs one floor down. It gets dark up above, better return to the light.
ONI: Sword Base	Legendary	Communication can get rocky. Looks like the walkway collapsed.
Nightfall	Easy/Normal/Heroic	You won't have to go far, but don't step in the guano.
Nightfall	Legendary	The rebels warn you to stay dry when the levee breaks.
Tip of the Spear	Easy/Normal/Heroic	Those shelves are mine. Shiny weapons may distract you.
Tip of the Spear	Legendary	One hell of a parking job. Sure hope it didn't get run over.
Long Night of Solace	Easy/Normal/Heroic	Perhaps Major Tom knows where it is? A room with a launch pad view.
Long Night of Solace	Legendary	Don't liftoff without it. Of course, reaching it is another thing altogether.
Exodus	Easy/Normal/Heroic	A cargo port Jet Pack jump. We suggest you eliminate all of the Brutes first.
Exodus	Legendary	At least Traxus employees have air conditioning. Although they probably don't have to make jumps like this.
New Alexandria	Easy/Normal/Heroic	Near a rooftop exit not far from the helipad. You'll have a nice view of ONI Tower from here.
New Alexandria	Legendary	How low can you go? A building on the outskirts of town.
The Package	Easy/Normal/Heroic	Look around before you leave. Sword Base has sure seen better days.
The Package	Legendary	It sees your good deeds and kisses you windy. Sure hope a tram doesn't come!
The Pillar of Autumn	Easy/Normal/Heroic	Break glass in case of emergency. At least there aren't any Covenant in the area.
The Pillar of Autumn	Legendary	On a hot tin roof. Best to get it before meeting Keyes.
Lone Wolf	Legendary	Somebody call the plumber! Better find it before the end comes.

HALO®

REACH

OFFICIAL LICENSED MERCHANDISE AVAILABLE NOW

APPAREL AND ACCESSORIES

BioWorld
Changes
LevelUp Wear

TOYS AND COLLECTIBLES

Diamond Toys
McFarlane Toys
NECA/WizKids
NKOK
Square Enix

POSTERS AND ART PRINTS

Acme Archives
GB Eye
Trends

To All our Faithful Fans -
Thank you for playing Halo: Reach.
Over the past decade, we've shared some of our most memorable experiences together, inside the far reaching expanses of the Halo universe. It's been one hell of a ride. And we couldn't have done it without you.
As we continue marching toward our ultimate goal of World Domination, Bungie remains inspired and fueled by you, our passionate fan community. So Play. Forge. Film.

We'll see you starside.

BUNGIE: Aaron LeMay, Aaron Lieberman, Adrian Perez, Alex Bezman, Alex Chu, Alex Pfeiffer, Andrew G Davis, Andrew Harrison, Andrew Solomon, Andy Firth, Artem Volchik, Ben Thompson, Ben Wallace, Bill O'Brien, Blake Low, Bob Glessner, Brad Fish, Brendan Walker, Brent Abrahamsen, Brian Frank, Brian Jarrard, Brian Sharp, C Paul Johnson, Cale Haskell, Cameron Pinard, Chad Armstrong, Chad Foxglove, Charlie Gough, Chris Alderson, Chris Butcher, Chris Carney, Chris Gossett, Chris Opdahl, Chris Tchou, Christian Diefenbach, Christine Edwards, Christopher Barrett, CJ Cowan, Curtis Creamer, Cyril Saint Girons, Dan Miller, Dave Dunn, Dave Matthews, David Aldridge, David Allen, David Candland, David Gasca, David Helsby, David Hunt, David Lieber, David Stammel, Davina Chan , Derek Carroll, Domenic Koeplin, Dorje Seattle Bellbrook, Drew Shy, Eamon McKenzie, Eric Elton, Eric Osborne, Forrest Soderlind, Frank Capezzuto, Gayle d'Hondt, Graham Bartlett, Hao Chen, Harold Ryan, Isaac Hannaford, Jacob Miner, Jae Parks, Jaime Griesemer, Jaime Jones, James Haywood, James McQuillan, James Phillips, James Tsai, Jamie Evans, Jason Jones, Jason Robertson, Jason Sussman, Javier Burgos, Jay Weinland, Jerome Simpson, Jessica Coombs, Jessica Owens, Joan Toigo, Joe Spataro, Jon Cable, Jon Weisnewski, Jonty Barnes, Joseph Staten, Joseph Tung, Josh Hamrick, Josh Rodgers, Justin Hayward, Justin Klaassen, Justin Truman, Ken Malcom, Kentarou Taya, Kurt Nellis, Lars Bakken, Lee Wilson, Leo Martinez, Lorraine McLees, Luis Villegas, Luke Ledwich, Luke Smith, Luke Timmins, Marcus Lehto, Mark Flieg, Mark Goldsworthy, Mark Noseworthy, Marke Pedersen, Martin O'Donnell, Mat Noguchi, Matt Bennier, Matt Kelly, Matt Priestley, Matt Richenburg, Matt Sammons, Matt Segur, Max Dyckhoff, Michael Means, Michael Williams, Michael Wu, Michael Zak, Mick Buckmiller, Mike Baldwin, Mike Buelterman, Mike Hoffman, Mike Milota, Mike Tipul, Milton Cadogan, Natasha Tatarchuk, Nick Gerrone, Niles Sankey, Ondraus Jenkins, Pat Jandro, Patrick O'Kelley, Paul Bertone Jr., Paul Lewellen, Paul Russel, Paul Vosper, Petar Kotevski, Pete Parsons, Peter O'Brien, Phil Kauffmann, Raj Nattam, Ray Broscovak, Renae Wetsig, Richard Lico, Rob Adams, Roberta Browne, Robt McLees, Roger Wolfson, Ryan Ellis, Sage Merrill, Sam Arguez, Samuel Jones, Scott Bilas, Scott Shepherd, Sean Shypula, Shauna Sperry, Shawn Taylor, Shi Kai Wang, Steve Chon, Steve Cotton, Steve Lopez, Steve Reddoch, Steve Scott, Stosh Steward, Tam Armstrong, Tim Williams, Tom Burlington, Tom Doyle, Tom Gioconda, Tom Saville, Travis Brady, Tristan Root, Troy McFarland, Tyson Green, Vic DeLeon, Xi Wang, Yaohua Hu, Yongjoon Lee, Zach Russell **ADDITIONAL MUSIC AND RECORDING:** Halo 2 Soundtrack "Never Surrender" appears Courtesy of Niles Rogers and Nataraj, Michael Salvatori (TOTALAUDIO), Northwest Sinfonia, Stan Lepard (PANTHER MODERN), Studio X **CONTACTORS: Aquent:** Anthony Vacarro, Dan Mod, Dan Phillips, David Henry, David Liu, Gene Blakefield, Jason Keith, Jason Pate, Jesse Hall, Lionel Ward, Loren Broach, Matt Lichy, Sam Heine, Tomas Jech **Comsys:** Andra Niculescu, Andy Howell, Annamaria Stolfo, Jason Shifley, Richard Chen, Thomas Coldwell **Excell:** Cullen Bradley, Andrew Hopper, Anton Feist, Cory Blakslee, Dan Callan, Justin Ewert, Karley Donnell, Michael Allen, Mike Axworthy, Ron Running, Tomonori Kinoshita, Uwe Krahe **Filter:** Esequiel Garcia, Kevin Dalziel, Kyle Hug, Matt Turner **FrameShift:** Sanjay Chand **Fxville:** Jeff Palmer **Independent:** Bryen Hensley, Dave Atherton, Nik Kleverov, Robert Goldberg **Kaarbo Design:** Noah Kaarbo **Perhapsatron:** Erik Bertellotti **Volt:** Alan Tseng, Chad Hale, Chiaki Isono, Eddie Nunez, Eric Carter, Jeff Mattson, Jeffrey Kleinman, Joe Sifferman, Jonathan Green, Jooyoung Lee, Joshua Anderson, Mariana Feddersen, Michael Durkin, Michael Sechrist, Robert Kehoe, Rolando Cisneros, Ryan Ladeen, Schuyler Ko **Xversity:** Andrew Saturn, Andy Xiao, Aviv Arad, Benjamin Wommack, Chris Daltas, Chris Fivash, Darren McKee, David Parker, Donnie Taylor, Eric Huang, Eric Kramer, Erick Reyes, Gary Huang, Gordon Lee, Jason Jones, Jeremiah Pieschl, John Stvan, Johnny Renquist, Joseph Ainsworth, Justin Lakin, Kayl Myers, Kevin Gordon, Kevin Hanschen, Mark Uyeda, Martin An, Matthew Lumb-Mielke, Merritt Filban, Micah Jelmberg, Michael Tea, Nathan Rodland, Nicole Warner, Nina Saldana, Pat Gillette, Ryan Eames, Ryan Klaverweide, Sean Kellogg, Sergey Mkrtumov, Tadd Foote, Tanner Johnson, Will Christiansen **ART, ANIMATION AND FX VENDORS:** House of Moves, Image Metrics, NewBreed Visual FX, Pearl Digital Entertainment, Polygon, Schematic, Vicon **BUNGIE SPECIAL THANKS:** Abigail Harris, Allen Murray, Christian Allen , Clifford Garrett, David Shaw, Don McGowan, Eric Neustadter, Francois Boucher-Genesse, Frank Pape, Glenn Israel, Jean-Charles Cullandre, Jefferson Ng, Jim Charne, Jim Veevaert, John Gronquist, Justin Yorke, Kevin Salcedo, Matthew Burns, Noah Bordner, Oliver Miyashita, Seth Gibson, Shane Kim, Stephen Toulouse, Steve Dolan, Steve Theodore, Theo Michel, Victor Tan, Xbox Live Air Marshals **CAST:** Aisha Tyler, Alona Tal, Amanda Phillipson, Bob O'Donnell, Carol Roscoe, Carole Ruggier, Chris Edgerly, Coby Bell, Courtenay Taylor, David Scully, David Scully, Freddy Bosche, Gavin McLean, Greg Grunberg, Hakeem Kae Kazin, Jamie Hector, Jeff Steitzer, Jen Taylor, Joe Staten, John Patrick Lowrie, Jon Huertas, Ken Boynton, Marcella Lentz-Pope, Nathan Fillion, Pat Duke, Patrick Galagher, Pete Stacker, Pete Stacker, Phillip Anthony Rodriguez, Ron Hippe, Ron Livingston, Steve Downes, Sunil Malhotra, Tim Gouran, Todd Licea, William Mapother, Zachary Levi **MOTION CAPTURE AND FACIAL PERFORMERS:** David Hogan, Deborah Fialkow, Hans Altwies, The Bungie Auxillary Players **CASTING AND VOICE OVER PRODUCTION SERVICES:** Blindlight **COMMUNITY:** 7th Column, Brian Morden, Bungie.net Forum Ninjas, Burnie Burns, Claude Errera, Good Game Network, Halo.Bungie.Org, Major League Gaming, Miguel Chavez, Rooster Teeth

THANKS AND ACKNOWLEDGEMENTS

DOUG WALSH

Writing a book of this magnitude simply isn't possible without the support of an army of people almost too numerous to list. My two months spent working on-site at Microsoft were made far more productive and enjoyable than I ever dared imagine thanks to the amazing help of Corrinne Robinson, Tyler Jeffers, Christine Finch, and Michelle Ballantine. Corrinne's team helped shepherd this project along from start to finish and sought to it that I had access to every resource possible. Thank you all for your hospitality, your support, and most of all your patience! I want to also thank Chris Shaules, Desmond Murray, and Jeremy Patenaude for answering all of my Campaign and Firefight questions; Andrew Schnickel, Alex Cutting, and Alex Liberman for their technical support; and Jacob Benton and the entire Waypoint Team for their help in creating the Firefight strategy videos. There was a true vision for this book from start to finish and Chris Hausermann and Keith Lowe of BradyGames deserve a ton of credit for pulling it all together. Joe "The Not-So Silent Cartographer" Epstein and Areva Ragle deserve special thanks for their fantastic work assembling the campaign maps—great work to both of you. I'd like to also thank Leigh Davis of BradyGames for assigning me this project—this was truly a remarkable book to be a part of—and providing such a great crew of co-authors to work with.

Lastly, I want to thank my dog Kimo for the wonderful memories he left me with. Together, we wrote nearly a hundred strategy guides over the past decade and though he couldn't be with me through the end of *Halo: Reach*, his spirit will forever be curled at my feet, just like always. We'll never forget you Kimo.

BRADYGAMES

WOULD LIKE TO GIVE SPECIAL THANKS TO THE FOLLOWING PEOPLE WHO MADE THIS GUIDE POSSIBLE:

From Bungie Studios: Ryan Eames, Marcus Lehto, Lorraine McLees, Robt McLees, James McQuillan, and Eric Osborne.

From MGS and 343 Industries: Steve Alliston, Alicia Brattin, Michelle Ballantine, Jacob Benton, M.E. Chung, Bill Clark, Alex Cutting, Deacon Davis, Kyle Dolan, Jeff Dubrule, David Ellis, Christine Finch, Kevin Franklin, Jon Goff, Paul H. Gradwohl, Eric Helbig, Chris Howard, Josh Lindquist, Tyler Jeffers, Steven Jones, Alex Liberman, David McMahon, Matt Mills , Gregory Murphy, Desmond Murray, Carlos Naranjo, Jeremy Patenaude, Veronica Peshterianu, Adam Pino, Corrinne Robinson, Tony Santos, Andrew Schnickel, Eric Schuh, Jonathan Schwartz, Scott Sedlickas, Chris Shaules, Alyson "Zippy" Szymanski, Brad Welch, The *Halo: Reach* Test Team, Gray Team, and Everyone at 343 Industries.

PHIL MARCUS

If you're a vet, from the moment you stepped on the Pillar of Autumn to the moment you rode a Warthog across an exploding Halo, you may have been wondering about Reach. Now you can discover that story. Whether you're old or new, the multiplayer in Halo: Reach is massively expansive, there's a lot to explore, and a lot to like. I hope this guide helps your enjoyment of the experience in some small way.

I'd like to thank the dedicated *Halo: Reach* team that helped put this book together, Doug Walsh, Rich Hunsinger, Joe Epstein, my editor Chris Hausermann, and our heroic designer, Keith Lowe, it was a pleasure.

Very special thanks to our welcoming hosts at Microsoft, 343 Studios, and of course, Bungie. Corrinne Robinson made us feel very welcome for the weeks spent on site, and Tyler Jeffers and the rest of the team greatly assisted us, thanks for your multiplayer assistance, advice, and good humor.

SEA SNIPERS

This guide's multiplayer section was created in part by the Sea Snipers, www.seasnipers.net

Thanks to [SS]Midnight aka Ammon Terpening for his attention to detail and hard work throughout this project and thanks to all of the Sea Snipers who contributed.

[SS]Rator aka Rich Hunsinger
[SS]Midnight aka Ammon Terpening
[SS]Snakebite aka Dale Pittman
[SS]Showstoper aka Alejandro Rosas

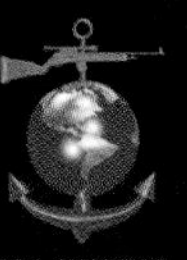

The Sea Snipers are:

[SS]Bassani	[SS]Midnight	[SS]Showstoper	[SS]Wally
[SS]Chief	[SS]Rator	[SS]Snakebite	
[SS]Grunt	[SS]Sabotage	[SS]SportoFu	
[SS]Hobo	[SS]Shooter	[SS]Switters	

We would like to thank BradyGames for the opportunity to work on this project especially Leigh Davis and Chris Hausermann. Thanks to Corrine Robinson and Tyler Jeffers for their hospitality and help while hosting us at Microsoft too.

The Sea Snipers are always appreciative and honored to be called in to work on projects with BradyGames. We try to deliver the most accurate and detailed content possible in every project we work on. We hope you can use the content provided in this guide to get more out of your game.

Special thanks to Phil Marcus and Doug Walsh for their work on guide, and to my wife for her unending patience and love throughout all of my work. I love her.

OFFICIAL STRATEGY GUIDE

By Doug Walsh, Phillip Marcus, Rich Hunsinger, and Sea Snipers

DK/BradyGames, a division of Penguin Group (USA) Inc.
800 East 96th Street, 3rd Floor
Indianapolis, IN 46240

ISBN: 978-0-7440-1232-3

Printing Code: The rightmost double-digit number is the year of the book's printing; the rightmost single-digit number is the number of the book's printing. For example, 10-1 shows that the first printing of the book occurred in 2010.

13 12 11 10 4 3 2 1

Printed in the USA.

BRADYGAMES STAFF

Editor-In-Chief
H. Leigh Davis

Licensing Manager
Mike Degler

International Translations
Brian Saliba

Project Coordinator
Stacey Beheler

CREDITS

Senior Development Editor
Chris Hausermann

Title Manager
Tim Fitzpatrick

Senior Book Designer
Keith Lowe

Designer
Dan Caparo

Production Designer
Areva

The Silent Cartographer
Joe Epstein

Editorial Assistant
Angela Blau

343 INDUSTRIES

General Manager
Bonnie Ross

Franchise Development Director
Frank O'Connor

Managing Editor
Kevin Grace

Business and Strategy Analyst
Alicia Brattin

Lead SDET
Chris Shaules

Halo IP Licensing Manager
Christine Finch

Program Manager
Corrinne Robinson

Sr. Attorney
David Figatner

Paralegal
Carla Woo

BUNGIE

VISUAL ID AND DESIGN

Creative Director
James McQuillan

Senior Graphics Designer
Lorraine McLees

Content Coordinator
Ryan Eames (Xversity)

Graphics Designers
John Stvan (Xversity)
Ryan Klaverweide (Xversity)

3D Artist
Darren McKee (Xversity)

Editor
Eric Osborne

Contributing Editors
Brian Frank
Chris Opdahl
Dan Miller
Josh Hamrick
Lars Bakken
Luke Smith
Matt Sammons
Michael Tipul
Niles Sankey
Sage Merrill